KEROUAC ON RECORI

'*Kerouac on Record* is a tantalizing new collection of essays and interviews on the interrelations between Jack Kerouac and music – both the music he heard and was inspired by in his "bop prosody", and the music later artists have been inspired by him to produce, either as settings of his works or as intertextual companion pieces extending the life span of those works by recontextualizing them for new generations of listeners and readers. Warner and Sampas have brought together some of the most engaging writers in the fields of literary and cultural Beat Studies, as well as some of the most articulate voices within the music community: critics, producers, music archeologists, and lyricists. This blend of perspectives and registers makes for an unusually engaging reading experience as one traipses through the manuscript, high on "life, joy, kicks, darkness, music" as Kerouac himself memorably put it in *On the Road*.'

Bent Sørensen, Associate Professor of English, Aalborg University, Denmark, and Member of the Advisory Council of the European Beat Studies Network

'Warner's and Sampas's encyclopedic collection represents a vital contribution to Beat scholarship. This is not just because the range of interactions between Kerouac's work and genres of popular music – from jazz to country to punk – is dazzling, but also because it insists on seeing the Beats' creativity as interdisciplinary from the start, and on the need for Beat criticism to follow suit. As a model of this approach, it is exemplary, with contributions from poets, rock critics, literary scholars, playwrights and many others. This is a book with a wide appeal to anyone interested in Kerouac, the Beats and popular music, and one that will quickly become indispensable to scholars in these fields.'

James Peacock, Senior Lecturer in English and American Literatures, Keele University, UK, and co-editor of The Clash Takes on the World: Transnational Perspectives on the Only Band That Matters

'With his ear for language, accents, riffs, and affinity for the spontaneous improvisation of the highly trained musician, Kerouac's prose and verse dances with an undeniable musicality that has kept readers across the globe coming back to his works again and again. Many of these readers, as it turns out, have been musicians. This collection brings together a series of essays that, taken together, strive to convey the profound, long-lasting, and yet underappreciated, force of inspiration Kerouac represents to a half-century of recorded music.'

Jean-Christophe Cloutier, Assistant Professor of English, University of Pennsylvania, USA

'Following *Text and Drugs and Rock 'n' Roll: The Beats and Rock Culture* (2013), Simon Warner partners with Literary Executor of the Estate of Jack Kerouac, Jim Sampas, to go deeper into his exploration of the connections between the great figures of the Beat Generation and the music of the so-called "rock era". Interspersed with exclusive interviews of the likes of Lee Konitz, Graham Parker, Lester Bangs, and Allen Ginsberg, the 20 chapters are signed by an impressive array of journalists, music industry professionals, rock critics, writers, film makers and academics from all over the world. Addressing such issues as the influence of jazz on Kerouac's "spontaneous prose" style, the lineage between his "Beat bop prosody" and Patti Smith's "punk rock poetry", or his inspiring "the myth of the American road" in Bruce Springsteen's lyrics, they shed light on what appears to be a two-way relationship between popular music and the work of the author of *On the Road*. As Warner puts it: "If, for Kerouac, it was jazz that would have the principal impact, then it was rock on which the writer would have the main effect."'

Olivier Julien, Lecturer in the History and Musicology of Popular Music,
Paris-Sorbonne University, France

KEROUAC ON RECORD

A LITERARY SOUNDTRACK

Edited by Simon Warner and Jim Sampas

BLOOMSBURY ACADEMIC
LONDON • NEW YORK • OXFORD • NEW DELHI • SYDNEY

BLOOMSBURY ACADEMIC
Bloomsbury Publishing Inc
1385 Broadway, New York, NY 10018, USA

BLOOMSBURY, BLOOMSBURY ACADEMIC and the Diana logo are trademarks
of Bloomsbury Publishing Plc

First published in the United States of America 2018

A catalog record for this book is available from the Library of Congress.

ISBN: HB: 978-1-5013-2334-8
       ePDF: 978-1-5013-2336-2
       eBook: 978-1-5013-2337-9

Typeset by RefineCatch Limited, Bungay, Suffolk
Printed and bound in the United States of America

To find out more about our authors and books visit www.bloomsbury.com
and sign up for our newsletters.

CONTENTS

Contents

ACKNOWLEDGEMENTS

Simon Warner would like to thank the following for their input to and support on this project: my wife Jayne Sheridan; Charlotte Heslop for her invaluable editorial assistance and crucial work on the index; Jed Skinner for transcription help; Dave Moore for frequent advice; all contributors for their submissions and particular appreciation to those interview subjects featured in the book; my co-editor Jim Sampas; and members of the wider academic community – both those involved in Popular Music Studies and Beat Studies (with special reference to the European Beat Studies Network) – for their continued efforts to open up new and interesting areas of enquiry, particularly that place where popular music and Beat literature intersect.

Jim Sampas would like to thank: my co-editor Simon Warner for his exceptional work and dedication to this project; each of the incredibly talented and accomplished contributors to this book; Paul Marion and David Greenberg for their great guidance and advice; Jerry Cimino, David Stanford and Mark Bliesener for their steadfast enthusiasm and encouragement; and all the heirs of Jack Kerouac for their support of the film and album projects over the years. I also want to thank my daughters, Gemma and Chloe, for their endless inspiration.

The co-editors would also like to pay due credit to the New York team at publishers Bloomsbury for their attention and guidance on this journey – Ally Jane Grossan, who initially commissioned this title, and her successor as Music editor Leah Babb-Rosenfeld, who has continued to support us, plus those dedicated assistants Michelle Chen, Susan Krogulski and Katherine De Chant who also helped in getting this project over the line. In addition, much appreciation to Giles Herman in Bloomsbury's London office and to Merv Honeywood and Ronnie Hanna of RefineCatch for their diligence and patience.

PERMISSIONS

FOREWORD

He was the leading light of the Beat Generation writers and the most dynamic author of his time, but Jack Kerouac also had a lifelong passion for music, particularly the mid-century jazz of New York City, the development of which he witnessed first-hand during the 1940s and 1950s with Charlie Parker, Dizzy Gillespie and Thelonious Monk to the fore.

The novelist, most famous for his 1957 book *On the Road*, admired the sounds of bebop and attempted to bring something of their original energy to his own writing, a torrent of semi-autobiographical stories he published between 1950 and his early death in 1969.

Yet he was also drawn to American popular music of many varieties – from the blues to Broadway ballads – and, when he came to record albums under his own name, he married his unique spoken word style with some of the most talented musicians on the scene.

Kerouac's musical legacy goes well beyond the studio recordings he made himself: his influence infused generations of music makers who followed in his wake – from singer-songwriters to rock bands. Some of the greatest transatlantic names – Bob Dylan and the Grateful Dead, Van Morrison and David Bowie, Janis Joplin and Tom Waits, Sonic Youth and Death Cab for Cutie, and many more – have credited Kerouac's impact on their output.

In *Kerouac on Record*, we consider how the writer brought his passion for jazz to his prose and poetry and to his own record releases, the ways his legacy has been sustained by numerous more recent musical talents, those album tributes that have kept his memory alive and the scores that have featured in cinematic adaptations of the adventures he brought to the printed page.

INTRODUCTION
Simon Warner

We'd stay up twenty-four hours drinking cup after cup of black coffee, playing record after record of Wardell Gray, Lester Young, Dexter Gordon, Willis Jackson, Lennie Tristano and all the rest, talking madly about that holy new feeling out there in the streets.

Kerouac, 1994a, pp. 47–8

This collection explores the rich association between literature and music which exists so clearly in that terrain carved out by the novelist Jack Kerouac, an American writer who lived a relatively short but intense life, much of it infused by the sound of songs, listening to and vocalizing with records at home and in others' apartments, the playing of and accompaniment by instruments at parties, engagement with live performances in bars, clubs and theatres and the pleasure of hearing new hits on the radio, in cars on road trips, on jukeboxes, in cafes and restaurants, the riffs and solos of jazz and the ballads of Broadway and Hollywood, the melodies and lyrics of blues and country. These multiple sources provided a potent soundtrack to this prolific observer of the US in all its varied character – urban and rural, the plains and the mountains, the seas and the forests. This book endeavours to illustrate those musical connections he made throughout his 47 years, but also extrapolate them beyond his life. For if Kerouac was so influenced by the many kinds of musical experience he enjoyed himself, here was a writer who would also influence several generations who followed in his wake, popular musical artists who found in his stories, his adventures, his poetry, from the mid-1960s to the end of the century and beyond, a pulse of inspiration so powerful that they could not help but bring some of his spirit, some of his craft, to the art they themselves created.

If, for Kerouac, it was jazz that would have the principal impact, then it was rock on which the writer would have the main effect. In this book we will pay most attention to the way recorded materials developed from these interactions. These examples can be categorized in various ways: albums that Kerouac recorded himself, two emerging from his close relationship to jazz, one centred on a medium we would now call spoken word; albums that are actual tributes to the novelist – either creations by specific bands or compilations featuring various acts; soundtracks to films and documentaries that have been based on Kerouac's work – from *Pull My Daisy* in 1959 to *Big Sur* in 2013; and work on record which displays a sense of association with themes expressed in his literary imagination – compositions and compilations that appear to rise from, even pay homage to, the creative aspirations, the cross-country odysseys and the bohemian lifestyle that the *On the Road* author pursued between the early 1940s and the end of the 1960s.

Alongside these descriptions and dissections, we will encounter the symbolic power of music to writer, and the emblematic inspiration of writer to music. Jazz, particularly in the 1940s as bebop commenced its artistic rise, became a potent symbol of rebellion to white men – and some women – in the US, individuals who wanted to shake off the dust of the conventional mainstream and experience the excitement and danger of life on the urban edges. Bop – its clubs, its instrumentalists – represented an ideal of outsiderdom when America was experiencing the post-war confusions of race and politics. In this thrilling, marginalized milieu, it was possible for those rejecting the narrow confines of expected social and economic existence to experience something wilder, something perhaps even dangerous, particularly when drugs of various kinds became part of this semi-hidden enclave. Out of this allegiance to the outlying fringes would emerge subcultures like the Beats. For rock musicians, from the mid-1960s particularly, as that platform of expression began to extend its visions, its horizons, beyond the moon-in-June simplicities of the singles charts and mere commercial motivation or the visceral rhythms of dance, Kerouac's ideas and ideology, his unique imaginative impulse, provided a model for music-makers who wanted to escape the formulaic straitjacket of love's vicissitudes, framed in three minutes of plastic, and, further, transcend the constrictions of celebrity and show business, rejecting the standard pop star tropes of the day for those of the thinking and engaged artist.[1] In this transformation they attempted to make art that commented not just on the romantic threads of life but also on social and political ones and they found in this writer's words – and those of his other Beat associates – a template on which they could build. Thus, talents as diverse as Bob Dylan, the Fugs and the Grateful Dead, the Doors and Van Morrison, Jethro Tull and David Bowie, made sometimes elusive, occasionally even explicit, references to this writing world as they concocted their experimental lyrics and sounds during a particularly productive decade. Nor were those influences dispelled once, in the 1970s and 1980s, punk and new wave, indie and grunge came along, with the Clash's Joe Strummer, Sonic Youth's Thurston Moore and Lee Ranaldo, REM's Michael Stipe and Pearl Jam's Eddie Vedder to the fore, as others continued to fly that identifying flag.

There has been a gradually growing body of writing investigating these genre-breaking connections in recent times. To identify a selection of these, jazz and Kerouac has been addressed in books by Roy Carr et al. (1987), Stephen Ronan (1996), Lewis MacAdams (2002), John Leland (2004 and 2007) and Nancy M. Grace (2007), articles by Jim Burns (1993), Brian Hassett (1999), John Swenson (1999), Douglas Malcolm (2004), Larry Kart (2004) and Michael Hrebeniak (2017), and Sam Charters' 1982 address at the Naropa Institute on 'Jack Kerouac's jazz'.[2] Rock and Kerouac has been more tentatively approached, but some authors have begun to explore this relationship, too. Dave Perry (1990), Ronan (1996), Steve Turner (1996), Holly George-Warren

(1999), John Leland (2004), Laurence Coupe (2007), Simon Warner (2013) and Brian Hassett (2015) are among those who have started to analyse this Beat/rock entwining.

Kerouac on Record will engage further still with these musico-literary overlaps, these intertextual and trans-generational extensions, these multi-generic instances, these intriguing disruptions to long-standing understandings that assumed a natural divide between high and low culture where literature and popular music were barely nodding acquaintances, in a number of ways and via a range of different voices. Kerouac and his fellow travellers – the so-called Beat Generation, christened in a Manhattan conversation he had in 1948 with John Clellon Holmes, the writer who would publish the first recognized Beat novel, *Go*, in 1952 – were more than happy to straddle the worlds of the literary and musical, particularly the area of jazz, an especially fertile sector at a time when racial tensions remained high and music associated with black artists was regarded with caution, if not downright fear, its earthy sensuality often regarded as subversive and threatening. The Beats enjoyed the tensions this implied: in the black American life they perceived possibilities unavailable to white Americans and sought experiences in the company of those at the ethnic margins. As Kerouac famously wrote in *On the Road*:

> At lilac evening I walked with every muscle aching among the lights of 27th and Welton in the Denver coloured section, wishing I were a Negro, feeling that the best the white world had offered was not enough ecstasy for me, not enough life, joy, kicks, darkness, music, not enough night.
>
> 1972, p. 169

By straying from the accepted path, the Beats marked themselves as outsiders to the mainstream but also, by their actions, early integrationists, progressive souls to a small minority but irresponsible transgressors to many,[3] a decade or so before the Civil Rights movement began its earnest and organized quest to dispel the deep-held reservations of the white population that the granting of equal status to those of different skin colour in society might be fatal to the stability of the national community, still profoundly separated by the dictates of race, to a greater or lesser degree, across all the states.

Just as Kerouac and the Beats set out to disrupt norms – whether literary, cultural, social or racial – this collection will perhaps challenge some pedagogic ones. It will be eclectic in its enquiry, not only drawing on academic analysis but also journalistic readings; involving cultural historians and novelists, lyricists and playwrights; incorporating input from critics, broadcasters and biographers; showcasing recollections from musicians and producers; featuring essays on various phases in this panoramic story, including chapters focusing on key individuals but also on important genres; embracing conversational exchanges and interviews with significant figures attached to the scene but also with notable authors who have written about this world, that productive intersection of the fictional and the poetic with the realm of the musical. It will, indeed, even feature poems that reflect on that association, a piece of intertextuality actually commenting on that intertextuality.

The transatlantic, indeed the global, academy has been quite slow to recognize that there are cultural practices of importance which lie outside the traditional architecture of elite art, an issue with which that Anglo-American quality journalism has been comfortable for rather longer. But as we canter deep into the second decade of the post-millennium century, those heavily-defended precepts in the halls of learning have been considerably undermined. In the years since the Second World War, there has been a gradual liberalization in the lecture room, and vistas have broadened. The mass media, a pejorative term still when applied by the educated establishment even as recently as the middle of the last century, finally prised open the well-guarded door of academe, when, first film from around the 1960s, then radio and television in the 1970s, then an overarching discipline of media or communication studies, tentatively began to acquire a recognized study status that broke the older rules of engagement. Within these mass produced and massed consumed formats, it was eventually deemed that they possessed worthwhile, even complex, meanings transcending concepts of mere transient entertainment. Yet even within this more liberal learning atmosphere, there were anomalies.

The writings of the Beat Generation, initially emerging for public consumption in the 1950s,[4] gained a wide readership but still generated a deep suspicion within many of the ivory towered literary departments of the following 30 or so years. Whether for reasons of style, intent, language, inclusion of drug use or rejection of traditional mores, there was a reluctance to regard this literary subset as serious or substantial, perhaps too shocking on the one hand but maybe too accessible or populist, or even popular, on the other. Popular music – and by that I use the broad umbrella embracing rock, pop and folk, blues and country, soul, hip hop and reggae, and multifarious other genres, including even jazz – also had a slow and difficult gestation in terms of its earning serious scholarly consideration. It took until the end of the 1980s in the UK, and longer elsewhere, for dedicated degree programmes focusing upon the historical, cultural and sociological significance of these musical developments to appear within universities, a trend initially prompted, I do believe, by the output of new waves of singers, songwriters and groups, particularly from the mid-1960s, which clearly had a gravitas, a gathering of insights, that went beyond the trivial and ephemeral confines of adolescent life, teen love and loss, and strayed into territory once assumed to be the exclusive domain of the dons and the policymakers – politics, culture and society.

The maturity of engagement between popular song and an era of high drama – the threat that Cold War would ignite into something more ferocious, Civil Rights demands and anti-war demonstrations, headline-grabbing assassinations to the emergence of fervent calls for notions of individual identity, from gender to sexuality and ethnicity, to be properly regarded, student attacks on the accepted educational canon and the reorientating effects of narcotic stimulation – sowed the seeds that would blossom in university courses and campus classes around 20 years later. In other words, it was eventually realized that to seriously study the times, you also had to understand the sounds. If important sub-fields of study, like punk and metal, hip hop and grunge, for instance, would follow in time, it is hard to see how these specialized foci could have existed without the unique circumstances engendered by the 1960s and its cataclysmic and globally influential musico-political interaction.

I do not think it is any coincidence that the tentative acceptance of popular music as a substantial thread of expression and creativity – solidified in the study terrain of Popular Music Studies – happened within a similar timeframe to the rather grudging agreement that Beat literature possessed worth and value, potential and impact, beyond the confines of the courts of censorship,[5] characterised in the consolidation of Beat Studies.[6] In fact, although Kerouac found nothing agreeable about the 1960s revolution, particularly not its aggressive campaigning against the Vietnam War, the elision of rock as a force of protest with Beat as a platform of resistance provides a fascinating lens for our deeper understanding of the last third of an increasingly open-minded, if still somewhat chaotic, last century. In Allen Ginsberg, who took a quite alternative view of that volatile era of demonstration and psychedelia to his long-time friend, many of the most impressive of the new rock stars identified their guru (most felt the same, too, about Kerouac, and his vision of a freewheeling America where the individual could pursue his, maybe possibly her, destiny, even if the often idolized author had by now abandoned such wide-eyed, near childlike, optimism, embodied in the vivid descriptions of his travels); in Dylan, the Beatles, the Grateful Dead, the Doors and later others, Beat poets – including Michael McClure, Lawrence Ferlinghetti, Gary Snyder, Gregory Corso and Ginsberg, naturally – perceived a fresh generation of energetic, inventive mavericks ready to sound the same trumpets of rebellion that the versifiers had initially played with such discordant majesty some ten years before, challenging the status quo to change. How do we know this?

Let us share a few pertinent examples. Ginsberg befriended Dylan and McCartney, appeared on the Rolling Stones's 'We Love You' (1967) and Lennon's 'Give Peace a Chance' (1969) and later became an ally of the latter in his Green Card fight in the early 1970s; Ginsberg, Ferlinghetti and a multitude of Bay Area Beats welcomed Dylan to San Francisco and City Lights bookstore, the so-called 'Last Gathering of the Beats', during the difficult touring months following his controversial electric set at Newport, in December 1965; Neal Cassady was part of the Dead entourage and members of that Haight-Ashbury band paid Herbert Huncke's Chelsea Hotel rent in later years; McClure collaborated with Jim Morrison; McCartney organized recording facilities for Burroughs in mid-60s London and, with his fellow Beatles, chose the writer as a celebrated face to feature on the cover of *Sgt Pepper's Lonely Hearts Club Band*; Ginsberg, McClure, Ferlinghetti, Snyder and Lenore Kandel joined the Human Be-In cast in January 1967 in a Golden Gate Park demonstration against the war in Vietnam when the stage was shared with the acid rock battalions of the Grateful Dead, Jefferson Airplane, Quicksilver Messenger Service, Country Joe and the Fish among others; and McClure and Ferlinghetti were on the bill when the Band played their final gig at Winterland in San Francisco, a commemoration that became Martin Scorsese's movie *The Last Waltz* in 1978. Kerouac is one of the few absentees – and a very notable one – from this parade of alliances. It would take until November 1975, when Ginsberg and Dylan, a long-time fan, visited the writer's grave as part of the Rolling Thunder Revue, for this particular Beat legend to be, posthumously, the focus of a high-profile rock celebration. Yet, as this book in many of its chapters will show, popular musicians of many stripes would ensure the Kerouac name would ultimately possess, we might argue, the greatest legacy value of all.

So, the evidence is there: once academicians were ready to make genuine sense of the huge stories of that pivotal period, they realized they could not be interpreted without regarding the power of Beat writing and an increasingly literate rock music as crucial components in this complex network of disturbed power relations between the mid-1950s and on to the present day. As we have more than hinted, Kerouac, who came of age as a writer in the 1950s, would be an unwilling participant in the activities that the following decade generated, with a new version of the politically aware rock as its ubiquitous soundtrack. But if the 1960s was a period of extraordinary change, the man who had penned *On the Road*, to some positive reviews but also, perhaps more importantly, to the acclaim of a rising generation of mostly young men, who found in its pages a blueprint to challenge the stifling orthodoxies of that era when Eisenhower's America enjoyed unequalled economic benefits but lived in the constant shadow of possible nuclear annihilation, regarded the US, in the dozen years after the appearance of his signature text, as a worrying place indeed.

These waves of baby boomers, including those very folk and rock musicians who would help to orchestrate and solidify the new vision from their appearances at the March on Washington, in 1963, to the festival of Woodstock, in 1969, and many places in between and beyond, saw in the pages of his attention-grabbing books[7] the possibilities of freedom through travel, through adventure, through music, sexual escapades, religious quests and drug experiences, too. Yet Kerouac believed his idealized account of two young men – Sal Paradise, his own alter ego, and Dean Moriarty, a thinly-veiled portrait of the real-life Neal Cassady, whom he had first met 1946 – traversing his homeland, his continent, in the late 1940s, seeking meaning, spiritual understanding and a father figure in the open West, was no conceivable excuse for the revolutionary behaviour that crackled across the US nation in what we might call the long 1960s. From Greensboro in 1960 to Wounded Knee in 1973,[8] and on regular occasion in those intervening years and since that seminal time, rebels and demonstrators have laid the inspiration for their resistant strategies at the door of the Beats, very often *On the Road* itself.

William Burroughs, a principal and founding Beat protagonist, may have stated of Kerouac that 'Woodstock rises from his pages' (2010, p. 324), and Ed Sanders, one of the key players in the counterculture as poet/musician in the Fugs, might have identified Kerouac – in front of the writer himself on live television in 1968[9] – as a catalyst for his own personal rebellion against the US establishment, but also for the hippy nation that became such an incandescent symbol in the later 1960s. However, the man who conceived the Duluoz Legend – the overarching Proustian umbrella he devised for the autobiographical tales recounting fictional retellings of his picaresque life – had no time for such assertions or claims. He believed that LSD, that extraordinary chemical compound which promised mind-expanding visions and even personal revelation, was a Soviet plot to sabotage America, an intriguing turn of the tables considering that the Beats had been marked by some commentators in the later 1950s as little more than unwashed, workshy commies, and possibly entryists, operating on behalf of the feared Russian regime.

The term beatnik, conceived by *San Francisco Chronicle* journalist Herb Caen in 1958, was a reflection of this paranoia. As the USSR launched Sputnik, a radio satellite, into space late the previous year, with the implication that the US could now be spied on from up above, Caen added the Russian suffix '-nik' to Beat to stress, in a jokey fashion the journalist later claimed, this guilt by association. But the satirical nickname well and truly stuck and Kerouac spent much of the time subsequently trying to disassociate himself from this particular allusion, even going as far as writing articles that acknowledged that Beat had various connotations but one he particularly wanted to stress was strictly religious: beatitude and the beatific, or behaviour linked to saintliness, a deep-seated reflection on the writer's lifelong, and almost unflinching, commitment to the Roman Catholic creed.[10] Connecting Beat to the good works of Rome may have been seen as a means to deflect some of the harsher criticisms he and his writing allies were by now attracting. When he made his famous appearance on *The Steve Allen Show* in 1959, he strove to maintain this charm offensive. His host asked him what Beat meant. 'Sympathetic,' he replied, a long way from the 'beat up', 'beat down' and 'beaten' suggestions that had been in mind when the street hustler and junkie Herbert Huncke introduced Kerouac, Ginsberg and Burroughs to this term in the all-night, neon cauldron of Times Square around 1944.

For Kerouac, as we have already outlined, this volatile state of affairs that gripped the US, and indeed much of the West, during 1960s was not going to meet his approval. By then, his alcoholism had reached a point of no return and this was certainly a factor in his disgruntled demeanour towards events and even to former close friends, like Ginsberg and Cassady. The latter inevitably became identified with the Moriarty persona that Kerouac had ascribed to him on the page in *On the Road*, and, in the wake of the novel's bestselling stature and widespread publicity, drew the negative attention forces of law and order leading to his jailing after undercover police officers sold him marijuana in an act of entrapment in 1958. Although this seriously damaged their friendship, Cassady bounced back from his incarceration, befriending a younger novelist, the West Coast-based Ken Kesey, who had, in 1962, published an acclaimed work of fiction entitled *One Flew over the Cuckoo's Nest*. In the wake of its critical and financial success, Kesey, who had been part of a an LSD test programme as a university student at the end of the 1950s, decided to spread the news about this psychedelic wonderdrug to a largely unsuspecting American public in a series of so-called Acid Tests from 1964 onwards. Kesey employed Cassady, in a move that had more than a symbolic ring to it,[11] to drive the school bus, adapted and floridly decorated, that would deliver the writer and his clan of fellow travellers – friends, artists, musicians – around the country, distributing their lysergic cargo to townspeople across the breadth of the nation, an audacious but not illegal jamboree as the drug was only banned in the US in 1966.

On this initial trek, Kesey and Cassidy and their crew – the so-called Merry Pranksters – invited Kerouac to Manhattan as that drug-fuelled odyssey hit the East Coast and, although the older novelist, by now living out of the city on Long Island, did turn out to meet this harlequin gang, Kerouac's suspicion of the crowd of protesters, the proto-hippies who would preface the gathering the tens of thousands of freaks and flower children in San Francisco and across the US from around 1966, was already deep-seated. Kerouac's conspiracy concerns, in respect of LSD, continued to invoke the spectre of the 1950s when the Soviets' undermining of the US was regarded as a very distinct possibility, a perception far from dispelled as the next decade began, with the erection of the Berlin Wall in 1961, the Cuban Missile Crisis of 1962 and growing tension in South-East Asia, which would quite quickly see an ideological struggle between communism and capitalism played out militarily in the jungles and paddy fields of Vietnam, as matters escalated from 1964. This conjunction of impending war, psychedelic mischief-making and the onset of alcohol reliance turned Kerouac into a scathing critic of this carnivalesque subcultural regime and the rest of the decade would see the *On the Road* creator play out a deep and dark psychodrama in which figures like Cassady and certainly Ginsberg – a vocal figurehead of the anti-war movement – would be demonized by their one-time soulmate. His conservative instincts roused, his Republican tendencies confirmed, his pro-war position entrenched, Kerouac even took his mother's anti-Semitic cue, attacking Ginsberg's Jewish affiliation in a way that characterized the fading writer's disturbed and deranged condition as he hurtled towards a drink-soaked death, in October 1969 in Florida, before his burial in the cemetery of his childhood home in Lowell.

Kerouac and jazz

Bop began with jazz but one afternoon somewhere on a sidewalk maybe 1939, 1940, Dizzy Gillespie or Charley [sic] Parker or Thelonious Monk was walking down past a men's clothing store on 42nd Street or South Main in LA and from the loudspeaker they suddenly heard a wild impossible mistake in jazz that could only have been heard inside their own imaginary head, and that is a new art. Bop.

Kerouac, 1994b, p. 113

Kerouac's real interest in jazz was cultivated after he left Lowell to head to New York City on a football scholarship, with Columbia University awaiting him, in 1939. On the cusp of a European war that would eventually suck him, his Manhattan friends and all-America into its drama in various ways, he would undertake a year of preparatory study at a prestigious private institution called Horace Mann School for Boys. There he would meet more knowledgeable aficionados of this vibrant musical form, like Seymour Wyse (see Moore, 1986, pp. 79–88). Together, they attended shows by musicians up and down the isle, at venues such as the Apollo and the Savoy.

With his friends, Kerouac would encounter jazz players at the height of their powers, meet and talk to some, even conduct interviews and write about those musicians – Count Basie and Glenn Miller, for example – for his school magazine, a clear sign that even from his late teens there was going to be a crossover between this musical style and a distinctive writing voice that was developing in such an interesting way.

Not only was the young Kerouac beginning to express himself through reportage and fiction but, intriguingly, he was also in the city where jazz music was also about to undergo some extraordinary changes. The swing bands, which had become dominant by the end of the 1930s, with many of these ensembles led by white musicians, faced a fresh creative challenge. At the start of the 1940s, black musicians, who had been at the heart of the birth of this musical form a quarter of a century or more before in the city of New Orleans, endeavoured to reassert control once again over this fluid métier. The ubiquitous swing sound was about to be tested by a quite different approach to jazz music-making – bebop, often shortened to simply bop.

Some of the most talented players of the New York scene – such as saxophonist Charlie Parker, trumpeter Dizzy Gillespie, pianist Thelonious Monk and drummer Kenny Clarke – began to formulate a new musical language that resisted the predictable dance rhythms of big band swing and, instead, within a small group format, extemporized on structures and scales that were far too complex to dance to but rather encouraged a thinking audience to test their cerebral reflexes in the hothouse clubs in Harlem and, in time, on 52nd Street.

At Minton's Playhouse, founded in 1938 at 118th Street, this novel and dynamic musical form, testing for players and listeners, began to make its mark. Bebop confused existing jazz fans, triggering fierce debate in the pages of magazines like *Down Beat* and *Metronome* (see Gendron, 2002, pp. 150–1), but attracted new waves of followers who were tired of the bland predictability of swing tempos. The location of the theatre made it an obvious draw to young black audiences, but living not far away in an apartment on the edge of the ghetto district were Kerouac and his largely Ivy League clique, a motley gathering of would-be writers who, by the mid-1940s, were ambitious and indeed confident enough to have developed a so-called 'New Vision', a manifesto that would proclaim radical approaches to making art, writing prose and penning poetry, a gospel that preached anti-establishment positions and unconventional solutions to the creative process. They identified 'uncensored self-expression' as the seed of creativity, looked to expand artistic consciousness 'by non-rational means' and believed that art superseded 'the dictates of conventional morality' (see Watson, 1995, p. 40).

For Kerouac and his closest allies – the more senior figure, Harvard graduate Burroughs, and their younger protégé, Columbia undergraduate Ginsberg, among others – the city of New York, by now caught up in the global crisis of war but filled with a near reckless, almost existential, urge for pleasure and gratification, from its upper echelons to its febrile street community, provided an extraordinary laboratory for these uncompromising early experiments in life and literature to be played out.

In the abstract and frenetic stylings of the new bebop, there appeared to be a fragmented mirror to the kind of energies that Kerouac and co. were bringing to their subterranean existences. The fact that drugs – as marijuana gave way to harder addictions like heroin for so many of the leading instrumentalists – were part of the scene provided a further parallel, as these white dropouts from conventional society also saw in narcotics a potent emblem of contumacy, a disorientating means to add stimulation and invention to their lives and their nascent experiences, in conversation and on paper.

In time, for a writer like Kerouac, however, jazz would become more than just a symbolic force. He would aim, particularly in his 1950s output, to emulate the very rhythmic shapes, the actual syntax, of those ground-breaking and influential jazz stylists – like Parker, Lester Young, Lee Konitz – to whom he was so drawn. He speculated that his writing, built on his own original notions of 'spontaneous prose',[12] could be as thrilling and inspiring as the improvised solos of the musicians. And so this musical form became not just a source of content – often specific individuals and bands and named songs from the jazz world regularly appear in his novels and his poetry – but also a catalyst for a distinctive style of prose and verse. His passion for this scene is well conveyed in his essay 'The Beginning of Bop', which originally appeared in *Escapade* in April 1959, an entertaining, if imaginative and somewhat fanciful, retelling of the founding of that musical style.

This relationship between jazz and Kerouac's literary outpourings is very much the focus of the first section of this book. In Jim Burns's opening chapter, this long established poet, editor and commentator, on matters both Beat and musical, explores the very evidence we find of jazz in the author's novels – instrumentalists and performers from George Shearing and Slim Gaillard in *On the Road* to Charlie Parker in *The Subterraneans* and many more beside, who bring a verve and verisimilitude to the action of many of the novels. Then we include that classic Kerouac essay on how the musical seeds were sown to flourish as the sounds of his beloved bebop.

Next, Larry Beckett, poet and rock lyricist, examines Kerouac's own jazz poetry from *San Francisco Blues* to *Book of Haikus*, then the UK-based Canadian Marian Jago explores Kerouac's relationship to the work of Lee Konitz, a saxophonist whom the writer held in high regard and saw as a key catalyst in his construction of his spontaneous prose theory. The veteran Konitz is also interviewed about this connection.

To follow, US academic and poet Jonah Raskin explores the history, content and context of Kerouac's own three key album releases, while eminent scholar-critic of Beat A. Robert Lee pursues another body of significant poetic output, *Mexico City Blues*, a cycle of verses drawing quite deliberately on the intertextuality of poetry and jazz, specifically the notion that instrumental solos can be emulated through poetic passages.

We proceed with an interview with jazz musician, cinematic and symphonic composer David Amram, Kerouac's friend and collaborator, the subject of a conversation with countercultural historian Pat Thomas. Finally in this section, Michael J. Prince, the Norway-based American academic, examines the place of jazz and its meanings in the significantly reconstituted 1960 film version of *The Subterraneans*.

Kerouac and rock

> Then we sailed down into the Irish Sea, laid anchor off Belfast, waited there for some British convoy boats, and crossed the Irish Sea that afternoon and night straight for Liverpool. 1943. The year the Beatles were born there, ha ha ha.
>
> Kerouac, 1982, p. 204

Although Kerouac wrote an essay celebrating the greatest rock 'n' roll icon and even considered the possibility of calling *On the Road*, *Rock and Roll Road* instead (Brinkley, 1999, p. 115), there is no real evidence that rock music had a direct bearing or impact on the writer, even if he does briefly namecheck the Beatles in his late book *Vanity of Duluoz* (1968). In 1957, screen icons James Dean and Marlon Brando who had attracted accolades for their performances in movies aimed at young adult and late adolescent audiences – filmic representations of a rebellious spirit chimed with a new age and assurance of the increasingly visible and economically assertive teenager – were praised by Kerouac in a piece called 'America's new Trinity of love: Dean, Brando, Presley', narrated by the alternative comic Richard Lewis on the 1997 tribute collection *Kicks Joy Darkness*.

Although, in this brief piece, Kerouac spoke of a hero already dead – James Dean, killed in a car crash in 1955 – and touches upon Presley only tenuously, he does talk of 'three young men of exceptional masculine beauty', adding '[n]ow the new American hero ... is the image of compassion in itself', so he found clear sympathy with these new developments. It is perhaps worth adding, too, that if his most discussed title had indeed been *Rock and Roll Road*, it would have been, for sure, an anachronistic choice, as the pleasures and travails of the journey recounted had been played out some years before rock'n'roll was first used to describe a new brand of music, a hybrid of blues and country, on a Cleveland radio station around 1951, as Alan Freed, the seminal if later discredited DJ,[13] borrowed a black euphemism for the sex act and applied it to an energetic hybrid form of white-tinged rhythm and blues.

This apparent disconnection between the writer and the musical style of rock'n'roll – quickly abbreviated to rock even from its early eruption in the mid-1950s – has been no discouragement to later musicians flying the banner of rock and linking their output with Kerouac and his influence on them. Although it would be the mid-1960s before rock cast off its role as mere good-time dance music, when it did, many of the most influential players felt comfortable in revealing the importance of literary inspiration, with Kerouac frequently identified as a writer who had shaped their songwriting, even their wider lives. As we will discover in this very volume, major creative figures in the field from Bob Dylan and Jerry Garcia to Janis Joplin, Jim Morrison and Tom Waits to Ryan Adams and Death Cab for Cutie have found the *On the Road* author a totemic figure in their artistic and personal development. As Steve Turner wrote, 'One of the achievements of Kerouac and his Beat contemporaries was in making literature, whether spoken or written, as "sexy" as movies, jazz and rock 'n' roll' (1996, p. 19).

Still others carry traces of the Kerouac aura – John Cale, Joni Mitchell, the Incredible String Band, Warren Zevon, Patti Smith, Bruce Springsteen, Rickie Lee Jones, 10,000 Maniacs, Steven Tyler, Morphine, Uncle Tupelo, Jeff Buckley, the Raveonettes, the Hold Steady, the Gaslight Anthem and Hurray for the Riff Raff – in the work they have produced. The late, great David Bowie said that *On the Road* 'showed me I didn't have to stay in Bromley' (Turner, 1996, p. 21), the suburban London borough of his youth. Many too have recorded material that pays tribute to the author – from Ramblin' Jack Elliott to Mark Murphy, King Crimson to Ulf Lundell and the Waterboys – and literally hundreds of songs (see the voluminous listing in Appendix V) mention Kerouac in their titles or their lyrics. Leading young actors – Johnny Depp, Matt Dillon and Keanu Reeves – at the height of their credibility in the 1990s pinned their colours to the Kerouac mast. And the trail of acknowledgement continues. The young British band the 1975, much touted in their homeland and around the world at the present time, borrowed their name from a handwritten inscription in a Kerouac paperback that their lead singer Matty Healy picked up in a second-hand store.

It seems most unlikely that Kerouac would have been appreciative of this kind of near canonization, but he might have been pleasantly surprised. He would have been more taken aback, perhaps, when respected UK rock journalist Tony Parsons told readers of the *New Musical Express* (*NME*), at the height of the British punk explosion in 1977, in an article celebrating the novelist, 'Acknowledge your roots, kid – the counterculture starts here.' Yet cult authors and the independent spirit of the best rock music seem to share a cause in mind: making art on the fringes, often reflecting on the underbelly of life, relating to the renegades and rulebreakers rather than mainstream society. Kerouac did all of those things and, actually, at certain points in his erratic career almost achieved stadium status – when the reviews were almost hysterically good and the sales were capable of achieving a place on the bestseller charts – but his final years, his ugly decline and his premature death damaged his reputation and almost extinguished the kudos his golden years in the later 1950s had secured. But, if in the 25 or so years after his passing his work was little regarded and much fell out of print, there were several generations of intelligent songwriters and music makers who could not ignore his effect. Even when he was being little read, he was, paradoxically, still being sung about and listened to, not to mention being commemorated by music journalists on both sides of the Atlantic.

The mid-1990s would see him and all the members of the Beat Generation revivified, as a major nationwide touring exhibition of the US, 'Beat Culture and the New America, 1950–1965', helped to contextualize their achievement and influence, and, somewhat paradoxically, the deaths of Ginsberg and Burroughs in close succession in 1997 further regenerated interest in their lives and work and those of other novelists and poets who were part of the prolific circle, Kerouac, of course, included.

The essays that deal here with a sequence of significant rock bands and singer-songwriters consider those who were drawn to the writer during his lifetime, those who remained intrigued by him even during the more fallow years that followed his demise, and those who have discovered him in more recent times, the younger composers and lyricists who remain adherents of the Kerouac vision. It seems several generations of music-makers with aspirations beyond mere Top 40 acceptance have found in this writer, in the Beat ethos more generally, an authentic and authenticating source, a blueprint to rebel yes, but also a template on which to build a body of songs of substance, material that may still deal with human relations but which goes beyond the formulaic, adopting socially minded, political and spiritual positions that question the world as these artists find it, just as Kerouac and his clan of radical poets who preceded them did in the 1950s.

Journalist Michael Goldberg contributes a section on Bob Dylan, charting his Kerouac-like journey from his early college days in Minneapolis, on to New York and from folk to rock. Lowell-based writer Paul Marion offers a short, personal account of the aura surrounding Kerouac's grave, the visitors it has attracted, and still draws, to its stone. Canadian Brian Hassett, whose life of journeying has echoed that of his literary hero, contemplates the relationship of the Grateful Dead to the Kerouac legend. And Mark Bliesener, rock band manager and Denver resident, draws on local knowledge to portray the musical tastes of Kerouac's closest compadre Neal Cassady.

Playwright Jay Jeff Jones grapples with the brief and brilliant flame that was Jim Morrison, while British lecturer Peter Mills considers the enduring impact of Kerouac's writing on Van Morrison's work from his early days in Them right up to the present day. Journalist and Beat specialist Holly George-Warren describes an extraordinary exodus of Texan beatniks who headed west to California with Janis Joplin the star turn, while UK-based academic Douglas Field explores the unique manners of Tom Waits and his commitment to the Kerouac code.

Established US Beat expert Nancy M. Grace unravels the Kerouac strains in the output of Joni Mitchell, and fellow American scholar and Beat movement specialist Ronna Johnson pursues a similar course in relation to Patti Smith. Journalist and lecturer Simon A. Morrison engages with the influence that the writer has brought to

Bruce Springsteen's style and his musical content, while Japan-based American academic Matt Theado considers the ways in which country music has picked up and run with many of the themes that the novelist brought to the page. The highly reputable rock critic James Sullivan offers an account of the evidence in punk and new wave of the writer's sustained influence.

The final chapter, with rock in mind, revisits a sequence of tribute albums to Kerouac which have emerged in the last 20 years, a cycle of releases overseen by one of this book's co-editors, music and film producer Jim Sampas. He offers a personalized account of the creation of this gathering recordings, but also engages in conversation with his fellow co-editor Simon Warner to cast further light on the development and realization of this body of work: tributes, homages and also movie and documentary soundtracks that have been conceived and released over the previous two decades.

In the midst of these essays you will also find interviews with the Kerouac-influenced legend of rock criticism Richard Meltzer; a conversation with Jim DeRogatis, biographer of Lester Bangs, an acclaimed journalist much shaped by the novelist, by James Sullivan; an exchange between Allen Ginsberg and Pat Thomas, who also interrogates new wave survivor Graham Parker; and the sharing of thoughts between Tom Waits biographer Barney Hoskyns and Simon Warner. Further, two poems by Marc Zegans consider the relationship between rock music, the Beats and verse itself. To conclude, the appendices incorporate a new and comprehensive Kerouac discography compiled by independent Beat scholar Dave Moore; a detailed discographic overview by Jim Sampas of his own tribute productions; and an updated listing of those songs that mention or reference Kerouac and Cassady, overseen by Moore and Horst Spandler, alongside two classic Kerouac texts on his own writing method.

Notes

1. For example, both Bob Dylan and the Beatles appeared to pursue potentially career-damaging trajectories – the singer rejecting his folk fan base in his controversial electric set at Newport in summer 1965 and the group abandoning touring the following year – but each became all the more credible having made those huge artistic decisions in the face of commercial logic. Dylan was a committed fan of Kerouac and friend of Allen Ginsberg; McCartney first, then Lennon, were close to Ginsberg.

2. Sam Charters, 'Jack Kerouac's jazz', talk given at Naropa Institute, Boulder, CO, 26 July 1982, 25th anniversary of *On the Road* conference, the Allen Ginsberg Project, http://ginsbergblog.blogspot.co.uk/2014/08/sam-charters-jack-kerouacs-jazz-1-intro.html (accessed 17 March 2017).

3. Norman Mailer's essay 'The White Negro: Superficial Reflections on the Hipster', published in the Fall 1957 edition of *Dissent*, controversially explored the rise of a new phenomenon where young white men were attracted to the lifestyle and values of black men at the margins. It appeared almost simultaneously with Kerouac's *On the Road*, which was published that year in September. Note that the latter's description of his Denver visit has attracted criticism for over-romanticizing the condition of the black US community.

4. Kerouac's *The Town and the City*, his debut, appeared in 1950 but is not generally regarded as a Beat novel. Holmes's *Go* (1952), then Burroughs's *Junkie* (1953), Ginsberg's *Howl and Other Poems* (1956), *On the Road* and Burroughs's *Naked Lunch* (1959) might be regarded as landmark moments in this history.

5. Although Kerouac did not face the stress and strain of legal action over his writings, his two main colleagues, Allen Ginsberg and William Burroughs, did. Proceedings initiated in the US on obscenity grounds against the former's poem 'Howl', in 1957, and the latter's novel *Naked Lunch*, in 1965, brought widespread publicity to the Beat Generation circle but also prompted negative reactions and public criticism.

6. It is perhaps interesting to note the early convening of researchers in these areas. IASPM (the International Association for the Study of Popular Music) was launched in 1980; the BSA (the Beat Studies Association) was founded a little later in 2004; and EBSN (the European Beat Studies Network) was established in 2010.

7. After *On the Road*, numerous titles would follow in quick succession, among them *The Dharma Bums* (1958), *The Subterraneans* (1958), *Doctor Sax* (1959), *Maggie Cassidy* (1959), *Lonesome Traveller* (1960), *Big Sur* (1962) and *Desolation Angels* (1965).

8. At Greensboro in North Carolina, four young black Americans took places in the whites-only cafeteria of F. W. Woolworth as the non-violent struggle against racial inequality gained purchase. At Wounded Knee, in South Dakota, members of AIM (the American Indian Movement) seized and occupied the town in a rights dispute amid corruption claims, an incident which galvanized the Native American population in their wider protests. Terry H. Anderson's fine history, *The Movement and the Sixties* (1995), uses those very historical markers in his subtitle to delineate the range of his enquiry.

9. William F. Buckley Jr's talk show *Firing Line* featured a drunk Kerouac and an eloquent Sanders debating the hippy phenomenon in the 3 September broadcast. Academic Lewis Yablansky completed the line-up.

10 Although Kerouac took an important and substantial interest in Buddhism from the 1950s – experiences particularly recounted in *The Dharma Bums* (1958) and reflected in his adoption of the haiku as a verse form, his prose poems in *The Scripture of the Golden Eternity* (1960) and the extensive meditative notes of *Some of the Dharma* (1997) – he never abandoned an allegiance to Catholicism, a religious paradox that engaged the author into the 1960s and fed into his work.

11. Cassady's astounding feats of skill and endurance at the wheel of an automobile became an enduring motif of Kerouac's fictional account.

12. See Jack Kerouac, 'Essentials of Spontaneous Prose', Appendix I.

13. Freed faced payola charges – allegations he had been paid to play particular artists' records – at the end of his breakthrough decade which seriously damaged his career, though he remains an important figure in the history of rock'n'roll and subsequent popular music incarnations.

Bibliography

Anderson, Terry H., *The Movement and the Sixties: Protest in America from Greensboro to Wounded Knee*, New York: Oxford University Press, 1995.

Brinkley, Douglas, 'King of the road', in Holly George Warren (ed.), *The Rolling Stone Book of Beats*, London: Bloomsbury, 1999, pp. 109–22.

Burns, Jim, 'Jack Kerouac's jazz scene', *Transit* 3 (Summer 1993).

Burroughs, William, *Word Virus: The William Burroughs Reader*, London: Fourth Estate, 2010.

Coolidge, Clark, *Now It's Jazz: Writings on Kerouac & the Sounds*, Albuquerque, NM: Living Batch Press, 1999.

Carr, Roy, Brian Case and Fred Dellar, *The Hip: Hipsters, Jazz and the Beat Generation*, London: Faber, 1987.

Coupe, Laurence, *Beat Sound, Beat Vision: The Beat Spirit and Popular Song*, Manchester: Manchester University Press, 2007.

Farrell, James J., 'The Beat of personalism', in James J. Farrell, *The Spirit of the Sixties*, London: Routledge, 1997, pp. 51–80.

Gendron, Bernard, *Between Montmartre and the Mudd Club: Popular Music and the Avant Garde*, Chicago: University of Chicago Press, 2002.

George-Warren, Holly (ed.), *The Rolling Stone Book of the Beats*, London: Bloomsbury, 1999.

Grace, Nancy M., *Jack Kerouac and the Literary Imagination*, New York: Palgrave-Macmillan, 2007.

Hassett, Brian, 'Abstract Expression: From Bird to Brando', in Holly George-Warren (ed.), *The Rolling Stone Book of the Beats*, London: Bloomsbury, 1999, pp. 22–6.

Hassett, Brian, *The Hitchhiker's Guide to Jack Kerouac*, n.p.: Gets Things Done Publishing, 2015.

Hrebeniak, Michael, 'Jazz and the Beat Generation', in Steven Belletto (ed.), *The Cambridge Companion to The Beats*, New York: Cambridge University Press, 2017, pp. 250–64.

Kart, Larry, 'Jazz and Jack Kerouac', in *Jazz in Search of Itself*, New Haven, CT: Yale University Press, 2004, pp. 330–5.

Kerouac, Jack, *On the Road*, Harmondsworth: Penguin, 1972 (1957).

Kerouac, Jack, 'Aftermath: The philosophy of the Beat Generation', in *Good Blonde & Others*, San Francisco: Grey Fox Press, 1994a; *Esquire*, March 1958.

Kerouac, Jack, 'The Beginning of Bop', in *Good Blonde & Others*, San Francisco: Grey Fox Press, 1994b, *Escapade*, April 1959.

Kerouac, Jack, *The Vanity of Duluoz: An Adventurous Education, 1935–1946*, London: Penguin, 1982.

Leland, John, *Hip: The History*, New York: Ecco, 2004.

Leland, John, *Why Kerouac Matters: The Lessons of On the Road*, New York: Viking, 2007.

MacAdams, Lewis, *Birth of the Cool: Beat, Bebop & the American Avant Garde*, London: Scribner, 2002.

Mailer, Norman, 'The White Negro', in Gene Feldman and Max Gartenberg (eds), *Protest: The Beat Generation and the Angry Young Men*, London: Panther, 1960, pp. 288–306.

McNally, Dennis, *Desolate Angel: Jack Kerouac, the Beat Generation and America*, Cambridge, MA: Da Capo Press, 2003.

Malcolm, Douglas, '"Jazz America": Jazz and African American culture in Jack Kerouac's *On the Road*', in Harold Bloom (ed.), *Jack Kerouac's On the Road*, Philadelphia: Chelsea House, 2004, pp. 93–114.

Monson, Ingrid, 'The problem with white hipness: Race, gender, and cultural conceptions in jazz historical discourse', *Journal of American Musicological Society* 18, no. 3 (Fall 1995): 396–422.

Moore, Dave, '"My Really Best Friend and collaborator . . ." an interview with Seymour Wyse', in John Montgomery (ed.), *Kerouac at the "Wild Boar" & Other Skirmishes*, San Anselmo, CA: Fels & Firn Press, 1986, pp. 79–88.

Nicosia, Gerald, 'Kerouac as musican: Notes and interpretations of *Readings by Jack Kerouac on the Beat Generation*', booklet essay, *The Jack Kerouac Collection*, Rhino Records, 1990.

Parsons, Tony, 'The legend of Jack Kerouac, Beat chronicler supreme', *NME*, 8 January 1977.

Perry, David, 'The Jack Kerouac Collection', booklet essay, *The Jack Kerouac Collection*, Rhino Records, 1990.

Phillips, Lisa (ed.), *Beat Culture and the New America, 1950–1965*, New York: Whitney Museum of American Art, 1995.

Ronan, Stephen, *Disks of the Gone World: An Annotated Discography of the Beat Generation*, Berkeley, CA: Ammunition Press, 1996.

Roszak, Theodore, *The Making of a Counter Culture*, London: University of California Press, 1995.

Swenson, John, 'Beat jazz: The real thing', in Holly George-Warren (ed.), *The Rolling Stone Book of the Beats*, London: Bloomsbury, 1999, pp. 27–31.

Torgoff, Martin, *Bop Apocalypse: Jazz, Race, Beats And Drugs*, Boston: Da Capo, 2017.

Turner, Steve, *Jack Kerouac: Angelheaded Hipster*, London: Bloomsbury, 1996.

Warner, Simon, *Text and Drugs and Rock'n'Roll: The Beats and Rock Culture*, New York: Bloomsbury, 2013.

Watson, Steven, *The Birth of the Beat Generation*, New York: Pantheon, 1995.

Weinreich, Regina, 'The Beat Generation is now about everything', in Josephine G. Hendin (ed.), *A Concise Companion to Postwar American Literature and Culture*, Oxford: Blackwell, 2004, pp. 72–94.

Whaley, Preston, *Blows Like a Horn: Beat Writing, Jazz, Style and Markets in the Transformation of US Culture*, Cambridge, MA: Harvard University Press, 2004.

Discography

Kerouac, Jack, 'Fantasy: The early history of bop', orig. in *Escapade*, April 1959, *Readings by Jack Kerouac on the Beat Generation*, Rhino Records, 1990.

Kerouac, Jack, 'America's new Trinity of love: Dean, Brando and Presley', *Kicks Joy Darkness*, Ryko, 1997.

Webography

Charters, Sam, 'Jack Kerouac's jazz', talk given at Naropa Institute, Boulder, CO, 26 July 1982, 25th anniversary of *On the Road* conference, the Allen Ginsberg Project, http://ginsbergblog.blogspot.co.uk/2014/08/sam-charters-jack-kerouacs-jazz-1-intro.html (accessed 17 March 2017).

CHAPTER 1
JACK KEROUAC'S JAZZ SCENE
Jim Burns

Writing in *Escapade* in December 1960, Jack Kerouac ran through a long list of jazzmen he considered of importance at the time. He got a few of the names slightly wrong (Al Macusik instead of Hal McKusick, for example), but generally demonstrated that he was aware of what was going on in the jazz world, and that his enthusiasm for the music was as great as it had always been. If there is one thing that constantly comes through in his books, it is the fact that he understood and loved jazz and the music of the big bands of the 1930s and 1940s. And it does need to be made clear that the two were heavily interconnected in the period that was Kerouac's most active in terms of influences and interests. This covers roughly a 20-year time frame – 1935 to 1955, give or take a year or two either way. One of the advantages of examining the music in question is that it has been well documented on record, so it is possible to listen to the bands, soloists and singers that Kerouac frequently mentioned; and, by doing so, to understand how his writing reflected the sounds and the moods of particular periods.

But let's go back to the beginning, to the years when the young Kerouac was starting to take notice of the bands, musicians and vocalists. In *Maggie Cassidy* (1959) there is a passage where Jacky Duluoz and friends visit the Ritz Ballroom. There is nothing really glamorous about the place, but to them it seems exciting and different. They see 'lights playing polka dots around the hall' and catch sight of 'the sudden group of jitterbugs with long hair and pegged pants'. One of the jitterbugs tell them, 'Oh, Gene Krupa is the maddest drummer in the world. I saw him in Boston! He was the end!' In Kerouac's description of the scene there is the buoyancy of initiation into the seemingly magical world of dancehalls, jitterbugs and heroes like Gene Krupa. Now it is true that, in his reaction to the dance-band music being played in the ballroom, and the reference to Krupa, Kerouac was doing little more than registering what many 16-year-olds would have thought and felt at the time. But this is, of course, what gives his writing its appeal. It refers to both the personal and the general, and in doing so neatly hints at things to come, in this case a fascination with jazz, its fans, their enthusiasms and their language.

Still, it was quite a long way from jazz, even allowing for Krupa's name being used. He was, in 1938, just launching a band of his own after three years with Benny Goodman, and he had been lucky enough to be in at the birth of the swing craze. In the words of George T. Simon, Krupa was, 'quite a showman . . . with his gum chewing and his hair waving and his grimaces and his torrid drumming' (Simon, 1967, p. 306).

It was more than probable that Kerouac read Simon's articles about Goodman, Krupa and others, as he was a leading commentator on the music scene between 1935 and 1955. Simon was employed by *Metronome* magazine, and as Dennis McNally remarked of Kerouac and his friends, 'The whole gang went to Lowell's City Auditorium to hear Harry James, bought *Metronome* with the gravity of stockbrokers purchasing *The Wall Street Journal*, and disputed fine points with the subtlety of diplomats' (McNally, 1979, p. 27). *Metronome* was an influential jazz and popular music journal in the 1930s and 1940s. It helped spread the word about bands, musicians, singers and their records to the small towns of America, and its annual polls, in which readers voted for their favourite performers, were an indication of popular tastes.

Radio was a major factor in shaping those tastes, and Kerouac's reminiscences of the period are full of references to radio programmes. To quote George T. Simon again, 'big bands headlined numerous top radio series' (Simon, 1967, p. 56). One of the most popular shows was *Make Believe Ballroom*, which used recordings to create the atmosphere of a dance-hall so that people could clear the furniture to one side and shuffle around their living rooms. Other programmes (the *Fitch Bandwagon*, for example, and those sponsored by Camel, Old Gold, Raleigh-Cool and Chesterfield) featured live broadcasts by top bands such as Glenn Miller, Woody Herman and Tommy Dorsey. Kerouac would have heard these broadcasts and so picked up on the different styles in evidence, the talents of the soloists and the qualities of the singers. It needs to be remembered that what many of the bands were playing was mostly popular music and not out-and-out jazz.

The swing bands did have a wide range of music at their disposal, and the better ones – Goodman, Dorsey, Artie Shaw, Charlie Barnet – had first-rate soloists in their ranks. But a glance through discographies, or better still, a sampling of the actual records, will soon indicate that they churned out commercial material much of the time. Novelty numbers abounded, as did routine arrangements of popular songs. Some of the songs were of superior quality, but there were hundreds of others which were soon forgotten. Does anyone now recall 'In a Little Hula Heaven' or 'Our Penthouse on Third Avenue' (both recorded by Tommy Dorsey in 1937)? And how about 'There's Honey on the Moon Tonight' (Gene Krupa, 1938)? Or 'You're a Sweet Little Headache' (Benny Goodman, 1938)? Nostalgically, these discs do have a certain amount of charm, and Kerouac could well have heard and enjoyed them, but only the most dedicated collector of old dance-band records would bother trying to find copies.

So, in the late 1930s, what Kerouac was listening to was essentially popular music with a degree of jazz colouring. The jazz was primarily of a white big band kind, because it was the white bands which tended to get the publicity and the peak radio times, plus the booking for theatres and dance halls. It was possible to hear some black bands on the radio, but far easier to tune in to white ones. Kerouac's experience of black big band music, and especially jazz, was limited in the 1930s, as it was for most people of his age growing up in towns like Lowell. Even black teenagers outside the big cities often found it more convenient to hear music by Artie Shaw or Benny Goodman than by Count Basie or Duke Ellington.

Here's Kerouac himself describing what he was hearing: 'At the last minute I'd stand undecided in my room, looking at the little radio I just got and in which I'd started listening to Glenn Miller and Jimmy Dorsey and romantic songs that tore my heart out . . . "My Reverie", "Heart and Soul", Bob Eberle, Ray Eberle . . .'. Miller's band was definitely one of the more commercial of the time, and so was Jimmy Dorsey's. As for the singers mentioned, they were competent vocalists in the big-band context, but neither had the individuality to assert themselves sufficiently to succeed in the way that Frank Sinatra did after he'd served his apprenticeship with Harry James and Tommy Dorsey.

There are other references of relevance in *Maggie Cassidy*, and one curious aside in which a character called Pauline Cole is said to have later sung with Artie Shaw's orchestra: 'Some day she'd sing for Artie Shaw, some day little gangs of coloured people would gather around her microphone in Roseland Ballroom and call her the white Billie.' The real identity of this person was a mystery for many years until Beat scholar Dave Moore established that Kerouac was referring to Margaret (Peggy) Coffey, a friend from his boyhood days in Lowell. She sang with Bobby Byrne's band in 1946 and recorded at least two tracks with him. The band played at the Roseland Ballroom in New York, which might explain Kerouac's reference to it. Peggy Coffey also sang with the Vic Roy Band, a local outfit in the Nashua area, but doesn't appear to have had a lengthy career in show business. She may have auditioned for Artie Shaw's orchestra, but never actually worked with it.

Kitty Kallen and Helen O'Connell, both band vocalists, are mentioned, and then, in the final pages of *Maggie Cassidy*, some newer names creep in which suggest that Kerouac's move to New York brought a broadening of his jazz awareness. He tells, as Jacky Duluoz, how he is introduced to 'Lionel Smart' (Seymour Wyse), who recommends Count Basie's band, and so, 'it's rush to the Savoy, talks on the sidewalks of the American night with bassplayers and droopy tenormen with huge indifferent eyelids (Lester Young)'. To be fair, Kerouac also refers to Frank Sinatra singing 'On a Little Street in Singapore' (hardly a great song), Glenn Miller at the Paramount, and Artie Shaw. But Basie and Ellington and Lester Young had entered his consciousness, and it's at this point that he begins to touch on the kind of sounds which gave a foretaste of what was to come with the bop revolution of the 1940s.

Count Basie's band was, in the late 1930s and early 1940s, one of the most influential, at least insofar as musicians and more knowledgeable fans were concerned. As one jazz historian put it, 'For the perceptive, the hip, and the aspiring jazz musician, appearances of the Count Basie orchestra became the most exciting events of those years' (Russell, 1971, p. 142). Tenorman Lester Young became the idol of numerous young saxophone players, and the small but growing army of hipsters. His personal behaviour, as well as his musical approach, caught the imagination of these dissidents, and he became a kind of 'underground' hero.

A fictional treatment of Young in this role can be found in John Clellon Holmes's *The Horn* (1958), demonstrating that other Beats, besides Kerouac, were impressed by him. Kerouac was convinced enough about Young's importance to have interviewed him for the *Horace Mann Record*, something that he refers to in *Vanity of Duluoz* (1968), where he also recalls 'Lionel Smart' insisting that he listens to Lester. And in his *Escapade* article about jazz, Kerouac mentioned that he and Wyse had collaborated on an article, 'Lester Young is ten years ahead of his time', which they submitted to *Metronome* without success. To stress that Wyse was his guide in those days, Kerouac said in another *Escapade* piece, 'The Beginning of Bop' (1959), that Young was an important figure and that there was a 'strange English kid hanging around Minton's who stumbled along the sidewalk hearing Lester in his head'.

Kerouac's tastes in jazz were clearly expanding, and in 'The Origins of the Beat Generation' (1959) he recalled visiting Minton's Playhouse when Young, Ben Webster, Charlie Christian and Joe Guy were playing, which suggests he was one of a small group of genuine enthusiasts. Minton's was a 'seedy box on One Hundred Eighteenth Street. It was owned by a peripheral musician named Henry Minton who had been the first black delegate to New York's famous Local 802' (Collier, 1978, p. 348). At some point in 1940, Minton asked Teddy Hill, a one-time bandleader, to become manager of the club, which he did, organizing a small house band (Thelonious Monk, Joe Guy, Nick Fenton, Kenny Clarke) and running the place as an after-hours hangout for musicians and the hipper fans. Within a few weeks of its opening it had become the place to jam. Jazzmen, known and unknown, frequented Minton's to relax after their jobs with bands and in clubs had finished for the night.

All accounts agree that Minton's, and another club called Clark Monroe's Uptown House, were the places where bop was, if not exactly born, at least starting to take on a clearer form. Kerouac must have been in a position to evaluate the new music as it developed. He did say, in 'The origins of the Beat Generation', that, in 1944, he still 'didn't like bop', though he was obviously listening hard, because he added that he first heard Charlie Parker and Dizzy Gillespie in a small 52nd Street club called the Three Deuces. I don't think that we need to place too much emphasis on Kerouac's admission that his first experience of pure bop (as opposed to the mixture of swing and bop he would have heard at Minton's) had left him a little confused. Many people felt that way initially, and that includes a large number of musicians.

The music at Minton's often included early bop ideas, but the recorded evidence demonstrates that they were within an established framework, and that the experiments were tentative enough to often seem to be personal eccentricities rather than major innovations in jazz. But by 1944–6, when Kerouac was visiting the Three Deuces (and presumably other clubs on 52nd Street), bop had blossomed, and the kind of group that Parker and Gillespie led made few or no concessions to anyone unable to adapt to their musical revolution. One either took the music to heart or left it alone. That it could even baffle musicians is evident from the account by drummer Dave Tough of a visit to a 52nd Street club: 'As we walked in, see, these cats snatched up their horns and blew crazy stuff. One would stop all of a sudden and another would start for no reason at all. We could never tell when a solo was supposed to begin or end. Then they quit all at once and walked off the stand. It scared us' (Stearns, 1968, p. 159).

Kerouac did come to terms with bop, and by the mid-1940s was involving himself in the hipster milieu of New York. He probably saw the new music as reflecting the mood of his friends, as well as paralleling the social and artistic theories they were expounding. The 1946–7 period was when bop established itself. Billy Eckstine's big band – wilder and far more daring than any of the white swing bands had ever been – was spreading the word. In New York, Los Angeles, Chicago and other cities, small groups of boppers were coming together to take their music into clubs. On record, too, the new music was gaining ground. A number of small companies – Guild, Savoy, Blue Note – were recording bop groups, and even the established companies like RCA started to take chances with the new sounds. I'm not suggesting that there was a complete acceptance of the music. Bop was always a minority interest, and it never appealed to the public in general, even though there was a short-lived commercialized bop craze around 1949. It resulted in a few bop references being used in popular songs; 'Bop Goes My Heart', sung by Frank Sinatra, was one example. But even though Charlie Parker was a great jazz innovator, and looked on as a god by the hipsters, most people had no idea who he was, and cared even less.

In 'The Origins of the Beat Generation', Kerouac stated that 'by 1948 it was all taking shape', and while this can be seen as referring to the general development of his involvement with Ginsberg, Burroughs and the rest, it is significant that he went on to bring in a number of jazz references. Symphony Sid's all-night modern jazz and bop show was always on', he wrote, and 'it was the year I saw Charlie Bird Parker strolling down Eighth Avenue in a black turtleneck sweater with Babs Gonzales and a beautiful girl'. Then he added, 'In 1948 the "hot hipsters" were racing around in cars like in *On the Road* looking for wild bawling jazz like Willis Jackson or Lucky Thompson (the early) or Chubby Jackson's big band while the "cool" hipsters cooled it in dead silence before formal and excellent musical groups like Lennie Tristano or Miles Davis.'

In this handful of references, Kerouac really evokes a range of jazz styles from the late 1940s. Symphony Sid was a disc-jockey who specialized in playing bop and related music. Babs Gonzales was a bop singer and noted character around the scene. His book, *I Paid My Dues: Good Times, No Bread, A Story of Jazz* (1967), is a racy account of his own participation in the activities of the 1940s, and puts forward the highly debatable claim that he was the 'creator of the bop language'. Willis Jackson was a tenor saxophonist with a penchant for hard-blown performances. Dennis McNally records that Kerouac took John Clellon Holmes to a bar with a juke-box and enthused about Jackson's 'Gator Tail'. Lucky Thompson was a far better jazzman, and, though Kerouac doesn't do him justice by linking him with Jackson, he could play with great vigour. At his best, however, he used a rhapsodic style which had warmth and invention, and an individual sound which made him stand out. He often played alongside bop musicians, both in clubs and on records, but was not a bopper himself. Chubby Jackson, one-time bass player with Woody Herman, was definitely an extrovert, and his shouted encouragements to other musicians can be heard on recordings from the time. He had a short-lived big band of his own around New York, and it's possible that Kerouac heard it in the clubs. It often displayed more enthusiasm than finesse, but it was exciting and it's easy to see why Kerouac linked it to the 'hot hipsters'.

Pianist Lennie Tristano never reached the front ranks of the jazz fraternity, but he did have some critical success as the leader of a small group of white jazzmen who played in what was thought of as an extremely cerebral style. Tristano made some gestures in the direction of 'free form' jazz, and his recording of 'Intuition' (1949) created something of a minor sensation among intellectuals who liked jazz. John Clellon Holmes, reminiscing when interviewed, referred to Tristano as 'a mostly forgotten genius of the jazz piano' (Knight and Knight, 1981, p. 28). On another occasion, he noted, 'one of our passions just then was the work of pianist Lennie Tristano, who was, perhaps, the most avant-garde of the younger jazzmen of that year, and who, a month before, had recorded the first attempt at total, free form, atonal improvisation, a record called "Intuition", not yet released but played occasionally by Symphony Sid on his all-night radio show'(Charters, 1975, p. 110). It's also of interest to mention the reference to Lee Konitz, an alto saxophonist associated with Tristano, which occurs in *Visions of Cody* (1972). Kerouac's semi-humorous description of Konitz playing as 'if the tune was the room he lived in and was going out at midnight with his coat on' catches some of the complexity of his style.

Miles Davis is a familiar enough name, but it's often forgotten that, in the late 1940s and early 1950s, he was often linked with the so-called 'cool school' of playing. Working with Charlie Parker's group, he had not attempted to compete with the more-flamboyant work of Dizzy Gillespie, Fats Navarro and other bop trumpeters, but instead had fashioned an approach which allowed him to operate mainly in the lower and middle registers of his instrument. In 1949 and 1950, he teamed up with the highly-influential arranger Gil Evans, and the baritone saxophonist Gerry Mulligan, to record a number of sides which avoided the freneticism of bop and aimed more towards tight arrangements, relaxed improvising and a generally calm and thoughtful air. Kerouac's reference to the 'cool' hipsters is accurate, and jazz historian Marshall Stearns, discussing such types, noted that 'the proper pose when listening to a Miles Davis record was one of despair' (Stearns, 1968, p. 158).

On the Road also deals with the late 1940s period and inevitably gets around to bringing in jazz of various sorts. There are several brief references to records that jazz fans of the period would have been familiar with, among them Billie Holiday's 'Lover Man', Lionel Hampton's 'Central Avenue Breakdown' and Red Norvo's 'Congo Blues', the latter featuring Charlie Parker and Dizzy Gillespie. Curiously, Kerouac invents the name of the drummer, calling him 'Max West', whereas it was actually J. C. Heard. 'Max West' may have been made up from the names of Max Roach and Harold 'Doc' West, two other drummers active with bop groups in the 1940s.

One of the more significant references is when Dean Moriarty visits Sal Paradise's relatives in Virginia: 'They ate voraciously as Dean, sandwich in hand, stood bowed and jumping before the big phonograph, listening to a wild bop record I had just bought called "The Hunt" with Dexter Gordon and Wardell Gray blowing their tops before a screaming audience that gave the record fantastic frenzied volume.' This particular performance was long by the standards of the day (it lasts around 18 minutes and was originally released on several 78rpm discs) and was recorded at a concert/dance in Los Angeles in 1947. It particularly spotlighted Gordon and Gray, two popular tenormen on the West Coast, but also had solos by other bop stalwarts such as trumpeter Howard McGhee, altoist Sonny Criss and pianist Hampton Hawes.

Its determined, almost wild atmosphere is expressive of much of the feeling of *On the Road*. The same urgency and excitement comes through, and the suggestion, in both music and writing, is that it's necessary to 'Go'. That very word, used in the 1940s as an expression of approval and encouragement, can be heard shouted from the audience throughout 'The Hunt'. And in referring specifically to the record, Kerouac knew what he was doing. It caught the tone of the times perfectly, and as John Clellon Holmes put it: 'listen there for the anthem in which we jettisoned the intellectual Dixieland of atheism, rationalism, liberalism – and found our own group's rebel streak at last' (Clellon Holmes, 1968, p. 199). Holmes, of course, called his novel about the Beats in New York *Go*. Kerouac perhaps didn't have Holmes's precise intellectual appreciation of what the music represented, but he recognized intuitively that it matched Dean Moriarty's mood, as well as the frame of mind of many of his other friends.

Later in *On the Road* there is an intriguing comment about George Shearing, the blind English pianist who had settled in the United States in the 1940s, and who had a fair amount of popular success when he formed a group which specialized in playing quiet, relaxed jazz. The music was light, often using well-known popular songs as a basis for improvising which was largely confined to a chorus or two of attractive embroidery. It was, in other words, an innocuous form of jazz, pleasant and undemanding. Kerouac had heard Shearing – a skilled musician and quite capable of producing good bop-style playing – prior to his popular period. As he says, 'those were his great 1949 days before he became cool and commercial'.

One of the best-known jazz references in *On the Road* occurs when Sal and Dean go to a night club to listen to Slim Gaillard, 'a tall thin negro with big sad eyes who's always saying "Right-oroonie", and "How 'bout a little bourbon-oroonie"'. Gaillard was not a bop musician, despite being linked to the music and using bop musicians like Gillespie, Parker, Howard McGhee and Dodo Marmarosa on his records. He had been active in jazz since the 1930s, and the duo, Slim and Slam, which paired Gaillard with bassist Bam Brown, had produced discs which, because of their novelty appeal, reached a fairly wide audience. But Gaillard's influence as a hipster hero relates to the mid-1940s and after. He made a large number of records for minor labels on the West Coast, some of which attained an 'underground' status. At one time Gaillard's music, along with that of another cult figure, Harry 'the Hipster' Gibson, was banned by a number of radio stations on the grounds of bad taste, supposed drug links and encouraging anti-social behaviour. The 1940s were, as Robert Creeley once said, 'the time of the whole cult of the hipster' (Creeley, 1946, p. 46).

Before leaving *On the Road*, I want to briefly discuss the passage where Sal and Dean listen to 'a wild tenorman bawling horn across the way'. This is the section of the book which appeared, in slightly different form, as 'Jazz of the Beat Generation' in *New World Writing* in 1955. The 1940s were peak years for saxophonists of the kind described by Kerouac. There were jazzmen like Dexter Gordon and Gene Ammons who could play good jazz and arouse audiences. And Illinois Jacquet and Arnett Cobb were noted for hard blowing while retaining a measure of worthwhile jazz content in their music. But there were also dozens of others, mostly now forgotten, who were never major jazzmen but had some connection to the music. As LeRoi Jones outlined it in his short story, 'The Screamers', 'All the saxophonists of that world were honkers, Illinois, Gator, Big Jay, Jug, the great sounds of our days. Ethnic historians, actors, priests of the unconscious' (Jones, 1967, p. 76).

Jones shows how jazz and rhythm-and-blues intermingled, just as jazz and big-band music had, by including Illinois Jacquet and Gene Ammons ('Jug') with Big Jay McNeely and Willis Jackson ('Gator'). It has always struck me that Kerouac, in the *On the Road* passage, was more likely writing about a rhythm-and-blues style tenorman than about an authentic jazz soloist such as Dexter Gordon or Wardell Gray. Some of the sweat and power of rhythm-and-blues comes through in the prose. The action takes place on the West Coast, and recordings from the 1940s and early 1950s by local artists like Big Jay McNeeley and Big Jim Wynn do match in music what Kerouac described in words.

The early 1950s found Kerouac still actively involved with jazz in terms of listening to it and writing about the musicians. *The Subterraneans* is supposedly set in San Francisco, but the events it describes took place in New York, a switch being thought necessary for legal reasons. A bop tenorman, 'Roger Beloit', is one of the characters, and Kerouac says, 'or, while listening to Stan Kenton talking about the music of tomorrow and we hear a new young tenorman, Ricci Commuca, Roger Beloit says, moving back expressively thin purple lips, "This is the music of tomorrow?"'. Beloit is actually Allen Eager, a noted tenor-saxophonist of the 1940s who, in the early 1950s, had fallen on hard times, like many bop musicians. His cryptic comment about the supposed 'music of tomorrow' is understandable in that 'the new young tenorman, Ricci Commuca' (real name, Richie Kamuca) played in a style perfected several years previously by musicians like Allen Eager and Zoot Sims, and with Lester Young as a major influence on them all.

If one listens to Stan Kenton's 'This is an Orchestra', recorded in late 1952 and probably heard often on the air in 1953, when the action of *The Subterraneans* takes place, it is possible to hear him talking about Kamuca with enthusiasm, and generally suggesting that his orchestra was playing 'the music of tomorrow'. It was the sort of hyperbolic statement Kenton was prone to making. Kamuca, incidentally, was a good jazzman, but hardly original, and it's easy to see why 'Beloit' (Eager) was reluctant to accept him as such.

There are other jazz musicians in *The Subterraneans*. Charlie Parker is there, and so is Gerry Mulligan who, in 1953, was enjoying success with a series of records featuring him with Chet Baker. The fact that the group didn't include a pianist was considered unusual at the time. Tracks like 'My Funny Valentine', 'Walking Shoes' and 'Bernie's Tune' would have been heard regularly on radio programmes. So would Stan Kenton's 'Yes', which Kerouac mentions as featuring the voice of Jerry Winters, female vocalist with the band in 1952. Her name was actually Jeri, but that's a minor point. He also refers to Jeri Southern, whose recordings of 'When I Fall in Love' and 'You Better Go Now', though not jazz, were popular with some jazz enthusiasts. She had the same smoky quality as Jeri Winters, June Christy, Chris Connor and others who Kerouac describes as 'the new bop singers'. That he was following jazz trends closely is apparent from the names he mentions. The 'cool' tendency of the early 1950s was becoming more dominant.

When he came down from his sojourn on Desolation Peak in 1956, one of his first acts was to visit a jazz club, as recounted in *Desolation Angels*: 'So we go out and get drunk and dig the session in the Cellar where Brue Moore is blowing on tenor saxophone, which he holds mouthpieced in the side of his mouth, his cheeks distended in a round ball like Harry James and Dizzy Gillespie, and he plays perfect pretty harmony to any tune they bring up – he pays little attention to anyone, he drinks his beer, he gets loaded and eye heavy, but he never misses a beat or a note because music is his heart, and in music he has found that pure message to give the world.'

The saxophonist named was Milton 'Brew' Moore, a white musician who, like Allen Eager, appeared on the scene in the 1940s with a style derived from Lester Young. Moore was reputed to have once said that 'anyone who doesn't play like Lester is wrong'. He was never a well-known jazzman, though he was quite active in the New York area in 1949/1950. By the mid-1950s he had drifted to San Francisco. As Kerouac noted, Moore liked to drink beer, hence his nickname 'Brew'. Photographs bear out the accuracy of Kerouac's description of how he held his saxophone when playing.

Moore's performances could be variable because of his drinking, but Kerouac does capture some of the wistfulness that was in evidence when he was at his best, as well as the fact that he played with a great deal of swing. In some ways Moore paralleled Kerouac's prose. He could be gentle, almost sentimental, and then good humoured and lively. And, also like Kerouac, drink brought about his death. He spent his last years in Europe, and died after a fall, probably when drunk. If, as someone said, 'all poets have broken hearts', then both Moore and Kerouac bore out the truth of that statement. It does seem accurate to say that musicians like Allen Eager and Brew Moore appealed to Kerouac because of an inherent quality in their music that was also present in his prose. Larry Kart described it as 'a meditative, inward turning linear impulse that combines compulsive swing with an underlying resignation – as though at the end of each phrase the shape of the line dropped into a melancholy "Ah, me", which would border on passivity if it weren't for the need to move on, to keep the line going' (Kart, 1983, p. 27).

I began this chapter by referring to something that Kerouac wrote in 1960. Jazz was then only just starting to move beyond what had been developed in the 1940s and 1950s, so Kerouac wasn't faced with the problem of having to say whether or not he liked anything that was radically different. He was essentially still dealing with music that was a natural extension of what he had known and loved since the 1930s, and from the evidence of his writing there is nothing to suggest that he ever went much further than that. The 1935–55 period was, as I suggested earlier, the key one insofar as his jazz and popular music tastes were concerned, with the death of his idol, Charlie Parker, in 1955, almost bringing an era to an end.

I haven't attempted to be totally comprehensive when detailing Kerouac's references to jazz, and I'm aware that he names many other musicians and singers in his novels, poems and articles. There's a poem about Dave Brubeck, for example, and in *The Town and the City* he mentions Anita O'Day. The 'New York Scenes' section of *Lonesome Traveller* brings in John Coltrane, and the little-known trumpeters Don Joseph and Tony Fruscella, as well as altoist Charlie Mariano. *Vanity of Duluoz* covers the swing bands again, with Jimmy Lunceford, Charlie Barnet and many more accurately placed in the time scale and often described in a way that evokes the kind of music they played.

The point is that Kerouac's interest in jazz was something which influenced him in the sense of propelling him to write, and to attempt to inject an improvisational feeling into his prose. 'I want to be considered a jazz poet' he stated, and though arguments will always exist about how far it's possible to parallel music in writing, it has to be accepted that jazz was clearly important to him. With this in mind we can see, from what was said in his books, how the music provided a background to the events that he described. It could even be suggested that the best way to read Kerouac is with the music of the particular period he is discussing providing an accompaniment to the rhythms of his prose.

Further reading

The literature of jazz has expanded substantially since I wrote the first version of this chapter in 1983. However, it seems to me that some of the books I then recommended are still among the best for providing background and information to Kerouac's jazz interests.

His novels have appeared in various editions, but the scattered writings, such as the *Escapade* columns and 'The Beginning of Bop' are not as easy to find. *Last Words & Other Writings* (n.p.: Zeta Press, 1985) has the *Escapade* material, and *Good Blonde & Others* (San Francisco: Grey Fox Press, 1994) has 'The Beginning of Bop'.

George T. Simon's *Simon Says: The Sights and Sounds of the Swing Era, 1935–1955* (New Rochelle, NY: Arlington House, 1971) is a selection of material from *Metronome*, and provides a good guide to the kinds of bands and singers Kerouac would have listened to.

Among the best histories of the bop movement are Ira Gitler's *Jazz Masters of the 40s* (New York: Macmillan, 1966) and *Swing to Bop* (New York: Oxford University Press, 1985). If a copy can be found, Leonard Feather's *Inside Be-Bop* (New York: J.J. Robbins & Sons, 1949) has the genuine period feel. It was reissued as *Inside Jazz* (New York: Da Capo, 1977.) Scott Deveaux's *The Birth of Bebop: A Social and Musical History* (Berkeley: University of California Press, 1997) is a good general history of the early days of the music.

An insight into the world of New York night clubs is in Arnold Shaw's *The Street That Never Slept* (New York: Coward, McCann & Geoghegan, 1971). Shaw's *Honkers and Shouters: The Golden Years of Rhythm & Blues* (New York: Macmillan, 1978) documents the importance of the tenor saxophone to the music of the 1940s and early 1950s.

Ted Gioia's *West Coast Jazz: Modern Jazz in California, 1945–1960* (New York: Oxford University Press, 1992) and David H. Rosenthal's *Hard Bop: Jazz & Black Music 1955–1965* (New York: Oxford University Press, 1992) are both of relevance.

There are numerous biographies of individual jazzmen, and perhaps the most relevant in relation to Kerouac are Robert Reisner's *Bird: The Legend of Charlie Parker* (New York: Citadel Press, 1962) and Ross Russell's *Bird Lives: The High Life and Hard Times of Charlie 'Yardbird' Parker* (London: Quartet Books, 1973), though the accuracy of some of the information in Russell's book has been questioned. There are later biographies of Parker, but Reisner and Russell both knew him. However, Brian Priestley's *Chasin' The Bird: The Life and Legacy of Charlie Parker* (Sheffield: Equinox Publishing, 2005) is a well-informed guide to Parker's music.

Douglas Henry Daniels' *Lester Leaps In: The Life and Times of Lester 'Pres' Young* (Boston: Beacon Press, 2002) is a well-documented work. Stan Britt's *Long Tall Dexter* (London: Quartet Books, 1989) is about Dexter Gordon. Art Pepper's *Straight Life* (New York: Schirmer Books, 1979) is informative about a life in jazz in the 1940s and 1950s, as is Hampton Hawes' *Raise Up Off Me* (New York: Coward, McCann & Geoghegan, 1973). Dizzy Gillespie's *Dizzy: To Be or not to Bop* (London: W. H. Allen, 1980) is a lively account of his activities. *Infatuation: The Music and Life of Theodore 'Fats' Navarro* by Leif Bo Peterson and Theo Rehak (Lanham, MD: Scarecrow Press, 2009) and *Drummin' Men: The Bebop Years* by Burt Korall (New York: Oxford University Press, 2002) are informative for the bebop period.

There are few convincing fictional accounts of bop. John Clellon Holmes's *The Horn* (London: André Deutsch, 1959) has characters based on Lester Young, Dizzy Gillespie and others. Ross Russell's *The Sound* (New York: Dutton, 1961) uses the life of Charlie Parker as a basis for a story about a brilliant but wayward trumpeter. It's colourful and Russell knew the music at first-hand, having recorded Parker for his

Dial label. The short story 'Dance of the Infidels' in Alston Anderson's *Lover Man* (London: Pan Books, 1961) has an authentic ring to it. Elliott Grennard's 'Sparrow's Last Jump' in *Jam Session: An Anthology of Jazz*, edited by Ralph J. Gleason, Peter Davies (London: Putnam, 1958) is a short story based on the notorious 1946 Dial recording session when Parker collapsed. Grennard was present in the studio.

Bibliography

Allen, Donald (ed.), *Robert Creeley: Contexts of Poetry: Interviews 1961–1971*, Bolinas, CA: Four Seasons Foundation, 1973.

Charters, Ann, *A Bibliography of Works by Jack Kerouac*, New York: Phoenix Bookshop, 1975.

Clellon Holmes, John, *Nothing More to Declare*, London: André Deutsch, 1968.

Jones, LeRoi, *Tales*, New York: Grove Press, 1967.

Kart, Larry, 'Jack Kerouac's "Jazz America" or who was Roger Beloit?', *Review of Contemporary Fiction* 3, no. 2 (Summer 1983).

Knight, Arthur and Kit Knight, *Interior Geography: An Interview With John Clellon Holmes*, Warren, OH: The Literary Denim, 1981.

Lincoln Collier, James, *The Making of Jazz*, New York: Granada Publishing, 1978.

McNally, Dennis, *Desolate Angel: Jack Kerouac, the Beat Generation and America*, New York: Random House, 1979.

Russell, Ross, *Jazz Style in Kansas City and the Southwest*, Berkeley: University of California Press, 1971.

Simon, George, T., *The Big Bands*, New York: Macmillan, 1967.

Stearns, Marshall, *The Story of Jazz*, New York: Mentor Books, 1968.

CHAPTER 2
THE BEGINNING OF BOP[1]
Jack Kerouac

Bop began with jazz but one afternoon somewhere on a sidewalk maybe 1939, 1940, Dizzy Gillespie or Charley [sic] Parker or Thelonious Monk was walking down past a men's clothing store on 42nd Street or South Main in LA and from the loudspeaker they suddenly heard a wild impossible mistake in jazz that could only have been heard inside their own imaginary head, and that is a new art. Bop.

The name derives from an accident, America was named after an Italian explorer not after an Indian king. Lionel Hampton had made a record called 'Hey Baba Ree Bop' and everybody yelled it and it was when Lionel would jump in the audience whale [sic] the saxophone at everybody with sweat, claps, jumping fools in the aisles, the drummer booming and belaboring on the stage as the whole theater rocked. Sung by Helen Humes it was a popular record and sold many copies in 1945, 1946. First everyone looked around then it happened – bop happened – the bird flew in – minds went in – on the streets thousands of new-type hep cats in red shirts and some goatees and strange queerlooking cowboys from the West with boots and belts, and the girls began to disappear from the street – you no longer saw as in the Thirties the wrangler walking with his doll in the honkytonk, now he was alone, rebop, bop, came into being because the broads were leaving the guys and going off to be middleclass models. Dizzy or Charley or Thelonious was walking down the street, heard a noise, a sound, half Lester Young, half raw-rainy-fog that has that chest-shivering excitement of shack, track, empty lot, the sudden vast Tiger head on the woodfence, rainy no-school Saturday morning dumpyards. 'Hey!' and rushed off dancing.

On the piano that night Thelonious introduced a wooden off-key note to everybody's warmup notes, Minton's Playhouse, evening starts, jam hours later, 10 P.M., colored bar and hotel next door, one or two white visitors some from Columbia some from Nowhere – some from ship – some from Army Navy Air Force Marines – some from Europe – The strange note makes the trumpeter of the band lift an eyebrow. Dizzy is surprised for the first time that day. He puts the trumpet to lips and blows a wet blur –

'Hee ha ha!' laughs Charlie Parker, bending down to slap his ankle. He puts his alto to his mouth and says 'Didn't I tell you?' – with jazz of notes . . . Talking eloquent like great poets of foreign languages singing in foreign countries with lyres, by seas, and no one understands because the language isn't alive in the land yet – Bop is the language from America's inevitable Africa, *going* sounded like *gong*, Africa is the name of the flue and kick beat, off to one side – the sudden squeak uninhibited that screams muffled at any moment from Dizzy Gillespie's trumpet – do anything you want – drawing the tune aside along another improvisation bridge with a reach-out tear of claws, why be subtle and false?

The band of 10 PM Minton's swings into action, Bird Parker who is only 18 year old has a crew cut of Africa looks impossible has perfect eyes and composures of a king when suddenly you stop and look at him in the subway and you can't believe that bop is here to stay – that it is real, Negroes in America are just like us, we must look at them understanding the exact racial counterpart of what the man is – and figure it with histories and lost kings of immemorial tribes in jungle and Fellaheen town and otherwise and the sad mutts sleeping on old porches and big Easonburg woods where just 90 years ago old Roost come running calling 'Maw' through the fence he'd just deserted the Confederate Army and was running home for pone – and flies on watermelon porches. And educated judges in horn rimmed glasses reading the *Amsterdam News*.

And the band realized the goof of life that had made them be not only misplaced in the white nation but mis-noticed for what they really were and the goof they felt stirring and springing in their bellies, suddenly Dizzy spats his lips tight-drum together and drives a high screeching fantastic clear note that has everybody in the joint look up – Bird, lips hanging dully to hear, is turning slowly in a circle waiting for Diz to swim through the wave of the tune in a toneless complicated wave of his own grim like factories and atonal at any minute and the logic of the mad, the sock in his belly is sweet, the rock, zonga, monga, bang – In white creamed afternoons of blue Bird had leaned back dreamily in eternity as Dizzy outlined to him the importance of becoming Mohammedans in order to give a solid basis of race to the ceremony, 'Make that rug swing, mother, – When you say Race bow your head and close your eyes.' Give them a religion no Uncle Tom Baptist – make them wearers of skull caps of respectable minarets in actual New York – picking hashi dates from their teeth – Give them new names with zonga sounds – make it weird –

Thelonious was so weird he wandered the twilight streets of Harlem in winter with no hat on his hair, sweating, blowing fog – In his head he heard it all ringing. Often he heard whole choruses by Lester. There was a strange English kid hanging around Minton's who stumbled along the sidewalk hearing Lester in his head too – hours of hundreds of developing choruses in regular beat all day so in the subway no dissonance could crash against unalterable choruses in implacable bars – erected in mind's foundation jazz.

The tune they were playing was 'All the Things You Are' . . . they slowed it down and dragged behind it at half tempo dinosaur proportions – changed the placing of the note in the middle of the harmony to an outer more precarious position where also its sense of not belonging was enhanced by the general atonality produced with everyone exteriorizing the tune's harmony, the clonk of the millenial piano like anvils in Petrograd – 'Blow!' said Diz, and Charley Parker came in for his solo with a squeaky innocent cry. Monk punched anguished nub fingers crawling at the keyboard to tear up foundations and guts of jazz from the big masterbox to, make Charley Parker hear his cry and sigh – to jar the orchestra into vibrations – to elicit gloom from the doom of the black piano. He stared down wild eyed at his keys like a matador at the bull's head. Groan. Drunken figures shaded in the weaving background, tottering – the boys didn't care. On cold corners they stood three backs to one another, facing all the winds bent – lips don't care – miserable cold and broke – waiting like witchdoctors – saying, 'Everything belongs to me because I am poor.' Like 12 Century monks high in winter belfries of the Gothic Organ they wildeyed were listening to their own wild sound which was heralding in a new age of music that would eventually require symphonies, schools, centuries of technique, declines and falls of master-ripe styles – the Dixieland of Louie Armstrong sixteen and New Orleans and of bif Popa Forest niggerlips jim in the white shirt whaling at a big scarred bass in raunchy nongry New Orleans on South Rampart street famous for parades and old Perdido Street – all that was mud in the river Mississippi, pasts of 1910 gold rings, derby hats of workers, horses steaming turds near breweries and saloons, – Soon enough it would leap and fill the gay Twenties like champagne in a glass, pop! – And crawl up to the Thirties with tired Rudy Vallees lamenting with Louis who had laughed in Twenties Transoceanic Jazz, sick and tired early Ethel Mermans, and old beat bedsprings creaking in that stormy weather blues when people lay in bed all day and moaned and had it good – The world of the United States was tired of being poor and low and gloomy in a line. Swing erupted as the Depression began to crack, it was the year marijuana was made illegal, 1937. Young teenagers took to the first restraint, the second, the third, some still wondered on hobo trains (lost boys of the Thirties numbered in the hundreds of thousands, Salvation Armies put up full houses every night and some were ten years old) – teenagers, alienated from their parents who had suddenly returned to work and for good to get rid of that dam [sic] old mud of the river – and tear the rose vine off the porch – and paint the porch white – and cut the trees down – castrate the hedges – burn the leaves – build a wire fence – get up an antenna – listen – the alienated teenager in the 20th Century finally ripe gone wild modern to be rich and prosperous no more just around the corner – became the hepcat, the jitterbug, and smoked the new law weed. World War II gave everybody two pats of butter in the morning on a service tray, including your sister. Up from tired degrading swing wondering what had happened between 1937 and 1945 and because the Army'd worked it canned it played it to the boys in North Africa and raged it in the Picadilly [sic] bars and the Andrew sisters [sic] put the corn on the can – swing with its heroes died – and Charley Parker, Dizzy Gillespie and Thelonious Monk who were hustled through the chow lines – came back remembering old goofs – and tried it again – and Zop! Dizzy screamed, Charlie squealed, Monk crashed, the drummer kicked, dropped a bomb – the bass questionmark plunked – and off they whaled on Salt Peanuts jumping like mad monkeys in the gray new air. 'Hey Porkpie, Porkpie. Hey Porkpie!'

'Skidilibee-la-be you, – oo, – e bop she bam, ske too ria – Parasakiliaoolza – menooriastibatiolyait – oon ya koo.' They came to their own, they jumped, they had jazz and took it in their hands and saw its history vicissitudes and developments and turned it to their weighty use and heavily carried it clanking like posts across the enormity of a new world philosophy and a new strange and crazy grace came over them, fell from the air free, they saw pity in the hole of heaven, hell in their hearts, Billy Holliday [sic] had rocks in her heart, Lester droopy porkpied had hung his horn and blew bop lazy ideas inside jazz that had everybody dreaming (Miles Davis leaning against the piano fingering his trumpet with a cigarette hand working making raw iron sound like wood speaking in long sentences like Marcel Proust) – 'Hey, Jim', and the stud comes swinging down the street and says he's real *bent* and he's *down* and he has a *twisted* face, he works, he wails, he bops, he bangs, this man who was sent, stoned and stabbed is now *down, bent,* and *stretched-out* – turn the microphone on mouse click he is home at last, his music is here to stay, his history has washed over us, his imperialistic kingdoms are coming.

Note

1. This essay has appeared under a number of different headings since its debut in print. As independent Beat scholar Dave Moore explains: 'The original title of the piece was "The Beginning of Bop", published in *Escapade* magazine, April 1959. This is also the title of the same piece in the 1993 Kerouac collection *Good Blonde & Others*. On the 1959 Verve LP, *Readings by Jack Kerouac on the Beat Generation*, it is called "The Beginnings of Bop" on the sleeve, but "History of Bop" on the record label. There, Kerouac reads the complete article in that recording. On the 1990 Rhino reissue of that album the track is called "Fantasy: The Early History of Bop". So, all the articles are the same; only the title has been changed.' Email to the co-editors, 10 October 2017.

CHAPTER 3
2ND CHORUS: BLUES: JACK KEROUAC
Larry Beckett

There are writers who achieve equally at poetry and prose, like Johann von Goethe and Boris Pasternak, but it's easier to tag a writer as a master at one of these forms and ignore their work in the other, then hide this expedience behind the assumption that no one can achieve at both. And so there are American writers whose verse is eclipsed by their fiction, but not because it's unworthy, and these include Herman Melville, Stephen Crane and Jack Kerouac. This prejudice accounts for the fact that Kerouac, author of the Beat novel *On the Road*, though he had poetry published, did not see his splendid *Book of Haikus* in print during his life, as it came out in 2003, 42 years after it was written. He contended that he didn't distinguish between poetry and prose: in a letter to Ginsberg, he said, 'You guys call yourselves poets, write little short lines, I'm a poet but I write lines paragraphs and pages and many pages long' (Kerouac, 1992).

Consider this passage from *On the Road*, completed in 1952:

> We wheeled through the sultry old light of Algiers, back on the ferry, back toward the mud-splashed, crabbed old ships across the river, back on Canal, and out; on a two-lane highway to Baton Rouge in purple darkness; swung west there, crossed the Mississippi at a place called Port Allen. Port Allen – where the river's all rain and roses in a misty pinpoint darkness and where we swung around a circular drive in yellow foglight and suddenly saw the great black body below a bridge and crossed eternity again.
>
> Kerouac, 1957

And Regina Weinreich's poetic analysis:

> The repetition of 'back' develops in a typical build-up so that the pacing of the unconscious exposition that follows gains momentum. This momentum is further triggered by the assonance and alliteration that move the line of Kerouac's free prose. The initial *w* and long *e* sounds lead into the slant rhymes of 'ul', 'ol', and 'Al'. The short *a* of 'back' is echoed in 'splashed' and 'crabbed', all intended to emphasize the 'wheeling' motion that he is describing. The use of prepositions – 'on', 'toward', 'out' – reinforces 'wheeling' so that a great deal of ground is covered in a compact motion.
>
> Note the pacing in the 'unconscious' exposition that follows ... First, the repetition of 'Port Allen' creates force. Second, the poetic effects are tighter. The

rolling *r*'s of 'where', 'river', 'rain', 'roses', are picked up by 'darkness', with 'where' again creating a circular motion. The word 'swung' is repeated; 'around' picks up the rolling *r* as does 'circular drive', which actually states what the writing accomplishes at the levels of both sound and sense . . . And the alliteration of the *b*'s in 'black body below a bridge' suggests something still mysterious as the passage comes full circle in crossing the Mississippi (and eternity) again.

Weinreich, 2001

In theory, Kerouac may consider prose and poetry as the same, but in practice his prose has narrative and characters not found in his poetry, though it can intensify in description through rhetoric and sound into a poetic texture. His poetry, unlike his prose, loosens into free association and free verse. It has the music and compression expected in that genre.

In 1953, Kerouac wrote his first poetic cycle, 'Richmond Hill Blues' (Kerouac, 1995b), 22 lyric poems with titles, and in the next year he extended that experiment with the 80 choruses of *San Francisco Blues* (Kerouac, 1995b). Like Ferlinghetti's *Pictures of the Gone World* (1955), it's a numbered series of word paintings of the city, in which individual poems may stand alone or be considered stanzas in a cycle, and whose form is determined spatially. Kerouac says:

In my system, the form of blues choruses is limited by the small page of the breastpocket notebook in which they are written, like the form of a set number of bars in a jazz blues chorus, and so sometimes the word-meaning can carry from one chorus into another, or not, just like the phrase-meaning can carry harmonically from one chorus to the other, or not, in jazz, so that, in these blues as in jazz, the form is determined by time, and by the musician's spontaneous phrasing & harmonizing with the beat of the time as it waves & waves on by in measured choruses.

Kerouac, 1995b

In a May 1954 letter to Ginsberg, Kerouac describes the origin of what he calls his first book of poetry: 'This is from my new book of poems *San Francisco Blues* that I wrote when I left Neal's in March and went to live in the Cameo Hotel on Third Street Frisco Skidrow – wrote it in a rockingchair at the window, looking down on winos and bebop winos and whores and Cop cars' (Kerouac, 1995c).

70th Chorus

    3rd St is like Moody St
Lowell Massachusetts
It has Bagdad blue
    Dusk down sky

And hills with lights
And pale the hazel
  Gentle blue in the
    burned windows
Of wooden tenements,
  And lights of bars,
    music brawl,
'Hoap!' 'Hap!' & 'Hi'
In the street of blood
And bells billygoating
  Boom by at the ache
    of day
The break of personalities
  Crossing just once
  In the wrong door

Each chorus is a quick sketch, looking out of the window and, in 70th Chorus, into the sundown sky and rundown street. In 1951, the painter Ed White had suggested to Kerouac, 'Just sketch in the streets like a painter but with words' (Clark, 1984), and a few days later he attempted this new technique. Here's an example from *Visions of Cody*:

A sad park of autumn, late Saturday afternoon – leaves by now so dry they make a general rattle all over and a little girl in a green knit cap is squashing leaves against the wire fence and then trying to climb over them – also mothers in the waning light, sitting their kiddies in swing seats of gray iron and pushing them with grave and dutiful playfulness – A little boy in red woodsman shirt stoops to drink water at the dry concrete fountain – a flag whips through the bare bleak branches – salmon is the color of parts of the sky – the children in the swings kick their feet in air, mothers say *Wheee* – a trash wirebasket is half full of dry, dry leaves – a pool of last night's rain lies in the gravel; tonight it will be cold, clear, winter coming and who will haunt the deserted park then?

Kerouac, 1974

70th Chorus is a sketch in verse: offhand, on the spot, spontaneous sight and sound notations, connected paratactically by a dash or 'and', but in short, two- to eight-syllable lines, and with the connotative language, compression and music of poetry. This technique abjures revision, and assumes that a poet can improvise as successfully as a jazz musician: 'It's all gotta be non stop ad libbing within each chorus, or the gig is shot' (Kerouac, 1995b). In a letter written when preparing the manuscript for publication, Kerouac notes that he's restored 'original lines that I had tried to erase and write over of [sic] in 1954!' (Kerouac, 1995c). Improvisation had existed in oral poetry, in primitive song, in Homer's interpolations, where pre-existing material helped shape the poem, and in written Japanese *renga*, from which the independent haiku emerged, where complex rules were meant to assure form.

Notice that the opening lines of the following chorus:

> Nevermore to remain
>> Nevermore to return

can be read as a natural continuation of the last lines of 70th Chorus, where two people cross paths and don't connect. Then there's a dash, and 71st Chorus veers off into an evocation of other rooms in the hotel; however, the riff about Third Street and Moody Street is restated. This raises the question of whether 70th Chorus should be read alone, or with the first two lines of 71st Chorus, or do both choruses make a poem, or the whole cycle? Kerouac said in a June 1961 letter, 'I see it is a beautiful unity' (Kerouac, 1999b) and, in the introduction to *Mexico City Blues*, 'I want to be considered a jazz poet blowing a long blues in an afternoon jam session on Sunday' (Kerouac, 1959). Kerouac blurs the line between prose and poetry, between one poem and the next, and between life and art, because he's not imagining, he's sitting in the rocking chair in the Cameo Hotel, improvising.

The poetry wavers between evocative phrases, 'and hills with lights', and light metaphor, 'the street of blood'. Besides the parallels with Ferlinghetti already outlined, the chorus seems to be influenced by the rich and quick-changing language of Shakespeare in *Hamlet*:

> And I, of ladies most deject and wretched,
> that suck'd the honey of his music vows,
> now see that noble and most sovereign reason,
> like sweet bells jangled, out of tune and harsh . . .

Shakespeare, 1604, III.i.158–61

in phrases like

> music brawl,
> 'Hoap!' 'Hap!' & 'Hi'
> In the street of blood
> And bells billygoating

by translations of Japanese haiku by R. H. Blyth (Blyth, 1942):

> Not a single stone
> To throw at the dog –
>> The wintry moon!

Taigi, 18th C.

The silence!
The voice of the cicada
    Penetrates the rocks.

Basho, 17th C.

On the sandy beach,
Footprints:
    Long is the spring day.

Shiki, 19th C.

in its five triads by indentation:

It has Bagdad blue
    Dusk down sky
    And hills with lights

and by Ginsberg's 1953 long poem, 'The Green Automobile':

But first we'll drive the stations of downtown,
    poolhall flophouse jazzjoint jail
    whorehouse down Folsom
        to the darkest alleys of Larimer

paying respects to Denver's father
    lost on the railroad tracks,
    stupor of wine and silence
        hallowing the slum of his decades,

Ginsberg, 1963

in its short lines and downbeat city images:

Gentle blue in the
    burned windows
Of wooden tenements,

acknowledged by Kerouac: 'Allen had influenced me with mad image-makings and crazy "oops!" writing' (Kerouac, 1995c).

San Francisco Blues was written, according to an April 1962 letter, 'with that fuckyou freedom' (Kerouac, 1999b), which means, 'in poetry, you can be completely free to say anything you want, you don't have to tell a story, you can use secret puns' (Kerouac, 1999a). One consequence of freedom from considering the reader is private reference, and the poem begins by comparing the present street with one in memory, whose importance is clear only when it's known that it's his teenage street, and by associating 'Bagdad' and 'blue', as though from an illustration in a childhood copy of *The Arabian Nights*. The collocation of San Francisco, Lowell and Bagdad suggest that it doesn't matter what city he's living in, there's always a rundown street, as in Ferlinghetti's 'The Long Street':

> The long street
> which is the street of the world
>
> Ferlinghetti, 1958

The introduction to the street is one sentence, and the rest of the poem another; light punctuation increases the ambiguity of the phrases. The body of the poem, using alliteration on *b* for all major words, is divided into an evocation of the serenity of nature – 'blue dusk', 'gentle blue' – and a meditation on the fury of humanity – 'brawl', 'blood', 'billygoating', 'boom', 'break'. The poem is unified by other music, of assonance on *a*, as well, in 'pale the hazel', 'ache / of day / The break'. The alliterative sequence 'Hoap!' 'Hap!' & 'Hi', which are nonsense, is a Kerouac signature, coming from his love of language before semantics; in almost every poem, there is a series of pure sound syllables.

After the peace of the sky at dusk, the poem turns at the 'burned windows' in the 'wooden tenements', which can be seen as reflecting blue sky and red sunset, or as having been literally burned, or as burning with the fire of neglect. Violence emerges, as out of the bars comes 'music brawl', which can be loud music, or music followed by a fight. '"Hoap!" "Hap!" & "Hi"', which sound like jazz scat singing, are half-heard words from below, or symbols, monosyllabic and meaningless, of people who fail to communicate, yelled 'In the street of blood'; the meanings of the homonyms, hope, hap and high, are there in undertone.

The bells are the evening angelus, ringing a call to prayer in the down and out Mission district; however, they don't evoke prayer or restore peace: they are 'billygoating', an image associated with the devil, or bells on animals, and 'boom', like explosions. 'The ache of day' is a poignant play on 'the break of day'; 'break' is then picked up in 'The break of personalities', as possible friends or lovers 'cross', one going in, one out, in a verb alluding to crucifixion, and fail to connect in their one chance at the entry to the harsh bar, which is 'the wrong door'.

The name Beat was originally intended by Kerouac to mean beat down; he later revised it to include beatific – in his words, 'beat, meaning down and out but full of intense conviction' (Kerouac, 1995a). The 'tenements' and 'bars' evoke the earlier sense, and 'bells' and 'crossing' the latter. The poet looks out of the skid row hotel window and plays a downhearted solo on the saxophone of our language. That he's not in the street, but at the window, gives a natural aesthetic distance, important to art.

In his *Paris Review* interview, Kerouac equates a stanza with a breath:

... a tenor man drawing a breath and blowing a phrase on his saxophone, till he runs out of breath, and when he does, his sentence, his statement's been made ... That's how I therefore separate my sentences, as breath separations of the mind ... I formulated the theory of breath as measure, in prose and verse ... in 1953 at the request of Burroughs and Ginsberg.

Kerouac, 1999a

If 70th Chorus is rewritten in possible breaths:

> It has Bagdad blue dusk down sky and hills with lights
>> and pale the hazel gentle blue in the burned
>> windows of wooden tenements,
> and lights of bars, music brawl, 'Hoap!' 'Hap!' & 'Hi'
>> in the street of blood, and bells billygoating
>> boom by at the ache of day, the break of
>> personalities crossing just once in the wrong door

it's the sound of Ginsberg's 'Howl':

> who walked all night with their shoes full of blood
>> on the snowbank docks waiting for a door
>> in the East River to open to a room full of
>> steamheat and opium,
> who created great suicidal dramas on the apartment
>> cliff-banks of the Hudson under the wartime
>> blue floodlight of the moon & their heads shall
>> be crowned with laurel in oblivion

Ginsberg, 1956

Kerouac was invited by Ginsberg to read at the Six Gallery event, but said no, 'I won't do it because I'm too bashful' (Kerouac, 1995c). But he did show up:

... the big mad capping final night of the great poetry reading with Allen on the stage before a hundred eager Raskolniks in glasses crowding in from the rear of the reading hall, with wine in my hands a gallon jug I'm drinking yelling 'Go', Allen is howling his HOWL pome and other crazy poets there, it's mad, it will never end ...

Kerouac, 1995c

In October 1957, with Philip Lamantia and Howard Hart, and accompanied by the musician David Amram, Kerouac gave the first New York poetry and jazz reading, at the Brata Art Gallery, of these and other poems. He considered *San Francisco Blues* a major book; with its connections to jazz and oral poetry, it's fitting that though choruses appeared in literary journals, it was rejected by publishers, and appeared, as choruses 1–23, on his 1959 recording *Blues and Haikus* (Kerouac, 1990a), with two saxophones – Al Cohn and Zoot Sims – counterpointing and harmonizing; five more choruses appeared in 1960 on *Readings by Jack Kerouac on the Beat Generation* (Kerouac, 1990b). In 1983 it was bootlegged in Bristol, and in 1995 officially published in Kerouac's own anthology of eight blues cycles, *Book of Blues* (Kerouac, 1995b), which includes 'San Francisco Blues', 'Richmond Hill Blues', 'Bowery Blues', 'MacDougal Street Blues', 'Desolation Blues', 'Orizaba 210 Blues', 'Orlanda Blues', 'Cerrada Medellin Blues', but not 'Berkeley Blues', 'Brooklyn Bridge Blues', 'Tangier Blues', 'Washington DC Blues', 'Earthquake Blues'. *Mexico City Blues* (Kerouac, 1959), the longest cycle, was published in 1959. They are sketches improvised in the places they name, occasionally moving into inward meditations, ordered by the mystery that governs the days in which they were written.

Blues and Haikus[1] has the composite quality seen in many Beat poetry texts, which shows radically different ways of poetry side by side. Kerouac's 'blues' are redefined by him, and only have improvisation and low-down feeling in common with the musical form. In the same way, his haikus are redefined by him, and may only have the stanza, three short lines, in common with the Japanese poetic form:

> The 'haiku' was invented and developed over hundreds of years in Japan to be a complete poem in seventeen syllables and to pack in a whole vision of life in three short lines. A 'Western Haiku' need not concern itself with the seventeen syllables since Western languages cannot adapt themselves to the fluid syllabic Japanese. I propose that the 'Western Haiku' simply say a lot in three short lines in any Western language.
>
> Above all, a Haiku must be very simple and free of all poetic trickery and make a little picture and yet be as airy and graceful as a Vivaldi Pastorella. Here is a great Japanese Haiku that is simpler and prettier than any Haiku I could ever write in any language: –

> A day of quiet gladness, –
> Mount Fuji is veiled
> In misty rain.

Basho, 1644–1694

Here is another . . .

> She has put the child to sleep,
> And now washes the clothes;
> The summer moon.

Issa, 1763–1827

And another, by Buson (1715–1783):

> The nightingale is singing,
> Its small mouth,
>   Open.

Kerouac, 1971

He is outlining his inspirations, discovered in volumes of haiku translated by R. H. Blyth (Blyth, 1947–52). He read these books with his friends Gary Snyder, Allen Ginsberg and Philip Whalen in Berkeley in 1955. Kerouac, from the East, found himself as a poet in the West, and improvised street poetry, called blues, but he also worked in the tight form of Western 'haikus', as he acknowledges in his essay 'The Origins of Joy in Poetry':

> The new American poetry as typified by the SF Renaissance (which means Ginsberg, me, Rexroth, Ferlinghetti, McClure, Corso, Gary Snyder, Philip Lamantia, Philip Whalen, I guess) is a kind of new-old Zen Lunacy poetry, writing whatever comes into your head as it comes, poetry returned to its origin, in the bardic child, truly ORAL as Ferling said, instead of gray faced Academic quibbling . . . But SF is the poetry of a new Holy Lunacy like that of ancient times (Li Po, Han Shan, Tom o Bedlam, Kit Smart, Blake) yet it also has that mental discipline typified by the haiku (Basho, Buson), that is, the discipline of pointing out things directly, purely, concretely, no abstractions or explanations, wham wham the true blue song of man.

Kerouac, 1971

Here are ten consecutive poems from *Book of Haikus*:

> Missing a kick
>   at the icebox door
> It closed anyway

> Perfect moonlit night
>   marred
> By family squabbles

> The Spring moon –
>   How many miles away
> Those orange blossoms!

> When the moon sinks
>   down to the power line,
> I'll go in

> Looking up at the stars,
>> feeling sad,
> Going 'tsk tsk tsk'

This July evening,
  A large frog
On my doorsill!

> Dawn, a falling star
>> —A dewdrop lands
> On my head!

In back of the Supermarket,
  in the parking lot weeds,
Purple flowers

> Protected by the clouds,
>> the moon
> Sleeps sailing

Chief Crazy Horse
  looks tearfully north
The first snow flurries

Kerouac, 2003

Earl Miner, author of *Japanese Court Poetry*, notes that haiku in the West keep the concreteness and compression of their Japanese models, but that they're an attempt to graft the exotic Eastern form onto the Western lyric, which doesn't take, and the results are trivial: 'Haiku is too reduced a form and grows too complexly out of its cultural background to be adaptable as a whole into Western languages' (Miner, 1974). He is referring to haiku's roots in the larger forms of *renga* and *tanka*, its syllabic music and its allusiveness. But Kerouac transforms all he touches. Given modern prose, he improvises sketches; given the blues, he writes notebook page poetry; and so, given haiku, rather than repeating the failure Miner points out, he tries to reinvent it as a Western form. It isn't about seasonal words or 17 syllables, but it keeps the Zen objectivity praised in Basho by his favoured translator, R. H. Blyth (Blyth, 1942), whether Basho is looking at the object:

By the roadside,
  A Rose of Sharon;
    The horse has eaten it.
... (There is colour, there is movement; the horse's strange, rubber-like nose nuzzling the flower; no poet anywhere to be seen)

or the subject:

> Leaves of the willow tree fall;
>> The master and I stand listening
>>> To the sound of the bell.
> … (The ear full of sound; the heart full of silence; the communion of saints).

Kerouac, in a notebook, describes this method: 'Keep the eye STEADILY on the object' (Kerouac, 2003). This leads to concreteness, where the senses are always engaged; when he says 'pack in', this leads to compression, where the music is in the scarcity of syllables. In so few words, distributed alliteration, as in 'moonlit night / marred', and assonance, as in 'Horse / looks tearfully north', are intensified. In 'Perfect moonlit night / marred / By family squabbles', we imagine outdoors and indoors, see the moon's grace and hear the husband and wife, or father and son, yelling; we feel the distance between the moon on its way, and the family in disharmony. Kerouac's haikus span the worlds of nature: moon, blossoms, stars, frog, dewdrop, weeds, flowers, clouds, snow; and man: icebox, family, power line, doorsill, supermarket, Crazy Horse.

'Missing a kick / at the icebox door / It closed anyway' appears to lack imagery from nature, until it's seen that the physics of the spring that closes the door is natural, and that the point is that, as the *Tao Te Ching* says, inaction when appropriate is fine, since 'Good government comes of itself' (Bynner, 1944). The haiku 'Chief Crazy Horse / looks tearfully north / The first snow flurries' which Kerouac thought his best, is an historical epic in three lines that hold the uncertain stand, the nobility and the final grief of the American Indians.

Kerouac speaks of discipline in relation to haiku, and invokes concreteness and compression. It's a revelation to find that this writer, associated with spontaneous prose and poetry, recommends revision when writing in this form: 'haiku is best reworked and revised' (Kerouac, 1999a). In this interview, he goes on to compose a haiku, recasting and paring the lines. This artifice can be seen inside one haiku, or the whole series. There is a sequence in the haikus quoted: kitchen, home in moonlight, moon, stars, evening, morning, flowers, the moon and sleep, a dream of history. *Book of Haikus* is composed. He follows, not the laws, but the spirit of the haiku, knowing that a masterpiece makes its own laws.

The modernists were influenced by haiku, with a few memorable results: Ezra Pound's 'In a Station of the Metro' (1912), Wallace Stevens' 'Thirteen Ways of Looking at a Blackbird' (1917), William Carlos Williams' 'The Red Wheelbarrow' (1923). Earl Miner asserts that Pound's idea of 'super-position', where the objective transforms into the subjective, was modelled on haiku, and informs his later work (Miner, 1974). But Kerouac devoted himself to haiku, and wrote and rewrote hundreds of them, arranging them into books.

The 'haikus' written from 1956 to 1961, in the shirt pocket notebooks with sketches and blues, were selected, revised and sequenced for *Book of Haikus*, which was rejected by publishers, and published, in part, on the same 1959 recording as *San Francisco Blues, Blues and Haikus* (Kerouac, 1990a). His performance there, with saxophone players alternating at improvising responses, is extraordinary. Talking about the Beat poets reading out loud to jazz, David Meltzer says, Kerouac 'had the truest ear and spirit for it, his language responding to the music easily. His work on record with Al Cohn and Zoot Sims displayed some lovely possibilities' (Silesky, 1990). Because I could no longer wait for the publication of Kerouac's lost book, I selected and calligraphed *American Haikus*, in 1992. The complete *Book of Haikus* (Kerouac, 2003), with 213 poems on a world of subjects, was published in 2003 as one of the sections of *Book of Haikus*, with two later manuscripts, *Desolation Pops* and *Beat Generation Haikus*, and uncollected haikus gathered from his notebooks and prose.

Regina Weinreich summarizes Kerouac's achievement, in form: 'the purposeful caesura or cut of Japanese haiku as key to its sound and sense'; and in content: 'the rendering of a subject's essence, and the shimmering, ephemeral nature of its fleeting existence' (Kerouac, 2003). Both can be seen in the haiku:

> In back of the Supermarket,
>   in the parking lot weeds,
> Purple flowers

Kerouac, 2003

where the cut comes between 'weeds' and 'Purple flowers'; the nature of flowers, 'born to blush unseen', is encountered in the neglected lot. Kerouac's *haikus* are like those flowers: everyone's in the supermarket, and they bloom anyway. Ginsberg says of Kerouac, 'In addition he has the one sure sign of being a great poet, which is he's the only one in the United States who knows how to write haiku' (Kerouac, 1999a). There is nothing like *Book of Haikus* in our literature: it's an American classic. What did Kerouac say? 'Come back and tell me in a hundred years' (Kerouac, 1992).

Notes

1. In Japanese and English, haiku is both the singular and plural form. Kerouac consciously violated this convention by saying haikus, in an effort to Westernize the form.

Bibliography

Blyth, R. H., *Zen in English Literature and Oriental Classics*, Tokyo: Hokuseido Press, 1942.

Blyth, R. H., *Haiku*, Volumes 1–4, Tokyo: Hokuseido Press, 1947–52.

Bynner, Witter, *The Way of Life According to Laotzu*, New York: Farrar, Straus and Giroux, 1944 (1978).

Clark, Tom, *Jack Kerouac*, New York: Harcourt Brace Jovanovich, 1984.

Ferlinghetti, Lawrence, *Pictures of the Gone World*, San Francisco: City Lights Books, 1955 (1995).

Ferlinghetti, Lawrence, *A Coney Island of the Mind*, New York: New Directions Books, 1958.

Ginsberg, Allen, *Howl and Other Poems*, San Francisco: City Lights Books, 1956.

Ginsberg, Allen, *Reality Sandwiches*, San Francisco: City Lights Books, 1963 (written 1953–60).

Kerouac, Jack, *On the Road*, New York: Viking Press, 1957 (written 1951–2).

Kerouac, Jack, *Mexico City Blues*, New York: Grove Press, 1959 (written 1955).

Kerouac, Jack, in Lawrence Ferlinghetti (ed.), *Scattered Poems*, San Francisco: City Lights Books, 1971 (written 1954–65).

Kerouac, Jack, *Visions of Cody*, New York: McGraw-Hill, 1974 (written 1951–2).

Kerouac, Jack, *Pomes All Sizes*, San Francisco: City Lights Books, 1992 (written 1945–66).

Kerouac, Jack, 'About the Beat Generation', in Ann Charters (ed.), *The Portable Jack Kerouac*, New York: Viking Press, 1995a (written 1957).

Kerouac, Jack, *Book of Blues*, New York: Penguin Books, 1995b (written 1954–61).

Kerouac, Jack, 'Letter to Donald Allen', in Ann Charters (ed.), *Selected Letters*, Vol. 1, New York: Viking Press, 1995c (written 1940–56).

Kerouac, Jack, 'Jack Kerouac', in George Plimpton (ed.), *Beat Writers at Work*, New York: Modern Library, 1999a (1968).

Kerouac, Jack, 'Letter to Allen Ginsberg', 'Letter to Don Allen', in Ann Charters (ed.), *Selected Letters*, Vol. 2, New York: Viking Press, 1999b (written 1957–69).

Kerouac, Jack, 'Book of Haikus', in Regina Weinreich (ed.), *Book of Haikus*, New York: Penguin Books, 2003 (written 1956–61).

Miner, Earl, 'Haiku', in Alex Preminger (ed.), *Princeton Encyclopedia of Poetry and Poetics*, enlarged edn, Princeton, NJ: Princeton University Press, 1974.

Shakespeare, William, *The tragicall historie of Hamlet, Prince of Denmarke*, London: James Roberts, 1604.

Silesky, Barry, *Ferlinghetti: the Artist in His Time*, New York: Warner Books, 1990.

Weinreich, Regina, *Kerouac's Spontaneous Poetic: A Study of the Fiction*, 2nd edn, New York: Thunder's Mouth Press, 2001.

Discography

Kerouac, Jack, *Blues and Haikus*, The Jack Kerouac Collection, Rhino Records cd, Disc 2, New York: Hanover, 1990a (recorded 1959).

Kerouac, Jack, *Readings by Jack Kerouac on the Beat Generation*, The Jack Kerouac Collection, Rhino Records cd, Disc 3, New York: Verve, 1990b (recorded 1960).

CHAPTER 4
DUET FOR SAXOPHONE AND PEN: LEE KONITZ AND THE DIRECT INFLUENCE OF JAZZ ON THE DEVELOPMENT OF JACK KEROUAC'S 'SPONTANEOUS PROSE' STYLE
Marian Jago

I wanted to put my hand to an enormous pean which would unite my vision of America with words spilled out in the modern spontaneous method.

> Kerouac, *Visions of Cody*, Preface

I knew that they [the Beats] were there, but I didn't know how much they were listening.

> Lee Konitz, letter to author, 2001

An examination of Kerouac's writings and letters details an evolution in style which sought to emulate creative practices found in jazz improvisation. By his own repeated admission, Kerouac expressed a desire to be considered a jazz musician who played with words, who sought to transcend the rigid boundaries of the written page and to exist 'in the moment' alongside the passages of jazz he found so compelling. In September of 1945, Kerouac wrote to Allen Ginsberg of his artistic frustrations and ambitions, stating, '[remember] . . . last summer how I was searching for a new method in order to release what I had in me . . . Fact was, I had the vision . . . I think everyone has . . . what we lack is the method' (Charters, 1995, p. 98). In 1951, Kerouac would come to discover that the method he was seeking – the approach he would come to call 'spontaneous prose' – lay in the conscious emulation of certain jazz practices. A longstanding jazz fan who had heard the likes of Billie Holiday, Lester Young and Charlie Parker at various New York clubs, Kerouac found himself profoundly affected by the musical approach of altoist Lee Konitz, mentions of whom litter Kerouac's journals, letters and novels written post-1951 when utilizing or attempting to describe his new 'spontaneous prose style'.[1] As late as 1957, when writing to editor Donald Allen, Kerouac would say of his inspiration to adopt a 'spontaneous prose' method that, '[l]ike Lee Konitz in 1951 I want to blow as deep as I want' (Charters, 1999, p.18).

Much has been written over the years about the connection between the Beats and the aesthetic of post-Second World War jazz expression in general, as well as a reasonable amount on the importance of jazz to Kerouac's writing style especially, though very little of this has dealt with Lee Konitz's influence specifically. As a very small sampling of work in this area, one may find John Shapcott's examination of 'spontaneous improvisation' and the ways in which bebop's emphasis on immediacy, spatial intimacy and spontaneous outbursts of appreciation or encouragement during the course of a jazz performance are replicated conversationally in the taped conversations that formed the basis for Kerouac's *Visions of Cody* (1972). Shapcott draws attention to the ways in which the linear and referential structure of the taped speeches resemble improvised jazz solos, and how Kerouac undertook the task of representing the spontaneity of everyday conversation in a manner which bore the speaker's distinct psychological signature. Shapcott further suggests that the difficulties Kerouac encountered in trying to capture the improvisational nature of conversation can be seen as similar to the ways in which the expressive nuance of idiomatic jazz expression resists musical notation (Shapcott, 2002, p. 236).

James Campbell (1999) reconsiders Kerouac's love for jazz in light of his seeming ignorance of the black American literary tradition (Campbell, 1999, p. 367), while James Hopkins's thought-provoking article, 'To Be or Not to Bop: Jack Kerouac's *On the Road* and the Culture of Bebop and Rhythm 'n' Blues' (2002), seeks to unravel the convoluted timelines involved in the life experiences, drafting and redrafting of *On the Road* in the context of historical developments in jazz and jazz reception.[2] Douglas Malcolm (1999) considers some of the wider implications of this jazz influence, and looks at the extent to which the mapping of musical theory/practice onto literary practice is possible, before suggesting that the role of jazz to Kerouac might be most important not in the practical application of its stylistic principles, but in its 'ideological, behavioral, and semiotic' effect (Malcolm, 1999, p. 85). These prescient insights are clouded somewhat by his confluence of improvised compositional *practice* with the eventual stasis of words (post-composition) on the page,[3] and by a lack of expertise with regard to jazz performance practice, about which he makes several assumptions that might charitably be considered problematic. In wondering why Kerouac did not give equal consideration to other forms of jazz practice beyond those tied to the breath – overlooking that Kerouac's model was a saxophonist[4] – Malcom then compounds this oversight by relying on saxophonist Larry Teal's interpretation of desirable saxophone phrasing (Malcolm, 1999, p. 91) without pausing to consider that Teal is a classical rather than jazz saxophonist, and that the various idioms may well have competing or incompatible notions of style. Kerouac, of course, would have been concerned with tone, phrasing and delivery appropriate to jazz, not classical performance.

Michael Jarrett, in his excellent work on tropes in/of jazz writing, is right to remind us that perhaps improvisation, in a literary context, ought best to be considered emblematic of a creative problem and possible methodological approach, rather than as a tangible solution or product – as process, for how can writing be improvised once it has been transcribed (Jarrett, 1994, p. 341)? This sort of wider thinking on the linkage between jazz and improvisational practices and literary endeavour is reiterated by Meta Du Ewa Jones who, in writing about African American poetry, suggests that we move toward an approach which might yield

> an appropriate sense of the dynamic interplay between vocal and visual characteristics in musically influenced Black poetry. A scholarship that recognizes the oral and textual as imbricated, not disparate, elements [and] . . . how the vocal and the visual are performed across the geographic space of the page.
>
> Du Ewa Jones, 2002, p. 66

Of these and myriad other works which explore in some fashion the linkage between Kerouac and jazz, only three have specifically considered the role that alto saxophonist Lee Konitz has had on Kerouac's methodological development, despite Kerouac's frequent referencing of Konitz in his works of fiction and personal correspondence. Preston Whaley's *Blows Like A Horn: Beat Writing, Jazz Style, and Markets in the Transformation of U.S. Culture* (2004) mentions Konitz only in passing, concentrating instead upon the recording, in 1949, of the firstly freely improvised jazz tunes ('Intuition' and 'Digression') by the Lennie Tristano Sextet, of which Konitz was a part, and which may have had some affective impact on Kerouac's conception for *Visions of Cody*. Sterritt (2000) too mentions Konitz only in passing (as the 'lyrical-alto' source of Kerouac's early-1950s inspiration), on his way to considering various definitions of improvisation (revision, prevision) and the ways in which the allure and mystique surrounding (jazz) improvisation in the mid-twentieth century might have served as an attractive bulwark of 'aesthetic and psychological authenticity' against uncertainties and suspicions regarding the authenticity of artistic works and practices in an era of technological reproduction and manipulation (Sterritt, 2000, p. 164).

Indeed the only significant consideration of Konitz's influence on Kerouac comes from Tim Hunt, whose '"Blow As Deep As You Want To Blow": Time, Textuality, and Jack Kerouac's Development of Spontaneous Prose' (2012) repeatedly underscores the importance of Konitz to Kerouac's developing style and work on *On the Road*. Though reference to Konitz has long been available in Kerouac's published novels (*Desolation Angels*, *Visions of Cody*) and collected letters (Charters, 1995, 1999), Hunt benefitted from access to the Jack Kerouac Archive, from which additional journals mentioning Konitz were released in 2016 (*The Unknown Kerouac: Rare, Unpublished & Newly Translated Writings*). Here for the first time we might read the full and unadulterated journal entry in which Kerouac describes an evening listening to Konitz at Birdland as one of the great discoveries of his life, a profoundly affective moment which helped Kerouac past frustrations and hesitation in the development of his writing style (Kerouac, 1951, in Tietchen, 2016, pp. 137–40).

Despite widespread recognition of the role of jazz in the development of Kerouac's prose and to the Beat aesthetic more generally, the view of Kerouac's relationship with jazz has oftentimes been something of a limited or myopic one. For instance, one track from *Poetry for the Beat Generation* (Kerouac, 1959) has done much to propagate the notion that, of all jazz players, Charlie Parker spoke most immediately to Kerouac and figured as his most prominent jazz influence. Entitled simply 'Charlie Parker', it is one of Kerouac's jazz / poetry attempts (along with 'October in the Railroad Earth' from the same recording session) to have survived with any sort of mainstream popularity.

> Charley [sic] Parker, who recently died
> Laughing at a juggler on the TV
> after weeks of strain and sickness,
> was called the perfect musician.
> And the expression on his face . . .
> . . . The expression that says 'All is Well'
> – This was what Charley Parker
> Said when he played, All is Well.
> You had the feeling of early in the morning
> Like a hermit's joy, . . .
> . . . Charley Parker the secret unsayable name
> That carries with it merit
> Not to be measured from here
> To up, down, east or west

Kerouac, 1959, 239–41

Though one of the most eloquent literary tributes to Charlie Parker, the poem's worth as a signifier of Kerouac's own personal jazz aesthetic has perhaps been overstated. One cannot deny the influence of Parker upon almost every jazz musician and enthusiast since his emergence on the scene in Kansas City during the late 1930s. Nonetheless, I would deny that Parker exercised any significant *direct* influence upon Kerouac's writing style beyond his hand in the invention of bebop, the formalization of which stands as the basis for Kerouac's literary attempts at jazz-styled improvisation. Though Kerouac adored Parker, referring to him as 'the Only' (Kerouac, 1993, p. 358), and crediting him (quite correctly) as a major force in the creation of modern jazz (Kerouac, 1993, p. 370), Kerouac would instead take pains to align himself specifically with the white alto saxophonist Lee Konitz,[5] who, in the late 1940s and early 1950s, was developing a tone and style on the alto saxophone independent of Parker's pervasive influence. In Konitz, Kerouac found a particular and direct inspiration as he sought to develop his own literary voice, and in the process, a new form of American prose. In Konitz, Kerouac saw not only *that* such visions could be achieved, but *how*.

Though never afforded much widespread or mainstream popular appeal, within jazz circles, Lee Konitz has been highly regarded by both fans and critics since his emergence on the scene in the 1940s, first with the Claude Thornhill Orchestra and then with pianist Lennie Tristano, with whom he would form a significant working relationship.[6] In addition to his idiomatic jazz playing, Konitz has been a driving, albeit at times subliminal force in the avant-garde, recording and performing with Tristano on some of the first 'free jazz' recordings in 1949,[7] an improvisational aesthetic that he has repeatedly returned to during his career both live and on record, and which deeply informs his performance practice.

Though Kerouac peppers his novels and letters with direct references to jazz and to some of its key players, it was Konitz who served as a specific inspiration for Kerouac's 'spontaneous prose' method – Kerouac's attempt not to *write* novels in the classical sense, but to *blow* life through his pen as he saw Konitz do through his horn, constantly chasing the new idea. In particular, Konitz's trademark use of extended eight-note lines marked by an unorthodox use of accents and poly-rhythmic effects parallels Kerouac's own use of long-line technique in prose, and of idiosyncratic punctuation. Throughout Kerouac's novels and correspondence Konitz is alluded to, lionized and, most tellingly, assumed by Kerouac as a musical alter ego (Charters, 1995, p. 327; Charters, 1999, p. 18). It was the distilled immediacy of the moment which compelled Kerouac, and it may be why he turned to Konitz, one of jazz's master improvisers.

In all of Kerouac's mature work,[8] great effort is made to approximate the improvisational nature of jazz on the written page. In his short essay 'Essentials of Spontaneous Prose' (Kerouac, 1958), Kerouac comments that when writing, 'language is undisturbed flow from the mind of personal secret idea-words, *blowing* (as per jazz musician) on subject of image' (Kerouac, 1958, p. 72) and that, in terms of a particular methodology, there should be 'No periods separating sentence-structures already arbitrarily riddled by false colons and timid usually needless commas – but the vigorous space dash separating rhetorical breathing (as the jazz musician drawing breath between outblown phrases)' (Kerouac, 1958, p. 73).

Further, in the liner notes to *Poetry for the Beat Generation* (Kerouac, 1959), we receive the oft quoted remark by Kerouac that he 'want[ed] to be considered a jazz poet/blowing a long blues in an afternoon jam/session on Sunday'.[9] Kerouac as well took pains to inform his audience that all of the tracks on *Poetry for the Beat Generation* (Kerouac, 1959) had been completed in single takes, hoping, one assumes, that his jazz-literate audience would make the obvious methodological connection and equate his efforts with the immediate creativity of improvised jazz performance.[10] Such declarations made public Kerouac's long-harboured desire to be equated as an artist with the jazz musicians he admired and, through the evolving nature of his literary method, to reinvent not only the manner in which an author manipulated words upon the page, but how those words were conceived and expelled. With conscious purpose, Kerouac sought to forge a new form of literary expression through a direct attempt to mirror the creative practices of jazz players.

It becomes clear when reading Kerouac's correspondence that his artistic ethos was based nearly entirely upon a musical aesthetic. In seeking analogies and examples to express his editorial frustrations and to detail his concept of the creative process, Kerouac repeatedly draws upon the musical metaphor:

... I can't possibly go on as a responsible prose artist and also a believer in the
impulses of my own heart and in the beauty of pure spontaneous language if I
let editors take my sentences, which are my phrases that I separate by dashes
when 'I draw a breath', each of which pours out to the tune of the whole story its
own rhythmic yawp of expostulation, & [sic] riddle them with commas ...
ruining the swing [of the work/idea] ...

Kerouac, 1957, in Charters, 1999, p. 17

That the music in question is specifically jazz becomes clear through Kerouac's
repeated allusions to writing, and indeed to most forms of spontaneous creativity,
as 'blowing' (jazz parlance for improvising/soloing), and to punctuation as being
akin to drawing breath. Kerouac's idiosyncratic use of punctuation signalled not a
conventional pause in the structured narrative, but rather a necessary halt in the
writer's own thought process – a momentary pause for air or inspiration, a physical
break in the writing/inspirational process itself, much as a horn player is required to
do when drawing breath, forming and punctuating phrases with pauses that accentuate
and drive the rhythmic impetus of both the piece as a whole and that instrumentalist's
particular commentary upon it when soloing.

Much as the jazz musician practises scales and exercises daily, cultivating a musical
vocabulary to be drawn upon without thought during an actual performance, Kerouac
wrote constantly, carrying around a pocket notebook to record his observations,
many of which later appeared in his novels and poetry. For Kerouac, it followed that
a writer could practise his skill in the same manner that a musician did, and could
then draw upon his talents to produce an uncorrected, intuitive and truthful
representation of place and feeling. Kerouac's well-known practice of 'sketching', an
activity wherein the writer would recall a place, person or event and then write a non-
stop, uncorrected, flowing description of the recalled image, reflects in some ways the
process of improvising over chord changes. Memory, much like the melodies and
chord structures of standard tunes, would play a vital role in Kerouac's methodology,
functioning as source material to which he would frequently return (Sterritt, 2000,
p. 168). Biographer Gerald Nicosia details that Kerouac would often 'write in his head'
during participation in daily events, simultaneously transcribing his felt experience in
order that the act of putting words on paper at a later date became a mechanical
extension of this embodied process (Nicosia, 1983, p. 521). This process again mirrors
in some ways the compositional practices of jazz musicians, wherein the musical
gestures are often noted on paper only long after they have been sung or played into
being.

Kerouac's use of the pocket notebook was not limited to the purposes of practice
however, and served to tie the day-to-day realities of Kerouac's methodology to his
inspirational model of the jazz player by using the size of the notebook to mimic the
compact structure of blues and standard chord progressions (most often 12 and 32
bars, respectively). Composed in such pocket notebooks, Kerouac's book of poetry

San Francisco Blues (1954) gained its lyrical form and structure therefore not from the *accidental* nature of the small pages upon which it was written, but, along with its later counterpart *Mexico City Blues* (1959), from a *conscious* attempt to approximate the form and function of the standard 12-bar blues, a popular vehicle for jazz improvisation. Pages could have been conjoined at a later date to form longer lines and larger works rather than the loosely interconnected series of poetic 'choruses' that comprise the work's final form, but were not. Rather, Kerouac used the limited size of the notebook as a means of creative limitation or structure, much in the way that chord structures and song forms function for jazz musicians.

> In my system, the form of blues choruses is limited by the small page of the breast pocket notebook in which they are written, like the form of a set number of bars in a jazz blues chorus, and so sometimes the word-meaning can carry harmonically from one chorus to the other; or not, in jazz, so that, in these blues as in jazz, the form is determined by time, and by the musician [or poet's] spontaneous phrasing & harmonizing with the beat of the time as it waves & waves on by in measured choruses. It's all gotta be non stop ad libbing within each chorus, or the gig is shot.
>
> Kerouac, 1961, in Charters, 1999, p. 337

Kerouac sought to be constrained merely by subject matter and the breadth of his creativity, stretching out within forgiving boundaries much as he saw jazz musicians do nightly, limited within tune structures only by their own creative stamina; winding and reworking the 'standard' repertoire endlessly, evening after evening. If *San Francisco Blues* (1954), *On the Road* (1957) and *Visions of Cody* (1960) can be seen as reasonably successful attempts at realizing an improvisatorial model for literature based upon jazz playing, it should be recognized that Kerouac sought such a model specifically. But more than simply borrowing forms from the jazz tradition, Kerouac turned for inspiration and methodological guidance to Lee Konitz, one of the music's most original and masterful improvisers as he searched to develop his own voice and distance himself from the existing American literary canon.

One of the few works to include close musical analysis and transcription in a discussion of the connections between jazz and poetry in America post-Second World War, Charles O. Hartman's *Jazz Text: Voice and Improvisation in Poetry, Jazz and Song* (1991), features Lee Konitz as the work's first topic of discussion. Indeed, the only other jazz musician to rate an entire chapter is noted free jazz pioneer Ornette Coleman. Hartman as well unwittingly furnishes, in his cogent and striking examination of Lee Konitz's 1953 rendering of 'All the Things You Are', a description of Konitz's style which well reflects those elements seized upon by Kerouac. In discussing how Konitz's rendering of this Jerome Kern tune, a standard in the jazz repertoire, differs from the original as penned, Hartman informs us that Konitz, through his radical restructuring of the tune creates an

... irregular rhythm [which] combine[d] with the much increased fragmentation of phrases ... heighten[s] the sense of fast time, of events crowding together. Rhythmic displacement, which the listener felt previously only in relation to the unheard, remembered melody, here comes more directly into your awareness – less an idea, more an immediate sensation.

Hartman 1991, p. 17

In nearly every way, this eloquent description of Konitz's playing reflects assessment that followed the publication of *On the Road* (1957), and, indeed, which seems to invade any discussion of Kerouac's literary contributions to this day. As Konitz sought to displace associations common to certain tunes in terms of rhythm, melody and emotional context, so too did Kerouac seek, through a similar self-conscious manipulation of conventional phrasing techniques, to reinvent the American novel. His spontaneous prose method is often described as a 'rush of ideas' which conspire to force events together, create strange juxtapositions and prompt unique emotional responses to the events described. Indeed, the events of a narrative to Kerouac often seem to be (as chords and melody are to Konitz) more a vehicle for the abstract expression – the hows and whys of playing and writing – rather than as ends entirely in and of themselves.

Blessed with a lithe, effervescent, yet business-like tone, in the late 1940s and 1950s, Konitz developed an approach which reclaimed the alto saxophone from the sole possession of Charlie Parker, a style which stressed long running lines of eight notes, unique accent placement and a melodic, or horizontal approach to harmony which, for the most part, eschewed lick and pattern-based playing. Konitz's style favoured a more introverted exploration of tonal colours, phrasing and rhythmic placement to detail a tune, rather than the more extroverted displays of (often macho) virtuosity prevalent in much bebop of the time and exemplified by the Blue Note 'blowing session' records of the 1950s and 1960s.

Lee Konitz arrived in New York [from Chicago] playing Charlie Parker's horn [the alto saxophone] at a time when Parker was not only the most influential altoist, but the most influential musician in jazz. When not only fellow alto players, but tenor men, pianists, even drummers were trying desperately to sound like Bird – he became the only altoist to develop and retain a unique style in that atmosphere. Which ain't too shabby for a kid of 21.

Tesser, 1980, p. 16

This passage from *Down Beat* provides a commentary that perhaps helps to explain more fully Kerouac's particular identification with Konitz as he sought to free himself from the influence of the American literary canon and forge a new, historically resonant literary style (Weinreich, 1987, p. 19).

When one considers not merely what Konitz played, but rather *how*, in relation to his contemporaries, Kerouac's choice of him as stylistic role model becomes easy to understand. Indeed, the way Konitz's lithe, mercurial phrasing perpetually jaunts across the top of the rhythm section may have seemed to Kerouac the distilled essence of his own obsession with notions of movement and immediacy. Polar opposites which ultimately pulled Kerouac apart, motion and presence nonetheless appeared to sustain Konitz (the jazz musician) – seemingly able to be at once truly present in the artistic moment, yet never tied to it; ever reaching and creating, yet not chained irrevocably to the prior note played, the prior instant experienced.

On Monday, 8 October 1951, while actively searching for a methodology which resonated with his artistic ambitions yet still simultaneously worried about reception, reputation and literary success, Kerouac recorded in his journal that he had encountered one of the 'great discoveries of [his] life'. Kerouac was at Birdland, and though he had almost certainly heard Konitz on prior occasions in groups led by Lennie Tristano, Konitz's playing that evening prompted the epiphany that the saxophonist was doing 'exactly what I am ... but on alto'.[11] In a performance of 'I'll Remember April', Kerouac heard that Konitz:

> ... foresaw the tune straight through, took complete command of it, let measures
> of it carry it along on its own impetus while he busied himself *within it* with his
> own conception of it – a conception so profoundly interior that only the keenest
> ear could tell what he was doing ... beautiful, sad, long phrases, in fact long
> sentences that leave you hanging in wonder what's going on and suddenly he
> reveals the solution and when he does, with the same vast foresight that he
> brings to a tune. You now understand it with vast *hindsight* – a hindsight that
> you wouldn't have gotten without his foresight, and a hindsight that at last gives
> you the complete university education in the harmonic structure of 'I Remember
> April' [sic] ...

> Kerouac, 1951, in Tietchen, 2016, pp. 136–7

Not only did Kerouac hear in Konitz's phrasing something which resonated with his own literary approach, but in Konitz's idiosyncratic approach to jazz improvisation, he saw a way to see past concerns about reception and contemporary comparisons.

> ... here I've been worried all along that people wouldn't understand this new
> work of mine because next to Daphne du Maurier it is almost completely
> unintelligible (for instance)! – *does LEE KONITZ worry about VAUGHN
> MONROE?* ... Konitz's interest is artistic or shall we say *laborious*, workaday,
> *genuinely hung-up* in the art, the craft, the agony of the thing ... Does Konitz try
> to tone down his imagination to make his music more understandable to the
> masses? – he's not playing for the masses, he's playing for musicians and listeners

...and he knows that the masses or a least masses of listeners would catch up and listen in the future and find their souls transformed ...

Kerouac, 1951, in Tietchen, 2016, p. 137

Emboldened, Kerouac then wrote the phrase he would later reiterate in a variety of forms and places.[12]

I noted down in pencil in the gloom of Birdland at 2 a.m. – 'Now – BLOW AS DEEP AS YOU WANT TO BLOW.' Because I saw then, watching Konitz, master of all the musicians except Charlie Parker & mad Miles Davis, the interior laws of art ... that it develops constantly and anybody who holds himself back, tones himself down, for reasons of success of even just popularity or love of his circle (my reason?) is simply backing away from the forefront of what everybody will be doing years from now and will thereby lose his power ... Naturally, no more than Lee Konitz, I mustn't expect to get rich ...

Kerouac, 1951, in Tietchen, 2016, p. 138

On 13 October 1951, Kerouac followed up on his experience – 'now what am I going to do about that Lee Konitz business!' – underscoring both the impact of Konitz's performance as well as an ongoing confusion as to how to implement in writing the processes he was so drawn to in jazz performance (Kerouac, 1951, in Tietchen, 2016, p. 141). The day following his encounter with Konitz at Birdland, Kerouac wrote an excited letter to Neal Cassady concerning revisions to the working manuscript of *On the Road*, in which he exclaims that he has written to 'show [Cassady] ... my finally-at-last-found style & hope', and that Cassady ought, from that moment on, 'just call [him] Lee Konitz' (Kerouac, 1951, in Charters, 1995, p. 327).

In Konitz's approach to the navigation of the jazz standard and in his preference for improvised, and therefore occasionally hesitant and unpolished, playing over the security offered by the lick-based language of bebop, Kerouac perhaps heard someone successfully threading the needle – offering a solution to the seeming dichotomy of composition on the one hand (the written word) and improvisation on the other (process). In Konitz, Kerouac encountered an artist moving beyond his materials toward an improvised expression of the interior self. A process, Tim Hunt suggests (see also Jago 2011, 2013, 2015), made possible by the fact that Konitz's approach, his absolute familiarity with the sonic materials, enabled him to:

...use the 'tune' not as something to express by playing it (performing the composition), nor as something to elaborate by generating variations from it (improvising from composed elements), but as a means to engage and enact his own interiority. In the performance, as Kerouac perceives it, Konitz plays himself through the music rather than playing the music and thereby manages something deeper than improvisatory elaboration. Moreover, through engaging his material with such great depth of knowledge and trust in his artistic power, Konitz is able to enact, not merely to comment on, 'rushing interiority' so that some in the club 'could tell what he was doing' and respond.

Hunt, 2012, pp. 67–8

In addition to Konitz, Kerouac makes specific and frequent reference to another reasonably obscure jazz figure: blind pianist and educator Lennie Tristano.[13] Though known for his extensive use of counterpoint, polytonal and poly-rhythmic effects, long running lines and advanced harmonic reworkings of the standard repertoire, Tristano largely resisted an active playing career, preferring to play and record in his home studio and to teach. By 1951, Tristano's studio in Manhattan had become a de facto headquarters for a talented group of students including Konitz, tenor saxophonist Warne Marsh, guitarist Billy Bauer, pianist Sal Mosca and others.[14] Tristano did enjoy an active playing career and relatively high profile in New York during the 1940s and 1950s however, and Kerouac, who was something of a jazz insider (friends with Jerry Newman, a regular attendee at Minton's and other uptown after-hours clubs)[15] was a fan of his work.[16] In January of 1948, Kerouac saw fit to include a lengthy passage about Lennie Tristano in a letter to Allen Ginsberg:

Incidentally, if you're still dubious about Tristano's greatness, ask Freddy Gruber and Vicki about him. And when I went to see Tristano I overheard some of the cats discussing him in the john – cats with beards and artistic-looking manners and real Bohemian hipness, etc. – and they were saying that they couldn't stand anybody else any more … They agreed that Tristano was more profound than Stravinsky, which I think is a gross understatement. He is very close to Beethoven, as all the musicians agree … The guy is standing the music world on its ear.

Kerouac, 1948, in Charters, 1995, p. 141

Kerouac's initial offhand remark about Tristano indicates that both he and Ginsberg were already sufficiently familiar with the pianist's work that a comment about a 'Tristano style' possessed critical worth. Further, Kerouac's comment about Ginsberg's possible continuing doubts as to Tristano's greatness suggests prior conversations or correspondence in which both the state of modern jazz and Tristano's role within it figured prominently. That Kerouac could frame such discussions, and sought out the pianist on his opening night at an unnamed New York nightclub, suggests that Kerouac had been exposed to the pianist's early recordings and had witnessed earlier nightclub performances (at which he would have almost certainly have heard Lee Konitz).

In 1949, with a group that included Lee Konitz, Warne Marsh, Billy Bauer, Arnold Fishkin and Denzil Best, Tristano recorded the first examples of what would come to be known as 'free jazz'. At the conclusion of a recording session for Capitol, Tristano had his group record four 'free' compositions. Though only two sides ('Intuition' and 'Digression') survived and saw limited release, the incident marked the first time that such experimental jazz had been recorded for posterity. The tunes were navigated with no set melodic or rhythmic pattern, and the only constraints placed upon complete artistic freedom were the approximate three-minute time limit imposed by 78rpm records and the order of entrance, which was discussed briefly in advance. Tristano's group had included one free composition nightly during an extended gig at Birdland the same year, and its members were accustomed to playing in such a fiercely improvisatorial manner during their tutelage with Tristano. Kerouac, already an admirer of Tristano's by 1949, may well have heard the sides on the radio,[17] and may well have witnessed live renderings of the 'free' aesthetic at nightclub performances that same year. Sections of *On the Road* which detail a wild, all-night conversation between Dean Moriarty and Carlo Marx, along with the heavy experimentation of *Visions of Cody*, suggests that Kerouac had some experience of free improvisation, if not a direct knowledge of the 1949 sides (Shapcott, 2002; Whaley, 2004).[18]

Though comprising a different aesthetic from that espoused by many of the free jazz experimentalists of the 1960s, freedom and form may indeed coexist harmoniously, a notion repeatedly remarked upon by Konitz and Tristano in interviews, and closely mirrored by Kerouac in discussions of his craft. 'Freedom and discipline concur / only in ecstasy, all else / is shoveling out the muck' wrote Hayden Carruth in his poem 'Freedom and Discipline' (1993, p. 16), expressing in poetic form his belief that jazz stemmed from the 'concurrence of discipline and freedom' (Carruth, 1993, p. 29), a rare yet attainable conjunction which produces, as an inevitable by-product, the ecstasy of art. Such an ethos was similarly detailed by Barry Ulanov in the liner notes for *The New Tristano* (Tristano, 1962), Lennie Tristano's second LP for Atlantic:

Lennie calls what he does here 'stretching out in the forms'. Within the jazz forms, simple as they are, he has sought the utmost limits of spontaneity of the improvising imagination. He is never enslaved to any sequence of notes or chords, He is almost completely free – though not completely. That is part of the joy in it, he explains: 'to see how far you can stretch out in a given frame of reference'. The possibilities, he says, are 'practically infinite, endless even in the most simple forms. You are constantly creating form on form, a multiplicity of lines, a great complex of forms.'

Ulanov, 1962

It is deceptively easy to play standard tunes – seemingly braced by tradition and familiarity – when in fact one is constantly required to reinvent oneself within a predictable form, to play a shifting game of chicken with expectancy and pattern, and to lay to rest notions of entropy and stagnancy. Indeed, to flirt continually with cliché and repetition is perhaps inherently more difficult than to confront a blank musical canvas, free to paint with unfettered strokes of sound, and thus is, in the accomplishment, perhaps the more profound. In 1957, Lee Konitz would confirm his adoption of Tristano's musical philosophy in the liner notes to his album *The Real Lee Konitz* (Konitz, 1957):

> I feel that in improvisation, the tune should serve as a vehicle for musical variations and that the ultimate goal is to have as much freedom from the harmonic, melodic and rhythmical restrictions of the tune as possible – but the tune must serve to hold the chords and variations together. For this reason, I have never been concerned with finding new tunes to play. I feel that I could play the same tunes over and over and still come up with fresh variations.
>
> Konitz, 1957

More than 30 years later, Konitz would reconfirm his 1957 assertions regarding the nature of improvising:

> As soon as I hear myself playing a familiar melody I take the saxophone out of my mouth. I let some measures go by. Improvising means coming in with a completely clean slate from the first note. The process is what I'm interested in. You can turn the most familiar standard into something totally fresh. The most important thing is to get away from fixed functions.
>
> Zwerin, 1999

When Kerouac spoke of Tristano 'setting the music world on its ear', and of wishing to blow as deeply as Lee Konitz, he may well have been expressing an identification with these notions of freedom, whole and total, within form, and of escaping boundaries while residing within them, for surely this is what Kerouac set forth to do with his writing: reinvent and reassess a pre-existing literary form (the American novel) from within.

The evidence of jazz's influence upon Kerouac is evident from as early as 1945 (Charters, 1995), a preoccupation which culminated with his conscious adoption of Konitz as improvisatorial role model, but which did not fixate upon the altoist to the exclusion of other jazz performers, some of whom, like Red Allen, Al Cohn and Zoot Sims, were pressed into service as accompanists on Kerouac's jazz/poetry record sessions. Large tracts of Kerouac's letters are devoted to the discussion of jazz records, and the majority of Kerouac's explanatory metaphors, regardless of situational employment, are rooted in the jazz idiom. If Konitz was the inspirational catalyst for Kerouac's 'spontaneous prose' style, he was part of a concerted and deeply felt interest in jazz more generally.

In 1947, Kerouac, in an episode later related in *On the Road* (1957), was forced to take a job as a security guard. Writing to Neal Cassady of the terms of his employment,

Kerouac begs of him, 'whatever you do, don't think ill of me for being a cop ... I do not do my duty. I am a cop looking like some fugitive from Charley [sic] Ventura's Sextet' (Charters, 1995, p. 113). By 1947, it is clear that jazz had been imbued with serious and immediately communicable ideological connotations by Kerouac and his group of companions and associates. Indeed, Kerouac's reliance upon the jazz-based metaphor to express himself often spilled over from letters to his presumably jazz literate contemporaries to fill the pages of letters to book publishers and academics. Though we are at a loss to determine how well received these exhortations were, it becomes increasing clear that Kerouac felt unable to adequately express himself in any other terms.

In 1951, Kerouac wrote to well-known literary critic Alfred Kazin to solicit his support for a Guggenheim Fellowship. In expressing his admiration for Kazin, Kerouac writes, 'Besides I consider you "creative" more than critic, as did everyone else in 1948–49 when you "blew" on Whitman, Melville, Twain, Thoreau and Emerson so marvelously'(Charters, 1995, p. 312). Kazin should perhaps have counted himself lucky that Kerouac saw fit to add explanatory quotes around the term 'blew' to indicate that its meaning extended beyond the dictionary definition, and their inclusion seems to suggest that Kerouac feared or anticipated some level of immediate cultural misinterpretation. Those who plunge into Kerouac's letters, or even published works such as *Visions of Cody* (1972), without at least some background in jazz are missing much of the artfulness of Kerouac's expression, and indeed must fail to comprehend much of Kerouac's work as it was intended.

Visions of Cody (1972) was conceived and written in 1951 as an experiment in spontaneity following Kerouac's creative epiphany at Birdland, and as a possible way to chink some of the gaps he perceived in the *On the Road* manuscript. Large sections were transcribed directly from tapes of casual conversation, and the work is fraught with references to jazz not merely in passing, but as a conscious attempt to form associative connections between the music, Kerouac himself and his friend Neal Cassady. *Visions of Cody* contains references to jazz as varied as Billie Holiday being compared to the sound of Texas, intimate and enthusiastic discussions of jazz records, and extended descriptive passages about Lester Young which serve to link Neal Cassady to the mystique and tradition of the pioneering jazz stylist:[19]

> ... it was Lester started it all, the gloomy saintly serious goof who is behind the history of modern jazz and this generation [...] what doorstanding influence has Cody gained from this cultural master of his generation? what [sic] mysteries as well as masteries? what [sic] styles, sorrows [...] the beauty goof – Lester is just like the river [...] is like the vibration of the entire land sucked of its gut in mad midnight, fevered, hot, the big mudhole rank clawpole old frogular pawed-soul titanic Mississippi from the North, full of wires, cold wood and horn [...] This had no effect on Cody? he who stood with me listening to Lester's Children in Chicago ...
>
> Kerouac, 1993, pp. 392–3

And:

> 'You Can Depend on Me', man, that's the name of the record [...] when Lester
> was really blowing and generated this excitement which was so tremendous,
> I've never known anything like it here in the United States – expect, perhaps,
> maybe, man, you know, when Cody, on his last trip, when he came for no reason,
> and went back, remember?
>
> Kerouac, 1993, p. 395

Kerouac indeed often sought to appropriate and adapt the image of certain jazz
players for his own use. In *Visions of Cody*, Neal Cassady becomes, by association both
indirect and unequivocal, Lester Young, the tragic pioneer of a new jazz idiom,
romantic and misunderstood. In *On the Road*, Allen Ginsberg, in the guise of Carlo
Marx, becomes an unnamed tenor player (Kerouac, 1957, p. 201); Charlie Parker
becomes Herman Melville, titan of American prose; Lennie Tristano becomes equated
with Nathaniel Hawthorne (Charters, 1995, p. 367); and, of course, Kerouac himself,
as indicated earlier, assumes Lee Konitz's creative mantle. When Kerouac writes to
John Clellon Holmes in 1952 (while still working upon the manuscript that would
become *Visions of Cody*) that 'jazz musicians most perfectly epitomize the often sorry,
and fabulous, condition of the artist in America ... the sad sick night of subterranean
America blowing ecstasy by the Moon of Eternity ... the shadow of a golden horn on
a nightclub wall' (Charters, 1995, pp. 367–8), he is describing himself as he wishes to
be seen, crafting for himself the image of the jazz musician to be worn as an identity.

Written in the wake of his 1951 Birdland experience, *Visions of Cody* is loaded with
references to Lee Konitz. The book is related in the first person, and much of its
contents follow a conversational 'and-this-is-what-I-did-today' examination of the
novel's characters and of Kerouac himself, the disembodied 'I'. Thus an extended
passage concerning Lee Konitz from the novel's opening section may be considered at
best a dramatization of fact, and at worst wishful thinking, rather than as a wholly
invented literary diversion:

> Following Lee Konitz the famous alto jazzman down the street and don't even
> know what for – saw him first in that bar on the north-east corner of 49th and
> Sixth Avenue [...] Lee, who wouldn't talk to me even if he knew me, was in the
> bar ... waiting with big eyes for his friend to show up and so I waited on corner
> to think and soon I saw Lee coming out with his friend who'd arrived and it was
> Arnold Fishkin the Tristano bass player – two little Jewish gazotsky fellows they
> were really as they cut across the street and Konitz in that manner that was
> forceful and I said to myself 'He can take care of himself even though he goofs
> and does "April in Paris" from inside out as if the tune was the room he lived in
> and was going out at midnight with his coat on' – (but I haven't heard him for
> weeks and weeks) [...] and where d'you think they go but Manny's the music

store of hipsters and Symphony Sid...And Konitz goes completely unrecognized [...] though the ... owners know Lee so well they don't say to him, as I would, 'Where you playing now, great genius?'

Kerouac, 1993, p. 23[20]

Kerouac here again marks himself as one of the jazz initiate, having seen Konitz regularly it appears, though not, and with some sadness, 'for weeks and weeks'. In order to reinforce his position as privileged initiate, Kerouac is sure to demonstrate that he is able to recognize relatively minor jazz figures such as bassist Arnold Fishkin on sight, and sees fit to include idiosyncratic references to disc jockey Symphony Sid, and Manny's music store. Kerouac is the 'jazz insider' (and thereby like-minded artist), one who recognizes Konitz (authentic artistic genius) where others do not. Kerouac revels in the exclusivity of his knowledge, and uses jazz fluency as a means of glorifying his fictional characters. Cody Pomeray (the hero of *Visions of Cody*) and his friends thus become, in their wild and romanticized youth, possessed of

... the same robe of refined dissipated excitement [that] everyone else's dumb about ... like Miles and Lee Konitz cutting into a bar together ... so tragic and hidden from the city, right there, the vision, what you get, what there is.

Kerouac, 1993, p. 81

However, this self-conscious name-dropping belies an insecurity as well, for Kerouac was not, despite all his longings, a jazz musician, nor would he ever be. Thus, forever excluded, he bemoans that Konitz would not talk to him, even if he knew him.[21]

When waxing rapturously in *Visions of Cody* about a short-lived attempt to play the tenor saxophone, Kerouac, who had earlier displayed a wealth of knowledge and understanding about the great tenor saxophonist Lester Young, would invoke Konitz's name in the same breath and make associative connections between the two players which initially seem to defy explanation:

I was not only on my first day as a tenor man but understanding all music as I lay either flat on my back or stood up aslump with my sweet old horn, learning the first modified woodshed rudiments of raw wild joy which is American jazz, the *song*, the great whistling song, whistling into your horn and holding your horn high, aware all the time of all the mistakes you can make ... then raising your horn, horizontal like Lester and Lee Konitz...

Kerouac, 1993, p. 328

Though Lester Young was famous for the peculiar horizontal angle at which he held his saxophone (a position some say developed in order to better project his thin, vibratoless tone over the brass sections in the big bands he first worked in), Konitz has never been associated with such a trademark stance.[22] Konitz is, however, deeply indebted to Young stylistically, and it is possible that Kerouac was attempting to make clear this lineal, stylistic connection. Further, Konitz's inclusion in this paragraph from *Visions of Cody*, which goes on to list a myriad of tenor saxophonists such as Brew Moore, Sonny Stitt[23] and Stan Getz, is surely a reflection of Kerouac's fondness for him, and a desire therefore to include him in his rapturous discovery of actually blowing into a saxophone. Crafting a linkage between Konitz and Lester Young also enabled Kerouac to allude to a connection between himself (with Konitz as creative alter ego) and Neal Cassady, who had been linked in the narrative to Lester Young. By placing Konitz in this paean to Young/Cassady, Kerouac was, in effect, staking his claim, through a symbolic identification with Konitz, to Cassady as much as to jazz.

In a letter to Neal Cassady in the autumn of 1950, we find our first evidence that Kerouac's initial infatuation with Tristano was waning, though, as later mention in his voluminous correspondence will indicate, it was never to vanish entirely:

> ... John Holmes ... et al ... are ... cool, as opposed to fellows like you and me ... no word for it, but it sounds like RAW. A raw mind and a cool mind are two different minds. The raw mind is usually associated with the physical life ... Our feeling for music is raw, too ... The reaction is more physical, more jumping-minded, and tends from the art-of-art Tristano groove to favour the art-of-life ... Lucky Thompson or Trio Shearing (not sextet) ...
>
> Charters, 1995, p. 232

Kerouac, in admitting that his fondness for the 'art-of-art' stylings of Lennie Tristano had grown beyond the limits of intellectualism to find expression in the more accessible playing of Thompson and Shearing, was abandoning the literary and intellectual framework which had produced *The Town and the City* to wrestle with the free form construct of *On the Road* at the same time that Lee Konitz was extricating himself from the confines of the Tristano school to strike out on his own musically. Konitz's first album as leader, *Subconsciouslee*, was released in 1949 and featured Tristano, but Konitz was also beginning to work frequently without direct connection to Tristano,[24] and would leave New York in 1952 to tour with the Stan Kenton Orchestra, a decision which would place considerable strain on his relationship with Tristano for some years.

It becomes clear that in seeking to craft a new methodology for prose and poetry, Kerouac was consumed by potential creative parallels to jazz, an art form which seemed to him in many ways to be an ideal and uniquely American form of expression. Having completed five novels utilizing his spontaneous prose method (*On the Road, The Subterraneans, Doctor Sax, Maggie Cassady* and *Visions of Cody*), yet still unsuccessful at finding a publisher willing to print them, Kerouac wrote to Alfred Kazin in October of 1954, after having seen the critic deliver a television lecture on

Herman Melville. In the letter, Kerouac quotes sections of text from *The Subterraneans* which abandoned conventional punctuation and structure nearly entirely, and then seeks to explain his methodology:

> Alfred, this whole paragraph [from *The Subterraneans*] was written in one breath as it were, and the 'Lord' at the end of it is like its period, dot, more like the sometimes 'Bop' at the end of Modern Music (Jazz) and intended as a release from the extend of the phrase, the rhythmic paragraph is one phrase. I don't use periods and semicolons, just dashes, which are interior little releases as if a saxophonist drawing breath there. The effect is good prose, don't you think?
>
> Charters, 1995, p. 451

As jazz was to Kerouac the encompassing embodiment of 'Modern Music' in its entirety, his spontaneous prose method was to assume the mantle of 'Modern Prose' (Charters, 1995, p. 450) and would establish its own unique manner of expression though intentionally misplaced or misspelled words, a subversion of conventional punctuation and an overarching emphasis upon rhythm and authenticity of expression.

Likewise, in a letter seeking to explain spontaneous prose to Malcolm Cowley, his editor at Viking Press, Kerouac wrote that:

> If it isn't spontaneous, right unto the very sound of the mind, it can only be crafty and revised, by which the paradox arises, we get what a man has hidden, i.e., his craft, instead of what we need, what a man has shown, i.e., blown (like jazz musician) – the requirements for prose & verse are the same, i.e., blow – What a man most wishes to hide, revise and un-say, is precisely what Literature is waiting and bleeding for ... I foresee a new literature on account of this – but it's hard ... you must learn to answer questions spontaneously with no recourse to discriminating thinking.
>
> Charters, 1995, p. 516

Indeed, so important was jazz to Kerouac's aesthetic that in 1961, following the publication of *On the Road* and the fame which ensued, he answered an inquiry from a student at the University of Pennsylvania somewhat tersely:

> 'Original members' of Beat Gen. means it started out in 1948 a group of poets, beardless, with no political beefs, no idea of 'non-conformity', just poets. Today's 'beatnik' can't even recognize Stan Getz when he hears him, or even tell the tune he's playing ...
>
> Kerouac, 1961, in Charters, 1999, p. 324

To Kerouac, the movement's reluctant figurehead, jazz was integral to the existence of the Beats and became a cultural and artistic identifier, a rejection of ignorance which was tantamount to a modern atheism. Indeed, so closely had Kerouac bound himself to the jazz aesthetic that he may well have perceived an ignorance of the music as a personal rejection. To Kerouac, his artistic motives and methodology were identical in ideal, if not in execution, to those of a jazz musician.

As a man telling a story in a bar without interruption, as he once described his style (Kerouac, 1995, p. 280), Kerouac perhaps hits on the most apt analogy for his craft and for the musical model upon which it was based. There stands a dedication to the story (tune) – to telling it as well as you can from start to finish, full of description and with all the elements of plot and purpose, complete with dramatic pauses, colour, inflection and appropriate digressions all crafted immediately without respite or time to pause and assess one's own place in the narrative as it is being told. One must trust one's training, one's technical mastery of the language (instrument) and one's knowledge of the subject at hand (harmony and melody) to compose spontaneously an outcome which may well rest upon practice, but must exist without backtracking, and *with* error. In many ways such a process is the inheritance of all our ancient oral traditions. It does not, however, mean to suggest that given the opportunity to tell the same story (tune) in the same bar for the same audience, one would not choose to tell it differently. In fact, the art (jazz or storytelling) demands that you invest in variation, are able to reinvent the story while remaining true to the integrity of the idea in light of an audience of repeated listeners. It is not, as often erroneously suggested, that Kerouac did not revise, but rather that the aim was not to have to.

Konitz, as the jazz improviser, cannot stop to consider, cannot track backwards in time to erase or revise, but rather must be wholly present in the moment – the note, the measure, the chorus, the tune being constructed *as it is being constructed*. Kerouac sought to approach these heights of immediacy, of required residence *in the moment* by reducing, if not erasing, the customary lag and distance that existed between a notion conceived in the writer's head, and the final much edited and reworked finished product. Kerouac sought to eliminate the gap of time which commonly stood between author and audience, in many ways requiring that his readership share the moment with him, rather than be told about it afterwards with polished assurance. Though not required by the genre of print, Kerouac imposed upon himself the same restrictions (and their corollary freedoms) which faced the jazz improviser, and trained himself to perform under them. In June of 1951, with *On the Road* finished and awaiting publication and Kerouac anticipating the fame he had sought for so long, he would, in speaking of a planned retreat to the solitudes of Mexico, indicate that all that he would take of his New York life, all he could not, or did not yearn, to leave behind, were his jazz recordings; the embodiment of the heartbroken soul of America he so loved, and had so long searched for (Charters, 1995, p. 319).

Notes

1. Konitz is mentioned in *Visions of Cody* (1972) at length, and also in *Lonesome Traveller* (1960). Additionally, the Tristano group featuring tenor saxophonist Warne Marsh (named) and Konitz (not named but most certainly included in the ensemble) is mentioned in *Desolation Angels* (1965).

2. A very interesting and helpful article, Hopkins nonetheless does make what I would consider some mischaracterizations of jazz, including a suggestion that a 'big solid foghorn blues' has no place in the history or development of bebop (282), which I would counter with Hawkins, Webster, Young, Gray and Gordon, and then chase with Mobley, Griffin, Rollins and Coltrane, among others. Hopkins also questions or limits the use of repetition in bebop vs pop and R&B (282) while overlooking the role of the blues (and other standard forms) as a vehicle for improvisation; one taken up in earnest by Kerouac as a writing tool.

3. In the same way a jazz solo, once recorded and played back or transcribed and then read might be considered 'un-improvised'. Generally speaking, we rather accept that the process of the solo's creation – its being played into being – was improvised, a process which is not diminished by our after the fact re-creation or rebroadcast of the solo by mechanical means (recording, sheet music). Kerouac's prose methodology may well have been improvised in terms of its process, and its transmission after-the-fact via print media is perhaps not particularly relevant.

4. Beyond Konitz, Kerouac mentions saxophone players in his work more than any other form of jazz instrumentalist; from unnamed tenor players to Lester Young, Brew Moore, Charlie Parker, Wardell Gray, etc.

5. That Konitz is a white player is no doubt of some interest, particularly when considered along with some of the ways in which Kerouac handled issues of race throughout his body of work. However, a detailed examination of the racial issues embedded in Kerouac's treatment and understand of jazz is beyond the scope of this work.

6. Konitz is also well known for his work with Miles Davis and Gil Evans in the ensemble (1949/1950) which would become known as 'The Birth of the Cool' nonet. Konitz was a pupil of Tristano (along with noted tenorist Warne Marsh, pianist Sal Mosca, bassist Peter Ind, etc.) as well as a featured soloist in Tristano's ensembles and leader in his own right. Though he has a limited popular profile today, in the 1940s and 1950s Konitz (along with Tristano) was well regarded and critically acclaimed, featuring frequently in the yearly polls conducted by the major jazz periodicals, though his idiosyncratic style and unwillingness to adopt more mainstream, less improvisational forms of jazz eventually limited his commercial and popular appeal. Konitz was named an NEA Jazz Master in 2008, has received numerous other honours and awards, and has amassed a discography hundreds of titles deep. For more on Konitz, see Hamilton, 2007; Jago, 2011, 2015. In 2017, at the age of 90, Konitz remains remarkably active on the global jazz scene.

7. The original 1949 sides 'Intuition' and 'Digression' are available on, Lennie Tristano and Warne Marsh, *Intuition*, Capitol Jazz CDP 7243 8 527771 2 2, 1996. Those interested in later examples of Konitz's 'free' playing could consult *Lee Konitz: Unaccompanied Live in Yokohama* (1996), *Self Portrait* (1998), *French Impressionist Music from the Turn of the Twentieth Century* (2000), *Gong with the Wind* (2002) and *Duos with Lee* (2009). Additionally, it should be noted that even Konitz's idiomatic playing of jazz standards adheres to an ideology which renders them truly improvisational efforts. About this, one could consult Hamilton, 2007; Jago, 2011, 2015.

8. For argument's sake, all those works composed following *The Town and the City* (Kerouac 1950), which was written between 1946 and 1948 using more conventional writing methods and narrative structure.

9. *Mexico City Blues*, note on introductory page (Kerouac, 1959).

10. At the time most jazz recordings were taken 'live off the floor' without recourse to overdubs or multi-tracking.

11. It is unclear what sort of a group this was, and who the leader might have been. The group apparently also featured baritone saxophonist Cecil Payne, but the rest of the group went unnamed in Kerouac's journal entry.

12. Not least of these as item #7 – Blow as deep as you want to blow – on his list of 30 guidelines in 'Beliefs and Technique for Modern Prose' originally written as a letter to Donald Allen and then published first in 1958 in *Heaven & Other Poems* (Grey Fox Press) and, most famously, in the Spring 1959 issue of the *Evergreen Review*.

13. For more on Tristano, see Shim, 2007; Jago, 2011, 2013, 2015.

14. 317, E. 32nd Street was the address, and also served as the title to one of Tristano's most famous jazz compositions. Kerouac was aware of the school and mentions it in his 8 October 1951 journal entry, speculating that Konitz must have made much of his living teaching at the school, rather than playing (Tietchen, 2016, p. 137).

15. Jerry Newman owned a record store in Greenwich Village called Esoteric at which Kerouac spent time, and ran an independent record label of the same name, recording for which Newman made by hauling a portable disc-cutting recorder to various jazz clubs. His recordings of Charlie Christian, Thelonious Monk and others live at Minton's in 1941 are important documents of bebop's development.

16. Indeed it is very likely that Konitz caught his ear initially as part of one of Tristano's groups.

17. Despite attempts by Capitol to prevent their release, copies were obtained by disc jockey Symphony Sid who played them regularly on his popular radio programme. As a result of his support, 'Intuition' was eventually released in 1950, and 'Digression' in 1954 (Shim, 2007, p. 52).

18. Despite the landmark recordings of 1949, Lennie Tristano is not often immediately associated with the free jazz movement which arose in the 1960s, the title of free jazz pioneer conferred instead upon Ornette Coleman, whose *Something Different!* was not released until 1958. Though it would have a more lasting resonance than Tristano's initial experimentation with the free aesthetic, Coleman's work simply emerged too late to have had any major impact on Kerouac's developing style. Not a single mention of him can be found in either Kerouac's fiction or published letters. Further, the furore that ensued following Coleman's breakthrough engagement at New York's Five Spot in 1959 gives some indication of how revolutionary the nature of the Tristano group's efforts would have been in 1949. In reference to Tristano's relative exclusion from discussions of the avant-garde movement in the 1960s, Konitz has commented that, 'No one . . . hardly ever mentions [the 1949 date]. And you know damn well that these cats have heard that record somewhere along the line. It [the free jazz experimentation of the 1960s] doesn't just come from no place' (Gitler, 2001, p. 235). One possible reason for this exclusion may lie amidst the politics of race which, in the militant 1960s, saw hitherto unprecedented delineations along racial lines within the jazz community itself.

19. Kerouac, 1960 /1993, pp. 135, 142–4, 156–64, 183, 358, 391–3, 395–6, 372–3.

20. Konitz was shown this passage in 1992 by journalist and jazz critic Francis Davis, who asked him to comment on Kerouac's characterization of him:

> Gazotsky? Says Konitz . . . 'He means Arnold and I were little dancing guys, I guess. It's a real word, Russian or maybe Yiddish. It has to do with being cute in some way, like when the grandmother pinches the cherubic cheek of the child and says, "Zotsky!" Applied to me, I don't know.' After observing that he never played 'April in Paris' in the 1950s ('He must have been thinking of "I'll Remember April"'), and being assured that Kerouac used 'goofs' to signify hanging loose, not screwing up, Konitz concedes that the image of him playing a standard 'inside out . . . like [it] was the room he lived in and [he] was going out' was apt.
>
> Davis, 1992

21. In fact it seems as if Konitz did speak to Kerouac; anecdotes abound that it was Konitz who provided Kerouac with some encouraging words during his disastrous engagement at the Village Vanguard in 1957, though Konitz has no recollection of ever speaking to him (communication with author, 11 April 2017). Guitarist Billy Bauer, who often played with both Tristano and Konitz, reported in his autobiography *Sideman* (Bauer, 1997) that Kerouac once helped him carry his amplifier up the stairs and onto the street, and it is likely that many more casual encounters occurred.

22. Konitz has been known on occasion to hold his saxophone at unorthodox angles to manipulate the instrument's sound, so it is possible, though quite unlikely, that Kerouac witnessed Konitz hold his alto in a fashion similar to Young at some point.

23. Though well known as an altoist as well, Stitt developed his most distinctive sound on tenor, an instrument which enabled him to avoid being compared to Charlie Parker.

24. Miles Davis' 'Birth of the Cool' nonet 1949/50, a tour of Scandinavia 1951, with George Russell 1951, etc.

Bibliography

Bauer, Billy, *Sideman: The Autobiography of Billy Bauer*, New York: William H. Bauer Publications, 1997.

Campbell, James, 'Kerouac's Blues', *Antioch Review* 57, no. 3 (1999): 363–70.

Carruth, Hayden, *Sitting In: Selected Writing on Jazz, Blues and Related Topics*, Iowa City: University of Iowa Press, 1993.

Charters, Ann (ed.), *Jack Kerouac: Selected Letters 1940–1956*, New York: Penguin Books, 1995.

Charters, Ann (ed.), *Jack Kerouac: Selected Letters 1967–1969*, New York: Penguin Books, 1999.

Davis, Francis, 'The Beat goes on for jazz's Lee Konitz, still cool at age 65, Europe was interesting for Konitz. He had never tap-danced with a cellist before', *Philadelphia Inquirer*, 2 December 1992.

Du Ewa Jones, Meta, 'Jazz Prosodies: Orality and Textuality', *Callaloo* 25, no. 1 (2002): 66–91.

Feinstein, Sascha, *Jazz Poetry: From the 1920s to the Present*, Wesport, CT: Praeger, 1997.

Gitler, Ira, *Masters of Bebop, The: A Listener's Guide*, New York: Da Capo Press, 2001.

Hamilton, Andy, *Lee Konitz: Conversations on the Improviser's Art*, Ann Arbor: University of Michigan Press, 2007.

Hartman, Charles O., *Jazz Text: Voice and Improvisation in Poetry, Jazz and Song*, Princeton, NJ: Princeton University Press, 1991.

Holmes, John Clellon, *The Horn*, New York: Thunder's Mouth Press, 1999.

Hopkins, David, 'To Be or Not to Bop: Jack Kerouac's *On the Road* and the Culture of Cebop and Rhythm 'n' Blues', *Popular Music* 24, no. 2 (2005): 279–86.

Hunt, Tim, '"Blow As Deep As You Want To Blow": Time, Textuality, and Jack Kerouac's Development of Spontaneous Prose', *Journal of Beat Studies* 1 (2012): 49–87.

Jago, Marian, 'Musical Koryu: Lineal Traditions in Jazz: Lennie Tristano/Lee Konitz', *MUSICultures* 38 (2011): 205–27.

Jago, Marian, 'What is a Jazz Record Anyway? Lennie Tristano and the Use of Extended Studio Techniques in Jazz', *Journal of the Art of Record Production* 8 (2013).

Jago, Marian, 'Dig-It: The Musical Life of Ted Brown', *Journal of Jazz Studies* 10, no. 2 (2015): 95–118.

Jago, Marian, 'Jedi Mind Tricks: Lennie Tristano & Mental Approaches for the Practice of Jazz Improvisation', *Jazz Research Journal* 7, no. 2 (2015).

Jarrett, Michael, 'Four Choruses on the Tropes of Jazz Writing', *American Literary History* 6, no. 2 (1994): 336–53.

Kerouac, Jack, 'Essentials of Spontaneous Prose', in Barney Rossest and Donald Allen (eds), *Evergreen Review*, New York: Grove Press, 1958.

Kerouac, Jack, *Mexico City Blues*, New York: Grove Press, 1959.

Kerouac, Jack, *On the Road*, New York: Penguin Group, 1991 (1957).

Kerouac, Jack, *Visions of Cody*, New York: Penguin Group, 1993 (1960).

Kerouac, Jack, *Desolation Angels*, New York: Riverhead Books, 1995.

Litweiler, John, *The Freedom Principle: Jazz After 1958*, New York: William Morrow and Company, 1984.

Malcolm, Douglas, '"Jazz America": Jazz and African American Culture in Jack Kerouac's "On the Road"', *Contemporary Literature* 40, no. 1 (1999): 85–110.

Nicosia, Gerald, *Memory Babe: A Critical Biography of Jack Kerouac*, New York: Penguin, 1983.

Shapcott, John, '"I didn't punctuate it!" Locating the Tape and Text of Jack Kerouac's "Vision's of Cody" and "Doctor Sax" in a Culture of Spontaneous Improvisation', *Journal of American Studies* 36, no. 2 (2002): 231–48.

Shim, Eunmi, *Lennie Tristano: His Life in Music*, Ann Arbor: University of Michigan Press, 2007.

Sterritt, David, 'Revision, Prevision, and the Aura of Improvisatory Art', *Journal of Aesthetics and Art Criticism* 58, no. 2 (2000): 163–72

Tesser, Neil, 'Lee Konitz Searches for the Perfect Solo', *Down Beat* 47, no. 1 (1980). Thomas, Lorenzo, '"Communicating by Horns": Jazz and Redemption in the Poetry of the Beats and the Black Arts Movement', *African American Review* 26, no. 2 (1992): 291–8.

Weinreich, Regina, *Kerouac's Spontaneous Poetics: A Study of the Fiction*, New York: Thunder's Mouth Press, 1987.

Whaley Jr, Preston, *Blows Like A Horn: Beat Writing, Jazz Style, and Markets in the Transformation of U.S. Culture*, Cambridge, MA: Harvard University Press, 2004.

Zwerin, Mark, *Lee Konitz: How to Get Away From Fixed Functions*, Paris: Culturekiosque Publications Ltd, 1999.

Discography

Kerouac, Jack, *Blues and Haikus*, Hanover-Signature Record Corporation, LP 5006, 1959.

Kerouac, Jack, *Legends of the 20th Century*, EMI 7243 5201882, 1959.

Kerouac on Record

Kerouac, Jack, *Poetry for the Beat Generation*, Hanover-Signature Record Corporation, LP 5000, 1959.

Kerouac, Jack, *Readings by Jack Kerouac on the Beat Generation*, Verve Records, 1960.

Konitz, Lee, *The Real Lee Konitz*, Atlantic LP 1273, 1957.

Tristano, Lennie, *Descent Into the Maelstrom,* East Wind (J) EW 8040, 1953.

Tristano, Lennie, *Lennie Tristano*, Atlantic LP 1224, 1955.

Tristano, Lennie and Warne Marsh, *Intuition*, Capitol Jazz CDP 7243 8 527771 2 2, 1996.

Ulanov, Barry, *The New Tristano*, Atlantic LP 1357, 1962.

INTERVIEW 1: LEE KONITZ

Marian Jago

Alto saxophonist Lee Konitz (b. 13 October 1927) is a significant figure in the history of jazz. As well as having had a remarkable solo career, he was a member of various groups led by pianist Lennie Tristano (himself of considerable interest to Jack Kerouac) in the 1940s through to the 1960s, appeared on the first recorded examples of 'free jazz' in 1949 ('Intuition', 'Digression'), was a member of the innovative Claude Thornhill Orchestra and the Miles Davis nonet now known as the 'Birth of the Cool', and in general presented a unique alternative to the saxophone sound and phrasing of Charlie Parker at a time when the influence of Parker-inspired bebop was nearly inescapable.

Despite his frequent and continued use of jazz standards as a performance vehicle, Konitz was, and is, committed to the ideals of musical improvisation above all else; finding the challenge of seeking 'freedom-within-form' to be inspiring rather than limiting. In his development of a highly personal approach to improvisation and the melodic line, Konitz had a profound impact upon Jack Kerouac's concept of 'spontaneous prose', an influence alluded to frequently by Kerouac in his writings (in particular *Visions of Cody*), his letters and, most explicitly, in a journal entry from the autumn of 1951.

I've known Lee Konitz for more than 15 years and, from time-to-time, we've discussed Kerouac, though Lee never seemed quite sure how to take Kerouac's interest in either him specifically, or jazz more widely. It was clear he'd not spent much time with any of Kerouac's writings, and had picked up what he knew of the Beats by word of mouth. Given the frequency with which bad poetry was paired with jazz in the wake of the Beats, it's hardly surprising that his opinion of Kerouac and the rest of the movement was immediately less than positive.

In 2002 I wrote to him with some of the information contained within the preceding chapter, and he wrote back to me, 'My! My! Whoever thought!! I knew they were listening, but never met any of them, including Jack; and I certainly would have said something to him, if I had.' Some 14 years later, I conducted the following interview over the phone (via Skype) – me in England and Lee in New York – on 10 April 2017.

MJ: Kerouac was profoundly impacted by hearing you play one night at Birdland in 1951 . . .

LK: I have some idea about that. Not that [night] specifically, but it sounded like he reacted [to me].

MJ: How aware were you of what I'll call the Beat movement in New York during those years? The 1940s and 1950s.

LK: Well, not very aware, as I wasn't of most things. I was just in my little world trying to make sense out of what I was doing, and that entered into it, and I got interested [in the Beats briefly] and then lost interest soon. I couldn't follow it.

MJ: You read some of the books?

LK: Yeah. [Kerouac's] book. I don't think I read the whole thing, but I got an impression. Which I can't really recall right now.

MJ: Now the book – *On the Road* – was written quite a while before it was published. He composed it late 1940s . . . 1951. But it didn't get published until 1957. Were you conscious of those guys being on the scene then?

LK: They weren't genuinely genuine to me, somehow.

MJ: In what way?

LK: I guess they were just trying to make effects, and I wasn't really impressed with the results. It just seemed they were staying high and trying to make something happen, and it wasn't happening.

MJ: What do you mean by when you say 'trying to make effects'?

LK: Well . . . just in general it sounded like they were jiving a little too much.

MJ: With some of them that was probably true, but I think with Kerouac it might have been a bit different. Certainly it seems he had a long-standing and legitimate interest in jazz. He knew quite a lot of people on the scene at the time, and if you read his letters, his enthusiasm for the music comes through. And he was fairly well informed. He was a big fan of Lennie [Tristano] . . .

LK: I didn't get that impression [at the time] . . . about Lennie. I didn't read about that. But I heard little stories about him being at the Half Note club when we were playing and afterwards kind of walking up behind us or something, following what we were doing? And it became kind of weird. [*This is probably the story related in* Visions of Cody, *about which Konitz was interviewed by Francis Davis in 1992.*] It was as if he wasn't interested enough to find out how to talk to me, you know?

MJ: I think he was intimidated.

LK: Well … that's the way it seems to have turned out. But that didn't impress me. With all the effect he was having, to become intimidated by a saxophone player, somehow seems a little strange.

MJ: Do you have any recollection of talking to him?

LK: No. I have no remembrance of ever shaking hands, or anything like that. It was a distant relationship.

MJ: He went to a lot of gigs, it seems. And gigs of Lennie's.

LK: I didn't know that.

MJ: And in 1951, you had a profound effect on the methodology he was developing for writing …

LK: I wish I had known that … [at the time] it just sounded like they were showing off, and that didn't ring a bell for me.

MJ: Showing off in what way?

LK: I mean, just … like, saying things that would cause an effect, rather than what they really felt.

MJ: What do you think about this idea that a lot of his mature style and approach to writing were, according to him, kind of prompted by what he thought he heard in your approach to improvisation? That you were being truly original, and truly yourself, and he was impressed that particular night by the fact that you were obviously doing things musically because you believed in them, and not because you were attempting to be attractive, commercially.

LK: Well that registers with me. And I appreciate that, and I wish I'd know that better [at the time]. I just heard a bit of a reaction from somebody about Kerouac's interest in me, and didn't pay much attention to it, I guess.

MJ: [*I read some excerpts from the journals about the night at Birdland in 1951.*]

LK: I never heard anything like that, okay. Nothing that specific, no.

MJ: I think a little bit he might have been impressed with you moving away from Lennie, too. I think that inspired him, as well … maybe to break away from literary influences he was feeling …

LK: You're saying that when I was I doing whatever he [might have thought] I was doing to get away from Lennie, that that was . . . commendable?

MJ: Yeah, I think he found it inspirational.

LK: Not criticizing me, for leaving Lennie's influence?

MJ: No, I think he was inspired by hearing you as an original voice opposed to Charlie Parker, initially, and then sort of to be doing your own thing outside of Lennie.

LK: Well, all I can say from this distance is that if I had heard some of that really happening . . . I never had an impression that it was more, on Kerouac's part or whoever he was hanging out with, that [an interest in jazz] was just part of the things we do when we get together and get high and get talking about things. I never got those facts that you just read to me.

MJ: That's kind of a shame. Kerouac's interest in jazz was, I think, pretty legitmate. And I think it's neat that most people think his big jazz influence was Charlie Parker or Dizzy Gillespie, but if you read his letters [and journals], it was actually you.

LK: Well, thank you for telling me that; how many years later? But I thank you for the insight. Thank you, and I will try to get to know them better.

CHAPTER 5

JACK KEROUAC GOES VINYL: A SONIC JOURNEY INTO KEROUAC'S THREE LPS – POETRY FOR *THE BEAT GENERATION*; *BLUES AND HAIKUS*; AND *READINGS BY JACK KEROUAC ON THE BEAT GENERATION*

Jonah Raskin

The 27 March 2017 cover of *The New Yorker* magazine testifies to the longevity of the Beats. 'Shelf Life' is the name of the piece that graces the issue. Luci Gutiérrez is the name of the artist who did the drawing that depicts a tall, narrow bookcase. At the top, there are albums by Count Basie, Dizzy Gillespie and Billie Holiday. Near the bottom there are books by Jack Kerouac, Allen Ginsberg and Patti Smith, plus another with the title *Beat Generation*. No generation in popular culture has had more longevity than the Beats, and no generation has gone on recreating itself, from the age of Kerouac and Ginsberg to the age of the neo-Beat, Patti Smith. Moreover, in the annals of American literary history, no group of writers has ever recorded itself more than the generations of Beat writers.

It seems unlikely, however, that anyone who was alive in 1957 and who was paying attention to cultural signposts would have predicted that the Beats would be alive and well 60 years later, and, what's more, featured on the front cover of *The New Yorker*. Not only are the Beats alive today. So is the jazz that sustained them. Gillespie, Holiday, Ginsberg and Kerouac are all in the pantheon of popular culture that spans the Americas and Europe. Sixty years seems like a long time ago in the world of tweets, Twitter and emails. But in some ways it seems very much connected to our own world.

The year 1957 was a big one for the history books, the airwaves and the written word. The Russians launched their satellite, Sputnik, into outer space. That same year, legendary DJ Alan Freed launched his primetime TV show *The Big Beat*, and also appeared in the movie *Mr. Rock and Roll*, along with headliners such as Chuck Berry, Little Richard and Screamin' Jay Hawkins.

And Viking published a picaresque novel titled *On the Road* by Jack Kerouac, a 35-year-old author who straddled the worlds of music and literature and who was known, if he was known at all, for his first novel, *The Town and the City* (1950). He also attracted a following for a story called 'Jazz of the Beat Generation' (1955) in which he introduced Neal Cassady and Allen Ginsberg, who appears under the name Carlo Marx. There's also a large cast of African American characters who 'dig' the blues and jazz. 'Jazz of the Beat Generation' gave readers a taste of what was to come in *On the*

Road, though the story didn't catapult Kerouac into the world of fame. His 1957 novel brought him both acclaim and notoriety.

Indeed, beginning in the autumn of that year and then again all though 1958, Kerouac left obscurity behind him, and watched, with a sense of alarm, as the media turned him into the King of the Beats and the father of beatniks. Along with Ginsberg's 'Howl' (1956) and William Burroughs' *Naked Lunch* (1959), his road book became the bible for the counterculture. In the 1960s, it inspired the hippies and their ilk who turned to rock'n'roll, marijuana, rebellion, and to sex outside the boundaries of matrimony. Kerouac and the Beats had shown the 1960s generation a way beyond American norms.

On 5 September 1957, in the pages of the *New York Times*, Gilbert Millstein praised Kerouac for his excellent writing about jazz. Near the end of his review, Millstein noted that *On the Road* offered 'some writing on jazz that has never been equalled in American fiction, either for insight, [or] style of technical virtuosity'. He also called Kerouac's book a 'major novel'. Not surprisingly, it landed on the bestseller list. The timing couldn't have been better. Jazz was at a peak and the Beats were news. The conjunction between the two electrified both listeners and readers.

Not only was the late 1950s a good time for jazz, for jazz-inflected novels and recordings by writers, it was also a good time for jazz criticism that expanded the audience for the music that had originated in New Orleans, made its way up the Mississippi to Chicago and then to New York and California. Kerouac offers a vivid capsule version of that history in *On the Road*, though it doesn't take the place of Marshall Stearns's *The Story of Jazz*, a comprehensive account of the music and the musicians that appeared in 1956. Three years later, Eric Hobsbawm, the British historian and Communist Party member, published, under the pseudonym Francis Newton, *The Jazz Scene* in which he noted that the Beats combined a passion for jazz and for Buddhism. He also observed that Kerouac's novel symbolized the 'fate of the beat generation'. Hobsbawm thought that the 'jazz-steeped writing', as he called it, was primarily of interest from a sociological rather than a literary point of view. Moreover, he enjoyed jazz as the music of the people not for an avant-garde.

For Jack Kerouac, 1957 was the best of times and the worst of times. The high school football player and college dropout imbued with a sense of wanderlust found himself and lost himself, embraced fame and ran from it. By 1957, in his mid-30s, he had been married twice and divorced twice. He was also the father of a daughter named Jan whom he would not acknowledge and rarely saw, but who followed in his footsteps and became a writer. Jan Kerouac loved her father. 'Even people who can't get through his wild run-on prose on paper are instantly captured by his voice' she wrote. She certainly was entranced with his recordings.

In 1957 Kerouac fell in love with Joyce Glassman (later Joyce Johnson) and also broke up with her, though he asked her to serve as his eyes and ears and report to him all the gossip she heard concerning him. 'Miss Grapevine', he called her. She was a good listener and information-gatherer. One night in December 1957, Joyce attended

Jack's debut as a 'nightclub performer' – that was his phrase – at the legendary Village Vanguard in Manhattan. *The Nation*, the liberal-left weekly, panned his performance. Glassman watched in a kind of horror. Kerouac, her lover, could barely stand up straight or find the microphone, though he managed to hold onto a bottle of booze and to take occasional sips. Many of those who saw the show said that only the last-minute intervention by TV personality and pianist Steve Allen salvaged Kerouac's performance and provided him with a modicum of dignity.

At Christmas and New Year, he was down, but he wasn't out. Indeed, he had a way of finding beauty in sadness, which was perhaps why he loved the blues and wanted to write like the jazz greats of his era, including the saxophonist Lee Konitz. 'Just call me Lee Konitz', Jack told Neal Cassady. Konitz's music influenced him profoundly, though he also admired Charlie Parker, Lester Young, Thelonious Monk and Billie Holiday, the Harlem-born vocalist who died in 1959 at the age of 44.

After the debacle at the Village Vanguard, Kerouac was eager to rise above the naysayers and rebuff his critics and competitors, including the poet Kenneth Rexroth, whom he called a 'square' and accused of wanting 'to grab off the Beat Generation as his own invention & baby'. Once upon a time, Jack and Kenneth were friends in San Francisco. Then politics and ego got in the way. Then, too, by the late 1950s Kerouac was disenchanted with California, its culture and its radicals including Rexroth, an anarchist and pacifist.

Rexroth and Lawrence Ferlinghetti, the poet, publisher and bookstore owner, collaborated on an album titled *Poetry Readings in the Cellar* (1957), with liner notes by Ralph Gleason, who reviewed *On the Road* favourably for *The Saturday Review*. Ferlinghetti explained that *Coney Island of the Mind* (1958), his collection of poems, was 'conceived specifically for jazz accompaniment'. Kerouac would say much the same thing in a note at the beginning of his *Mexico City Blues* (1959): 'I want to be considered a jazz poet blowing a long blues in an afternoon jam session on Sunday.' In his cosmology, jazz would take the place of the church and the choir.

In January 1958, after a rough month in New York, Kerouac saw a way to compete with Rexroth and Ferlinghetti and become a player again in the world of the spoken word. Bob Thiele, the Vice President at Dot Records, suggested that Kerouac and Steve Allen get together in a recording studio, 'repeat their performance' at the Vanguard and make a record 'for posterity'. Kerouac's advance against royalties acted as a stimulant, and, while he liked Allen as a person and considered him a friend, he didn't relish a repeat performance with Steve at the piano. Indeed, his music struck him as 'pretty'. Kerouac didn't want pretty, but rather something he called 'beautiful in an ugly graceful new way'. Still, with or without Allen, he knew that recording in a studio could not and would not be a repeat of his performance at the Vanguard, then one of the prime venues for jazz in New York.

It's not clear what actually happened at the Vanguard during the week that Kerouac appeared on stage there. No one took photos or recorded him, though at least two newspaper reporters were present: Howard Smith and Dan Wakefield who came to opposite conclusions about Kerouac's performances. Smith raved about it while Wakefield panned it. One night, Kerouac forgot to bring a copy of *On the Road* that he had planned to read from, and instead dipped into the manuscripts he had with him, including work by Ginsberg and Corso. He could adapt quickly when he had to.

Still, while there is no authentic account of his performances at the Vanguard, it seems fair to say that on the first night Kerouac performed with J. J. Johnson and his quartet. That collaboration didn't go well. It ended abruptly. Kerouac told *Village Voice* columnist Howard Smith after the first night that he 'decided not to read to music because I feel they don't mix'. Then, he apparently changed his mind, and read with Steve Allen, though for much of his life he did, indeed, feel that music and poetry should not mix. Howard Smith loved his unaccompanied performances. 'He is the prince of the hips, being accepted in the court of the rich,' he exclaimed. Other observers, including David Amram, were far less enthusiastic.

One of Kerouac's closest friends in this period, Amram felt that the cold audience and the cavernous room chilled Jack's enthusiasm. Joyce Johnson reported in *Minor Characters* that the overheated groupies dampened his spirits. She rescued him and took him to a hotel inhabited by old bohemians and drunks.

No doubt about it, Kerouac didn't like to be put on the spot at the Vanguard, or feel that he had to satisfy the demands of the anonymous members of an audience he couldn't see in the dark. In this same time period, TV was felt to be even less hospitable than the Vanguard. On *Nightbeat*, when host John Wingate asked Jack what he wanted, he said that he was 'waiting for God to show his face'. He meant well, though viewers couldn't figure him out. Not even friends like Allen Ginsberg's father, Louis, understood Jack's remarks, and not even Norman Mailer, who published his controversial essay 'The White Negro' in 1957, spoke as enigmatically as he did.

Now, in January 1958, Wingate was behind him. The Village Vanguard was behind him. The reporters who had ridiculed him had moved on to other prey. An LP with a real record company beckoned. An LP with his name on it was something he had wanted for a very long time.

Jack departed from Orlando, Florida, where he lived with his mother, Gabrielle. His sister and his brother-in-law had a home nearby. He took the train to New York and carried with him what he described as 'a huge suitcase of un-typed manuscripts of prose and poetry'. No doubt the suitcase and the manuscripts were real, though no one today knows if they still exist and if so where they might be located. In 1959, Robert Frank, the co-director of the Beat movie *Pull My Daisy*, took a photo of Kerouac in Florida holding in his right hand what must be the very same suitcase. Frank added a caption that reads, 'Jack at the home of his brother-in-law ... His suitcase filled with manuscripts and notebooks'. Steve Allen also saw the suitcase and its contents when Kerouac arrived for their recording session sometime in the winter of 1958.

The exact date for that session is unknown, though the authoritative text in the booklet for Rhino Record's big boxed-set – *The Jack Kerouac Collection* – states that

Poetry for the Beat Generation was 'possibly recorded March 1958'. *Poetry for the Beat Generation* was the first of three LPs that Kerouac made in the late 1950s, one after the other, without knowing where they might land in the vast world of the spoken word just then expanding rapidly. Rhino Records released those three albums as CDs in 1990.

The booklet that goes with *The Jack Kerouac Collection* offers photos of the author himself – one of them shows him with his ear glued to the radio – plus tributes by Jerry Garcia, Allen Ginsberg and William Burroughs who noted of the author of *On the Road*, 'Woodstock rises from his pages.' An exaggeration, indeed, but it contained an element of truth. Kerouac influenced Dylan and Garcia, too, who noted in 1989, 'I can't separate who I am now from what I got from Kerouac.'

Rhino Records was the first to reissue Kerouac records, but it was not the last company to do so. In 2011, Chrome Dreams released a two-CD set of Kerouac recordings. Then in 2016, Hoodoo Records released its own version of Kerouac's audio work with yet another booklet that offers photos of Jack and his accompanists, Steve Allen and Al Cohn and Zoot Sims, plus an insightful essay about Kerouac and his work by Paul Gerard. There are many ways these days to hear Jack's polyphonic voice.

The recording session that took place in the winter of 1958 happened almost by accident. That seems to be the way Kerouac wanted it, in homage to bebop that was born, he would say, because of a 'goof' on the part of Charlie Parker. Kerouac wanted his own album to be a kind of 'goofing'. Steve Allen, who goofed on his own TV show, liked the idea of a goofing session with Jack. 'There was no rehearsal,' Allen said. He added, 'We had no idea what would happen.' Track six on *Poetry for the Beat Generation* is called 'Goofing at the Table'.

Kerouac did show up on time for the session and put his suitcase on top of the piano that took up much of the space in the studio. According to Allen, Jack opened the suitcase, removed 'a roll of paper . . . long and white' and 'a lot of little scraps of paper'. Allen explained that Kerouac 'gradually got together a pile of papers on the music stand'. He was not in a hurry and neither was Allen.

When Jack remembered the occasion, he said that he reached into his suitcase 'as if blindfolded', then picked out a few things to read, and showed them to Allen who said, 'Anything you want.' That was part of the 'goof': the randomness of the selection process. Spontaneity was clearly at work, though at home in Florida assembling the texts from which he read might have been a matter of deliberate sifting and careful sorting.

In a way, taking the texts from the suitcase was like unpacking his own volatile and adventurous life. The selections he read add up to an audio self-portrait of the artist as an often lonely white man who loved Buddhism and the blues, his mother, New York and a certain cool 'slouch hat' which he celebrates in a six-minute ode. Hipster accessories, including hats and dark glasses mattered to him. They were the Beat tribe's badges of honour.

Kerouac remembered that Steve Allen sat down at the piano, started to play, then gave a signal to an engineer who 'turned on the tape'. Neither Allen nor Kerouac had a game plan for the afternoon session, though the recording with Allen seems to have taken Kerouac back to the informal occasions when he taped himself reading, singing and playing jazz with friends. They included the novelist John Clellon Holmes, author of *Go* (1952); the piano player and record collector extraordinaire Tom Livornese; and the legendary New York record storeowner Jerry Newman. As his letters from the 1940s and 1950s show, the tape recorder never terrified Jack, nor did reading aloud in an intimate circle of friends. In fact, he greatly enjoyed singing and reading with a tape going.

That winter day in 1958 when he arrived in New York from Florida, there were only two microphones in the studio. One of them was designated for Kerouac, who read while he stood with his manuscripts in hand. The other microphone was for Allen, who played what critic David Perry has described as 'graceful accompaniment fitting Kerouac's reading'. Perry also hailed the sessions as 'a spontaneous recording experiment' and characterized Kerouac's voice as 'rough-hewn'. Allen added, 'He did not give a dramatic reading . . . I was the performer, he wasn't.'

One wonders what Allen meant by 'dramatic' or why Perry made Kerouac out to be an unpolished poet. Neither of those comments seems to be accurate. For the CDs on the Hoodoo label, critic Paul Gerard listened to the same tape and heard something else: a 'spellbinding performance' that was 'musical'. Gerard also called it 'one of the crowning achievements of recording in the 1950s'. In 60 goofy and yet beatific minutes, Allen and Kerouac taped 14 tracks, the shortest under a minute, the longest over seven minutes that added up to a total of 35 minutes of poetry and jazz that provide a real sampler of Jack's work.

At the end of the hour, one of the engineers announced, 'That was a great first take.' Kerouac replied, 'It's the only take.' Allen added, 'That's right.' They all packed up and went their separate ways. *Poetry for the Beat Generation* was not released until June 1959, 15 months or so after the initial recording session took place, though Dot Records made and distributed 130 albums (catalogue number 3154). Then, the company's president, Randy Wood, stopped production and distribution. Call it corporate censorship. Place it on the same spectrum that led to the prosecution for obscenity of Ginsberg's 'Howl' and Burroughs' *Naked Lunch*.

In Randy Wood's view, certain passages on the album that he didn't specify were 'in bad taste', 'off colour', 'obscene' and 'not clean family entertainment'. He would not allow his 'diskery' to be associated with the project. The word 'diskery' itself suggests his priggishness, his inability to move with the times, and his failure to hear the promise of things to come in Kerouac's lively performance. Wood seems to have wanted to save American youth from the Beats. Indeed, he insisted that he would not permit his son to listen to any of the tracks on the album lest he be corrupted.

Thiele fought back tactfully, politely, and as though he might have been arguing before a judge in a courtroom. He agreed that the album was not meant for kids, but he argued that 'such great poets as Walt Whitman and e.e. cummings have works not suitable for children but are respected as works of art'. Wood didn't budge, refused to express regrets and offered no apology. He probably didn't see himself as censorial, though Thiele did. He resented Wood's heavy hand and resigned from Dot.

Thiele also explained that when he signed up to work for Wood he was never told that all records had to be clean entertainment for the whole family. 'I was never aware of any policy at Dot concerning matters of this type,' he wrote. Wood's refusal to release the album might have reminded Jack of his long battles with the publishing industry and its refusal to recognize his genius and make his work available to the public. Now, however, he had friends and allies. Now, he wasn't anonymous any more, but rather a published author with friends who had connections and who were eager to advance his career, and perhaps add to their own lustre.

Thiele and Allen formed Hanover, their own record company, secured the master tape and recruited *New York Times* critic Gilbert Millstein to write the liner notes for the album. Once again, Millstein sang the praises of Jack Kerouac, this time as a recording artist not as a novelist, or as the 'avatar' of the Beat Generation. To Millstein's ear, *Poetry for the Beat Generation* (Hanover no. 5000) was definitely not obscene, but rather 'another reminder, if only a small one, of the enduring oneness of human beings'. Indeed, Kerouac had aimed to be all-embracing, to include the sacred and the profane, the noisy and the sonorous and to link Beats, bohemians, subterraneans and 'jazzniks', as he called them. He added to the argot.

Jack's inclusivity is apparent in his poems to the white California-born jazzman Dave Brubeck and to the African American saxophonist Charlie Parker, who was known as 'the Rimbaud of modern jazz' and who died at the age of 34 in 1955. In the mid-1950s, Dave Brubeck was playing jazz piano on college campuses. His first album for Columbia, which was released in 1954, is titled *Jazz Goes to College*.

On *Poetry for the Beat Generation*, Kerouac's brilliance comes through in his long prose piece 'October in the Railroad Earth', that was published, in a slightly different form, in *Lonesome Traveller* in 1960 under the title 'The Railroad Earth'. That single track – the first on the album– celebrates jazz, the blues, bebop and 'The Negro' as 'the essential American'. Kerouac had long endorsed the idea that to understand America one had to understand the 'Negro' and 'Negro music' as sung by the likes of Billie Holiday and Sarah Vaughan, and as performed by Count Basie, Duke Ellington, Lester Young and Charlie Parker.

In 'October in the Railroad Earth', he illustrated his idea about the 'Negro' as the essential American with a cast of African American characters, including a black pastor whose voice he mimics in the line, 'Why yes Mam but de gospel do say that man was born of woman's womb.' Even black pastors, Kerouac suggests, can't help but use earthy language and be of the Earth itself. On the same track, he also takes on the persona of a young woman and sings plaintively, 'Mama, he treats your daughter mean.' He sounds like he feels her pain.

In 'One Mother', he expresses his tender and unabashed love for Gabrielle Kerouac, the woman who brought him into the world, raised him, defended him, protected him and supported him as a writer, perhaps more than anyone else he knew save for Ginsberg. Gabrielle was his saint. He was the sinner, though he takes a humorous look at his own sins of the flesh in 'I'd Rather Be Thin than Famous'. In fact, Kerouac had gained weight; the extra pounds made him feel uncomfortable in his own body and about himself. Fame proved to be far trickier than he had imagined. But he still loved old New York, the New York of bums and bohemians. In homage to that past, he recorded two jazzy pieces: 'Bowery Blues' and 'McDougal Street Blues'.

When he looked back at *Poetry for the Beat Generation*, Kerouac called it 'a little gem'. Indeed, the album shows that he was a performer with many different voices: sad, joyful, nostalgic and impassioned. It shows that he had mastered the art of rhyme, repetition and alliteration. The album also reveals him as an empathetic human being who accepted suffering and recognized the beauty of the world. At times, Allen's accompaniment seems at odds with Kerouac's words and voices. It might have worked better for a lounge singer in Las Vegas than for Kerouac in a recording studio in New York. Still, it's helpful to remember the words of the critic, Bruce Eder, who noted that 'Kerouac's readings are in a class by themselves, and separate from Allen's'. Eder added, 'The two performances co-exist and weave together without ever really joining ... Kerouac did his thing, Allen did his.'

Not surprisingly, when Thiele suggested a second album, Kerouac wasn't eager to have Steve Allen accompany him. In fact, he asked specifically for Zoot Sims and Al Cohn, two white jazz saxophonists whom he knew well and whose work he admired. Thiele was afraid that two saxophones would drown him out. He tried to persuade Jack to change his mind, but Jack was adamant. He said that he would only make the recording with Sims and Cohn and no one else. Thiele went along with Jack's request and the project moved ahead.

On the album, Sims and Cohn don't overpower Kerouac, in part because he insisted on being heard and because Sims made sure that he stood in front of the microphone and spoke directly into it. At one point, Sims stopped playing and said to Cohn, 'we're definitely overshadowing Jack'. No engineer expunged that comment or others like it. From that juncture on, Sims and Cohn were careful not to overpower Jack's voice. Kerouac's personality shone through on one occasion when Zoot told Cohn to play 'Western Jazz'. Jack replied, 'Let him play what he wants.' He didn't like the idea of a boss of any kind telling anyone what to do.

According to the information in the Rhino boxed set, *Blues and Haikus* was 'possibly recorded' in the spring of 1958 and then not released until October 1959. The title itself surely belongs to Kerouac. Indeed, the concept had to have been his: marry the music of African Americans to the poetry and philosophy of Japan. Kerouac's 'American haikus', as he called them, can be bluesy, much as his blues can sound like *haikus*. The tracks on the second album are shorter than on the first, with brief bursts of intense energy, the music jabbing at the words and the words inviting cries from the musicians. At times, *Blues and Haikus* sounds like traditional call and response which is sometimes described as the 'sound of collaboration'. Sims and Cohn aren't as brilliant as Lester Young or Charlie Parker, but they definitely enhance the poet's words.

Kerouac waited for a year and a half for the release of *Blues and Haikus* (Hanover no. 5006). Afraid that the album would never be circulated, he was sure that Norman Granz – the jazz entrepreneur and the executive producer for the album – intentionally delayed distribution because he was afraid of a lawsuit on the grounds that the album appealed to 'prurient' interest. Kerouac had heard the criticism before. Even Ginsberg complained that Jack's books were 'so full of sex language' that they never would be published. Censorship and rejection were in large part the story of his career as writer and a creative artist.

Still, he kept going and didn't slow down. Moreover he looked to jazz musicians for inspiration; they persevered even when they were ignored and their music rejected. 'Jazz musicians most perfectly epitomize the often sorry, and fabulous, condition of the artist in America,' Kerouac told John Clellon Holmes in a letter from June 1952 in which he also explained that he was going to write a novel about Lester Young and Billie Holiday that he would call *Hold Your Horn High.*

At times, *Blues and Haikus* sounds raunchier than *Poetry for the Beat Generation.* The album teases listeners with glimpses of girls – Kerouac called his method of making word pictures, 'sketching'. Moreover, the two saxophonists paint musical pictures of birds, bees and a lonely businessman on his way home. To borrow from the jazz lingo that had become an integral part of Kerouac's vocabulary, Cohn and Sims really 'blew'.

Jack, Zoot and Al redid some of their initial takes. On the LP, as well as on the CD, an attentive listener can hear Zoot say, 'Take one.' Later he adds, 'Do that over.' A real surprise on *Blues and Haikus* is Jack's rendition of a soulful song that's not listed on the album. The brief lyrics tell a poignant love story: 'Oh baby, baby / oh baby baby / I'm going to give you / the railroad blues.'

Listening to those lyrics and, indeed, to the entire album, one can't help but sense that the blues had gotten under Kerouac's skin and that they had made him the person he had become. He doesn't seem to be channelling anyone on *Blues and Haikus*; he's not trying to be Frank Sinatra or Billie Holiday, which he had done and could do. Rather, his voice comes from his own heart.

At the end of the session, Kerouac wanted Sims and Cohn to sit down and hear the tape. They weren't interested. Then, after they took their instruments and left the studio, he 'cried in a corner' and then wailed, 'My two favorite musicians walked out on me. They didn't even want to hear this back.' He and Thiele descended on an Eighth Avenue bar and got drunk; Jack ended the evening by tossing beer bottles into the street.

To Ginsberg, he boasted that on all three albums, 'I really read like a bitch.' As of that moment, none of his recordings were for sale or in circulation, though Jack had his own copies that he played on a brand new state-of-the-art record player that he had just bought. It was 'a Webcore three-speed', he told Ginsberg, who knew a lot about tape recorders and recordings. In 1959, he made his own album, *Howl*, for Fantasy Records. He, too, had been recording himself for a decade.

Kerouac heard Ginsberg's album and raved about it. He especially enjoyed his reading of the poem 'Footnote to "Howl"', which turns the word 'holy' into a profane chant. Jack told Allen that it was 'the most beautiful thing I've ever heard'. In the 1940s, they started out as amateurs. Now, they were professionals. Jack shared his new-found glory with his old friend. Still, he wanted Ginsberg to know that his three albums – *Poetry for the Beat Generation*, *Blues and Haikus* and *Readings by Jack Kerouac on the Beat Generation* – were 'the greatest poetry records since Dylan Thomas'. He was the greatest and he wanted everyone to know.

Kerouac made his last LP for Verve, created in 1956 by Norman Granz, who had watched Kerouac perform at the Village Vanguard in December 1957. Granz offered Kerouac a three-record deal with Verve, though nothing came of it, perhaps because Jack was busy writing novels and working on the goofy movie *Pull My Daisy* (1959), which demonstrates that the Beat aesthetic touched nearly all the arts. The cast includes musician and composer David Amram, photographer and filmmaker Robert Frank, plus the poets Ginsberg, Gregory Corso and Peter Orlovsky, the painters Larry Rivers and Alice Neel and the dancer Delphine Seyrig. Kerouac provided the narration, yet another avenue for him to use his voice.

It is too bad he didn't record more of his work; after all, by 1959 he had become an accomplished performance artist in the studio if not the stage. He might have rivalled Dylan Thomas who died in New York in 1953 at the age of 39. By the end of the 1950s, the Caedmon recordings of Dylan served as the gold standard for poets who wanted to tape themselves.

Beginning in 1952 and all through the 1950s, Caedmon revolutionized the spoken word and helped to pave the way for Kerouac's recordings, as well as for Ginsberg's and Burroughs'. Indeed, no literary movement in the twentieth century recorded with more passion and precision than the Beats, though they had competition. By 1959, the year Kerouac made his last album, revenue at Caedmon topped half a million dollars. Dylan Thomas's records outsold Jack's. His booming Welsh voice proved hard to resist. Plus his early death contributed to his legendary status as one of the twentieth century's great poets.

Whether Kerouac's third last album – *Readings by Jack Kerouac on the Beat Generation* – is his best is a matter of debate. At over 41 minutes it's the longest of his LPs. Moreover, there's no musical accompaniment, which means that Kerouac's voice stands out and perhaps sounds more musical than on the first three albums. At the same time he was exceedingly photogenic. The brilliant cover photo, by musician and photographer John Cohen, shows Jack with his ear glued to a radio, turning the dial and tuning into the music. The image is quintessential Kerouac.

Bill Randle, who produced *Readings by Jack Kerouac on the Beat Generation* and who wrote the liner notes for the album, linked Kerouac to James Dean, Charlie Parker and Dylan Thomas, whom he called 'luminous'. Randle saw Dean, Parker and

Thomas as 'martyrs' who belonged to the pages of 'stark tragedy'. He didn't specifically add Jack's name to that trio of artists and performers, but he seems to have felt that he shared their martyrdom.

Before the recording session, Randle spent 'hundreds of hours' with Kerouac, sifting through published and unpublished material, though where and when he doesn't say. Then, Jack made the final selections. In his liner notes, Randle calls Kerouac's readings 'crude' and 'unpolished', though he also admits that they provide an 'aural experience' that's 'almost hypnotic'. That's strong praise, indeed, though Randle also wrote to Kerouac and called him a 'sloppy craftsman'. Randle suggested that Jack ought to have edited *before* he read, and not 'as he read'. The phrase 'sloppy craftsman' must have hurt Jack, though editing while he read gave him a jolt that editing in advance just didn't provide.

Kerouac biographer Gerald Nicosia took issue with Randle. Indeed, what he missed, Nicosia argues in an essay (included in *The Jack Kerouac Collection*) titled 'Kerouac as Musician', was 'that the essence of Kerouac's artistry lies in a spontaneity that is totally faithful to his own impulses at the moment of creation or utterance'. Listening to *Readings by Jack Kerouac on the Beat Generation* it seems likely that Kerouac changed the texts at the microphone in the act of performing, even if it was only to pause for a moment or two or to change the cadence of a line. As he knew, a little pause could make a big difference.

But without the texts that he carried in his suitcase and that he held in his hands when he recorded, it's difficult to say how much or how little he actually followed his 'own impulses', as Nicosia calls them. Moreover, it might be helpful to remember that 'improvisation' means the 'art of improving', not merely divagating from the original. In that sense, Kerouac was an adept improviser. He recycled his own work; descriptions that first showed up in his journals later appeared in improved ways in his novels.

Moreover, it might be helpful to borrow the key word – 'virtuoso' – that Gilbert Millstein used in his review of *On the Road*. Indeed, Kerouac's virtuosity seems as important as his ability to improvise. A comparison between the LP *Readings By Jack Kerouac on the Beat Generation* and the published texts shows that there's some ad-libbing and some changes that were made in the moment. Indeed, Kerouac turned improvisation into an art form.

It's probably also worth saying that Kerouac discovered the literary form that worked for him and that he used in *On the Road* after listening extensively to jazz records in Mexico with William Burroughs. Not surprisingly, he called it *'wild form'* and put those two words in italics. In a letter written in June 1952 to John Clellon Holmes, with whom he shared his passion for jazz, Kerouac described a marathon session when he played record after record of Miles Davis, Shorty Rogers, Stan Getz and a couple of Swedish jazzmen, Bengt Hallberg and Lars Gullin. Then he explained to Holmes that 'Wild form's the only form [that] holds what I have to say'. Kerouac books are indeed 'wild' though they also have form. His LPs are also an example of 'wild form' – there's freedom and there's also shapeliness. As he noted, 'Something that you feel will find its own form'.

What makes the third album, *Readings by Jack Kerouac on the Beat Generation*, significantly different from the first two albums is the subject matter. Kerouac insisted on reading hefty portions from the book that he was calling *Visions of Neal* and that would be published as *Visions of Cody* three years after his death, in 1972, with an introduction by Ginsberg.

For years, Kerouac had tried to distance himself emotionally from the real Neal Cassady, who appears as Dean Moriarty in *On the Road* and as Cody Pomeray in *Visions of Cody*. After 1957, the two men drifted further and further apart, though for nearly a decade they were connected by a love of jazz, as *On the Road* shows. Jack and Neal saw each other for the last time in 1964, the same year Kerouac gave a drunken performance at Harvard. When Cassady died in 1968, he and Kerouac were no longer travelling the same road.

The literary links between Sal Paradise and Dean Moriarty proved impossible to separate. They were immortal fictional characters seeking the hottest of jazz from New York to California. Still, Kerouac made significant changes that distanced his characters from the real life people who inspired them. Viking insisted that he not use actual names in *On the Road*. The change from Neal to 'Dean' (and then again from Neal to 'Cody') might have provided Kerouac with a modicum of closure on their intense on-again, off-again relationship. The name changes also would have provided a shield of sorts against a libel suit. They also helped to transform the real Neal into the mythological characters and western heroes Dean Moriarty and Cody Pomeray.

On his third and final album, Kerouac allocated more time to Neal/Cody than any other individual, including Lucien Carr who appears on two substantial tracks, both titled 'Lucien Midnight: The Sounds of the Universe in My Window'. Those two tracks add up to about three minutes and 20 seconds. The texts were published as 'Old Angel Midnight' in the magazine *Big Table* in the spring of 1959. Clearly, Kerouac wanted to remember and honour the friends he met in New York in the 1940s and who were among the founding brothers of the Beat Generation. 'I love Allen Ginsberg,' Kerouac shouts on 'Lucien Midnight'. He sounds like he loved Allen as much as he loved his mother.

Kerouac also wanted to remember and honour the birth of bop and the Beat Generation. 'Fantasy: The Early History of Bop', track 8 on the third album, is one of Kerouac's most passionate essays about jazz, as well as one of his most coherent pieces about the genesis and evolution of African American music. It appeared in print under the title 'The Beginning of Bop'. The differences between the text and the recording are illuminating. On the recording, Kerouac uses the word 'girls'. In the text, the word 'broads' takes its place. The word 'niggerlips' (which sounds like Lenny Bruce) disappears entirely, as does the phrase 'steaming turds'. The revisions, which were presumably made by Kerouac himself, suggest that he wanted to make the album sound inoffensive, albeit without changing the tenor of the piece itself. Had he become more sensitive to 'off-colour' language? It would seem so. Was the excision of the made-up word 'niggerlips' a real loss? No, probably not.

The major difference between the album and printed text is that on the album one can hear Kerouac's seductive and compelling voice. On the printed page, one can only imagine Jack's voice. Some of the sounds can only be appreciated on the recording, especially when Jack sings 'Skidilibee-la-bee you, -oo, – e bop she bam, ske too ria – Parasakiliaoolza – menooriastibatiolyait-oon ya koo.' Was he ad-libbing at the microphone, or were those sounds in the written text that he held in his hands? Once again, without the manuscripts themselves the answer to that question is anyone's educated guess. Still, Kerouac's virtuoso recordings are a wonder to listen to and hear.

His career in front of the microphone (and the TV camera) culminated in November 1959 when he appeared on *The Steve Allen Plymouth Show* that was broadcast nationally. Since he had started his act as a nightclub performer with Allen in New York, it seems appropriate that he concluded with Allen in Los Angeles, where he read from *Visions of Neal*, as it was then called, and then from *On the Road*, the book everyone was eager to hear from the lips of the legendary author himself.

For the TV audience, Kerouac created a smooth segue that viewers might not have heard and appreciated. After he ended the excerpt from *Visions of Neal*, and before he started to read from the conclusion of *On the Road*, he explained, 'A lot of people have asked me why did I write that book or any book.' He added, 'All the stories I wrote were true because I believed in what I saw.' Then came the kind of observation that had long been a part of his repertoire, and that would become even more frequent as he aged: 'I wrote the book because we're all gonna die.' Mortality stalked him all his life and infused his novels. Jazz sometimes seemed like his antidote to death.

When he read from *On the Road* on TV, he included the vivid description of Dean Moriarty wearing his moth-eaten overcoat. On TV, Kerouac skipped the section that follows it probably because it doesn't add an essential element to the mood or the narrative itself. Kerouac picked up the thread in the next-to-the-last paragraph in which his inimitable style emerges and his voice caresses his words. The last paragraph begins, 'so in America when the sun goes down . . .'.

On TV, Kerouac read the last five words in the novel, 'I think of Dean Moriarty.' Then, after a brief pause he read them once again, only more slowly the second time and with a sense of solemnity that seems to accord with his comment, 'we're all gonna die'. Over the years, he had learned the power of repetition, and, while he didn't change his words, he changed the delivery. When he echoed those five words, 'I think of Dean Moriarty', he suggested both the absence and the presence of Dean Moriarty, as well his adventurous life and his certain death.

Kerouac's conclusion to the novel – 'I think of Dean Moriarty' – was as good a way as any to say hello and goodbye to the TV audience. It was also a good way to say hello and goodbye to the real Neal Cassady and the fictional Dean Moriarty.

Between 1957, when *On the Road* was published, and 1959, when he read from his big, breakthrough novel on TV, Kerouac had mastered the art of performing before a live audience. In those two years, he had learned how to make records, work with professional jazzmen and reinvented himself. The man who had grown up with a love for the blues found a way to express his love anew, in a new medium for a new age: the age of TV, rock'n'roll, Sputnik, vinyl and the LP, which, in the 1950s, replaced the 78rpm record.

It was not the age into which he was born and raised – the age of the Victrola, swing, Frank Sinatra and the big bands. But it was the age in which he made his mark with recordings and with the spoken word. Indeed, on the three LPs known as *The Jack Kerouac Collection*, the author of *On the Road* conveyed, through the instrument of his own personal voice, the vision and the wisdom of the Beat Generation.

One final comment about jazz and Kerouac seems necessary. Indeed, probably the most pernicious comment that was ever made about Kerouac wasn't Truman Capote's dismissal of his writing as merely 'typing'. No, the most pernicious comment came from Kenneth Rexroth in a review of *The Subterraneans* which was published by the *San Francisco Chronicle* in 1958. 'There are two things Jack knows nothing about – jazz and Negroes', Rexroth wrote. Unfortunately his remark has been repeated as though it's the gospel. Rexroth doesn't seem to have read *On the Road* or *The Subterraneans* carefully. Both novels testify to Kerouac's deep understanding of jazz and his keen appreciation of African American music and culture. Moreover, Kerouac's sense of himself as a writer derived to a large extent from his immersion in jazz and the blues neither of which can be dissociated from African American life. No writer in the English language in the mid-twentieth century felt jazz as intensely as Kerouac, except perhaps African American writers like Langston Hughes, Ralph Ellison and James Baldwin. To use the colloquial once again, Kerouac could 'blow blow blow' with the best of novelists and poets.

Further reading

Long gone are the days when Kerouac's work was unavailable. Now, almost all of it is in paperback. Still, there is no book about Kerouac and jazz, though there's plenty of material available to make a big book on the subject. Students, teachers and scholars can dig into Kerouac's letters, in two volumes, both edited by Ann Charters and published by Viking. There are extensive comments about jazz and jazz musicians all the way through both books. Also useful is *The Unknown Kerouac*, edited by Todd Tietchen, that contains an essay about Frank Sinatra and another titled 'On Contemporary Jazz: "Bebop"' from 1947 that shows Jack was thinking about jazz a decade before *On the Road* was published. That volume also contains Kerouac's journal from 1951 in which he writes extensively about jazz, plus two works of fiction which were originally written in French and that are translated here into English by Jean-Christophe Cloutier. The Library of America publishes *The Unknown Kerouac*. The volume is so new – it was published in 2016 – that scholars, biographers and critics have not yet, as of this writing, had time to absorb all the information it contains, though I have made ample use of it for this chapter. It's the best place to begin for anyone eager to learn more about Kerouac and jazz.

Discography

There are three CDs of Kerouac's recordings from the late 1950s on three different labels: Rhino, Hoodoo and Chrome Dreams. They can all be purchased online. The boxed-set from Rhino comes with a large booklet that has extensive information about Kerouac and his three LPs, plus the original liner notes. Hoodoo and Chrome Dreams provide smaller booklets that are not as comprehensive as Rhino's. Chrome Dreams offers three tracks not on the other labels: Kerouac's interviews with the conservative author William Buckley; Fernanda Pivano, an Italian journalist; and Ben Hecht, the screenwriter and novelist. Charles Waring's essay in the Chrome Dreams CDs is eloquent, as is Paul Gerard's essay in the Hoodoo label. They all have unique strengths. It's hard to say which one is indispensible. If I had to recommend one it would be Rhino's *The Jack Kerouac Collection*.

CHAPTER 6
ART MUSIC: LISTENING TO KEROUAC'S *MEXICO CITY BLUES*
A. Robert Lee

I want to be considered a jazz poet blowing a long blues in an afternoon jam session of Sunday. I take 242 choruses; my ideas vary and sometimes roll from chorus to chorus or from halfway through a chorus to halfway into the next.

Jack Kerouac, Note to *Mexico City Blues*, 1959[1]

This could hardly sound a more winning prospectus: Kerouac's poem pitched as 'a long blues', a multi-chorus of riffs, scats, improvisations. The aim of creating a Sunday's 'afternoon jam session' adds its own flavour, the suggestion of spontaneous and easy-on-the-ear composition. Yet, oddly, *Mexico City Blues* (1959) has never in truth captured a huge readership, not by the standard of *On the Road* (1957) or *The Subterraneans* (1958). For the question often enough arises of the poem's accessibility, the in-house allusions, various skeins of wordplay and tics of syntax, the seams of Buddhist and Catholic religious philosophy. Even the poem's Mexico can at times challenge instant recognition, the elusive snippets of Aztec-ism and local folklore and language. How truly and readily is the whole given to ease of access? How best to take on the 'jazz' fashioning of the poem, its overall music?

Written in the summer of 1955 at 212 Orizaba Street, Mexico City, in a roof hut up above the first floor lodging of Maynard Garver, a Burroughs acquaintance and addict of 20 years and whose narcotics-driven voice speaks in a number of the choruses, 'Mexico City Blues' was first drafted in pencil and within the page limits of one of Kerouac's ever-present Notebooks.[2] Kerouac himself had been reading sutras and it cannot surprise that the poem was conceived as a species of Buddhist meditation or even dream. The link to Ginsberg's 'Howl' also rather emphatically comes into play. On returning from Mexico City to San Francisco it was he, after all, who came up with the name 'Howl'. Given, too, that he and Ginsberg had been discussing their respective poems by mail, vision and tactics, there can be little doubt that *Mexico City Blues* and 'Howl', for all their considerable difference, give grounds to be thought of as Beat counterparts. One epilogue worthy of mention has to be Ginsberg's recording of the entire text, a reading full of winning and evidently sympathetic voice.[3]

In this regard both compositions belong also in the classic American Long Poem tradition. One hears Whitman, 'Song of Myself', for sure, but it is far from out of keeping to invoke a circuit of, say, Pound's *Cantos* (1970), Berryman's *The Dream Songs* (1969) or Zukovsky's *A* (1978). From the Beat orbit, Kerouac's own 'The Scripture of the Golden

Kerouac's Eternity' (1960) or Ginsberg's own 'Kaddish'(1961) can justly be invoked; but so, also, and perhaps however uncustomary, can a number of epic Beat-feminist classics to include Diane di Prima's *Loba* (1973) sequence, Joanne Kyger's *Tapestry and the Web* (1965) or Anne Waldman's *Iovis* (1992) poems. In other words, *Mexico City Blues* remains only provisionally situated – Beat, Buddhist, Catholic, extended religious and secular chant, rhapsody (hard not to invoke Gershwin's 'Rhapsody in Blue'), poetic auto-fiction, but for immediate purposes Kerouac's own word-jazz.

Two cross-bearings give highly useful points of entry to the imaginative workings of *Mexico City Blues*. Ted Joans's 'The Wild Spirit of Kicks', written on Kerouac's death in October 1969 and in deliberately capitalized script, not only recalls a warm interethnic friendship but the jazz dynamic that played so huge part in drawing them one to another:

> JACK IN RED AND BLACK MAC
> RUSHING THROUGH DERELICT STREWEN
>   STREETS OF NOTH AMERICA
> JACK IN WELLWORN BLUEJEANS AND
>   DROOPSYWEATHER OF SMILES
> RUNNING ACROSS THE COUNTRY LIKE A
>   RAZOR BLADE GONE MAD
> JACK IN FLOPPY SHIRT AND JACKET
>   LOADED WITH JOKES
> OLE ANGEL MIDNIGHT SINGING MEXICO
>   CITY BLUES
> IN THE MIDST OF BLACK HIPSTERS AND
>   MUSICIANS
> FOLLOWED BY A WHITE LEGION OF COOL
>   KICK SEEKERS
> POETRY LOVERS AND POEM GIVERS
> PALE FACED CHIEFTAIN TEARING PAST
>
> THE FUEL OF A GENERATION
> AT REST AT LAST
>
> JK SAYS HELLO TO JC
>   JOHN COLTRANE, THAT IS

Mexico City Blues itself is given explicit acknowledgement with Kerouac denominated 'Ole Angel Midnight' and a key presence for hipsters black and white. How, too, to resist the chain of images of Kerouac as 'A Razor Blade Gone Mad', a 'Pale Faced Chieftain Tearing Past' and, perhaps above all and with an eye to Kerouac's on-the-road impact, 'the fuel of a generation'. It is also more than some wry witticism that Joans should envision the late Kerouac headed into the afterlife company of a sax maestro like John Coltrane. The closing couplet aptly serves to remind of Kerouac's religion of jazz, an affiliation he shares not only with Joans but Beat's leading African American voices of the early Jones/Baraka, Bob Kaufman, A. B. Spellman and a jazzman-poet (and University of Massachussetts music professor) like Archie Shepp.[4]

Joans's tribute can, and to considerable profit actually should, be read alongside any number of explicit 'jazz' choruses in Kerouac's own poem. But the 239th Chorus, in particular, gives a guideline, a passkey, to the jazz aesthetic in play throughout *Mexico City Blues* as a whole. Almost needless to say, the presiding deity is another stellar name, that of Charlie Parker, Yardbird/Bird (1920–55). Parker's perfection of his art, whatever the drug-taking and sad-comic occasion of his death, is to be linked to Buddha's transcendence. For all his turbulent life, Parker shares the creative genius which bespeaks 'All is Well':

Charley Parker. Looked like Buddha.
Charley Parker, who recently died.
Laughing at a juggler on the T V
after weeks of strain and sickness,
was called the Perfect Musician.
And his expression on his face
Was as calm, beautiful, and profound
As the image of the Buddha
Represented in the East, the lidded eyes.
The expression that says 'All is Well'
This was what Charley Parker
Said when he played, All is Well.
You had the feeling of early-in-the-morning
Like a hermit's joy, or like
      the perfect cry
Of some wild gang at a jam session
'Wail, Wop' – Charley burst
His lungs to reach the speed
Of what the speedsters wanted
Was his Eternal Showdown.
A great musician and a great
      creator of forms
That ultimately find expression
In mores and what have you.

This is the Parker for whom Kerouac's accretions of praise take on not only Buddhist resonance ('calm, beautiful, and profound') but who, in the same chorus, he also designates 'the Perfect Musician'. The encomium has Parker 'Musically as important as Beethoven', 'a leader of music' and the virtuoso of 'perfect tune & shining harmony'. He so embodies enduring best jazz ('the perfect cry / Of some wild gang at a jam session'). But is there not also a necessary reflexivity in Kerouac's terms of reference? If Parker, as the 239th Chorus proposes, is 'a great / creator of forms', then assuredly that has to be equally Kerouac's own ambition, art music that aspires to its own triumph of form. Time and again throughout *Mexico City Blues*, jazz serves as this kind of reflective mirror, or perhaps more appositely, as a kind of enactive echo chamber.

If the 241st Chorus will go on to eulogize Parker as 'the perfect horn', others in the jazz gallery win their dutiful (and warm) recognition. Big band jazz, for instance, is summoned as follows in the 23rd Chorus:

Sing you a blues song
      sing you a tune
Sing you eight bars
      or Strike up the Band . . .
Yes baby Count Basie
Basie's fat old Chock
Wallopin Fat Rushing
What a wow old saloon man

Basie as pianist-bandleader in the career that spans Harlem, Kansas, Chicago and the European-tour years, and Rushing, Oklahoma City-born, the 'shouter' blues vocalist with Basie and at his height in the 1940s, clearly stir especial esteem for Kerouac. His own spoken-sung lines, accordingly, again seek virtually to re-enact the music they recall. In this, *Mexico City Blues* connects with a body of African American poetry which aims to do likewise, notably Ted Joans's *Black Pow-Wow: Jazz Poems* (1969), Jayne Cortez's *Pisstained Stairs and the Monkey Man's Wares* (1969), Michael Harper's *Dear John, Dear Coltrane* (1970), and latterly, Yusef Komunyakaa's *Testimony, A Tribute to Charlie Parker* (2013).

Blues allusion, necessarily, saturates the poem, typically in the figure of Leadbelly (Huddie William Leadbetter, 1888–1949), the legendary genius of the 12-string guitar. The 221st Chorus links him to the folkloric Old Man Mose (Louis Armstrong's recording would be apropos), with a touch of off the cuff wordplay in the name:

Old Man Mose
Early Jazz pianist
Had a grandson
Called Deadbelly . . .
Old Man Mose is Dead
      But Deadbelly get Ahead
         Ha ha ha

Blues, as with the jazz in general in the poem, supplies both motif and cadence. The 197th Chorus fuses blues and race ('Blue, black, race, grace. / face, I love ye'). The 202nd Chorus apostrophizes the making of a perfect poem to a 'Honey Land / Blues'. Vernacular Mexico, its gods, serpents and feathers, becomes an 'Aztec Blues'. The 171st Chorus offers a kind of summary, the bond of Kerouac's own voice with those who have peopled the blues across time and to whose refrains and measure he has been drawn to from the outset:

> So I'm with you
>   happy once again
> and singing all my blues
> in tune with you
>   with you.

This jazz-blues orchestration underwrites all of the poem and, in reading through, one meets it across the various planes of experience explored by Kerouac. Let five or so do duty, both serious and playful, and starting with Beat itself and its antecedents as a working roster. The 5th Chorus is early to announce partnerships, the fellahin circle ('KIND KING MIND / (Allen Ginsberg called me'). The at the time pseudonymous 'William Lee' is revealed as Burroughs, Kerouac's own co-author of *And The Hippos Were Boiled in Their Tanks* (1946), their collaborative narrative based upon Lucien Carr's killing of the dangerously obsessional David Kammerer. Gregory Corso is pronounced 'The Italian Minnesinger' and 'Haunted Versemaker/King/of Brattle Street' in memory of Corso's early verse. Neal Cassady is summoned in passin' in the 27th Chorus, a seeming slur but actually a fond nod to 'Nuts like Carl Solom'

Others at the Beat periphery include the 74th Chorus's Gore Vidal with its know reference to sexual tease ('This is for Vidal / Didn't know I was / a Come-Onne you?'). The literary company extends into the yet larger circuit of William (Williams (83rd Chorus), and Thomas Wolfe, Whitman, Melville and Twain Chorus). But the operative name has again to be Ginsberg, explicitly name 213th Chorus – 'Poem dedicated to Allen Ginsberg'. The chorus itself might scat ('loose my shoetongue ... Fill my pail well ... ding my bell'). The eff more a two-way inter-media exchange, Beat as jazz, Jazz as beat.

Mexico, legendarily, holds a special place in Beat mythology. All of the l spent time there, whether on narcotics and sex runs, in escape from US p' or simple adventuring. Each had cause to be taken up with *latinidad* and yet also with Aztec and other indigenous flights of mythology anc *Junky* (1953), Burroughs, assuming prime observer status, writes ((trickling) down to Mexico' (p. 143). In his 116th Chorus, Keroua 'fellaheen Mexico' and speaks of listening to 'Aztec radio'. In fact *N* a widest bandwidth of Mexican culture under jazz-improvisatio' extends from the street and children's 'Indian songs' of the 1'

Thes
his S
Mich

Chorus's references to the volcano myth of Popocatapetl (as Kerouac spells it) and the 207th Chorus's to Quetzacoatl and the lure of the 'Feathered Serpent' along with each topographical flood myth. Nor does Kerouac deny Mexico's draw for him of getting *borracho* (drunk) in 'old sour Azteca' (13th Chorus). All of these aspects of Mexico he aggregates into an overall 'music' in his repeated term. Mexico so transfigures into 'Mexico', itself as it were a south-of-the-border jazz-blues.

Family, for Kerouac, was always a pressing dimension, parents, dead brother, his own daughter, and even when about his road and boxcar-hopping itineraries. The trajectory runs from upbringing in joual-speaking township Lowell to New York City and Columbia and from Beat California (whether City Lights and other San Francisco or the mountain fire watch-outs at the instigation of Gary Snyder) through to the Florida of his eventual alcoholic collapse and death. Gabrielle Kerouac, his mother, Leo Kerouac, his father, perhaps above all his elder brother Gerard, and Jan Kerouac, the daughter he was late to acknowledge, all assume pertinent roles in the poem, figures of actuality yet also of near-myth. The now several Kerouac biographies, few still more exigently than Ann Charters's pioneer life-history (1973) and Gerald Nicosia's compendious *Memory Babe* (1994), have set out the narrative in serious detail, albeit that subsequent accounts have been advantaged by new archival and correspondence findings. *Mexico City Blues*, however, contributes its uniquely particular take on the dynasty and again as a world, a time-and-place memorial history, given through musical filtering.

Kerouac, ironically, at one point even affects to speak as though a family of one, the figure of 'Ti-Jean', or *Petit Jean,* as he specifies in the 148th Chorus. 'I was the first crazy person / I'd known' avers the 88th Chorus. In filling out detail of actual kin, he rarely leaves doubt of a blues texture, intimate memory pitched as though jazz-sung or given sax-like inflection. His father, in the 103rd Chorus, is remembered half-belonging to a dream, a figure at once real and unreal, 'straw hat, newspaper in pocket, / Liquor of the breath, barber shopshines' yet to be recalled 'like a shadow' and 'hurrying to his destiny which is death'. His mother in the 237th Chorus ('Ma mere, tu es la terre') is to be likened not only to the Virgin Mary of the vestigial family Catholicism but also 'Demema', 'mother of the Buddhas'. But hauntingly there is his beloved elder sibling Gerard, dead at nine of rheumatic fever, whose image Kerouac, in the 19th Chorus, turns to as though a fusion of Blake and spiritual:

> Christ has a dove on his shoulder
>> My brother Gerard
>> Had 2 Doves
>> And 2 lambs
>> Pulling his Milky Chariot.

e familial dimensions entwine with the poem's overall shaping religious layers. In *ratching the Beat Surface: Essays on New Vision from Blake to Kerouac* (1982), el McClure offers a pertinent observation:

In Kerouac's *Mexico City Blues* a self-created substrate – a surpassing religious vision was born – or was blown, as one blows a saxophone! It's the surpassing religious visionary poetic statement of the twentieth century.

(p. 75)

Buddhism suffuses the poem, but not as though a belief system so esoteric as to risk eluding common grasp. Indeed, in the 65th Chorus, Kerouac veers into a folksy route-map:

> To understand what I'm sayin
> You gotta read the Sutras.
> The Sutras of the Ancients, India
> Long ago . . .

Buddha himself is to be seen, 'Discoursing in the middle, / Sitting lotus posture, / Hands to the sky, / Explaining the Dharma / In a Sutra so high'. The Buddhism within reach is 'folded magnificence' (102nd Chorus), a Beat-spiritual vector of enlightenment and compassion. But however consequential the prospect, Kerouac can at the same time return to being jazz-playful, affectionately colloquial as in the 190th Chorus and its explanation of Dharma:

> What I have attained in Buddhism
>   is nothing
> What I wish to attain
>   is nothing . . .
> No matter how you cut it
>   it's empty delightful boloney.

Catholicism as legacy holds equal status with Buddhism throughout the poem, be it liturgy, intercessory Holy Family, Christly peace or forgiveness. Gabrielle Kerouac he elides not only with Damema, Buddha's mother, but with the Messiah. In this respect, his relationship with Jan Kerouac comes again into play, the daughter he had with Joan Haverty Kerouac, born in February 1952 and author of *Baby Driver* (1981) and *Train Song* (1988). Improvising on the theme of 'a home for unmarried fathers' (166th Chorus), he opens his poem to the idea of universal paternity and maternity, the generic human family, especially in Choruses 68–71. 'Mary / Who's my mother?' he asks in the 69th Chorus. The universalist impetus he has then extends into the opening of the 70th Chorus:

> Who *is* my father?
> Who is my mother?
> Who is my brother?

Who is my sister?
I say you are all my father
   all my mother
   all my sister
   all my brother

It is this kind of inclusivity, that of an evident spiritual variety, that leads James T. Jones, author of the diligent *Map of Mexico City Blues* (1992), to summarize the poem's religious turn as follows:

> What makes *Mexico City Blues* such a remarkable religious poem is its Christlike gesture, its Buddhalike gesture, of presenting itself as the story of every human being. Ultimately Kerouac wishes to escape paternity in the way the great figures of religion, by accepting his relationship to all people and assuming responsibility for the human family.

It may well be that so generous a stance lets Kerouac off the hook about his denial of Jan Kerouac. Understandably that has been a source of some controversy. But granted its prevailing religiousness of feeling, it also sounds a tacit footfall of the blues or a spiritual, the shared and endemic musical 'grace' he so often insisted upon as the very hallmark of a set by Parker or Coltrane.

One returns, finally, to the poetics, the jazz fashioning, of *Mexico City Blues*. Chorus 31 calls upon another reflexive note, Kerouac as self-aware 'Singer of . . . Angel Sounds and Singer of Religion'. He makes his credential a blend of poet, believer, and one of the world's absurd:

Convulsive writer of Poems
And dialog for Saints
Stomping their feet
On Pirandelloan stage

In the 43rd Chorus the link to music, to bebop and its Beat following, is made emphatic, a fusion of expressive impulses (and with a smattering of scat):

Mexico City Bop
I got the huck bop
I got the floogle mock
I got the thiri chiribim . . .

He also figures the poet-singer as indeed a jazzman, the orchestrator of sound, measure, performance, the call to what in round-midnight argot he calls 'SLIPPITY BOP':

Like, when you see,
the trumpet kind, horn
    shiny in his hand, raise
    it in smoke among heads
    he bespeaks, elucidates,
    explains and drops out,
    end of chorus . . .

Mexico City Blues allows for a range of points of entry, themes and voice. The 34th Chorus has long held one kind of sway with its 'I have no plans / No dates . . . so I leisurely explore / Souls and Cities' and its half-teasing question 'That's enough, isn't it?' The concluding 242nd Chorus has served as a rally with its 'Stop the murder and suicide! / All's well! I am the Guard.' But it remains crucial to take the poem within the terms of its own titling, a jazz-blues, a music boldly and at times even startlingly pressed into word.

Notes

1. All references are to Jack Kerouac, *Mexico City Blues* (New York: Grove Press, 1959). Given subsequent editions and reprints I have opted to give references by Chorus rather than pagination.

2. These Notebooks, together with Kerouac letters and artworks, were acquired in 2001 by the New York Public Library for their Albert A. Berg collection.

3. This recording is to be found as *Mexico City Blues (242 Choruses) Read by Allen Ginsberg* (Boulder, CO: Shamballah Lion Readings, 1996). I thank Jim Sampas greatly for helping me get access to the discs.

4. For a helpful context, see Michael Hrebeniak, 'Jazz and the Beat Generation', in Steven Belletto (ed.), *The Cambridge Companion to The Beats* (New York: Cambridge University Press, 2017), pp. 250–64.

Bibliography

Berryman, John, *The Dream Songs*, New York: Farrar, Straus and Giroux, 2014.
Burroughs, William, *Junky*, New York: Ace, 1953.
Burroughs, William and Jack Kerouac, *And The Hippos Were Boiled in Their Tanks*, New York: Grove Press, 1945 (2008).
Charters, Anne, *Kerouac: A Biography*, San Francisco: Straight Arrow Books, 1973.
Cortez, Jayne, *Pisstained Stairs and the Monkey Man's Wares*, New York: Phrase Text, 1969.
Di Prima, Diane, *Loba*, New York: Penguin, 1998.
Ginsberg, Allen, *Howl and Other Poems*, San Francisco: City Lights Books, 1956.
Ginsberg, Allen, *Kaddish and Other Poems (1958–1960)*, San Francisco: City Lights Books, 1961.

Harper, Michael, *Dear John, Dear Coltrane*, Pittsburgh: University of Pittsburgh Press, 1970.

Joans, Ted, *Black Pow-Wow: Jazz Poems*, New York: Hill and Wang, 1969.

Joans, Ted, *Teducation: Selected Poems*, Minneapolis: Coffee House Press, 1999.

Jones, James T., *A Map of Mexico City Blues*, Carbondale: University Southern Illinois Press, 1992.

Kerouac, Jack, *On the Road*, New York: Viking, 1957.

Kerouac, Jack, *The Subterraneans*, New York: Grove Press, 1958.

Kerouac, Jack, *Mexico City Blues*, New York: Grove Press, 1959.

Kerouac, Jack, *The Scripture of the Golden Eternity*, Chevy Chase, MD: Corinth/Totem Press, 1960.

Kerouac, Jack, *Baby Drive*, New York: St Martin's Press, 1981.

Kerouac, Jan, *Train Song*, New York: Henry Holt, 1998.

Komunyakaa, Yusef, *Testimony: A Tribute to Charlie Parker*, Middletown, CT: Wesleyan University Press, 2013.

Kyger, Joanne, *The Tapestry and the Web*, San Francisco: Four Season Foundation, 1965.

McClure, Michael, *Scratching the Beat Surface. Essays on New Vision from Blake to Kerouac*, San Francisco: North Point, 1982.

Nicosia, Gerald, *Memory Babe: A Critical Biography of Jack Kerouac*, Berkeley: University of California Press, 1994.

Pound, Ezra, *The Cantos*, Berkeley: University of California Press, 1948–69.

Waldman, Anne, *The Iovis Trilogy: Colors in the Mechanism of Concealment*, Minneapolis: Coffee House Press, 2011.

Zukovsky, Louis, *A*, Berkeley: University of California Press, 1978.

INTERVIEW 2: DAVID AMRAM
Pat Thomas

David Amram (born in 1933) is a composer and multi-instrumentalist (piano and French horn amongst others). He wrote and recorded the scores for such classic films as *Splendor in the Grass* and *The Manchurian Candidate*. He is best known to Kerouac scholars for appearing in and composing the music for the 1959 film *Pull My Daisy*.

But his connections to Jack run deeper than that – they performed together in Manhattan jazz clubs and art galleries in the late 1950s. Amram recalled just after Jack's death in 1969, 'He would sing while I was playing the horn, sometimes making up verses. He had a phenomenal ear. It was like playing duets with a great musician.' And they socialized at Amram's home: 'He used to come by and play the piano by ear for hours. He had some wonderful ideas for combining the spoken word with music.' Amram has written extensively about his relationship with Kerouac, most notably in his book *Offbeat: Collaborating with Kerouac*.

But Amram's Beat-cred is not limited to just Jack – he also collaborated with Allen Ginsberg in 1971 (along with Bob Dylan), later released as an album titled *First Blues*.

I first encountered the warm and affable David when I compiled an expanded version of *First Blues* in 2016. His memory for people and places and what they said and did decades ago is remarkable – so it was with great joy and ease when I connected with Amram (on 28 April 2017) to discuss the wild and wonderful world of Jack Kerouac.

PT: I know that Jack was, you know, a big music fan and I wanted to talk a little bit about the artists and musical styles that excited Jack as a fan.

DA: Well, fortunately Jack answered that question himself in so many things that he himself wrote. So, when people ask 'What was Jack Kerouac like?' I say, 'Read his books.' That's exactly what he was like. And secondly, he mentioned in that famous sketch of 'What is Beat' that he was being supposedly nailed to the wall by a playwright who became a journalist and was interviewing Jack and was kind of almost sarcastic as to why would someone who got this enormous recognition all of a sudden be so gracious and kind and that Jack of itself was not portraying what was supposed to be Beat, even though he's supposed to be the granddaddy of Beat. And he said, among other things, that he admired Buddha, Lao Tse and Mohammed, the Star of David and Jesus Christ. He said the greatest composer was Bach, for emphasis, a German. He loved Bach and he loved the Brandenburg Concertos, which we both dig. And the people that he mentioned say in the wonderful part of I always read, that he also used to read, we called 'The Children of the American Bop Night'. He starts mentioning King Oliver, Louis Armstrong and the great New Orleans masters. And he loved Lester Young and Billie Holiday. He loved Gerry Mulligan, who he mentions quite a bit. And of course Charlie Parker, Dizzy Gillespie and Thelonious Monk and he also appreciated a singer named Lee Wiley, who was terrific, who Jack used to hear and picked up on – a lot of jazz people still haven't discovered her.

We would go places and he always had that power of being a great listener and made you listen harder. And when I used to play and he would be there before I really got to know him – and when we finally actually formally met in 1956 at a bring your own bottle party, and he just handed me a piece of paper that said, 'Play with me' and took the paper back. I remember seeing him in places where I was playing. I always would see him because there'd be a whole bunch of people lying around stoned out of their heads or falling off the table or trying to buy some dope or hang out or have some romance or just mumbling to themselves or were so spaced out and there would always be one person that you could feel who was listening, and that was always Jack. He was a great listener and observer and also was able, when we wrote, to capture that musical feeling that he was absorbed in and somehow bring you into the world he was writing about, just the way a great musician or singer suddenly brings you into their world and makes you part of it.

He also was a terrific scat singer and, when I played with him, it was just like being with another great musician. Sometimes we would go to parties and he'd play the piano and I would do my freestyle rapping, rhyming nutcase stuff, and I'd sit down at the piano. He could not only do Beowulf, Chaucer – we didn't even know what the words meant – and he'd not only memorize it, but he could explain and translate it for us – and Thackeray, and Charles Dickens. He could do Baudelaire, and Racine – in French! He knew all the stuff from memory and he could recite those things in a way that was so beautiful and one of our favourites, who was the guide, I think, to both of us for reading, was Dylan Thomas and his *A Child's Christmas in Wales*. That whole LP was something we all wore out because it was just so beautiful. He was a great singer like Frank Sinatra, who we loved. When Jack read, you could understand every word and he managed to make each word, whether it was his work or someone else's, or something he was making up on the spot, he was able to paint a picture through the words. His narration for *Pull My Daisy*, which was magical – I was there when he was doing it – he was doing that spontaneously. In 1959 we did that. Columbia Records wanted to put out a 30-minute recording of Jack reading with my spare music just the way we did it on the film, just as a soundtrack without our bad acting. I meant 'bad acting' because I was in the film at Jack's request and I proved – as Allen Ginsberg and Gregory Corso and everybody else there, by our non-heightened performances – that we were not actors. We had a good time doing it and meanwhile massacring a beautiful play that Jack had written. So, what we did was, after we were done clowning around, someone edited 50 hours of stoned-out clowning around in something resembling almost a story. Jack saw the wreckage of his play – because I saw the play[1] finally, in 2012, at Lowell, the premiere, and it was terrific. There's one scene in *Pull My Daisy*, that was supposed to be about me, that was really interesting. In fact, I saw my character, Mezz McGilliCuddy, was really done by a good actor and was actually interesting and *we* were just goofing around.

Anyway, all that being said, it was so great how Jack was able to take something and instead of stopping and saying, 'Jesus Christ, this isn't what I wrote! What are you guys doing?!' He somehow made that into what looked like something that made sense with this crazy, spontaneous narration, including the voices of the characters that we were supposed to be and he did that off the top of his head. So he was able to do that like a great jazz improviser and he also could read European classics, and his own works, and the works of Gregory Corso and other people – and Philip Whalen – from memory and make them sound great. I just mention that because that's not something that I see in many books about Jack except my own that I wrote called *Offbeat: Collaborating with Kerouac*. But anybody that ever knew him or any recording almost that you hear of Jack's, you can hear what a brilliant guy he was and what a musical guy he was.

PT: This is leading into my next question because in his lifetime Jack recorded and released those three albums with various collaborators and I wanted to get your opinion of those records.

DA: Well, the one that was with Al Cohn and Zoot Sims, I don't remember the name of the record [*Blues and Haikus* – Editor's note] but that was wonderful and Jack loved Zoot and Al. At the time, they were best when they were making a lot of recordings in New York and sometimes you could make two or three recordings in a day if you were lucky since nobody, at that time, made very much money playing in the jazz clubs – although, you could at least get something to eat and a meal and get to see a lot of old friends, and then half the time, the money you did get you'd have to pay other people's halves when they came to hear you and walked out. So you could be a big jazz star and usually have a day job or, let's just say, live very modestly. Fortunately in New York at that time you could live modestly and have a great time because the rents enabled you to have a modest way of living. So, if someone could make two or three records a day, that was where you could actually get enough to survive, pay a few bills, and maybe even go out and have a nice meal with your partner or your wife or your girlfriend or whatever.

When Al and Zoot were done, Jack wanted to hang out with them, as he did with everybody that he met, and they were in a hurry because they had another record take and Jack felt terrible because he thought they were snubbing him. Actually they really liked him and liked what he did, and they were very proud to have been on the record long after he passed away. They loved him and what he did but they had to go on to the next gig! The recording was wonderful and I enjoyed every second of it. Everybody liked Zoot and Al. Since they came out of the Lester Young school, it made Jack feel good because he would have loved to do one with Lester Young as well. After we did *Pull My Daisy*, we thought ours was going to come out and that's finally out now, 58 years later – actually 59 years later – in the States it's coming out now, in 2017, finally on a five CD box set with my music from *The Manchurian Candidate*, *Splendor in the Grass*, 60 years of my recorded music.

PT: Oh, I got that as an import on your recommendation.

DA: I think one of them is *Pull My Daisy* without the acting, just with the sound, and you could hear what Jack was like. It was almost like hanging out with him with all that stuff he was making up. He was watching the film as he was making it up. He's making a film that you can make in your head by listening to it. The other one that he did that was terrific was the one with Steve Allen playing. Steve's thing was … he would just sort of play his wonderful, almost like cocktail piano, and then Jack would just read over that and use that as the atmosphere to make you feel like you were just sitting somewhere and suddenly Jack was starting to talk to you or making up a poem on the spot, even though he was reading stuff that he had already written, it was just so beautiful. But he used Steve's cocktail piano the way if the radio was on or he just started reading, because he liked to do that as well. When I played with him I tried to have my music accompany the music that was already in his words because Billy Collins told me once, 'I usually play with musicians because the music's already there in the poetry.'

In Jack's case, he could do it either way so when you hear the one with Steve Allen you see another side of Jack, of how he was, as if he was reading a poem in someone's place in the middle of a party and there was a lot of talking going on, and he used the background sounds of something else to accompany – he was accompanying and enriching the ambience that was already there. That's a wonderful recording. Then he has some of them reading on *Blues and Haikus* and other parts of things that he wrote. The thing I love doing with Jim Sampas was *Jack Kerouac Reads On the Road*, when we had his works 'Washington, D.C. Blues' and 'Orizaba 210 Blues', where he actually just made up that stuff himself. Those were fantastic. There's another one, too – I can't remember which one that is – but those ones with Al Cohn, Zoot Sims and Steve Allen are the ones that fortunately had been available since they came out and somehow didn't end up in the cut-out bin.

PT: That's right, they've been reissued on CD several times. I want to talk about the musicality of Jack's writing. You hear rhythms in poems like *Mexico City Blues* and then, in *Visions of Cody*, he's describing in one spot having breakfast in the diner of having bacon and eggs and toast in the same way a musician might solo. His 'first thought, best thought' is very much like a jazz improv.

DA: He was just being conversational. One time I went over, in my book *Offbeat: Collaborating with Kerouac* I think I mention that, he called up and I was with a friend, he called up about ten o'clock at night and said, 'Hey, David, why don't you come over with your friend. I'm here at someone's house and we can hang out.' I said, 'Well, you know, I'm copying a kaddish which they're going to be doing as part of my Friday night sacred service and this was one part of the sacred service that never got written in time. They're going to be doing it in Jersey and they want to have that as part of it.' I said, 'I've finished writing it but I've got to write it out clearly so the poor singer and their accompanist can, you know, be able to read it and play it and not have to have an anthropologist come in and figure out what I meant.' And that just requires putting it down neatly. So I had my pen and ink and ruler – it was just a mechanical thing really – and putting in the final touches of dynamics and stuff like that because there were no computers in those days. I don't wear a white powdered wig but I still do it the old-fashioned way, the way Beethoven did it, and try to write it down so that the singer or the person won't say 'I wonder what he meant by that.' It'll be clear. So, Jack said, 'Come on over, bring your stuff.' So I said to my friend, 'Let's go over,' because she loved Jack's writing, so I said, 'Let's go over and try to see Jack just for an hour.' She said, 'Man, I have to go to work in the morning. You're going to be there all night!' I said, 'No, no, I'll just be there an hour or two.' She said, 'Come on, I know you guys. You'll be there all night.' I said okay and I went by myself. He sat down and I got out my piece of paper and pen and music and I started copying.

He started telling me a story about when he was over visiting Burroughs and the Algerian struggle was still going on and the French barracks were still there. He was in the French barracks with all these French cats speaking this Quebecois. He was talking to them then all these kids who were also sort of the equivalent of draftees in the other army, they were young guys, off-duty, they were hanging out with the French guys. They were just kids, teenagers or in their twenties. They didn't care about the politics, they didn't want to go to war with each other, they were just young guys in the army. They were hanging out together drinking tea and talking and telling jokes. Jack, speaking French, Quebecois-style, they spoke French – a lot of kids at that time in Algeria also spoke French – so they were having a good time. Jack told all these amazing stories and I'm sitting there copying away. I could listen to him because I was just copying at the same time. Suddenly, he ends this fantastic story and I look out and it was light out. It was already daytime. It was seven in the morning! I said, 'My God, Jack, you've been talking for like seven and a half hours. I wish I had a tape recorder. That was a whole book you just rapped out!' He said, 'That's what I try to do when I'm writing. To have people feel that I'm talking right to them, telling them a story.' He said, 'I can never quite get it but that's what I try to do.' And that blew my mind. That was, I thought, so much more important than so many things I read about what his literary style was. It was just that simple: he was telling a story. When I wrote *Offbeat*, Kurt Vonnegut was supposed to give a great quote for it but he said, 'David, I'm glad you did it that way because it's the same thing that Jack would've said to you.' He said,

'Write the way you talk.' In other words, Jack was showing everybody that the idea is just what Lester Young – one of Jack's favorites – said to someone when they came out and played ten minutes of fantastic solos setting new Olympic world records for speed, more notes than were necessary in a lifetime and blasting down the house, and Lester Young, in his inimitable, gracious style, said, 'That was most impressive. Now I'd like to hear *your* story.'

It was always a thing about the idea of telling your story. Since we all realize everyone has a story, everyone has a song in their heart, everyone has a heartbeat, everyone has a heritage, everyone has something precious to offer, Jack and a lot of these people's stuff we revere told their story just as the first great jazz poet Homer did when he rapped out the whole *Iliad* and *The Odyssey* accompanied by whatever guy or gal – or guys or gals – had to back him up playing the lyre, that little lap harp they used to play. Or when King David did his song to Solomon accompanied by a harp player or maybe two or three harp players if two of them got tired, or when Socrates was sitting under that olive tree and Plato wrote a bunch of stuff down that Socrates had said – I don't know if he had a backup player or not – but the idea of telling stories … Jack even used to say, 'I guess they haven't read Cervantes. They haven't read *Don Quixote*. That's just like two guys wandering around hanging out having these crazy adventures. There's nothing new about that!' He said, 'It's always interesting because it's telling stories of stuff.'

Of course, the Eastern seaboard establishment in the 1950s were so horrified when Jack just broke it all down and tried to explain it. He was just someone from Lowell, Massachusetts, who'd been all over the world, voluminous reader, lover of life, of people, of art, of music, of everyday people, telling his stories. Of course, that's what all the wonderful writers had done and I think he understood, somehow, that all those lyric artists who were not trying to be mysterious Dr Freakenstein, but just simply telling a great, great story were really the artists whose works survive and that's the greatest art of all. He didn't fulfil the role of the Great American Novelist of the minute, or the month, or – in his case – the year by putting on a tweed coat, having a fake British accent, having a nervous breakdown and getting writer's block. He was just someone who could go hang out with anybody and everybody, listen to their stories, tell his stories, and then lock himself up in a room and write until he would just about drop dead, finish a book, be exhausted and then start on his next book. He wrote up until the day he died, he was still writing. He never stopped writing.

PT: What are some of your particular favourite works of Jack's?

DA: I'm so often asked this question and my answer – I hope you forgive me – would be what Thelonious Monk said, which you can see on the internet, he was interviewed and they said, 'Monk, you've written so many wonderful songs and melodies, which are your favorite?' Monk's response was, 'All of them.' Then they said, 'What happens if you write one that isn't a favorite, one that you don't like?' He said,

'Then I don't put it out.' There was another huge pause and then he ended the interview by saying, 'I have standards.' I can't think of anything of Jack's that I don't like and each one that I read, even if it's that wonderful book of letters of his, and things that keep being discovered and rediscovered, all have a special flavour and paint a special picture. I can't really distinguish because all of them relate to the body of work, the body of life, and his idea which was to have sort of the legend of Duluoz and knowing his family in Quebec, they have a whole 400-year history of the Kerouac family, and Jack is part of that legend of Duluoz that he was talking about.

I think he knew that as a kid from his father, Leo, that he was part – and the Kirouac family in Quebec, they're very proud of him as one of the members of the family who went south and did real well – but he's part of the larger picture of that whole family. He somehow had a sense of that[, and] while it was very hard to figure out, his sister always said he wrote in English and dreamed in French, how he could get out his identity in a new land, in Lowell. When he lived there, the French-Canadian enclave, rather than be in the loyal Kirouac family presumed to be – pardon the expression – ethnic, which was code word for subhuman, the ethnic folk of that particular area, and Jack felt connected to a large family that was hundreds of years old that he'd never really known about and to the families of all the people that he met. He was kind of like Woody Guthrie, who came from Okemah, Oklahoma, but was a worldwide person after his travels as a merchant seaman. Jack had a worldwide, global image and that was before they had a thing called World music, or the internet, or the global village or any of that stuff. He was always there, but once people couldn't see beyond their shoelaces, so it was hard.

PT: I think for me, and many Kerouac fans, you're like the living legacy. You and when Ginsberg was still alive, you guys are both incredible artists in your own right and both of you have been very generous in talking about Jack. Obviously, when Allen passed, that was the end of that. Whenever I saw documentaries in the '70s and '80s and '90s, the two guys that you could always count on who actually really truly knew Jack were you and Allen. I think it's great that after all these years you're still willing to share all this Kerouac knowledge with the rest of us.

DA: I was just blessed. I was just lucky. Allen was lucky; we were all lucky just to know him. Thing about him is that he shared everything with everybody. People alive like Willie Nelson who were that way – and I play with him for Farm Aid and Willie's two or three years younger than me – he's that way with everybody. All the people that I knew, Dimitri Mitropoulos, to whom I dedicated my first book, was the conductor of the New York Philharmonic, he was about the most generous person I ever met in my life. Charlie Parker was that way. Most of the people I've known and loved to be with are about that and realize that the 'full greed ahead' philosophy only leads to an endless, competitive competition of who can be the most narcissistic and disgusting and whoever the most disgusting person that strikes fear in you and acts like a superstar is, every single time you get to be with someone like that, they're miserable. They're unhappy and they get no satisfaction.

If you're lucky to get to know somebody that made a contribution and they enriched your life with their generosity, you realize when you get older, you're happy if they even bother to hang out with you, that they shared what they had. When you do that, what you get back from not being that way, comes back to you and your kids and everybody that you're with, and each day becomes a new adventure. Also, when you get older, rather than staring in the mirror – because when you get enough wrinkles, and you figure the mirror's not broken – you get interested in looking at something else and thinking about something else other than yourself; that's much more rewarding, when you get to that point where you can see that the joy as Mitropoulis, the great conductor, told me, 'The joy is in the giving.' The joy that you get back from that is so good for your health, you can feel good and be healthier and it's much more fun and then you can also be more creative [than] when you're sitting in that room saying, 'Why should I bother to write a symphony when no one wants to hear it?' and this and that – well, forget about all that crap and just go ahead and follow your hopeless dreams anyway. Still try to become a better artist. The final thing is that will foster creativity in others.

That was what Jack was about. I never heard him put down another writer or another artist. He would always encourage people. I always mention that he would find the most insecure person in the room after he became a famous person, which he never wanted to be. He would purposely spend time with them and try to make them feel good. I was just lucky to know him and I'm lucky now to know a lot of other people by trying to remain open myself. I keep getting reinvigorated and keep learning more. I recommend to everybody who likes Jack that if he can establish something in your heart, you can find that we all are put here for a purpose and if we feel we were put here to do something, we should go ahead and do it. When you're told it's a waste of time or there's no demographic and there's no future, do it anyway and follow your career death wishes to the max. I'm still doing that at the age of 86! Following all my hopeless courses has given me, and continues to give me, a wonderful life. I can survive. All my kids grew up, they're not in jail, they have their own lives and I'm still healthy enough to keep doing stuff I love to do and I just thank God every day I'm able to do that.

Note

1   The play was called *The Beat Generation*.

CHAPTER 7
BEAT REFRAINS: MUSIC, MILIEU AND IDENTITY IN JACK KEROUAC'S *THE SUBTERRANEANS*, THE METRO-GOLDWYN-MAYER FILM ADAPTATION

Michael J. Prince

Music in film may perform several functions, establishing the particular time and place of a setting, setting the mood or 'atmosphere' of the work or a scene; it can flesh out characters with musical cues to persons and their momentary psychological and emotional disposition, as well as intensify action, enmity and romance within the cinematic narrative. In films which rely on historical settings, including adaptations, the emphasis on the historical authenticity of the period may take precedence, be it a minuet in a Jane Austen adaptation, or the actual pieces played by a string quartet as the Titanic sinks (Kalinak, 2010, pp. 1–8). In film adaptations of the works of the Beat writers, this issue is made more complex by the fact that the Beat poets themselves invoked a particular musical style, bebop jazz, as a 'marker' for that coterie of like-minded writers and their readers. Jack Kerouac, in particular, is frequently associated with jazz. Alto saxophonist Charlie Parker plays an iconic role in his extended poem series, *Mexico City Blues*, and the prosody of his writings frequently aspires to the bebop aesthetic, with significant passages employing non-semantic sounds to drive the poetry rhythmically and tonally forward. Kerouac was known to be an enthusiastic and capable amateur percussionist and his shared appreciation of bebop with his muse and soul mate Neal Cassady is a feature of *On the Road* and other works. This chapter deals chiefly with a film inspired by the writings of Jack Kerouac in the most direct sense of being *adaptation*, by examining a particular aspect that has been derived from the source text and adapted for the needs of the film.

Most of Kerouac's works in his extended Dulouz series involve the Beats and their milieu, at least insofar as it orbits the poet Kerouac. In broad terms, four films can be considered adaptations of Kerouac's prose; this chapter will discuss the first one in depth and refer to the others by way of contrast at the end. *The Subterraneans* was adapted to film shortly after it was published. The 1958 novel invokes deep references to musical experiences, as audience of a Charlie Parker performance and as tonal and rhythmic identity marker for the subject formation of the narrator's object of desire, Mardou. Arthur Freed's 1960 Metro-Goldwyn-Mayer musical had an almost insurmountable task reflecting that on screen.

To facilitate this discussion, I must ask the reader to ascend to a relatively secure ledge among Gilles Deleuze and Felix Guattari's lofty historical materialist edifice, *A Thousand Plateaus* (published in French, 1980). This volume, along with its precursor, *Anti-Oedipus* (1972), provides an epistemology from the molar to the cosmic, and a phalanx of neologisms (as they use them) that may deter even the most stalwart of cultural critics. My analysis here will only occasionally leave the province of speculation in which I use the term 'refrain' to mean a sound that determines a milieu. This will aid us in several ways. First, Deleuze and Guattari's chapter on the refrain addresses both written literary expression, such as those of Romanticism, and musical articulation. Since an adaptation generally originates in prose, and frequently incorporates sound and music in the film version, the concept 'refrain' is especially apt to discuss a work which dedicates considerable prose to musical expression, as well as the musical expression itself in the adaptation. Second, they show how sound can engender affinity in the subject and create a milieu. The history of the Beats is one of an extremely unlikely coterie who sought first and foremost prose publication, but who also inspired a countercultural expression that swept the United States in the visible presence of beatniks and, later, hippies. Music was the seed kernel around which these countercultures crystalized – though not the same music – and at the outset, the music and the counterculture, while not precisely cognate, were considered to overlap. While not every fan or practitioner of bebop was a Beat or beatnik, every Beat or beatnik could be identified with bebop jazz. These types of affinities and the establishment of their attendant milieux is something Deleuze and Guattari's notion of the refrain does exceedingly well. In short, this paradigm suggests that music is integrally involved in establishing a terrain, or sense of place in time, out of a period of relatively chaotic indeterminacy. And, finally, within the subject positions taken on in conjunction with the refrain, the improvisational and spontaneous elements of Kerouac's Beat refrain, literarily as well as musically, can be examined in terms of what sort of world it ascribes to.

The refrain is a marker and creator of a milieu, as initially defined by Deleuze and Guattari, '*any aggregate of matters of expression that draws a territory and develops into territorial motifs and landscapes*; ... we speak of a refrain when an assemblage is sonorous and "dominated" by sound' (Deleuze and Guattari, 2013, p. 376). Since their discussion of this phenomenon is principally based upon ethology – birdsongs and procreative territories play a major role here – applying this to the Beat poets, and the attendant bohemian trend in postwar US society, presents some interesting parallels. While developing the concept, they point out that 'the bird sings to mark its territory. The Greek modes and Hindu rhythms are themselves territorial' (p. 363). A milieu is determined by its 'cutting edge', and this can be a refrain (p. 391). This 'cut' can be inclusive, attracting all those who resonate sympathetically; but it may also be exclusive in its execution, something akin to the blaring of a particular genre of music in a clothing shop or a café as a prophylaxis against an undesired clientele. The character of this refrain in my discussion is music, and much of the following analysis will depend on bebop jazz, and references to it in Kerouac's literary works and how this featured refrain that came to determine a literary and cultural milieu has been adapted to film via plot elements, characters and the soundtrack.

With this in mind, this chapter discusses the transfer and tension between Kerouac's 1958 novel *The Subterraneans* and the feature-length film. This will involve the character of these musical articulations and how they succeed as refrains to suggest and demarcate the Beat milieu and the affinity and identity of characters within it; in terms of genre, as a marker of realia in a historical period; or as a signal of intimacy and authenticity between characters, and even between the filmmakers and the viewers.

* * *

It may strike one as odd that the first film adaptation of a Kerouac novel was a *musical*, but with a little reflection, it makes sense. Arthur Freed's production of *The Subterraneans* (1960) was released at a time well before rock'n'roll had completely captured the popular culture imagination. What could be more natural than that the author most readily identified as a 'Beat' poet should have his narratives enshrouded in jazz beats, a musical genre that Kerouac expresses a great love for? The Beats represented the most authentic, and most recognized, countercultural pulse in post-war America up to that time, and the milieu of the Beats is a major part of many of the films based upon Kerouac's work.

However, as a source for the film adaptation, Kerouac's *novel* has relatively little music performed in it, and that which is mentioned is certainly of a type less sanitized and more musically challenging than what is prevalent in the film. So, as an adaptation, this signifying nod in the direction of authenticity of the milieu is committed at the expense of what at first glance appears as a lack of fidelity to the original novel. Yet, music saturates the novel, mostly by reference to jazz artists, comments on performance and in accounts by which the characters themselves relate to and identify with bebop. Count Basie is mentioned in the opening pages to characterize an incidental character Leo Percepied hung around with in San Francisco, Larry O'Hara; and Leo's staring 'straight into the sadglint of my wallroom at a Sarah Vaughn Gerry Mulligan radio KROW show' (Kerouac, 1958, p. 2) or 'while listening to Stan Kenton and talking about the music of tomorrow' (p. 6) all indicate an interest and concern for the music in his milieu; but movie actors, such as Charlie Chaplin, are invoked in the same register.

But when describing his object of desire, Mardou Fox, particularly her voice, the references to contemporary music take on a specificity which only the hippest of contemporary readers would appreciate: 'it's charming but much too strange, and a sound I had already wonderingly heard in the voice of new bop singers like Jerry Winters especially with Kenton band on the record *Yes Daddy Yes*'[1] (Kerouac, 1958, p. 7). Bearing in mind that, aside from setting the narrative in the North Beach of San Francisco,[2] Jack Kerouac, via his Percepied persona, is committed to telling the most truthful narrative possible, this reference to the character of the refrain of the 'new bop generation' is clearly a marker. Knowledge of Kenton, and Jerry Winters' laconic, almost sneering vocal delivery demarcates a border, one within which the narrator and his lover, Mardou, are included, but also the implicit audience for the novel. In this sense, Mardou is credited with expressing the refrain, her vocal articulations those of the 'new' generation, demarcating in time what the refrain also does in space.

Spatially, the evening in the jazz bar the Red Drum with Mardou, Adam Moorad[3] and others is, while not dominated by Charlie Parker's performance per se, strongly integrated in that performance, expressing something of 'that excitement of San Francisco bop in the air' (Kerouac, 1958, p. 12):

> ...and up on the stand Bird Parker with solemn eyes who'd been busted fairly recently and had now returned to a kind of bop dead Frisco but had just discovered or been told about the Red Drum, the great new generation gang wailing and gathering there, so here he was on the stand, examining them with his eyes as he blew his now-settled-down-into-regulated-design 'crazy' notes.
>
> Kerouac, 1958, p. 13

Implicitly, the 'great new generation gang' is in some measure unified by, or even created out of, Parker's mellifluous alto sax articulations, which have also become somewhat 'regulated', and located within the club. But in addition to providing the refrain for the Beats in this novel, Parker and Leo occupy the same space of the gaze as Leo notes that 'Bird, whom I saw distinctly digging Mardou several times also myself directly into my eye looking to search if really I was that great writer I thought myself to be as if he knew my thoughts and ambitions' (Kerouac, 1958, p. 14). This perspective of Leo and Mardou from the point of view of 'the king and founder of the bop generation', all the while with his 'great lungs and immortal fingers at work' embeds Percepied in this milieu, and, as will be mentioned again below, already lays the foundation for the young author's claim to be 'the bop-writer' (Kerouac, 1958, p. 98). While the stylistic character of novelistic prose is a difficult metre to specify, *The Subterraneans* was Kerouac's freest prose up to that time, and the long run-on sentences, paragraphs that frequently run over three pages, and the vibrant stream-of-consciousness cohesion within the narrative stream, all suggest that this novel was composed with the musical self-consciousness of jazz rhythms.

This may be due to the Kerouac's need to render Mardou's dialogue, which expresses a profound awareness of musical qualities, as well as her being credited with bebop musicality in the way she spoke and sang. The role of bebop in the crucial episode of her subject (re)formation illustrates this. As she relates her psychotic meltdown, the 'naked babe ... on the fence episode', Mardou's journey during which she goes mad and then reconstructs her own identity is rich in musical resonances in her reported series of conversations. For instance, her awareness of 'every intonation in his speech and mine and the world of meaning in every *word*' in her exchange with the man in the wheelchair (Kerouac, 1958, p. 30), and her sense of 'obligation [to]

communicate and exchange this news, the vibration and new meaning that I had'
(p. 32) with the man in the swivel chair. The significance of musical expression comes
out not only in Kerouac's prose as he describes the last of Mardou's 'flips' of insanity,
but also in an evaluation of Mardou's levels of awareness when she arrives at her
sister's house. She recalls:

> ... the Negro chickenshack jukeboxes and she stood in drowsy sun suddenly
> listening to bop as if for the first time as it poured out, the intention of the
> musicians and of the horns and instruments suddenly a mystical unity
> expressing itself in waves like sinister and again electricity but screaming with
> palpable aliveness the direct *word* from the vibration, the interchanges of
> statement, the levels of waving intimation, the smile in sound ...
>
> Kerouac, 1958, pp. 34–5

This is the signal episode for Mardou's psychosis, and as a result of this auditory/
visionary hallucination, she is 'taken to the hospital, [where she] pulled out of it fast'
(Kerouac, 1958, p. 35). So, the Beat refrain of bebop is not just a marker of a milieu,
but the key to the subject (re-)formation of Leo's beloved. In this sense, the Mardou
whom he loves is in some measure made out of jazz. This episode is the most
significant in the book, if for no other reason than its monumental verbiage: it runs
for a single paragraph over 11 pages, composing over a tenth of the original Grove
Press edition, a full quarter of the first of two chapters.

Mardou is not only inscribed in Parker's identity-imparting gaze as mentioned
earlier, but she is also the only character in the novel who *herself* articulates bebop
music. Mardou's subjectification is bop-inspired, but she also has the music in her; Leo
is enchanted by 'the amazing fact she is the only girl I've ever known who could really
understand bop and sing it' (Kerouac, 1958, p. 67). Furthermore, in the second chapter
she refers back to the above episode when she was 'flipping', and then graces it with a
musical articulation, her refrain of intense subjective experience: 'I can't describe it, it
not only sent waves – went through me – I can't, like, *make* it, in telling it in words, you
know? "OO dee bee dee dee" singing a few notes, so cutely' (Kerouac, 1958, p. 67).
Mardou's shift to scat-singing marks her transcendence; it may be 'cute', but it is also a
cue that refers to a refrain element that ascends, or at the very least complements, the
romantic attraction with one of pure aesthetics. As the young lovers stroll in San
Francisco, they were 'singing wild choruses of jazz and bop, at times I'd phrase and she
did perfect in fact interesting modern and advanced chords ... and at other times she
just did her chords as I did the bass fiddle' (Kerouac, 1958, p. 67); on the following page,
Percepied revels 'in the glee of it', of his scatting bop with Mardou. In Kerouac's world,
and the relationship that Percepied is describing, this is not merely incidental praise
but the pinnacle of subjectification within this milieu that the refrain is demarcating.
Indeed, in these impromptu duets, a grudging equality obtains between the author and
the object of his desire which later in the narrative morphs into her superiority.

For Percepied, too, identifies with bebop, with its understanding and with its production. First and foremost, this is obvious in the rhythm of his prose in this novel; *The Subterraneans* is itself a series of choruses, similar in articulation, at times, to *Mexico City Blues*, published the following year, with its run-on syntax and associative semantics. One notes in the narrative flow of the entire book that jazz, and particularly bop music phraseology, permeates the work. At the end of the first chapter, Leo reflects on the activity of writing, 'when the vision of great words in rhythmic order ... go roaring through my brain', and his prose (d)evolves into the playful phonetic gibberish that is also used for great effect in *Mexico City Blues*, and with even more subtlety in the closing poem of *Big Sur*, 'Sea'.[4] In this case, however, the passage reminds one of a squawking saxophone or something by Slim Gaillard, 'damajehe eleout ekeke dhdkdk dldoud' (Kerouac, 1958, p. 42). And while Percepied's prose is itself a bop-artefact, he also wants to be considered a bop poet. In his meeting with Balliol Mac-Jones, a thinly veiled figure for John Clellon-Holmes, Percepied implicitly takes some credit for Mac-Jones's literary triumph. At the same time, Leo is jealous of the attention that Mardou has lavished on his literary rival: 'I say "What are you talking about in there bop? Don't tell *him* anything about music" – (Let him find out for himself! I say to myself pettishly) – *I'm* the bop writer!' (Kerouac, 1958, p. 98).

Leo as the bop writer is then, himself, articulating a refrain that determines the Beat milieu, but in prose, not music. Kerouac, through his novelistic persona, is excluding readers who may not be familiar with, say, Stan Kenton, simply by using such a narrow musical reference to describe Mardou's voice, or by giving alto saxophonist Charlie Parker a major role in his own identity formation. In this respect, Kerouac's writings also determine a milieu: reading and enjoying his writings brings one into that milieu. It is almost a commonplace today to say that *On the Road*, Kerouac's most famous work, was the 'beatnik bible', but Kerouac's prose and poetry experiments were on the cutting edge of literary expression at that time, and Kerouac functioned for the Beat literature milieu in an analogous fashion as to how Charlie Parker did for Leo Percepied, Mardou Fox and the subterraneans in their milieu. *The Subterraneans* itself is a refrain.

* * *

With the be-bop refrain so clearly demarcating the Beat milieu from the 'straight', and its also serving as the major identity anchor for the subjectification of the two principal characters, it may now come as less of a surprise that Arthur Freed, when faced with the task of adapting this novel to film, decided that a musical would be a proper vehicle for the story. Film Historian Hugh Fordin writes, 'Freed's intention was to make this low-budget, black-and-white avant-garde picture, without the Metro gloss'; and the production, as it gelled, was intensely aware of the role that music was to play: 'The milieu depicted in the film demanded on-screen as well as off-screen contemporary jazz. André Previn was the obvious choice as musical director, composer and performer' (Fordin, 1996, pp. 497–8). Obvious to Arthur Freed and

Metro-Goldwyn-Mayer is undoubtedly not so obvious to people outside of Hollywood. Previn composed and conducted the music for numerous well-known Hollywood films, but he also recorded a jazz piano version of the soundtrack of Freed's *Gigi* in 1958. His inclusion of alto saxophonist Art Pepper, Art Farmer on trumpet and Gerry Mulligan on baritone sax may have given the ensemble a more West Coast, lyrical jazz vibe than the at times frenetic bebop mentioned in the novel, though Gerry Mulligan does indeed hold a special place in Kerouac's book – he is mentioned four times; his music is to be a feature of Mardou and Leo's future cohabitation in Mexico (Kerouac, 1958, p. 40); and his music functions as an audio soundtrack to their lovemaking (Kerouac, 1958, p. 51).

As I have written at length elsewhere, when it comes to the typical scale of fidelities of a film adaptation, Freed's *The Subterraneans* takes astounding liberties with the original. Mardou is changed from a black woman to French; the character Roxanne in the film is derived from a cursorily mentioned person in the novel; the street preacher, the Reverend Joshua Hoskins, is simply inserted with no analogue in the original; and Leo and Mardou agree to marry at the end of the movie, a characteristic Hollywood permutation to the heart-wrenching break-up at the end of the novel (Prince, 2016, pp. 1–22). However, the role of the bebop refrain is intriguingly implemented in the film by director Ranald MacDougall, writer Robert Thom and producer Arthur Freed. While specific pieces of music do not cross the adaptive synapse, music, *jazz* music, is still a strong marker of the milieu.

The viewer meets this in the first scene at Leo's mother's apartment: the interior shot after the credits focuses on a 45 record spinning out a bebop tune on a portable phonograph. The associative link between Leo's prose and bebop is made first by Leo (George Peppard) ripping his day's writing from the typewriter in disgust and then his mother (Anne Seymour) removing the tone arm from the record, asking why he 'can't play something more gentle, like "The Blue Danube"'. With the bebop/jazz refrain positioned in opposition to tamer bourgeois tastes in the very first exchange of dialogue, the viewer is unambiguously positioned within the Beat milieu of the phonograph's refrain which continues throughout the first part of his mother's criticism of Leo's life-choice as an author, before she again interrupts the piece. He is revealed to be a searcher who is looking to find something. And, not surprisingly, what he finds is linked to this type of music; Leo's storming out of the house to go to the library is accompanied by the tense strains of melancholy strings, the mood music that Previn is also extremely adept at writing, and Leo is ushered into his car with some blue notes from an alto sax. While he is driving the music is peppier, with challenging tonalities in the horns as Leo searches.

Yuri (Roddy McDowall) ushers him into the club Daddy's Catacomb to revel with the subterraneans, and jazz music is a key part of this milieu. During the minor tiff between Mardou (Leslie Caron) and her former lover the music is energetic, but when Leo finally gets a chance to meet Mardou, the jazz ensemble is playing a smoother melody. It is unclear whether this is recorded music or live, and with dialogue establishing characters being spoken above it, the casual viewer really has little opportunity to enjoy it. It is literally background music, even if it is jazz. When Mardou's spontaneous suggestion impels the party to leave their drinks, at the next cellar bar, there is no music at all: rather the characters present themselves between chants of 'Go! Go! Go!' until Leo announces to Mardou and the world that he wants her. Then there is a cut to another night spot with Previn's jazz ensemble *in media res*. Mardou casts affectionate glances at Leo, who obviously is enjoying the music.

Here in this third locale of Leo's nocturnal wandering, Carmen McRae performs the only vocal piece, 'Coffee Time'. Kerouac's novel is rich with references to alcohol – indeed it was a major problem – but here, the milieu is established with an anthem to the coffee house, also a recognized milieu of the Beats, if not within the source novel. McRae sings Freed's lyrics promising jazz, coffee and good conversation, but her performance is interrupted by Adam Moorad's (Jim Hutton) monologue on Cézanne. As Leo traipses through the San Francisco night with his new-found friends, a plate of spaghetti is suddenly placed in his hand by a sweatshirt-clad parson with an eight-inch crucifix, the Reverend Joshua Hoskins (Gerry Mulligan), who played jazz saxophone for years till 'he got the long distance message and joined the church'. This locale is the Poet and Painter's mission, and it, too, is implicitly demarcated by a jazz refrain, in the person of the well-known baritone saxophonist.

The viewer has to wait through considerable intrigue before this is made clear, but Mardou's 'flip', her running abroad naked, is transferred from a psychotic episode that resolves itself into Mardou's madness being managed by the Reverend and his wife, who clothe her in a blanket and shoo away the police. The strong subject formation through bebop of the original is thereby perverted by her taking refuge in the Poet and Painter's mission. So, indirectly, music, in the form of the jazz musician turned street priest, may still be considered a part of Mardou's recovery of identity. Outfitted in Mrs Hoskins's conservative dress, Mardou subsequently informs her analyst (Ruth Storey) that she is pregnant, but wants to keep the baby. Leo, for his part, wants to marry Mardou, and after a disturbing phone call with his mother, there is a quick cut to a bar, where Leo is implausibly propped in front of a half empty beer and an overfull ashtray, while on stage baritone saxophonist Mulligan, as the Reverend, plays a soulful blues. Ultimately, Mardou and Leo's mutual cruelties resolve into a bourgeois couple, to Previn's and Mulligan's closing jazz strains.

Freed's movie may be counted as an unqualified disaster artistically as well as at the box office. The problem may have been that few who would have responded to the innovative prose and the authentic confessional character of a memoir would have much enjoyed such a compromised adaptation of the film. Some few vestiges of the refrain from the original do make it into the film, albeit obliquely. Leo's identification with bebop is attenuated to some appreciative nodding and careful table drumming to McRae and Mulligan's performances. Mardou's almost spiritual connection to bebop which marked her subject reformation, and was so crucial to it that it merits two references in the novel, is oddly deflected into her being 'saved', perhaps even spiritually, by the good Reverend Hoskins and his wife. Given that this character is played by Gerry Mulligan, one could suggest that Mardou's cure and successful subjectification after her psychotic episode in the film was due to a musician, if not to music, but it would be a stretch. However, the baritone saxophonist with the crucifix does reflect Kerouac's spiritual connection to bebop, to be sure, in a rather ham-fisted way. Jazz is holy to the Beats, but no amount of free spaghetti served up at the Poet and Painter's mission will even approach the role of bebop as a refrain for the Beat milieu expressed in the novel.

* * *

With a single exception, subsequent adaptations which have tried to portray the Beat milieu via the bebop refrain have also fallen flat. Twenty years later, John Byrum adapted Carolyn Cassady's memoir *Heart Beat* to film. While some portion of Mrs Cassady's book actually makes it into the film, much of the background and action comes from Jack Kerouac's *On the Road*. In Cassady's book, the agenda is to recount a ménage à trois between her, her husband and the famous author. The novel establishes its place in the Beat milieu primarily through epistolary references (including correspondence to renowned Beat poet Allen Ginsberg), but not through music. However, her memoir does contain references to Kerouac as a drummer. The slim volume begins with a letter in which Neal Cassady's wife urges Kerouac to 'be sure and bring your Bongo drums, or you'll have to go down on O'Farrell and see the gone drums there' (Cassady, 1978, p. 15). And an episode later in the narrative positions Kerouac *as a musician* at a 'pay the rent' party; one either contributes to the rent or performs for the guests. Jack wants to play, but he ends up destroying a new set of bongos in his effort to tighten the skin of the drum heads over a gas flame. This episode, or any episode of Kerouac's musicality, is missing from Byrum's adaptation. The film music consists of relatively sparse sequences of Jack Nitzsche's music for mood, but the film otherwise uses primarily period pieces to inform the viewer that this is 1950s America. The opening credits include a nuclear explosion and suburban tract housing to the Four Aces version of Fain and Webster's 'Love Is a Many Splendored Thing'. Far outside of the province of the book, Neal's piloting of Ken Kesey's bus at the end of the film is musically introduced with a sweeping sitar arpeggio that shifts to Jimi Hendrix's 'Purple Haze'. While certainly a refrain for the heirs of the Beats, it is improbable that this was a refrain for Cassady in that milieu.

The year 2013 gave us two Kerouac film adaptations: *On the Road* and *Big Sur*. While *The Subterraneans* and *On the Road* are about the creation of a milieu from Kerouac's perspective, *Big Sur* is more about the dissipation of the Beats, and especially the telling burden upon the poet to try to maintain his artistic integrity, as well as the duties foisted upon Kerouac to sustain the milieu. Those highly divergent novelistic discursive tasks have been reflected in the music at work in those respective films. The music used with Michael Polish's *Big Sur* features the Aaron and Bryce Dessner indy-vibe combined with classically trained, yet iconoclastic German composer Kubilay

Üner to defuse the power of the jazz-based refrains around which the Beats as a movement crystallized. The scene at the beginning of the film with Kerouac in a North Beach bar includes a frenetic bebop piece as background, but not so much as a refrain of a milieu which includes Kerouac, but rather one which destroys him. Contemplative and confessional, much of the film really is of Big Sur, the woods, the ocean and clouds. In short, this film concerns a dissolution, of sorts, and the music is not a refrain of the Beats, but totally in service of Polish's film. Cinematically dominated by nature, and tamely paced, the film at times invokes associations to a Ron Fricke work, and the soundtrack matches this expansive perspective.

In Walter Salles and José Rivera's *On the Road*, Kerouac's novel has inspired a variety of refrains: there is the period realia of Arlen and Koehler's 'I've Got the World on a String' in Ella Fitzgerald's 1950 Decca version, as Camille and Sal Paradise dance together in the cowboy bar in Denver; there are solemn unaccompanied vocal solos, such as Kerouac's own 'Sweet Sixteen' performed in the back of a flatbed truck; and between jazz clubs, bars and parties, there is enough bebop and blues to fill a movie soundtrack CD, along with the more contemporary (yet timeless) incidental music composed and performed by Gustavo Santaolalla and the capable hands of veteran jazz bassist Charlie Haden. This variety, while not a major feature of the Beats, is a virulent refrain around which a present day audience for Beat adaptation cinema can crystalize. Much of the musical episodes portrayed in Kerouac's novel are included. The scene at the start of the film with Dean and Sal in a Negro jazz bar establishes jazz as the Beat refrain that links the two main characters. For some reason, the repeated references to pianist George Shearing in the original are absent, and Slim Gaillard becomes a strong musical presence in the film. Gaillard's lyrics provide a whimsical analogue to some of Kerouac's phonetic renderings, but I do not wish to over emphasize the possible intertextuality, as that aspect of Kerouac's prose and poetry is never presented in the film.

In a sense, Salles and Rivera's *On the Road* selection of music is so successful due to its inclusiveness. Kerouac's seminal novel is an important part of whatever one recalls when one thinks about post-war America. The filmmakers were aware of this, but were caught in the quandary of making a novel that was originally exclusive in terms of its prose and its dominant refrain into a mainstream film. The musical selection here works as a more general refrain for that space and time. The novel *The Subterraneans* is particular: integrally linked to a single romance, the unique prose itself marks a border similar to the bebop jazz from the time it was written. Kerouac's *On the Road* is a refrain for post-war America.

Notes

1. The song 'Yes Daddy Yes'.
2. In the vast majority of Jack Kerouac's writing he adopts an autobiographical and confessional style which involves people that he has met and interacted with. Therefore,

The Subterraneans, one of the rawest of Kerouac's confessions, was set not in New York where the story actually occurred, but in North Beach. This, plus the name changes, provided the distance of plausible deniability (for legal reasons), or at least made it more difficult to put real names and faces to his character gallery.

3. The pseudonymous Allen Ginsberg in this novel.

4. In the prefacing note at the beginning of *Mexico City Blues*, Kerouac writes 'I want to be considered a jazz poet blowing a long blues in an afternoon jam session on Sunday'. The 239th, 240th and 241st choruses are about Charlie Parker, and on occasion throughout the body of this work, Kerouac employs foreign language words and purely phonetically rendered sounds for poetic effect. See the 215th chorus for an extreme example (Kerouac, 1959). In the poetic postscript to *Big Sur*, 'Sea', the extended phonetic renderings are more sibilant and nasal, less percussive, since this work employs extended onomatopoeia of the sea at Big Sur. See Kerouac, 1992, pp. 217–41.

Bibliography

Cassady, Carolyn, *Heart Beat*, New York: Pocket Books, 1978.

Deleuze, Gilles and Félix Guattari, *A Thousand Plateaus: Capitalism and Schizophrenia*, London: Bloomsbury, 2013.

Fordin, Hugh, *M-G-M's Greatest Musicals: The Arthur Freed Unit*, Da Capo Press, 1996.

Kalinak, Kathryn, *Film Music: A Very Short Introduction*, Oxford: Oxford University Press, 2010.

Kerouac, Jack, *The Subterraneans*, New York: Grove Press, 1958.

Kerouac, Jack, *Mexico City Blues*, New York: Grove Press, 1959.

Kerouac, Jack, *Big Sur*, London: Penguin, 1992.

Prince, Michael J., *Adapting the Beat Poets: Burroughs, Ginsberg, and Kerouac on Screen*, Lanham, MD: Rowman & Littlefield, 2016.

Filmography

Big Sur, dir. Michael Polish, Ketchup Entertainment, 2013.

Heart Beat, dir. John Byrum, Warner Brothers, 1980.

On the Road, written and dir. Walter Salles and José Rivera, Lionsgate / MK2, 2013.

The Subterraneans, dir. Ranald MacDougall, Metro-Goldwyn-Mayer, 1960.

CHAPTER 8
BOB DYLAN'S BEAT VISIONS
(SONIC POETRY)
Michael Goldberg

Jack Kerouac never got a Nobel Prize for Literature, but Bob Dylan did. Oh yeah, Bob got one, finally, later, way later, 2016 later. When the Prize was announced, it was hard not to think of Kerouac, one of those who, as Dylan put it, 'left the rest of everything in the dust', hard not to think of the other Beat writers who so profoundly influenced Dylan and each deserved their own Nobel Prize. Poet/publisher Ferlinghetti, whose 'I Am Waiting' is echoed in 'It's Alright Ma (I'm Only Bleeding)', and Burroughs, whose extreme imagery was reimagined in Dylan's mid-1960s songs, and Ginsberg, whose 'Kaddish' Bob said he dug so much, and whose 'Howl' helped Dylan birth 'Like a Rolling Stone'.

The Prize was awarded to Dylan 'for having created new poetic expressions within the great American song tradition'. Yeah, but that kinda sold him short. The real Big Bang theory: Dylan made a new *kind* of poetry, a sonic poetry that took the lightning flash images of Beat writing and merged them with the raw, wild sounds of primal rock'n'roll. A new kind of poetry that you could hear on the radio or at a concert hall. Poetry freed from the page. 'My songs are pictures', Dylan said at the beginning of 1966, the very peak of his creative powers, 'and the band makes the sound of the pictures.'[1]

In this chapter I'll talk about how Dylan came to create that sonic poetry, and the profound influence the Beat writers, and in particular Jack Kerouac, had on Dylan. Much has been made, over the many decades since Dylan first appeared on our radar in the early 1960s, of the influence of Woody Guthrie, and how Dylan journeyed to New York in 1961, and then went to Greystone Psychiatric Hospital in New Jersey to visit and sing to Guthrie, who was suffering from Huntington's Disease, a fatal, degenerative nerve disorder. Dylan himself, who was very closemouthed about influences when interviewed in the 1960s, made a point of playing up his connection to Guthrie, writing 'Song to Woody' in February 1961, and a poem, 'Last Thoughts on Woody Guthrie', which he read at his 12 April 1963 concert at New York's Town Hall.[2] But in terms of Dylan's breakthroughs in songwriting, it was the work of Kerouac and some of the other Beat writers that provided much of the inspiration (and in some cases the actual phrases) that resulted in Dylan's most groundbreaking songs. The focus here will be on the words, not the music. Others have written about how Dylan and various studio musicians forged the music, and anyway, there's simply not space for me to discuss that aspect of Dylan's creative process.

Dylan had many influences, and it would be simplistic (and wrong) to only credit the Beats. A huge trove of songs, poems, novels, films, theatrical productions and paintings, as well as lived experience, reside behind the hundreds of songs Dylan wrote during the past five-plus decades. But in terms of his WOW! POP! BLAM! CRASH! recordings, mostly made in 1965 and 1966, the Beats were the heart of the matter.

Voice of a generation redux

I always had the feeling that his true love of the [Beats] period were the works of Jack Kerouac.

David Amram, musician, composer and friend of both
Jack Kerouac and Bob Dylan[3]

It's not surprising that Dylan identified with Kerouac. Both men grew up at a serious distance from the sophistication and power centre that is New York City – Dylan at a literal remove in Hibbing, Minnesota; Kerouac at a kind of world-view remove in Lowell, Massachusetts. Both moved to New York City and lived there for decades. In their youth both felt like outsiders, Kerouac because his parents were French Canadian, because he spoke French, not English, until he was five or six, and because he was Catholic; Dylan because he was Jewish. Both were populists. Kerouac wrote of hanging around skid row when he arrived in a town or city, and expressed his compassion for the common man in his novels; as a teenager in 1958 Dylan wrote a paper analysing John Steinbeck's *Grapes of Wrath*, a novel about the plight of a poor family during the Great Depression, for a time idolized and imitated Woody Guthrie of 'This Land Is Your Land' fame, and later wrote songs about hobos, immigrants, refugees, oppressed African Americans and other social injustice. Kerouac, as the writer/photographer John Cohen, who knew and photographed him, wrote, 'found his artistic persona as a trouble-raiser and provocateur within literary intellectual circles';[4] Dylan did the same within the worlds of folk and rock music, as well as 'literary intellectual circles'. Both were seen as the voice of a generation, and both struggled with the aftermath of that kind of fame.

As a kid, Dylan felt like an outsider even at home. In an interview for Martin Scorsese's 2005 documentary, *No Direction Home*, Dylan spoke of discovering that the big radio he and his family sat around listening to also had a phonograph, and on it one day he found a gospel recording, Bill Monroe's 'Drifting Too Far From the Shore'. 'The sound of the record made me feel like I was somebody else,' Dylan said. 'That I was maybe not even born to the right parents or something.' In August of 1949 Kerouac wrote in his journal, 'Some people are just made to wish they were other than what they are, only so they may wish and wish and wish. This is my star.'[5]

As outsiders, Kerouac and Dylan rebelled against their white privilege and the materialism that dominated American society; both, as young men, were on a search for authenticity. 'He [Kerouac] was an outsider, he was on the streets, and everyone reading his book [*On the Road*] was an insider, sitting by their fire, and the idea of the outsider as being the originator was interesting to Kerouac and was interesting to Bob,' filmmaker D. A. Pennebaker, a friend of Kerouac's who made the Dylan documentary *Dont Look Back* in 1965 and also filmed Dylan's 1966 tour of England, told me during a March 2017 interview. 'It still is. He [Dylan] still thinks he's an outsider who has worked his way in.'

Pennebaker, who also told me he's read all of Kerouac's books, noted other reasons that Dylan related to Kerouac. 'I think the fact that he [Kerouac] was able to thumb his nose at the rules,' Pennebaker said. 'He was besetting the world of writing as it existed. And he was getting away with it. Also, his writing appeals to Dylan because it has a kind of poetic and musical quality, and Dylan responded to that. The whole thing of sleeping on the beach and the waves, that's the kind of thing Dylan liked.'

'I'm a poet, and I know it. Hope I don't blow it'

> Remember, Bob Dylan's a poet, man. So when he writes, it's a poet writing, and when he talks, it's a poet talking.
>
> Bob Neuwirth, Dylan's friend and former road manager

'I'm a poet, and I know it. Hope I don't blow it,' Dylan sang in 1964's 'I Shall Be Free No. 10'. 'My poems are written in a rhythm of unpoetic distortion,' Dylan wrote in the liner notes to 1965's *Bringing It All Back Home*. He told the Canadian Broadcast Corporation's (CBC) Martin Bronstein in February 1966, 'For a while I did consider myself a poet. [Now] I don't like to consider myself a poet because it puts you in a category with a lot of funny people.'

Beat poet Michael McClure, a friend of both Kerouac and Dylan, wrote in a 1974 article for *Rolling Stone*:

> By the time I met Bob [1965], his poetry was important to me in the way that Kerouac's writing was. It was not something to imitate or be influenced by; it was the expression of a unique individual and his feelings and perceptions.
>
> There is no way to second-guess poetry or to predict poetry or to convince a poet that the very best songs in the world are poetry if they are not. Bob Dylan is a poet; whether he has cherubs in his hair and fairy wings, or feet of clay, he is a poet. Those other people called 'rock poets', 'song poets', 'folk poets', or whatever the rock critic is calling them this week, will be better off if they are appreciated as songwriters.[6]

Dylan's first book, 1971's *Tarantula*,[7] is the work of a poet captivated by the Beat writers, as are his liner notes for *The Times They Are a-Changin'*, *Another Side of Bob Dylan*, *Bringing It All Back Home* and *Highway 61 Revisited*.

'He was a poet first,' Lawrence Ferlinghetti told me in February of 2017. 'He wanted to be a published poet. But luckily he had a guitar and he knew how to make it into music. His early songs [in the 1960s] were long surrealist poems.'

At Hibbing High School, a grand building completed in 1923 at a cost of a then astounding $4m in Hibbing, Minnesota, the town where Robert Zimmerman spent more than a decade of his youth, there is, as Greil Marcus noted, poetry on the walls – quotes from Tennyson's 'Oenone'. Dylan's high school English teacher was B. J. Rolfzen, who another Hibbing teacher, Aaron Brown, described as a 'gentle man who loved poetry, and preached poetry almost like a religion'. Teenage Robert Zimmerman sat in the front row of Rolfzen's class (room 204) for two years as Rolfzen lectured about Shakespeare, Keats, Shelley, Byron, Wordsworth, Frost, William Carlos Williams and others. Zimmerman considered Rolfzen, now deceased, a mentor and in the years following his success as Bob Dylan, the rock star spoke to Rolfzen during at least two of his infrequent visits to Hibbing.

Zimmerman had a rock'n'roll band when he was in high school, but even before then he wrote poetry. He told CBC's Martin Bronstein that he started writing poems when he was eight or nine 'about the flowers and my mother and stuff like that'. One of his teenage poems that survives, 'Bad Poem', was written in 1956 (and exhibited in the Experience Music Project's travelling exhibition, *Bob Dylan's American Journey, 1956–1966*, which was at various museums from 2004 to 2008).[8] The handwritten poem reads in part:

> Waiting in the house, was Raatsi on the bed
> 'I'm gonna pin Boutang's arm', Melvin, then said
> A noise outside! and Raatsi's face had gleem [sic]
> Ah ha, it was Dale coming on his machine

'It's really like a Bob Dylan song,' John Cohen told me. Cohen, in addition to being a photographer and writer, is a filmmaker and member of the New Lost City Ramblers; he photographed Kerouac in 1959, and became friends with Dylan and photographed him in 1962 before Dylan's first album, *Bob Dylan*, was released. 'So this is from 1956. What he was messing around with in terms of language in '56. Whew! It's a wonderful missing link, well a link, and it's so early, '56. It's wild.'

'I came out of the wilderness and just naturally fell in with the Beat scene . . .'

Was Bob Dylan influenced by the Beats? Well, yeah. Was he influenced by Robert Frank photographs and films, yeah. Bob, you know, he's like a sponge. He's influenced by everybody.

Bob Neuwirth

In September 1959, when he arrived in Minneapolis, Robert Zimmerman began calling himself Bob Dylan. It was another poet, Dylan Thomas, from whom Zimmerman borrowed his new last name, as he finally admitted, after decades of denying it, in his 2004 memoir *Chronicles: Volume One*. He was in Minneapolis to attend the University of Minnesota, but his true education came in the bohemian cafes of Dinkytown, a three-block area centred at the intersection of Fourth Street and Fourteenth Avenues. 'I came out of the wilderness and just naturally fell in with the Beat scene, the bohemian, bebop crowd, it was all pretty connected . . .', Dylan told writer Cameron Crowe during an interview for the liner notes included in the 1985 *Biograph* boxed set. 'I had already decided that society, as it was, was pretty phony and I didn't want to be part of that . . .'

'It [the Beat scene] was Jack Kerouac, Ginsberg, Corso and Ferlinghetti – *Gasoline, Coney Island of the Mind* . . . Oh man, it was wild – *I saw the best minds of my generation destroyed by madness* – that said more to me than any of the stuff I'd been raised on,' Dylan continued. '*On the Road*, Dean Moriarty, it made perfect sense to me . . . Anyway, I got in at the tail end of that and it was magic . . . It had just as big an impact on me as Elvis Presley.'

Among the books Dylan read while hanging around Dinkytown were Ferlinghetti's *A Coney Island of the Mind*,[9] Burroughs' *Naked Lunch*,[10] Ginsberg's *Howl and Other Poems*[11] and two by Kerouac, *On the Road*[12] and *Mexico City Blues*.[13] Later, according to Kerouac biographer Dennis McNally, a friend gave Dylan copies of *Doctor Sax* and *Big Sur*, and in his memoir, *Chronicles*, Dylan references *The Subterraneans*.

According to Ginsberg, Dylan told him, 'Someone handed me *Mexico City Blues* in St. Paul [Minnesota] in 1959 and it blew my mind. It was the first poetry that spoke my own language.'

Ginsberg told McNally that when Dylan read an article in the 9 February 1959 issue of *Time* magazine, 'Fried Shoes', about a reading Ginsberg and Corso did in Chicago, Dylan realized there were 'other people out there like me'.

'Talkin' New York'

'I suppose what I was looking for was what I read about in *On the Road* – looking for the great city, looking for the speed, the sound of it, looking for what Allen Ginsberg called the "hydrogen jukebox world",' Dylan recalled in *Chronicles*.

Maybe I'd lived in it all my life, I didn't know, but nobody ever called it that. Lawrence Ferlinghetti, one of the other Beat poets, had called it 'The kiss proof world of plastic toilet seats, Tampax and taxis' [actually, Ferlinghetti wrote, 'a kissproof world of plastic toiletseats, Tampax and taxis']. That was okay, too, but the Gregory Corso poem 'Bomb' was more to the point and touched the spirit of the times better – a wasted world and totally mechanized – a lot of hustle and bustle – a lot of shelves to clean, boxes to stack. I wasn't going to pin my hopes on that. Creatively you couldn't do much with it. I had already landed in a parallel universe, anyway, with more archaic principles and values; one where actions and virtues were old style and judgmental things came falling out on their heads. A culture with outlaw women, super thugs, demon lovers and gospel truths ... streets and valleys, rich peaty swamps, with landowners and oilmen, Stagger Lees, Pretty Pollys and John Henrys – an invisible world that towered overhead with walls of gleaming corridors. It was all there and it was clear – ideal and God-fearing – but you had to go find it. It didn't come served on a paper plate.[14]

Less than a year and a half after arriving in Minneapolis, in January of 1961, Bob Dylan got a ride to New York and quickly made his presence known. He met and hung out with Guthrie, and got to know numerous musicians including Dave Van Ronk, Ramblin' Jack Elliott and the New Lost City Ramblers (who included John Cohen); he played Greenwich Village clubs, eventually landing a primo two-week gig (that began on 11 April 1961) opening for bluesman John Lee Hooker at Gerde's Folk City.

Both before and after he got to New York, Dylan read many other poets in addition to the Beats. Dave Van Ronk told Dylan biographer Robert Shelton that when he brought up the French Symbolist poets Dylan feigned ignorance; but Van Ronk said he found a well 'thumbed through' book of translations of poems by the French Symbolists on Dylan's shelf (likely *An Anchor Anthology of French Poetry*,[15] published in 1958, which is currently included in the 'Books' section of Dylan's official website). 'I think he probably knew Rimbaud backward and forward before I even mentioned him,' Van Ronk said, and, in *Chronicles*, Dylan wrote about Rimbaud, noting that when he read one of Rimbaud's letters, 'Je est un autre' ('I is someone else') the 'bells went off'.

The Symbolists were, of course, a major influence on the Beats. 'I met Jack on the sidewalk outside my loft and told him how I liked his book, *On the Road*, and added that it reminded me of Woody Guthrie's writing,' John Cohen wrote in his book of photographs, *There is No Eye*. 'There was a resemblance between their rambling sentences, free grammar, and the long list of places and titles that evoked images of America ... Jack was indignant. "Woody Guthrie's just a folk singer. I'm a poet, like Rimbaud and Verlaine".'

Dylan also read the fifteenth-century French poet François Villon, and he wrote in his memoir that after he got to New York he read long poems including Lord Byron's 'Don Juan' and Samuel Taylor Coleridge's 'Kubla Khan'. 'I began cramming my brain with all kinds of deep poems,' Dylan wrote.

Dylan also dug the ultra-cool monologist and comedian Lord Buckley, whose hip wordplay and controversial raps anticipated the Beats. Buckley, a cult figure who began performing in the 1930s, made his first recordings in the early 1950s, but his albums continued to be released throughout the 1960s (following his death in October 1960). A 1961 live recording by Dylan of 'Black Cross' (a poem by Joseph S. Newman that appeared as a Buckley monologue on the 1959 album *Way Out Humor*, describing the lynching of an African American, and which has been described as one of Buckley's 'signature pieces') was included on the *Great White Wonder*, the Dylan bootleg, and Dylan also performed 'Black Cross' at the Gaslight Café on 15 October 1962.[16] In the cover photo for *Bringing It All Back Home*, the album *The Best of Lord Buckley* sits on the fireplace mantle. In *Chronicles*, Dylan described Buckley as 'the hippest bebop preacher', and wrote, 'With stretched out words, Buckley had a magical way of speaking. Everybody, including me, was influenced by him in one way or another.'

Sometime in 1961, Lawrence Ferlinghetti, whose book *Starting From San Francisco* was published that year by New Directions Press, finished up his business at New Directions (then with offices on the eleventh floor of 333 Sixth Avenue), took one of the two elevators in the old building down to the lobby and there he saw this kid who he later [after Dylan's success] realized was Bob Dylan. 'He was hangin' around the elevator with his guitar in the building where New Directions was,' Ferlinghetti told me. 'And as I walked past him he says, "How do you git up there?" So he wanted to be published as a poet first. New Directions in those days was the ivory tower for poets.'

Neither man – Ferlinghetti nor, Ferlinghetti believes, Dylan – recognized the other that day. Dylan was already a fan of Ferlinghetti's poetry. In addition to *A Coney Island of the Mind* (also published by New Directions), Dylan had read Ferlinghetti's first poetry collection, *Pictures of the Gone World* (which is included in *A Coney Island of the Mind*). Ferlinghetti's poems influenced Dylan. 'It's Alright Ma (I'm Only Bleeding)' is the stepchild of Ferlinghetti's 'I Am Waiting',[17] a poem that includes such lines as:

and I am waiting
to see God on television
piped onto church altars
if only they can find the right channel

and:

and I am waiting
for the human crowd
to wander off a cliff somewhere
clutching its atomic umbrella

Numerous poems in *A Coney Island of the Mind* name-drop high-profile personages from history and fiction, something Dylan would soon do in such songs as 'I Shall Be Free', in which he mentions President Kennedy, Anita Ekberg, Brigitte Bardot, Sophia Loren, Ernest Borgnine, Willy Mays, Yul Brynner, Charles de Gaulle and Robert Louis Stevenson.

'He [Ferlinghetti] is the Beat poet whose work most noticeably includes constant allusions to others' texts and titles – a feature we recognize as characteristic in Dylan's 1960s poetry, in *Tarantula* and throughout his songs,' Dylan authority Michael Gray wrote in his *The Bob Dylan Encyclopedia*.

'So throw a match on it'

On 29 July 1961, Suze Rotolo, 17 at the time and active in the Civil Rights movement, met Bob Dylan at an all-day folk festival held at the Riverside Church in Manhattan. They soon became a couple, and as Rotolo recounts in her 2008 memoir, *A Freewheelin' Time*, she took Dylan to the Museum of Modern Art, turning him on to her favourite paintings. They saw plays together, including the Living Theater's *The Brig* and LeRoi Jones' *Dutchman*, and art house films. In late 1962 or early 1963, Dylan and Rotolo viewed photographer Robert Frank and Alfred Leslie's *Pull My Daisy*. Filmed in 1959 (the year Frank's initially controversial book of black and white photographs, *The Americans*,[18] was published in the US by Grove Press with an introduction by Kerouac) and premiered in November of that same year, *Pull My Daisy* was based on the third act of Kerouac's play, *Beat Generation*,[19] and featured an improvised narration by Kerouac; actors included Ginsberg, Corso and Amram, who scored the film and became a friend of Dylan in the 1960s. In his book *Like A Rolling Stone: Bob Dylan at the Crossroads*,[20] Greil Marcus writes that Dylan's voice in 'Visions of Johanna' and 'Desolation Row' is 'partly Jack Kerouac's voice in his narration for [the] life among-the-beatniks movie *Pull My Daisy*. "Look at all those cars out there", Kerouac says. "Nothing there but a million screaming ninety-year-old men being run over by gasoline trucks. So throw a match on it".'

On 26 September 1961, Dylan began a series of shows opening for the Greenbriar Boys at Gerde's, and on 29 September, Robert Shelton's now-famous review of Dylan ran in the *New York Times*. The next day, Dylan played harp on a Carolyn Hester (then married to novelist Richard Fariña) session being produced by legendary Columbia Records A&R man/producer John Hammond (Billie Holiday, Charlie Christian, Aretha Franklin), who signed Dylan in October. (Hammond oversaw the 1961 release of Robert Johnson's mid-1930s recordings on LP for the first time, as *King of the Delta Blues Singers*; that album's cover is also among the many cultural artefacts in the photo on the cover of *Bringing It All Back Home*. Dylan wrote in his memoir that when Johnson started singing – Hammond gave Dylan an advance acetate of the Johnson album – 'he seemed like a guy who could have sprung from the head of Zeus in full armor'. Dylan also wrote, 'Johnson's words made my nerves quiver like piano wires.')

Dylan already understood that you could take an existing song and fuck with it and end up with a new song. This was the folk tradition. Robert Johnson, for instance, had turned two of Skip James's songs, 'Devil Got My Woman' and '22–20', into 'Hellhound On My Trail' and '32–20'. Typically, new words were layered on existing melodies. But Dylan would take a postmodern approach, combining his own words with words and phrases he picked up from films, magazine and newspaper articles and books, utilizing them as raw materials to tell his own stories.

Dylan's first album, released in 1962, was nearly all covers of blues and folk songs, but there were two originals, 'Song to Woody' and 'Talkin' New York', and both showed that Dylan was aware of the folk tradition. In the case of 'Song to Woody', the old song was Woody Guthrie's '1913 Massacre' (which in turn used a tune likely borrowed from the English folk song 'Hear the Nightingale Sing', which goes under a number of names including 'One Morning in May' and 'The Nightingale'). Dylan's 'Talkin' New York' was based on Guthrie's talking blues, and borrows or reworks phases from Guthrie's 'Talkin' Subway' and other songs on *Talking Blues*, an album by folklorist John Greenway released on Folkways in 1958. Greenway's version of 'Talkin' Subway' includes verses written by Guthrie but never recorded by him.

It wasn't until his second album, *The Freewheelin' Bob Dylan* (1963), which Dylan spent a year, off and on, writing and recording, that we saw the first evidence of Bob Dylan the revolutionary songwriter. 'Blowin' in the Wind' gave Dylan songwriting cred when Peter, Paul and Mary's version reached no. 2 on the *Billboard* pop chart in August of 1963. Dylan took the melody for his song from the old spiritual, 'No More Auction Block for Me', which musicologist Alan Lomax said originated in Canada and was sung by former slaves who went there after Britain abolished slavery throughout the British Empire in 1833. Dylan likely heard Odetta's version (he was a major fan of the woman whom Martin Luther King Jr called 'the queen of American folk music'), which appeared on her 1960 album, *Odetta at Carnegie Hall*. But it was another song Dylan wrote for the *The Freewheelin' Bob Dylan* that was his first step into a whole new dimension of songwriting.

In September of 1962, Dylan was upstairs in what folkie Tom Paxton called a 'hang-out room' above the Village Gaslight Café, a club where Beat writers including Ginsberg and Corso had appeared in the late 1950s. By 1962, Beat poetry readings were giving way to folk music performances, and the Gaslight was the premier folk club in the Village (Dylan performed at the club a month later, in October of that year). 'Dylan was banging out this long poem on Wavy Gravy's typewriter [he was still Hugh Romney at the time],' Paxton said. 'He [Dylan] showed me the poem and I asked, "Is this a song?" He said, "No, it's a poem." I said, "All this work and you're not going to add a melody?"' Romney, who has corroborated Paxton's story, was the Gaslight's poetry director at the time (earlier drafts of 'A Hard Rain's a-Gonna Fall' were handwritten in a notebook).

John Cohen, who also frequented the hang-out room, told me, 'I came back from making my film, *The High Lonesome Sound*, in Kentucky. He [Dylan] showed me the words to "Hard Rain". This was as he was writing it. And I said, if you're going to write stuff like that, this isn't Woody Guthrie, this is more like Rimbaud. He claimed he didn't know who I was talking about.'

Soon Dylan turned that 'poem' into a song.

One of the Beat poets who Dylan admired, Allen Ginsberg, was blown away when he heard the recording of 'A Hard Rain' in 1963. 'When I got back from India, and got to the West Coast, there's a poet, Charlie Plymell – at a party in Bolinas – played me a record [*The Freewheelin' Bob Dylan*] of this new young folk singer,' Ginsberg said during an interview for *No Direction Home,*

> And I heard 'A Hard Rain', I think. And wept. 'Cause it seemed that the torch had been passed to another generation. From earlier bohemian, or Beat illumination. And self-empowerment … There's a very famous saying among the Tibetan Buddhists, if the student is not better than the teacher then the teacher's a failure. And I was really knocked out by the eloquence, particularly, 'I'll know my song well before I start singing', and, 'where all souls shall reflect it' and 'I'll stand on the mountain where everybody can hear'. It's sort of this biblical prophecy. Poetry is words that are empowered that make your hair stand on end that you recognize instantly as being some form of subjective truth that has an objective reality to it because somebody's realized it. Then you call it poetry later.

Ginsberg also said he thought Dylan's writing was 'an answering call or response to the kind of American prophecy that Kerouac had continued from Walt Whitman'.

Although based on the old Anglo-Scottish border Child ballad 'Lord Randall' (also known as 'Lord Randal'), 'A Hard Rain' displayed what would mark Dylan as unique among his peers at the time, his ability to write song lyrics that were literature. It is no surprise that Dylan was writing a poem, and only after he'd written several drafts did he transform it into a new kind of song.

As Dylan expert Clinton Heylin wrote in his book *Revolution in the Air: The Songs of Bob Dylan, 1957–1973*, what is also unique about 'A Hard Rain' is

> … the relentless rivulet of images, pouring down on one another in a stream so unending that in the final verse he cannot stop himself from breaking the very bounds of song form itself in order to 'tell it and think it and speak it and breathe it' like it is. Such a freewheelin' verse structure was not something he acquired from either Woody Guthrie or Robert Johnson. It smacked of Ginsberg's 'Howl' or the speed rapping of Kerouac – and it transformed Dylan into a folk modernist.

It was in the winter of 1963 that Dylan met Kerouac's good friend, Allen Ginsberg, who Dylan would describe to Robert Shelton in a March 1966 interview as 'holy'. They were introduced at a party held in Ted Wilentz's apartment in the Village upstairs from the Eighth Street Bookshop (which Wilentz co-owned with his brother Eli, and where in the early 1950s you could, on occasion, find Kerouac, Corso and other Beats browsing) and spoke about poetry. It was the beginning of a friendship that would last until Ginsberg died on 5 April 1997. The night after Ginsberg's death, Dylan dedicated his performance of 'Desolation Row' to his friend.

David Amram told me in February 2017 that he thinks the initial motivation for Dylan, who never met Kerouac, to become friends with both Ginsberg and himself was their friendships with Kerouac. 'After 1959 Jack had bailed out of New York except for an occasional visit,' Amram said. 'So when Dylan came [to New York] loving Jack's work, I think the only two people who had been part of that [friends of Kerouac] were Allen Ginsberg and myself. I always wondered what interest he could possibly have in what I was doing as a jazz player who wanted to write symphony music and I realised that probably the closest he could get to Jack was through Allen and me.'

'The great American road trip'

In February 1964, Bob Dylan literally went on the road, travelling for 20 days across the country in a Ford station wagon. It was what his road manager at the time, Victor Maymundes, called, in reference to Kerouac, 'the great American road trip'. They were joined by folksinger Paul Clayton and *Daily Mirror* reporter Pete Karman (a friend of Suze Rotolo), who was there, according to Maymundes in his book, *Another Side of Bob Dylan*, 'to record the journey south into the dark and dangerous country of America'. 'I think it was in the back of everybody's mind that this was sort of an *On the Road* redux,' Karman told Dylan biographer Howard Sounes.

This Kerouacian journey – in which they picked up a hitchhiking miner and tried unsuccessfully to talk to Hamish Sinclair, secretary and strike leader for the National Committee for Miners in Harlan County, Kentucky; played pool and went bowling in Asheville, North Carolina; and had a brief, awkward conversation with Carl Sandburg at his home in Flat Rock, North Carolina – would be the catalyst for the next stage of Dylan's writing. He worked on two transformative songs in the back seat during the trip, songs that were a piece with his transition to writing Beat influenced picture poems: 'Chimes of Freedom' and 'Mr. Tambourine Man'. And he heard the Beatles on the radio.

'When we were driving through Colorado we had the radio on and eight of the top 10 songs were Beatles songs. In Colorado! "I Wanna Hold Your Hand", all those early ones,' Dylan said during a 1971 interview with one of his biographers, Anthony Scaduto. 'They were doing things nobody was doing. Their chords were outrageous, just outrageous, and their harmonies made it all valid ... But I just kept it to myself that I really dug them. Everybody else thought they were for the teenyboppers, that they were gonna pass right away. But it was obvious to me that they had staying power. I knew they were pointing the direction of where music had to go.'

Dylan was also taken with Rimbaud at this time. He told Karman, 'Rimbaud's where it's at. That's the kind of stuff means something. That's the kind of writing I'm gonna do.' In fact, it would appear that Dylan's 'magic swirling ship' in 'Mr. Tambourine Man' was inspired by Rimbaud's poem *The Drunken Ship* (included in *An Anchor Anthology of French Poetry*), which includes the line, 'Now I, a little lost boat, in swirling debris'.

When Dylan and his road buddies arrived in the Bay Area, Karman split and Bob Neuwirth, a musician and painter who Dylan had met at a folk festival in 1961, joined the entourage before they headed to Carmel, and then on to LA. For the next few years Neuwirth would be one of Dylan's closest friends as well as his road manager. Before they left the Bay Area, Dylan wanted to make contact with Ferlinghetti. He attempted to visit the poet/publisher but he wasn't at home; Dylan left a note.

Back in New York in March 1964, Dylan rented an electric guitar. A month later, he dropped acid for the first time. Producer Paul Rothchild told Dylan biographer Bob Spitz he was present when Dylan took his first hit of LSD at his manager Albert Grossman's mansion in Woodstock. Although Dylan has denied it, his experiences on acid clearly affected his songwriting (as well as the poetry he wrote for *Tarantula* and his liner notes).

In the months that followed there must have been some kind of contact either between Dylan and Ferlinghetti, or Grossman and Ferlinghetti – in which the possibility of Ferlinghetti's City Lights Books publishing Dylan's writing was discussed. Ferlinghetti told me he had hoped to publish Dylan at that time. In April, the month he dropped acid, Dylan wrote a long 118-line prose-poem letter to Ferlinghetti, which is now part of the City Lights Archive at the University of California, Berkeley, Bancroft Library, in which Dylan expressed the hope that he would get some material to Ferlinghetti 'one of these days'. The letter reads, in part:

> . . . have t look thru all my pants pockets
> an collect things t send t you.
> as of now I am in the midst of destroyin all I've
> done (I've even crashed my old typewriter t pieces an have burned my
> pens into little tiny plastic statues)
> I know I will send you something one of these days.
> all I have t do is finish something t send you.
> in any case, if I am poisened or framed or kilt or ratted on
> I will will will you some edgar lee masters?
> type (bob dylan written) poems of grand embarassment.
> thelonius monk grand style grand (me upright)
> the world's fair begun down there.
> I'm gone . . .

Dylan didn't write a book for City Lights. Instead, Grossman made a deal for Dylan with the Macmillan Company. As Ferlinghetti told me, there was no way City Lights could compete with Macmillan. Dylan completed *Tarantula* in 1966. It was written in a stream-of-consciousness, at times hallucinogenic, Beat style like the liner notes Dylan had been writing for his albums.

Tarantula was to be published in the autumn of 1966, but following Dylan's motorcycle accident he put the book on hold; it wasn't until 1971 that it was published.

That year Dylan told *Rolling Stone* publisher Jann Wenner, 'Boy, they were hungry for this book. They didn't care what it was. They just wanted ... people up there were saying, "Boy, that's the second James Joyce", and "Jack Kerouac again" and they were saying "Homer revisited" ... and they were all just talking through their heads.'

During that summer of 1964, while up in Woodstock, New York, where his manager had a mansion and where Dylan sometimes rented a cabin from the mother of folksinger Peter Yarrow of the group Peter, Paul and Mary, Dylan wrote a song that broke more new ground, another song that clearly showed the Beat influence, 'It's Alright, Ma (I'm Only Bleeding)'.

The song begins with a rush of images:

> Darkness at the break of noon
> Shadows even the silver spoon
> The handmade blade, the child's balloon
> Eclipses both the sun and moon
> To understand you know too soon
> There is no sense in trying

and later:

> Old lady judges watch people in pairs
> Limited in sex, they dare
> To push fake morals, insult and stare
> While money doesn't talk, it swears
> Obscenity, who really cares
> Propaganda, all is phony

'It's Alright, Ma' appeared on Dylan's first rock album, *Bringing It All Back Home*, released in March of 1965. Most, if not all, of the songs on that album, including 'Subterranean Homesick Blues' and 'Mr. Tambourine Man', show the influence of the Beats, and Dylan underlines that by including a mention of Ginsberg in his liner notes and a photo of Ginsberg wearing Dylan's top hat on the back cover. Among the many cultural artefacts in the front cover photo is a copy of *GNAOUA*, a one-shot magazine published in 1964 that focused on exorcism and Beat-era poetry (including writing by Ginsberg and Burroughs) edited by the poet Ira Cohen.

'A hundred-mile-an-hour clip'

The documentary filmmaker D. A. Pennebaker was asked by Albert Grossman to film Dylan's spring 1965 acoustic tour of England. Pennebaker had, in the late 1950s, been given the rights by Kerouac himself to make a film of *On the Road*; he had those rights for about a decade, he says, until the end of the 1960s or early 1970s. Pennebaker had become friends with Kerouac years before the Beat writer wrote *On the Road*.

'Well I had the rights to it [*On the Road*] only because Kerouac wanted me to do it,' Pennebaker told me during a March 2017 interview. 'I kept telling him I didn't know how to do that kind of film. I said, "If you guys can put on your wading boots and stand by the highway up at Bear Mountain I'll stand with you [and film it] and we can ride out to California. 'Cause I don't know how to make a film with actors acting like you guys." And he said, "Well you can figure that out. You can get somebody to help you do that."'

Pennebaker had concluded that he didn't want to make fictional films, and had already made a handful of cinema vérité documentaries. In late 1964 Pennebaker agreed to make the documentary film that became *Dont Look Back*, which in its own way is a kind of homage to Kerouac and *On the Road*.

'I knew there had to be some way to translate Kerouac's particular angst, his fidgety enthusiasm, and love of things around him, people around him, in film terms,' Pennebaker told Dylan biographer Bob Spitz. 'From watching Dylan's absolute compulsion to somehow evolve from Kerouac, I began to understand how to approach the film [*Dont Look Back*]. Kerouac and Neal Cassady lived a hundred-mile-an-hour clip; Dylan and Neuwirth enjoyed their own fantastic life-style, and in a way, their essences were intertwined.'

During the mid-1960s, Dylan and Neuwirth were a kind of Kerouacian pair, getting their own kicks in Manhattan and during Dylan's tours in the US and Europe (when Andy Warhol gave Dylan one of his Double Elvis paintings, Dylan and Neuwirth tied it to the roof of Dylan's Ford station wagon 'totally unprotected', according to writers Tony Scherman and David Dalton's book, *Pop: The Genius of Andy Warhol*, and drove up to Woodstock, depositing the canvas at Grossman's mansion), but also, like Kerouac himself, searching for truth in a world where truth is often buried beneath a mountain of lies and misdirection. One gets a good idea of the Dylan–Neuwirth dynamic in *Dont Look Back*, where the duo ceaselessly make fun of Donovan, who had a hit record while Dylan toured England.

'I think Bob always, without voicing it, always considered himself a Kerouac kid,' Pennebaker said at the outset of our interview. 'Kind of a jail kid that's gotten loose. He would often refer to stuff that Kerouac had done or written.'

Writing about Neuwirth in *Chronicles*, Dylan made a Kerouac reference: 'Like Kerouac had immortalized Neal Cassady in *On the Road*, somebody should have immortalized Neuwirth. He was that kind of character. He could talk to anybody until they felt like all their intelligence was gone ... I got a kick out of everything he did and liked him ... We liked pretty much all the same things, even the same songs on the jukebox.'

Dylan and Neuwirth, according to Pennebaker, spoke about Kerouac when they were all in England in late April and early May 1965 making *Dont Look Back*. 'Dylan would say something [about Kerouac],' Pennebaker said. 'Neuwirth knew the book [either *Dharma Bums* or *Desolation Angels*]. Dylan liked that idea, of the mountain time [Kerouac's time as a fire lookout on Desolation Peak in the North Cascade Mountains of Washington state in 1956]. Dylan liked that idea of the mountain and got intrigued by it. So there were mentions of the book.'

Dylan appears to have considered making a film of *On the Road*. In a letter to his agent Sterling Lord dated 29 February 1968 (published in *Jack Kerouac: Selected Letters 1957 – 1969*), Kerouac wrote, 'Let me know what develops with Jack Geoghegan [editor-in-chief and president of Coward-McCann, the company that published *Desolation Angels* and *Vanity of Duluoz*] selling Vanity reprint, and with the movie Bob Dylan plan for ROAD.'

Dylan himself no longer has any memory of wanting to make a film of *On the Road*, according to his manager. Neither does Sterling Lord. Responding to an email I sent him, Lord wrote, 'I do not recall anything about that situation' and in another email, 'I do not remember anything Jack Kerouac said about Dylan. I never heard him talk about Dylan.'

Kerouac actually did say a few things about Dylan. Kerouac's friend, writer John Clellon Homes, interviewed by Kerouac biographer Dennis McNally, said that at first Kerouac thought Dylan was 'another fucking folksinger', but changed his mind and 'gruffly conceded' to Holmes, 'Well okay, he's good.'

'Writ for my own soul's ear'

'Like a Rolling Stone' probably owes more to Allen Ginsberg's 1955 'Howl' than to any song.

> Greil Marcus, *Like a Rolling Stone: Bob Dylan at the Crossroads*

It is 1955. Allen Ginsberg sits at his desk in his North Beach apartment. On his wall he's tacked his friend Jack Kerouac's 'Belief and Technique for Modern Prose', a list of 30 suggestions for getting to the heart of things in one's writing.[21] (And now for a two-paragraph digression, but an important digression.)

Kerouac had struggled for several years trying to write his second novel, after *The Town and the City*. Much had been written, but Kerouac wasn't satisfied. Finally, in April of 1951, partially inspired by a letter wild man Neal Cassady had written him, and with his notebooks and journals next to the typewriter, he started over and wrote what would become the most famous and influential of Beat novels, *On the Road*, in three intense weeks at his apartment on West 20th Street in the Village, onto a 120-foot 'scroll', as Kerouac called it, of tracing (*not* teletype) paper. Typing at breakneck speed, fuelled by many cups of black coffee, Kerouac was like a jazz musician improvising late into the night, letting the facts of his road trips with Cassady blur into the fictional account of Dean Moriarity (Cassady) and Sal Paradise (Kerouac). There were three additional drafts (typed on conventional typing paper, not scrolls), before the book was eventually published by Viking Press on 5 September 1957.

As Ginsberg wrote (quoted in Howard Cunnell's essay for *On the Road: The Original Scroll*), Kerouac had developed a style that was

> ...a long confessional of two buddies telling each other everything that happened, every detail, every cunt-hair in the grass included, every tiny eyeball flick of orange neon flashed past in Chicago in the bus station; all the back of the brain imagery. This required sentences that did not necessarily follow exact classic-type syntactical order but which allowed for interruption with dashes, allowed for the sentences to break in half, take another direction (with parentheses that might go on for paragraphs). It allowed for individual sentences that might not come to their period except after several pages of self reminiscence, of interruption and the piling on of detail, so that what you arrived at was a sort of stream of consciousness visioned around a specific subject (the tale of the road) and a specific view point ...[22]

Some of Kerouac's writing suggestions on that sheet tacked to Ginsberg's wall freed Ginsberg to write 'Howl', the poem that essentially launched the Beat movement and which was also named by Kerouac, who read early drafts.

As poet, songwriter (for Tim Buckley and others) and Beat expert Larry Beckett noted in his book, *Beat Poetry*,[23] writing about the genesis of 'Howl', Ginsberg makes reference to a number of Kerouac's techniques:

1. Scribbled secret notebooks, and wild typewritten pages, for your own joy

...

4. Be in love with your life

...

8. Write what you want bottomless from bottom of the mind

...

24. No fear or shame in the dignity of yr experience, language & knowledge

'I thought I wouldn't write a poem,' Ginsberg wrote in *Howl: Original Draft Facsimile*, 'but just write what I wanted to without fear, let my imagination go, open secrecy, and scribble magic lines from my real mind – sum up my life – something I wouldn't be able to show anybody, writ for my own soul's ear.'

The result was a draft of the first part of 'Howl' which begins:

> I saw the best minds of my generation
> destroyed by madness
> starving, mystical, naked,
> who dragged themselves through the angry streets at
> dawn looking for a negro fix

In 1956 Ferlinghetti published Ginsberg's first book of poetry, *Howl and Other Poems*, which, thanks to an obscenity trial, brought Ginsberg widespread notoriety and brought attention to the Beat scene, which turned into a national fad after *On the Road* was published on 5 September 1957 (Ginsberg, acting as an informal agent for Kerouac and William Burroughs, is credited with helping get Kerouac's first novel, *The Town and the City*, published by Harcourt Brace in 1950).

'Well the language which they [the Beats] were writing, you could read off the paper, and somehow it would begin some kind of tune in your mind,' Dylan told John Cohen during a 1968 interview for *Sing Out!* 'I don't really know what it was, but you could see it was possible to do more than that ... not more ... something different than what Woody and people like Aunt Molly Jackson and Jim Garland did.'

'Hey, you dig something like cut-ups?'

On 3 May 1965, the day Jack Kerouac's eleventh novel, *Desolation Angels*,[24] was published, Bob Dylan sat in a room of the Savoy Hotel in London, and with Joan Baez providing harmony vocals, sang Hank Williams's 'Lost Highway'. Dylan started with the third verse, followed with the fourth and then seemed at a loss before Bob Neuwirth called out, 'There's another verse, "I'm a rolling stone ..."'

Dylan then sang, 'I'm a rolling stone all alone and lost / For a life of sin I have paid the cost ...'

And that was the moment, Greil Marcus said during a conversation with D. A. Pennebaker about *Dont Look Back* for the 24 November 2015 Blu-ray edition of the film, 'when the notion of "Like a Rolling Stone" first appears'.

Dylan wanted to break free of traditional song structures. He told journalist Paul Jay Robbins in March 1965, 'I've written some songs which are kind of far out, a long continuation of verses, stuff like that – but I haven't really gotten into writing a completely free song. Hey, you dig something like cut-ups? I mean, like William Burroughs?'

He went on to tell Robbins, who interviewed him for the *Los Angeles Free Press* when Dylan was in Southern California in late March of 1965 playing the Santa Monica Civic Auditorium, that he wrote *Tarantula* because

> ... there's a lot of stuff in there I can't possibly sing ... all the collages. I can't sing it because it gets too long or it goes too far out. I can only do it around a few people who would know. Because the majority of the audience – I don't care where they're from, how hip they are – I think it would just get totally lost. Something that had no rhyme, all cut up, no nothing, except something happening, which is words.

Drugs certainly played a part in the next phase of Dylan's songwriting. In a February 1966 interview with Nat Hentoff, Dylan's comments about LSD might explain the anger and desire for revenge expressed in some of his *Highway 61* songs. 'I wouldn't advise anybody to use drugs – certainly not the hard drugs; drugs are medicine,' Dylan told Hentoff. 'But opium and hash and pot – now, those things aren't drugs; they just bend your mind a little. I think *everybody's* mind should be bent once in a while. Not by LSD, though. LSD is medicine – a different kind of medicine. It makes you aware of the universe, so to speak; you realise how foolish *objects* are. But LSD is not for groovy people; it's for mad, hateful people who want revenge. It's for people who usually have heart attacks . . .'

The Beats were decidedly on Dylan's mind during his spring 1965 British acoustic tour. He hung out with Allen Ginsberg, who appears in the short film Pennebaker shot in London for 'Subterranean Homesick Blues' (seen at the start of *Dont Look Back*), spoke to a reporter about Burroughs and repeatedly brought up Kerouac in Pennebaker's presence.

In out-takes for *Dont Look Back* shot in England in late April and the first two weeks of May 1965, Dylan is seen showing a journalist how he attempted to use Burroughs 'cut-up' technique to write a song, but said it hadn't worked for him 'because the rhyming scheme sounded so weird'.

During Dylan's stay at the Savoy Hotel he was constantly writing in his room, typing away, as seen in *Dont Look Back*, and described by Marianne Faithfull in her autobiography. 'For a while he had a roll of that waxy English toilet paper in the machine,' Faithfull wrote. 'It was just the right width for song lyrics, he said. A little bit of *un homage à Kerouac*, too, of course.'

Back in the US in June of 1965, a decade after Ginsberg wrote 'Howl', at the cabin in Woodstock that Dylan sometimes rented from Peter Yarrow's mother, Dylan finally did what Kerouac and Ginsberg had done: he put aside the 'rules' of traditional songwriting and let words flow in a rush from his subconscious onto the page. The result was the words he would edit into what some believe is his greatest song, 'Like a Rolling Stone'.

Sometime in early June while he was working on 'Like a Rolling Stone', Dylan bought a large 11-room, two-storey arts and crafts house called Hi Lo Ha in Byrdcliff, New York, not far from both Woodstock and Bearsville, where his manager Albert Grossman had the big house in which Dylan had often stayed. Still in Woodstock, he completed the lyrics and set them to music.

With 'Like a Rolling Stone' and possibly other new songs written, Dylan called guitarist Michael Bloomfield and asked him to come up to Woodstock to stay with him and wife Sara at the new house and learn the songs during the weekend of 12 –13 June. 'And I went to Woodstock, and I didn't even have a guitar case, I just had my Telecaster and Bob picked me up at the bus station and took me to this house where he lived . . .,' Bloomfield told Larry 'Ratso' Sloman in November 1975; Sloman quoted him in his 1976 book, *On the Road with Bob Dylan*:

He taught me these songs, 'Like a Rolling Stone' and all those songs from that album and he said, 'I don't want you to play any of that B. B. King shit, none of that fucking blues, I want you to play something else,' so we fooled around and finally played something he liked, it was very weird, he was playing in weird keys which he always does, all on the black keys of the piano, then he took me over to this big mansion and there was this old guy walking around and I said, 'Who's that?' and Bob said 'That's Albert' . . . We fucked around there for a few days and then we went to New York to cut the record . . .

Dylan described the song – recorded with Dylan's producer, Tom Wilson, on 15 and 16 June 1965 at Columbia Studio A in Manhattan (the keeper take was cut on 16 June) and released as a single on 20 July – as a 'breakthrough'. And it was! Dylan had made something brand new. He had fused the dense, vivid and at times surreal imagery of the Beats' writing to the wildest rock'n'roll. The result: a kind of sonic poetry.

'Like a Rolling Stone' was Dylan's first pop hit, reaching no. 2 on the *Billboard* Hot 100 on 4 September 1965 (the Beatles' 'Help' was no. 1 that week).

'You have to vomit up everything you know,' Dylan told Ginsberg and journalist Ralph J. Gleason just five months later, in December of 1965, while in San Francisco. 'I did that. I vomited it all up and then went out and saw it all again.'

Dylan was asked by CBC's Marvin Bronstein, during an interview in Montreal on 20 February 1966, to name the song he remembered being a breakthrough. 'Do you mean the most honest and straight thing which I thought I ever put across?' Dylan said. 'That reached popularity, you mean . . . If you're talking about what breakthrough is for me, I would have to say, speaking totally, it would be "Like a Rolling Stone". I wrote that after I had *quit*. I'd literally quit, singing and playing – I found myself writing this song, this story, this long piece of vomit, twenty pages long, and out of it I took "Like a Rolling Stone" and made it as a single.'

Dylan, in talking about his process to Bronstein and others was, as usual, taking poetic licence. He told other interviewers his 'long piece of vomit' was ten pages (Jules Siegel), or six pages (Robert Shelton). Whatever.

'And I'd never written anything like that before and it suddenly came to me that that was what I should do,' he told Bronstein. 'Nobody had ever done that before . . . Anybody can write a lot of the things I used to write, I just wrote 'em first because nobody else could think of writing them – but that's only because I was hungry . . . I'm not saying it's ["Like a Rolling Stone"] better than anything else . . . After writing that I wasn't interested in writing a novel, or a play. I want to write *songs*. Because it was a whole new category.'

During his February 1966 interview with Jules Siegel, while talking about 'Like a Rolling Stone', Dylan brought up 'hatred' and the desire for 'revenge', two of the emotions he told Hentoff he associated with LSD, a drug he had taken within the previous two years. 'It wasn't called anything, just a rhythm thing on paper all about my steady hatred directed at some point that was honest,' Dylan said.

In the end it wasn't hatred, it was telling someone something they didn't know, telling them they were lucky. Revenge, that's a better word. I had never thought of it as a song, until one day I was at the piano, and on the paper it was singing, 'How does it feel?' in a slow motion pace, in the utmost of slow motion following something. It was like swimming in lava. In your eyesight, you see your victim swimming in lava. Hanging by their arms from a birch tree. Skipping, kicking the tree, hitting a nail with your foot. Seeing someone in the pain they were bound to meet up with. I wrote it. I didn't fail. It was straight.

'No rhyme, all cut-up, no nothing, except something happening, which is words'

I couldn't have written those songs back then. If I had just come out and sung 'Desolation Row' five years ago I probably would have been murdered.

Bob Dylan to Nat Hentoff, autumn 1965,
unpublished interview for *Playboy*

Following the 3 May 1965 publication of *Desolation Angels*, the publisher, Coward-McCann, a subsidiary of G. P. Putnam's Sons, ran full-page ads in the *Sunday Times Book Review*, the daily *New York Times*, the *New York Review of Books* and elsewhere. If you were in New York, and dug Jack Kerouac, it would have been hard not to know that the 'King of the Beats' had a new novel in the stores.

Hi Lo Ha, Dylan said, was where he wrote the rest of *Highway 61 Revisited* in the six weeks between the 15 and 16 June sessions in Manhattan where 'Like a Rolling Stone' was recorded, and the late July and early August sessions at which the rest of the *Highway 61 Revisited* album was completed. (Dylan, ever the poet, said that in one interview, but in another with Jann Wenner for *Rolling Stone* he said he wrote the *Highway 61* song 'Desolation Row' 'in the back of a taxicab' in New York.)

More interesting than where the songs that comprise *Highway 61 Revisited* were written is that just six weeks after *Desolation Angels* was published, Dylan used the book as a major source of raw material for his new songs. 'Desolation Row' took the first half of its title from Kerouac's new book, and Dylan seems to have gotten the idea for the song's main theme from Kerouac as well. In *Desolation Angels*, Kerouac writes about 'Surrealistic Street',[25] and describes a wild cast of characters that he sees out on skid row. What is 'Desolation Row', as Dylan describes it in his song, if not a dark, at times horrific version of Kerouac's 'Surrealistic Street'?

In *Desolation Angels*, Kerouac writes about 'the sisters from Arkansas who'd seen their father hanged'.[26] Dylan's song begins, 'They're selling postcards of the hanging . . .', a reference to the lynching of three African American circus workers on 15 June 1920 in Duluth, Minnesota, the city where Dylan was born; Dylan's father was nine years old in 1920 and lived two blocks from where the hangings occurred. Shockingly, postcards with a photo of the dead men hanging from a tree were later sold there.

There's much more: Dylan slightly reworked four of Kerouac's phrases for his song. Kerouac wrote, 'They sin by lifelessness',[27] which Dylan turned into 'Her sin is her lifelessness'. 'Cabinets with memories in them'[28] became 'memories in a trunk'. 'The perfect image of a priest'[29] became 'a perfect image of a priest'. 'Get his letter'[30] became 'received your letter'. Historical figures that were in Kerouac's book appear in Dylan's song: Romeo, Einstein, Noah and the Phantom of the Opera. Kerouac writes about a hunchback; Dylan name-drops the Hunchback of Notre Dame.

And still more: 'Completely in a trance'[31] becomes 'got him in a trance'. 'Asking for cigarettes' becomes 'bummed a cigarette'. Kerouac writes about a 'heart attack' and 'fornicating machines'; Dylan sings about a 'heart-attack machine'. 'Tell your fortune' becomes 'fortune-telling lady'. 'Blow up' becomes 'blow it up'. Kerouac writes of a girl 'getting upside down ready before her stagedoor mirror'; Dylan sings of the Good Samaritan 'getting ready for the show'. Kerouac writes 'Death is our reward'; Dylan, 'Death is quite romantic'. Kerouac's 'vests and ironed pants' became Dylan's 'iron vest'.

There are also many duplicated words. 'Postcards', 'sexless', 'painting', 'passports', 'sailors', 'blind', 'circus', 'restless', 'moaning', 'riot', 'sweeping', 'ambulance', 'jealous', 'monk', 'immaculate', 'electric', 'patients', 'peeking', 'nurse', 'agent', 'factory', 'sniffing', 'kerosene', 'castles', 'insurance', 'escaping', 'captain', 'fishermen' and 'flowers' are in both the book and the song.

Near the end of 'Desolation Row', Dylan sings, 'I had to rearrange their faces / And give them all another name'. This was exactly what Kerouac had done in all of his novels; changing names so the real people his characters were based on wouldn't be identified.

Other songs borrowed from Kerouac as well. In *Desolation Angels*, Kerouac describes a trip he took with his mother to Juarez;[32] Dylan started 'Just Like Tom Thumb's Blues' with his narrator in Juarez; and in that same song Dylan borrows a phrase from Kerouac's book: 'Housing Project hill'.[33] Near the end of *On the Road*, Sal Paradise, Kerouac's narrator, after visiting a Mexican whorehouse with his friend Dean Moriarty, is sick and alone, abandoned by Moriarty; once Sal recovers, he returns to New York. Dylan's narrator in 'Just Like Tom Thumb's Blues' is sick and alone in Juarez and has been ground down by his dealings with prostitutes and others, and his friends, who 'said they'd stand behind me', are gone; he intends to return to New York. Kerouac writes in *Desolation Angels*, 'As Cody wins he really loses, as he loses he really wins',[34] which seems relevant to Dylan's 'Up on Housing Project Hill / It's either fortune or fame / You must pick one or the other / Though neither of them are to be what they claim.' Dylan's 'fortune or fame' also echoes Kerouac's 'poverty and fame'. There were other influences in addition to Kerouac. The inclusion of 'Tom Thumb' in the title is an obvious reference to Rimbaud's poem 'Ma Bohème' ('My Bohemia'),[35] with the line 'Little Tom Thumb, I dropped my dreaming rhymes', a poem included in the same book of French Symbolist poetry Dylan likely owned in the early 1960s.

In *Desolation Angels*, Kerouac writes, 'I was 24 sitting in my mother's house all day while she worked in the shoe factory';[36] the chorus to 'Tombstone Blues' is 'Mama's in the fact'ry / She ain't got no shoes'. Kerouac writes about a burlesque house skit in which a woman talks of having sex in a graveyard;[37] in 'From a Buick 6', Dylan says he has 'this graveyard woman'. Kerouac mentions both junkyards and angels; Dylan sings about a 'junkyard angel'.

There is, of course, a long history of repurposing ideas and even words in art and literature; T. S. Eliot in his epic poem 'The Waste Land' does just that. Dylan was quite familiar with Eliot, and included him in 'Desolation Row', 'fighting in the captain's tower' with Ezra Pound. He also named Eliot's two wives, Valerie and Vivien, in 1967's 'Too Much of Nothing'. 'Desolation Row' has been compared to 'The Waste Land'.

In his book *The Sacred Wood: Essays on Poetry and Criticism*,[38] published in 1920, T. S. Eliot wrote, 'Immature poets imitate; mature poets steal; bad poets deface what they take, and good poets make it into something better, or at least something different. The good poet welds his theft into a whole of feeling which is unique, utterly different than that from which it is torn; the bad poet throws it into something which has no cohesion.'

Dylan's brilliance as an artist has always been his ability to absorb art 'like a sponge', as Neuwirth put it, and in the case of the *Highway 61* songs, to take Kerouac's phrases and ideas and words and utilize them to write something only Dylan could write. *Desolation Angles* may have been where Dylan got the idea to sing about the Duluth lynchings, but it took Dylan's genius to turn that idea into such a moving opening line.

Highway 61 Revisited, released in 1965, is a masterpiece, but there were more breakthroughs. Without even coming up for air, Dylan would write and record his greatest album, the following year's *Blonde On Blonde*, which contains his greatest song, 'Visions of Johanna' (and during the summer of 1967 Dylan and his band members would record the now infamous and revelatory 'Basement Tapes'). Tellingly, 'Visions of Johanna' (and much of the rest of *Blonde On Blonde*) would also borrow from the dense imagery of Ginsberg and Kerouac and would even draw its title from another Kerouac novel, 1963's *Visions of Gerard*.

That the Beats continued to be on Dylan's mind is evidenced by the photos he had taken by Larry Keenan of himself with Michael McClure and Ginsberg in the alley outside City Lights Books on 5 December 1965. Dylan had planned to use at least one of the photos for the *Blonde On Blonde* album artwork, but changed his mind. (Photos by another photographer who was there, Dale Smith, show Ferlinghetti standing next to Dylan, Ginsberg and McClure.)

'Visions of Johanna' was such a breakthrough for Dylan because with it he reached his goal of writing a 'completely free song'. There is no message, only the vague hints of a story, hints that leave the mystery intact. The song captures a state of mind as the narrator recalls being in a particular room at a particular time. It is also a song packed with amazing word images: 'the ghost of 'lectricity howls in the bones of her face'; 'But Mona Lisa musta had the highway blues / You can tell by the way she smiles'; and 'Oh, jewels and binoculars hang from the head of the mule'.

Dylan conveys what it was like to be in that room with the heat pipes coughing, music from the country music station playing softly as a surreal scene – word pictures – flash through the narrator's mind. His earlier political songs are transparent; 'propaganda songs' as The Minutemen would sing. 'Visions of Johanna' is deep. Multilayered, it catches the atmosphere, the moment, what it was to be in that room, thinking those thoughts, feeling those feelings. With that song, just as with Ginsberg's poems and Kerouac's novels, Dylan was not trying to make some big statement, he wasn't trying to fabricate something, he was simply laying out his truth. Art allows us to see through the façade to what's beneath it. That is what the Beats did, and that is what Bob Dylan did (and still does) with 'Visions of Johanna' and many of his other songs.

Dylan would, in the years that followed, write some excellent songs. But, as he eventually acknowledged, as time passed, he could no longer write the kind of free, hallucinatory songs he'd written in the 1960s. 'To do it, you've got to have power and dominion over the spirits,' he wrote in *Chronicles*. '[You had to be able to] see into things, the truth of things – not metaphorically, either, but really see, like seeing into metal and making it melt, see it for what it was and reveal it for what it was with hard words and vicious insight.'

'An unmarked grave'

Dylan and Ginsberg visiting Jack's grave was an honoring of Jack's importance to them.

John Cohen

In November of 1975 Allen Ginsberg stood with Bob Dylan at Kerouac's grave at Edson Cemetery in Lowell, Massachusetts. Ginsberg opened Kerouac's book of poetry, *Mexico City Blues*, and read from the 54th Chorus. Dylan then read a line from the 230th Chorus:

The quivering meat of the elephants

Ginsberg finished the line:

. . . of kindness

Then Ginsberg jumped to the last two lines:

Like kissing my kitten in the belly
The softness of our reward.

After that the two of them, Dylan and Ginsberg, made music, Dylan with his Martin, Ginsberg with his harmonium; they played what Sam Shepard described in his book, *Rolling Thunder Logbook*, as a 'slow blues', trading verses, right there at the grave, the grave of Jack Kerouac, right there in Lowell, Massachusetts, where Kerouac was born.

'This gonna happen to you?' Ginsberg had said with a nervous laugh, before the jam session, as they stood looking at the grave, looking at the tombstone that says 'Ti Jean, John L. Kerouac, Mar. 12, 1922–1969 – He Honored Life'.

A nervous laugh, as if Ginsberg wasn't so sure he shoulda said what he said.

'Nah,' Dylan said, 'I'm gonna be in an unmarked grave.'

Notes

1. Jonathan Cott (ed.), *Bob Dylan, The Essential Interviews* (New York: Wenner Books, 2006), p. 97. *Playboy* magazine interview, published March 1966.

2. Bob Dylan, 'Last Thoughts on Woody Guthrie', https://bobdylan.com/songs/last-thoughts-woody-guthrie/ (accessed 17 March 2017).

3. All unattributed quotes are from interviews conducted by the author during January, February and March 2017.

4. John Cohen, *There is No Eye: John Cohen Photographs* (New York: powerHouse Books, 2001), p. 118.

5. Jack Kerouac, 'On the Road again', *The New Yorker*, 22 June 1998, p. 56.

6. Michael McClure, 'The Poet's Poet', *Rolling Stone*, 14 March 1974, p. 32.

7. Bob Dylan, *Tarantula* (New York: Macmillan, 1971).

8. Robert Zimmerman, 'Bad Poem', http://www.bonhams.com/auctions/23878/lot/64/?category=list&length=10&page=7 (accessed 17 March 2017).

9. Lawrence Ferlinghetti, *A Coney Island of the Mind* (New York: New Directions Publishing Corporation, 1958).

10. William S. Burroughs, *Naked Lunch* (New York: Grove Press, 1959).

11. Allen Ginsberg, *Howl and Other Poems* (San Francisco: City Lights Books, 1956).

12. Jack Kerouac, *On the Road* (New York: Viking Press, 1957).

13. Jack Kerouac, *Mexico City Blues* (New York: Grove Press, 1959).

14. Bob Dylan, *Chronicles, Volume One* (New York: Simon & Schuster, 2004), pp. 235–6.

15. Republished as *The Anchor Anthology of French Poetry From Nerval to Valery in English Pranslation*, ed. Angel Flores (New York: Anchor Books, 1958).

16. 'Black Cross' by Joseph S. Newman, and Lord Buckley's version: http://keever.us/blackcro.html (accessed 17 March 2017).

17. Ferlinghetti, *A Coney Island of the Mind*, p. 50.

18. Robert Frank, *The Americans*, intro. Jack Kerouac (SCALO Publishers; original New York: Grove Press, 1959).

19. Jack Kerouac, *Beat Generation* (Cambridge, MA: Oneworld Classics/ Da Capo Press, 2005).

20. Greil Marcus, *Like A Rolling Stone: Bob Dylan at the Crossroads* (New York: PublicAffairs, 2005).

21. Jack Kerouac, 'Belief and Technique for Modern Prose'. See Appendix II.

22. Howard Cunnell, *On the Road: The Original Scroll, Jack Kerouac* (New York: Viking, 2007), p. 22.

23. Larry Beckett, *Beat Poetry* (New York: Beatdom Books, 2012)

24. Jack Kerouac, *Desolation Angels* (New York: Coward-McCann, 1965).

25. Ibid., p. 116

26. Ibid., p. 131

27. Ibid., p. 405

28. Ibid., p. 67

29. Ibid., p. 208

30. Ibid., p. 107

31. Ibid., p. 134

32. Ibid., p. 382

33. Ibid., p. 164

34. Ibid., p. 187

35. *The Anchor Anthology of French Poetry*, p. 106

36. Kerouac, *Desolation Angels*, p. 315

37. Ibid., p. 118

38. T. S. Eliot *The Sacred Wood: Essays on Poetry and Criticism* (London: Methuen, 1920; Kindle version location 1376).

CHAPTER 9
CARRYING A TORCH FOR 'TI JEAN'
Paul Marion

We were talking about Bob Dylan getting the Nobel Prize for Literature last week and ole Jack Kerouac having received nothing in his life by way of awards and prizes, and so my friend and I went to the famous gravesite in Edson Cemetery and presented to dead Jack a gold trophy-top from my grandfather-in-law's jewelry-store left-overs in my cellar in recognition of Jack's contribution to world literature, an athlete-figure in a cape and holding a torch, maybe some kind of Prometheus, after all, for the man who stole fire from his book-writing heroes to light the literary underbrush in America in the mid-twentieth century, including a blaze that warmed the fervid heart of young Robert Zimmerman from the Iron Range in upper Minnesota, young Bob who was a crow stealing rag bits to make a brilliant nest when Kerouac and friends were rising, when the Beats and others he said offered 'more to me than any of the stuff I'd been raised on' (as big as Elvis, he said), Joan Baez's 'unwashed phenomenon' and Anne Waldman's 'ear-poet' who drilled into Kerouac's sound hive, the same Bob who was excited to read Kerouac's 'breathless, dynamic bop poetry phrases' even after he set aside his once-bible *On the Road*, and gave a nod to Jack in his towering 'Desolation Row', the through-story Bob who is living his solo legacy in his 70s on the Endless Tour that has run from the White House to Las Vegas and quite a few truck stops in between, an Endless Tour that recapitulates Henry Thoreau and his brother John on the Concord and Merrimack Rivers, Walt Whitman intent on the open road, Woody hopping freight cars, and Jack in the 1940s front seat, passenger side, memorizing the national road of prairie pavement and coastal turns, and then the middle-time Bob who sat on the ground with Allen Ginsberg saying poems from *Mexico City Blues* (where my friend stood today) back in November 1975 barnstorming the city with his Rolling Thunder Revue, which I was lucky enough to see-and-hear just down the street from my apartment in Pawtucketville, that neighbourhood of tenements and broad boulevards across the river from centre-Lowell and just this side of the Dracut wild woods, the neighbourhood where young Jean/John/Jack patrolled the streets and invented his Doctor Sax atop the sandbank in earshot of the bashing foamy Merrimack, another young guy from a small American place who wanted to go big with what filled him, all this in mind in the autumn sun amid dry leaves red and also gold like the shiny trophy that we notched into the earth right by the simple flat granite marker that bears John L. Kerouac's name and dates, a name that was not spoken from high podiums for his benefit, a name that was not pulled from a sealed envelope at any New York or Swedish ceremony, a name that only rose in the chorus of his readers then and again today, a name and a presence that was strong when we stopped by to say 'Take this for what you gave us.'

And when we turned to go more readers from two cars parked nearby were heading Jack's way. Cemetery staff will deny it but swear Dylan sneaks in whenever he plays Lowell's arena to pay his respects and again close the loop between Willy Purple of *Tarantula* and 'girlsinger' Lee Anne Burns from *Old Angel Midnight*. Maybe some month on an extended intermission the Laureate will don his masked welding helmet and produce a grand gate with keys and strings to mark the path to the quiet, maple-shaded, sweet spot at Seventh and Lincoln.

INTERVIEW 3: RICHARD MELTZER
Michael Goldberg

Riffing on Jack Kerouac and his 'bop prosody'

Richard Meltzer – or R. Meltzer, as in the early days of his writing career he bylined his essays, reviews, articles and books – came to Jack Kerouac late, and to be more specific, his 'late thirties'. By then he was an established 'rockwrite guy', as Meltzer put it, or 'rock-crit', with more than a decade and a half of published words, who just happened to also write about boxing, tattoos, Eve Babitz, TV, bottle cap collecting, tampons, cigars, robot toys, his disaster of a date with a college girl poet, and on and on and on. Point being, Meltzer has always been a WRITER, a writer whose books belong on the shelf next to other important writers, not relegated to the rock-crit ghetto.

From his first writings for *Crawdaddy!* in 1967 (*Crawdaddy!* being the first magazine of serious rock criticism and news, predating *Rolling Stone*) he had his own Meltzerian style, a way of writing (looking at the world) unlike any other writer of that time. Basically, he had fun. Writing was one way he got his kicks (others being sex, drugs and rock'n'roll). (Also, he was often very funny – and still is.) (Also redux, he is considered to be the first critic to take rock'n'roll seriously, that is, the first *real* rock-crit.)

Meltzer is a serious (often not-so-serious) intellectual, and he's brilliant (he can write circles around most of us). His first book, *The Aesthetics of Rock* (begun in 1965 when he was 20), an academic treatise which developed during his undergraduate studies in philosophy at New York State University at Stony Brook (an excerpt of which was published in *Crawdaddy!* in early 1967), made him the first writer, as Greil Marcus put it in his introduction to the 1987 edition of the book, to 'simultaneously run rock'n'roll through all of Western philosophy, and vice versa . . .' Meltzer was a grad student at Yale in 1966 until he was booted out for attempting, as he puts it in the 'New Foreword' to the 1987 reprint (there was no foreword or introduction to the original 1970 edition), 'to "extend the text of philosophy" by dosing it silly with rock'n'roll'. He continued:

> Well, as long as you're asking, *The Aesthetics of Rock* (get your felt-tip marker) is the nearly verbatim transcript of my first three years, 1965–68, of beating my head against various walls, personal and systemic, in an unguided, utterly ingenuous, unrestrainedly passionate attempt to make even *provisional* mega-sense out of something, far as I can tell even today, no one previous had particularly cared to 'explore', verbally, much more than the frigging surface of: rock, rock, rock (and ROLL). Of which I was – gosh – a frigging, unwashed 'disciple'.

As time went on (1971, maybe), Meltzer entered his Beat period (writing-wise), which you can check out throughout his second (and brilliant/hilarious) book, 1972's *Gulcher* (as I write this you can pick up a used copy via Amazon in good condition, at least according to one seller, for $2.32 plus another $3.99 for shipping – and a bargain at that). Only he hadn't read the Beats when he wrote *Gulcher*. Still, even as a teenager in the late 1950s/early 1960s the Beat aesthetic, as caricatured on such TV shows as *The Loves of Dobie Gillis* and *77 Sunset Strip*, shattered the surface façade of 1950s life. 'Just seeing even an approximate reality of an actual people with beards and black sweaters was the polar opposite of the dress code in the McCarthy '50s,' Meltzer told me. 'This totally conformist madhouse that was America.'

When Meltzer finally did read Kerouac – *Vanity of Duluoz*, *Big Sur* and *On the Road* for starters – WOW!!#!! 'Well I felt we were brothers,' Meltzer told me. 'Our writing, especially our so-called stream of consciousness, long lines, long sentences – I felt there were a lot of similarities and it really pleased me to see that.'

In 1975, Meltzer wrote a lengthy essay, 'Another Superficial Piece About 176 Beatnik Books' (which I reprinted in my online rock'n'roll magazine, *Addicted To Noise*). Meltzer wrote:

> Apropos of nothing (and everything), in multifarious non-frivolous ways, Kerouac, Ginsberg and Burroughs are to Beat what Charlie Parker, Dizzy Gillespie and Thelonious Monk were to Bebop. Parker and Kerouac: universe-blazers, stripminers of personal pneuma, and easily the finest (most consistently exciting) soloists. Ginsberg and Gillespie: the behavioural flamboyance, the scene-manifesting definition-starts-here show-and-tell, scene-steering sometimes to the point of trivialization, of bric-a-brac horseshit on dotted lines as hokey as any their respective scenes were born to kill but still, much work of seminal muscle and technical brilliance. Burroughs and Monk: the odd men out, stylistically and attitudinally different enough to be 'not really beat', 'not really bop' (just majorly, transcendently significant and 'of the time'), reassessors, dynamiters of prevailing form (and challengers of audience forbearance).

Yeah, Meltzer has a lot to say about the Beats, and so late last year I contacted him to see if he wanted to shoot the shit about the greatest Beat of them all, Jack Kerouac. As you already know since this intro would not be in this book if he hadn't responded in the positive, yes, he was up for it. Meltzer and I spoke on 9 December 2016 for nearly two hours. In a rambling, improvised conversation true to Meltzer's writing style, he touched on everything from the bebop recordings that Kerouac loved to the unique qualities of Kerouac's writing to tangents about those in Kerouac's circle of friends and acquaintances.

Enjoy.

MG: I believe you told me you didn't read Kerouac until your forties.

RM: Late thirties. I was aware of him. I must have glanced at some pages, you know. I didn't read anybody in those years. But my writing it seems to me was always informed by a certain Beat ethos. A rejection of all dogma. Especially literary dogma, and a warrant to just go, make a mess. So when I finally did read Kerouac and Burroughs, etc., mischief and trouble making were already part of my modus operandi.

MG: Do you remember when you were first hearing about the Beats?

RM: I was in junior high. Mid-'50s.

MG: What kind of impact did what you heard about the Beats have on you at that time.

RM: Well you see this hogwash on TV like Maynard G. Krebs on *Dobie Gillis* [originally *The Many Loves of Dobie Gillis*]. Kookie on *77 Sunset Strip*. They were supposed to be beatniks, hipsters, whatever, and there was something appealing about them, but it certainly didn't seem real. Even just seeing this *Life* magazine expo of these horrible filthy beatniks, showing them in their pad, in their milieu. Just seeing even an approximate reality of an actual people with beards and black sweaters was the polar opposite of the dress code in the McCarthy '50s. This totally conformist madhouse that was America. Even in just the slightest glimpses I saw a rejection of that. I wasn't motivated to go read the stuff any more than I'd be motivated to read *War and Peace*. But I just, I became a writer, and I would say, and probably to this day, I still consider myself too young to be classed as a beatnik and [Anne] Waldman, who was somehow classed as one, she was close to Ginsberg at Naropa [University], she's only a month older than me, so maybe I'm on the cusp anyway, and Ed Sanders is eight years older than me, he's still alive. But basically my writing – I always felt sympathy for the nakedness and presumed honesty of what they were about. I saw no reason to put any brakes on my own impulses in those directions.

MG: What do you think your writing has in common with the Beats, and Kerouac in particular?

RM: I don't know if my writing is any more like Kerouac than Philip Whalen or Gregory Corso. There is no, what's the word, beatnik style sheet anyway. They all wrote not only different from each other, they were fairly different book to book, chapbook to chapbook. There's a lot of ground – continents' worth of text covered – but there are certain things they all had in common. They all wrote about each other. Their friendships were the content of what they wrote and that to me was – I love that. The notion of what they all stood for, in a way, what they represented, was an intersection between kicks and cellular concern, like universal compassion, at least try it on for size. Kerouac was so concerned with the dignity of all beings. He was asked once in an interview – he tried Buddhism on for size for at least ten years, tried to wean himself off his Catholicism – and some interviewer asked him how do you see karmic responsibility, what is your karmic responsibility?, and he said, 'No rest until every sentient being is redeemed.' If you heard something like that on the floor of Congress it would blow a hole off the top of the universe. He was dead serious – every little mouse, every sparrow. He wrote the greatest piece I ever read on bullfighting [a section of the prose piece 'Mexico Fellaheen' in the book *Lonesome Traveler*]. He hated it. He loved the bull, he just couldn't imagine that the spectacle was popular. He ends by saying: a bull is a sentient being. And that's what appeals to me most about Kerouac over and above the others. He takes in whatever 'love' is. I don't know what it is, really. I've loved but I don't know what it means – sexual love, love of mankind, all that stuff. I have no idea what it is except it's some kind of visceral relation to others of various species. And once in awhile you get a certain disingenuousness about it when it's discussed – in general – but it just seems to be much more palpable and urgent among the Beats, and Jack in particular. Just the whole torment of being alive and trying to love and emote and all the stuff. Love and friendship. It comes to a head in *Big Sur*, his masterpiece, where he has encounters with several of his colleagues, his beatnik brothers, for the last civil time, including his last civil encounter with Neal Cassady, and Cassady unloads his girlfriend on him, which drives Jack completely mad. Michael McClure asks Jack at some point, 'Tell me, you were going to give me the address of your editor at the *Paris Review*.' 'Fuck you!' And he puts it in the book. 'This is the account of my last civil encounter with this gentleman,' and so forth. And Philip Whalen, on the other hand – Jack gets drunk in San Francisco, in Golden Gate Park, falls asleep, and he wakes up several hours later and Philip Whalen is still there. They'd been drinking together. And he calls him saintly Phil Whalen. He wanted to make sure nobody would pick Jack's pocket, and years later – I don't know exactly when he wrote it – didn't Whalen die around 2000 or something? – somewhere early in the twenty-first century [2001] they put out a collection of Whalen's writings [written in the late 1950s and/or first year or so of the 1960s] called *Goofbook for Jack Kerouac.*[1] It has all this stuff that Jack encouraged him to write including at about page four he has this, he writes, 'cunt', and he does this little drawing of one, and it's the kind of thing – Jack encouraged everyone to go as extreme as their hearts would allow, but somehow it wasn't published while Whalen was still alive, like they were embarrassed for him. But when it came out it was called *Goofbook for Jack Kerouac*. And William Burroughs says Jack never appears as a character in anything by Burroughs, though Burroughs does appear in Jack's books – Bill was asked about this, he said, 'He's in everything I write. He's the spirit looking over my shoulder at every word I write to make sure I keep it honest.' And that's quite a role to play in the career of somebody like Burroughs. He gave Burroughs the name, 'Naked Lunch'. He told him years before he wrote it, 'You will write a book called "Naked Lunch".' But anyway, you want to talk specifically about Jack's books?

MG: Which of his books did you read first?

RM: I read *Dharma Bums* first. It just happened I got some used paperbacks, and *On the Road* was I think the third or fourth that I read. I read *Vanity of Duluoz*, which was the last of his books published while he was still alive. And I love that. And then I read *Big Sur*, and then I think I read *On the Road*.

MG: A lot of people think that *On the Road* is his best book but you really disagree with that.

RM: It was his hit, it was his bestseller. His only bestseller. I think it's a terrific book but it's far from his best. And one of the reasons it is – he did several takes on Neal Cassady, his original muse. Some people prefer *Visions of Cody*, which didn't come out until he was dead, and in which Neal is the star, and which I think is just a big hunk of kitsch like *Moby Dick*. Neal also appears in *Dharma Bums*, he appears in *Big Sur*, and basically Jack had so many unresolved misgivings about Neal and they show even in *On the Road*. Jack ends up sick in Mexico City and Neal abandons him. Still he ends up praising Neal to the skies. And I think the reason I like *Dharma Bums* at least as much is because Gary Snyder is his character, his protagonist, and he doesn't have as much invested in getting Gary right and in fact Gary thought that he got him wrong. But I think it's, I think he got him quite right, and if not for *Dharma Bums*, we would not know that this stodgy nature poet Gary Snyder, who is still alive, we would never know without Jack that he was a wild and crazy kid. Jack told that tale, I think quite well. But anyway, that's that one, and *Desolation Angels* is from the same time and goes all the way up to the moment when *On the Road* was released, and I really dislike *Desolation Angels*. It's one he wrote late in life. It was something he wrote for money, essentially. I mean he had some stuff lying around but he added new text, it's the 1960s already and he, Jack, couldn't care less about the burgeoning counterculture, and he keeps saying things like he doesn't care for Freedom Riders. He talks about how much he loves his mother, and if you can't dig it, tell it to Mao. It's a very sour book but it covers, remarkably, the only trip he ever took on the road with just him and a woman, and the woman is his mother. He takes her to a church in Mexico and she's crying, 'I couldn't believe that Mexicans were even humans, Jack. Thank you for showing me that they're good Catholics,' and so forth. But *Dharma Bums* is a more viable take on his San Francisco days, some of the San Francisco days. And then his other stuff, I think there are very few things that came out after he died that are any good. One of them is this play that he wrote called *Beat Generation*, which is pretty much a description of an encounter with Neal and his wife. [The Robert Frank/Alfred Leslie film *Pull My Daisy* is adapted from the third act of *Beat Generation*.] Neal wants to bet on the horses and his wife doesn't like that. The play is pretty lively and he meant business when he wrote it, and it was in the hands of his agent, Sterling Lord, and ten years ago they found it and put out a decent printing of it and it's a good book, as is the souvenir book from *Pull My Daisy*, which has the text that he improvised – the narrative that he did for the movie as he was watching the footage. It's a good movie. Another thing they put out since he died, *Kerouac at Bat: Fantasy Sports and the King of the Beats*. It's a book of writings he did on baseball. He actually made up his own fake baseball league, named all the players, he was still doing this in the late '50s, and there's a very nice coffee table book with some of his drawings and writings on baseball. But getting back to *On the Road*, Neal is fine as a muse and all of that, he's perfect, but Jack is really too ambivalent about who Neal ultimately fucking IS. It reads like hype, hagiography, which is diametrically opposed to who JACK fundamentally is, in literature or in lore. He's much more honest about Neal in *Big Sur*, much more definitive. (For his final take on Neal, chronologically, take a look at his last letter to him, on pages 306–9, in *Jack Kerouac Selected Letters 1957–1969*).

MG: When you did start reading his books, do you remember how you felt reading them. Do you remember the impact?

RM: Well I felt we were brothers. Our writing, especially our so-called stream of consciousness, long lines, long sentences, I felt there were a lot of similarities and it really pleased me to see that. Last time we spoke you brought up *Mexico City Blues* in terms of imagining it as he did, as a bunch of jazz solos, and my feeling is that his prose is much better jazz solos than his so-called poetry – he does longer lines. If you look at *Mexico City Blues*, they're very short lines. It's like he's stopping to take a breath every three or four syllables in some places.

MG: The first book of his that I read was *On the Road*, and aside from the story which was exciting to read when I was a teenager, and the whole idea of freedom, and just hitting the road, that whole thing, but the language! There are points in that book where he starts a sentence and he's just going and going and going. There's a section when Neal is driving across the country and Jack and Marylou are in the car that is incredible. And his descriptions, both in that book, and in *The Subterraneans*, when he's going to jazz clubs, the writing is amazing, whether it came out spontaneously or whether he ultimately worked it over, when you read it, it feels so natural, and you just want it to keep going.

RM: That's what I'm saying. He takes much longer solos in his prose then he does in his poetry. The poetry just seems to me mainly, especially *Mexico City Blues*, it's kind of like a send-up of poetry as a form. 'I don't want to write poetry like anybody else does, let's see what I can do.' But there are a lot of short poems that he wrote that are good too. *Pomes All Sizes* has some good stuff and *Scattered Poems*, but basically it's in his prose that he gets to, it's beyond making music, it's what he called bop prosody, he's thinking in poetic form, musical/poetic form, and it's not important whether it was one take or he worked it over.

Another one that's great is *The Subterraneans*, which he wrote in three days on Benzedrine inhalers, and I think it's just a whale of a good book, just the flow and the stops, the starts. It takes place, he wrote it to take place in New York, and the publisher made him change it to San Francisco, so there are some problems in how it's presented, changing street names and stuff like that, but basically it's – there are pages when he's choking on his own spit, it's an amazing document of his writerly oompah, his literary record in something like real time. I mean the lines that fizz out are as interesting as the ones that continue. It's not a studio album. It's a warm-up in the back room before going onstage maybe. Which is certainly good enough.

MG: So you felt a kindred spirit when you read Kerouac's stuff. At that point did his writing have an impact on your own writing?

RM: I could tell you some of the people that my writing was influenced by when I was 17, 18 years old. I'd say the first writer, the first two writers that ever influenced me were Muhammad Ali – just the way he talked, everything was all caps, exclamation points, just incredible. His press conference after beating Sonny Liston the first time is one of the greatest pieces of oral literature anywhere ever – and the other influence was LeRoi Jones [who changed his name to Amiri Baraka] – at the time all I knew was his reviews of albums and concerts for *Down Beat*. He would just say totally obnoxious and utterly reasonable things about the hand as dealt by consumer generatrix central, and a lot of his attitude I just ate up, and his sentence structure I copped from too, even though some of that today reads a little arcane and clunky. It's hard to say what influenced me, writers and language, other than those two. Basically I read philosophers – I was a philosophy major, I could say Aristotle, Plato, but that didn't make for credible writing. My first book, *The Aesthetics of Rock*, is largely unreadable because I didn't really think about prosody, myself, about how does this read, and when I got to my second book, *Gulcher*, by then I'd had a few years of rock writing where essentially the places where I wrote would take anything I gave them because they were paying like $12.50, they couldn't ask for much, so I basically went whole hog in a totally anti-academic direction and that's where I essentially think I had a parallel, what's the word, windfall inspiration like the Beats did. Just go for the jugular, if even just for kicks. Truth would be nice but kicks is basic too. I mean really when I started reading in my late thirties, part of it was because I wasn't going to rock shows as much anymore. I had time on my hands – okay, I'll try to read. I read a lot of Faulkner at first because I knew that he was a tough read, he was hard to read, and I loved it. I love the kind of mischief he was doing in that direction, creating unreadable pages where you had to – you'd need a pickaxe to get it, what was going on. And I read William Burroughs, who seemed to me to be the playful version of Faulkner but even more unreadable at times, and then I read James Joyce, Joseph Conrad and I read Kerouac a whole bunch. I think the first full novel, the first one that I finished, that struck me as creative and powerful as anything I could imagine in the English language was

Big Sur, the great now-I-begin-to-die novel, and it's like he goes back, he tells this tale of absolute misery and the end of the road. It has an account of the last time he ever tries to hitch, on the road to San Francisco, and nobody picks him up and the road is hot, he gets blisters on his feet, and by the end of the book he's got the DTs. And of course he goes home to his mother to write the book. He was somebody who was driven to write from an early age, whatever that's about. I still don't know what that's about. If you're addicted to it you do it, but I wouldn't wish writing on a dog, but still I go on. But in any case he told Burroughs that by the time he was 21 he'd already written over a million words and that's the stuff, the junk they're putting out these days, his apprentice novels, like *The Sea Is My Brother* and so forth, stuff that he didn't even regard as especially publishable when he was alive. But he had to, to get to the point where he could write a novel in three days, he had to have done a lot of, you know, crap, and so he did, he did the backstory, he served his time as an apprentice and even to the end he was writing a lot of silly things and great things and whatever, but mainly he just had to write, and as a writer myself I still don't know what that's about.

MG: It sounds like from what you just said – I mean I was going to ask you if you think he was an important writer – but it sounds like you definitely do.

RM: Sure. I mean he wrote some garbage. I think *Satori in Paris* is just a waste of time. It's like Grove Press gave him some money, he had an inkling that his ancestors came from Brittany, so he was going to go to some archive in Paris and check out his family background. He ends up in Paris and he's just drunk and drunker and drunker and he ends up coming back without a story. It's quite sad but in a way it's a very fun account of being a drunk, and yet I can read it, having heard Jack read his own stuff aloud – there's about three or four albums worth of material, you hear his voice, you hear his cadences – and I was able to read *Satori in Paris* in his voice and it was bearable. Like *Pic*, which was the first thing to come out after he was dead, which is an account of – it's told in dialect – a southern black kid who's running away from home or whatever, and it was something he'd done years before that was lying around, he wasn't making a dime anymore so Grove Press paid him to finish *Pic*, in which this kid is on the road and his idea of the ending was, wow, this kid is on the road and he runs into Jack and Neal, wouldn't that be great, and his mother says, 'No, Jack,' his mother says, 'Why don't you have him become a Catholic?' 'Great ending, ma,' and that's what he does. And so it's a fairly absurd project all together, but I read it hearing Jack's voice and it was great. Ad hominem.

MG: Why do you think Kerouac's an important writer?

RM: Well, who is? I'd say my favourite writers in the English language are Faulkner, Joyce, William Burroughs, Kerouac, Beckett, Joseph Conrad and I don't know too many others who are on that scale, there's just something – I can't include Dostoyevsky because I don't speak Russian, but a translation, who knows? But my sense of all the people who've eaten the English language for breakfast and spit it out, shit it out, he's certainly up there with a short list of people.

Another one that I think is way up there, slightly better than *On the Road*, is *Tristessa*. It's less than a hundred pages. He has another one called *Old Angel Midnight* that's about 65 pages, that's his *Finnegans Wake*. At his very best it's magic, an alchemy of words.

MG: What do you think it was about his books that really moved you, that makes you put him up there among your favourite writers?

RM: Well, as I said, *Big Sur* is the great now-I-begin-to-die novel and *The Subterraneans* is a terrific book about heartache, and some of them are very funny. I spoke to Aram Saroyan about ten years ago, William Saroyan's son, and he mentioned that he was in on one of Kerouac's last interviews. Ted Berrigan, Aram Saroyan and Duncan McNaughton went to visit Jack [and interview him for the *Paris Review*] up in New England, and on the ride up they said to each other, ah, Kerouac is old hat, we'll just talk to him, no big deal, and they got there and in less than a minute the three of them realized that he was speaking to them more openly, offering more intimacy than any of them had with each other. He just opened his veins and was so frighteningly real that they were dumbfounded and pleased to discover this. That he was just so willing to be naked on the dotted line.

MG: And normally we experience so little of that –

RM: – in our lives. But it's also – he died very young: 47. He was an alkie and the serious junkies way outlived him. Burroughs made it into his eighties. And Neal Cassady was 41 when he died – he wasn't quite an alkie, did a lot of speed. And the other one, Lew Welch, was 42 when he killed himself. You know Lew's story? He was one of the Reed College beatniks with Philip Whalen and Gary Snyder. His family had had some money once upon a time, but they didn't anymore. He went to Reed on the GI Bill. And Whalen and Snyder – Snyder ended up going to Japan to study Zen. Whalen became a San Francisco poet, and Lew's mother says, 'Lewie, get a job.' She gets him work at an ad agency in Chicago, and while he's there he comes up with 'Raid kills bugs dead', for which he hated himself and he said, 'I can't hold a job that kills the human spirit,' and so forth. He ends up as a longshoreman in San Francisco, doing things that paid enough to keep him alive and thus write poetry, but he still hated himself for 'Raid kills bugs dead', and Allen Ginsberg says, 'Lew, it's terrific, it's all consonants: Raid. Kills. Bugs. Dead. Beautiful.' And in *Big Sur*, Lew is Kerouac's driver (Neal is the past). He drove twice across the country with Jack, and there's a late interview where Jack identifies himself and Neal, they're both Celts, and Lew as well. The three of them are Celts in Jack's mind. They were brothers. His [Lew's] final girlfriend was the mother of Huey Lewis, whose real name was Hugh Cregg. He became Huey Lewis in honour of Lewis Welch. This is true. So when Lew can't take it anymore he writes his greatest poem, 'Song of the Turkey Buzzard', addressed to a buzzard, a California vulture. And he runs into the woods with his gun, he leaves the poem, and Snyder and some people find it. Snyder organizes a posse of 40 people and they go in the woods and never find him. So Lew is assumed to have died at 42. He was a drunk; he was a terrible drunk, just like Jack. They were two very sympatico characters. Jack, Lew and Cassady are the three earliest deaths of all the Beats. Drinking had something to do with that, plus speed for Cassady.

MG: Music plays a big part in both *The Subterraneans* and *On the Road*. Can you talk about the different ways that music was part of Kerouac's trip? He obviously was a huge fan of jazz. And that's in some of the books. But just in the words and the sentences . . .

RM: Well, the jazz of his early twenties was bebop. Charlie Parker, Dizzy Gillespie, Miles Davis, etc., etc. Which was in my lifetime. I was born in 1945, and I think of that as the musical high point of my life, the bebop era. When I was a day old – I checked the recording date for 'Salt Peanuts' – Dizzy Gillespie and Charlie Parker – and it was recorded on 11 May 1945. When I was one day old, in the city where I was born [New York]. To me that's everything. And Jack understood. And why shouldn't he like the most important music in the world? It's right there in his midst. Bebop and Abstract Expressionist painting, both of which were happening in New York at the same time, for a complete tilting of the earth on its axis. And rock'n'roll came much later. I mean when I was writing about music myself I felt – and I read Kerouac writing about jazz – I realized that I felt, writing for *Crawdaddy* and all that kind of stuff, as an insider. I was not a neutral observer or any kind of observer. I was a participant in rock'n'roll. The thing with Jack and his era was, I don't think jazz musicians ever accepted the Beats as insiders, and it's a pity. Jack talks somewhere about a conversation he had with Philly Joe Jones, the drummer; he had encounters with these people, but I think he was very daunted by what they did. They were just total musician magicians. LeRoi Jones went on to have one of his many careers as a music writer, and he wrote some terrific pieces about everything from the 1940s onward. He wrote the greatest piece about Albert Ayler ('It Ain't about You', which appears in the book *Digging: The Afro-American Soul of American Classical Music*) that I think is one of the single greatest descriptions of what jazz is by anybody ever, but he was – by that time he'd had a career developing the nuance, the oompah of what there was to say about his favourite music.

Jack was basically just – it was the first time through [Jack writing about jazz]. But I think for the first time through it's fantastic. Better than people writing reviews of the Grateful Dead and the Jefferson Airplane in silly local 'zines in San Francisco. Which was claptrap mostly, and it was a while before anybody was able to come to grips with psychedelic music, but Jack writes cogently about Dexter Gordon, Wardell Gray, he writes about R&B (he mentions Wynonie Harris in *On the Road*) . . . And later some of these bios claim that he liked George Shearing. Well, Neal liked George Shearing – a blind English piano player, wasn't even viable cocktail music. But like many things white in the '50s, it was popular. So Neal goes hogwild over George Shearing and tolerant Jack doesn't burst the bubble.

MG: It's interesting how bebop is happening while Jack is writing, and while he was living the stuff that he then wrote about, and then when he wrote about those times bebop influenced how he wrote.

RM: I don't know how directly, or specifically, it influenced his prosody, the structure of his word spew, but I used to imagine when I was writing on different keyboards how it would feel, I'd put on music, way before I had a computer, I'd be playing Thelonious Monk or Cecil Taylor while I wrote, because it felt like an accompaniment for what I was doing with my fingers. And sometimes I put on tenor sax music and I had to take it off because it felt too much like a human voice speaking to me and it was, what's the word, it didn't enable me to occupy my own mind. It drew me out. So I felt that keyboard music was the most effective, and least distractive while I wrote. As far as what I listened to when I wasn't writing, I listened to everything.

MG: So you don't think that the rhythms of music, the improvisational ways that a solo might go in jazz, you don't think that . . .

RM: Well, certainly it affected Jack but I don't think that one-to-one you could say, oh, this feels more like Wardell Gray than Illinois Jacquet, you know. In general, sure. He was writing improvised prose.

MG: Had anyone done that before him?

RM: Once you had the radio and the Victrola, I'm sure writers listened to music while they wrote. I would think. Ginsberg wrote an account of how he met Jack and the whole crew. First he met Lucien Carr, he was in the university dorm, he hears something at the end of the hall, someone's playing a classical record, 'I wonder if that's the Brahms Quintet?' Brahms' Piano Quintet. And he knocks on Lucien's door and says, 'Is that the Brahms Quintet?' 'Oh yeah, come on in.' And through Lucien he [Ginsberg] met Burroughs and Jack, and in any case I'm sure Lucien also went to see Charlie Parker, but likewise Jack mentions *Fidelio*, Beethoven's opera, 40 pages into *On the Road*. Jack was worldly and 'cultured' enough, but he was drawn to bebop and R&B.

MG: You once compared Kerouac's writing to the playing of Charlie Parker.

RM: Sure.

MG: Can you talk about that?

RM: Well, there's a solo Charlie Parker did when he was 24 years old, a session I think in early '45, with Red Norvo, the vibes player (Norvo actually appears as himself in the original *Ocean's 11*), but anyway, it was a sextet. Charlie, Dizzy Gillespie and a bunch of swing era people, and he did a lot of takes, maybe six sides, several takes of each, and there's this one called 'Congo Blues', which is credited to, it's a Dizzy Gillespie composition. And it opens – and early Dizzy is my favourite Dizzy, because he doesn't know exactly what he's doing – he's just breathing in large gulps of ideas and sometimes he even sounds like Mozart and he takes this very decent solo and then Parker comes in [RM imitates a sax solo] and it's like vroom, blowing the roof off, he just ascends into this roar of joy and he's 24 years old and he'd probably already played a million hours himself, he was fully formed at 24 and he could do many, many kinds of utterance and nuance and syntax and leaps of logic and all of that, and then he had this whole period, he went West, he ended up in Camarillo, he's living a fairly dangerous life, to be black visiting Hollywood in 1947 was dangerous. Hollywood was one of these don't-let-the-sun-set-on-you – he'd play a gig in Hollywood and then they'd escort him to the boundaries of some other municipality. And Jack honoured more than just the art of the black man, the very day-to-day oompah of black life had its direct appeal to him. There are some who think his writings about that kind of thing straddle racism, but Eldridge Cleaver in *Soul On Ice* quotes Jack from *On the Road* going to some black part of Denver and just says it's remarkable writing. That this white guy could understand and dig it. And everything about Jack and company, it was just the full frontal embracing of everything. Everything they deemed to matter. But as far as the music that he mentions, he saw Ornette Coleman and he liked him. He liked Cecil Taylor. The people he would still go see, like at the Five Spot or wherever, by the late '50s early '60s, I just think that he was – I don't know that he ever embraced rock'n'roll. He was probably too old for it by then. It was a teenage music. He was never more than an adolescent in many ways anyway, but topically I don't think he would have listened to Sonny and Cher.

MG: If you were going to suggest some jazz albums that represent the music that Kerouac was into, what would they be?

RM: Well anything that Charlie Parker did on the Dial label. There are all kinds of CD collections. Dial and Savoy, those two labels. There might even be a four-, five-CD collection of the Dial and Savoy combined.

MG: Are there other albums by other artists that you would suggest?

RM: Well, Dexter Gordon and Wardell Gray did a series of things with names like 'The Chase' and 'The Steeplechase'. Kerouac specifically mentions 'The Hunt' in *On the Road*.

MG: What about Lester Young?

RM: Well, Lester Young had been playing with Count Basie in the late 1930s when Jack would have been at Horace Mann (Horace Mann School in the Bronx), where they sent him for prep for Columbia. Lester Young was a principal influence on Charlie Parker. Lester Young was a guy who took the entire lower register of tenor sax and turned it upside down. Lester once said to Coleman Hawkins (who played this deep meaty lower body kind of thing), 'You play like everything is connected to your stomach. I'm playing from my head.' And it would sound very ethereal, if that's the right word, compared to other people who played tenor. And Charlie Parker, who played alto, was influenced by Lester on tenor. He said, 'Everything that Lester played was out of this world.' He was older than Parker and the boppers. He ended up being brutalized during World War II. They drafted him, he was already in his late thirties, they drafted him and stationed him in some white town in the South where all these white sergeants beat the shit out of him, clubbed him, things like that, and he never really recovered. His playing went from being very ethereal to very heart-on-his-sleeve, welcome-to-my-pain. But I'm sure all of that appealed to Jack.

MG: In *The Subterraneans* Kerouac has this incredible scene where he's (Leo Percepied in the novel) describing Charlie Parker. '... up on the stand Bird Parker with solemn eyes who'd been busted fairly recently and had now returned to a kind of bop dead Frisco but had just discovered or been told about the Red Drum, the great new generation gang wailing and gathering there, so here he was on the stand, examining them with his eyes as he blew his now-settled-down-into-regulated-design "crazy" notes – the booming drums, the high ceiling ...' And then Percepied imagines that Charlie Parker can see from the stand his budding love affair with Mardou and how it will end. He, Parker, knowing it won't last.

RM: He's just feeling very self-conscious there. Jack is. I mean it always seemed like it was doomed to him. But I'm trying to think of others – in *Big Sur* there's this character who hangs around in the beginning who is just some hipster kid that Jack hates, he's trying to sing like Chet Baker, trying to imitate Chet Baker, and this just offends Jack no end, and I'm sure that Chet Baker offended Jack as well. Like a matinee idol who imitates Miles Davis passing for the state of the art. I mean to this day there are people who regard Chet Baker as a hipster icon. He probably did more heroin, all the days of his life combined, than anybody else.

MG: At one point in *The Subterraneans* he describes Mardou hearing bop as this mystical enlightenment:

> ... She stood in drowsy sun suddenly listening to bop as if for the first time as it poured out, the intention of the musicians and of the horns and instruments suddenly a mystical unity expressing itself in waves like sinister and again electricity but screaming with palpable aliveness the direct *word* from the vibration, the interchanges of statement, the levels of waving intimation, the smile in sound, the same living insinuation in the way her sister'd arranged those wires wriggled entangled and fraught with intention ...

RM: He's looking for – I know what that's about. He wants to imagine this woman he loves as being everything she could possibly be. I had a wife for five years; I projected everything onto her. And Mardou, she was never self-conscious of any of those things, yet Jack saw her as being at one with that consciousness. I just think that he's a fool in love.

MG: As you were talking, I was thinking, seeing her so unselfconscious in that way, perhaps he was wishing he could be that unselfconscious.

RM: Well, sure. His relationship to her, she [Alene Lee] said later on in interviews, that she never had any idea that he took her that seriously. 'Like what? You're in love with me?' And they broke up when she fucked Gregory Corso. Jack just couldn't live with that. [*Laughs*] He forgave Gregory of course. It was a very dubious relationship at all times, and I think it's terrific. It's his only 'true love forever' novel. I mean compare it to Philip Roth, one of his early novels, *Goodbye Columbus*. He has this relationship and the girlfriend gets a diaphragm and the mother discovers it. Ooh, how terrible! That's Philip Roth's boy–girl novel, and *The Subterraneans* is the real thing, i.e. revelatory of the crazy fool's gold that is love.

MG: The late Lester Bangs, at least initially, was probably more influenced by Kerouac ...

RM: He read much more of that stuff early on than I did.

MG: You and Lester pioneered a distinctive, some might say gonzo, writing style *before* Hunter S. Thompson.

RM: Sure.

MG: So in a way the Beat aesthetic, through the two of you, went on to influence a whole genre of rock criticism.

RM: I would guess. But Lester also read more. We'd have these arguments. He read but didn't like Henry Miller. He thought that Bukowski was the better Henry Miller, and he'd read these things like *Les Chants de Maldoror*, classic French – I never read any of those books but he read a bunch and he read for kicks at a time when I didn't read for kicks. But then again he would use the word 'beatnik' in a very pejorative sense. Once I had a column in *Creem*, he was my editor, and I sent him a bunch of poems and he rejected them saying I will not print any beatnik shit in this magazine. Okay.

MG: So what was that about?

RM: He was just no fun. [*Laughs*] Ultimately. And that's the other thing, I mean a lot of Beats per se, at least some of them, were real squares. Regardless of their dedication to this, that and the other, some of them were unreconstructed academics, like John Clellon Holmes, who shared a birthday with Kerouac, and they got together every year and got drunk together and he wrote several memoirs about Jack and it really just seems like they had nothing in common except a birthday. Jack wouldn't pass up an opportunity to get drunk. And Holmes did a chapbook about Kerouac visiting him. The last time Kerouac visited, he lived in Old Saybrook, Connecticut, and all Jack did was drink. They didn't have one conversation, and Holmes said 'How sad, how sad.' He was looking for Jack to be something of a serious academic, at heart, which he never was. Or maybe was quite early, but not later. They would say to each other: Kerouac was Thoreau and Holmes was Emerson. They were both from New England, so they compared themselves to these New Englanders, but there was no mesh to it, it was just talk and speculation. Holmes had the first official beatnik novel published, *Go* – Jack was very jealous. And it's a book where he has Ginsberg, Cassady, all those people are characters, and it's very academic, it's a very dreary book. It just ends up dismally. Holmes did not see the joy in these people's lives. Even the occasional joy. Some of these other people – Ginsberg became an academic as the years passed. And he won a National Book Award and began wearing sports coats more often. And his writing got much less, there was much less of the feral in his poems. Which reminds me, Ginsberg and HIS relationship to jazz. Allen could hear it, but what was he hearing? His great masterpiece 'Howl', a dandy poem, game changer in world poetry, but he claimed he got it from 'Lester Leaps In', Lester Young's quasi-R&B rave-up. The 'best minds of my generation' opening, that was supposed to be – 'Lester Leaps In' was supposed to be its rhythmic basis. Nope. No way. Allen had a tin ear!

MG: When *On the Road* was published it very quickly became really popular, but critics at the time wrote some pretty nasty things about it.

RM: Right. You know what John Updike wrote in his review for the *New Yorker*? It was called 'On the Sidewalk'. 'Oh this crazy kid, he's driving his tricycle in the street, get it back on the sidewalk.' He thought these people Jack wrote about were just a bunch of uncouth children.

MG: Some of the critics couldn't separate what was in the book, the story of the book and the people in it, from the writer. On a certain level there wasn't a separation, but if you look at it as a novel, even at that time, there would have been a lot to appreciate about it.

RM: Sure, but most book reviewers are creeps. Always were, always will be. I would say about myself, I have gotten very few fair reviews. The only time I got reviewed in the *New York Times*, they said, 'He seems so intelligent, why does he write like he comes from the gutter?' Okay? Somebody else called me, another critic out of New York called me 'a Hunter Thompson without hope'. I would hope that Hunter Thompson had no hope. But anyway, Jack was, throughout his life he was disturbed by the press. I mean he's lucky he got the original review in the *New York Times*. Their regular reviewer was on vacation. So the backup reviewer did the review and he was delivered to the world. Could have easily not happened.

MG: Not only was how he was writing different, but what he was writing about was different.

RM: Anybody can write about anything. Saul Bellow, once in a while, would write about things on the seamy side of life, but Jack's writing persona, his narrative voice, was of the other side as well.

MG: Right. He was inside it. He was inside it and he's telling you about it.

RM: Burroughs, whose all-time favourite writer was F. Scott Fitzgerald strangely enough, he thought Jack had the impact of Fitzgerald. Fitzgerald wrote about the Jazz Age to a bunch of jokers in the '20s and Jack delivered the whole counterculture and beyond to the '50s.

MG: Do you think that interest in Kerouac at this point is, on some level, nostalgia for the past?

RM: Everything today in the purview of the youth of America, or whoever it is that anything is being marketed to, is that superficial. I mean it's for people who think everything went to hell when they shot Kennedy, that that's American history. You know, that Richard Nixon ended the Vietnam War, as opposed to being its major protagonist. The movies they've made lately based on Kerouac – they did a terrible, terrible version of *On the Road* that's almost like a feminist sob story in some areas. Doesn't matter if Kerouac was a misogynist at times, but that simply wasn't the oompah of *On the Road*. They made a movie of *Big Sur*, it's just absolutely terrible, but it has an actor I didn't know who looked like Jack, so they got that, but they had George Peppard play Jack in the film version of *The Subterraneans*. John Heard in *Heart Beat*. For one thing, literary figures, nostalgia for literary figures – what do you think?

MG: I think there are many levels. Nostalgia probably is a factor for some readers. I think there are people who appreciate the writing. I can only imagine if someone today is 16 and they happen to read *On the Road* then things are going to appeal to them about that book that are different than someone who is 40 or older ...

RM: There was a book that came out in '72 by Emmett Grogan, *Ringolevio*. A lot of people read it when it came out, and it's a very forcible, intentional hard sell on the kind of things Jack Kerouac just had fun with. It's just telling you until it's maddening about how – he's [Grogan] already complaining about Abbie Hoffman, about how dare Abbie Hoffman do something called *Steal This Book*, we won't be able to steal food and give it out free anymore. It's a good book but it's not – it's a manifesto. I mean *On the Road* is not a manifesto. I think more people should read *Ringolevio* and they don't. There was a book called *I, Jan Cremer* that Grove Press published, about a guy's sexual exploits, it was a Grove Press bestseller in 1965 or so, but nobody remembers it. He's Dutch or something. Translated by Alexander Trocchi – the Scottish Beat.

I wrote this book in 1995. It was my novel. *The Night Alone*. It was my version of my mess and welcome to it. Here we go. And it got me nowhere. The book starts out where I say if you want to kill me, and I know you do, and give a bunch of suggestions for how you can kill me. And the best review I got was from someone who could really understand what fun I was having from the word go with this opening. 'Oh just like any novel, it begins with suggestions for killing the author.' But all the other reviews I got were like 'Where is this guy coming from?' I spent six years on it. My mother taught me, she really had no right, she taught me that merit is rewarded. Yeah, right. And so I grew up with that. Jack grew up with that. And it's possible that today's kids have not grown up with that. All the better. Jack was a French-Canadian Catholic who didn't speak English until he was five [some sources say age six]. So in some ways you could say he's like Joseph Conrad. English is his second language. It's one reason he had such glee dancing with words. But in any case, whatever he was, in 2000 I had this other book, *A Whore Just Like the Rest*, my collection of rock writings. I did a reading at City Lights for that, and I got to share a bottle of red wine with Ferlinghetti, who is one of the bigger squares of the whole bunch, and we talked about Jack and various things. Like he posthumously published Jack's book, *Pomes All Sizes*, but the first printing left Jack's name off of the spine and everybody thought this was intentional, because in *Big Sur* Jack refers to Ferlinghetti not as one of his fellow writers but an affable entrepreneur, and Ferlinghetti was very pissed about that. So I asked him. 'Oh no no no,' and he says Jack looks better than ever today. This is the year 2000. And I don't know how he looks now, but I'd be happy if he looks like anything at all.

MG: Any other thoughts?

RM: I was looking at Jack's letters, his two-volume set of letters. They're not the complete letters. There's plenty of other stuff. But some of it, the letters to Cassady towards the end are very very telling. He just came to loathe Cassady. Like whatever year it was when Kesey's bus came to town and Neal was driving, they stopped at Millbrook to meet with Tim Leary, and next they were in New York and they had a big party. Ginsberg invites Jack. 'Neal's going to be there' – and that's where you get these famous photos. At some point, Abbie Hoffman took an American flag and wrapped it around Jack's shoulders, and Jack was pissed off and folded the flag – so there are photos of him holding the flag. If you see the whole contact sheet he had a little fun himself with that, but the ones they print, they want it to indicate that Jack was exasperated with these people. In any case, he hooked up with Neal; Jack was living in Northport on Long Island at the time, and Neal and his girlfriend drove out to visit Jack and his mother, and Jack has a letter to Neal about that: 'You motherfucker, how do I know that your car wasn't stolen, imagine if my mother got into all kinds of trouble because of you. Your girlfriend stole some really good chocolates out of the refrigerator,' and on and on. That's his last words to Neal. So. There are a lot of letters like that that are very telling about the way his friendships went in the final years, and a lot of the letters are, you would say, depressing.

Note

1   Philip Whalen, *Goofbook for Jack*, Michael Rosenberg (ed.), Guerneville, CA: Big Bridge Press, 2001.

CHAPTER 10
THE GRATEFUL DEAD: JACK MANIFESTED AS MUSIC
Brian Hassett

The Grateful Dead were Jack manifested as music.

Their essence was born of the road and adventures. They worked in improvisational music much like spontaneous prose. They broke every rule in showbiz . . . then broke every concert record there is – just as Kerouac broke every rule of grammar then had over 50 books in print.

Like Jack, the band had a prolific career whose output spanned multiple genres and decades, had many different co-conspirators, and found inspiration in the mythical characters of the West and the open Road. And they both considered Neal Cassady their driving force – in fact he literally drove each of them On the Road.

Both the Beats & the band had a core member who drank himself to an early grave, and others who spent considerable time & effort exploring the benefits of psychotropic drugs. Both groups were largely based out of San Francisco, and both had New York as their other home. And in fact it was the very same neighbourhoods of both cities – North Beach and Greenwich Village – where each came of age before growing out into the rest of the city and world.

San Francisco has a centuries-old history of radicals, rebellion and reinvention. From Jack London to John Muir, Haight-Ashbury to Silicon Valley, the Bay Area has nurtured iconoclasts and outcasts, fostering new paradigms since its founding, be they environmental or cyber, free love or free jazz, gay rights or immigrants' plights. Hence, when Carolyn Robinson first moved to the city and planted the flag that would beckon her future husband Neal Cassady, years before Lawrence Ferlinghetti or any other Beats ever set foot in the place, it was a town that already personified everything the burgeoning movement was about. It was an outsiders' oasis, a North American version of a European masterpiece of architecture to inspire every walking breath, a multi-hilled town of innumerable little villages, each with a thousand stories pouring out of every three-storey Victorian house.

Jack fell in love – not only with Carolyn and his life-brother Neal: and so much so that he actually moved there briefly with his mother in 1957 – but also with the mirror city spirit of his beloved New York: the jazz clubs, the neighbourhood bars, the openness and effervescent ever-changing characters and concepts that sprung from every 5-cent coffee or 10-cent beer. And just as the Beats' work brought this open-minded life-embracing sense of Adventure to the rest of the world, so too did the music that manifested there in the mid-'60s. Bob Dylan may have gone electric on the

East Coast, but the real electricity of the kool-aid of cool rock came from the West, young man.

The Dead were proud flag-waving Beats who were keeping the beat in a whole new way. Just as Jack took a novel approach to novel construction, the band did the same with song structure. Just as Jack soloed on the keys, stretching his flow and ideas to places heretofore unseen, so did that other J, Jerry, play his lines into a whole new space unheard in music save for the best of Jack's beloved bebop. The Dead were not only the natural progression of the music of the Beats – but also of the very city that was home to both. In fact, Jack was so comfortable with each, he easily recast *The Subterraneans* events from New York to San Francisco in just three days of storytelling.

* * *

Unlike most bands and authors, both the Grateful Dead and Kerouac's popularity only grew after their primary heartbeat stopped – with the Dead's 2015 Fare Thee Well shows in Chicago breaking TicketMaster, pay-per-view and Soldier Field all-time records, and Kerouac having roughly four times as many books in print today as he did the day he died. Not to mention the thousands of Dead-based bands playing around the world as you're reading this, or the hundreds of copies of *On the Road* that will be bought every day that you have this book in your hands.

Yet they both had inauspicious professional debuts (the Dead's first album and Jack's *The Town and The City*) – which in most cases would have presaged an undistinguished career, and certainly not be indicative of an artist who would end up changing their medium and worldwide culture.

And both had an unusually strong affinity for the other's form. Garcia was a voracious reader of books, and few novelists lived a life with as strong a connection to music as Jack. And the Grateful Dead were the only band that either Jack or Neal ever sat in with.

Really it was – as it always seems to be – Neal Cassady at the centre of the whole damn thing. No other rock band can claim anywhere near as close a connection to any one of the key Beats as the Grateful Dead can with their brother Neal. He lived at their house, ate at their table, drove their bus, performed on stage with them, and directly inspired some of their most oft-performed songs – including 'The Other One' and 'Cassidy'. Not to mention that 'Truckin'' is a musical *On the Road*, or 'Wharf Rat' is their *Big Sur*, or 'Attics of My Life' their *Book of Dreams*, or that 'Mexicali Blues' echoes *Mexico City Blues*, or that 'China Cat Sunflower' could have been lifted from *Old Angel Midnight*, and on and on.

But Cassady . . . Cassady . . . Cassady . . . the guy Jack most wanted to impress, ditto Allen – the Mighty Muse – and just as with them, he was there from the beginning with the Dead – on the bill or on the stage at many of the original Acid Tests including their now-legendary first big-venue gig – The Trips Festival – at the Longshoremen's Hall in S.F. in January '66.

On hanging with Neal, Jerry Garcia told *The History of Rock n Roll* (1995) documentarians:

> Cassady was such an overwhelming ... *trip!* He was *so* singular. For one thing, he was *the* best sight-gag / physical comedy person. He had an incredible mind. He would do this thing, he did it to everybody – where you might not see him for months, and he would pick up *exactly* where he left off the last time he saw you. Like, *in the middle of a sentence!* First of all, you'd go, 'What the hell?' And then you'd realize, 'Oh yeah, this is that story he was telling me last time!' It was so mind-boggling, you couldn't believe he was doing it.
>
> He was also the first person I met who he himself was the art. He was an artist, and he was also the art. And he was doing it consciously. He worked with the world. His face could go through millions of expressions and contortions, and his body language was *so* communicative. It was *amazing.* He was like a musician in a way ... It was an art form that hasn't been discovered yet ... something between philosophy and art.
>
> Off and on he stayed in our attic when we were at 710 [Ashbury St]. He had a little camp up there with a mattress and his old chinos, and he'd come in and live there for a week or so, every month or couple of months.

And it wasn't just Neal Cassady they housed. Further on down the road the band began to cover original Beat Herbert Huncke's rent at the Chelsea Hotel until the day he died.

And it wasn't just Neal and Huncke they were in bed with, but right from the get-go, at that Trips Festival, the group was sharing the bill with Allen Ginsberg and Michael McClure, and the following January of '67, they were the climactic band at the pivotal '60s birthday party – the Human Be-In in Golden Gate Park – sharing the stage with Allen, Michael, Gary Snyder, Lawrence Ferlinghetti and Lenore Kandel.

But as much as they were born directly out of the general Beat milieu, it was Jack and Neal specifically who were their core influence. As Jerry told Al Aronowitz: 'After I read *On the Road*, I began to hear rumors that it was about real people. When I heard that,' and Jerry broke into a grin, 'I *had* to meet them.' After first meeting a few North Beach imposters who were scamming their dinner off being 'the real Dean Moriarty' he finally encountered the genuine article. Jerry went on:

> It was Neal who taught Kerouac how to write. Jack was trying in very orthodox ways until Neal got him off of it. Jack learned from Neal's manuscripts. I've read them. He wrote like he talked. He could keep me spellbound for hours. Nobody could tell a story like Neal. He had the best timing. Someday his manuscripts'll all be published and recognized.

In fact, it was going 'on the road' with the real Moriarty a few years later that caused Garcia to make the commitment to the band instead of painting. As he told Ken Babbs for his and Kesey's magazine *Spit in the Ocean* special Neal issue:

Cassady did something that changed my life. It was after the Acid Test in Watts. I hit him up for a ride back to our house, and it was just me and him for some reason. He was mellow Neal, just a guy, just like us. But there was a mysterious thing there. I had a feeling that I was involved in a lesson.

I was flashing on Neal as he was driving that he is one of these guys that has a solitary kind of existence, like the guy who built the Watts Towers, one person fulfilling a work. And I made a decision that night to be involved in something that wasn't a solitary pursuit. I was oscillating at the time. I'd originally been an art student and was wavering between one-man/one-work, or being involved in something that was dynamic and ongoing, and something in which you weren't the only contributing factor. That night I decided to go with what was dynamic and more than one mind was involved with. The decision I came to in the car with Neal was to be involved in a group thing – and I'm still involved in it.

Further, the very last question in the very last interview Garcia ever gave on camera (to the Silicon Valley Historical Association, on 28 April 1995) was about Neal Cassady:

I got to be good friends with him. He was one of those guys that truly was a very *special* person. In my life, psychedelics and Neal Cassady are almost equal in terms of influence on me.

Neal *was* his own art. He wasn't a *musician*, he was a 'Neal Cassady'. He was a set of one. And he was it. He was the whole thing – top, bottom, beginning, end, everything. And people knew it. And people would be drawn to it. He was an unbelievable human being – the energy that he had, and the vocabulary he had of gestures and expressions – oh boy he was funny! Phew! I really loved him. [These were the last words Jerry Garcia ever spoke on camera.]

The Dead's main lyricist, Robert Hunter, who actually met Cassady before Kesey did at a communal house nicknamed 'The Chateau' in Menlo Park not far from Kesey's Perry Lane scene in Palo Alto, said of Cassady to *Relix* magazine:

He was flying circles above me. He used to visit me a lot. He paid me the compliment of saying that when he goes to New York, he visits Bill Burroughs and when he comes here, he hangs at my house.

He was Mr. Natural for us. He would say things and, if you had him on tape and could listen back, you could hear replies you hadn't heard before – multifaceted replies. The man was phenomenal, a phenomenal brain. Yeah, he was a *wonderful* guy.

It was hard *not* to be Neal after he was around. He was such a master of any social situation that you'd learn it yourself, and when he was away it would take weeks before you'd stop being Neal. This was true of all of us. He was such . . . an original. He had such a dynamic life and it was just *packed*. He just enjoyed the *hell* out of it.

Of the music in Jack's writing, Hunter said, 'That's bop!' And he later put his voice where his heart was and read from *Visions of Cody* as part of the *Kicks Joy Darkness* CD, and was the voice of Dr Sax on the audio recording of Jack's play *Doctor Sax and the Great World Snake*.

John Perry Barlow, the Dead's other lyricist, who wrote the words to 'Cassidy' among many others, called Neal 'The Most Amazing Man I Ever Met' (capitalization his). Bassist Phil Lesh phrased it, 'Neal was the closest thing to poetry in motion I've ever seen.' Garcia called him 'the 100% communicator' and 'the powerhouse of the Acid Tests'. And those were gatherings with a lot of power! Imagine yourself at an evening with Neal Cassady, Allen Ginsberg, Ken Kesey, the Merry Pranksters, the Grateful Dead and a barrelful of Owsley's freshest!

At one of those early Tests, rhythm guitarist and band youngster Bob Weir discovered that Ginsberg 'was pretty damn amazing, the stuff he would say and do. So I figured, okay, I'm gonna sit next to this guy, which was okay with him.' To *Garcia* biographer Blair Jackson, Weir said:

> When I fell in with Ken Kesey and Neal Cassady, it seemed like home sweet home to me, to be tossed in with a bunch of crazies. There was some real serious crazy stuff going on . . . For one thing, I had to abandon all my previous conceptions of space and time . . . I thought I was pretty well indoctrinated into the 'anything goes' way of life, but I found much more than anything goes with the Pranksters. There was a world of limitless possibilities. It was . . . God, it's hard to say anything that doesn't sound clichéd, but it was really a whole new reality for this boy. We were dealing with stuff like telepathy on a daily basis.
>
> We picked up a lot from those guys. Particularly from Cassady. He was able to drive 50 miles-an-hour through downtown rush-hour traffic, he could see around corners – I don't know how to better describe it. And that's useful if you're playing improvisational music; you can build those skills to see around corners, 'cause there are plenty of corners that come up. We gleaned that kind of approach from Cassady. He was one of our teachers, as well as a playmate.

Another time Weir went even further – 'We're all siblings, we're all underlings to this guy Neal Cassady. He had the guiding hand.' Describing hanging with Neal, he said, 'It was pretty freeform, but it was also – I hate to use the word cosmic, but I don't know how else to describe it. We were together in this big mind meld, and he would be having a conversation with what was going on in your head.'

At their first show after hearing the news that Neal had died (4 February 1968) – on Valentine's Day at the Carousel Ballroom in S.F. – Garcia made a special announcement, something he *never* did, and dedicated their show to Cassady.

As Phil put it in his Grate book *Searching for the Sound*, 'I truly believe we were channeling Neal that night. The music was such a living thing: growing and changing from bar to bar, with his turn-on-a-dime responsiveness to context and novelty. When we listened back to the show, it was spectacular – vivid, protean, and relentless.' In fact, right away they realized the Neal-channeled series of songs that flowed out that night should be the sequence for their upcoming studio/live amalgam album *Anthem of the Sun* released later that year. And that's what they did, including with live tracks from this Neal show as part of it.

Phil devoted much ink in his memoir to this milestone moment in his life, including, 'It hardly seemed credible that a life force like his, so generously endowed with the *rhythm* of motion through time, could be smothered and shut down at such an early age . . . Neal's death had hit me harder than I knew; I'd been obsessing on the loss of one of the most inspiring people I'd ever known personally . . . I vowed to myself that in the future I would live up to Neal's inspirational example.' When Neal and Carolyn Cassady's only son John heard this passage read aloud he broke down at his palace and started crying.

'His life is nowhere near over,' Weir told *On the Road* director Walter Salles decades after Neal's passing. 'He lives in me and through me, especially when I'm on stage. He was more present than any human I've ever met. What I didn't learn I just osmoted from him. Living purely and completely in The Moment. What he saw in the present was an accumulation of all things past and future. "Now" is all he was really involved with. That's what I've always drawn from when I'm playing – forget everything and just be there.'

And speaking of forgetting everything, Weir often tells the miraculous story of how he wrote the last verse of 'The Other One' with the now-famous line – 'The Bus came by and I got on, that's when it all began; There was Cowboy Neal at the wheel of the Bus to Nevereverland' – on the very day Neal was busy dying in Mexico. He further elaborates that at their first show back in S.F. (when Garcia made the stage announcement) they debuted the just-written Neal verse. Great story. Only problem is, pretty much every Dead show was recorded, and you can hear him singing that verse in every version for months before Neal died. Which, on the upside, means Neal coulda heard them sing it.

A much more reliable songwriting story is lyricist Barlow's account of the song 'Cassidy' – in his essay 'Cassidy's Tale' – where he describes writing it about both Neal's death and the birth of a daughter within the Dead family named Cassidy:

This is a song about necessary dualities: dying & being born, men & women, speaking & being silent, devastation & growth, desolation & hope. I didn't actually meet Neal Cassady until 1967, by which time the Furthur bus was already rusticating behind Kesey's barn in Oregon, and the Grateful Dead had collectively beached itself in a magnificently broke-down Victorian palace at 710 Ashbury Street.

Cassady was still very much Happening. Holding court in 710's tiny kitchen, he would carry on five different conversations at once and still devote one conversational channel to discourse with absent persons and another to such sound effects as disintegrating ring gears or exploding crania. To log into one of these conversations, despite their multiplicity, was like trying to take a sip from a fire hose.

With a face out of a recruiting poster (leaving aside a certain glint in the eyes) and a torso, usually raw, by Michelangelo, he didn't even seem quite mortal. Though he would shortly demonstrate himself to be so.

The front room of the second floor had once been a library and was now the location of a stereo and a huge collection of communally-abused records. He had set up camp on a pestilential brown couch in the middle of the room, at the end of which he kept a paper bag containing most of his worldly possessions.

In the absence of other ears to perplex and dazzle, Neal went to the music room, covered his own with headphones, put on some Be-Bop, and became it, dancing and doodley-oooping a cappella to a track I couldn't hear. While so engaged, he juggled the 36 oz. machinist's hammer which had become his trademark. The articulated jerky of his upper body ran monsoons of sweat and the hammer became a lethal blur floating in the air before him.

The Dead's most obvious Kerouac-reflective song is their anthemic Road ode 'Truckin''. Like Jack's *romans à clef*, the song is autobiographical, and was literally written *on the road* by Hunter, with music by Jerry, Phil and Bob. And like Jack's *Road*, it largely defined their entire oeuvre to the general public. The song unabashedly celebrates Road life, Adventure, travelling, drugs, sleeplessness, getting into and out of trouble, and heading out to the streets just to see what you could find.

And just as Jack's *Road* line 'the only people for me are the mad ones' became his most quoted, this Road song's phrase 'What a long strange trip it's been' became the Dead's, and has become so much a part of American vernacular it's been used by congressmen on the floor of the House of Representatives, appeared in headlines on all manner of non-Dead-related stories and in book titles ranging from law to nature, and is even a level to achieve in some online video games like *World of Warcraft* (of all things)!

And speaking of lines that lasted, Bill Graham's quote that was ultimately painted onto the outside of Winterland – 'They're not the best at what they do, they're the only ones that do what they do' – is their default epigram and seems to still get proven by the day.

Another line from 'Truckin'' worthy of Kerouac – 'Chicago, New York, Detroit it's all on the same street' – is brought to life in part by the playful use of the preposition 'on'. Besides the wonderfully surreal psychedelic visual of cities weaving in and out on the same street – all blurring into one as you travel them – but also that they're all on the same road – as in 'all roads lead to Rome'. From most anywhere in North America,

New York (and Adventure!) is on the street outside your front door – you just have to make a few turns to get there.

The song also has a reference to 'soft machine' – quite possibly Burroughs' novel being name-checked. After all, as Weir revealed in a 1966 interview, they considered calling themselves Reality Sandwich at one point! But this song – that never would have existed without the band members' mutual love of *On the Road* – was so resonant it never dropped out of their live repertoire from the time it debuted in August 1970 through to their final shows with Garcia in July 1995.

As their drummer Bill Kreutzmann said in his book *Deal*, he'd read *On the Road* even before he'd met the rest of the band, and described how 'It became influential to me in the same way that certain music was influential. It was jazz, on the page ... it was a boarding pass out of Palo Alto and into destinations unknown – my life's great adventure ... that there was something greater out there, and even if it didn't appear within my reach, I could grab ahold of it anyway, just by believing it was possible. That's really important. Because after that, I started reaching for it. And sure enough, I was able to grab ahold.'

Or as their first co-manager Rock Scully sketched the band's North Beach birth in his memoir *Living with the Dead*, 'The hungry i, Vesuvio's, and City Lights were our shrines. Kerouac, Kesey, Corso, Burroughs and Ginsberg were our holy madmen. We idolized the Beats ... Jerry was 15 when *On the Road* came out, and it became his bible ...'

And what would you say if I told you the most important poetry reading in Beat history was brought to you by the most important teacher in young Garcia's life?

It's true!

Wally Hedrick was the connecting rod. He was one of the six artists and poets who opened the Six Gallery on Fillmore Street in San Francisco in 1954. By the following summer, Wally had emerged as their event director, staging what years later would be known as 'happenings' – poetry and music performances in the middle of an art gallery with a rainbow of participating creative people, many in an altered consciousness. By the summer of '55 he asked a young on-the-scenester Allen Ginsberg if he wanted to put on a reading there. According to Wally, Allen said no. Then he finished 'Howl'. Then he said yes.

On 7 October 1955, with young Ginzy as the catalyst and publicist, Wally and The Six put on a 'charming event' (as Allen called it) – 'Six Poets at Six Gallery' – which became the coming-out party for the Beats. What the Human Be-In and London's International Poetry Incarnation were for the generation a decade later, this was the moment the participants all first realized there was a larger community of like-minded souls than they thought. These were The Big Three public events ... which were followed by Monterey Pop, Woodstock, the US Festival, Live Aid and so on ... but these were the first magic mass moments that spawned a cultural / consciousness revolution.

M.C.ed by the unofficial poet laureate of San Francisco at the time, Kenneth Rexroth, it featured a 23-year-old Michael McClure in his very first poetry reading (who also writes about the evening extensively in his *Scratching The Beat Surface*); a couple of Philips, Whalen and Lamantia; a young nature lover named Gary Snyder raving on about 'A Berry Feast'; and one Allen Ginsberg reading 'Howl' in public for the first time. 'It drew a line in the sand,' as McClure put it, for confessional, honest, candid, sexual, rebellious Beat poetry, and prompted attendee Lawrence Ferlinghetti to send Allen a telegram the next day – 'I greet you at the beginning of a great career. When do I get the manuscript?', reprising Ralph Waldo Emerson's famous letter to Walt Whitman upon experiencing *Leaves of Grass*.

Kerouac himself was also present, but in the capacity of a 'Go' yelling cheerleader and Go-for-wine running ringleader, gathering up change from 'the rather stiff audience' and nipping out to score 'three huge gallon jugs of California Burgundy and getting them all piffed', as he vividly described the night in his Northern California adventure novel, *The Dharma Bums*, where he also mentions how a reserved Neal Cassady and his girlfriend-of-the-moment Natalie Jackson (one month before her death) were also present at this historic evening that's widely and rightly regarded as the public Birth of the Beat Generation.

And wouldn't you know it, but Doctor Wally who delivered this baby became an art teacher at the California School of Fine Arts where a couple of years later a wayward young artist named Jerry Garcia would enroll in what he described as the only school he was proud of attending. Hedrick became not only his teacher but a guiding force in Garcia's discovery of the Bohemian arts, at one point telling the young rebel who was still without applause that he and his friends were the real Beat Generation.

The historian Dennis McNally wrote such a Grate biography of Kerouac and the world around him, *Desolate Angel*, that Jerry anointed him to be the band's publicist and write the official history of the Grateful Dead, which he eventually did, called *A Long Strange Trip*. (There it is again!) In it he shares the detail of how Hedrick 'sent Garcia over to City Lights Bookstore to pick up Jack Kerouac's *On the Road*, a book that changed his life forever. Kerouac's hymn to the world as an explorational odyssey, an adventure outside conventional boundaries, would serve as the blueprint for the rest of Garcia's life.'

Then there was Jack's '"secret" skid row hotel' as he described S.F.'s Mars Hotel in *Big Sur* that the Dead would later immortalize as the title and cover of their 1974 studio album, and which was seen (sadly) being demolished in *The Grateful Dead Movie* (1977).

The way Garcia himself remembered his transformation, as captured in the liner notes for the 1990 Rhino re-release of Jack's three records put together by James Austin:

> I recall in 1959 hanging out with a friend who had a Kerouac record, and I remember being impressed – I'd read his stuff, but I hadn't *heard* it, the cadences, the flow, the kind of endlessness of the prose, the way it just poured off the page.

It was really stunning to me. His way of perceiving music – the way he wrote about music and America – and the road, the romance of the American highway, it struck me. It struck a primal chord. It felt familiar, something I wanted to join in. It wasn't a club, it was a way of seeing. It became so much a part of me that it's hard to measure; I can't separate who I am now from what I got from Kerouac. I don't know if I would ever have had the courage or the vision to do something outside with my life – or even suspected the possibilities existed – if it weren't for Kerouac opening those doors.

Or there was the time later in life when Jerry was looking back in a *Rolling Stone* interview and said:

I read *On the Road* and fell in love with it, the adventure, the romance of it, everything. I owe a lot of who I am and what I've been and what I've done to the Beats from the fifties. I feel like I'm part of a continuous line of a certain thing in American culture, of a root . . . I can't imagine myself without that – it's what's been great about the human race and gives you a sense of how great you might get, how far you can reach. And I think the rest of the guys in this band all share stuff like that. We all have those things, those pillars of greatness to lean on. If you're lucky, you find out about them, and if you're not lucky, you don't. And in this day and age in America, a lot of people aren't lucky, and they don't find out about these things.

Rolling Stone, 1993

Or there were the liner notes Robert Hunter wrote for the *One Fast Move or I'm Gone* DVD where he said:

We have the scriptures of a butterfly dreaming he is a man dreaming himself a butterfly.

Jack captured the guts of his own soul, if not the soul of our times, in torrential cloudbursts of exalted prose, egotistical letters, improbably immature journals – both drunken and sober – for all to see. And he did want us to see. Why? God knows . . . but he did, and we have, and there you go. Maybe so that, despite all, we would love him. And we do. Case closed.

Another uncanny brotherly commonality between Jack and Jerry (besides both losing their fathers at a relatively young age) was how they both meticulously archived and preserved their own work. Whether due to an awareness of their legacy or simply for practical creative purposes, you're hard-pressed to find a writer who maintained better records or a band who recorded more performances. Jack regularly drew on his filing cabinets full of letters and notebooks to produce his next book, and the Dead would listen to how their alchemy sounded out in the room beyond the circle of players. And both these archives would also turn out to be invaluable historically and financially as there were vaults of material that could be drawn on in the years after their passing.

* * *

And then there were the drugs.

Lots and lots of drugs. Miracle drugs. Drugs that could make you see through walls and time and space. Drugs no one outside small circles had even heard of. Drugs like yagé (aka ayahuasca) that Bill and Allen travelled to South America to experience, then wrote *The Yage Letters* about, or mescaline that Aldous Huxley did the same with in *The Doors of Perception*. And wouldn't you know it, but just as the young Warlocks were beginning to stir their cauldron, a great big Bear ambled out of the woods and poured in a bucket of LSD.

Both Kesey and Hunter participated in the government's early tests on the drug at the Veterans' Administration Hospital in Menlo Park circa 1959/60, and a young chemist on the scene named Augustus Owsley Stanley III, aka Bear, knew how to decipher formulas in science books and recreate them in his basement. Suddenly the mind-altering that Jack and Neal and all the Beats had gone out of their way (and into jail) in pursuit of was available in 3D rainbows on the corner for a dollar.

As Carolyn Cassady describes in her rivetingly real *Off the Road*, Jack and Neal first experimented with peyote (to not much effect) in 1952. Jack had another less-than-satisfactory experience on ether with the artist Jordan Belson in 1955, but a much more successful trip was taken on mescaline (the active ingredient in peyote) in October 1959, prompting him to write a 5,000-word 'Mescaline Report', and tell Allen in a letter right afterward that he planned to take mescaline monthly 'and am rarin to try lysurgic next' (after Allen's recommendation following his first trip in May '59 – although Jack never followed through on either as far as we know). He also added, 'if everybody in the world took mescaline but once there would be eternal peace'.

He wrote Allen again about the trip in June the next year, still raving, 'When on mescaline I was so bloody high I saw that all our ideas about a "beatific" new gang of worldpeople, and about instantaneous truth being the last truth, etc., etc. I saw them as all perfectly correct and prophesied, as never on drinking or sober I saw it – Like an angel looking aback on life sees that every moment fell right into place and each had flowery meaning.'

Allen also mentioned that Jack took ayahuasca/yagé in October 1960, and claims he said, 'This is one of the most sublime or tender or lovely moments of all our lives together'; but in a later letter Jack referred to 'visions of horror as bad as the Ayahuasca vision', so it seems he didn't process it very positively.

He also took psilocybin with Timothy Leary at Allen's apartment on East 2nd Street in January '61, and although he arrived already drunk and caused Leary to have 'my first negative trip' (as he later confessed to Allen), Jack described the experience quite favourably to Leary in a letter. 'The faculty of remembering names and what one has learned, is heightened so fantastically that we could develop the greatest scholars and scientists in the world with this stuff . . . There's no harm in Sacred Mushrooms if taken in moderation as a rule and much good will come of it.' This was also the trip where Jack said the now widely quoted 'Walking on water wasn't built in a day.'

He also wrote to Allen about taking mushrooms one last time (in December 1961), and wanting to send a telegram to Winston Churchill, 'thinking, on psilocybin, one baron to another, he'd understand'. And although there's a photo of Jack by Allen taken in his 5th Street apartment in the autumn of 1964 captioned 'a moment on D.M.T. visions', Kerouac ultimately concluded of tripping 'I wrote nothing of value on it,' and never went back.

Where Jack and the Beats had come of creative age breaking open Benzedrine inhalers and scrambling to find leafy ditchweed, their younger brothers were handed a silver platter with a psychedelic splatter. It was the same pursuit of higher consciousness, but at a new '60s Space Age pace. Just as Jack was making leaps his father could never understand, so too did he have trouble keeping up with his offspring.

* * *

Starting before Jack left us and continuing decades afterwards, no single creative entity in America caused more people to go 'on the road' than did the Grateful Dead. They were Jack and Neal writ large. They were 'The World's Largest Travel Agency' – both physically and psychically. Where Cassady expanded the Road trip from a Hudson to a school bus – the Dead turned the bus into a *Space* ship.

They were the music of Jack's writing. There could be lulls and less-than-polished passages, but they were always leading to explosions of unequalled colour and light and joy and life. And like Jack's books, the Dead's performances were not formulaic, conventional, predictable or repetitious, and their songs celebrated the lives and aspirations of the American Everyman, the workingman – like one of their definitive albums, *Workingman's Dead*. They both painted American Beauty, lived on the American Road, sang songs of The Road like Whitman before them, and spawned a trip that more adventurers jumped on than any other in history. Jack may have written the book, but the Dead extended his vision into a functioning Road lifestyle that then birthed a festival culture that is the thriving nationwide Six Gallery of the twenty-first century.

And the band put their money where their heart was – including being primary funders of the On the Road Jack Kerouac Conference in Boulder in 1982 (that I wrote a whole first-hand Adventure Book about, *The Hitchhiker's Guide to Jack Kerouac*). That summit – which included Ken Kesey and fellow core Merry Pranksters Ken Babbs and George Walker, plus Abbie Hoffman, Timothy Leary and every living Beat from Allen to Gregory to Bill to Holmes, along with all the key women from Carolyn Cassady to Edie Kerouac to Jack's daughter Jan, not to mention three shows by the band at nearby Red Rocks Amphitheatre – ended up changing the world's perception of Kerouac which had plummeted to near irrelevancy in the '70s. But that genius of organization and promotion – Allen Ginsberg – in his wisdom, brought together the '60s offspring, as well as all the living original Beats, to rally the troops and share love stories with the next generation of scholars, journalists, academics, acolytes, practitioners and pranksters. The result was an author who had been largely out of print and out of mind began a resurgence that has continued unabated to this day – all stemming from an event funded by the Grateful Dead.

And the commitment didn't end with Garcia's passing in 1995 and the retirement of the Grateful Dead entity. *Kicks Joy Darkness* with Robert Hunter was in 1997, his Dr. Sax portrayal in 2003, and the *One Fast Move or I'm Gone* doc was in 2009. Phil Lesh's tribute to Neal came out in 2005, and Kreutzmann's reverential remembrance was in 2015. In 2007, Bob Weir did a Kerouac-themed show in Jack's birthplace of Lowell, as well as a talk and Q&A with Jack and Dead biographer Dennis McNally. And both Weir and McNally gave extensive filmed interviews to Walter Salles in 2010 for a documentary about *On the Road* that has yet to be released.

They're still on about it to this day.

Love for real not fade away.

CHAPTER 11
DRIVER: NEAL CASSADY'S MUSICAL TRIP
Mark Bliesener

Archetypal Beat writer Neal Cassady and a small group of like-minded friends helped liberate literature and culture from the stale old, pre-pop world it was shackled to. By kicking in these doors, the Beat writers ensured that future generations would never have to endure the restraints of the old. In the process, they would inspire and challenge generations of writers and also musicians to come, as they helped define a more in-your-face, and ultimately more American style of writing. But what music drove the Beats? And more specifically, what music motivated the 'driver' of all things Beat – Neal Cassady of Denver, Colorado?

Angel Headed Hipster or Damaged Angel? Holy Goof or American Muse? To call Cassady complicated is beyond understatement. He truly lived in the moment, embracing the promise of each second to hold a potential epiphany. Neal was the driver. He got you from here to there. An unforgettable, magnetic persona to all who encountered his frenetic force field. Cassady personified action, and his musical soul was equally alight and engaged.

Neal was not a musician. He never attempted to stake a claim in that field (or really any other). But throughout his short life, Cassady was influenced and infatuated by the cornucopia of music all around him. The master of all, he truly was all things to all people. Whatever it was you wanted – Neal was it. And *he* wanted it all.

Cassady and Denver would provide the style, setting and substance for important early Beat tomes and explorations. Colorado's exhilarating big skies and optimistic attitude helped liberate both a way of writing and a lifestyle corralled within the gray urban corridor of the American Northeast.

At the precise moment that the post-war earthquake of modern art and culture was crowning New York City as its undisputed capital, Jack Kerouac, Allen Ginsberg and others departed on the road to Denver – a journey of 1,780 miles from New York City and nearly 2,000 miles from Jack's Lowell – to 'brood and lone' in that Colorado cow town set 5,280 feet above sea level, and isolated by its geography at the foot of the Rocky Mountains. Theirs was a mad quest for all things Neal, and his particular kind of kicks – both literary and libidinous.

Denver was a boom town, wealthy, war-wearied but pumped up. America rushed to the gas pumps. Go, go, go. The direction of the country, and most who ventured on the road, was west. Neal's west. Why trek to this Mile High City? Neal met Jack and Allen while visiting Denver friend Hal Chase and his fellow Denverite Ed White at Columbia University in 1946. Via this meeting and through Neal's voluminous letters,

Jack and Allen found inspiration and more in his amphetamine addled writing style and, most of all, his cool. Denver cool.

Ed White, who would maintain a friendship with Kerouac until he died, and features as Tim Gray in *On the Road*, recalls, 'Neal arrived in New York at the Greyhound Bus Station, I think Hal Chase encouraged him to come with little Luanne' (Cassady's then wife Luanne Henderson).

'I remember waiting with Hal for Neal to arrive,' White said:

I think Jack may have been there with us. We went up to campus and introduced Neal to everybody. That's when Allen Ginsberg was in my class at Columbia. Jack was very much at ease on the campus and had friends who lived in the neighbourhood, though he was not a student as they had dropped him from the football team and his scholarship. We got to be very good friends. When Jack came to Denver it was his first time across the country. He had never been east of the Mississippi and was so excited!

Neal's uniquely Denver lower downtown neighbourhood would provide them with an ideal base for their exploits. In the 1940s, Denver's fabled Larimer Street alone hosted 29 blocks of cheap booze, girls and flop houses serving thousands of cowboys, drifters and non-transient bums on their own endless road trip. These spit-stained streets comprised Neal's world. And Neal was certainly a product of an environment filled with a myriad of distractions and attractions, some previously unavailable to his more uptight East Coast brethren.

Plus, there was music in Denver. Historically Denver was a city of immigrant neighbourhoods with local German halls like the Turnverein and Tivoli pumping out enough oom pah pah music to nearly drown out the choruses of Italian folk songs and Mexican rancheras which filled the leafy city blocks as the sun went down and tired workers found a moment of solace in music.

The live commercial music scene in the 1940s was a jumble of mainstream pop and swing music provided for the youth of Denver at venues like the Rainbow Ballroom, which hosted Harry James and Benny Goodman, and the Trocadero at Elitch Gardens, where the sounds of local boy Glenn Miller kept crinoline skirted Denverites and their dates swooning into the night. Radio stations like KLZ and KOA filled the airwaves with mellow pop and syndicated national broadcasts on their CBS and NBC networks. And, in 1940, KVOD began a continuous broadcasting legacy as one of the nation's first full-time classical music stations. This was also the time when it was commonplace for music to be made at home. The percentage of dwellings with a piano, guitar or other instruments in the parlour was quite high throughout the city.

Neal's friendship with his Denver boyhood pal Al Hinkle spanned four decades. Hinkle, who may be best remembered as Big Ed Dunkel in *On the Road*, also figures in *The Subterraneans* and numerous other Beat texts. Hinkle recalls his first exposure to music coming in his Westside living room.

'My oldest brother played the drums,' said Hinkle. 'My grandfather played the violin, though he really strummed it more like a fiddle. We also had a ukulele and my sister Josephine played that and my mother made up songs. Her favourite were Western songs.'

Simultaneously the Western Swing sounds of Bob Wills and his Texas Playboys poured out of jukeboxes in working-class bars, while true cowboy songs were sung around campfires in numerous hobo camps down by the railroad tracks along the Platte River. Adventurous radio listeners could also find the Carter Family's country music at the end of the dial pumped in via 250,000 watts from Tijuana on border radio station XERA. Or on a night clear enough for the broadcasting signal to bounce across miles of prairie, they discovered *The Grand Ole Opry* chiming in on Nashville's WSM or Chicago's WLS's *National Barn Dance*. And of course, Gene Autry ruled the cowboy music range on the big screen at downtown movie palaces like the Paramount and Center theatres. And perhaps most importantly – there was jazz.

Segregated Denver's Five Points neighbourhood (the Harlem of the West) provided the only safe haven for blacks between Kansas City and Los Angeles, and featured a variety of hot spots jumpin' with jive. The Rossiarian Hotel, which hosted Ella Fitzgerald, Charlie Parker, Billie Holiday, Louis Armstrong and many others, was just one of the dozens of bars, music venues and clubs which dotted Welton Street.

Celebrated composer and musician David Amram, who was also a Cassady and Kerouac pal and collaborator, looks back on that neighbourhood which held so much allure and promise. 'Neal took Jack to Five Points when he first came to Denver in 1947 and on other trips in '47 and '49,' Amram recalls. 'He introduced him to a whole world he never knew. Though Jack had been to Harlem and heard jazz on Moody Street in Lowell and had heard all different types of ethnic music in neighbourhoods growing up, he had never really spent time in the environment that Neal took him to. You can't teach spontaneity and you can't teach joyous overcoming of adversity. When Jack went to Five Points with Neal, that's what he saw over and over again. All kinds of people were there partying together in their world,' explains Amram. 'It was a place where Neal could be accepted for who he was. Everybody was accepted there for who they were and what they were. Not for status or how much money they made or any of that sort. It was much more down to earth and profound at the same time.'

Amram thinks it was in Five Points where Neal may have first met the brilliant and often underrated musician, actor and multi-track recording pioneer Slim Gaillard. 'Slim was an amazing singer, songwriter, pianist, percussionist who spoke so many languages and was a brilliant guy,' recalls Amram. 'He was conversive with all the street cultures, neighbourhoods and people who created the music you would hear in Five Points. His scat singing and improvisation was very similar to the way Neal spoke and wrote – of the moment, spontaneous and most erudite. There was a whole level of sophistication, brilliance and fun there, which is often not acknowledged as part of that picture.' Amram concludes, 'Because of Neal's friendship and mutual admiration with people like Slim, he was able to expose Jack to all of this.'

The saxophone and Charlie Parker in particular would strike a life encompassing chord with Cassady. Al Hinkle recalls Neal's passion for music – and particularly Parker or 'Bird' – in their shared youth. 'Even when driving, Neal was making music,' he laughed. 'Banging his hands on the steering wheel and dashboard, radio or not. And if there was a radio in the car, he'd tune in a station with a strong enough signal listening for anything with a strong beat, especially if it had a saxophone on it. Charlie Parker was his favorite.'

Cassady's daughter Jami Cassady Ratto recalls that, 'As a child our whole house was full of different kinds of music.' In addition to her own early exposure to this tremendous variety of sounds, Ratto has distinct memories of her father 'playing' sax around their Los Gatos, California, home.

'Music was on all day, every day,' remembered Ratto. 'My sister [Cathy Cassady Silvia] and I would play classical music and dance – we kids were always dancing. We had routines we would break into at parties too! Mom taught us all to dance and I seriously studied ballet. My brother John would play the Beatles and Mom would be listening to the great jazz albums or Russian folk dance music. Dad loved it all especially jazz and the sax. He had this old sax, I don't know where he got it or where it ended up,' she said. 'But I remember him fooling around with that thing. Dad would sit there in the living room playing in his own way. He never had a lesson but the sax spoke so eloquently to him.'

David Amram sees the sax, and Neal's infatuation with the instrument as 'endemic to American life in the 1930s and 40s, as it provides a sense of yearning'. He believes that

> ...the saxophone expresses the late hours of urban life in a haunting style which is also a kind of paean to the new world and the people who came here with an understanding that we are living in an Indian nation. As Woody Guthrie said, 'Way down yonder in the Indian Nation ridin' my pony on the reservation.' We're living in what basically was, and still is spiritually to an extent, a Native-orientated nation – people who have been here 50,000 years. Neal understood that.

Amram recalls the late Native American saxophone player Jim Pepper telling him that 'the sax and jazz were so linked with his Native heritage that it was difficult to deal exclusively with, and find a welcoming place, to be creative'. Amram concludes, 'There's something so powerful about the saxophone.'

Yet, Cassady's taste in music, and the arts in general, was hardly limited to forays into Five Points in search of solace, sounds and kicks. In a 10 August 1948 letter to his Denver friend Bill Tomson, Neal expounds at length on the absolute necessity of a catholic appreciation of music in particular, and of the arts in general:

> Don't let the huge, foolish triteness everywhere about you come to be a cause of frustration and drag to you: sleep with Dante, feel with Shakespeare, work with

Eliot and Auden, play with Goethe and Proust, sin with Dostoevsky and Kafka, study and see all Paris 50 years ago, Van Gogh, Cezanne, Gaugin, Lautrec, Matisse, Picasso, etc. Do the same with music; with your knowledge of Western music (not hillbilly of course) but western swing. Now forget that Western stuff and convert your rhythm to an intellectual feeling for Eastern Jazz, personified by Dizzy, Howard,[1] Lester Young, Coleman Hawkins, Dexter Gordon, Illinois Jacquet, Vido Musso, Wardell Grey on the tenor saxophones. Charlie Parker, Willie Smith, King Perry, Boots Mussilli, etc. on the alto saxes ... Once you are in touch and familiar with modern music and its place, its problems, its potentialities, etc. you must then dig the classics. Mozart, Beethoven, first, then Stravinsky, Mahler, second, then, flit about from one to another, one composer to another, one century to another, past masters to present masters (like Ellington, Kenton, Gillespie, etc.). By that time, you'll have evolved you own real tastes and desires, and perhaps, do something yourself in furthering today's music.

Cassady concluded the letter saying, 'Just as you are being advised to really dig Literature, Art, Music by me, so too, you must delve into theatre just as fully. The art of drama dear Bill, is our mutual love, with perhaps Literature a close second.' He referred to Tomson as his 'younger blood brother', and obviously felt quite fraternal with him despite, or perhaps because of the fact, Tomson had dated Cassady's future wife, Denver University student Carolyn Robinson.

David Amram saw in Cassady the admirable characteristic of aspiring to better himself as well as all those he came into contact with. 'Despite his difficulty and troubles in trying to figure out a path for himself in life, he always fostered creativity in other people,' states Amram. 'When I spent time with him, I was amazed by Neal's knowledge of composers like Hector Berlioz who had such a handle on what we now call World music and also wrote autobiographically. Neal had a great knowledge of classical music, of baroque music. Music where every note was emotional.'

In 1959, Cassady and Amram both had a hand in crafting what is perhaps the ultimate Beat film, *Pull My Daisy*. Narrated and written by Kerouac, and directed by Robert Frank and Alfred Leslie, the short film is loosely based on an incident in the life of Neal and his wife Carolyn. The cast included Allen Ginsberg, Peter Orlovsky, Gregory Corso, Richard Bellamy and others. *Pull My Daisy* featured a score by David Amram with Allen, Jack and an uncredited Cassady joining them in composing the title song.

'There was a big open book, we all would all contribute a line or two,' recalled Amram:

A lot of Allen's lines were more of his romantic exploits, which is fine. But Neal and Jack both liked the more spiritual aspects of what it was about, 'Seraph hold me steady'. That was all Jack and Neal's Catholic background which they loved and cared about, and which meant so much to Jack in particular. In the film, artist Larry Rivers took the role of Neal. So he had on Neal's railroad brakeman's outfit, and he also played Neal's saxophone.

In this time frame, rock'n'roll struck its claim on American music and culture, and the guitar began to eclipse the sax as a lead instrument. Evidence suggests that Neal didn't think any more or less of this new style than of any other musical form. However, it would be in the rock songwriting explosion lurking beyond an impending psychedelic horizon, where Cassady and the Beats may have had their longest-lasting impact.

In the later Eisenhower and early Kennedy era it was a rite of passage for teens to read *On the Road*. As the 1950s faded, many of the young songwriters and musicians who would go on to write the soundtrack of the late 1960s and early 1970s clandestinely read this book, which was banned in many American schools. Inspired by, and writing about Cassady, Kerouac provided a ride away from home for these songwriting runaways. *On the Road*'s romanticized notion of hitchhiking alone launched thousands of road trips and their resultant songs.

By painting vivid pictures of an alternate reality existing just beyond the safe, suburban borders from which these hitchhikers sought escape, Jack (and Neal) provided both radical relief and inspiration. Via this exposure to the real grit of life, young songwriters like Lou Reed, Paul Simon, Joni Mitchell, Bob Dylan and others not only created a leaner, more romantic lifestyle, but also discovered a cadence and freedom illuminating the way to a leaner lexicon, which would serve them, and the music to come, well. And, in the process, they helped detonate the youthquake of the late 1960s. Though for some who would pick up a guitar and a pen to express their feelings, the influence of the Beats was more peripheral – until the Acid Tests.

In the summer of 1962, Cassady first met author Ken Kesey, then flush with money on the heels of the success of his novel *One Flew Over the Cuckoo's Nest*. Kesey and Cassady were attracted to the spontaneous spirit and quest for enlightenment embraced by both. Neal was quickly drafted as the driver and motor-mouthpiece for their adventures. Kesey and his gang, quickly dubbed the Merry Pranksters, initially held Acid Tests on his La Honda, California, farm and later at venues throughout the Bay Area.

The Tests featuring live, loud rock music and a fledgling light show, were centred on the distribution and use of LSD. Cassady's personal and spiritual impact on Acid Test house band the Warlocks, later to be rechristened the Grateful Dead, is unmistakable and well documented in that band's music. Neal also spent time with Jefferson Airplane and other San Francisco groups. However, his appreciation of this new music scene seems to have been focused more on the live event rather than recorded work. Originally dubbed 'dance concerts', the explosion of these live shows in San Francisco during the 1960s was a direct descendant of the Acid Tests.

In 1964, the Pranksters left the West Coast headed for the World's Fair in New York City, to be followed by a trip upstate to commune with Tim Leary and Richard Alpert in Millbrook. Their psychedelically painted school bus named 'Further' was well stocked with numerous doses of LSD. Alternatively called 'Furthur', this was the worlds first painted 'hippie bus'.

Neal Cassady's impact as Kesey collaborator and driver of the bus, for this initial dissemination of LSD to the American populace, was arguably of far greater influence on music and songwriting than his most visionary early letters, or role as literary muse.

Neal's son John Allen Cassady recalls his dad's immense appreciation of, and emotional involvement with, all styles of music including rock'n'roll. 'His mind was a sponge,' said the younger Cassady. 'Though I never saw him buy a record, he was really very knowledgeable about every kind of music known to man. He'd get so excited listening to music that he'd lean over the speaker as it was playing and point out all the details of what was going on.'

John also remembers an evening during his early adolescence listening to Chuck Berry on the radio with his dad, as they cruised Highway 17 on the way to watch car races at the Speedway in San Jose. 'He was driving a '49 Pontiac,' John recalls. '"Maybelline" came on the radio and he cranked it up loud, swinging the steering wheel from side to side to the beat and banging on the dashboard, all the while driving with his knees. "Maybelline" was kind of the story of his life.'

There was a natural affinity between the cars and girls-centric lyrics and staccato phrasing of Chuck Berry, and Cassady's writing and lifestyle. Neal almost single-handedly invented the notion of the non-stop, 24-hour sex, drugs and rock'n'roll modus vivendi. Back in the days before the music business was reduced to a series of talent contests, when real rock stars walked amongst us, they were a similar force to Neal as master of all things cerebral and sensual.

In his aptly titled song 'Go Go Go', Chuck Berry cites his own influence by, and admiration for, jazz masters mutually appreciated by Cassady, when he name-checks Ahmad Jamal, Stan Kenton and Errol Garner. Also, Berry's duck walkin' stage moves and lyrical humour borrowed more than a little from Slim Gaillard. Did the late Chuck Berry read *On the Road*? Probably not. But Chuck and Neal Cassady both dug Slim Gaillard. And the influence of these innovators still has an impact on the young, hungry post-rock generation via hip hop, rap, spoken word and whatever's to come. This great continuum of American music, now truly a global music, rolls on – and Neal, you know, is still in the driver's seat.

Note

1. A possible reference to Howard McGhee, a trumpet-playing associate of Lester Young.

CHAPTER 12
JIM MORRISON / ANGEL OF FIRE
Jay Jeff Jones

Believing that the secret was simply knowing the right place to turn up; they were mostly young lads, too young and nervous looking, cutting school to hang out in fabled North Beach; in search of a scene to dig, an anxious proximity to chicks, kicks and poetic heroes. Some were so determined they kept coming back for years, got thrown out of bars using fake IDs, discovered narcotics at Mike's or the Hot Dog Palace or the Swiss-American Hotel and were lost and gone long before anyone ever heard of hippies.[1]

Jim Morrison's Navy officer father was posted to Alameda Naval Air Station in northern California in 1957, Alameda being a pleasant island community on the Oakland side of the Bay and within easy bus or ferry travel of San Francisco. Morrison (sometimes with his coolest school friend, 'Fud' Ford) began to make the trip across. When Morrison went by bus, he would have alighted at the 7th Street bus terminal where a morose Allen Ginsberg had once been a baggage handler in the basement. From there he could have taken a long hike across meat rack Market Street, through the Tenderloin sleaze, aromatic, secretive Chinatown and finally down Adler Alley around the side of City Lights Bookstore. Even at 14, Morrison hoped that a carefully composed appearance (crumpled Levis, sweatshirt with cut-off sleeves and sandals) would make him look like he belonged.

From an early age, Morrison was a voracious reader, gripped by books far beyond his years and family social background. During his freshman year in high school, he claimed Norman Mailer as his favourite writer. In City Lights, he would come across titles that no one he knew even knew existed and discovered Jack Kerouac's *On the Road* shortly after its publication in 1957.

Kerouac's foundational Beat odyssey enthralled him, and Dean Moriarty, in all his Dionysian goofiness, was a pure inspiration. In their early teens, introspective boys are often tentative, but Morrison had a prodigal waywardness and would be well remembered as a show-off and classroom joker. Dean/Neal's boyhood circumstances (fractured, violent, drunken family) had shaped him into a feral pool-hall desperado. It was an irresistible type for Morrison; to imitate and method act, juggling buffoonery with soulful poet moods that baffled and charmed school mates. In due course, those routines would equally attract and then disquiet his girlfriends.

As part of his library of Beat authors, Morrison included some of Fantasy Records' zany red vinyl LPs, a mixture of jazz and Bay Area poets reading their work. One of these was *Poetry Readings in the Cellar* (1957), with the Cellar Jazz Quintet accompanying Lawrence Ferlinghetti and Kenneth Rexroth.[2] Rexroth recited a single long poem, 'Thou Shalt Not Kill', beginning with the sparse, angry beat of a snare drum.

> They are murdering all the young men.
> For half a century now, every day,
> They have hunted them down and killed them.
> They are killing them now.
> At this minute, all over the world . . .

For a boy who had spent all his life as a child of the US Navy's 'family', Beat poetry's pacifist sympathies were illicit goods, and he defiantly took them to heart. Eleven years later, conscious of his father's part in the Tonkin Gulf incident, possibly a US government manipulated confrontation to escalate the Vietnam War, Morrison would create his own anti-war mini-drama, 'The Unknown Soldier', and perform it at Doors concerts across the country.

Promoted and posted to the Pentagon, the captain moved the family to Alexandria, Virginia, a long way from North Beach's hip frissons. Washington, DC, had its own, small bohemian scene and Morrison began to spend his spare time there. In his favourite hangout, a cellar café called Coffee'n'Confusion, he gave his first poetry reading, reciting one short poem, then making sure to declare himself as the author.[3]

Growing older, Morrison's clowning around could turn into something more disturbing. Friends who had been attracted to his easy charm and unusual intelligence, felt that he was testing them. The family's affluence and his father's absences at sea gave him the means and the time to form an independent personality and he refused his parents' plan to enrol him at Annapolis (to be followed by a career in the US diplomatic service). The compromise reached was attending junior college at Clearwater, Florida, where he could room with, and be supervised by, his church-going, teetotal grandparents.

At Clearwater, followed by Florida State University, in Tallahassee, Morrison felt liberated, resisted supervision by anyone, and did his best to appear 'mad to live' and 'desirous of everything at the same time', the type of audacious Libertine that Sal Paradise/Kerouac eulogized in *On the Road* and would have wanted to know.[4] When he drank alcohol, which was often, there was no moderation. When he travelled, he hitchhiked, even when his parents sent the plane fare to visit them at their new home in Southern California.

The course that engaged him most at FSU explored the philosophers of protest: rebels against received beliefs. The star turn, for Morrison, was Frederic Nietzsche. Along with Arthur Rimbaud and the Beats, Nietzsche helped add intellectual framing to his instinctive attraction to disorder and intoxication, his indifference to prudence, accountability or self-control.

Deciding that he wanted to be a filmmaker, Morrison transferred to UCLA's College of Fine Arts. His parents didn't approve but continued to support what they thought was education. Although some of their money was spent in bookshops, it mostly went on alcohol and supplies of increasingly available hallucinogens. Instead of studying, Morrison would hang out at Venice Beach, a mixture of faded Beat Generation resort and tinsel town favela. At night he roamed the Strip, the short, pulsating stretch of Sunset Boulevard that would eventually shape his future.

In 1965, with UCLA behind him, Morrison told everyone he was off to New York, where he would attach himself to Jonas Mekas and the Film-Makers' Cooperative. Instead, he drifted back to Venice and settled into psychedelic suspension, mostly camping out on the rooftop of an abandoned office building. In the resolved attitude of his literary idols, he began to fill notebooks with the poetry that came to him as he hallucinated on grass, acid and lack of food. Some of the words came as song lyrics, with imagined, fully formed musical backing.

* * *

In July 1965, on the beach in Ocean Park, Morrison bumped into Ray Manzarek, a friend and former co-student at UCLA. Manzarek was from Chicago and three years older. He had hoped that his Master's degree would secure a directing career. Instead, he lost confidence in his movie ideas and was feeling aimless. Sometimes working as a semi-pro musician in a bar band, he otherwise lay around in the sun, wondering what to do next.

Manzarek had his first encounter with Kerouac's writing in 1959, through the pocket-sized, Signet paperback of *On the Road*: the illustrated montage cover previewed the 'frenetic search of Experience and Sensation' contained within. He remembered, 'it was wild and hip and cool and dangerous and sublime all at the same time ... The first I ever read that said, "There is another way to live, kids. You don' have to put on the yoke of conformity."' He credited Kerouac for inspiring his move to California.[5]

On the day of their oceanside reunion, Morrison was reluctant to reveal that he had been writing songs. With a little encouragement, and in a quiet but unfaltering voice, reminiscent of Chet Baker, he half sang, half recited his lyrics for 'Moonlight Drive', 'My Eyes Have Seen You' and 'Summer's Almost Gone'. Not only did Manzarek see possibilities, but in his head, began to spin accompanying arrangements. He would later declare that moment the inception of psychedelic rock, ignoring corresponding developments going on in San Francisco. He had also glimpsed an embryonic magnetism, a hint of the mojo, that would make Morrison a star. By the end of the afternoon, they agreed that they were going to make 'a million dollars'.[6] In later accounts Morrison preferred stressing a more avant-garde provenance for the Doors' beginnings: between jazz poetry and rock infused experimental theatre.

Ray and his girlfriend Dorothy Fujikawa – the only one with a job – rescued Jim from the rooftop, squeezing him into their one bedroom apartment. Manzarek had thoughts of *Jules et Jim*. Considering the tight space, it was helpful that the Morrison library had been cut down to one box of essential texts, including all of Rimbaud, *On the Road*, *Doctor Sax* and *The Town and the City*, several of Allen Ginsberg's collections and Mailer's *The Deer Park* and *Advertisements for Myself*. At this point, there may have still been occasional money from home, but once Morrison wrote to his parents and said that he was in a rock'n'roll band, the admiral cut him off.

* * *

Sudden, luminous, coast-to-coast fame came to Morrison almost exactly two years later, at the age of 24, thanks to a song he mostly didn't write. In July 1967, 'Light My Fire' became *Billboard* magazine's top single for three weeks. The idea and lyrics that conflated drug-taking with sexuality were drafted by Doors guitarist Robby Kreiger, a well-timed step beyond pop's usual flirtatious burbling. What really made the difference was Morrison's delivery, honed over and over by hundreds of performances, filling the song with a sultry, determined persona. There were also his leather pants, the 'look' that New York-based Warhol 'superstar' and poet Gerard Malanga would accuse him of stealing.

By the time that Jack Kerouac was 24, the certainties that had carried him to New York had come to nothing. The major achievement of his twenties, not fully appreciated until much later, was falling into the clutches of the much-documented Libertine Circle. Among the Libertines, Kerouac had also found Arthur Rimbaud, a further exciting corruption of his wholesome, provincial aspirations. When he came to write a tribute to Rimbaud, he identified his own discord with the inner conflict of the belligerent boy: a poet who would disorder his senses with anything or anyone that came to hand, set against the Catholic, peasant-class pragmatist who became a white trader in Africa. There would never be a divided intention for Morrison; no hesitation concerning excess and sensory derangement. The model of the Beats and, through them, his wholehearted embrace of Rimbaud and Artaud seemed to be all he needed.

When 'Light My Fire' established the Doors as a major new act, the formula of its success was an ace melody, showy but raunchy instrumentation and a photogenic singer, the most commercial track on an album that became a turning point in American rock music. The second Doors album, *Strange Days*, released in September 1967, pushed the boundaries further. By then, the band had a better grasp of the experimental studio possibilities and an increased confidence in its own originality. When Morrison managed to keep his pretty face off the cover, it didn't appear to hurt the album's sales.

Although not quite the singer/songwriter that he sometimes claimed, Morrison turned out to be in the right place at the right time. In 1965–6, Bob Dylan had burned his folk roots bridges and become an underground comet, but in 1967, as far as the public knew, he had burnt himself right out of sight. What the cultural revolution of the mid-1960s presented to the more arriviste rock stars, especially Morrison, was the rise of a glossier rock music media and an increasingly commercialized underground press. It was the opportunity to be taken seriously. Growing readerships meant more money, attracting smarter writers and interviewers. The arrival of New Journalism also suited the subject: becoming part of the story, on the tour jet, under the sheets, in the back of the police car. Writers were sharing champagne, doing lines and feeling the warm edge of rock's limelight. The days of asking pop musicians about their favourite flavour of jellybean were done.

With interviewers that he took to, Morrison's literate and uninhibited conversation was appreciated. He could flex some hip lingo, had a well-stocked intellect and a line in playful cynicism. He could be easier and less abstruse than Dylan. Prior to hiding away in Woodstock, Dylan did everything he could to beat the 'generation spokesman' rap. Morrison saw that another way, a corrective to being perceived as a pop idol poster boy. Despite the much-witnessed misbehaviours – expulsions from clubs and lushed-out performances – Morrison usually kept his head during interviews. A drink might never be far away, but he took care to tend to business. Not the Doors' business, but the venture of himself; to be seen as a writer, a thinker and renaissance man in the making. Long in the future, Richard Goldstein would look back and write:

> Whatever his limits, Morrison was engaged in the same struggle radical intellectuals were waging: to confront both the banality of mass-culture and the sterility of art.[7]

What Morrison thoughtfully took from Kerouac, Ginsberg, Ferlinghetti and other Beats helped him find the tone for much of his fragmentary material: word snapshots and erotic reveries of the American night, lowlife and wild side character studies; America in dissolute and abandoned moods; the underside, the impulses of the fugitive and recusant. 'Our heroes drove at night along highways that rolled on forever,' wrote the Doors' official photographer Frank Lisciandro, recalling a road trip he took with Morrison through the Deep South. At the end of the road, in a New Orleans' French Quarter blues club, the unrecognized Morrison had gigged with the house band.[8]

When Morrison began to make changes in his image, they were a declaration against stardom's superficialities as much as his abdication from the absurdity of being the Lizard King. Alcohol calories had padded him out. The careless beard and vagabond outfit of unwashed jeans, army surplus jacket and battered boots took him comfortably back to a boho asceticism. It also gave him the camouflage to go drinking below the social tideline, down among the authentics, in the run-down streets and bars of the more soulful America that Kerouac had poeticized for him.

Show business exigencies – tour schedules, interviews, performances, photo calls – always kept Morrison in motion. Crisscrossing the country by air, sometimes abroad, he always packed his notebooks and, even when drunk, jotted down the ironies and acerbic revenge of a reluctant pop icon – the alter ego of a frustrated poet.

Morrison's lyrics never amounted to Beat narratives in song, but outlaws and rebels would continue to be key figures, especially in the sulky, bluesy atmospheres of *Morrison Hotel/Hard Luck Café* and *LA Woman*, the final albums of his life.

* * *

> Somewhere along the line I knew there'd be girls, visions, everything; somewhere along the line the pearl would be handed to me.[9]

The problem wasn't just the launch of a novel, exalted by one sensational review in the *New York Times* (and much put-down elsewhere), but the fact that a book and its artlessly sincere, unassuming author could turn the Beat Generation, an often-mocked sideshow of ruffians, into . . .

> . . . *what was happening* . . .
> . . . *what you absolutely <u>must</u> know about* . . .
> . . . *what had outflanked the whole, bloated frontline of culture militia.*

Kerouac couldn't have seen what was coming to him, even after Gilbert Millstein's review had fingered him as the Beat Generation's 'principal avatar'. He had expected the licence of success to open a civilized dialogue with the world. He could then state the case for his bop solo, thought-to-page literary invention, a form he had created for portraying the lives and voices of American outsiders, who would be resolved in the magnitude of his Wolfean tapestry, work-in-progress. The last thing he expected to be was 'King of the Beats'.

Amid all the excitement, John Clellon Holmes came into New York City, invited to attend Millstein's publication party for Kerouac. Instead, he had to track the guest of honour down to Joyce Glassman's apartment where he had been hiding out, shaking and hung over, reeling from constant interviews. In the days ahead, Holmes, who was beset by people who thought they could use him to get to Kerouac, said:

> Most books that come out are contained. That is 'I want to read that book'.
> But what happened when *On the Road* came out was . . .
> 'I've got to meet this man. *Got* to . . .'.
> 'What are you talking about? Read his book'.
> 'No, no. It's not that. He knows everything . . .'.
> . . . for the rest of his life he never, never got his needle back on true north. Never.[10]

Glassman did what she could to support Kerouac through his crisis. She believed that he was feeling obligated; had to live up to the myth, the autobiographical legend that he had already invested years in. Its moment had come and it was up to him to see it through. The problem was, an act of literary genius had implicated the author with Dean Moriarty's demon brio and prodigious appetites. 'All the men wanted to fight him. All the women wanted to fuck him, not in a nice way, but in an aggressive way ...'[11]

* * *

The darker side of Morrison's character had emerged long before it could be blamed on his success. To Manzarek, the other Doors and producer Paul Rothschild, his Mr Hyde was someone they called 'Jimbo': a redneck, sadistic and destructive personality. Jimbo would often appear when their friend Jim was more than usually drunk, quite often when he was in the company of a fluctuating entourage of buddies (or as the Doors saw them, freeloaders, fame groupies and sex jackals); a less formal equivalent to Elvis's Memphis Mafia. Morrison was unknowingly duplicating Kerouac's decline, and his audacious exploration of the American night city had come down to: 'You go out for a night of drinking and you don't know where you are going to end up the next day ... It's like a throw of the dice.'[12]

In 1968, on the back of *Waiting for the Sun*, their third studio album, the Doors were enjoying the high point of their commercial success. They had been working on the new album, *The Soft Parade*, and struggling to make progress. Artistically they had lost touch with their original edge and the material was flimsier and less adventurous. Morrison turned up one day at the Doors' offices and announced that he couldn't go on, that he was 'having a breakdown' and was quitting the group. It was clear, as much as anything, that he wanted to quit being 'Jim Morrison'. Manzarek persuaded him to carry on, at least for another six months.

Waiting for the Sun had used up the best of what was left from Morrison's early, Venice rooftop notebooks. The demands of their new schedules, including stadium dates, and his self-impelled, erosive lifestyle, left him little time or energy to expand or even organize his jottings. More of the lyrics were being written by Robby Krieger, and Morrison wasn't happy about some of them. By this time, he was also reluctant to sing the early, pop chart, crowd-pleasing Doors songs. The old spirit of jazz prosody, riffing improvisations, untamed words from unknown places, continued to whisper in his ear. More and more, his live performances would go off at a tangent, challenging the band to stay close behind, but now and then it was all they could do to save their own skins.

Morrison's erratic behaviour and verbal assaults on audiences resulted in a war of attrition. Some crowds were even drunker and more stoned than he was and they dared Morrison towards transgressions they could hardly imagine. Sometimes he still gambled on poetry, usually 'The Celebration of the Lizard' and, mostly, they called his bluff. What he could have used was William Burroughs' lethal conviction as he insisted on an answer to the line 'Is everybody in?', but that wouldn't be heard until 30 years later, on *Stoned Immaculate*, a Doors tribute album.

Greil Marcus gave the cross Morrison had to carry a sneering proverb: 'Forget about art. You're a sausage. I'm a sausage. The world is meat.'

… sometimes babbling, lashing out, sometimes at the crowd sometimes at phantoms only he could see; he appeared on stage in a fog of self-loathing, and he could hate the songs he had to sing as expansively as he could hate his bandmates, his audience, and himself.[13]

The uncontrollable side of Morrison was also fed by a hatred of authority. Although he could explain himself in scraps of philosophy, his reactions were closer to Tourette's. The presence of authority figures, whether menial officials, airline cabin crew, club bouncers or police officers, were irresistible targets of scorn. He would give them a certain look, not from the insolence of fame, but straight from his heart. Morrison's unpredictability gave Robby Krieger more than a little grief, but he never doubted the conviction beneath it all.

He lived his whole life right on the edge, and people could sense that when he was onstage; there was always something under there, ready to happen … he was totally committed to living the life of the revolution.[14]

The Living Theatre in this prime period was possibly the most exotic embodiment of the generational juncture declared in *On the Road*: itinerant, tribal, revolutionary, communal, audaciously sexy, stoned and disturbing. Their intention was changing the world through electrifying ritual spectacles. The Living captured supporters and enthusiasts wherever they went, and Jim Morrison was one of the most ardent. Introduced to Julian Beck and Judith Malina by Michael McClure at Lawrence Ferlinghetti's flat, he anted up $2,500 so that they could make a move back to Europe.

In LA, Morrison had watched the performance of the Living's production *Paradise Now* five nights in a row, and then caught a flight to Miami for a Doors concert at the Dinner Key Auditorium. His thoughts were charged with the Living's physical disinhibition and utopian wrath and, by the time he arrived at the arena, he had been drinking most of the day. From backstage, the Doors saw a full house packed like sheep into an overcrowded space where, without their agreement, seating had been removed to increase the promoters' profits. The audience was putting up with grim conditions to be in the presence of whatever showbiz hype and marketing voodoo had convinced them the Doors were. It was too much for a drunken Morrison and all he had to offer the fans was disillusion and provocation. 'You're all a bunch of fucking idiots … Maybe you love getting your face stuck in the shit … You're all a bunch of slaves!' He either pretended or attempted to expose his penis and the show exploded, not into utopian bacchanal, but a pathetic riot.

***

A meeting between Morrison and Michael McClure was arranged by the poet's agent and they got together in an Irish tavern in New York City.

We disliked each other at first sight – both with long hair and leather pants – and began sullenly drinking Johnny Walker, which quickly turned to talk about poetry . . .[15]

Since the evening ended better than it started, they met again in LA and then London, when Morrison and his tempestuous, but most enduring, girlfriend Pamela Courson were there for a long break. McClure flew over so he and Morrison could meet with the producer Elliot Kastner about a proposed film version of McClure's play *The Beard*. Instead, they were commissioned to co-write a script based on *The Adept*, an unpublished McClure novel.

With this, Morrison momentarily had almost everything he could have wished for: the comradeship and encouragement of a major Beat poet, one who had featured in three of Kerouac's novels. He was engaged on a writing project that combined an uber-cool tale of motorcycles, coke dealing, anarchy and a mystical journey, with legitimate Hollywood movie making. His co-authorship would be fully credited and there was a sneaky possibility of being cast in a lead role. It mattered so much that he kept himself alcohol-free during all their working days. McClure described the collaborative process as pretty laid back:

Jim'd say, 'You remember that violinist we saw in Sloane Square, man? The kid with the rag hat?' And I'd say, 'Yeah'. 'I want him right here, playing down below the street while the protagonist of *The Adept* comes to the window and looks down'. I'd say, 'Okay man'.[16]

And so it went: the script opened with the busker now placed in front of Carnegie Hall. The scene cuts to a penthouse apartment where someone wakes up and climbs out of a sleeping bag. He's wearing leather trousers and goes to the window, where he looks down. The actual location of this 'penthouse' POV was from a small, walk-up apartment on West 57th Street that belonged to the American actor Tom Baker.

Baker was one of Morrison's other best friends . . . and also one of the worst. He had qualified for friendship through his appreciative knowledge of Kerouac's books, but also by being acquainted with Norman Mailer. When he was studying at New York's Actors' Studio, Mailer had recruited him to help with the stage adaptation of his novel *The Deer Park*. It was a caustically anti-Hollywood book that Morrison especially admired. As their relationship progressed, Baker took it on himself to shake Morrison up and challenge his complacency, not unlike Cassady's effect on Kerouac. When Morrison couldn't think of a way to get into trouble, Baker would usually do it for him. They first met in LA through Pamela Courson, with whom he had a fling when the Doors were out of town. Their compatibility included not only literature and underground culture, but a shared contempt for show business and conformity. Their intellectual exchanges always gave way to eventful prowls through the LA dolce vita: hitting on groupies and getting 86'd from clubs. In the time they knew each other,

Morrison's career went inexorably higher and Baker struggled to get cast in mediocre TV series and biker movies.

To celebrate the completion of *The Soft Parade*, the Doors held a gathering at their upgraded offices and studio. Following his 'breakdown', Morrison had carried on with the album, but disliked the results. The songs lacked substance and had been pimped-up with horn and string section backings to provide a middle-of-the-road lushness. At the debut party, Baker gave Morrison a dressing down, criticizing the expensive set-up, the shiny new IBM typewriters and filing cabinets, remarking:

> Jesus, look at the place Morrison, it's fucking disgusting. You did this, Jim. You financed this whole round-haircut establishment. Why'n fuck don't you just move your whole corporate operations up to Sacramento with the rest of the bureaucrats?[17]

Morrison took a slow look around and then jumped up on a desk and began to kick and stomp on one of the new typewriters. He finished off by pouring beer over the files and papers. The following day, everything had been replaced, as good as new.

* * *

In interviews, Morrison would drop hints of a possible change of occupation, the elusive show business second act. He even acknowledged, in the custom of the times, that pop bands were on a limited ticket; musical fashion changed and a new generation would put them aside. He mentioned he had wanted to become a writer from an early age, initially a playwright. 'There's a lot of acting,' he told Richard Goldstein, referring to his singing performances. 'And it has this one other thing . . . a physical element . . . a sense of the immediate. When I sing, I create characters.'[18] He liked the idea of starting his own theatre group and for a while got close to LA's Company Theatre, until they produced a satire about a pop star that might have been about him. He cultivated one of Mailer's ideas, that the interview was a new artform, and the self-interview was a concept he would pursue. He also discussed writing a column for an underground newspaper, which would have been his observations of life in LA, perhaps 'Notes of a Dirty Young Man' (an interview with the Doors appeared in a September 1967 issue of *Open City*, pages away from Bukowski's regular column). And then the movies, the ones he may or may not have had offers to act in and the ones he wanted to write and direct himself. *HWY*, he considered a good start.

HWY: An American Pastoral was a dark abstraction of life and death on the road, an ART film in search of a point, attributed collectively by Morrison to himself and the friends who worked on it. The completed movie lingers largely on him, the only credited actor and an arbitrary 'killer on the road'. There is too much inconsequential footage, although not enough to make it a Warhol homage. *HWY* is Morrison's half-baked memo of the full-scale, serial killer road movie he said he wanted to make in the future, something existential, reckless and desperate. If he had still been alive in

1994, Stephen Wright's stunning, chameleon psychopath-at-large novel, *Going Native*, would have made him sick with envy, especially when the *New York Times* called it an *On the Road* for the '90s.[19]

After he had some experience abroad, brief band tours and recuperative stays in London and Paris, Morrison professed that he only felt right when he was at 'home' in America. He appreciated the character, the native moods of his own country, and it had provided the fibre of his material. When, at last, a return to Paris, for an indefinite stay, seemed an option, it was the ghost town of Bohemia that drew him, the evidence he had gathered from books that exile in Paris could bring a poetic talent to the boil. But Paris was a muse that ran on metropolitan vitalities; vintage hedonism and constant joie de vivre. It was one of the least likely detox destinations possible. In 1965, five years after an escape to Big Sur failed to restore Kerouac's psychic balance (largely because he couldn't resist North Beach carouses), he set off for Paris, but the Satori he claimed to find there failed to convince anyone but himself.

Once Morrison and Courson had set up in Paris, there was limited contact with the Doors or other friends back in LA. In a rare phone call 'home', speaking to John Densmore, he gave an upbeat report about his state-of-mind and productivity. In Paris, the people around him thought he was depressed and ill at ease. To them he sometimes spoke of not going back, to the Doors or to LA. He had arrived with a list of projects: writing new lyrics, new poems, an opera, a book about the Miami trial, another film idea. The best films, he understood, were as unpredictable as dreaming, but there's a point when alcohol suppresses dreams, or makes the ones that come, unpleasant. What he was really doing, apart from drifting from bar to bar, was staring into blank pages. Nagging ill health didn't help; he had chest problems and discomforts from damages unknown. His beverage of choice, cognac, was a taxing way to drink.[20]

He brought to Paris copies of his films; the finished two – *Feast of Friends* and *HWY*. Thanks to his French film contacts, Alain Ronay and Agnes Varda, these were given courtesy consideration, but no follow-up interest. He wanted them to be shown, so that the people he met in Paris, the people he wanted to know, would realize who he really was. Meanwhile, he used a Super 8 camera to make movie tourist snaps: places that he and Courson went to visit; possibly the later discovered, but unverified one of her dressed in white and running ahead, among the tombstones.

In the apartment, they projected these home movies on the walls, but must have yearned to see his real films again: *Feast of Friends*, for all that was gone (the discarded snakeskin jacket); *HWY*, for all that had yet to happen (the endless road; all that freedom, mystery and chance).

The appeal of cinema lies in the fear of death.[21]

On the evening of 2 July 1971, Jim Morrison went into the Action Lafayette cinema, possibly with Pam Courson; possibly alone; possibly not at all. There are many versions of what happened that night and likely to be others still unheard. If he went, he watched *Pursued*; what has been called a 'Freudian' western, about an orphan boy / man, played by Robert Mitchum. While he was in Paris, Morrison had been offered the role of 'D.J.', the lead character in a film adaptation of *Why Are We in Vietnam?*, Norman Mailer's Burroughsian novel. The director had suggested that Mitchum would be in the film, playing D.J.'s tycoon father, but Morrison thought he would turn it down, saying that he preferred to stay in Paris.[22]

Following the movie, he went back to his apartment, where he and Courson watched their travel films again, then listened to Doors albums. During the night, he felt unwell and decided to soak in the tub. Or he became drunk and ingested heroin, either knowing what it was, or thinking that it was cocaine. Or he went out again, on his own, to a sleazy club, the aptly called Rock'n'Roll Circus. He purchased a bag of heroin and, due to its purity, took an overdose in the club toilet. Two drug dealers carried him home.

All the versions we know have the same ending. Shortly after dawn, Courson woke up, or came to, or came home and discovered Morrison's body in the bath. Firemen were called and lifted him from the water, tried to revive him and then placed the body on the bed. Among the very few friends who knew that he was dead, there was shock, denial, confusion and perhaps a little remorse. Four days later he was quietly buried in Père Lachaise cemetery and most of the world didn't know he was gone.

> regret for wasted nights
>   & wasted years
> I pissed it all away
> American music[23]

Notes

1. Observations from author's experience, North Beach, 1960–5.

2. Ken Layne, 'The Lizard King Next Door', *Gawker*, 17 September 2013.

3. Mark Opsasnick, 'Coffee, Confusion and Jim Morrison: The Forgotten History of Hip Coffee Houses and Beatnik Poets in the Nation's Capital', *Beltway Poetry Quarterly* 3 (2008).

4. Jack Kerouac, *On the Road* (New York: Compass Books / Viking Press, 1959), p. 8.

5. Ray Manzarek, *Light My Fire: My Life with the Doors* (London: Century, 1998), pp. 67–8.

6. Ibid., pp. 93–104.

7. Richard Goldstein, 'Jim Morrison Plays Himself', *Village Voice*, 26 February 1991, p. 36.

8. Frank Lisciandro, *An Hour for Magic* (London: Eel Pie Publishing, 1982), p. 80.

9. Jack Kerouac, *On the Road* (New York: Compass Books/Viking Press, 1959), p. 11.

10. John Clellon Holmes, in Barry Gifford and Lawrence Lee (eds), *Jack's Book* (New York: St Martins Press, 1968), pp. 240–1.

11. Joyce Glassman, in ibid., p. 241.

12. Bob Churish, interview, in Jerry Hopkins (ed.), *The Lizard King/The Essential Jim Morrison* (London: Plexus, 1992), p. 260.

13. Greil Marcus, *The Doors: A Lifetime of Listening to Five Mean Years* (London: Faber & Faber, 2011), p. 20.

14. Robby Krieger quoted in ibid., p. 98.

15. Anis Shivani, 'Exclusive: Beat Poet Michael McClure on Jim Morrison, The Doors, Allen Ginsberg, Jack Kerouac', *Huffington Post*, 3 March 2011.

16. Michael McClure, in Frank Lisciandro, *Morrison: A Feast of Friends* (New York: Warner Books, 1991), p. 112.

17. Tom Baker, *Blue Centre Light* (New York, 1981), manuscript given by Baker to the author.

18. Goldstein, 'Jim Morrison Plays Himself', p. 36.

19. Michiko Kakutani, 'Books of The Times; On the Road Across the Alarming 90's Landscape', *New York Times*, 7 January 1994.

20. Jerry Hopkins, *The Lizard King: The Essential Jim Morrison* (London: Plexus, 1992), p. 160.

21. Jim Morrison, *The Lords and The New Creatures* (New York: Touchstone / Simon & Schuster, 1971), p. 55.

22. Stephen Davis, *Jim Morrison: Life, Death, Legend* (London: Ebury Press, 2004), p. 435.

23. Jim Morrison, *Wilderness, Volume 1* (New York: Vintage Books, 1989), p. 208.

CHAPTER 13

LIGHT IS FASTER THAN SOUND: TEXANS, THE BEATS AND THE SAN FRANCISCO COUNTERCULTURE

Holly George-Warren

'Just like a regular old beatnik on the road.' That's how 27-year-old Janis Joplin, at the height of her fame in 1970, described herself to TV's Dick Cavett, after she'd spent a few weeks hitchhiking around northern Brazil with her then-beau David Niehaus. Thirteen years earlier, in the Gulf Coast town of Port Arthur, Texas, she'd read *On the Road* and had reimagined her life in the shadow of Sal Paradise and Dean Moriarty.

Among the children of the 1950s who read Kerouac's *On the Road* and started their own journeys, many, like Joplin, lived in the most conservative regions of America: in Texas, for example, segregation remained entrenched after Civil Rights legislation and a Supreme Court ruling. A racist educational system and a repressive moral code kept most young women in their place. Yet out of this restrictive environment, Janis Joplin emerged as a free-thinking blues fan, soon to become the most emotive white blues singer in rock. Other like-minded young Texans were having similar epiphanies after reading *On the Road*, including Chet Helms, founder of the Family Dog concerts at the Avalon Ballroom and manager of Big Brother and the Holding Company; Travis Rivers, publisher of underground paper *The Oracle*, proprietor of poster shop The Print Mint and manager of the band Mother Earth (ME); ME member Powell St. John, writer of songs by pioneering psychedelic band 13th Floor Elevators and Big Brother; Dave Moriaty, founder of Rip-Off Press (publisher of underground comics); and Gilbert Shelton, creator of the Fabulous Furry Freak Brothers comics. Together, they formed in San Francisco's Haight-Ashbury in the 1960s a loose sort of 'Texas Mafia' – prominent members of a scene there greatly inspired by, a generation earlier, the Beats in North Beach.

It was *Time* magazine that originally alerted 14-year-old Janis Joplin to Kerouac and the Beats in the autumn of 1957. A bookworm since she could read, she'd become a member of a group of high-school malcontents – teenage boys a year older – who were all immersed in *On the Road*. One of them, Jim Langdon, a jazz musician who would become a music critic and journalist, lent Joplin his copy. She devoured it, taking pause at Kerouac's mention of her Golden Triangle region:

We took a chance on one of the dirt roads, and pretty soon we were crossing the evil old Sabine River that is responsible for all these swamps. With amazement we saw great structures of light ahead of us. 'Texas! It's Texas! Beaumont oil town!' Huge oil tanks and refineries loomed like cities in the oily fragrant air.

Crammed into the backseat of Langdon's car with the bookish Dave Moriaty and other boys, Joplin cruised the Triangle from Port Arthur to neighbouring towns Orange and Beaumont. Joplin and her friends found hope on the open road. They, too, could be Kerouac's 'sordid hipsters of America, a new beat generation', with their 'real straight talk about souls'. For Joplin, *On the Road* was 'a revelation', according to Karleen Bennett, her closest girlfriend in high school. Another friend recalled, 'We were just book-reading, rebellious, and hell-raising, and we all eventually wanted to go to North Beach to join the Beat Generation.'

Among her crowd, Joplin was the first to make it there. During the summer of 1961, she dropped out of college in Beaumont and moved to Los Angeles to live with an aunt. Before long, she'd relocated to Venice Beach, to partake of the Beat lifestyle. She got there just in time for the last gasp of the Gas House, the Beat hangout where impoverished poets and artists found a venue for their work since 1959. Locals had demanded it closed due to the continual sound of bongos and other such nuisances; the city revoked its permits, so it had become primarily an art gallery with the occasional clandestine performance. Joplin would later tell friends she'd sung there.

Eric Nord, aka Big Daddy, who had run the Gas House in its heyday, was spending much of his time back in North Beach, where he'd opened the Coexistence Bagel Shop. Venice's most prominent Beat poet Stu Perkoff, who'd sold his Venice West Espresso Café, had become addicted to heroin and rarely made the scene. His café, under new ownership, continued to thrive, however, and Joplin became a regular. Her new friends encouraged her to sing and make art. But several of her pals were junkies, who had no qualms about stealing from their friends.

Disillusioned, Joplin hitchhiked to San Francisco, heading straight for North Beach. She hung around the City Lights Bookstore, staying in cheap hotels and sleeping on park benches. Jim Langdon recalls, 'I got a letter from her and I talked [a friend] into going with me to meet Janis out in San Francisco. We hitchhiked from Austin. [Getting a ride to Denver], I looked at a map of the Union Pacific line at the freight yards there and figured we could go from Denver up to Wyoming, across to Salt Lake City. But we ended up in the Green River, Wyoming jail, just shy of the Utah line, so that was the end of our adventure.' Adds Langdon, 'We identified with the beatniks. It was pre-hippie. I remember reading a quote Janis gave to somebody, and she said, "I ain't no hippie, man. I'm a beatnik".'

In North Beach, Joplin approached Dave Archer, doorman of the Fox and Hound coffeehouse, on Grant Avenue. He remembered that she asked him in her strong Texas accent if she could 'sang' inside. In a 2002 memoir, Archer recalled that she was smoking a cigar and wearing a sheepskin and leather vest over a work shirt and blue jeans. Archer, who'd moved to San Francisco as a self-described 'wannabeatnik', recognized a kindred spirit. He recalled that she sang 'Silver Threads and Golden

Needles' that night. Soon after, Joplin used the last of her cash to take a bus home to Port Arthur.

In 1962, Joplin enrolled at the University of Texas in Austin, after a visit to 'the Ghetto', a decrepit off-campus apartment building filled with bohemians, including her buddy from Port Arthur Dave Moriaty. Another resident, Powell St. John, was an art student and harmonica player from West Texas. 'When I moved into the Ghetto, my apartment had just been vacated by a beatnik', St. John recalls. 'When I came to the university in 1959, I fancied myself a beatnik.' He'd soon invite Joplin to join his acoustic folk-bluegrass group, the Waller Creek Boys. With the trio, she'd sing blues and folk tunes in public for the first time.

Through their frequent appearances on campus and the beer joint Threadgill's, Joplin met Chet Helms, who thought of himself as a 'beatnik on the road'. A year older than Joplin, Helms spent much of his youth in Fort Worth. His mother's family were fundamentalist Baptists, so his strict upbringing included 'no dancing, no dating'. In 1960, he entered the University of Texas as a member of the Reserve Officers' Training Corps and the Young Republicans. But he soon became a Civil Rights activist and left-leaning progressive, joining the Students for Direct Action (SDA) and working to integrate the city's movie theatres and lunch counters. He'd experienced racism in Fort Worth when epithets were hurled at his Asian stepfather. A voracious reader, Helms became a regular at the Ghetto, discovered peyote and pot, and made friends with a bisexual black student who turned him onto Ornette Coleman and other jazz players.

'At the University of Texas', Helms recalled, 'I had been with a crowd of bohemian fringe people who lived at the Ghetto. We had red wine parties and peyote tea parties. These people were referred to by everybody else at the university as beatniks, and so we identified as beatniks, and we read the literature, and we read *On the Road*, and we had to hitchhike to California. Part of earning your stripes as a beatnik was hitchhiking from coast to coast several times.' Helms quit UT in the spring of 1962, and began travelling like his hero Jack Kerouac: 'I came to California for a few months', said Helms. 'I was very enamored of the Beat Generation in San Francisco, which was the mecca for the Beats. I couldn't get there fast enough. But I went back to Austin, hooked up with Janis again, started talking about the West Coast, and she shared a lot about her experiences in Venice in '61. She was very well-read in the Beat literature, as was I, and she was very attracted to San Francisco for that reason, of course being where Lawrence Ferlinghetti and all these folks were.' In January 1963, Joplin quit UT and joined Helms on the road, hitching together to San Francisco.

'When I think about Janis, I think about what it was like to grow up in Texas in the Fifties', Helms once reflected, 'and I think about a couple of lines from a couple of her songs.'

One of them is 'Why why is it so hard breathing in the air' ['Oh, Sweet Mary'] cause that's what it was like in Texas. It's hard to convey, and I don't think it was just Texas, I think it was America of the Eisenhower years. Texas was an extreme example of it. I've always thought the reason why so many extraordinary singers, writers, performers, musicians and so on came out of Texas, was because it was such a repressive environment and the only space you had was what you created for yourself with your imagination. That paid off in manifold ways in terms of artistic expression. The other line is from the Kris Kristofferson song ['Me and Bobby McGee'], 'Freedom's just another word for nothing left to lose'. That's in many ways the way we felt, and I think the way Janis felt in Texas at the time. [Kristofferson was born in Brownsville, Texas.]

In San Francisco, Joplin and Helms crashed at a friend's apartment in a rundown neighbourhood. 'If we could have afforded it, we'd have stayed in North Beach,' Helms recalled, 'but because of the publicity of the Beat era, the rents had gone sky high there, and so we were forced out to the Haight Ashbury, a cheap rent district.' Joplin spent much of her time, though, hanging out in North Beach coffeehouses. The Fox and Hound had become Coffee and Confusion, where Joplin soon became a regular. Co-editor (with Allen Ginsberg) of the Beat 'zine *Beatitude*, biracial poet Bob Kaufman was still in the neighbourhood. Joplin ran into him in a bar one night, where he was flying on speed and rapping to anyone who would listen. Soon after, following a run-in with the police, he took a vow of silence that lasted 15 years.

In addition to playing the Coffee Gallery for a few dollars, Joplin joined panhandlers at the corner of Grant and Green, singing for spare change, and taking a cue from poets who stood outside City Lights Bookstore, at Broadway and Columbus, where sandwich boards offered poems in exchange for a donation. Joplin wandered inside to thumb through chapbooks and volumes of prose and poetry. She had started writing her own lyrics to songs like 'What Good Can Drinking Do' and 'So Sad to Be Alone'. Next door, a few Beats and musicians still gathered at Cafe Vesuvio's bar. She'd visited these landmarks during her earlier visit to San Francisco; this time she felt more like she belonged. A few doors up the street from Coffee and Confusion, the Coffee Gallery at 1353 Grant was a larger club that had hosted readings by Ferlinghetti and Kaufman in 1959. Though Joplin was underage, she managed to get into the place, with the help of friendly bartender Howard Hesseman, a member of the improv comedy troupe the Committee. She wowed the owners on hoot night and booked a gig there as well. Four years after its heyday, the Coffee Gallery and other North Beach haunts were frequented by tourists as much as folk music fans and bohemians.

Joplin was in and out of San Francisco from 1963 to 1965, leaving for a while to live in New York's East Village. While there, she checked out some of the Beats' old haunts in the West Village. Along the way, she picked up a nasty drug habit: shooting methamphetamine nearly killed her. By the time she boarded a bus home to Port Arthur, she weighed less than 90 pounds. After a year back in Texas, Joplin was beckoned again to San Francisco by Chet Helms, who'd started organizing psychedelic dances with the loose-knit Family Dog and managing Big Brother and the Holding

Company. The improvisational Big Brother wanted a female lead singer, and, in June 1966, Joplin joined mutual friend Travis Rivers on a road trip West.

Originally from San Antonio, Rivers had run an antiquarian book shop in Austin, between attending classes at UT and partaking in peyote. Drawn to the Beats, books and the blues, he and Joplin had an on-again-off-again relationship that fizzled after a few weeks in the Haight. Rivers became the publisher of the underground newspaper *The Oracle*; the paper's operation was in a backroom of The Print Mint, a shop Rivers opened to sell psychedelic posters by artists like Stanley Mouse, Alton Kelley and Rick Griffin. Rivers would put together the roots-rock band Mother Earth, featuring Powell St. John, who'd relocated to San Francisco, and vocalist Tracy Nelson. St. John's song 'Bye Bye Baby' would become part of Big Brother's repertoire, after he taught it to Joplin before she left Austin.

As lead singer of Big Brother and the Holding Company, Joplin found her tribe. Its members – bassist Peter Albin, drummer Dave Getz and guitarists James Gurley and Sam Andrew – had been aficionados of Kerouac. Before Joplin joined, the band had played San Francisco's Trips Festival at Longshoremen's Hall in January 1966, with Neal Cassady, Ken Kesey and the Merry Pranksters as ringleaders. Light shows were created there and later projected at Helm's Avalon Ballroom by Southerner Bill Ham, an artist and jazz fan who'd moved to San Francisco in 1960.

Big Brother's Dave Getz had moved from New York to North Beach in 1960 to study art. Inspired by Kerouac and jazz musicians, Getz recalled that 'North Beach was my scene. San Francisco was just the best in the early '60s. I'd get off work at the Spaghetti Factory and walk down Broadway and go to the Jazz Workshop, and hear John Coltrane, Max Roach, and Art Blakey.' In 1965, he'd lived on Fillmore Street next door to artists Jay DeFeo and Wally Hedrick, who threw parties where the remaining Beats gathered.

Sam Andrew, who was raised in farflung places due to his father's career in the Air Force, had been studying linguistics and English literature at Berkeley before joining Big Brother. He disparaged the term 'hippie' as being a derogatory label given to those who travelled to San Francisco in search of the Beat forebears: rather than being 'hip' like the Beats, they were 'hippies'.

When Joplin arrived in the Haight in June 1966 to rehearse with Big Brother, she and the band immediately hit it off. She embraced their loud, improvisational music and songs like Peter Albin's 'Light Is Faster Than Sound', though she'd never performed with an electric band. 'When I first met Janis, she was not a stranger to me at all,' Sam Andrew remembered. 'Her accent, her attitudes, even her clothes made her seem like a sister or cousin from my mother's side of the family who were all from the same part of Texas as Janis was. We talked for hours into the night, every night, about "God and the Universe", a favorite phrase of hers . . .'

The band's other guitarist, James Gurley, whose avant-garde style was inspired by John Coltrane, had moved from Detroit to the West Coast in the early 1960s. 'There's something mysterious about San Francisco, an air, a spirit of something you just don't feel in any other cities,' Gurley once explained. 'Jack Kerouac had a lot to do with it. I'd been reading *On the Road* and *The Dharma Bums* and all his novels, so that was an inspiration to go to California. San Francisco especially, from reading his novels.' Gurley and Joplin briefly became a couple after she joined the band, but similar to relationships detailed in Kerouac's work, it didn't last and Gurley returned to his wife Nancy. Joplin retained a close bond with Andrew and Gurley after she left Big Brother in 1968.

By the late 1960s, others from Austin's Ghetto scene arrived in San Francisco. In addition to Powell St. John, Dave Moriaty relocated after a stint in the Marines and started the Rip Off Press, which published underground comics. Artist Gilbert Shelton, from Houston, had made his name in Texas via his work as editor of the UT humour magazine *The Ranger*, and primarily through his subversive comics. In 1968, his *Fabulous Furry Freak Brothers* comics first appeared in an Austin, Texas, underground rag, and, after moving to San Francisco, he continued to draw the iconic stoner characters.

As for Joplin, she clung to her identity as the progeny of the Beats – which sustained her from her dismal existence in her home state to the rigours of stardom. 'In Texas, I was a beatnik, a weirdo,' she told critic Nat Hentoff in 1968. 'Texas is okay if you want to settle down and do your own thing quietly. But it's not for outrageous people, and I was always outrageous ... I got treated very badly in Texas.' Hentoff noted her grim smile. 'They don't treat beatniks too good in Texas.'

Joplin's success as a singer meant constant touring; to the end of her life, she would stay on the road. Taking a break in Febuary 1970, she flew to Brazil for Carnival. There, she met David Niehaus, a young man from Ohio who'd been travelling through South America for a year and a half. Harkening back to her days hitching from Texas to California, she joined Niehaus on his adventure. 'Most people in her position at that point wouldn't be on the highway in Brazil, hitchhiking into the jungle,' says Niehaus. 'To go up there, with her position in the world, to already be so successful, that's a real unusual person. When we were on the road, she had compassion for people ... There's nobody I've ever met that had as much compassion as she did.' After a month together in Brazil, Niehaus would spend time in Marin County with Joplin before continuing his own journey, taking him around the world. Following his departure, Joplin would sometimes name-check his quest when she sang 'Cry Baby'.

Joplin's journey would end in October 1970, when she died of a heroin overdose, six weeks after a trip home to Texas for her high school reunion. While there, reporters questioned her about her outsider status growing up in Port Arthur. 'I felt apart from them,' she said, nearly breaking into tears. 'She was so sensitive to the world,' says Niehaus. 'That's what killed her. Cause she had to turn it off.'

CHAPTER 14
HIT THE ROAD, JACK: VAN MORRISON AND *ON THE ROAD*
Peter Mills

> For me, it was Kerouac. I was working with this geezer who was reading all this stuff so he gave me a few books by Kerouac and then Sartre, Nausea. Things like that. Initially you go – woh! – when you're older it's a different take but I suppose I still have the same influences. Even now, I can still see the direct line back to those kind of things.
>
> Van Morrison to Niall Stokes, Hot Press, 29 October 2003

A 1989 edition of the BBC arts show *Arena* focusing on the Beats contained an extraordinary tribute to Jack Kerouac by two people who owed much to him – the sui generis jazz-wanderer Slim Gaillard and Northern Irish singer and songwriter Van Morrison. Morrison read a section of Kerouac's 1957 work *On the Road* which describes the book's narrator Sal Paradise and his roadmate Dean Moriarty 'going mad together' on a night in San Francisco and visiting a club where they see a performance by Gaillard. Incredibly, Slim recreates the scene as described by Kerouac for the camera, sitting at Morrison's feet. The Irishman hurls himself into the words, delivering them with rousing animation:

> When he gets warmed up he takes off his undershirt and really goes. He does and says anything that comes into his head. He'll sing 'Cement Mixer, Put-ti Put-ti'.

The scene is both startling and ludicrous as Gaillard disrobes in front of us while Morrison reads Kerouac's wildly vivid description of the jazzman doing the same some three decades earlier. He first whips off his cap, then jacket, tie, shirt, while still keeping up a frantic rhythm on the bongos he has before him. All the while he chants in a mix of jazz-English, faux-Arabic and an invented scat-konnakol he called 'Vout-O-Reenee' – like other artists Morrison admired, such as Louis Prima, the balance between daring originality and borderline absurdity is tightrope'd before us.

Morrison sits, impassive, waiting for his cue which comes as Gaillard scales back the furious rhythm and the text addresses the musical dynamics of the scene:

> [Gaillard would] suddenly slow down the beat and brood over his bongos with fingertips barely tapping the skin as everybody leans forward breathlessly to

hear; you think he'll do this for a minute or so, but he goes right on, for as long as an hour, making an imperceptible little noise with the tips of his fingernails, smaller and smaller all the time till you can't hear it any more ... Dean stands in the back, saying, 'God! Yes!' – and clasping his hands in prayer and sweating. 'Sal, Slim knows time, he knows time.'

Kerouac, 2000b, pp. 166–7

Anyone who has caught Morrison on a good night (which, contrary to the received wisdom, is more often than not) might have noticed how he uses the dynamics of sound in this way, encouraging his band to 'bring it down' so a section of a song can be explored anew, sometimes even abandoning the mic altogether and singing from the back of the stage, unamplified. In both cases, the 'liveness' of the moment requires the audience to really *listen*. The segment read on *Arena* concludes as Gaillard's fingers gradually leave the surface of the bongos but still flutter above the skins; somehow we still feel the rhythm, even though we no longer hear it. There is clearly a double use of 'time' in Kerouac's prose – time as an idea for measuring human experience and time as a musical rhythmic element, and he returns to this theme throughout the book. For example:

And for just a moment I reached the point of ecstasy that I always wanted to reach, which was the complete step across chronological time into timeless shadows ...

Kerouac, 2000b, p. 164

This sense of breaching the river of time finds an echo, as we shall see, in Morrison's own work, as he explores the nature of time, place and memory in tracks such as 'Cleaning Windows' and 'On Hyndford Street'. It also suggests a connection between live musical performance and a directly spiritual experience as Sal 'clasps his hands in prayer': certain rituals are observed, but, if you're lucky, something new is discovered every time. As Morrison would sing in 2008's 'Behind The Ritual', 'behind the ritual, you'll find the spiritual'.

There is an edit-fade to the *Arena* reading and we see Morrison and Gaillard in the midst of conversation. Van asks Slim where he met Kerouac – he replies that he met him in jazz club in San Francisco, perhaps the same one mentioned in *On the Road*, and that Jack loved it so much he would come to the club 'eight days a week'. This mix of fact and fiction, swirled up so tightly together that it is impossible to separate them, makes the intersection of these memories and Kerouac's work itself something beyond mere storytelling – it feels like a new art form in itself, pure experience rendered live on the page. Morrison's interest in Slim Gaillard is that of a musical connoisseur and fan – who wouldn't want to watch an artist like him at work? – but he most probably will have first heard of him through the very words he reads aloud for the camera; the same pages that have conferred a different kind of fame on Gaillard, from Kerouac's *On the Road*.

Published in 1957, this book and the later *Dharma Bums* (1958) were extremely significant influences on the young George Ivan Morrison growing up in the late 1950s on Hyndford Street in East Belfast. The books seemed to function as part of a kind of information network that he picked up on via the jazz, blues and country records he heard in his neighbourhood, the sound of John Lee Hooker and Hank Williams, the words and voices of Mezz Mezzrow and Woody Guthrie speaking of a world beyond the tight grid of streets of his neighbourhood, and the possibility represented by the open road stretching to the horizon. All of this mingled with the local traditions of Irish music (though at the time, he later recalled, folk music was 'nowhere' to him and his friends) and add to this the nightly tuning-in to Radio Luxembourg and the radiogram-dial listed stations of Europe (beautifully caught in the 1990 song-poem 'In The Days Before Rock and Roll'). Once he began finding his way forward as a musician, all these influences sublimated and eventually emerged entirely distinctively in Morrison's music, the jazz, the poetry, the words, the sounds, the rhythm – even the static on the radio.

> I started … mixing black influences with Jack Kerouac – *On the Road*, *The Dharma Bums*. That was my starting point, the Beats putting poetry – spoken word – and jazz together.
>
> David Fricke, 2016

To some extent, that is what Morrison has been doing for over 50 years, the free spirit of jazz running through his words and music, a mood vividly embodied by Gaillard and Kerouac. So in this piece we will look at how his early reading of Kerouac has impacted upon his work, dividing such assessments into three distinct phases, guided by Morrison's own developing lyrical and musical styles: the unconscious influence permeating his very earliest work, then a more conscious deployment of its impact and finally a more reflective and contemplative assimilation of the enduring energies unlocked by his youthful readings.

Words and music

Morrison is perhaps unusual among musicians in that he has often cited books and writers as being as powerful an influence upon his own work as other musicians. Where we might have had to guess or deduce that, say, Bob Dylan had read Paul Verlaine, or that Morrissey had read Edith Sitwell, and that's why their work had taken a particular turn, this isn't really the case with Morrison, as he has developed the habit of dropping references into songs via direct mentions of names and even specific works. Kerouac is in there, but is by no means unique; rather, he is part of a unique mix. Among those Morrison has called to the table are a mix of American, Irish, English and European writers, of diverse periods and literary genres. These include Henry David Thoreau, Walt Whitman, Edgar Allen Poe, Oscar Wilde, W. B. Yeats, Seamus Heaney, James Joyce, Samuel Beckett, William Blake, John Donne, Samuel Taylor Coleridge, Lord Byron, Arthur Rimbaud – and there are others. We should note that he is equally likely to cite fellow musicians – John Lee Hooker, Chet Baker – and fellow Belfast 'homeboys' such as sportsmen George Best and Alex Higgins. He's also well aware of this habit of naming; at Glastonbury in 1987, only minutes after an epic performance of 'Rave On John Donne', which gathers together no fewer than five poets from across four centuries, he sent up his own habit in a song performed this one time only – the lyric of 'Max Wall' consisted of a chanted list of names of British and Irish radio and TV comedians from the '50s and '60s. Like Kerouac, Morrison finds humour as well as mind-bending glory in the things he loves.

Even so, some reviewers have often taken a dim view of this aspect of his work – well, it ain't what they call rock and roll – some referring to it is as mere 'namedropping'. Yet I'd argue that this unambiguous acknowledgement of interest, influence and connection is both a source of inspiration and also a kind of creative generosity – a wish to pass on this interesting stuff just in case anyone else feels like following it up, whether it's Khalil Gilbran or Allen Ginsberg, whom he would name-check in live versions of his epic 'Summertime In England' in the 1980s. It connects these works to his own and allows these connections to develop in the mind of the listener. He even addressed and overcame a period of writer's block by a smart little trick, placing it in a tradition of writerly experience by declaring himself 'Tore Down à la Rimbaud'.

So, from John Donne to Seamus Heaney, from Samuel Taylor Coleridge to Samuel Beckett, Morrison has brought his literary and his musical interests together and, perhaps unsurprisingly, he has paid particular attention to written works which spring from a mix of words and music, notably blues-influenced or 'jazz writing' such as Mezz Mezzrow's *Really The Blues* (1942), which was directly referenced in 1991's 'On Hyndford Street' from the *Hymns To The Silence* double album. Out of this throng of ideas and names and influences, one seems to have been constant from his earliest work to the present day and that is Jack Kerouac. Morrison's chief musical hero was Ray Charles and the neat coincidence of one of his biggest hits, 'Hit The Road Jack', effortlessly and accidentally referencing both Kerouac and the book's title might have appealed to the young man too, persuading him of hidden links and connections. Morrison may have been so familiar with *On the Road* that certain images stuck with him and emerged unconsciously in his songs: 'the clack of high-heeled beauties' (Kerouac, 2000b, p. 164) certainly reminds me of 'the click and clack of the high-heeled shoe' in 'Madame George', and even Morrison's famous stage-holler, 'It's too late to stop now', has something of the elemental energy of Kerouac about it. Let's begin with a look at how the mercurial energy of 'jazz and the spoken word' helped formulate his earliest work.

On the road

After serving his musical apprenticeship in skiffle groups, showbands and 'on the road' in West Germany with the Monarchs, Morrison formed Them in early 1964 with Billy Harrison, Ronnie Millings and Alan Henderson. The first Them album opens with an extraordinary musical statement, in its way as startling in its impact as *On the Road* itself – 'Mystic Eyes' was recorded at the Decca studios on Denmark Street, London's former 'Music Row' in the heart of the West End. It was apparently begun as an instrumental which lasted over ten minutes, and even though we can't hear it – the tape has been lost – it gives us a sense of how Them's legendary sets during their spring 1964 residency at Belfast's Maritime Hotel, where the band served their musical apprenticeship, must have sounded. Crash-edited down from its original sprawl, it is still startling, and the story of Morrison's improvised vocal – the one we hear on the track today – rings true. It is said he set his harmonica aside and began singing over the band using lyrics he had been working on, and that the track we can hear today was the result of that very 'live' moment. Dropping the needle on this track is like opening the door to a nightclub and feeling the hot rush of a band in full flight. This kind of responsiveness to and inhabitation of the immediate, 'lived' moment has strong resonance with Kerouac's ability to express such sensations, and to explore the freedom and possibility of the present instant:

> Out we jumped in the warm, mad night, hearing a wild tenorman bawling horn across the way, going 'EE-YAH! EE-YAH! EE-YAH!' and hands clapping to the beat and folks yelling 'Go, go go!' Dean was already racing across the street with his thumb in the air, yelling, 'Blow, man, blow!'. A bunch of coloured men in Saturday-night suits were whooping it up in front . . . In the back of the joint in a dark corridor beyond the splattered toilet scores of men and women stood against the wall drinking wine – spodiodi and spitting at the stars.
>
> Kerouac, 2000b, p. 185

Listen to Morrison's voice as he calls out those 'mystic eyes' and you'll hear that 'ee-yah', a kind of generational update on Walt Whitman's 'yawp' of life. For Morrison it came from Kerouac and jazz and blues and found its way through him into the music. Kerouac's prose is gasping to keep up with his perceptions and the speed of life as it flies across the field of vision, calling in a bit of Jerry Lee Lewis and Oscar Wilde at the last, the better to catch the joy as it flies. This kind of lustrous life-embracing howl would blow into later Morrison works such as 1971's 'Wild Night' and an earlier tune, the lewd, darkly-gleaming shadowshapes of 'The Back Room', recorded with and for Bert Berns in 1967.

Them's recorded output only stretched to two formal albums and a basinful of outtakes and variant versions, all now comfortably complied. We might pick up traces of the heat of Kerouac across a number of Morrison originals on those albums – try the bucolic lasciviousness of 'Hey Girl', the bluesthink of 'Philosophy' or, especially, the deathlessly beautiful and so very rarely performed 'My Lonely Sad Eyes' in which the vocal performance unfurls like a single-roll typescript. We could also look in on some of the out-takes that did not surface until many years later such as the 'The Story Of Them', which effectively writes the group into being in a very 'Beat' manner or – perhaps *the* great lost Morrison classic – 'Friday's Child', both of which languished in obscurity until the mid-1970s.

'Friday's Child' is the real bridge between the 'old' Van Morrison, the R&B beat boom pop star, and the reborn child of 1968 and *Astral Weeks*. It introduces a range of feelings and themes which previous work had hinted at and which would become more sharply focused and important in later work; consider its motifs of north and south, images of movement, evocation of place, leaving home and entering into exile, and references to folk tradition. It is a celebration of youth and adventure but one which is shaded in melancholy; in this it strongly echoes Kerouac's striving for ways to come to terms with the terrible beauty of existence. Musically the song opens on determinedly minor chords, suggesting ambiguity, and an almost elegiac atmosphere. This is not a rock'n'roll celebration of youth; its tone is one of unease, even loss. The lyrical reference to Notting Hill Gate links it with *Astral Weeks'* 'Slim Slow Slider'. The girl in both songs could perhaps be the same person, at first in a state of innocence (or 'Before' in *Astral Weeks* terms) and then in a state of experience (the 'Afterwards' of *Astral Weeks's* second side, which 'Slim Slow Slider' closes). The song is about the building up of dreams in a state of innocence, with 'rainbows round [her] feet', even when the girl is 'making out with everyone that [she] meets', and how those dreams are brought back down to earth not by the actions of others but by the dreamer, awakening into a condition of realism: 'I watched you knock 'em down, each and every one'.

The girl in both songs feels close kin to certain female characters who ghost through *On the Road*, notably Dean's girlfriend Marylou – what a famous name! – and how she relates, or doesn't, to Dean and Sal's quest for experience, or, as they have it, for 'kicks':

> Dean was having his kicks; he put on a jazz record, grabbed Marylou, held her tight, and bounced gainst her with the beat of the music. She bounced right back. It was a real love dance.
>
> Kerouac, 2000b, p. 119

Like the girl in 'Friday's Child' and 'Slim Slow Slider', she doesn't conform to the bravado-driven dream-vision, knocking down the idealized 'castles in the sun'.

> [Dean]: Ah it's all right, it's just kicks. We only live once. We're having a good time.
> [Marylou]: No, it's sad and I don't like it.
>
> Kerouac, 2000b, p. 119

This dichotomy of dream and reality, of innocence and experience, now feels like a familiar one in Morrison's work, but it is in 'Friday's Child' that he first begins to find the lyrical and musical vocabulary to express it properly. The song is perhaps best known from a famous live bootleg recorded at Pacific High Studios in San Francisco on 5 September 1971; Morrison relocates the song to the city of the Beats by changing Notting Hill Gate to 'the Gate', the city's iconic bridge.

The very last track recorded by Morrison as member of Them provides further evidence of the fire started by his readings of Kerouac. In 'The Story Of Them', first recorded in late 1965 but not issued widely until the mid-1970s, the choice of the talking blues form frees the vocal from the need to deliver a melody in the conventional sense, although Morrison's delivery is melodic in the way it plays around the tune's easy, rhythmic swing. It also rhymes, often very wittily, in a way that as a talking blues it doesn't necessarily have to. Why use this form? First, it sets the story of Them in a musical and cultural tradition the band adored and toward which they certainly aspired – the blues, of course. Therefore the story of Them and the blues are wedded and indivisible. It also permits picaresque rumination in the way a straight eight bar does not – after all, this is a self-proclaimed 'story' with all the authorial room for manoeuvre and invention that that suggests. This is not, in any sense, a pop lyric, although it celebrates one of the central narratives of popular music culture: the band as gang, starting as outsiders and eventually winning over the mainstream. That victory is of course a bittersweet one for Morrison, whose connoisseurial suspicion of commercial success informs the ambiguous conclusion to the song, kissing the past goodbye but also cleaving to its apparent simplicities.

The open structures of the blues facilitated truth-telling or, at least, a blues that is directly associated with and drawn from autobiography. Kerouac's recordings had explored similar territory and the readings from his unpublished *Book Of The Blues* illustrate this to fine and clear effect. This isn't a generic tale of heartbreak, or of a band striving, or a veiled and allusive encoding of a struggle for fame, but a completely specific piece, entirely and directly telling the story of Them. Autobiographical songs are rarer than one might think, and ones as directly autobiographical as this one are rarer still. What's even odder is its retrospective mood; assured of a place in history ('and that is how ... we made our name') while also inhabiting that vital present moment. Morrison was only just 20 when Them recorded this number, and it illustrates how powerfully the past and the power of memory exercised its influence over his imagination even then. It was early in a career to be summarizing a life and its events, especially from a band who had recorded 'Don't Look Back'. It's funny too, and while not quite Boyce and Hart's '(Theme From) The Monkees', it joins that tune in a select club of songs – ones in which the artists' subject is themselves. Amongst their peers the Rolling Stones never did it, nor did the Animals, and it took the Beatles until the late 1960s to reflect and compose in this way, allusively first in 'Glass Onion' and then directly with 'The Ballad Of John and Yoko'. It is a commonplace technique in hip hop of course, where solipsism is integral, but in rock and pop the explicitly autobiographical discourse is still relatively rare. So it is little wonder that 'The Story of Them' remained obscure (with the exception of a limited release in the UK and Netherlands in 1967 during Morrison's tenure with Dutch group Cuby and The Blizzards). How, Decca Records may well have asked, to sell a song like that?

You can see their point. By late 1965 the world had already taken the drama of the unusually lengthy 'House of the Rising Sun' to its bosom, but a 7'20 talking blues would be as unusual on a pop album then as it would be now. Its lyrical tone is by turns wry and amused, sly and affronted: telling the tale of how the band formed out of a social scene made up of people who didn't fit in anywhere else and as a consequence of being outsiders everywhere else in the city, they made their own scene, which then became *the* scene. As Morrison noted in the sleeve note to a 2015 reissue of Them's complete recordings, the song was an attempt to imagine themselves into a scene like those in San Francisco or New Orleans, 'only I changed it to be local'. The description of the Maritime Hotel is brief but reeks of reality, emphasizing the importance of the 'three J's' ('That's Jerry, Jerry and Jimmy . . . who helped us run the Maritime') and of doorman Kit. The description of the band makes use of the famous slogan coined to launch the band in ads in the *Belfast Evening Telegraph* – 'Who are, what are, Them?'. The answer, initially, is a purely musical one, with a blast on the harmonica before a lyrical sketch which is truthful to a level almost comedic; it always strikes me as a description a girl in the audience would have given had she been asked to describe the group onstage at the Maritime ('That little one sings and the big one plays guitar with the thimble on his finger and . . .') – that is, public personae (the singer, the guitar player, the bass player, etc.) began to form and that is both 'how they made their name' and also a cause for a form of sadness – the openness of the scene was already passing away. This is part of the reason Morrison was able to reminisce at such close quarters; it must have already felt like years ago. Yet it is not idealized: the adjectives used to describe the group are not flattering:

Wild, sweaty, crude, ugly and, and mad
And sometimes just, a little bit sad

That tough melancholia is the tune's final mood: after it takes one final look at the Maritime Hotel, the song advises itself to 'walk away . . . wish it well'. So while the memory is strong it is also behind; this is the duality of that which is lost and the influence it exerts over the present moment even if you don't look back. The trick is to keep the two forces in hand and not let one extinguish the other. By writing it down and recording it in both the literal and metaphorical sense, it sets these scenes in the past but makes them accessible through the controlled apparatus of the song: this is an early example of this technique, a key one in Morrison's methodology and one which developed from his early exposure to Kerouac's passionate defence of the passing moment. Yet while 'The Story Of Them' is pointedly specific and particular, it was perhaps a very widely known song which most closely connects his earliest work to the world of *On the Road*.

Route 66

> My first ride was a dynamite truck with a red flag, about thirty miles into great green Illinois, the truckdriver pointing out the place where Route 6, which we were on, intersects Route 66 before they both shoot west for incredible distances.
>
> Kerouac, 2000b, p. 17

Route 66, running 2,448 miles from Chicago, Illinois, to Santa Monica in California, was laid down in the mid-1920s and opened on 11 November 1926, although it remained unmarked until the following year. So while the actual road belongs to a previous era – Steinbeck used it as a central motif of *The Grapes Of Wrath* (1939) – it became a symbol of optimism and freedom post-1945, a moment where restructuring of society had yet to begin and suddenly the possibility of unrestricted movement offered itself to a new generation. Bobby Troup's 1946 song turned the road into 'Route 66', the symbol of freedom, possibility and the American love affair with the motor car: before the song, it was, well, just a road. Thereafter, it was *Route 66*. This is the power of the popular song, to change the meaning of place, and of the journey – now, to travel down Route 66 is to perform a form of pilgrimage, just as it is to follow Morrison's (scrambled) travelogue as laid out in his 1989 spoken word number 'Coney Island'. 'Route 66', the song, feeds into and draws from the same rich seam of post-1945 American appetite for movement and discovery in a pan-generation of youthful non-combatants and returning war veterans alike, and Kerouac's work describes Troup's imagined journey detail by detail from the inside out.

Them's version, on their first album, shows that the song was as much a standard of the tough young R&B/garage band then as 'Gloria' would prove to be later. The song has a more interesting history than might be expected. It belongs to a previous era, certainly, but importantly the post-war, post-1945 surge of optimism and freedom. The song was originally recorded by Nat 'King' Cole in his jazz trio days, shortly after its composition in 1946 by Bobby Troup, and, nodding to Nat, Them's version is (perhaps unexpectedly) led by a jazzy piano and while it has the mercurial flash befitting the song and the age of the musicians it is not the overdriven-amp missile of other versions. Them's musical sophistication was rooted in their stylistic eclecticism which saw them set at a distance from some of their peers while also connecting them to the experimental mood of the time and that is clearly evident here – compare this for example to the Rolling Stones' version, and the Stones come off second best by some distance. So Them's take combines a nod to its roots as a pianist's song (Cole was of course as superb a jazz pianist as he was a singer) and connects it up to the more muscular musical traditions from which they were then drawing directly.

In subsequent R&B and pop versions it became a theme song for the post-Kerouac Beat Generation and the possibilities of life beyond the place in which you stand; the place names, so evocative of states falling like dominoes before the individual will, and the sense of movement is strong. It is a kind of phenomenological travelogue, which evokes, describes and transforms the places in the moment of their naming in this litany of potential and possibility. In Kerouac, writing after Bobby Troup, Route 66 is one of these possibilities, these routes out of the self and into the future and adventure that America seemed to represent to Sal Paradise. He flirts with it but does not pursue it for its symbolic value, or cultural significance, inherently real or culturally conferred. Kerouac turned to the road to escape and reshape his possible futures; paradoxically he and Bobby Troup did it so powerfully that the road has become a cornerstone of the American Dream, not least as the road to Hollywood and the Hotel California. After all, as we have noted, Route 66 is no longer just a road, it's an idea, a dream, a myth: the Mother Road.

Within *On the Road* we see what the meaning is, or might be, of looking for America – as in Paul Simon's phrase – invoking the frontier spirit, heading west, pushing back the boundaries, discovery, mapping, seeing, *veni, vidi, vici*. Yet what might be overlooked is that Sal's initial journey to the West Coast is accomplished fairly rapidly, and proves unsatisfactory; it happens not how he wanted to do it, with his 'single red line across America', a la 'Route 66', but in fits and starts, looping back on himself, veering wildly north and south. Partly this is because he goes in cars or, less willingly, coaches and buses, not on the box cars of the previous generation's mythologies – that is, Woody Guthrie's America, where the mobile population was the itinerant one, and being on the road meant being homeless, workless or stateless, literally as well as metaphorically. Yet in *On the Road* he is also following Guthrie's suggestion – 'this land is your land, from the California desert to the New York island' – and this grand geographical sweep from the West to East is an indisputably romantic gesture, which plays upon the febrile imagination, and the curiosity of the young country. *On the Road* translates that line from Guthrie into a way of living. 'Route 66' is closer to Kerouac, recording with tangible, sensual care ('Don't forget Winona') and pleasure ('Oklahoma City looks mighty pretty'), whereas Guthrie's song records more impressionistically, evoking the spirit of the land without dropping a single name. Kerouac cross-references furiously, frequently from those two modern American inventions, the movies and the mass-produced popular song; he also, more mysteriously, cites bon mots and scenes from the life of W. C. Fields as though he were a nineteenth century philosopher or mythologized saint:

> The following ten days were, as W.C. Fields said, 'fraught with eminent peril'... I moved in with Roland Major... Major liked good wines, just like Hemingway. He reminisced about his recent trip to France. 'Ah, Sal, you could sit with me high in the basque country with a cool bottle of Poignon Dix-neuf, then you'd know there are other things beside boxcars.'
>
> 'I know that. It's just that I love boxcars and I love to read the names on them, like Missouri Pacific, Great Northern, Rock Island Line. By Gad, Major, if I could tell you everything that happened to me hitching here.'
>
> Kerouac, 2000b, pp. 41–2

Here we feel the textures and speeds of life in old, high Europe: stillness, contemplation, time ('Ah, Sal, you could sit with me high in the basque country with a cool bottle of Poignon Dix-neuf') are held for contrast and comparison with the direct reality of the functional emphases on movement, which in turn feeds the auto-mythologies of mid-twentieth century America ('then you'd know there are other things beside boxcars'). Sal knows the difference already, but sees and welcomes the beauty of the functional, and the impossible glamour of the place name – 'Route 66' uses the same feeling, the song's internal rhymes are the things that make it immediately memorable (best shown in the lines 'get your kicks on Route Sixty Six' and 'Wagstaff Arizona, don't forget Winona' for example), but here the names reek of the possibilities and possible futures that each one holds.

Morrison knew the difference too and of course the last of Sal's trinity, 'Rock Island Line', was immortalized in song just as Bobby Troup's song coalesced the meaning of 'Route 66'. Leadbelly's song, first recorded by him on 22 June 1937 in Washington, DC, for John Lomax's Library of Congress sessions, has been recorded by a whole host of artists but the versions Morrison was most likely to have encountered were one of Leadbelly's originals from the 1930s and 1940s, or Lonnie Donegan's skiffled hit version, sped up no end from a smartly cantering blues to a punky, sound-box bashing cannonball, with an extended spoken section enveloping the famous chorus. Donegan's lyric is much longer than Leadbelly's original, and the spoken intro is a reinforcement of the specific location of the song's subject (the 'boxcars') and also extends the potency of the surrounding mythology that transforms both the fact and the meaning of the railway line in the way that Route 66 does for the road: 'the rock island line is a mighty good line' / 'take my way, that's the highway that's the best'. The boxcars are a network of escape – they go where they go (it wasn't called a 'line' for nothing) where Sal found that using the roads was something else, a different, less communal yet more personal method of 'looking for America'; the contacts are more intense, less regulated – so where are the stops? Who gets on or off? What is the speed? And what happens when, in the words of another child of Kerouac, Bruce Springsteen, we reach the end of the road we have burned down – nowhere to run, nowhere to go?

Down the road

For Morrison, that place was a step away from fashioning responses to direct experience and into working with memory. The second phase of Kerouac's incarnation in his work comes through more overt reference, where he is actually mentioned in song, and where the processes his work helped set in train are reflected upon and reviewed. The very first direct mention of Kerouac in a Van Morrison song comes later than we might expect, in a song called 'Cleaning Windows' on 1981's *Beautiful Vision*. A bright sketch of Belfast adolescence, it references one of Morrison's earliest jobs as a window cleaner (he also mentions the job in the bejewelled textures of

'St. Dominic's Preview' from 1972), and this writer has been at gigs where the song's composer has taken time out to extend its performance by giving a very detailed spoken word guide to how to get a window really clean. In amongst this Dylan Thomas-style celebration of the ordinary life – 'the smell of the bakery from across the street got in my nose' – we also find a checklist of early influences:

> I heard Leadbelly and Blind Lemon on the street where I was born . . .
> Kerouac's *Dharma Bums* and *On the Road* . . .

This litany of the important music, literature and philosophy for the young man in the song is skilfully confined to one verse, giving the impression of these disparate influences jostling for his attention and providing explosive conjunctions and juxtapositions in his burgeoning imagination – he goes back to work with these influences swirling round his head, the sounds and words and the images they conjure up hurling together, to create something fresh when allied to his own, personal and parochial observations. They are brought all the way back home, and 'on the street where I was born' marks the influence out as fundamental in its impact as part of his life: the books, the music, the influences which transform the world we make around us every day. Every person reading this could name texts and songs that have done something similar for them and their view of themselves and in this Morrison is absolutely right to insist on not being remarkable – what is remarkable is where he took the impact of those influences.

Musically the track is atypical of the record, digging a different sort of groove, as opposed to the open, bluesy planes of, say, 'Beautiful Vision' and 'Northern Muse'; this track, to borrow an adjective which was originally coined I believe by John Fogerty, choogles. It is driven by the unmistakable yet here restrained chug of Mark Knopfler's signature red-Strat style, guesting here while fresh from playing with Bob Dylan and poised on the cusp of huge CD/MTV-fuelled success with his band Dire Straits. The rhythm is one of urgency but also one of repose and ease – of natural momentum, where everything seems to fall into place, just as the jalapeno-hot horns drop into the mix as he sings of blowin' saxophone in a funky club, precisely the kind of place in which Sal and Dean 'go mad together' and discover Slim Gaillard in *On the Road*, reimagined and relocated to Belfast. While this song presents a scene and a feeling of belonging and completeness, it is the growing influence of this final image that will end up making the change, and take the young narrator away from the certainties of his environment ('Number 126? Ok, we'll be round tomorrow'). Success means going on the road.

Within the lexicon of a musician, being 'on the road' has a very particular meaning – being on tour, moving from one place to the next, from one gig to the next. Indeed in the 1970s the 'road song' quickly became a cliché of a rock band's repertoire. This hop aboard the endless highway is something which, paradoxically, Morrison lost his taste for in the early 1980s and has since then tried to find alternative models for playing live – something which he still relishes. He has tried one-offs, residences, weekend only shows, flying back to Belfast immediately after every UK show – trying to stay 'off the road' but to still play where and when he can. Yet, avoid it as he may – and who can blame him after well over 50 years of it – the road also represents a community of sorts, even though the emphatic loneliness and singular experience of it is emphasized over and again in beautifully contemplative pieces like 1999's 'Philosopher's Stone'. Yet those who are on the road share, or are caught in, what travel writer Jan Morris called a 'web of fellow-feeling'. The title song of 2002's *Down the Road* is a case in point. The tune was originally (and somewhat improbably) demo'd in the sessions leading to the album which featured 'Cleaning Windows' – *Beautiful Vision* in 1981. This was Morrison's first album after moving back to Europe from over a decade based in the US – he lived in Copenhagen in the period leading up to album, a stay most clearly signalled by two of the album's tracks, 'Scandinavia' and 'Vanlose Stairway' about visiting a girlfriend who lived in a top floor apartment in the Vanlose suburb of the Danish capital. In 1981, the song was entitled 'Down the Road I Go', the melody and lyric scattered and sketchy but recognizably the same song as in the 2002 version. The twenty-first-century version is a blend of melancholy and optimism; this complex mix of emotions seems to capture the embrace and rejection of both movement and stasis, and trying to find a way of holding the two contrary positions together, and closes by asserting that the endpoint of the journey is its starting point – 'trying to find my way back home'. The song in all its modesty of form and melody still manages to evoke both the physicality of the road – the tiredness, the miles covered, the years passing – and the metaphysical spaces that it also maps:

> All our memories, dreams and reflections that keep haunting me Down the road

A blast of harmonica in the demo unexpectedly connects the song to the boxcars of Woody Guthrie's *Bound For Glory* and the idea of endless, perpetual movement planted in his garden by Kerouac – as the characters of *On the Road* discover, sometimes one needs to go backwards to go forward. Kerouac's America is a new one, and it has its roots, indeed its apparent rootlessness, in Guthrie's invocation of a different nation.

Down the Road's final song, 'Fast Train', contemplates the experience of rootlessness in a way which both expresses and refutes both Guthrie's songs and Kerouac's narrative, with the train seemingly going round in circles – or as the lyric ends, 'going nowhere!', rather than onto the next tomorrow. It is an existential image of failed impetus and fogged direction – more Sartre than Sal. This admission of the exhaustion of the mythopoeic imagery of being 'on the road' effectively acts as a disavowal of such mythologies while still acknowledging their attractive force. In that sense he has come to the end of the line with such notions, and henceforward they would prove useful to him as an aid to reflection.

Off the road

> I would like them to play behind me while I'm reading ... can you hear me
> while they're playing?'
>   Kerouac, at the opening of his recorded readings of 'Poems from the
> unpublished *Book of the Blues*', on *Blues and Haikus* CD, 2008.

Kerouac's question to producer Bob Thiele during the recording sessions which
resulted in 1959's *Blues And Haikus* album begets another – what of the different
dynamics of reading and amplified music? Mixing the two together as both
Kerouac and Morrison have done can be problematic – too loud, the subtleties and
shapes of the words are gone; too quiet and the music becomes at best an ambient
buzz, at worst an irritating distraction subverting efforts to concentrate. Morrison's
spoken word recordings have navigated this line with varying success – 'Coney
Island' is awash with sumptuous strings which both elevate and occasionally
threaten to oversweeten the memory, while 'Song of Being a Child', a spoken word
duet with June Boyce based on the poem we see being written in Wim Wenders' *Wings
Of Desire* (1987), succeeds because it is arranged very simply, the circling keyboard
riff and punctuating snares providing a firm-but-loose structure around which the
voices weave. His most complete union of words and music as a performance is
perhaps 1983's 'Rave On John Donne', which unifies spoken word, singing and
instrumental elements in a seamless invocation of time and place. Yet it is a much
more intimate and personal piece which finds his creative connection to Kerouac's
performances most capably realized. A track on side 3 of his 1991 double album,
Hymns To The Silence (the title of which I borrowed for my 2010 book on Morrison),
is perhaps the most rewarding incorporation of the early influence into his later, more
reflective style. The slow, drifting outro of the title track leads us into 'On Hyndford
Street', perhaps his most intensely realized exploration and inhabitation of memory,
achieved by a sense of focused concentration which is both intense and utterly
relaxed.

'On Hyndford Street' is a not quite free-form, stream-of-consciousness flow of
memory and harks back to his original claim on mixing spoken word and the
free spirit of jazz; it emphasizes hearing and the feeling of the memory of sound –
listening to Radio Luxembourg, the voices whispering across Beechie River, the
laughter, the jazz and blues records, Debussy on the radio, the internalized voices
of Mezz Mezzrow and Jack Kerouac (reading '*Dharma Bums* ... over and over again').
In this, the words of Kerouac on the printed page are treated as being as replayable as
any Hank Williams 78. This benign clamour of voices feeds into the sense of
contentment and calmness, and harmony is brought through the bringing together
of apparent cross-currents of sound, meaning and feeling. It is a work in pursuit of
stillness, in contrast to the fevered movement and restless energy we feel from his
earlier work:

Reading . . . *Dharma Bums* by Jack Kerouac, over and over again . . .
And it's always being now, and it's always being now . . . can you feel the silence?

It is in this track that the purpose of the pursuit of these moments of stillness and of silence is made manifest: 'and it's always being now . . . It's always now'. This is satisfying metaphysically, as a place seems to have been discovered, or created, in which the clocks are stopped and a different understanding of time ('Dear God, Sal! Slim knows time, he knows time') seems to come about: it's achieved not in a laboratory or via complex thought processes but simply through thinking about ordinary life in a particular way. It's quite a discovery, and owes as much to the *way* Kerouac wrote as it does to *what* he wrote. It is also satisfying as a listener because we are drawn into this mood, either by the cumulative effect of this track following the title song, or simply via listening to the blend of Morrison's rich, close-mic'd voice, and the unobtrusive yet absolutely integral synthesizer-playing of the late, great Derek Bell. Indeed the discovery of profundity through the uncomplicated details of a life is mirrored by the simplicity of Bell's synth lines which also suggest the richness of the mood – slow, warm, on the brink of dreams but fully awake to feeling and meaning. There is also meaning and pleasure in Morrison's pronunciation of the word 'now' in the Belfast manner, 'noi-er'. The very sound of this pronunciation locates the thought culturally and topographically, unmistakably Northern Irish and equally unmistakably East Belfast. Just as Kerouac wrote in *The Dharma Bums* that 'Finding Nirvana is like finding silence', Morrison seems to find a form of intense personal repose in the contemplation of stillness and silence such as this. The road seems to have led home.

Having achieved an artistic breakthrough of this sort does not mean the journey is at an end of course: the road goes on forever. A late variant on how these ideas, feelings and memories, reconnecting the 70-year-old man to the energy of the raging Belfast boy popped up in the late song 'In Tiburon', issued on 2016's *Keep Me Singing*. Morrison spent many years living in Marin County, just to the north of San Francisco, and Tiburon is a small town in that charmed area, looking south toward the city across the bay. In an interview for *Rolling Stone* in 2016, David Fricke commented to Morrison, 'You lived in Northern California in the Seventies. Another new song, "In Tiburon", is set in the Bay Area, with references to City Lights bookstore and seeing trumpeter Chet Baker at jazz clubs there. How true is that?' Morrision responded:

That's not about me. That's about a certain era – the Beat poets, North Beach. I met Lawrence Ferlinghetti way back. I met Chet Baker much later in London. But it started with an idea. I was in this house in Tiburon, and this guy was showing me around. He was talking about this woman: 'She likes to listen to your music and look out the window, and nobody can touch her.' I go, 'This is a fucking song.' I didn't start writing it until last year. But that had to be a song: She sits up here in the Bay and no one can touch her. It couldn't be anything else.

Fricke, 2016

Even though he truthfully says that the song is 'not about me', it is a world he has inhabited, having mooched around in San Anselmo and Marin County for several years and no doubt browsed the shelves of City Lights, the legendary Beat bookshop founded by Ferlinghetti at 261 Columbus Avenue in San Francisco; this is probably where he encountered him. His encounter with Chet Baker is a matter of record – they met at Ronnie Scott's in Soho in 1986 during the filming of Bruce Weber's film about Baker, *Let's Get Lost*. Morrison tagged along with Elvis Costello who was central to the film's production and ended up onstage with Baker and his band singing an off-the-cuff 'Send In The Clowns'. As a listen or look shows, his memory of the lyric wasn't perfect but it's a great watch and a great performance – Baker, however, was not impressed: 'he's just shouting', he supposedly said (James, 2003, p. 324). Morrison didn't hold a grudge though, name-checking Baker in the exquisite 'When The Leaves Come Falling Down' from 1999's *The Healing Game*, the same album that features 'Philosopher's Stone'. Morrison spoke further about 'In Tiburon':

> The second verse is about the Beats. I met people involved with that scene like Vince Guaraldi, who I did some gigs with, he was a great jazz player. I also met guys like Allen Ginsberg and Lawrence Ferlinghetti a few times. I tried to fit Slim Gaillard into the song. I got to know him quite well – he's the scat singer who is referenced in Kerouac's *On the Road*. Kerouac and all those guys were a big influence on me as a kid starting out.

Purden, 2016

In fact almost the whole lyric of 'In Tiburon' maps the city of the Beats: writers, poets, musicians, bookshops, clubs, hotels, streets. It is the combination of them – time, place – that made something happen, and the song seeks to reconnect with those moments where something special emerged and tries to call it back. The point of view is not one of wild experience anymore, but a steady contemplation back down the years from a point of stillness, from across the bay in Tiburon. The agent of this reflection for the woman who inspired the song was Morrison's music and 'In Tiburon's' musical mood matches this reflective sensibility, a quietly lush and verdant string arrangement, unmistakably the work of Fiachra Trench, fringing the tidal inlets of memory, and Morrison's vocal timbre matches this tone – in his early sixties he struggled a little, especially live, to reach notes he sailed across even a decade earlier. 'One day I will find the right words, and they will be simple,' Kerouac said in *The Dharma Bums* and, picking this up, since 2010's *Keep It Simple*, Morrison has scaled back and redirected his vocal delivery into a less demonstrative but still affecting baritone, heard to good effect on this track. Like the afterglow of the narrator's experience in the song, the voice he uses to tell the story shows what happens once the physical energy starts to leave us while the memory stays strong. The urgency is replaced by a more measured release of ideas and emotions, through memory. The act of singing embodies the experience, reanimating it and remembering for the listener, even as it is experience projected through the perceptions of another. 'In Tiburon', with apparent ease, holds together the white-hot experience of youth and energy – the wild night of Kerouac's San Francisco – with temperate, contemplative stillness borne of age and fading energy, the world seen as it is and as it was from a window overlooking the bay, looking back at the city lights gleaming across the water.

'You can't live in this world but there's nowhere else to go,' wrote Kerouac. Morrison has discovered that, by connecting energy and experience through music and words, there might be; all our memories, dreams and reflections put us on the road, one more time.

Bibliography

Fricke, David, 'Van Morrision: The Rolling Stone Interview', *Rolling Stone*, 26 September 2016.
Gavin, James, *Deep In A Dream: The Long Night Of Chet Baker*, London: Vintage, 2003.
Kerouac, Jack, *The Dharma Bums*, Harmondsworth: Penguin, 2000a.
Kerouac, Jack, *On the Road*, Harmondsworth: Penguin, 2000b.
Mezzrow, 'Mezz' [aka Milton Mesirow], *Really The Blues*, London: Random House, 1946.
Mills, Peter, *Hymns To the Silence: Inside the Words and Music of Van Morrison*, London: Bloomsbury, 2010.
Morris, Jan, *Trieste and The Meaning of Nowhere*, London: Faber, 2006.
Morrison, Van, *Lit Up Inside*, London: Faber, 2014.
Steinbeck, John, *The Grapes Of Wrath*, London: Penguin, 1939.

Discography

Jack Kerouac

Blues And Haikus (Hanover-Signature Record Corporation, LP #5006, 1959)

Van Morrison

Albums
Blowin' Your Mind (Bang, 1967)
Astral Weeks (Warners, 1968)
Tupelo Honey (Warners, 1971)
Common One (Mercury, 1980)
Beautiful Vision (Mercury, 1981)
Inarticulate Speech Of The Heart (Mercury, 1983)

A Sense of Wonder (Mercury, 1985)
Enlightenment (Polydor, 1990)
Hymns To The Silence (Polydor, 1991)
Back On Top (Virgin/Point Blank, 1999)
Down The Road (Exile/Polydor, 2002)
Keep It Simple (Exile/Polydor, 2008)
Keep Me Singing (Caroline, 2016)

Songs
'The Back Room' (Bang, 1967)
'Slim Slow Slider' (Warners, 1968)
'Wild Night' (Warners, 1971)
'Summertime in England' (Mercury, 1980)
'Cleaning Windows' (Mercury, 1981)
'Rave On John Donne' (Mercury, 1983)
'Tore Down a la Rimbaud' (Mercury, 1985)
'In The Days Before Rock and Roll' (Polydor, 1990)
'On Hyndford Street' (Polydor, 1991)
'Philosopher's Stone' (Virgin/Point Blank, 1999)
'When the Leaves Come Falling Down' (Virgin/Point Blank, 1999)
'Down the Road' (Exile/Polydor, 2002)
'Fast Train' (Exile/Polydor, 2002)
'Behind the Ritual' (Exile/Polydor, 2008)
'In Tiburon' (Caroline, 2016)
Note: 'Max Wall' performed once only, 11th Glastonbury Festival , Sunday, 21 June 1987,
    Pyramid Stage; unrecorded.

Them

All Them tracks referred to are available on *The Complete Them 1964–1967* (Sony Legacy,
    2015)
'Mystic Eyes' (Decca, 1965)
'Philosophy' (Decca, 1965)
'Route 66' (Decca, 1965)
'Hey Girl' (Decca, 1966)
'My Lonely Sad Eyes' (Decca, 1966)
'Friday's Child' (Decca, 1967)
'The Story of Them' (Decca, 1967)

Lonnie Donegan

'Rock Island Line' (Decca, 1956, available on *Singles Collection 1955–62*, Marmot Music,
    2016)

Leadbelly

'Rock Island Line' (RCA, 1942, available on *The Very Best of Leadbelly* , Music Club, 1993)

Bobby Troup

'(Get Your Kicks On) Route 66' (Liberty, 1957, available on *Tell Me When You Get Home*, Jazzology, 2007)

Videography

Arena: How High The Moon, first broadcast BBC2, 29 October 1989.
Let's Get Lost, dir. Bruce Weber, Little Bear Productions, 1988.

CHAPTER 15

DETECTING JACK KEROUAC AND JONI MITCHELL: A LITERARY/LEGAL (NOT MUSICOLOGICAL) INVESTIGATION INTO THE SEARCH FOR INFLUENCE

Nancy M. Grace

> Criticism is the discourse of the deep tautology ... Criticism is the art of knowing the hidden roads that go from poem to poems.
>
> Harold Bloom, *The Anxiety of Influence*, p. 96

Singer-songwriter Joni Mitchell, one of the queens of twentieth-century rock'n'roll, found Beat artists annoying. 'That whole pocket of modern art is my least favorite in art history,' she told Tom McIntrye in 1998. 'I was kind of a Dadaist to the Beats in a certain way. Musically, they annoyed me. In painting, they annoyed me, and I made no bones about it.' When McIntrye tried to link her to them via Beat irreverence and 'anarchistic spirit', Mitchell refused to take the bait: 'I never was an anarchist. Never. No, that's probably why I don't like them. You need rules and regulations, but you need just ones.' Three years later, in an interview with Robert Enright, she once again distanced herself from them:

> I wasn't a fan of the Beats. I didn't like to see the underbelly revered. I figured it had its place, but I didn't want to be an imitator of it. I'm not a book burner but I longed for something more wholesome. God knows why I longed for the impossible. In high school I did a lot of satire on the Beats ... (2001)

The literary likes of Agatha Christie and Dorothy L. Sayers, or A. S. Byatt and Julian Barnes, might find these declarations intriguing – such mildly venomous statements could well smack of disguise and subterfuge, especially since the public record reveals that Mitchell is not a denier of influence. Over the decades, she has identified artists from Stevie Wonder, Billie Holiday, Miles Davis, Ray Charles, Cab Calloway, Tom Wolfe and Charles Mingus to Pablo Picasso as having had an impact on her work. And she's even admitted to discovering influences as she's listened to recordings of her performances (Denberg, 1998). Then too, anyone who has both read Beat literature, especially the canonical work of Jack Kerouac, and listened to Mitchell's lyrics recognizes similarities in themes, imagery and voice – the focus on travel, the American landscape, and confessional introspection among the most recognizable.

So Mitchell's remarks trigger a literary mystery that generates a tantalizing set of investigative questions. For instance, could she be intentionally eschewing a particularly important component in her development as a songwriter? If so, what specifically might she be avoiding or denying or forgetting? And why? This chapter will tackle these questions through a quasi-literary/legal method of investigation to trace a process of gathering evidence with which one can answer the question 'Is Joni Mitchell "guilty" of using Beat writers – and Jack Kerouac in particular – as an aesthetic influence?' The use of the term *guilt* here strongly implies her alleged cognizance of the act of using Kerouac in her artistic production, and thus the answer to this key question lies in a search for the most compelling evidence possible *directly* linking her art to Beat/Kerouac art. In other words, the case 1) rejects any claim that Mitchell unconsciously absorbed and synthesized Kerouac's work into her own, since such a claim, while true to some degree of all human cognition, is fundamentally unverifiable, and 2) is aimed at the evidentiary standard of Beyond a Reasonable Doubt, used in criminal cases, rather than the Preponderance of Evidence or More than 50 Per cent (or a Single Grain of Sand), which is required in most civil cases.

That being said, a logical first step is to collect and assess whatever evidence is readily available on the topic, exculpatory, that is, in Mitchell's favour, and inculpatory, that is, not in Mitchell's favour. Doing so reveals, first, that Mitchell herself, despite her public acknowledgement of aesthetic influences, struggled to avoid influences altogether, de facto including Beat writers, as she told Jody Denberg in a 1998 interview for KGSR-FM out of Austin, Texas, 'all the time I'm trying to be un-influenced by anything including myself, not to steal from myself', crediting her invention of tunings as the vehicle by which she forced herself to make new discoveries. Second, again contrary to Mitchell's declarations, literary critics, those providing expert testimony, have repeatedly found that her lyrics, philosophies, spiritual practices and other characteristics echo simpatico with the Beat writing. For instance, Simon Warner, editor of this volume, rightly identifies Mitchell as a singer-performer whose engagement with multiple media, a confessional approach, an immersion in jazz production and performance, and 'her concern with the existential lure of movement' place her 'in a Beat framework' (2013, pp. 159–62). Laurence Coupe links her philosophically to Gary Snyder as an environmental prophet (2007, p. 174), which makes sense when one considers her iconic 'Big Yellow Taxi' and 'Woodstock'.

Miles Parks Grier interprets her image on the cover of *Hejira* (1976) – Mitchell with cigarette and black beret – as a 'bebop-inspired Beat [poet], on the road like Jack Kerouac'. However, Kerouac never wore a beret, a Euro-beatnik image transformed into a mass culture trope for the Beats.[1] More to the point, however, Grier amplifies the Kerouac–Mitchell connection with respect to race, concluding that 'she shared their wanderlust, anti-establishment cynicism, and deep investing in jazz music and black people as reservoirs of the physicality and spontaneity that white people lost as they traded manual labor and rural or urban community life for intellectual labor and suburban isolation' (2012, p. 9). Lloyd Whitesell, in *The Music of Joni Mitchell*, a scrupulously detailed interdisciplinary analysis of Mitchell's poetry and music, also sees a Kerouac connection in Mitchell's 'The Boho Dance' (*Hissing of Summer Lawns*): 'The wild rebel figure of earlier songs appears here in muted form as the second-person addressee, the "subterranean" in the parking lot (a reference to the Beat ethos by way of Kerouac's novel *The Subterraneans*)' (2008, p. 94). Interestingly, the wording of Whitesell's claim implies that it is evidence-based, but he provides no evidence, leaving the provenance of Mitchell's use of the word ('Subterranean by your own design'; 1997, p. 146) most likely to a broader cultural association. We also have an indirect link mediated by Allen Ginsberg, who as 'friend of the late Jack Kerouac' (according to Katharine Monk in *Joni: The Creative Odyssey of Joni Mitchell*), while on Bob Dylan's 1975 Rolling Thunder Revue, would frequently mention Chogyam Trunpga Rinpoche (2012, p. 159), founder of Naropa University in 1974 and Mitchell's Buddhist teacher who inspired her song 'Refuge of the Road'.[2]

The urge to link Mitchell specifically with Jack Kerouac, as do Grier, Monk and Whitesell, takes on added appeal when one considers that she has had important relationships with individuals who were significantly influenced by Kerouac's art, including Dylan and Leonard Cohen, both of whom she has identified as 'points of departure' for her art (Wild, 1991). She performed with Dylan on his 1975 Revue, but Leonard Cohen, with whom she had a brief but intense affair, was most likely the most influential. Cohen was nine years her senior and already a published poet and novelist when they first met, in 1963. Cohen, described as 'more of a leftover beatnik than a hippie' (Weller, 2008, p. 242), played the role of a mild-mannered Svengali or Professor Higgins, schooling Mitchell in the humanities. 'He gave me his reading list,' she told singer Malka Marom, 'wonderful books: Camus, *The Stranger*; the *I Ching*, which I've used all my life; *Magister Ludi*; *Siddhartha* [the last two by Herman Hesse]. A wonderful reading list' (2014, p. 36). Cohen has openly acknowledged his lyrical indebtedness to Kerouac's jazzy-accompanied readings of 'Deadbelly' and 'Charlie Parker', and perhaps a Kerouac novel was on a list that he gave Mitchell. Whether she read Kerouac and other Beat writers because of Cohen, we don't know, but she clearly knew enough about them to associate Kerouac with the jazz/Beat period when she was in high school – 'I was the school artist, and so I'd be given projects . . . Frequently, I was paid in jazz records because that was the beatnik Kerouac period' (McIntyre, 2001) – and to consistently throughout her life distance herself from them.

Interestingly, her connection to Bob Dylan and thus possibly to Kerouac has emerged recently at the much broader level of genre in the Nobel Prize organization's assertion that literature and popular song lyrics can indeed be of the same mettle, not a new insight by any means but still a somewhat controversial matter, as illustrated by the Nobel presentation speech recognizing Bob Dylan as the recipient of the 2016 Nobel Prize in Literature. 'In a distant past, all poetry was sung or tunefully recited, poets were rhapsodes, bards, troubadours; "lyrics" comes from "lyre",' declared Horace Engdahl, a Swedish historian and literary critic, his words constituting a truism that long guided Beat poetics, particularly that of Kerouac and Allen Ginsberg in their efforts to rescue the literary arts from the sterility of the academic page.[3] Directly explicating Dylan's contribution to humane letters, Engdahl announced that Dylan had 'changed our idea of what poetry can be and how it can work . . . [and] [i]f people in the literary world groan, one must remind them that the gods don't write, they dance and they sing'. Mitchell herself, in a 1991 interview for *Rolling Stone*, explicitly credited Dylan's 'Positively Fourth Street' – his ambiguous, accusatory and narrative-driven hit single – with her move into complex literary modes: 'I realized that this was a whole new ballgame; now you could make your songs literature. The potential for the song had never occurred to me . . . But it [had] occurred to Dylan . . . And I began to write. So Dylan sparked me' (Wild, 1991).

Music and literary critics recognized this spark early on in Mitchell's career, evidenced, for example, by Homer Hogan's *Poetry of Relevance* (1970), a conventional high school English textbook featuring as poetry the lyrics of the Beatles, Jim Morrison and Mitchell. Hogan praised Mitchell's ability to manage both melody and words; explicated her lyrics as poetry with respect to attitude, manner, style, thought, description/narration and representation; and paired selected Mitchell lyrics with poems by authors including Amy Lowell, William Wordsworth, William Blake and John Keats.[4] Treated as poetry itself, then, Mitchell's song lyrics are ripe for connection to not only an impressive line of American-British modernist/Romantic poets, as Hogan illustrates, but also to other possible precursor literary giants such as Kerouac.

Nonetheless, this assemblage of extant treatment of a Kerouac-Mitchell connection alone does not serve as prima facie evidence, that is, evidence that on the face of it proves 'guilt' or 'innocence'. None of the expert testimony comes from exhaustive textual analysis, not even Hogan's, and the remainder in conjunction with the former constitutes at best circumstantial or indirect evidence requiring inferences to form connections between and among them. For instance, one can deduce that Mitchell was influenced (or may have been) by Kerouac. One might also infer that Mitchell was influenced by Ginsberg and Snyder or by only Cohen and Dylan or by Walt Whitman or William Wordsworth or Emily Dickinson or Rinpoche for that matter.

However, Mitchell's 'guilt' as a plausible finding becomes more realistic when one takes seriously the substantial list of topoi that her lyrics share with Kerouac's prose and poetry, ambivalence toward their own race, as Grier suggests, being but one of these. What follows is by no means comprehensive, and some are aesthetically more substantial than others: Travel, Confession, Freedom, Anti-Materialism, Low Art/High Art Fusion, Jazz, Spontaneous/Improvisational Composition Method, Voice of Wisdom and Prophesy, Sexuality/Gender, Love, the Natural World, Bums/the Dispossessed, Nietzsche, Buddhism, Dreams, Native Americans, Painting, Canadian Heritage, Race and Love of Cats. Exploration of these as grounds of consubstantiality could prove fruitful. For instance, studying Mitchell's song lyrics to discern her approach to Buddhism, to which she was introduced in art school (Marom, 2014, p. 155), and Kerouac's, which he initially learned about through reading Dwight

Goddard's *The Buddhist Bible* in the early 1950s, might reveal commonalities and/or innovations in American translations and adaptions of Buddhist texts and practices.

Likewise, a study of the voice of wisdom and prophecy, itself associated with the topoi of Buddhism, could build on moments when a reader hears echoes, albeit faint, of Kerouac's Shakespearean-New Testament modulated speech in a Mitchell lyric, as one might with this passage from Kerouac's *Doctor Sax*: 'Beef is going into Eternity at his end without me – my end is as far from his as eternity – Eternity hears hollow voices in a rock? Eternity hears ordinary voices in the parlor. On a bone the ant descends' (1959, p. 105), and this excerpt from Mitchell's 'Hejira': 'We all come and go unknown / Each so deep and superficial / Between the forceps and the stone' (1998, p. 164). Similarly, Mitchell's use of serpent and bird imagery in lyrics such as 'Don Juan's Reckless Daughter' and 'Snakes and Ladders', eerily similar to Kerouac's Great Snake of the World in *On the Road* and *Doctor Sax*, could serve as a foundation for an archetypal and Gnostic element unifying the two artists' linguistic representations of themselves and American post-World War II culture – all held together by the contrapuntal movement of the pair, Kerouac's voice driving relentlessly away from the semantic and narratival into music toward an escape from sound altogether as we see in *Old Angel Midnight* and *Mexico City Blues*, Mitchell's moving away from folksy ballad melodies toward longer, more syntactically complex linguistic and narratival constructions, such as those on *Don Juan's Reckless Daughter* and 'The Reoccurring Dream' (a multi-vocal song that she has described as more 'textual' than melodic (Denberg, 1998)) from the later *Chalkmark in a Rain Storm* (1988). Finally, such studies grounded in close readings can lead to the topic of composition style, both artists employing idiosyncratic jazz-based improvisational methods. Mitchell, for instance, told Malka Maron in a 2012 interview that her, Mitchell's, composing process 'coming out of *Hejira*' was like 'improvising around a melody that only I knew' (2014, p. 155), something akin to Kerouac's method which featured a procedure that he described as 'undisturbed flow from the mind of personal secret idea-words, blowing (as per jazz musician) on subject of image' (Charters, 1995, p. 484). Both are on record comparing their composition process to painting/sketching with words.

Taking Grier's lead, one might also pursue a fuller exploration of race as it intersects with sex and gender. This research could pair Kerouac's desire to be African American 1) expressed through Sal Paradise's desire to be 'a Negro, feeling that the best the white world had offered was not enough ecstasy for [him]' (1979, p. 180) and 2) his novel *Pic* (1971) narrated by a young black boy, with Mitchell's long-time involvement with black musicians, leading to her strong self-identification as black and her performative transformation into the black male hipster Art Nouveau, who appears on the cover of *Don Juan's Reckless Daughter*. Both can also be analysed around the controversy created by the 2017 publication, in the venerable feminist philosophy journal *Hypatia*, of an essay by Rebecca Tuvel arguing that transracial can be considered as viable as transgender.[5] Following Zadie Smith's non-judgemental discovery of Mitchell's 'black period', such a study could also seek to move beyond superficial unease and embarrassment, even outrage, at white ambivalence toward whiteness itself – much of which constitutes the current political climate – revealing instead the subterranean realities of complex racialized identities (2012, p. 35).

Along this same line, and this is not insignificant, one can infer that Mitchell and the Beats/Kerouac co-existed at a time dominated by a particular cultural discourse in the West, a fairly simple case to make based on a substantial body of American literary and cultural history. Topoi such as many of those listed above signify not only salient features of twentieth-century American counterculture but also the very bedrock of American identity against which *and along with* Americans have always negotiated – and which have influenced Canadian cultures for centuries as well. One can even go so far as to liken the comparative evidence to the analogical recognition that 1) humans share approximately 60 percent of the same genes with the tomato and 2) individuals of European descent can trace themselves genetically back to seven females[6] – meaning that convincing evidence of distinction is instead a marker of the mundane, a revelation that a comparison of Kerouac and Mitchell *flattens and democratizes* rather than separates and distinguishes.

Further refinement of and attention to these topoi, and others, might prove useful case studies to Beat Studies, American Studies, North American Historical and Cultural Studies, Popular Culture Studies and others. But even so, generating new evidence through such comparative analyses, while portending valuable cultural insights as well as new visions of both artists, again serves as circumstantial/indirect evidence. These potential studies, without access to archival data, do not resolve a question of direct influence.

It appears then that we are left with a mystery that one can resolve at best through 'a death by a thousand cuts', meaning that the most likely solution is based not on confessions or unassailable direct evidence such as eye witness testimony (e.g., 'I saw Mitchell composing a song using Kerouac's poetry as a template') but on a barrage of circumstantial inculpatory evidence, that which the literary critic Ihab Hassan called 'facile claim[s]' (1955, p. 66). If an investigator assembles enough of such material, one may be convinced by at least a preponderance of evidence and perhaps to even beyond-a-reasonable-doubt – in other words, each facile claim in the context of more and more such claims exponentially accrues strength and credibility – that Mitchell, for reasons that remain a mystery, is 'guilty' of denying a credible and direct aesthetic association to Jack Kerouac, no matter how flat and mundane that may be. Case closed.

This is where many an investigator might leave it. But when one looks for the kind of evidence, whether direct or indirect, that would have the *greatest* chance of standing up in court, a high bar for which even the literary sleuth might strive, the case for a Kerouac–Mitchell connection begins to unravel. We have yet to find that lost photograph of Mitchell reading *On the Road*, a twin of the one of Jackie Kennedy reading *The Dharma Bums* or Marilyn Monroe reading James Joyce's *Ulysses*. We have no interviews or letters in which she remarks on the importance of reading his novels, nothing such as her statement that 'Both Sides Now' was influenced by Saul Bellow's *Henderson the Rain King*.[7] No detailed patterns in her lyrics of appropriated Kerouacian language, analogous to Kerouac's long poem 'Sea' that concludes *Big Sur* as homage to Joyce's 'Proteus' episode in *Ulysses*. No specific references to Kerouac in her lyrics, such as those in LeRoi Jones/Amiri Baraka's 'In Memory of Radio': 'Who has ever stopped to think of the divinity of Lamont Cranston / (Only Jack Kerouac, that I know of: & me' (Charters, 1992, p. 340). No notes on composition methods connecting her improvisational methods to his spontaneous prose. No copy of *On the Road* with her annotations. No tattered postcard to an art school chum saying that she's 'got to find herself like Jack' and signed with a big wobbly heart and smiley face. No images or stories of them meeting, hanging out – a young lithesome Mitchell, born in 1943, sitting starry-eyed beside the aging Kerouac, 21 years her senior and an American pop culture icon when she was still in high school in Saskatoon. No eyewitness accounts of anything explicitly Kerouacian. And note that even if such direct evidence existed it must be treated with great care and efforts to corroborate since decades of scientific research have shown that eyewitness testimony is often unreliable. In the same vein, research in psychology and neuroscience over the decades has found human memory to be fallible, in effect undermining Mitchell's own memories about the importance to her art of individuals such as Cohen and Dylan.[8]

We do have photographs of Mitchell with Allen Ginsberg on the Rolling Thunder tour;[9] an interview in which Anne Waldman states that Mitchell gave her a dulcimer to accompany her poetry on that same tour (Billotte, 1976); Ginsberg's 29 June 1976 letter to Bob Dylan and 'composed also is for eye of Joni Mitchell', requesting money to support the founding of the Jack Kerouac School of Disembodied Poetics (2008, p. 387); and a statement from the Canadian poet Fred Wah remembering Mitchell attending a Vancouver party in 1963 to meet Allen Ginsberg (Sornberger, 2013, p. 182). So with respect to the Beats as a coterie, we have a modicum of forensic evidence (the photographs at the 'crime' scene, so to speak) and direct evidence from at least two self-identified Beat writers, Ginsberg and Waldman, alluding to some kind of connection to (Ginsberg) or relationship with (Waldman) Mitchell, and one eyewitness statement (Wah). But with respect to Kerouac, we are left with no oral testimony, no witness statements, no tangible evidence, no forensic evidence, no documentary evidence – and not even hearsay evidence.

Add the fact that each worked in different media and the 'guilty' resolution becomes less viable. First it must be acknowledged that Kerouac never considered himself a musician and despite the fact that he informally studied jazz and later in life read his works to jazz accompaniment (the most famous being his reading from *Visions of Cody*, masked as *On the Road*, to Steve Allen's jazz piano in 1959 on *The Steve Allen Show*), he was by no means a singer, songwriter or instrumentalist.[10] Likewise and conversely, Mitchell long considered herself a painter before she began writing song lyrics, language intended to work as companion to music itself. In fact, she has stated that she frequently writes the music first and then constructs 'three sets of lyrics before [she's] satisfied' (Whitesell, 2008, p. 41), fundamentally the opposite of Kerouac's spontaneous method, to which only a small portion had music added much later as a secondary or cosmetic feature.

Then too – despite the worthy claims made by Horace Engdahl – the musicality of literary language is not identical to the musicality of the sound that comes from, say, a saxophone, a guitar or a human voice. Musical harmony is the simultaneous occurrence of tones and pitches written as chords in vertical form denoting simultaneous production of multiple sounds – and performed as such. Literary harmony, however, exists in de facto linearity as words or letters moving horizontally, vertically or diagonally across a page, the pleasing nature (i.e., harmony) of various sounds assembled, if at all, in the reader's mental transcription and translation of the written text – the sounds never occur simultaneously. Similarly, that which we recognize as a literary composition appears *and is* distinctly different from a musical composition. Even when an author such as Kerouac intentionally uses musical forms and concertedly moves literary discourse away from the semantic and toward pure sound itself, the product is distinctly different from a conventional musical score.[11] For instance, Kerouac's musical method of creating *Mexico City Blues* with recurring rhythms and phrases and 'the linking of sound units from line to line and chorus to chorus' (Grace, 2007, p. 164) ultimately produces the language of lyric poems, just as do his efforts to create poetic discourse that looks like words being sung or meant to be sung – as in these cases: 'Of o cean wave' and 'Ra diance!' (*Book of Blues*, pp. 98, 99) as well as 'A–mer–ri–kay' and 'ho / o / ome' (*Book of Blues*, 34th and 38th choruses from 'San Francisco Blues'). These are clearly not musical scores, no matter the extent to which he intentionally manipulated features of musical composition.

As John Leland, author of *Why Kerouac Matters: The Lessons of On The Road*, concluded in 2001, '[a]s poems, even good song lyrics often feel beholden to easy rhymes or predictable formulas. Taken out of [their musical] context, these songwriting conventions often feel exposed and mannered. Music is a soft lyric's best friend, and a lot of verses . . . can use the companionship.'[12] As for poetry succeeding as music, Benjamin Lempert argues in an essay on the jazz poetics of Langston Hughes and Charles Olson that 'the "dream" of a written poem's literally being a mode of music remains forever "deferred", and why the idealized overcoming of the divide separating poetry from music remains unrealizable in the poem' (p. 310). Perhaps, we may infer, the divide remains concretized in the musical lyric as well. Therefore, yes, Mitchell's lyrics can be (and have been) read as poetry, Whitesell's being the most convincing analysis available, but does that mean that Kerouac's prosody is a distinct and aesthetically significant influence on Mitchell's prosody/songwriting? Not directly, by any means. Ultimately, the links between Kerouac's and Mitchell's media prove vexing, rendering it a challenge for a critic to convincingly identify a direct or even indirect (i.e. via Cohen and Dylan) Kerouacian heritage in Mitchell's oeuvre. At this point, even the most amateur of detectives faces the fact that to date the evidentiary ledger stands as a glass half empty rather than one half full: A correlation can be argued but not cause and effect. Mitchell is found not guilty: case closed. Or perhaps we have a hung jury.

All that being said, if this were a real-life police procedure, one dependent on using the law to resolve the matter rather than the homespun genius of a Miss Marple or the Oxford-based superiority of a Lord Peter Wimsey, one ought to have already identified the relevant law(s), along with key terms and their definitions in said legislation, as well as how courts have interpreted them. None of which we have done up to this point, since in the world of literature and the arts, there is no set of laws governing how artists are to create, the materials they can use and the processes with which they use them, other than laws of copyright and trademark. In fact, Helmut K. Anheier and Jüigen Gerhards, in an esoteric yet informative quantitative study of late twentieth-century German authors' opinions on influence, astutely recognize that '[m]odern literature lacks universal criteria for evaluating and identifying art'. While the Zeitgeist demands 'innovations, originality, and breach of tradition', Western writers find themselves in what Anheier and Gerhards call 'a position of aesthetic uncertainty [which] may be reduced by using other writers as reference points ...' (1991, pp. 139–40). It is this concept of *influence*, then, a more capacious term than 'reference point', that stands as an aesthetic substitute for the rule of law.[13] It is to that point that the Kerouac-Mitchell investigation must turn for a restart or redirection. Without doing so, any assemblage of evidence linking Mitchell directly to Kerouac inevitably floats away unattached, as we have already seen with our compilation of indirect evidence.

Influence, however, proves complicated, as is often the case with legal language and other forms of discourse. A basic dictionary definition may seem straightforward: 'The capacity to have an effect on the character, development, or behaviour of someone or something, or the effect itself.' But when one turns to the use of the term in literary critical discourse, questions and contradictions arise. For instance, in *The Dictionary of Literary Influences, 1914–2000* (2004), a standard reference tool published by Greenwood Press, editor John Powell uses a broad brush, defining *influence* as '[t]he relationship between [one's] achievements and [one's] reading' (p. xv). It can also mean the relation between a writer and other writers, the relation between a writer and traditions or the relation between a writer and a metaphysical muse. It can be, and has often been, confused with inspiration, as the charming list in Ihab Hassan's still astute 1955 essay on influence attests, Hassan noting mores, climate, locale, historical events (e.g., the Black Death), literary genres and others, along with forms denoting influence, such as forgeries and borrowings (pp. 66–7). Influence can be interpreted as positive, or, as in the case of Oscar Wilde's literary presentation of it in *The Picture of Dorian Gray*, an immoral act whereby one loses one's very soul (Wilde, p. xx). Some, such as Hassan, find the term extremely ambiguous, 'called upon to account for any relationship, running the gamut of incidence to causality, with a somewhat expansive range of intermediate correlations' (1955, p. 67). He rightly concludes that to do influence justice one must follow a procedure something along the lines of Friedrich Schleiermacher's hermeneutics, a process so rigorous that to make the study of influence at all viable one should instead concentrate on *tradition* and *development*.

The most widely recognized treatment of influence, however, is Harold Bloom's *The Anxiety of Influence*, which, odd as it may sound to some twenty-first-century readers, proves most useful in an investigation into Mitchell's relationship to Beat poetics. Bloom tackles the matter in terms of the impact of a strong poet, one of genius, on the development of a younger strong poet. *Influence* for Bloom is the act of *misinterpretation* on the part of the younger poet, albeit a necessary act that creates imaginative space for poets to assert their own unique identities to counter obliteration as a poet (2003, pp. 5, 71). The process results in 'anxiety and self-serving caricature, of distortion, of perverse, willful revisionism without which modern poetry as such could not exist' (p. 30). Loosely applying a Freudian, or family romance, perspective, Bloom identifies six types of misrepresentation: a deliberate misrepresentation or corrective of a precursor (clinamen or swerve); complete and antithesis (tessera) in which the poet 'antithetically "completes" his precursor' (p. 14); a deliberate break with the precursor (kenosis); counter-sublime to the precursor (daemonization); purgation and solipsism (askesis); and a final 'return of the dead' (apophrades), in which the younger poet seems to have been able to write the precursor's work, that is, erasing the precursor historically and aesthetically. Bloom sought to create a method for effectively reading the work of one genius through the lens of another genius's work, or the younger poem as a 'deliberate misrepresentation' of the precursor poem. Doing so, he contends, is more productive than merely reading a single poem as a decontextualized, solitary unit. He disassociates his definition of influence both from non- poetical forces and from what he called 'the transmission of ideas and images from earlier to later poets, [to] the history of ideas ... the wearisome industry of source-hunting, of allusion-counting', about which, ironically, this investigation up to this point has been most concerned.[14]

In accordance with Bloom's paradigm, then, one can say that weaker, more mundane poets are those who allow themselves to become vessels of mechanical imitation, rather than using the contentious relationship to transform the precursor's work. Bloom's paradigm is not without its faults (his misogynist Oedipal father–son perspective being the most obvious), but as a tool of linguistic definition and application, the closest one can come to a legal principle, it takes our investigation in a, perhaps surprisingly, more fruitful direction with respect to Mitchell's own statements about the issue.

So we once again return to her own language about Beat writers, the quoted passages that introduce this chapter:

1. That whole pocket of modern art is my least favorite in art history. I was kind of a Dadaist to the Beats in a certain way. Musically, they annoyed me. In painting, they annoyed me, and I made no bones about it.

2. I never was an anarchist. Never. No, that's probably why I don't like [the Beats]. You need rules and regulations, but you need just ones.

3. I wasn't a fan of the Beats. I didn't like to see the underbelly revered. I figured it had its place, but I didn't want to be an imitator of it. I'm not a book burner but I longed for something more wholesome. God knows why I longed for the impossible. In high school I did a lot of satire on the Beats and on abstraction.

It is language that frankly denotes knowledge of Beat writers as precursors of a great enough magnitude that she, early on also heralded as an artist of great magnitude, positions herself in opposition to them. There is a relationship with them, Kerouac implicitly included under the term *Beat*, which she directly acknowledges. Most vehemently, she identifies herself as a Dadaist, a fascinating descriptor that despite Tristan Tzara's claim that the word had no meaning is also, according to his own words, amongst others, destructive action, including the destruction of logic, good manners and social hierarchy. Mitchell then claims that she used the Beats as fodder (my language, not hers) for satire out of her desire for a more wholesome view of the world. Her statements project an anxiety of influence that led her art in its earliest stages away from the Beat vortex rather than in alignment with or imitation of Beat writers, and one can argue that the force with which she expresses her opposition to Beat poetics suggests that it seriously threatened her vision of herself as an original artist, whether poet, painter, musician or songwriter. Perhaps she consciously or unconsciously feared the kind of influence Oscar Wilde wrote about, the possibility of losing one's entire self to the viral possession of past literary genius.

By applying Bloom's theory of misrepresentation to Mitchell's own claims regarding Beat influence, we find three categories that seem most appropriate to this case: the swerve, antithesis and completion, and discontinuity. While Bloom's theory suggests that the young strong poet will take one over the other five, he doesn't discount a combination of tactics, which is what we find in our investigation of Mitchell.

Swerve

The swerve is the foundational move of the anxiety of influence, the moment when the younger poet recognizes that she must move away from the precursor, exactly what Mitchell remembers she did as a teenager. Granted, her teenage satire is likely not the mature work of the younger poet, but it might stand as evidence that even at an early age, for her, Beat writing was significant enough in popular culture that she used it to practise and develop her own art as a swerve away from Beat poetics. Additional markers of this swerve are her statements about the nature of Beat writing as both anarchistic and a revelation of the cultural underbelly, neither an entirely inaccurate representation but a misrepresentation of Beat writing overall. Interestingly, Mitchell might have come to understand, at least during the 1975 Thunder tour, the broad and deep complexities of Beat discourse, including its beatific elements, which Kerouac as well as Ginsberg emphasized – enough to recalibrate her representation of them. But she did not, instead, still repeating 50-some years later a 'beatnik' vision of Beat Generation writers as a cultural abomination.

Antithetical completion

Bloom contends that poets of antithetical completion consider themselves to be a 'completing link' and that they must persuade themselves and their readers that as a poet the precursor's work must be 'fulfilled and enlarged' (p. 67). The young poet travels an oppositional path, all the time working to complete the precursor's work by making it something larger, more whole. With Mitchell, one can say that her desire for wholesomeness is a statement of belief that the anarchistic Beat focus on the cultural underbelly was but a small piece of a superior poetic reality and that poems complete that artifice instigated by the antithetical turn to wholesomeness along with just rules and regulations.

Discontinuity

Bloom argued that '"[u]ndoing" the precursor's strength in *oneself* serves also to "isolate" the self from the precursor's stance' while appearing to eradicate the younger one's own '"divinity" as well' (pp. 90–1). In other words, the young poet must strip the precursor of their power through self-abnegation that further distances the younger from the precursor. With Mitchell, her identification as Dadaist opposition may be the most explicit evidence of this kind of anxiety of influence. As a Dadaist, she tears down everything that Beat writers have created, refusing to be an imitator, but she also undermines her own poetic process by associating herself with a movement that declared itself essentially nihilistic in nature, if not at least anarchistic, which she denied. An additional marker of discontinuity is Mitchell's declaration that she was seeking wholesomeness, the opposite of the Beat 'underbelly', yet admitting that she was seeking the impossible, a linguistic manoeuvre that empties her work of Beat influence, while she separates herself from their poetic power through her admission that what she sought was impossible. In other words, in opposition she situates herself as a force significantly strong enough to destroy them, but her identity as poet remains tied to Beat prosody; consequently, she must empty herself of that oppositional identity to some degree in order to create her own imaginative space.

Textual evidence of Mitchell's anxiety of influence – a brief discussion

Examples of lyrics that transparently appear to represent Mitchell's swerve are 'Both Sides Now', 'Chelsea Morning', 'Big Yellow Taxi', 'Michael From Mountains' and

'Woodstock', all five of which counter the anarchistic, 'underbelly' focus of Beat texts such as John Clellon Holmes's *Go*, William S. Burroughs' *Naked Lunch*, Ginsberg's 'Howl' and even Kerouac's *On the Road* – texts emphasizing in various ways the hidden reality of America's dispossessed. However, since we don't know which specific Beat works Mitchell might have read, in order to pursue a Bloomian overture of textual evidence to demonstrate the reading of her poems as manifestations of her anxiety of influence, we'll take as an example the most obvious possibility, Kerouac's *On the Road*, looking specifically at the conclusion, that famous paragraph in which Sal Paradise declares that God is Pooh Bear before rhapsodizing about memory and the night:

> The evening star must be dropping and shedding her sparkler dims on the prairie, which is just before the coming of complete night that blesses the earth, darkens all rivers, cups the peaks and folds the final shore in, and nobody, nobody knows what's going to happen to anybody besides the forlorn rags of growing old, I think of Dean Moriarty, I even think of Old Dean Moriarty, the father we never found, I think of Dean Moriarty.
>
> (pp. 309–10)

Kerouac, at the peak of his literary powers, concludes the travels of his protagonist, Sal, which have led him ultimately into what he calls the fellaheen world of Mexico, a world seemingly void of authoritative structure in which he achieves ecstasy and self-reliance sufficient enough to allow him to return home where he settles down and marries the girl of his dreams. Sal's search for the indefinable 'It' has led him back to acquiescence in a world predicated on a mélange of just and unjust laws and regulations, to a version of 'wholesomeness' defined as heterosexual marriage. In that move, Sal has also gained knowledge about himself and others, the futility of human progress, the power of love and ultimately death, the only certainty a fellow human can rely on, as conveyed through his elegiac memory of his spiritual guide, Dean Moriarty. It is a beatific vision that situates freedom of the self in an unnamed transcendent space, leaving the material self in a state of semi-servitude and mourning.

In contrast, Mitchell, at the peak of her powers one can argue in her jazz-inspired 'Paprika Plains' (which fills the second side of *Don Juan's Reckless Daughter*), achieves an antithetical completion of Kerouac. Whereas Sal has to leave the comfort of his aunt's home for the hardships of the road and working-class life before returning home to gift his reader with a bleak vision of all-encompassing night and old age, Mitchell's first-person narrator leaves a grungy bar scene to take a transcendental space odyssey over the American plains, through history and without time, the self a floating Emersonian eye guiding the speaker/singer to slash her vision of the earth from 'space probe photographs' so that she can return to the bar of her departure, to a place of material certitude and human connection, her voice ecstatic as it anticipates her reunion with a nameless 'you':

As I'm coming through the door
I'm coming back
I'm coming back for more!
The band plugs in again
You see that mirrored ball begin to sputter lights
And spin
Dizzy on the dancers
Geared to changing rhythms
No matter what you do
I'm floating back
I'm floating back to you!

(1997, pp. 185–6)

A similar antithetical completion, conjoined with discontinuity, concludes 'Don Juan's Reckless Daughter', a poem that in its use of the symbol of the snake echoes that same archetypal trope in Kerouac's *Doctor Sax*, as we noted earlier. The speaker/singer repeats a Sal Paradise vision of bleakness – 'We are all hopelessly oppressed cowards / Of some duality / Of restless multiplicity' – but then erases that position in the final stanza: '*The spirit talks in spectrums* / He talks to mother earth to father sky / Self indulgence to self denial / Man to woman / Scales to feathers / You and I' (1997, pp. 192–3, emphasis mine). In effect, the poem empties itself of Kerouac and of Mitchell herself – the hallmarks of discontinuity – by first freely imitating the Kerouacian vision but then negating both it and her use of it by expanding – the antithetical completion – Kerouac's solipsistic dualism of the self and the ocean of night into the unity of the spectrum, a transcendental spirit world encompassing the 'You and I'.

Resolution of the case?

When I began this investigation, I was convinced that I might well have to conclude that the question of Mitchell's guilt or innocence relative to Kerouac as an influence was at its deepest level meant to discredit Mitchell's originality, a swerve of its own rooted in a kind of critical misogynistic anxiety of influence. That may well be true. But as the investigation gained momentum, the volume of circumstantial evidence persistently led me to think that the best 'Detecting Jack Kerouac and Joni Mitchell' could do was to find that Mitchell belongs in the Beat lineage, the lines of creation that inevitably exist in tombs and tangles that rarely see the light of day. Lineage is something that one recognizes and acknowledges, or it can be recognized by a second or third party, such as a literary critic or historian. The complex body of work created by Beat writers descends from a number of lineages, including British-American Romanticism; European-American modernism; European surrealism, Dadism and vorticism; Western cinema; Eastern religious traditions and practices; Judeo-Christian theology; world folklore, and others. Mitchell's lyrics fit relatively smoothly into these, as well as others, so I maintain that the lineage argument is accurate. Yes, to the extent possible as a branch on a tree of descent presses forward in time, Joni Mitchell was influenced by Jack Kerouac, however minimal that use or appropriation might be – and bearing in mind that the 'Jack Kerouac' who influenced her may be a phantom conjured by the readers and audience of Mitchell's lyrics or a hybrid composite of authors of American wisdom literature, a Kerouac far removed from the flesh and bone writer who introduced America to the Beat Generation. In this respect, then, Joni Mitchell is exonerated.

However, when I turned the investigative lens of Bloom's theory of the anxiety of influence toward Mitchell, the possibility of a genuine, direct Beat influence became more plausible. Mitchell's dogged denials of such a connection took on enhanced meaning, projecting an anxiety of influence. We're still left with little direct connection between Mitchell and Kerouac, but at least critical readers now have a viable starting point from which to legitimately examine Mitchell's work as *poetic misrepresentation*, or *misprision* as Bloom called it, of various Beat texts. The above brief discussion of *On the Road* and *Don Juan's Reckless Daughter* is just the beginning . . .

And one must remember, the search for literary influence has no statute of limitations: direct evidence may appear 50 years hence leading the Kerouac-Mitchell scholar-detective to declare without a reasonable doubt a definitive connection.

The case remains open.

Notes

1. This derogatory rebranding took place not only through San Francisco columnist Herb Caen's use of the term beatnik but also through Fred Macdarrah's Rent-A-Beatnik parties in the late 1950s and early 1960s contemporaneously with the dim-witted beatnik Maynard G. Krebs in the sitcom *The Many Loves of Doby Gillis*.

2. Researchers may easily come upon Carl Wilson's review of Monk's book for the *Literary Review of Canada* in 2013 in which he claims that Monk stated that Kerouac had been on the Revue tour: 'The book is based entirely on previous press coverage, so anyone who has followed Mitchell over the years will find much . . . of it familiar – and, in places, inaccurate. For example, Monk says that Mitchell had a Buddhist teacher recommended to her by Jack Kerouac during Dylan's Rolling Thunder Revue tour in 1975, when Kerouac had been dead for six years; Monk probably means Allen Ginsberg, who was on the tour' (http://reviewcanada.ca/magazine/2013/01/an-awkward-original/; accessed 17 March 2017). Monk, in fact, knew that it was Ginsberg and stated as much in her book. Wilson's claim appears to be an egregious misreading.

3. See my essay 'The Beats and Literary History: Myths and Realities' in the *Cambridge Companion to the Beats* (2017) for a discussion of how Beat writers often denied the importance of academic writing and education in the development of their art.

4. http://www.jonimitchell.com/Library/view.cfm?id=3349 (accessed 17 March 2017).

5. See 'In Defense of Transracialism' by Rebecca Tuvel, *Hypatia* 32, no. 2 (Spring 2017): 263–78. Grier's essay 'The Only Black Man at the Party: Joni Mitchell Enters the Rock Canon' for *Genders Online Journal* is an excellent starting point, in conjunction with Kevin Fellezs's 'Gender, Race, and the Ma(s)king of "Joni Mitchell"' in the *Cambridge Companion to the Singer-Songwriter*.

6. See *The Seven Daughters of Eve* (2002) by geneticist Brian Sykes.

7. Mitchell told Gene Shay in his 1967 interview with her that she'd been 'reading a book, and I [hadn't] finished it yet, called *Henderson the Rain King* [by Saul Bellow]. And there's a line in it that I especially got hung up on that was about when he was flying to Africa and searching for something, he said that in an age when people could look up and down at clouds, they shouldn't be afraid to die. And so I got this idea "from both sides now". There are a lot of sides to everything, and so the song is called "From Both Sides, Now"'.

8. Research on these topics is extremely extensive, but see, for example, as a good starting point https://www.innocenceproject.org/science-behind-eyewitness-identification-reform/ (accessed 17 March 2017).

9. http://ginsbergblog.blogspot.com/2014/09/joni-mitchell.html (accessed 17 March 2017).

10. For an extended discussion of Kerouac's mass media fame, see Ronna Johnson's '"You're putting me on": Jack Kerouac and the Postmodern Emergence', in *Reconstructing the Beats*, edited by Jennie Skerl.

11. See my chapter 'Songs and Prayers' in *Jack Kerouac and the Literary Imagination* for additional examples and discussion of this phenomenon.

12. http:jonimitchell.com/library/view.cfm?id=651 (accessed 17 March 2017).

13. Anheiser and Herhard's major finding was that 'the denial/absence of acknowledged influence is found among writers who are excluded from the professional networks where reputations are made in the world of literature' (p. 137), a contradiction to the general consensus regarding Anglo-American writers and influence.

14. He also expressed antipathy toward what we now call digital humanities: 'an industry that will soon touch apocalypse anyway when it passes from scholars to computers' (p. 31).

Bibliography

Anheier, H. K. and J. Gerhards, 'Acknowledgment of Literary Influence: A Structural Analysis of a German Literary Network', *Sociological Forum* 6, no. 1 (1991): 137–56.

Belletto, S. (ed.), 'The Beats in Literary History: Myths and Realities', in *Cambridge Companion to the Beats*, Cambridge: Cambridge University Press, 2017, pp. 62–76.

Billotte, L., *Berkeley Barb*, 17–23 September 1976, p. 11.

Bloom, H., *The Anxiety of Influence*, New York: Oxford, 1973.

Charters, A. (ed.), *The Portable Beat Reader*, New York: Penguin, 1992.

Charters, A. (ed.), *The Portable Jack Kerouac*, New York: Penguin, 1995, pp. 484–5.

Coupe, L., *Beat Sound, Beat Vision: The Beat Spirit and the Popular Song*, Manchester: Manchester University Press, 2007.

Denberg, J., 'Jody Denberg's Conversation with Joni Mitchell', 8 September 1998, http://jonimitchell.com/library/view.cfm?id=1362 (accessed 3 July 2017).

Engdahl, H., 'The Nobel Prize in Literature 2016 – Presentation Speech', 2017, Nobelprize.org, Nobel Media AB 2014, http://www.nobelprize.org/nobel_prizes/literature/laureates/2016/presentation-speech.html (accessed 14 June 2017).

Enright, R., 'Words and Pictures: The Arts of Joni Mitchell', *Border Crossings*, 2001, http://jonimitchell.com/library/view.cfm?id=624 (accessed 15 May 2017).

Fellezs, K., 'Gender, Race, and the Ma(s)king of "Joni Mitchell"', in K. Williams and J. Williams (eds), *Cambridge Companion to the Singer-Songwriter*, Cambridge: Cambridge University Press, 2016, pp. 199–200.

Ginsberg, A. and B. Morgan (eds), *The Letters of Allen Ginsberg*, Philadelphia: First DaCapo Press, 2008.

Grace, N., *Jack Kerouac and the Literary Imagination*, New York: Palgrave-Macmillan, 2007.

Grier, M. P., 'The Only Black Man at the Party Joni Mitchell Enters the Rock Canon', *Genders Online Journal* 56 (Fall 2012): 1–9, file://localhost/Users/mpg236/Library/Application%20Support/Firefox/Profiles/6j2j7c18.default/zotero/storage/ZRCZHWE4/g56_grier.html (accessed 29 June 2017).

Hassan, I., 'The Problem of Influence in Literary History: Notes Towards a Definition', *Journal of Aesthetics and Art Criticism* 14, no. 1 (1955): 66–76.

Hogan, H., *Poetry of Relevance*, London: Methuen, 1970, http://www.jonimitchell.com/Library/view.cfm?id=3349 (accessed 17 June 2017).

Johnson, R., '"You're putting me on": Jack Kerouac and the Postmodern Emergence', *College Literature* 27, no. 1 (2000): 22–38.

Kerouac, J., *Doctor Sax*, New York: Grove Press, 1959.

Kerouac, J., *On the Road: Text and Criticism*, ed. Scott Donaldson, New York: Viking, 1979.

Leland, J., 'It's Only Rhyming Quatrains, but I Like It: Do Songs Succeed as Poetry?', *New York Times Magazine*, 8 July 2001, http://jonimitchell.com/library/view.cfm?id=651 (accessed 1 June 2017).

Lempert, B. R., 'Hughes/Olson: Whose Music? Whose Era?', *American Literature* 87, no. 2 (2015): 303–30.

Marom, M., *Joni Mitchell In Her Own Words: Conversations with Malka Marom*, Toronto: ECW Press, 2014.

McIntyre, T., 'Untamed Tiger', *San Francisco Examiner*, 20 October 1998, http://jonimitchell.com/library/view.cfm?id=330 (accessed 29 June 2017).

Mitchell, J., *Joni Mitchell: The Complete Poems and Lyrics*, New York: Three Rivers Press, 1997.

Monk, K., *Joni: The Creative Odyssey of Joni Mitchell*, Vancouver and Berkeley: Greystone Books, 2008.

Powell, J., *The Dictionary of Literary Influences, 1914–2000*, Westport, CT: Greenwood Press, 2004.

Shay, G., 'Folklore Program', 12 March 1967, http://jonimitchell.com/music/song.cfm?id=83 (accessed 30 June 2017).

Skerl, J., *Reconstructing the Beats*, New York: Palgrave-Macmillian, 2004.

Smith, Z., 'Some Notes on Attunement: A Voyage Around Joni Mitchell', *New Yorker*, 17 December 2012, pp. 30–5.

Sornberger, L. and J. Sornberger, *Gathered Light: The Poetry of Joni Mitchell's Songs*, Toronto: Three O'Clock Press, 2013.

Sykes, B., *The Seven Daughters of Eve*, New York: Norton & Co., 2002.

Tzara, T., 'Dada Manifesto', 1918, http://391.org/manifestos/1918-dada-manifesto-tristan-tzara.html#.WUGjECMrLFw (accessed 14 May 2017).

Warner, S., *Text and Drugs and Rock 'N' Roll: The Beats and Rock Culture*, London: Bloomsbury, 2013.

Kerouac on Record

Weller, S., *Girls Like Us: Carole King, Joni Mitchell, Carly Simon – and the Journey of a Generation*, New York: Washington Square Press, 2008.

Whitesell, L., *The Music of Joni Mitchell*, Oxford: Oxford University Press, 2008.

Wild, D., 'A Conversation with Joni Mitchell', *Rolling Stone*, 30 May 1991, http://www.rollingstone.com/music/features/a-conversation-with-joni-mitchell-19910530 (accessed 27 June 2017).

Wilson, Carl, 'An Awkward Original: The price of refusing to fit into musical – or gender – boxes', *Literary Review of Canada*, 2013, http://reviewcanada.ca/magazine/2013/01/an-awkward-original/ (accessed 17 March 2017).

Discography

Mitchell, Joni, *Hissing of Summer Lawns*, Asylum, 1975.

Mitchell, Joni, *Don Juan's Reckless Daughter*, Asylum, 1977.

CHAPTER 16
KEROUAC AND COUNTRY MUSIC
Matt Theado

Country music is not a genre that comes immediately to mind when one reads Jack Kerouac's work, nor is it a genre that seemed to appeal to him. Dean Moriarty, the hero of *On the Road* (1957), dismisses a radio programme that plays 'cowboy hillbilly' as the 'worst program in the entire history of the country'. Kerouac writes corny dialogue for a hapless character in the novel, a 'moo-sician' who plays with 'Johnny Mackaw's Sagebrush Boys'. Yet Kerouac and country songwriters draw from many of the same American roots, and similarities can be found in their motifs of home, nostalgia and the road. In addition, some contemporary country songwriters refer directly to Kerouac in their lyrics to evoke a spiritual pursuit or the lure of the American highway.

Country music is a genre that lacks a clearly limited definition. In general terms, country is characterized by folk roots, Southern and Western influences, string instruments, comprehensible narrative lyrics (open vocals rather than schooled vibratos, often with a Southern accent), basic chords and song structures, and a reliance on traditional values – the importance of family, home, love and Christianity, although these are often thwarted by vice. In the first decades of the twentieth century, 'hillbilly' musicians might travel to urban areas such as New York City to record their music and seek their fame and fortune. Music historian Ted Olson points out that, at that time, 'hillbilly music' was 'a catch-all term for much of the white folk and popular music composed and performed in the southern United States'. A series of recording sessions in Bristol, Tennessee, in 1927 brought some of the influential artists such as Jimmie Rodgers and the Carter Family to large, record-buying audiences. The influence of these recordings has led to them being known ever after simply as 'The Bristol Recordings'. The term 'country' became increasingly prevalent for this music beginning in the 1940s, according to sociologist Richard A. Peterson, and is retroactively applied to the music that was first recorded in the 1920s (Peterson, 1997, p. 9).

In the past century, country music has absorbed existing styles and branched out into new areas that challenge traditionally accepted notions of the genre. Some of these areas include bluegrass, rockabilly, country and western, honky tonk, outlaw country, country rock and more. Country's breadth and inclusiveness account for the occasional appearance of performers such as Jon Bon Jovi and Lionel Richie on country-hit charts. For decades, Nashville, Tennessee, has been the commercial centre of country music, but the genre remains uncontained by Nashville. Independent musicians compose and perform music that is sometimes labelled alt-country, for example, yet it too is subsumed within the broad rubric of country. Some contemporary country stars, such as Carrie Underwood and Taylor Swift, have successfully crossed over to the category of pop music, blurring the line between the genres for many fans.

Kerouac and country music songwriters often focus on America as their subject. In fact, the term 'country' implies that it is music for and about the nation. In her 1994 book, *High Lonesome: The American Culture of Country Music*, Cecelia Tichi makes a case for country music's American-ness: 'It is not a trivia question to ask, What does country music have in common with Thomas Jefferson, Walt Whitman, American painters Thomas Cole and Edward Hopper, and twentieth-century writers like John Steinbeck and Jack Kerouac?' (Tichi, 1994, p. 6). Tichi believes that exploring this question reveals the degree to which country music is interwoven in the American fabric. By focusing on *On the Road*, we can see a few of the ways that Kerouac and country songwriters incorporate the subject of America. In the opening pages of *On the Road*, Sal Paradise yearns to travel across the country; he reads books about the pioneers and pores over maps, plotting his route west. Along the way, Sal marvels at the shifting ambience of the landscape and the changing characteristics of people as he recounts the delights and hardships of travel. His narrative parallels those of numerous earlier American writers, notably Francis Parkman in *The Oregon Trail* (1849), a book that helped establish a pattern: a traveller journeys from the comforts of the civilized East to the promised land of the West through an unforgiving wilderness.

This pattern is engrained in the American consciousness and in country music. 'Sweet Betsy from Pike' is a prototype of country music. Composed some time in the 1850s, the song narrates the westward adventure of Betsy and Ike, who set out from Pike County in the East and face numerous trials on their way to California where they are married, until Ike's jealousy leads to divorce. Carl Sandburg in *The American Songbag* claims that 'Sweet Betsy from Pike' 'has the stuff of a realistic novel' (Sandburg, 1997, p. 108). The genre is a handier format than a novel, though; the ballad's simple melody and tight rhymes made it easy for westward travellers to memorize and sing the song even as they identified with its hardships. Sandburg concludes, 'It was a good wagon song.' Many folk and country musicians have recorded the song, from Pete Seeger and Cisco Houston to Johnny Cash and David Allan Coe. 'Sweet Betsy from Pike' helped to establish a framework for the American odyssey that Kerouac would share: the comforts of the East, the American rural landscape, the lure of California, and the hardships of travel. Musician and music journalist Bob Stanley believes that the frontier myth is central to country music, 'the point at which settled domestic life and chaotic, perilous adventure meet' (Stanley, 2014, p. 290). For generations, people who never saw the Great Plains, let alone a live horse, would identify through country ballads with the pioneers, the cowboys and the gold-rush '49ers. By the time *On the Road* was published in 1957, Americans had been watching Hollywood westerns and hearing country songs for generations.

The Betsy and Ike western ballad delivered more than a mythic westward-ho spirit. The opening lines ('Oh, don't you remember sweet Betsy from Pike') suggest the listener's familiarity with a time recently gone. Nostalgia is a prominent and enduring characteristic of country songs; country frequently conjures an idyllic past when life was simpler, a longing shared by Kerouac in varying degrees throughout his work. The very timing of *On the Road*'s publication makes a kind of nostalgic statement. The book was popular in the late 1950s and early 1960s just as American travel was changing from a rural experience to one that was more homogenized and sanitized. The winding country highways that Sal and Dean navigated gave way to the Interstate highways that were forbidding to hitchhikers while at the same time providing sleek spots atop the exit ramps for franchise restaurants, nationwide service stations and chain hotels. In that sense, the novel portrays the haphazard road life that was quickly becoming a part of the country's past. Likewise, country music frequently evokes memories of the past's pleasures. For example, in 1982's 'Are the Good Times Really Over?', Merle Haggard longs for the days before the Vietnam War and the Beatles, while blaming the rise of cheaply built cars and microwave ovens for displacing the traditional lifestyle of the recent past. For Haggard, the quality of life has declined as people embraced low-quality, time-saving commodities. In popular culture, Kerouac's name often is evoked as a totem of an adventure-travelling, hitchhiking era in contrast to today's brisk SUV trips on superhighways where travellers watch DVDs and follow the directions given on their GPS.

On the Road summons nostalgia on more personal levels, too. Dean reminds Sal of his pleasant boyhood friends, rather than his current crop of metropolitan, derisive friends. When he hears Dean's voice, Sal recalls 'the wash-lined neighborhood and drowsy doorsteps of afternoon where boys played guitars while their older brothers worked in the mills' (Kerouac, 1957, p. 7). This theme of the simplicity of a small-town childhood is clarified in the title of Kerouac's first published novel, *The Town and the City* (1950). In both novels, Kerouac recreates the innocence of the childhood working-class home in a way that parallels many country songs where the singer longs for the simplicity of a personal past. From its roots, country has embraced nostalgic notions of home, often depicted in a small town or rural setting that contrasts with the tainted city. Bob Stanley points to country's identification with home as one reason that it 'predates and survives the modern pop age' (Stanley, 2014, p. 283). The genre's longevity, not to mention its popularity outside the US, 'is provided by an incredibly attractive shared canvas of memory', Stanley finds. 'It reminds people of home' (Stanley, 2014, p. 284).

In 1923, Fiddlin' John Carson made one of country's first recordings, 'Little Old Log Cabin in the Lane', which, according to music journalist Kurt Wolff, was country music's first big hit, selling more than 500,000 copies. The song shares a sentiment of the Plantation Myth: the workdays are long gone, the master and mistress are dead and the plantation is collapsing. The song's narrator, an old man who once worked on the plantation, longs to remain in his rundown cabin, his only connection to the past.

In fact, musicologist Travis Stimeling explains that 'one might read country music's occasional obsession with all things past and gone as an extension of the nineteenth-century plantation song', citing such seminal American tunes as Stephen Foster's 'Old Folks at Home' (1851) and 'My Old Kentucky Home' (1853). Considering various migration patterns in America – from South to North during the early 1900s, for example – Stimeling finds that nostalgia and a longing for one's past home have been mainstays of country music.

Cecilia Tichi also emphasizes the seminal importance of home in country music, offering as evidence the presence of 'Home, Sweet Home' picked out on a banjo on the first release of the Bristol recordings. It may be one of the most familiar lyrics in America – 'Be it ever so humble, there's no place like home' – and by just reading the lyrics one can hear the familiar melody. This song, Tichi declares, 'is virtually a country music keynote' (Tichi, 1994, p. 20). From its recorded origins, country was synonymous with the idea of home. The call to one's past home may reflect a deeper spiritual home as well. Sal suggests in *On the Road* that everyone starts life 'a sweet child believing in everything under [their] father's roof' (Kerouac, 1957, p. 97). Home represents safety, security and trust.

One of country's first stars, Jimmie Rodgers, recorded 'My Little Old Home Down in New Orleans' in 1928. Rodgers sings, amidst a run of pleasantly warbling yodels, of having travelled east and west and now longs to return to the land of his dreams, his old home. In the Carter Family's 'My Little Home in Tennessee' (1932), the singer is 'always lonely', yearning to return home. The fact that Sara and Maybelle Carter were cousins and sisters-in-law, with Sara's husband adding harmony, deepens the legitimacy of their sense of home. Through the decades, the homes of country songs typically are situated in peaceful rural areas and tended by the matronly care of mothers and grandmothers. In 1974, John Denver shared his 'Grandma's Feather Bed' with his listeners as a way of depicting a simple, untroubled past among extended family. Cousins, aunts, uncles, even barnyard animals, were all part of the carefree family as recalled by an adult who sifts through his childhood memories. In 1986 the Judds recorded 'Grandpa (Tell Me About the Good Old Days)' as a lament of their contemporary lives that moved too fast and with insufficient moral support.

In 'The House that Built Me', a number one hit on *Billboard*'s Hot Country Songs in 2010, Miranda Lambert revisits her childhood home, describing minute details of her past that her listeners might likewise share – her mother cutting out photos from *Better Homes and Gardens*, for example – in order to soothe her damaged emotions. Most pointedly, Kerouac's *Doctor Sax* (1959) is an exercise in reconstructing a personal past, replete with details of marble games and sandlot sports, that brings the past into the present for the purposes of reckoning with one's adult life.

Undoubtedly, the notion of home represents one of Kerouac's most persistent motifs. Although its representation often appears simple, as in Kerouac's descriptions of his childhood homes in *Doctor Sax* and *Maggie Cassidy* (1959), his use of home as a central motif can also be quite complex. In her analysis of *The Town and the City*,

Regina Weinreich describes Kerouac's 'myth of the ultimate Paradise or original home, in every sense as profound, spiritual, and unattainable as the Biblical one' (Weinrich, 2002, pp. 29–30). Weinreich points out that the characters in *The Town and the City* leave home because they are 'compelled by restlessness, by wanderlust, and by necessity' (Weinrich, 2002, p. 32), reasons that match the compulsions of characters in country songs.

The centrality of home in country music is contrasted by the lure of the road, which is another of Kerouac's themes as well. 'Sweet Betsy from Pike' established the motif of a goal at the end of the journey, and through the spectrum of country music's history and styles the road has maintained its fundamental allure. Dean's goal in *On the Road* seems to be as simple as it is stereotypical: 'a fast car, a coast to reach, and a woman at the end of the road' (Kerouac, 1957, p. 219). For Sal, though, the road is a circular journey that always leads back home. In fact, in most of Kerouac's novels – or 'true life stories' as he once called them – his alter ego is constantly seeking to return to his mother (or aunt, as in *On the Road*) at home, paralleling the situation in many country songs. One of the most famous country songs around the world continues to be John Denver's 'Country Roads (Take Me Home)', a worldwide hit in 1971 that continues to sell briskly as a digital download. This song describes a traveller's desire to return home, and as befits the traditional code for country lyrics, only 'country roads' can bring him to his 'mountain mamma', an alliterative conflation of geography and the mythic mother. Larry Gatlin's 'Houston (Means I'm One Day Closer to You)', a number one hit in 1983, concerns the protagonist's divided desires: his love of home and of the rodeo life. As is the case for Kerouac's narrator-travellers, the road connects one's home and one's aspirations.

Some country songs treat life on the road as destination in itself, and this lifestyle seems to be Dean's rationale and also one main reason for Sal's appreciation of him. Songs in this tradition include Willie Nelson's 'On the Road Again' (1980), centred on the singer's eagerness to travel with his musician friends to new places for new experiences. 'I've Been Everywhere' has been recorded by country singers such as Hank Snow, Lynn Anderson and Johnny Cash. The song consists of little more than a hitchhiker's rhythmic recitation of names of American cities. One gets the impression of the nation's towns blurring past the windows of a speeding car. Both touring as a musician and riding as a hitchhiker are common devices country songwriters draw on to provide a panorama of the country. Another popular device is to represent the truck driver's life. Jerry Reed recorded 'East Bound and Down' as a theme song for the 1980 movie, *Smokey and the Bandit*; the song went to number two on *Billboard*'s Hot Country Song chart. This song is representative of the many trucker songs in country music in the way it celebrates solo travel, speed and machismo. In this celebratory song, there is no sense of loneliness or desire for home; instead, there is the excitement of movement and the joy of the road. A similar theme can be found in Eddie Rabbit's 1980 number-one country hit, 'Drivin' My Life Away'. The driver in this song seems to have no destination; he only stops for coffee before heading out again, his psyche blending with the rhythms of the windshield wipers and the music on the radio. He realizes that the road holds no consolation, so he yearns for a better life.

One of the most enduring country songs about life on the road is Roger Miller's 'King of the Road'. A top crossover hit in 1964 and covered dozens of times since, the song depicts the life of a contented hobo. The hobo settles for a simple life of transitory pleasures, found in a handout or in the discovery of a half-smoked cigar. The hobo is content and friendly; when he rides on freight trains he is familiar with the engineers and even knows the names of their children. This kindness matches that of the hoboes whom Sal meets in *On the Road*; these are the good-hearted free-spirited men with whom Sal sympathizes. After Sal listens to Mississippi Gene sing a despondent love song, Sal wishes him well; Gene assures him that he will 'make out and move along one way or the other' (Kerouac, 1957, p. 27). Although Montana Slim is similarly revered by Sal, he also seems to be potentially dangerous, at one point hinting that he might assault a man to steal his money. Roger Miller's hobo claims to know of unlocked doors; although his boast suggests that he would commit robbery, he may also simply be looking for shelter, and, in any case, the context of the song makes him appear to be harmless. The chief hobo in *On the Road* is neither one that Sal meets along the way, nor one that he meets at all; it is Dean's absent father. At one point, Dean recalls that his father used to sing 'Hallelujah, I'm a bum, bum again' (p. 196). Carl Sandburg notes that this song, heard 'at the water tanks of railroads in Kansas in 1897', was widely adapted. The lyrics include the term 'handout', just as 'King of the Road' did decades later. Sandburg clarifies that a handout 'is food handed out from a back door' (p. 184). The song includes lines that may have been particularly appropriate for Dean's father: 'I'm just out of jail / Without any money / Without any bail' (Sandburg, 1927, p. 185).

Cecelia Tichi offers a broad view of the use of the road motif in country music that leads one to consider issues of 'individualism, identity, ambition, activism, the quest for a wider world, the assertion of a restless spirit' (Tichi, 1994, p. 58). She could as well be speaking of the road that rolls down the middle of *On the Road*. When Kerouac and many country music songwriters identify the road as a place of journey away from and toward home, as an escape, and as ritual of searching, they thus foster a fundamental and enduring American tradition.

Kerouac's life has been conveyed in numerous biographies and his writing skills have been analysed in dozens of book-length studies and hundreds of articles. These topics may lately be finding a larger audience among country music fans, too, for his reputation is conveyed in the lyrics of numerous contemporary country songs. The use of Kerouac as a subject in songs seems to fall into three primary categories: biography, questing spirit and escape.

Jimmy LaFave's 'Bohemian Cowboy Blues' (2005) includes references to Jack Kerouac setting out on Highway 6, a biographical fact that Kerouac used as Sal's route in *On the Road*. LaFave recounts that as Kerouac travelled, he wrote confessional books and poems, another real-life activity. In a similar way, Natalie Merchant draws on Kerouac's biography in her song 'Hey Jack Kerouac' (1987). Merchant wrote this song while a member of the indie rock group 10,000 Maniacs, but she has since embarked on a solo career that has moved clearly into folk and country. Merchant focuses on her sympathy for Kerouac's mother, whom she imagines worries about her son as he grows increasingly lost in the world of fame, alcohol and critical attacks.

In some songs, Kerouac's legend looms larger than his life; his legacy as a traveller and spiritual guide are more important than the facts of his actual life. In these cases, he may be summoned as an avatar of the questing or searching spirit, often as a companion for the singer. Take for example 'Souvenirs', written by country award-winning singer-songwriter Gretchen Peters and released by Suzy Bogguss in 1993. From the opening lines, the singer makes clear her emulation of Kerouac in her 'American car' as she begins her journey to discover America, equipped with only a dream and a road map. The map, the dream and Kerouac's name combine to form a totemic spirit. Jerry Jeff Walker, famous for his 1968 song 'Mr Bojangles', recalled in his later years his own youthful quest for Kerouac's spirit in 'The Man I Used To Be' (1982). He finds that as the years have gone by, the person who made those spiritual quests on the road with Kerouac's spirit is now a stranger whom he views with the self-deprecating humour of an older-but-wiser man. Kerouac seems to be a travelling companion who was fun for youthful joyrides, but now Walker is glad to have left him by the side of the road. Ellis Paul also has a mixed reaction to this open-for-adventure spirit in 'Blacktop Train' (2005). This song's point of view seems to be that of a farmer in the mid-twentieth century who resents the construction of the National Highway Route 66 through the middle of his cornfields. He watches the naïve travellers who are entranced by their awe for Jack Kerouac while they 'blow on by', although he admits that these fast drivers represent revolutionary changes in American culture. Paul has another interesting intersection with Kerouac; he lent his voice to the character of 'Lousy' on the recording of Kerouac's radio play *Doctor Sax and the Great World Snake*.

Songwriters draw on Kerouac's spirit as a means of escape as well. Even as the sense of home dominates country music, so does the desire to escape from home. In their analysis of the relationships of music and tourism, Chris Gibson and John Connell conclude that while most genres of music offer some degree of escape, the open freedom of the American landscape is especially pervasive in country music, a point they connect to Kerouac: 'Tracing the legacy of the blues and Jack Kerouac's Beat Generation, road songs emphasized the simple pleasures of escape and freedom, restlessness and divorce from weary, conventional lives' (p. 172). In that spirit, numerous country songwriters have relied on Kerouac to help express the sense of flight and getaway.

The message cannot be more emphatically made than Jake Owen makes it in 'Setting the World on Fire' (2011). Owens is a member of the new generation of urban country singers, according to one reviewer, who 'may sing about double-wide trailers, old dirt roads, and moonshine' while his songs are markedly designed for 'city folks who wish they somehow lived in the country' (Erlewine). The song bursts with the explosive need for speed and escape; a young couple are leaving behind a patch of burnt rubber as they blast out of town, 'blazin' down the road like Kerouac'. One wonders whether the songwriters (Derek George, Chuck Jones, Kip Moore) have read Kerouac's books, or whether they are simply grasping at a handy cultural connection associated with the open road. In this case, Kerouac's name is shorthand for shooting out of town in a fast car, serving as little more than a getaway driver.

Some of the more significant developments in recent country music have been in a category labelled alt.country, a digitized abbreviation for 'alternative country'. John Molinaro provides a helpful description: 'Alt.country designates primarily younger bands who have melded pieces of country, folk, and bluegrass with styles that are typically considered antithetical to the country tradition, like punk, indie, or garage rock.' Molinaro highlights the country aspects of alt.country's 'aggressive attitude and . . . anti-establishment spirit' by showing their adaptation to the traditional notions of nostalgia that are at the heart of country. Some alt.country performers find themselves cast outside the conservative parameters of country music due to their cultural or political stances, which Molinaro points out may include 'unrepentant drug abuse, refusal to conform to current trends in Nashville', and so on. Molinaro also distinguishes alt.country from mainstream country in part by these artists' 'lyrical literacy', which means that some are drawn to America's literary heritage for both inspiration and technique.

Ryan Adams, Bill Mallonee and Jay Farrar have been dedicated readers of Kerouac's works, and their inspiration from Kerouac comes close to collaboration. Ryan Adams is one of the most formative influences in the alt.country scene, coming to notice with the band Whiskeytown in 1994, before venturing out as a solo performer in 2000. While he does not include direct references to Kerouac in his lyrics, Adams readily acknowledges Kerouac's influence on his work and his life: 'Kerouac was a huge part of my developmental process as was Allen Ginsberg and William Burroughs and Lawrence Ferlinghetti's beautiful poems – that was a huge part of who I was and who I still am today'. His reading of Kerouac did not end with the obligatory *On the Road*; he read not only more books but also Kerouac's statements about his writing methods. As a result, Adams has built in aspects of Kerouac's aesthetic and his worldview into his own songs, a view that further confirms the Americanness of country music. Kerouac, Adams contends, 'had a lust for a romantic version of the United States and how it could be this transformative place' (Budnick, 2014). Adams's first solo release in 2000 opens with 'To Be Young (Is To Be Sad, To Be High)', a song that engages the kind of youthful melancholy that Kerouac explored in such novels as *Doctor Sax*. The use of the word 'high' may be understood initially to refer to the use of drugs such as marijuana, but in the context of the song, the connotations include a spiritual connection. Rain is a familiar and soothing touch that Kerouac often draws on, and here Adams offers rain as well as a way of lifting the singer's sadness toward consecration. Not to take the point too far, but the song is reminiscent of Bob Dylan's

'Rainy Day Women #12 & 35' not only for its musical texture, but also in its connotations of rain and in the use of a term frequently associated with marijuana (in Dylan's case, 'stoned'), whose connotation can be both personal and biblical.

Other alt.country songwriters have drawn Kerouac's influence more directly into their music. Singer-songwriter Bill Mallonee began as the centre man in the band Vigilantes of Love in the late 1980s but has been an independent artist since 2000. As a touring musician, Mallonee spends a lot time on the road, and also like Kerouac, he is a prolific writer, having conposed hundreds of songs. *Paste* magazine recognized him in 2006 as one of the '100 Best Living Songwriters'. His 2011 release *'Ti Jean' Hearts Crossing the Center Line* compiles songs Mallonee has written about Kerouac through the years. Mallonee particularly 'wanted to highlight Kerouac's reverent belief in the innocence of the American spirit'. Mallonee never uses the name 'Kerouac' nor does he quote any lines from Kerouac's works. Nonetheless, the connections are unmistakable in such phrases as 'scrawling visions buzzed in that five and dime notepad' and 'angels seemed so sad' (in 'Hard Luck & Heart Attack'). Mallonee sought to write the songs from Kerouac's perspective and to put his songwriting in the service of reforming Kerouac's status. 'Tenderness was one of Kerouac's overlooked qualities', Mallonee writes, and he hopes that by his development of this lesser known attribute 'some of that virtue of his tender spirit might be restored to his legacy' (Mallonee, 2011). Reviewer Chris Smith is impressed that Mallonee successfully 'depicts not only the familiar Kerouac but also draws upon lesser-known traits, such as his tenderness, that serve to make the Beat writer more robust, more human'.

Jay Farrar began his career with Uncle Tupelo, a seminal band that helped define alt.country. Farrar fittingly discovered Jack Kerouac and the Beat writers via music; he first learned about them by listening to Bob Dylan. Once his interest had been piqued, he went on to read Kerouac's books while working in his mother's bookstore. Jane Ganahl writes in SFGate, an online corollary to the *San Francisco Chronicle*, that 'Farrar's songs teem with Kerouac-like images of loneliness and redemption on the road.' Ganahl wrote her profile in 2004, five years before Jay Farrar would release, with Death Cab for Cutie's Ben Gibbard, *One Fast Move or I'm Gone: Music from Jack Kerouac's Big Sur*, an album that brings Kerouac's own words directly into the alt.country music scene. Farrar wrote the songs in association with a documentary movie of the same title, directed by Curt Worden (2008), by incorporating and rearranging Kerouac's words from *Big Sur*. As a result of this collaboration, Kerouac receives shared composer credit with Farrar (Ben Gibbard wrote the title track). Reviewer Stephen M. Duesner provides an insightful commentary on the connection between Kerouac and country music: 'Kerouac embodies certain notions of America and Americana that jibe with [Farrar's] post-Uncle Tupelo output; Kerouac is Woody Guthrie with a typewriter.'

Jack Kerouac's works share with country music the themes of the significance of home – with its attendant sense of nostalgia – and the vitality of the road with its promise of a better life, or at least an escape from the present life. In addition, these references to home and the road are grounded in American traditions of travel that often represent a spiritual quest while maintaining an affinity for one's family and one's past.

Kerouac also shares with country music a sense of American authenticity. Just as country songwriters are essentially professional composers, not cowboys or hoboes or outlaws, so is Kerouac essentially a professional author. To be successful as an author, his texts had to find their way to publication, and as much as Kerouac offered lyrical hymns and personal testimony, he also wanted to earn his living as a professional author. For decades, debates among country music fans question the authenticity of one branch or another: is this music the real deal, the true music of the people, or is it a manufactured style, commercialized by the recording industry? In the opening pages of *On the Road*, Sal complains that his city friends are negative, cynical and overly sophisticated. In Sal's eyes, Dean is a cowboy from the West who rushes into this decadent atmosphere with his natural, enthusiastic style, leading Sal to change his life. Kerouac also produced a new kind of prose that many establishment critics panned as unliterary. In *Creating Country Music: Fabricating Authenticity* (1997), Richard A. Peterson writes that in its early days, establishment music producers did not understand the reasons for country music's popularity due mainly to their genteel, middle-class refinement (Peterson, 1997, p. 6). The derogatory responses of these popular music producers parallels the disparaging responses that Kerouac's books often received from the establishment critics. Yet country music persists with no signs of weakening, and Kerouac's works endure while his influence and his readership continue to grow.

Bibliography

Budnick, Dean, 'Ryan Adams on Playing with Phil Lesh and Jack Kerouac Inspiration (Cover Story Excerpt)', *Relix*, 29 October 2014, www.relix.com/articles/detail/ryan_adams_talks_playing_with_phil_lesh_and_jack_kerouac_inspiration (accessed 17 March 2017).

Duesner, Stephen M., 'One Fast Move or I'm Gone: Music from Kerouac's *Big Sur*', *Pitchfork*, 30 November 2009, www.pitchfork.com/reviews/albums/13741-one-fast-move-or-im-gone-music-from-kerouacs-big-sur/ (accessed 17 March 2017).

Erlewine, Stephen Thomas, 'Barefoot Blue Jean Night', Review, *All Music*, allmusic.com/album/barefoot-blue-jean-night-mw0002185446 (accessed 17 March 2017).

Gibson, Chris and John Connell, *Music and Tourism: On the Road Again*, Aspects of Tourism 19, Clevedon, UK: Channel View Publications, 2005.

Kerouac, Jack, *On the Road*, London: Penguin Books, 1999 (1957).

Mallonee, Bill, '"Ti Jean" – Hearts Crossing the Center Line? – Songs Inspired by the Writings of Jack Kerouac', *Bill Mallonee Music*,14 January 2011, billmalloneemusic.bandcamp.com/album/ti-jean-hearts-crossing-the-center-line-songs-inspired-by-the-writings-of-jack-kerouac (accessed 17 March 2017).

Molinaro, John, *Urban Cowboys: Alt.country in the 1990s*, xroads.virginia.edu/~MA98/molinaro/alt.country/jm-thesis.html (accessed 17 March 2017).

Olson, Ted, 'Victor Talking Machine Company Sessions in Bristol, Tennessee: The Carter Family, Jimmie Rodgers, Ernest Stoneman, and others (1927)', *Library of Congress*, 2002, www.loc.gov/programs/static/national-recording-preservation-board/documents/Bristol. pdf (accessed 17 March 2017).

Peterson, Richard A., *Creating Country Music: Fabricating Authenticity*, Chicago: University of Chicago Press, 1997.

Sandburg, Carl, *The American Songbag*, New York: Harcourt, Brace, and Company, 1927, Internet Archive, archive.org/details/americansongbag029895mbp (accessed 17 March 2017).

Smith, Chris, 'Here's a Life . . . A Poured Out Cup', 'A Review of Ti Jean: Hearts Crossing the Center Line'. By Bill Mallonee, *Englewood Review of Books*, englewoodreview.org/featured-ti-jean-by-bill-mallonee-vol-4-7/ (accessed 17 March 2017).

Stanley, Bob, *Yeah, Yeah, Yeah: The Story of Pop Music from Bill Haley to Beyoncé*, New York: Norton, 2014.

Stimeling, Travis A., 'Nostalgia and the 2015 Academy of Country Music Awards', 16 April 2015, *OUPblog: Oxford University Press's Academic Insights for the Thinking World*, blog. oup.com/2015/04/nostalgia-2015-academy-country-music-awards/ (accessed 17 March 2017).

Tichi, Cecelia, *High Lonesome: The American Culture of Country Music*, Chapel Hill: University of North Carolina Press, 1994.

Weinreich, Regina, *Kerouac's Spontaneous Poetics: A Study of the Fiction*, New York: Thunder's Mouth Press, 2002.

Wolff, Kurt, 'Country Clichés Unraveled: Nostalgia and The Good Ol' Days', Radio.com, http://radio.com/2014/06/13/country-cliches-unraveled-nostalgia-songs/ (accessed 17 March 2017).

CHAPTER 17

'STRAIGHT FROM THE MIND TO THE VOICE': SPECTRAL PERSISTENCE IN JACK KEROUAC AND TOM WAITS

Douglas Field

> . . . the realm is haunted. *Man haunts the earth*. Man is on a ledge *noising* his life.
> The pit of night receiveth. God hovers over in his shrouds. Look out!
>
> Jack Kerouac, 'Notes of 1950, February', p. 58[1]

'*The Heart of Saturday Night* is where you need to begin if you go looking for the ghost of Tom Waits,' Patrick Humphries claims in *The Many Lives of Tom Waits*, adding, 'here are songs which ooze booze, love and loss, shrouded in a jazz style that speaks of Waits's enduring fondness for the fifties' (2008, p. 70). Waits has remained an elusive biographical subject; his multiple stage personas, honed over five decades, have frustrated journalists who are unsure where to locate the 'authentic' Waits, illustrated by the title of Humphries's biography, which draws attention to the many incarnations of the singer-songwriter. A seasoned interviewee, Waits frequently remains in character for the media, rarely offering more than spectral glimpses of his private self. As Erik Himmelsbach observed in a review of Barney Hoskyns's biography of Waits, the musician 'is an angry ghost here, shaking his fist at Hoskyns for daring to rummage through his life' (2009). And yet, as Humphries intimates, Waits's preoccupation with the 1950s – and in particular his enduring fascination with what the singer called 'the ghost of Jack Kerouac' – may be a way of tracking artistic cohesion or integrity in the singer's protean career (Lake, 1975). In 1973, Waits undertook a trip to 'locate the unmarked grave of Jack Kerouac, who had died less than four years before' (Maher, 2011, p. 5). Five years later Waits added that 'I still feel the ghost of Kerouac no matter where I travel. Real 'portant t'ave heroes' (Irwin, 1978).

In the early 1970s, Waits listed his literary influences as follows: 'Jack Kerouac, Charles Bukowski, Michael C. Ford. Robert Webb, Gregory Corso, Lawrence Ferlinghetti' and others, adding that he drives a '1965 Thunderbird that needs a valve job', and that his 'favorite album is Kerouac-Allen on Hanover Records', which I will return to (Maher, 2011, p. 28). In the press release for his second album, *The Heart of Saturday Night*, Waits drew attention to the influence of Kerouac, a figure that haunts his life and work:

I've tasted Saturday nights in Detroit, St. Louis, Tuscaloosa, New Orleans, Atlanta, N.Y.C., Boston, Memphis. I've done more traveling in the past year than I ever did in my life so far, in terms of my level of popularity, on the night spot circuit, I remain in relative obscurity and now upon the release of a second album, which I believe a comprehensive study of a number of aspects of this search for the center of Saturday night, which Jack Kerouac relentlessly chased from one end of this country to the other, and I've attempted to scoop up a few diamonds of this magic that I see.

Maher, 2011, p. 28

In a number of songs Waits directly references Kerouac and his close friend and muse Neal Cassady, including: '(Looking for) The Heart of Saturday Night' from *The Heart of Saturday Night* (1974); 'Bad Liver and a Broken Heart (in Lowell)' from *Small Change* (1976); and 'Jack and Neal' from *Foreign Affairs* (1977). While Waits invokes Kerouac in his early albums, his admiration of the Beat writer is clearly more than youthful infatuation, illustrated by the inclusion of 'Home I'll Never Be' on *Orphans: Brawlers, Bawlers & Bastards* (2006), a song penned by Kerouac, and also called 'On the Road', which Waits recorded.[2]

Waits was clearly indebted to Kerouac's restless spirit but the singer's relationship to the writer goes beyond a study of influence. Rather than solely focusing on how Kerouac inspired the music and persona that became Tom Waits, I want to tease out the ways in which both artists share several characteristics in their work which is a productive way, not only of hearing Kerouac in Waits, but is a useful way to read – and also hear – Kerouac's work through listening to Waits. As I explore later in this chapter, the work of both artists is frequently characterized by references to an unrecoverable past; a yearning or nostalgia, or, to paraphrase Raymond Williams, a structure of haunting (1977). As I argue, however, the structure of haunting in the work of Kerouac and Waits goes beyond subject matter alone. While a number of Waits's songs, including 'What's He Building?' and 'The House Where Nobody Lives' from *Mule Variations* (1999), or the 'Halloween album' from *Bone Machine* (1992) draw on the gothic genre, I am more interested in the ways in which the voice in the work of both artists haunts the reader and listener through the ways that it is manifestly present through the rendering of the past.

The work of Waits and Kerouac is characterized by a restlessness; not only in the sense of what Japhy Ryder calls the 'rucksack revolution' in *The Dharma Bums* (1958), but a compulsion in both artists to wander away from the confines of the respective art forms with which they are associated. Waits is lauded as a singer-songwriter, but also as actor and occasional photographer: 'If I'm tied down and have to call myself something,' he told Todd Everett of the *Los Angeles Free Press* in 1975, 'I prefer "storyteller"' (p. 46), adding elsewhere that 'Vocabulary is my main instrument' (Humphries, 2008, p. 32).[3] If Waits wants to be described as a storyteller, he was also aware of Kerouac's desire to be considered a jazz poet, noting how the writer 'had melody, a good sense of rhythm, structure, color, mode and intensity' (Hoskyns, 2009, p. 36). Kerouac's syncopated prose sounded, as Matt Theado puts it, 'like a typewriter keyboard' (2009, p. 14), a style that Tim Hunt calls 'type talking', (2014, p. 71), but Kerouac was also an accomplished singer, illustrated by his intimate and haunting recording of the song 'On the Road', as well as four songs on *Jack Kerouac Reads On the Road* (1999), including 'When a Man Loves a Woman', recorded variously by Billie Holiday and Ella Fitzgerald.[4]

In several interviews in the early to mid-1970s, Waits points out how important the Jack Kerouac–Steven Allen collaborations were to his direction as an artist. In 1958, Kerouac recorded a spoken word album, *Poetry for the Beat Generation*, where the writer sang or spoke his work accompanied on the piano by Steve Allen, a composer, comedian and variety show host. Waits recalled that 'the first time I heard any spoken word that I was really impressed with was an album called *Jack Kerouac/ Steve Allen* and he [Kerouac] talked while Steve Allen played some stuff and he just talked over the top of it and it was real, real effective' (Larman, 2011, p. 23). Waits later added that 'it frees you as a songwriter to be able to just throw down some color and not worry about any sort of meter at all' (p. 24).[5]

In one of his most striking early television appearances, Waits appeared on the short-lived *Fernwood Tonight* show in 1977, where he performed 'The Piano has been Drinking' in a tousled suit. Delivering a masterful performance of a 1950s down-and-out lounge singer, Waits slugged from a bottle of beer as he recounted stories of car mishaps in a series of scripted one-liners that showed glimpses of his skills as an actor. Nearly a decade earlier, in 1968, an inebriated and confused Kerouac had appeared on William Buckley's *The Firing Line* where he refused to play the role of the King of the Beats that had been foisted on him by the media. While Waits has continued to reinvent himself over five decades, Kerouac had drunk himself to death just over a decade after his most famous novel.

In a review of his first tour for over a decade, the 1999 'Get Behind the Mule', MTV News salivated over the way in which

> Tom Waits took on more than a dozen identities Wednesday night during the first show of his first tour in more than a dozen years: he played hobo poet, down-and-out boozer, testifying preacher, barroom crooner, grizzled balladeer, stand-up comedian, monologist, punk rocker and, maybe strangest of all, Tom Waits himself.
>
> Kaufman, 1999

At first glance, Waits and Kerouac seem diametrically opposed as artists: the protean and experimental Waits and the static, even conservative writer, illustrated by an interview conducted with Kerouac shortly before he died in 1969. There Kerouac recalls attending a party sometime in the mid-1960s with the writer Ken Kesey and a group of his LSD-taking friends, the Merry Pranksters, the progenitors of the hippie movement: 'Kesey came up and wrapped an American flag around me. So I took it . . . and I folded it up the way you're supposed to, and put it on the back of the sofa. The flag is not a rag' (McClintock, 1969). Kerouac's careful folding of the American flag, which he re-enacts during the interview ('Kerouac demonstrates how he took it, and the movements are tender') is an explicitly patriotic gesture, which sits at odds with his reputation as an iconoclast, a countercultural anti-hero whose work critiques the narrow nationalism of post-war US consumer-driven society.

On one level, Kerouac's sombre rebuttal of Kesey's playful gesture underscores the ways in which the author of *On the Road* was unable to adapt to the shifts in the counterculture that took place during the 1960s. For Barry Miles, during the 1960s, Kerouac was perceived as 'a right-wing, anti-hippie, anti-communist, pro-Vietnam redneck', an image far removed from his seminal place in contemporary counterculture (1998, p. x). Unlike his close friend and muse, Neal Cassady, who drove the Merry Pranksters' bus during a prolonged 1964 road trip, Kerouac was increasingly rooted to home, where he lived with his paralysed mother and later third wife. As Timothy Leary recalled, 'the Catholic carouser' and 'old-style Bohemian without a hippie bone in his body . . . opened the neural doors to the future, looked ahead, and didn't see his place in it. Not for him the utopian pluralist optimism of the sixties' (Hrebeniak, 2006, p. 4). By the mid-1960s, Kerouac had become a self-confessed 'orating drunken "author"', a fate narrowly avoided by Waits (Hrebeniak, 2006, p. 5). By his fifth album, 'Like the repetitive drunk he was in danger of becoming,' Humphries observes, 'Waits's music was stuck in a groove', a rut almost certainly turned around by his marriage to, and creative partnership with, Kathleen Brennan (Humphries, 2008, p. 107).

While much of Kerouac's work fictionalizes events and conversations, the incident with the flag underscores the difficulty in analysing the layering of his fiction, where the legend of Kerouac blurs and often overwhelms a critical reading of the Duluoz Legend, the name that Kerouac gave to his *roman fleuve* cycle. In much of Kerouac's fiction, his characters are spectral presences of actual people he encountered; his fictional writing is haunted by the memories of events that took place, but which can never be traced back once since they have been transformed from memory and history into fiction. According to Ed Sanders, the Merry Pranksters had placed the flag on the couch in a direct reference to an incident in *On the Road*, where Sal Paradise, working as a policeman in a barracks, mistakenly raises the flag upside down. Like Kerouac, Paradise is 'horrified' at the misplacing of the flag but – unlike the author's frequent fictionalizing of actual events – here the incident, recalled variously by Kerouac and Sanders, is borne out of fiction, resulting in a palimpsest of life imitating art. Such incidents reinforce 'the myth that Kerouac himself perpetuated: that the books tell the true honest story of his life' (Miles, 1998, p. xvii). Writing in the preface to *The Big Sur*, Kerouac explains:

> My work comprises one vast book like Proust's except that my remembrances are written on the run . . . Because of the objections of my early publishers, I was not allowed to use the same personae names in each work. *On the Road, The Subterraneans, The Dharma Bums, Doctor Sax, Maggie Cassidy, Tristessa,*

Desolation Angels, Visions of Cody and the others including this book *Big Sur* are just chapters in the whole work I call the Duluoz Legend. In my old age I intend to collect all my work and re-insert my pantheon of uniform names ... The whole thing forms one enormous comedy, seen through the eyes of poor Ti Jean (me)...

(2006, no pagination)

Kerouac's description of his fiction as 'remembrances', along with his claim that he was compiling a 'contemporary history record' downplays his innovative narrative technique, a practice that he developed during the cycle of the Duluoz Legend (Douglas, 2007, p. vi). Known as 'memory babe', or the 'great remember', biographers and his contemporaries have noted Kerouac's ability to recall details, as well as his obsession with recording events in notebooks (Ginsberg, 2012, p. 4), a characteristic shared by Waits, who describes himself as a 'professional eavesdropper' (Humphries, 2008, p. 67).[6]

Kerouac's recollection of folding the flag 'the way you're supposed to', a comment charged with the importance of tradition and conformity, serves as a productive point to consider the contradictory elements of this complex, frequently mythologized writer in relation to Waits, another complex and self-mythologizing artist. While Waits's performances and personae seem at odds with Kerouac's seeming inability – or refusal – to morph into different roles, both artists in fact share a number of characteristics. Fêted respectively as the 'King of the Beats' and inducted into the Rock and Roll Hall of Fame, Kerouac and Waits are nonetheless guarded outsiders whose work confounds generic expectations. Both artists are chroniclers of everyday American life; their work is shot through with haunting wistfulness – black and white snapshots of a mood that flickers between nostalgia and sentimentality.

In 'October in the Railroad Earth', the first track on *Poetry for the Beat Generation*, the album much admired by Waits, Kerouac recalls his time spent as a 'student brakeman' on the Southern Pacific Railroad in California. In 15 sections, Kerouac chronicles his experiences working on the railroad, along with impressionistic slices of everyday life in San Francisco. Like Waits, who professes interest in the ordinariness of details – 'I like to know that there was gum under the table ... how many cigarettes were in the ashtray, little things like that' (Humphries, 2008, p. 67) – Kerouac recounts bus numbers, street names and the crowd of bums 'spitting in the broken glass' (1959). 'October' flirts with sentimentality as Kerouac describes the role of the railroad in American culture and it winks at nostalgia through his recollections of 'the first run I ever made' (1959). By shifting his narrative gaze away from 'the impending rush of their commuter frenzy' and onto the 'poor grime-bemarked Third Street of lost bums even Negros so hopeless', Kerouac zooms in on the dispossessed and the downtrodden, characters frequently left out of mid-twentieth-century American writing (1959). Kerouac was, as one critic puts it – in what could be a description of Waits – an 'archivist of the marginal, the unfashionable, the self-doomed', who works 'against the general tenor of literary convention controlled by and for the benefits of academics, critics, and editors' (Hrebeniak, 2006, p. 18).

In a number of Waits's tracks, the singer tips his pork-pie hat to the Beat writer's intimate portrayals of what Greil Marcus has called 'weird old America'. Waits captures fragments of the inner lives of hobos, waitresses and barflies – the invisible republic of mid-twentieth century – figures who are traditionally on the margins of US culture. Many of Waits's early tracks, including songs from *Small Change*, are set in diners and bars. They are tender snapshots of protagonists who are down on their luck: so poor, as Waits puts it, they can't even pay attention, just as Kerouac's characters are frequently transient figures who have opted out of the American Dream (Humphries, 2008, p. 217). Waits's protagonists are isolated individuals holding out for a final chance of love; sonic echoes of the crumpled hope found in Raymond Carver's characters in *What We Talk About When We Talk About Love* (1981) and of Edward Hopper's painting *Night Hawks* (1942), a title that Waits invoked in his 1975 album *Night Hawks at the Diner*, where he sketches characters, like those in the painting, who inhabit a 'deeply shadowed America hidden behind the giant billboards and manicured lawns' (Thiesen, 2006, p. 8).

While Hopper's disturbing painting captures the mood of alienation, solitariness and late nights that characterize Waits's early albums, it is Robert Frank's pioneering photography book *The Americans* (1958/1959), celebrated by the art critic Peter Schjeldahl as 'one of the basic American masterpieces of any medium', that helps make sense of these fragmentary structures of nostalgia, sentimentality and haunting in the work of Waits and Kerouac (Dawidoff, 2015). For Waits, who was directed by Frank in *Candy Mountain* (1988), and who used the photographer's image on the back cover of *Rain Dogs*, the Swiss-born artist 'changed the face of photography forever' (Humphries, 2008, p. 187). Later collected as *The Americans*, Frank's photographs, taken during a nine-month road trip in 1955, eschewed the post-war positivism found in Edward Steichen's 1955 exhibition, *The Family of Man*, instead exposing the lives of hidden Americans. In his introduction to the book, Kerouac celebrated 'the agility, mystery, genius, sadness and strange secrecy of a shadow photographed scenes that have never been seen before on film', adding, in what could be a description of his own work – or that of Waits – 'the humour, the sadness, the EVERTHING-ness and American-ness of these pictures!' (2016c, no pagination). When Kerouac asks 'what poems can be written about this book of pictures someday by some young new writer high by candlelight bending over them describing every gray mysterious detail' (2016c, no pagination), it is hard not hear Waits's early albums as a response; his songs an accompaniment or soundtrack to Frank's seminal book.

Kerouac's effusive introduction to *The Americans* unlocks something of the force behind Frank's photography: he locates in Frank's work a slippage between a photographic record of hidden America and the ways in which the images are both in and out of time. Frank's photographs, like much of Kerouac and Waits's work, captures the mood of a time, but without overt political or historical details. In *The Americans*,

Frank leaves out captions, forcing the reader to piece together images, many of which are blurred and out of focus, just as the work of Kerouac and Waits captures the mood of the past but does so with little recourse to temporal signposts.

In fact, while Waits's immersion into the subterranean world of the 1950s is more notable, Kerouac's work is structured around a longing for the past. Indeed both artists refused to be rooted in their respective contemporary milieux: the work of Waits and Kerouac is haunted by poignant meditations on the vanishing world of freight trains, hobos and the unexplored West. 'I was always backwards in a lot of ways,' Waits recalled in reference to his teenage love of Frank Sinatra and Cole Porter (Humphries, 2008, p. 31).[7] In an essay called 'The Origins of the Beat Generation', published in *Playboy* in 1959, Kerouac claimed that the Beat Generation 'goes back to the wild parties my father used to have at home in the 1920s and 1930s in New England', adding that the spirit of the Beat Generation – gentleness, thoughtfulness – had been hijacked and commodified by 1957, the year that *On the Road* was published (1993, p. 57). As Loui Menand observes in a perceptive reading of Kerouac's second novel:

> The bits and pieces of America that the book captures, therefore, are snapshots taken on the run, glimpses from the window of a speeding car. And they are carefully selected to represent a way of life that is coming to an end in the postwar boom, a way of life before televisions and washing machines and fast food, when millions of people lived patched-together existences and men wandered the country – 'ramblin' round', in the Guthrie song – following the seasons in search of work.
>
> (2007)

Kerouac's novel not only documents a quickly evolving landscape, but he also pokes fun at the novel's narrator, Sal Paradise, who, like Joe Martin in *The Town and the City*, is out of temporal step. In Kerouac's first novel, Joe muses, 'I wish I could have lived in those days when you rode on horseback and all you had ahead of you was this big unexplored space' (2000, pp. 67–8). In *On the Road*, Sal had spent the winter 'reading of the great wagon parties that held council there', but the reality is 'only cute suburban cottages of one damn kind and another' (1992, p. 19). Thrilled to see a cowboy – 'by God, the first cowboy I saw' – the man looks the part in his 'ten-gallon hat and Texas boots', but Kerouac acknowledges that Sal's excitement stems from a glimpse of the past seen through the carnival of the present. The cowboy is moving, not horses, but two cars, just as Sal can only experience his idea of the West through the Wild West festival (1992, p. 19).

Indeed much of Kerouac's work, including *The Town and the City* (1950), *Doctor Sax* (1959), *Visions of Gerard* (1963), *Visions of Cody* (1972) and the incomplete *Memory Babe* (begun in 1957), can be read as an urgent memory document that seeks to capture the fabric and texture of childhood. In *Doctor Sax*, for example, where he makes reference to 'Proust's teacup' (2012, p. 21), Kerouac includes multi-sensory descriptions, including 'sound', 'smell', 'temperature' and 'month', to capture what he describes in *Visions of Cody* as the '"inexpressibly delicious" sensation of this memory' (1972, p. 40). Here and elsewhere Kerouac displays a compulsion, not only to disinter his childhood memories, but also to fix them through language, sound, smell and temperature, snapshots of vanishing youth.

The tendency in Waits and Kerouac to look back, to be wilfully out of time, is in part explained by Svetlana Boym, who argues that 'Modern nostalgia is a mourning for the impossibility of mythical return, for the loss of an "enchanted world" with clear borders and values' (2007, p. 12), something heard in Waits's early songs, which seem to hark to back to his version of the 1950s. In the case of 'Martha', from *Closing Time*, the youthful Waits, still in his twenties, plays the part of Tom Frost, presumably in his sixties, as he reconnects with his former lover after several decades. Some of the poignancy in 'Martha', and other songs from the early 1970s, comes from the yearning expressed in Waits's voice for what Boym calls 'better time, or slower time – time out of time, not encumbered by appointment books' (2007, p. 8). As Boym explains, there is a useful distinction between what she terms restorative and reflective nostalgia. While the former 'stresses *nostos* (home) and attempts a transhistorical reconstruction of the lost home', reflective nostalgia 'thrives on *algia* (the longing itself) and delays the homecoming – wistfully, ironically, desperately', or, as we might describe this condition in relation to Waits and Kerouac, 'home, they'll never be' (2007, p. 7). Thus, while Waits's first album in 1973 coincided with widespread nostalgia for the 1950s and early 1960s in US popular culture (*American Graffiti*, *Happy Days*, Sha Na Na), both Waits and Kerouac come close to reflective nostalgia since both understand 'deep down that loss is irrecoverable ... To exist in Time is to suffer through an endless exile, a successive severing from those precious few moments of feeling at home in the world' (Reynolds, 2012, p. xxviii).

Boym's theorizing of nostalgia goes some way to elucidating the preoccupation with the past in the work of Kerouac and Waits, but I want to go a little further by suggesting that there is something spectral in the reflective nostalgia of both artists. Their compulsion to look backwards, I want to suggest, is elusive and hard to pin down, precisely because it acknowledges the impossibility of recovery whilst simultaneously endeavouring to do so, illustrated by Kerouac's *Visions of Gerard* (1963), which can summon up images and memories of his beloved dead brother, but not of course his flesh and blood; or in *Satori in Paris*, where Kerouac attempts to track down the Brittany roots of his name, Jean-Louis Lebris de Kérouac. Like Derrida's trace, which gives clues to an origin that can never be knowable, Kerouac's work in is shot through with references to haunting, not least in the title of his recently recovered novella, *The Haunted Life*.[8]

As Erik Mortenson discusses in an insightful reading, *Doctor Sax*, Kerouac's fifth novel, which was published in 1959 but written in 1952, employs conventions of Gothic fiction to recreate memories from his Lowell childhood. It is, Mortenson argues, a novel 'told through a narrator clearly looking back on his childhood with nostalgia' (2016, p. 77). And yet the novel is much more than just an exercise in nostalgia, or a coming-of-age novel that mourns the loss of childhood innocence. While *Doctor Sax* clearly draws on the popular pulp and radio character, The Shadow, a 'mysterious man who comes out of the dark', who is part vigilante and part superhero – not unlike Hoskyns's description of the 'shadowy protean figure' in Waits's song 'Black Wings' – Kerouac's novel also draws on a recurring dream that he shared with Allen Ginsberg, which both referred to as the 'Shrouded Stranger' (Hoskyns, 2009, p. 393; Mortenson, 2016, p. 59). As Kerouac explained in 1949, the Shrouded Stranger, what he elsewhere called 'the dark haunted thing', is 'ever-present and ever-pursuing. One may swirl nearer and nearer to that shroud, *and it may only be* our haunted sense of that *thing*, which is ever unnameable and is really our chiefest plaint' (Mortenson, 2016, p. 105). For Mortenson, 'This attempt to communicate the "dark haunted thing" . . . is the driving force behind Kerouac's life and work' (2016, p. 109).

Although *On the Road* is frequently held up as an exuberant coming-of-age or coming-of-writer tale, it contains more than 30 references to the word ghost/s. The narrator, Sal Paradise, sees 'ghosts of old miners', reminders of an American past that refuses to go away, just as he sees a 'ghost-town hotel', 'a ghost-town' and the 'ghostly shapes of yucca cactus and organpipe' as the protagonists reach the Gulf of Mexico (1992, pp. 41, 51, 276). Here the vestiges of pre-Second World War America refuse to die out. Like the out-of-focus portraits in Frank's *The Americans*, the images haunt the contemporary reader, who cannot locate their whereabouts in the contemporary American landscape, underscored by the old hobo who is described as the 'Ghost of Susquehanna', who teaches Paradise that there is wilderness in the East, not just the West.

On the Road also contains two references to the 'Shrouded Traveler'. Early in part two of the novel, Paradise reflects:

> Just about that time a strange thing began to haunt me. It was this: I had forgotten something. There was a decision that I was about to make before Dean showed up, and now it was driven clear out of my mind but still hung on the tip of my mind's tongue. I kept snapping my fingers, trying to remember it. I even mentioned it. And I couldn't even tell if it was a real decision or just a thought I had forgotten. It haunted and flabbergasted me, made me sad. It had to do somewhat with the Shrouded Traveler.
>
> (1992, p. 124)

Paradise contemplates the figure; he at first explains that the 'Shrouded Traveler' was in fact himself, just as he refers to himself twice as a 'haggard ghost', but this theory is dismissed as he concludes that the figure is a reminder, not just of death, but also the connections between the two (1992, pp. 59, 83): 'the one thing that we yearn for in our living days, that makes us sigh and groan and undergo sweet nauseas of all kinds, is the remembrance of some lost bliss that was probably experienced in the womb and can only be reproduced (though we hate to admit it) in death' (1992, p. 124).

While Mortenson rightly observes that Dean's father, who is never found and whose 'ghost haunted' Moriarty and Paradise (1992, p. 242), 'remains something of an enigma, a riddle, and as such is inextricably bound with the nostalgic search for lost origins' (2016, p. 110), *On the Road* nonetheless complicates such a reading as Paradise understands time, not as a linear construct, but as cyclical:

> I realized that I had died and been reborn numberless times but just didn't remember especially because the transitions from life to death and back to life are so ghostly easy, a magical action for naught, like falling asleep and waking up again a million times, the utter casualness and deep ignorance of it.
>
> (1992, p. 173)

Echoing William Wordsworth's poem 'Ode: Intimations of Immortality', where the speaker reflects that 'our birth is but a sleep and a forgetting' (1993, p. 270), Paradise's conception of time troubles a reading of the novel as a straightforward search for lost origins. Kerouac recounts how Paradise saw his 'mother of about two hundred years ago in England', in the streets of San Francisco, which is accompanied by 'a whole host of memories leading back to 1750 in England and that I was in San Francisco now only in another life and in another body' (1992, p. 172). In Paradise's vision, he reaches, not origins, but – in a reference to his surname – 'the point of ecstasy that I always wanted to reach, which was the complete step across chronological time into timeless shadows, and wonderment in the bleakness of the mortal realm' (1992, p. 173). Paradise's vision is driven, not by nostalgia for lost origins, but by an imagined future of 'lotuslands falling open in the magic mothswarm of heaven' (p. 173).

In Paradise's conception of the world in which 'the transitions from life to death and back to life are so ghostly easy', characters are haunted, not only by others, but by themselves. Ed Dunkel 'has visions all the time' – including the apparition of his mother (p. 223). Dunkel recounts how 'Last night I walked clear down to Times Square and just as I arrived I suddenly realized I was a ghost – it was my ghost walking on the sidewalk' (p. 130), just as Paradise describes himself as 'just somebody else, some stranger, and my whole life was a haunted life, the life of a ghost' (1992, p. 17). Although Kerouac is not explicit about what he means, forcing the reader to make sense of his flickering set of images, he suggests that since the self is 'reborn numberless times', every life is haunted by its previous incarnation; that every life is an echo of previous existence.

Kerouac's preoccupation with haunting is inextricably bound to his deep-rooted sense of place. As Gerard Nicosia observes, 'Kerouac's whole life was a search for the home he never had' (1990, p. 19), illustrated by his first novel, *The Town and the City*: 'A family leaves the old house that it has always known, the plot of ground, the place of earth, the only place where it has ever known itself – and moves somewhere else: and this is a real and unnameable tragedy' (2000, p. 239). For Francis, who remembers his boyhood as he glimpses at the abandoned family home, 'Looking at that house makes me feel absolutely certain that I never belonged there anyhow' (p. 189), a yearning echoed in the song that Ray Smith sings in *The Dharma Bums*, 'Everybody's Got a Home But Me', and the poem that Paradise sings in Part 4 of *On the Road*:

> Home in Missoula,
> Home in Truckee,
> Home in Opelousas,
> Ain't no home for me.
> Home in old Medora,
> Home in Wounded Knee,
> Home in Ogallala,
> Home I'll never be
>
> 1992, p. 255

The poem's concluding line, 'Home I'll never be', encapsulates Kerouac's sense of longing for a home that never quite exists, or existed. Moreover, as Simon Warner has traced, Kerouac recorded the song, also called 'On the Road', some time in the early 1960s, where it was lost until Jim Sampas, Kerouac's nephew by marriage, discovered the tape in the 1990s. Sampas sent the tape to David Amram, the noted musician, arranger and composer, who had collaborated with Kerouac and other Beat writers in the 1950s and 1960s, most notably in the seminal 1959 Beat film *Pull My Daisy*. Remarkably, Amram managed to assemble the same instrumentalists from *Pull My Daisy* for Jim Sampas's 1999 album, *Jack Kerouac Reads On the Road*, a posthumous compilation album which featured, 30 years after the Beat writer's death, a thought-to-be lost 28-minute recording of the author reading a section of *On the Road*. The album not only included Kerouac singing his own song 'On the Road', posthumously recorded with Amram and his musicians, but the sleeve notes included photographs by Robert Frank. The result was a revenant album which brought together the ghosts of Kerouac's past. 'I felt like I was hanging out with him again,' Amram recalled, a comment echoed by Douglas Brinkley who recalled that 'Everybody present when the music was recorded and mixed at New York's Manhattan Beach Recording Studio felt Kerouac's spirit hanging around' (Warner, 2014, p. 333; Brinkley, 1999).

I want to conclude by exploring the ways that the recordings of 'On the Road' illuminate some of the claims I have made about nostalgia and haunting in the work of Kerouac, but also Waits, who recorded two versions of the Beat writer's song: first, titled 'On the Road', with the funk band Primus, which was included on *Jack Kerouac Reads On the Road*; and then a bluesier, folksier, version, 'Home I'll Never Be', on *Orphans*. Kerouac's intimate question to the listener nearly 50 years after his death, 'Can you hear me now?', haunts the recording: it is, to borrow from Roland Barthes's study of photography in *Camera Lucida*, a punctum, the image or object that jumps out at the person viewing a photograph, or in this case, the sound or words that affect the listener: 'that accident', Barthes writes, 'which pricks, bruises me', as well as being a reminder that 'Recording has always had a spectral undercurrent' (1993, p. 27; Reynolds, 2011, p. 312).

The links between photography and recordings are, I think, a productive way of making sense of the haunting qualities of these and other recordings I'll touch on. Susan Sontag's observation that 'Photography is the inventory of mortality … Photographs state the innocence, the vulnerability of lives heading toward their own destruction, and this link between photography and death haunts all photographs of people' (2010, p. 70) is also a useful way of considering the haunting quality of recordings, a connection further made by Barthes in *Camera Lucida*, who compared the melancholy induced by viewing photographs to the experience of 'listening to the recorded voices of dead singers' (1993, p. 79). As the catalogue text of the Guggenheim photography and video exhibition *Haunted* (2010) reminds us, all recordings, including photographs and tape, are 'ghostly reminders of lost time and the elusiveness of memory' (Reynolds, 2012, p. 329).

While the technology of recording enables temporal ruptures, which are frequently spectral, I want to suggest that there is something particularly haunting about the posthumous arrangements of Kerouac's work, but also in Waits's duet with an unnamed homeless man on 'Jesus' Blood Never Failed Me', a song which Gavin Bryars, looped and overlaid with string and brass harmonies. In the case of the Bryars compilation, the plangent looping lament haunts the listener, and even more so because Waits is duetting with someone from beyond the grave. As Simon Reynolds explains, 'the sample collage creates a musical event that never happened; a mixture of time-travel and séance … It's the musical art of ghost co-ordination and ghost arrangement' (2014, p. 333).

Kerouac's recording of 'On the Road', a fragment of a song about the impossibility of return, is transformed by the Waits-Primus version from Kerouac's shy intimacy into an authoritative growl-declaration, which is driven by the music; some of the power and force, we might discern, derives from the way in which Waits delivers the lyrics about finding his father in a gambling hall – 'Father, Father, where have you been?' – just as he would later pen the song 'Sins of My Father' in his 2004 album *Real Gone*. As Tim Perlich observes:

> Despite the song being credited to Beat poet Jack Kerouac, the forlorn hymn to the highway life turns out to be one of Waits's most personally revealing. When he poignantly sings the lines 'Father, father, where you been? I've been in this world since I was only ten', it's not really Kerouac's life he's singing about. Waits is calling out to his own father, who left home never to be seen again, after a divorce in 1960, when Waits wouldn't have been ten years old.
>
> (2006, p. 413)

Perlich in fact confuses Kerouac with his muse, Neal Cassady, who appears as Dean Moriarty in *On the Road*, and who searches for his lost father in the pool halls of Denver. Perlich nonetheless picks up on the yearning in Waits's delivery, which is complemented by 'Missing My Son', the hidden track that concludes *Orphans*, where Waits recounts a shaggy-dog story about a mother who pretends to mistake the narrator for her son.

In Kerouac's recording of 'On the Road', he frames his song by saying 'Straight from the mind to the voice with no hand intervening', a reference, we might glean, to the ways in which the tape recorder enabled Kerouac to compose directly, without writing or typing, a technique he had outlined in 'Essentials of Spontaneous Prose', first published in 1957, where he wrote, 'PROCEDURE: Time being of the essence in the purity of speech, sketching language is undisturbed flow from the mind of personal secret idea-words, blowing (as per jazz musician) on subject of image' (*Good Blonde*, p. 69). Kerouac's phrase, 'straight from the mind to the voice', suggests that recording is an unmediated process – the 'undisturbed flow from the mind' – but I want to suggest rather that that is precisely the breath, what Charles Olson famously described as 'the HEART, by way of the BREATH, to the LINE', which imbues the work of Kerouac and Waits with a visceral, haunting quality (2009).

As Barthes explains in 'The Grain of the Voice', by way of Julia Kristeva, while the pheno-song may be technically proficient, and while 'everything in the (semantic and lyrical) structure is respected and yet nothing seduces, nothing sways us to *jouissance*' (1990, p. 183). By contrast, the geno-song, while it may be less technically adept, compels the listener precisely because it incorporates the materiality of the song – 'the tongue, the glottis, the teeth, the mucous membranes the nose', a striking feature of Waits and Kerouac's recordings (1990, p. 183).[9] As Michael David Szekely argues in a reading of Waits that connects him to the geno-song:

> the evocativeness of the Beat-like musical poetics of Tom Waits is driven home by the gritty, strained, smoke-spattered and irreverent growl of his vocal delivery. In much of Waits' music, one has the feeling of stumbling upon these stories, these experiences, previously tucked away in the underbelly of the world, after some of the smoke clears. Notably, in Waits, the voice creates an atmosphere with the other instruments: a piano right out of the saloon, the rickety thumps and clangs of percussion, the twangs of ruddy guitars, etc. This soundscape beckons, intrigues and lures us – a traveling troupe that seems to stumble itself, giving us the sense of having lived the story that is being told.
>
> (2006)

As Szekely suggests, it is the material, visceral qualities of Waits's music which lures the listener into an immediately recognizable atmosphere which eschews musical convention. In his use of the saw and bullhorn, or his recording of traffic sounds on Cahuengea Boulevard used in 'Looking for the Heart of Saturday Night', Waits collapses the distinctions, not only between tools and instruments, or voice and instrument, but inside and outside, just as the distinctions between word and music, here and now, home and elsewhere, presence and absence, are frequently blurred in Kerouac's work. While much of Kerouac's work is haunted by the past, it is in his recordings where he appears as revenant because, like Waits, he is so present.

In his description of music, Kerouac recognized the ways which geno-recordings confront the reader with an absent presence, what Simon Reynolds has called a 'spectral persistence' (p. 307). As Alessandro Portelli observes, the 'graphic image retains the distancing implicit in the concept of representation, whereas the recorded voice appears as the thing itself' (2012, p. 217).[10] In *Doctor Sax*, Kerouac recalls having 'an old Victrola in my bedroom which was also ghostly, it was haunted by the old songs and old records of sad American antiquity', a quality that both he and Waits found in Sinatra (p. 45). For Waits, who cited *Wee Small Hours* as his favourite album in 2005, Sinatra's album transported you: 'The idea being you put this record on after dinner and by the last song you are exactly where you want to be' (Waits, 2005). Kerouac admires Sinatra because he is not a pheno singer who employs 'vocal tricks that impede the natural expression of feeling'; rather Sinatra expresses 'loneliness and longing' and 'poetic tenderness' because he 'sings in his natural voice' (2016a, p. 3). In Sinatra, like the qualities of Kerouac and Waits, 'his speaking voice and his singing voice are easily recognisable at once' (2016a, p. 3).

In 1950, Kerouac described his wish to evoke that 'indescribable sad music of the night in America – for reasons that are never deeper than *the music*' and it is the tension between music and text that haunts his work (2016b, p. 58). In the work of Waits and Kerouac, it is, as Barthes puts it, 'the very friction between the music and something else ... The song must speak, must *write*', what he calls, in a phrase that speaks to Kerouac and Waits, 'the sung writing of language' (1990, p. 185).

Notes

1. Epigraph comes from: *The Unknown Kerouac: Rare, Unpublished and Newly Translated Writings*, ed. Todd Tietchen, trans. Christophe Cloutier (New York: The Library of America, 2016).

2. Waits recorded two versions of Kerouac's song 'On the Road' on *Orphans* (2006). 'On the Road' was recorded with the band Primus while 'Home I'll Never Be' is a bluesier version of the same song. Waits draws explicitly or implicitly on Kerouac up to and including *Blue Valentine* (1978). Thereafter Kerouac's presence is less pronounced until Waits's 1999 recording of 'On the Road'.

3. For examples of Waits's photography, see http://www.tomwaits.com/photos/?page=2 (accessed 25 April 2017).

4. Kerouac recorded three spoken word albums released by Hanover and Verve between 1958 and 1960: *Poetry for the Beat Generation* (1959), where he breaks into song on 'October in the Railroad Earth', as well as 'I'd Rather Be Thin than Famous'; *Blues and Haikus* (1959); and *Readings by Jack Kerouac on the Beat Generation* (1960). On *Jack*

Kerouac Reads On the Road (1999), he also sings 'Ain't We Got Fun', 'Come Rain or Come Shine' and 'Leavin' Town'.

5. Among Waits's numerous spoken word tracks are the following: 'Army Ants', 'Children's Story', 'Emotional Weather Report', 'Putnam Country', 'Spare Parts' and 'Frank's Wild Years'. Waits includes a number of spoken word tracks on *Orphans*, including 'First Kiss', 'Nirvana' and 'The Pontiac'.

6. See *Visions of Cody*, where Kerouac recalls 'that great diary that temporarily saved me and started the international spectral and now lost Duluoz of Dolours' (p. 120) and how he is 'trying desperately to be a great rememberer redeeming life from darkness' (p. 130).

7. As an example of going backwards, Waits worked with Shelly Manne on *Small Change*. Manne had worked with a number of jazz greats, including Coleman Hawkins and Chet Baker.

8. Kerouac wrote *The Haunted Life*, which is set in the fictional town of Galloway, in 1944 and the novella was thought to be lost. It was published as *The Haunted Life: And Other Writings* in 2014.

9. Barthes argues that all individual voices have what he calls 'grain', but he distinguishes between two different types: in contrast to the pheno-song, which engenders 'plaisir' (pleasure), Barthes experiences 'jouissance' (joy, chaos, vitality) in the geno-song, in part because the listener is aware of the materiality of the voice, e.g. Waits's growling. While his theory cannot easily be summarized, the pheno-song is structured around technique and style, whereas the geno-song is about what Barthes calls the 'voluptiousness' of sound-language.

10. I am grateful to James Riley for drawing my attention to the Portelli article.

Bibliography

Allen. S. and J. Kerouac, *Poetry for the Beat Generation*, Hanover Signature Record Corp, 1959.

Barthes, R., *Image, Music, Text*, translated and selected by S. Heath, London: Fontana, 1990.

Barthes, R., *Camera Lucida: Reflections on Photography*, London: Vintage, 1993.

Boym, S., 'Nostalgia and its Discontents', *Hedgehog Review* 9, no. 2 (2007): 7–18.

Brinkley, D., liner notes, *Jack Kerouac Reads On the Road*, Rykodisc, 1999.

Dawidoff, N., 'The Man Who Saw America: Looking Back With Robert Frank, the Most Influential Photographer Alive', *New York Times Magazine*, 2 July 2015, https://www.nytimes.com/2015/07/05/magazine/robert-franks-america.html?_r=3 (accessed 12 April 2017).

Douglas, A., 'Introduction: "A Hoop for the Lowly"', in J. Kerouac, *The Dharma Bums*, London: Penguin, 2007, pp. v–xxv.

Everett, T., 'Tom Waits: In Close Touch with the Streets', in P. Maher Jr (ed.), *Tom Waits on Tom Waits: Interviews and Encounters*, London: Aurem Press, 2011 (1975), pp. 45–9.

Ginsberg, A., 'The Visions of the Great Remember', in J. Kerouac, *Visions of Cody*, London: Penguin, 2012 (1972), pp. 1–10.

Himmelsbach, E., Review of *Lowside of the Road: A Life of Tom Waits*, by Barney Hoskyns, *Los Angeles Times*, 21 May 2009, http://www.latimes.com/entertainment/la-et-book21-2009may21-story.html (accessed 19 April 2017).

Hoskyns, B., *Lowside of the Road: A Life of Tom Waits*, London: Faber and Faber, 2009.

5">

5">

Hrebeniak, M., *Action Writing: Jack Kerouac's Wild Form*, Carbondale: Southern Illinois University Press, 2006.

Humphries, P., *The Many Lives of Tom Waits*, London: Omnibus, 2008.

Hunt. T., *The Textuality of Soulwork: Jack Kerouac's Quest for Spontaneous Prose*, Ann Abor: University of Michigan Press, 2014.

Irwin. C., 'Guess You're Waits', *Melody Maker*, 29 April 1978, http://www.tomwaitsfan.com/tom%20waits%20library/www.tomwaitslibrary.com/interviews/78-apr29-melodymaker.html (accessed 10 April 2017).

Kaufman, Gil, 'Tom Waits Slips Into Multiple Personas at Tour Opener', *MTV News*, 1999, http://www.mtv.com/news/515186/tom-waits-slips-into-multiple-personas-at-tour-opener/ (accessed 10 April 2017).

Kerouac, J., *Satori in Paris*, London: Quartet Books, 1977 (1966).

Kerouac, J., *On the Road*, New York: Penguin Books, 1992 (1957).

Kerouac. J., 'The Origins of the Beat Generation', in Donald Allen (ed.), *Good Blonde and Others*, San Francisco: City Lights, 1993 (1959), pp. 55–65.

Kerouac, J., *The Town and the City*, London: Penguin Books, 2000 (1950).

Kerouac J., *The Big Sur*, London: Harper Perennial, 2006 (1962).

Kerouac, J., *Doctor Sax*, London: Penguin, 2012 (1959).

Kerouac, J., 'On Frank Sinatra', in Todd Tietchen (ed.) and Christophe Cloutier (trans.), *The Unknown Kerouac: Rare, Unpublished and Newly Translated Writings*, New York: Library of America, 2016a (1946), pp. 2–3.

Kerouac, J., 'Notes of 1950 February', in Todd Tietchen (ed.) and Christophe Cloutier (trans.), *The Unknown Kerouac: Rare, Unpublished and Newly Translated Writings*, New York: Library of America, 2016b (1950), pp. 58–61.

Kerouac, J., 'Introduction', *The Americans*, by Robert Frank, Göttingen, Germany: Steidl, 2016c (1959). No pagination.

Lake, S., 'The Great White Hope', *Melody Maker*, 4 October 1975, http://www.tomwaitsfan.com/tom%20waits%20library/www.tomwaitslibrary.com/interviews/75-oct4-melodymaker.html (accessed 10 April 2017).

Larman, H., 'Interview with Tom Waits', *Folkscene, KFPK*, in P., Maher, Jr (ed.), *Tom Waits on Tom Waits: Interviews and Encounters*, London: Aurem Press, 2011 (1974), pp. 20–6.

Maher, Jr, P., 'Closing Time', in P. Maher, Jr (ed.), *Tom Waits on Tom Waits: Interviews and Encounters*, London: Aurem Press, 2011 (1973), pp. 3–26.

McClintock, J., 'Jack Kerouac's Last Interview? Jack Kerouac is on the Road No More', *Tampa Bay Times*, 1969/2013, http://www.tampabay.com/features/humaninterest/jack-kerouac-is-on-the-road-no-more/2109689 (accessed 5 January 2017).

Menand. L., 'Drive, He Wrote. What the Beats Were About', *New Yorker*, 1 October 2007, http://www.newyorker.com/magazine/2007/10/01/drive-he-wrote (accessed 10 April 2017).

Miles, B., *Jack Kerouac, King of the Beast: a Portrait*, London: Virgin, 1998.

Mortenson, E., *Ambiguous Borderlands: Shadow Imagery in Cold War American Culture*, Carbondale: Southern Illinois University Press, 2016.

Nicosia. G., 'Kerouac: Writer without a Home', in P. Actil, L. Dupont, R. Ferland and E. Waddell (eds), *Un Homme Grand: Jack Kerouac at the Crossroads of Many Cultures*, Ottawa: Carleton University Press, 1990, pp. 19–39.

Olson, C., *Projective Verse* (1950), Poetry Foundation, 2009, https://www.poetryfoundation.org/resources/learning/essays/detail/69406 (accessed 12 April 2017).

Perlich, T., 'Tom Waits: Haunted Songster's Revolutionary Dispatch from the Twilight Zone', in P. Maher, Jr (ed.) *Tom Waits on Tom Waits: Interviews and Encounters*, London: Aurem Press, 2011 (2006), pp. 411–16.

Reynolds, S., *Retromania: Pop Culture's Addiction to its Own Past*, London: Faber and Faber, 2012.

Sanders, E., *Fug You: An informal History of the Peace Eye Bookstore, The Fuck You Press, The Fugs, and counterculture in the Lower East Side*, Cambridge, MA: Da Capo Press, 2011.

Sontag, S., *On Photography*. New York: Picador, 2010.

Szekely, M., 'Gesture, Pulsion, Grain: Barthes', Musical Semiology, *Contemporary Aesthetics*, 2006, http://www.contempaesthetics.org/newvolume/pages/article.php?articleID=409#FN31link (accessed 8 April 2017).

Theado, M., 'Revisions of Kerouac: The Long Strange Trip of *On the Road* Typescripts', in H. Holladay and R. Holton (eds), *What's Your Road, Man?: Critical Essays on Jack Kerouac's On the Road*, Carbondale: Southern Illinois University Press, 2009, pp. 8–34.

Theisen, G., *Staying up Much too Late: Edward Hopper's Nighthawks and the Dark Side of the American Pysche*, New York: Dunne, 2006.

Waits, T., 'It's Perfect Madness', *Observe*, 20 March 2005, https://www.theguardian.com/music/2005/mar/20/popandrock1 (accessed 19 April 2017).

Waits, T., 'The Heart of Saturday Night Press Release', in P. Maher, Jr (ed.), *Tom Waits on Tom Waits: Interviews and Encounters*, London: Aurem Press, 2011 (1974), pp. 28–9.

Warner, S., *Text and Drugs and Rock'n'Roll: The Beats and Rock Culture*, London: Bloomsbury, 2014.

Williams, R., *The Country and the City*, New York: Oxford University Press, 1973.

Wordsworth, W., 'Ode: Intimations of Immortality', in *The New Oxford Book of Romantic Period Verse*, ed. Jerome McGann, Oxford and New York: Oxford Univeristy Press, 1993.

Discography

Various Artists, *Jack Kerouac Reads On the Road*, Rykodisc, 1999.

Waits, Tom, *The Heart of Saturday Night*, Asylum, 1974.

Waits, Tom, *Night Hawks at the Diner*, Asylum, 1975.

Waits, Tom, *Small Change*, Asylum, 1976.

Waits, Tom, *Foreign Affairs*, Asylum, 1977.

Waits, Tom, *Blue Valentine*, Asylum, 1978.

Waits, Tom, *Bone Machine*, Island, 1992.

Waits, Tom, *Mule Variations*, ANTI-, 1999.

Waits, Tom, *Orphans: Brawlers, Bawlers & Bastards*, ANTI-, 2006.

INTERVIEW 4: BARNEY HOSKYNS ON TOM WAITS

Simon Warner

Barney Hoskyns is one of our leading rock historians, having served time as a writer and reviewer on *New Musical Express* in the 1980s and as US editor of *Mojo* during the 1990s. His biography *Lowside of the Road: A Life of Tom Waits* was published in 2009 to positive reviews.

The *Observer* said of it, 'His piecing together of Waits's formative years from such collective silence is a serious piece of investigative work,' touching upon the elusive nature of his subject and his lack of willingness to personally co-operate with the project. In the *Guardian* notice, the critic said that Hoskyns 'focuses considerable attention on the actual music, and some of the best passages in the book are his descriptions of the songs and, particularly, some of the ever-more outlandish sounds on the various albums'.

Despite the difficulties imposed by the figure at the heart of his enquiry and those in the artist's circle, Hoskyns remains a fan and is certainly intrigued by the ways in which Kerouac has helped to shape his output. He talked to me at the London headquarters of the rock journalism web archive Rock's Backpages, which he directs, on 24 November 2016.

In the interview, the author of numerous highly-rated volumes, including *Across the Great Divide: The Band and America* (1993), *Hotel California: Singer-Songwriters and Cocaine Cowboys in the LA Canyons* (2005), *Trampled Underfoot: The Power in Excess Of Led Zeppelin* (2012) and *Small Town Talk* (2015), concerning Dylan and the community of Woodstock, muses on Waits, rock lyrics and the novel and that Nobel Prize for Literature award.

SW: Let's start off by asking to what extent do you feel Tom Waits has been influenced by Kerouac and the wider Beat writers? Did you get a sense that this was a strong element in the man's make-up?

BH: Unquestionably. There's no question that Waits like so many of his contemporaries are young men like him feeling somewhat at odds with mainstream American society who fell into the spell really of, particularly, *On the Road* – this was the bible wasn't it? Usually the entrée and I think it was for Waits, I don't think he'd read anything else by Kerouac or any of the other Beat writers before *On the Road*.

SW: Do you think he'd read Ferlinghetti?

BH: Do I think he'd read Ferlinghetti before? So yeah okay, maybe those two things, but there's no doubt that *On The Road* blew his mind, blew his little suburban mind as it blew many minds as you know all too well. So I think [for] Waits it was a gateway, it was a portal to some wild adventure that he'd never really imagined possible, you know? Although it's always worth saying that Waits's own dad was somewhat of an adventurer.

SW: He disappeared quite early, didn't he?

BH: Yeah, so I think Waits has a complicated relationship with, a) fathers, and b) father figure influences and rebellion. He has a complicated relationship with those things because he didn't have, despite a somewhat conventional suburban upbringing, you'd say it was middle class – his mother was quite stable and middle class and conventional I think from what I gather – he didn't have a kind of archetypal sort of golf-playing, Rotarian sort of dad to rebel against, so I think Waits's rebellion was quite complicated, you know. We all have to rebel against our fathers, but he said in an interview that he was rebelling against a rebel, so there's a kind of interesting, that's an interesting thing, for a boy to go through I think.

SW: He was living in Southern California, wasn't he?

BH: He spent his first few years in greater Los Angeles in Whittier, and then moved down with his mother to San Diego after his parents separated. It was in San Diego when he discovered the literature and then started almost to kind of live Beat literature. I think when he started working at Napolioni's . . . it wasn't just Napolioni's, he worked in another pizza place and he used to frequent diners. The two things went hand in hand. He was falling under the spell of Kerouac and the other writers and at the same time as he was plunged into this nocturnal world that I don't suppose his mother planned for him.

SW: He tells a story about a trip up to San Francisco which was quite a long journey for a middle or late teenager, you can hardly conceive . . .

BH: He went up there, he went up to City Lights, did he talk to Ferlinghetti, I think he did – he had some exchange with him.

SW: Yes, he bought some copies of probably the famous City Lights poetry imprint, Ferlinghetti wasn't there, he went into Vesuvio's, said to the bar tender if Lawrence Ferlinghetti comes back, can you get him to sign books, and the next time he went to City Lights, Ferlinghetti had done so. Must have been very exciting. So clearly as, I guess he was 16 or 17, he tells the story in a radio interview, he starts to be drawn into this world of writing. Were there other literary influences on Waits? Was Kerouac the most important or were there others shaping his sensibility as he moved into his twenties?

BH: Yeah, I think you know Waits was quite a voracious reader from an early age, certainly from his mid-teens, you know, I think he read quite widely. I think he read in not a particularly methodical way, it would have been like, you know, he was not a university graduate after all, so I suspect he read in a kind of in that slightly 'what's cool' way, what would look cool to be moseying along the street with. I know, for example, interviewing people who had been with him in the Heritage Coffee House in San Diego, and he'd be on the door and he'd be reading, he would take the tickets and then once everyone was in and listening to whoever it was who was performing, he'd sit on the door and he'd always have a book, it would be like Kierkegaard, *Fear and Trembling*, because things like that were part of all the 1960s existentialist kind of pseudo-intellectual search weren't they?!

SW: The strange thing with Waits was that he was doing this about ten years after that Beat boom had happened, this would have been the late 1960s ...

BH: Waits is always slightly out of time and out of step. One of the things that was amusing to write about when I did my biography was how he kind of kicked against the trend: you know, he very much was his own kid – and that's really very rare and always somewhat admirable when somebody kind of says, well okay, you might think that Jimi Hendrix is cool but I'm not gonna be a kind of free festival junior hippie you know, I'm more interested in Frank Sinatra frankly, or indeed Kerouac. I think partly as a result of his difficult relationship with his dad. He was always looking for some sort of validation from his elders. He was more interested in older men really I think than in his own contemporaries, his own peer group. I think Waits always thought there was more to be learned from people of his dad's age because I think he hadn't got what he needed from his dad. He said this himself in interviews, he said Bukowski was a kind of substitute father figure, not the most obvious surrogate dad you would pick! But for him, he was a little bit like his dad, he had an alcohol problem, and therefore it was kind of like can I find something like my dad in Bukowski? I think Bukowski was older than Kerouac, but I don't know if Kerouac was in some sense a literary father figure for Waits, more like a significantly older brother figure, you would take off into the night with, you know.

SW: And I think Waits and *On the Road* as Neal Cassady or Dean Moriarty and Sal Paradise go searching for Dean's father, a strong sense that Waits felt echoes of his own life. Did he ever re-meet his father? I don't know.

BH: He stayed in touch with his dad.

SW: It was more metaphorical?

BH: He didn't see much of his dad. His dad stayed in LA when Waits moved with his mother and sisters to San Diego. What we do know is that Frank would come through San Diego, pick the kids up and take them down to Mexico, so this was a wild weekend with dad, and I imagine he was probably like this erratic stepfather. Having said that, he was a teacher, he wasn't a kind of bartender you know. He was a bon viveur, he was a bit reckless, and he was a bit of a boozing romantic and he would take the kids to Mexico, to his ex-wife's consternation – 'Please be responsible Frank, you shouldn't really be taking them to Tijuana' – but he would . . .

SW: A sense of a road trip being made there perhaps?

BH: Of course, 'road trip' is slightly overstating it, given that it doesn't take very long to drive from San Diego to Tijuana, depending on how long you stop at the border – it may post-Trump take rather longer! – but then it wouldn't have taken very long you know and I don't think it was just Tijuana. Frank would take them there, and Waits would talk about being in bars with Frank and little Tom is falling asleep at the bar he shouldn't be in anyway, and Frank's singing songs with Mexican singers and 'Drinks on me', and that's the feeling one gets. I didn't have a father like that. That must be quite a very different picture of the world if you have a dad like that, so I always think that Waits's internal psychology is always about the relationship between the kind of reckless, slightly irresponsible dad and the quite starchy hausfrau mum.

SW: It's interesting, without getting too Freudian here, it's as if Waits spent to [the] 1970s leading the wild life, and ever since the early 1980s has lived the other life, isn't it?

BH: He would say he stopped living that life as a kind of performance art and grew up, stopped drinking eventually and became a proper husband and dad. But he would say that his art, his writing, his music became so much wilder and freer, because his house was in order, metaphorically and literally speaking. He was able to really liberate his creative id, is probably what he would say.

SW: In terms of the kind of evidence of Kerouac maybe and his ilk, but mainly Kerouac, how do you think that writing is evidenced in Tom Waits's musical output?

BH: It was all too obvious from *The Heart of Saturday Night* through to *Blue Valentine*, you would say that Kerouac was woven into that music. I suspect it didn't come to an abrupt halt with *Heartattack and Vine* and it never comes to a total, abrupt halt. Kerouac is always in there, but I would say that from *The Heart of Saturday Night* – there's 'Bad Liver and a Broken Heart' – Kerouac is a touchstone and a reference point and a forefather the whole way through. And I think that's because there's no doubt that *On the Road* freed up that kind of romantic adventurer in the young Waits as it did in so many people. It's like 'Wow. America is an extraordinary place', you know, for all its small town limitations, it's this vast country with all kinds of very different people and very different landscapes, very different communities, very different experiences to be had, and that very romantic idea of being someone who instead of staying in his own community, settling down, getting a regular job, getting a wife and 2.4 kids and a white picket fence, you go off in search of the romance that's there, the romance that you wouldn't necessarily think was there, that ability to find romance in the dingiest, sleaziest, darkest corners of American life, and a particular sort of bar . . .

SW: Kerouac *and* Waits both do this, of course.

BH: . . . bars and diners, you know . . .

SW: Both writer and musician are interested in that nostalgia, aren't they?

BH: Absolutely and it stands out in Edward Hopper, you know, Hopper's paintings. It's a different sort of expression of that milieu, that night-time Americana, it's not reckless and Dionysian, but it's more [a] melancholy, lonesome flipside to that, to which I'm sure Kerouac felt drawn many times when he was hungover. Deliberation is in there, in the writing, in the prose, the riffing, the jazz-influenced, bursting of the seams really, and I imagine, or my sense is, that for Waits as for so many, it's like up to that point you've got some really boring English teacher teaching you about Longfellow and suddenly it's like, wow, this can be literature, this utterly kind of unfettered, spontaneous bebop self-expression almost without the super ego even editing it, it's just like a bebop sax solo and Waits has talked about the impact of that.

SW: I remember a sixth form teacher bringing in one of the Penguin Modern Poetry collections with Ferlinghetti and Ginsberg and Corso and reading that in class, and opening up fresh vistas, and until that stage I didn't know it existed. Perhaps it happened to Waits as well . . .

BH: Before I forget, because it's worth throwing it in there – yes, Waits as a younger man comes relatively late to the Beat revolution as you know, which shouldn't in any way minimize or invalidate the impact it had on him – and of course I think we need to throw Bob Dylan into the conversation at this point: I suspect that Dylan, a bit older than Waits, but here's a guy who's part of something new and also very influenced by the Beats, particularly by Ginsberg and Kerouac, too.

SW: Dylan's autobiographical *Chronicles* seems to suggest he eventually leaves that initial fervour behind . . .

BH: We do know that Waits was of course fascinated by Bob Dylan, mightily impressed by Bob Dylan, and for him, in Dylan's writing and verse, he formed a bridge between the 1950s Beat moment and the new '60s insurgency.

SW: There's that marvellous moment in 1965 where Ginsberg and Dylan meet in San Francisco and they're . . .

BH: Robbie Robertson [Dylan's guitarist] talks about how awkward he felt and how he didn't want to be in that picture, and he always does look in that picture so out of place like 'oh, I don't know why I'm here, I'm not worthy'.

SW: That's fascinating because I've been reading *Small Town Talk*, of course, but I don't think it touches upon San Francisco, but Robertson in *Testimony* does talk about that.

BH: He talks about that photograph and he was like 'No, I don't need to be in this picture', they were like 'Come on', and you can see Robbie looking very bashful and unworthy. When I started my research on Waits I didn't realize how much of a Dylan freak he was, and I suppose you could say everyone would have been at that time, but when Waits started out, he was just another fucking Dylan wannabe, and he dressed like Dylan and he had a harmonica round his neck, he'd sit on the grass and try and impress girls with Dylan songs or Dylan-esque songs. It's clear that Dylan's writing for Waits had a strong Beat component to it, but I think that moving forward into the next decade, into the archetypal Waits of the '70s, the shambling drunk at the piano, that's where Waits takes the Kerouac influence, melds it with a bunch of other elements and creates this Tom Waits persona which is like a character in a Kerouac novel; it's almost like the sort of archetypal Beat figure, Beat persona, I think.

SW: Do you think this use of the Beat influence, and we might raise that old authenticity word . . . What do you think about Waits doing that in the '70s, adopting this stage and recording persona? Does he remain an authentic musician in rock terms or is he just playing a part like an actor?

BH: I very much try to explore that theme, that puzzle if you like, in the biography *Lowside of the Road*. One of the chapters I think is called 'In character', and you know my feeling is that Waits created that persona as a sort of artistic channel, as a device in a way, so, on the one hand it's an artistic device, on the other hand it's a real statement of not being in step with the times, being at odds with his musical environment and so I think it's interesting that the first Waits album – the way he is packaged and marketed and managed and, at moments on the record, doesn't sound a million miles away from those kind of David Geffen artists of the period – it was all Canyon singer-songwriters. That's what clearly they wanted him to be, albeit with some jazzier elements and some nods to the past and so forth, a sort of urban romantic thing rather than anything country rock-ish or . . . so, on *Closing Time*, he looks like he belongs on the Asylum label and I think with the next record there's a very conscious turn away from that, then he starts putting on the kind of the rumpled suits and the fedora and the tie and flaunting the whisky bottle, and it's very much like 'In my head this is [the] 1970s, but I am not part of the world of the Eagles even if they're gonna cover my song and make me some decent money.' My heart is not in that Los Angeles, I live in my head, I get up at 6am and I go out to some bar on Hollywood Boulevard that's been there for 25 years and the bartender's been there for 20 and there's only old guys in there and there's no other kind of hip young Sunset Boulevard types. And I think that's what he felt that – and this was the paradox – he felt that he was more authentic, even if, to the outside world, he obviously seemed inauthentic. For a lot of people, certainly for critics, this was a shtick, this was phoney, phoney baloney. In some sense it is, but we've got far enough in pop culture to sort of say, I don't really care if by some criteria it's authentic or inauthentic. Is it any good? Does it move me? And there are songs which you know obviously are just kind of like piano, stand up bass, brushes and a saxophone, you just think fuck's sake, you know, are you kidding? But it's really irrelevant if the music speaks to you and there was still that, it wasn't as if that America had vanished completely, it was just an America that was more interesting to him: it was more soulful, it was more authentic, I think, to him and that ties with the idea of he was more interested in what older writers and older musicians did – he wasn't interested in who was the new cool kid on the block. He was always reading stuff that was old or listening to records that were old and, of course, Kerouac collaborations on albums.

SW: He brought Al Cohn in, the saxophonist who'd played on *Blues and Haikus* with the novelist . . .

BH: He did. Nothing was more thrilling to Waits than working with bona fide heavy hitter jazz guys, some of whom had been part of the original West Coast jazz scene, the cool sound; working with Shelly Manne on *Small Change* was huge for Waits and Al Cohn as well. He played with Zoot Sims, and that to him was like if these guys are taking it seriously, and I'm not saying that all of them were, some of them may have taken him with a pinch of salt like some did . . .

SW: It's funny you should say that, because some of the jazz guys took Kerouac with a pinch of salt as well, they were brought in for a session fee . . .

BH: They probably thought he was a wanker, a miserable wanker, an impossible man . . .

SW: Absolutely. I'm going to ask you one last question – you were a little critical, maybe sceptical, questioning the award of the Nobel Literature prize to Dylan a few weeks ago. How do you feel about what happens when literary influences are taken into the popular music realm? Do you see it as a valuable connection or is there still a veritable high–low divide that means that pop music, in some ways, by taking on a mock seriousness loses some of its spirit, some of its verve? How do you feel about that intersection?

BH: For me it's not a high–low issue. The issue for me is probably this, which is that I think poetry, and prose for that matter, are doing something very different from music, I just don't think that however good music lyrics can be, and sometimes they're extraordinary, they can't ever quite be – because they're always in the service of meter and cadence and they're there to be sung – on the page they often don't: it's like taking a dimension out of them and they don't have the internal music that makes them poetic when they're performed and arranged, so to me lyrics can never be poetry. Glyn Maxwell made that point, in a brilliant book called *On Poetry*, arguing that it wasn't being in any way reactionary or snobbish towards lyricists – he was just saying that it can't be the same. The greatest poetry has its own internal music and, that is, it's a different art and therefore when you see … my quibble with the Nobel Prize thing is that Dylan could get a Nobel Prize for something but I'm not sure that literature is really the right category. To me Dylan is not – he's not a writer in the sense that say Cormac McCarthy was a writer. I was interested that the Norwegian author Karl Ove Knausgaard said that 'I love Bob Dylan' but until either [Philip] Roth or [Don] DeLillo or [Cormac] McCarthy have won the Nobel Prize, Dylan shouldn't be winning it.' And I thought about Roth and to some degree about DeLillo but I'd forgotten about McCarthy and frankly – I'm sorry to say this – but you know when you read Cormac McCarthy, this is literature on a Shakespearean level, this is poetic prose that Dylan will never touch. He will never come close to its greatness in my opinion.

I came quite late to Cormac McCarthy but I've read most of his stuff now and to me it's just sort of intoxicatingly brilliant; it is at the moment as good as Shakespeare, I really believe that. I know his writing is very wild and bloody and a million miles from Roth or DeLillo or writers who are writing about the American human condition, but I just think in terms of the power and the vivid intensity of language, McCarthy is the greatest American writer and I don't think that, if there's a Nobel Prize for Literature, Dylan shouldn't be winning it when Cormac McCarthy hasn't won it. Let's just leave it at that. I would also say as a sort of side issue, I think there are better lyricists than Bob Dylan. Let's say you gave the Nobel Prize for music lyrics …

SW: … Would you put Leonard Cohen in that category? …

BH: I think Cohen is a better – I think Dylan has written some extraordinary lyrics, but he's also unbelievably sloppy and just like pretentious and unconvincing to me in many, many cases. I think a lot of his writing … doesn't really matter what I think about it. I think in different areas of lyrics writing I think there are better lyricists. I think Becker and Fagen are better writers than Bob Dylan. I think that Richard Rodgers and Cole Porter are better writers than Bob Dylan. I think Randy Newman is a better writer per se than Bob Dylan. I don't worship at the altar of Dylan. A lot of the songs from the '60s and so forth that people think are a work of genius, they're a bit sort of adolescent actually. But then I sort of have some problem maybe with – because the only thing I was ever good at was English and I studied English at university so I have a sense of what great writing is – and I love *On the Road* and Kerouac, but there is a sort of Oxford snob part of me that is sort of like, that's wonderfully free and intoxicating and 'bleugh!', you know, just unfettered, to use a word that I used earlier. But it's not necessarily great literature.

CHAPTER 18

FROM BEAT BOP PROSODY TO PUNK ROCK POETRY: PATTI SMITH AND JACK KEROUAC – LITERATURE, LINEAGE, LEGACY

Ronna C. Johnson

Kerouac is a major, perhaps seminal, poet of the latter half of the U.S. XX Century – and mayhap thru his imprint on Dylan and myself among others, a poetic influence over the entire planet. Jack Kerouac was above all a poet's poet, as well as a people's poet and an Ivory Tower poet, like Rimbaud legended to youth round the world.

Allen Ginsberg, 1992, p. vi

Punk as a concept began with the Beat poets. William Burroughs has been called the grandfather of punk.

Jim Fourrat, in Colegrave and Sullivan, 2005, p. 29

. . . they [punk musicians] all read Allen Ginsberg, William Burroughs and Jack Kerouac. From them they learned a certain style and attitude.

Leee Childers, in Colegrave and Sullivan, 2005, p. 29

Artists are born, yes, but all are also made: by environment, opportunity, personal origins, local and global history. Artists respond to cultural, political and artistic – literary, musical, visual – influences; 'imprints', we might say. Interviews and biographies educe an artist's formative attention to earlier arts, forms and art makers. Or claiming a hero or idol or beau ideal – claiming affinity with a precursor – divulges an artist's creative loyalties and legacy. But deliberate and disjunctive, impulsive and premeditated, conscious and unconscious, drives and designs and distortions expressed by an artist may betray unrecognized influences and alignments with precursor artists. Influences are at once woven and concealed; apparent textual relations denied or disallowed. This discussion seeks to affirm and explain the literary-cultural influence of Jack Kerouac (1922–69), poet, novelist, Beat movement poetics originator, on Patti Smith (b. 1946), poet, artist, punk rock innovator, however indeterminate and indirect that influence may be. This influence is evident largely through inferential argument and historical context. Close readings of relevant texts help reveal markers of Kerouac found in Smith's art, and suggest the extent to which such influence is 'imprinted' consciously or unconsciously. The connection between

Kerouac's and Smith's work is not overt or apparent; yet once perceived, its surprising ubiquity comes into view.

* * *

Music journalist Chris Sullivan rightly proclaims that 'nobody could denigrate or under-estimate the importance of Patti Smith' (Colegrave and Sullivan, 2001/2005, p. 209) to the punk rock era of her work's heyday, and to American art and music. Defining a pivotal moment in mid-century US art, a passing of and advance on prevailing artistic movements under the forward velocity of her punk rock poetry, Smith has significantly contributed to muso-literary history. Incarnating the continuation of Beat movement poetics and themes in mid- to late 1970s punk-rock, Smith is a Beat poet-cum-rock musician who carries Beat poetics into an era of her own making two generations later, her Beat legacy extending Kerouac's precursive position; Smith's art rides cultural-literary transitions of Beat (art of resistance) to pop (art of simulation) to punk (art of refusal).[1] Her first record album, *Horses* (1975), put music to Smith's poetry; her devotion to poetry, her 'primarily literary' emphasis (Bracewell, 1996, p. 1), casts her in what Sullivan termed 'the pre-punk era' as well as accounts for a future direction, as the title *Patti Smith: Complete Lyrics, Reflections, Notes for the Future* announces. She insists that whatever the significance of her music and art, 'Poetry would always be my guiding principle' (Colegrave and Sullivan, 2001/2005, p. 242). Just so, she is an American poet, visual artist, singer-songwriter, 1970s New York punk rocker epitome, activist for power to the people.

As this cursory description suggests, although Smith was a key figure in the punk rock movement – she has been widely and reductively dubbed by music journalists the 'godmother of punk' (quoted in DeLano, 2002, p. 5)[2] – her range and creativity, her immersion in numerous cultural movements, have led scholars and artists to propose more capacious characterizations. Michael Bracewell defines Smith as 'one of the most radical writers and performers' of her era; his Smith 'embodies the second wave of New York's pop avant garde: the punk scene of the early Seventies, based around [the legendary club] CBGBs, that took over the underground after Warhol had been forced to close the doors of his Factory' (Bracewell, 1996, p. 1). The Warhol coterie was a 'Factory' of undifferentiated assistants to/manufacturers of the master artist's master plans, while the second wave of the pop avant-garde restored a romantic individualism to creative expression and, more, catalyzed a simultaneity in which 'art, poetry and music were all plugged into the same circuit' (Bracewell, 1996, p. 1). Popular music studies scholar Simon Warner and journalists quoted in Warner's 2013 landmark book, *Text and Drugs and Rock 'n' Roll* (Warner, 2013, pp. 356–65), have labelled Smith 'post-Beat', a category which I take to signify an artist staking new ground beyond that movement yet with a palpable debt to it. In my view, she is not 'post-Beat', but certainly *of* Beat movement literature and *of* the Beat Generation.[3] Anne Waldman, a Beat acolyte and protégé of Allen Ginsberg with whom she co-founded the Jack Kerouac

School of Disembodied Poetics at Naropa Institute (now Naropa University) in 1974, places Smith 'in a post-Beat pantheon' of free form poetics and artistic process: Smith 'takes what she can use (like Dylan too). Like all of us poets she's a magpie scholar' and because she 'was not inside the Beat literary movement or culture in the early days', it seems that Smith was liberated from strict coterie obligations to 'recalibrate and invent herself in relation to various cultural icons and literary movements' (Warner, 2013, p. 365).

Building on these productive analyses, I view Smith as a third generation Beat poet of blunt visionary declamation and a second generation New York School poet of vatic punk authority from the perspective of her contemporaneity with such poets and musicians, writers and performers as Anne Waldman, Bob Dylan, Lou Reed, Laurie Anderson, Sam Shepard and Ed Sanders (Johnson, 2004, p. 17) and her formative reflection of Beat movement literature and kinship with/in Beat Generation artists.[4] As some, such as the scene chronicler Leee Childers, have noted, punk descends from Beat (Colegrave and Sullivan, 2001/2005, p. 29). Smith embodies the Beat–punk rock cusp in her first publications and recordings, between 1970 and 1979. Warner clarifies: she is 'part of a continuum, a carrier of a flame, a latter day vessel who may frequently cite her muses but one also capable of shaping fresh visions from that amalgam of influences' (Warner, 2013, p. 364). Thus situated, Smith emerges as an embodiment of an archetypal postmodern condition, a liminal figure contingently defining and illuminating its cusp and then seeking to cross over it. In this and in other ways, she occupies a later point along the modern–postmodern continuum, which Jack Kerouac, in his life and work, clarified as such by constituting a pre-postmodern moment, an era of transition and experimentation that both artists marked and embodied from their respective eras, and sought to transcend (Johnson, 2000/2002).

Not only do Smith and Kerouac occupy comparable positions; this chapter conceives her as a poet-musician descended from and influenced by Kerouac. Kerouac forms a periphery of literary practices and poetics her work expresses, consciously or unconsciously. Her postmodern merger of literary styles and movements, her fusion of punk rock music and lyric poetry, are evident in her first recordings – 'Hey Joe'/'Piss Factory' (1974), *Horses* (1975), *Easter* (1978) – and in her early poetry – *Seventh Heaven* (1972), *Babel* (1978), *Early Work, 1970–1979* (1994). Her linguistic and cultural hybridity, her ability to embody pop and high cultures simultaneously (Keith Richards and Rimbaud) align her work with Kerouac's through Beat's 1950s themes and visions, its bigeneric bop prosody, especially bop's rhythms: 'When we dream it when we dream it when we dream it / We'll dream it dream it for free free money free money free / Money free money free money free money free money' (Smith, 1998, p. 18). Her offhand vernacular colloquial poetics evoke the contemporaneous 1960s New York School: 'i haven't fucked much with the past but i've fucked plenty with the future' (Smith, 1998, p. 85). And her artistic admixtures of these anticipate the chaotic 1970s punk rock emergence: 'Baby was a black sheep baby was a whore / Baby got big and baby get bigger / Baby get something baby get more / Baby baby baby was a rock n roll nigger' (Smith, 1998, p. 89). Smith may 'mark ... out a bohemian legend', but being 'a visionary and an iconoclast' distracts from her core artistic drives: she is 'primarily [a] literary figure', Bracewell notes (Bracewell, 1996, p. 1), an essential condition of the Kerouac–Smith intergenerational lineage.

In turn, Kerouac's under-recognized Beat novel *The Subterraneans* (1953, published 1958), which he wrote the landmark 'Essentials of Spontaneous Prose' to explain, digs the hipsters, writers, jazz aficións, junkies, figures who are literary precursors to the poet rocker Smith. The cultural pluralities and hybrid language and style that mark the Kerouac novel's eponymous subterraneans animate the post-war 'cool' hipster generation embodied in the novel's avatars Mardou Fox, Roxanne and Julian Alexander. Smith, though a dramatic heir to the Kerouac novel's Roxanne, at least in her style and passions,[5] is often seen as removed or even disqualified from that milieu because of her poetry: 'She was a bit of a hippie. I didn't know what she was going on about anyway. The whole poetry thing kind of left me cold,' remembered Marco Pirroni (Colegrave and Sullivan, 2001/2005, p. 209); indeed, to divest of her 'folk singer'/hippie look, Smith sheared her hair to resemble a British Invasion rocker, Keith Richards. But Smith similarly divested of the hippie identity and updated the Beat Generation's slinky hipsters as embodied by Julian Alexander (based on a real-life model, Anton Rosenberg)[6] in her 'hot' Kerouacian 'Babelogue', the Rimbaudian 'babel field' (Smith, 1978, p. 193) and 'Rock N Roll Nigger' (Smith, 1998, p. 89). It is said that free jazz innovator Ornette Coleman 'almost played on "Radio Ethiopia"' (Bangs, 1987, p. 303), a testament to Smith's pan-period musicality; a concurrence that speaks to Kerouac's prescience in *The Subteranneans,* whose hipster binary 'me hot–them cool' (1958, p. 11) seeds and fosters the tonal and stylistic multiplicity of the cool 'american artist' ('Babelogue') and 'hot' Beat legatee Patti Smith.

Yet how Jack Kerouac is heard in Patti Smith is complicated, qualified in the manner of inferential, indirect connection discussed below. Whether as 'a Beat, a belated Beat, a current Beat, or a post-Beat' (Warner, 2013, p. 364), like all historic figures and culture-makers, Smith stands on the shoulders of her predecessors, and while she is first to identify and proud to admit those of whom she is aware, Kerouac does not occupy a firm place in her self-proclaimed lineage. A process of indirect influence via an intermediary poet or musician especially pertains to Smith's influence by Kerouac. He is unnamed in her panoply of early muses, and when she eventually mentioned him, she did so vaguely and abstractly. She noted she only knew him 'second hand', as a presence once removed given her by others' impressions. In a testimonial to Kerouac recorded in the 2009 film *One Fast Move or I'm Gone: Kerouac's Big Sur*, Smith offers a recognition of his somewhat concrete claim on her attention because he was her male friends' hero: 'almost every fella that I really liked had a love affair with Jack Kerouac; think I'd known Kerouac more second-hand through guys [Sam Shepard, Fred Sonic Smith] ... through his friends cause I knew

William [Burroughs] and Allen [Ginsberg] ... so I guess I knew Jack mostly through men' (quoted in Worden, 2009). She also recognizes him in a dreamier, more abstract and metaphoric way: 'Seems like he's sorta always been in the air.'[7] Kerouac's cultural and personal ubiquity in Smith's milieu ('air'), the 'second-hand' connection: these are the conduits by which Kerouac's influence was disseminated and, as her early work shows, absorbed. The cultural history of Smith's Kerouac connection is eerie and mystical: he was a ghost, what he himself called 'a predecessor dier' (Kerouac, 1958/1976, p. 89); when Smith repeats herself – 'It seems like he's always been in the air' – she elaborates the connection in enigmatic images: 'in the curve of a steering wheel, the circling mandala, the rim of a bottle and the tip of the tongue' (Worden, 2009, liner notes). More directly, Smith, speaking of herself, also makes Kerouac's influence hard to see: she began her 1973 chapbook *Witt* with a 'notice' that reads, in part, 'These ravings, observations, etc, come from one who, beyond vows, is without mother, gender, or country. Who attempts to bleed from the word. A system, a space base' (Smith, 1973/1994, p. 35). This is a poet's stance as orphan, *sui generis*, *tabula rasa*; someone without precursors. But Smith acknowledges that this posture was a tactical move: the 'notice' in *Witt* is 'just an artist statement. It has nothing to do with me personally ... but the rules in my heart are the rules of art which are almost no rules at all' (quoted in Gross, 1975). Smith's disregard of rules is fundamentally Kerouacian, although in a defiant register. For him, 'the best writing is always the most painful personal wrung-out tossed from cradle warm protective mind' (Kerouac, 1957/1992, p. 58), or '#10. No time for poetry but exactly what is' (Kerouac, 1957/1992, p. 59). This precursor paradoxically inscribes latitude for free invention in his rules for literary art.

While Smith's free invention incorporates Kerouac as a predecessor, it does so indirectly, through ideas about inspiration, through focus, through syntax, ethos, discursive patterns, sound and more. To tease it out I trace Smith's connections with direct and indirect poetic and musical intermediaries, listen for echoes between his work and practices and hers, and pay attention to references and allusions, however submerged. Tracing Kerouac's markers in Smith's work is complicated by several teasing, and distracting, matters. Smith knew and venerated three of the first generation Beat writers, and celebrated them in *Just Kids*, *Complete* and *M Train*. Kerouac, Allen Ginsberg, Gregory Corso and William S. Burroughs, progenitors of the Beat Generation literary movement, are 'Daddies' of Beat poetry (Ginsberg in Corso, 1989, p. xix), a tropic pun on 1950s cool ('daddy-o') that also implies lineage and heirs, which are assurances of literary, historical and artistic validity and import. Though artist coteries can be competitive (see Bloom, 1975), there is little evident oedipal conflict among these 'Daddies' of Beat poetry, and alternative routes seem to be always at the ready for generating mutual influences.

Corso became an icon of poetry for Smith; she accompanied him to poetry readings at the St Mark's Poetry Project, where he would 'heckle' poets who bored him. She sang movingly at his funeral in New York in 2001 (Johnstone, 2012, p. 214) and visited his grave adjacent to Shelley's (Sebring, 2008; Smith, 2011). 'Happily, Gregory was a bad influence on me' she proclaimed (DeLano, 2002, p. 18), as if his fabled obnoxious behaviours modelled a front for a positive stance for a punk rock poet: Corso 'did not always take himself seriously, but he was dead serious about his poetry', a respect for the art that extended to practical criticism, taught through Mallarme's maxim that 'Poets don't finish poems, they abandon them' (Smith, 2010, p. 137). Here, the modern open ending – just let it go – becomes postmodernism's abdication of resolve for de facto contingency. In recounting their innocuous first meeting in a way that suggests his portentous literary influence on her, Ginsberg bought a hungry Smith a sandwich, mistaking her 'for a very pretty boy'; later she covered for him with metaphor: 'I would say you fed me when I was hungry . . . And he did' (Smith, 2010, p. 123). He pulled her out of mourning for her dead husband Fred, her brother Todd and bandmate Richard Sohl to return to performing again in 1995; she was at his deathbed in 1997. William S. Burroughs interviewed Smith for *Spin* magazine in 1979 at the Chelsea Hotel just before her withdrawal from performance, and, again, Smith conceals his precursive, paternal influence in an euphemism, his 'generous nod' of recognition during her first sets at CBGBs in 1975, 'smiling at the notion that he was the spiritual father of another generation of Johnnys' (Smith, 1998, p. 29). The rich field of her relations with three Beat poets contextualizes her conclusion that they 'were all my teachers, each one passing through the lobby of the Chelsea Hotel, my new university' (Smith, 2010, pp. 137–8). Smith does not even note for the record Kerouac's obvious contributions to the literature of his friends, these 'Daddies' of Beat poetry.

But those Beat 'Daddies' felt enormously indebted to Kerouac. Allen Ginsberg parsed Kerouac's extensive literary influence. Ginsberg claimed in 1992 that his own writing has 'always been modeled on Kerouac's practice of tracing his mind's thoughts and sounds directly on the page' (Ginsberg, 1992, p. ii). The more well known influence that made a classic American poem out of a soul's wrenching utterance was Kerouac's demand that Ginsberg not revise the first draft of 'Howl' Ginsberg had sent him (Charters, 1973, p. 244), but Ginsberg recognized in that requirement a succinctly troped and now famous poetics, 'Kerouac's formulation "Mind is shapely, Art is shapely"' (Ginsberg, 1992, p. ii), sometimes formulated 'First thought, Best thought'; both suggest the innate value of 'no revision' of the uncensored mind/spirit/ consciousness as it erupts into language for the first time, a Buddhist-inflected stipulation aimed at 'writing the mind' by courting unmediated and uncensored spontaneous thought (see 'Essentials of Spontaneous Prose'). Ginsberg delineated other paradigms of influence 'indebted to Kerouac's bardic breakthru' that importantly emphasized intuition as well as deliberation: in which 'poet after poet [was] influenced consciously by Kerouac, or swept up unconsciously into the cultural stream of self-empowerment – initiated by Kerouac' (Ginsberg, 1992, p. vi). For Ginsberg, literary and artistic influence is a potent permeation, a *Zeitgeist* not necessarily recognized in which artists like Smith augment the Kerouac 'breakthru' deliberately or not.

Ginsberg's confidence in an 'unconscious' or unwilled perpetuation (a turn on the effects of a Rimbaudian 'dereglement du sens') of a literary arts heritage departs from the usual registers of influence: imitation, interpretation and homage. Ginsberg's is a particular departure from Harold Bloom's famous post-war anxiety of influence, a rational, intellectual argument of transhistorical oedipal joustings of strong poets, ephebes against each other and against established poets, for recognition in the intra-poetic relationships that comprise canonical literary lineage(s) Bloom tracks and establishes (Bloom, 1973, passim). The literary and cultural influence of Jack Kerouac does not stir 'anxiety of influence' or galvanize oedipal combat in his friends, but evokes a different patriarchal trope, one of familial, tribal sharing. This trope is palpable in Smith's early work about her sisters Linda and Kimberly, and at a remove in 'Birdland', her poem about Peter Reich, son of Wilhelm, and in 'Piss Factory', about the exploited poor, exemplifying Smith's claim that when she 'entered rock 'n' roll, I entered into it in a political sort of way, not as a career' (Burroughs 1979/1988); that is, as a community-building project, not a purely self-sustaining one. This tribal community is what Smith carries from Kerouac into her own art, regardless of consciousness, forethought or motive. And her work expands from that coterie to embrace the beaten world: '"Piss Factory" wasn't anything to do with punk rock … what is punk rock, anyway? … I wrote that because I was concerned about the common man [sic], and I was trying to remind them they had a choice' (Bracewell, 1996, p. 5).

Inferential influence, indirect and elusive, is one route for tracing literary heritage when direct claims are lacking, absent or resisted, as in the case of Smith's (non-) recognition of Kerouac. Ginsberg speaks of Kerouac's influence as an unintended legacy or bequest transmitted through writers such as Anne Waldman, who 'inherited some of Kerouac's energy and intelligence in [the] U.S. ordinary mind' (Ginsberg, 1992, p. v). The accent on 'mind' is repeated by Bob Dylan, who recalls that 'Someone handed me *Mexico City Blues* in St. Paul in 1959 [the year it was published] and it blew my mind' (quoted in Ginsberg, 1992, p. ii). The doubled usages of 'mind' merge Buddhist and popular cultures as wisdoms or cognizances or consciousnesses: Dylan explained that Kerouac's 'was the first poetry that spoke his own language' (quoted in Ginsberg, 1992, p. ii), a figure for influence that refuses hierarchy or oedipal jousting by inferring a mutuality of common tongue and lexis. This abstract and vague claim (what *was* 'his own language', after all?) allows for capacious connections, suggesting a paradigm for once-removed influence: Smith is influenced by Kerouac *through* his impact on Dylan, who is 'the one', she says, 'who has been an inspiration and influence on my work' (Bockris and Bayley, 1999, p. 273) and whose art 'mind' came to life in interplay with Kerouac's poetry.

Inferential or once-removed influence is a by-product of the influence of direct contact from poet to poet, also delineated by Ginsberg. He charts Kerouac's direct influence on Burroughs, for example, permitting the suggestion of Kerouac's indirect influence on Smith through Burroughs' influence on her. Confirming 'Jack's catalytic effect in encouraging Bill to write' (Ginsberg, 1992, p. viii), Ginsberg recalls that 'Kerouac was a catalyst' also when he 'collaborated' with Burroughs in his 'first "hardboiled" fiction back in 1945 and passed the romantic "gemlike flame" of sacred prose-poetry, homemade, personal, spontaneous, to Burroughs himself' (Ginsberg, 1992, p. v). In turn, Burroughs was a seminal influence on Smith on her debut recording, *Horses*: 'I owed no small debt to him [Burroughs], for the hero of "Land" was truly a descendent of his Johnny in *The Wild Boys*' (Smith, 1998, p. 28). As Smith's Johnny descends from Burroughs' Johnny, a figure descended from Burroughs' 'hardboiled' fiction, which was catalyzed by Kerouac and shaped by the literary qualities Kerouac carried and passed to Burroughs in their collaboration, Smith is influenced by Kerouac. His absence in Smith's personal history – 'I had never read his books,' she admits (Worden, 2009, liner notes) – or history of references becomes a presence when strained or filtered through Burroughs the intermediary. Smith herself conceptualized literary influence as indirect contact with predecessor artists: she recounts that in 1968 people 'assumed she was influenced by Allen Ginsberg but in fact she had not yet read him. "I liked Walt Whitman and Bob Dylan. And Whitman was the father of Ginsberg"' (DeLano, 2002, p. 21). The implication is that via a qua-familial/paternal ('father') connection through a mutual appreciation of Whitman, Smith was influenced by Ginsberg though she had not yet read or met him, the model for once-removed influence.

* * *

this reading is dedicated to all that is criminal

> Patti Smith, from 'Introduction' to St Mark's Church on the
> Bowery Reading, 10 February 1971, *Complete*, 1998, p. xxi

Anyway, the hipsters, whose music was bop, they looked like criminals but they kept talking about the same things I liked, long outlines of personal experience and vision, nightlong confessions full of hope that had become illicit and repressed by War, stirrings, rumblings of a new soul . . .

> Jack Kerouac, 'The Origins of the Beat Generation',
> June 1959, *Playboy*

Jack Kerouac's poetics are evident in Patti Smith's literary rock'n'roll style, in her characteristic pastiche of cultural and linguistic associations and in her narrative swerves or unexpected juxtapositions in the pre-punk pop-rock milieu from 1970 to 1979. Her long hiatus from performing, from around 1979 to 1995, a distinctive passage in her journey as poet and artist, recalls Rimbaud's abandonment of poetry at age 19. But unlike Rimbaud, an influence for both Kerouac and Smith, as well as for Dylan, Smith returned to making and performing her art. Kerouac burned out before he could leave (Worden, 2009). Smith's connection to Kerouac is established in two ways: through the subjects and culture of her early poetry, and through her work's overall poetics. Smith's prototypical subjects of northeastern urban post-war life ('Piss Factory', written 1972; *Collected* 26; recorded 1974) and the existentialism of later romantic hallucinogenic pre-punk stories ('Birdland', 1974), her lyrical and vehement oratory and self-authorization ('Oath', 1970; *Complete*: 7; 'Rock N Roll Nigger', 1978; *Complete*: 89; and 'Babelogue', 1978; *Babel*: 193), all call forth Kerouac in his Lowell novels and hipster stories, such as *The Subterraneans*. These compositions also align with techniques Kerouac enumerated in his manifesto 'Essentials of Spontaneous Prose' (1957), as well as forms and poetics of the 242 choruses that constitute *Mexico City Blues* (1959, published 1995). Smith's Beat literary heritage of hipster cool helps obscure her work's powerful likenesses to Kerouac's distinctively unhip and even sentimental Lowell novels. Smith's poignant despair over young death and loss ('Redondo Beach', recorded 1971, in Smith, 1998, p. 10) and romantic apocalyptic sentiment for a baby sister and a dead man's son – 'Kimberly' (recorded 1975, in Smith, 1998, p. 21) and 'Birdland' (recorded 1975, in Smith, 1998, pp. 15–17) – resound a generation later with Kerouac's novels about his birthplace and hometown (Lowell, MA), called the Lowell novels, which include *Visions of Gerard* (1956, published 1963), *Maggie Cassidy* (1953, published 1959) and *Dr. Sax* (1952, published 1959). These novels are lyric testaments to his working-class Catholic family and the liminal identity of a first-generation Franco-American writer captivated by American writing and the hipster culture of Charlie Parker and bebop, in ways that are analogous to, and resound with, Smith's Jehovah's Witness upbringing, Bible education, blue collar identification and first lightning-bolt of cultural infatuation with Little Richard and 'Tutti Frutti' (Smith, 1998, p. xix). Textual readings of the literatures of both Kerouac and Smith – the 'longer, more detailed work of lexicographical archaeology' that Simon Warner judiciously recommends (Warner, 2013, p. 364) – illuminate Smith's poetry and musical productions as they extend paths grounded in and sustained by Jack Kerouac, and reflect both writers' mutual artistic stakes and occupations in building mid-century US literary art.

It is into this context of practical literary criticism and background that Smith's earliest poetry and recorded work are entered for study. Here, the Kerouac influence is inverted but corresponding. Kerouac takes musicians for models in composition of his prose and poetry – 'sketching language is undisturbed flow from the mind ... *blowing* (as per jazz musician) on subject of thought' and recommends for punctuation or rhythm the 'vigorous space dash separating rhetorical breathing (as jazz musician drawing breath between outblown phrases)' (Kerouac, 1957, in Charters, 1992, p. 57). Smith makes her music model her poetry. In 'Piss Factory' (written 1972, recorded 1974, in Smith, 2015a, p. 26), her recording of the poem with pianist Richard Sohl demands that his music follow the increasingly hectic and emphatic pace of Smith's chanting and ranting of the poem's lines (1974, Mer Records). In the 1960s, and beyond, poetry and music, words and melodies, mutually and inversely were found interacting in art projects. As Warner notes, artists such as Dylan and Baez 'were applying literary thoughts in musical settings, musical ideas in literary ones' (Warner, 2013, p. 168). An example of the latter process is 'Piss Factory', of which the three extant versions – typescript holograph (Smith, 1998, n.p.); prose poem and typescript holograph (Smith, 2015a, pp. 25–7); and the track recorded to Richard Sohl's dynamic jazz (not bebop) piano collected on *Land (1975–2002)* (2002) – provide exceptional opportunity to study the poet's poetry mind as she develops her claim to high art in the production of a popular music that would yet contain still enough 'art'. The photographer Robert Mapplethorpe, 'her soul twin, spiritual brother and part-time boyfriend' (Bracewell, 1996, p. 6), had complained that this first single, 'Hey Joe'/'Piss Factory', was not music they could dance to (Smith, 2010, p. 242), but in a later collaboration with Bruce Springsteen, the recording 'Because the Night' made Patti Smith and the Patti Smith Group (PSG) danceable. The presence of Jack Kerouac's influence in 'Piss Factory' is as powerful as that of Rimbaud, who is the occasion for the closing sentiments of the typescript version, a passage that was apparently edited out of the published print and the performed versions; never mentioned at all, Kerouac is palpable indirectly, in the poem's aesthetic form and high-low cultural subjects and finish.

Patti Smith's first recording was the single, 'Hey Joe' (J. Hendrix)/'Piss Factory' (P. Smith) on the independent label, Mer Records, in 1974. Other sources list the PSG pianist Richard A. Sohl as co-author of 'Piss Factory', and it is he who provides the propulsive jazz piano backing to Smith's declamation of the prose/poem, undoubtedly the purest Beat spoken-word composition that Smith recorded. Mapplethorpe gave Smith a thousand dollars to record this single at Electric Ladyland in Greenwich Village, the studio built by Jimi Hendrix just before his death (Bockris and Bayley, 1999, p. 104; Tarr, 2008, p. 13). Although Smith's choice and treatment of Hendrix's 'Hey Joe', the single's A-side, offers evidence of Kerouacian stylistic influences, with Smith's improvisational pastiche of the kidnapping of heiress Patty Hearst by the revolutionary Symbionese Liberation Army and her subsequent participation in a bank robbery, this recording is not accessible to study. 'Piss Factory' is easy to access, even in an archival version, a holograph typescript that Smith published from her personal archive in *Complete* (1998, n.p.) and a CD track of the Smith/Sohl recording, the rare original on Mer Records included on disc two of *Land (1975–2002)* (2002) (Tarr, 2008, p. 89). There is considerable variation between the typescript and the recorded track of 'Piss Factory' included on *Land*, a variation that highlights and exposes more of its Kerouacian and Beat influences.

The 'Piss Factory' track presents as a 1950s-style Beat Generation lyric poetry-and-music improvisation. It has been characterized by the journalist-critic Joe Tarr as a 'beatnik-style meditation on life in the factory' without the romantic 'Jack Kerouac eulogies of the working class' (15), but a eulogy is not what either poet is up to here. It brings to mind Kerouac's voice-over narration to David Amram's music track in the 1959 experimental film *Pull My Daisy* based on the song 'Fie My Fum' (1950) and the poem 'Pull My Daisy' (1948–50; 1961) collected in *Scattered Poems* (1970, 1971). Fifteen years separate 'Piss Factory' and *Pull My Daisy*, yet these poems by poets who never met resonate on the subjects of poverty, blue collar labour, and urban/suburban/ rural northeast origins, but even more so on the best ways to tell their stories of this life as true and as art; in Smith's case, the role of the artist is emphasized. Smith's early work such as 'Piss Factory' and 'Oath' (1970) powerfully display what Ginsberg would term an 'unconscious' influence of Kerouac, and to Smith's advantage. Tarr notes that when the 'Hey Joe'/'Piss Factory' single was released, Smith 'was still a nobody, some weird beatnik chick, a controversial poet known only by the scenesters in New York's underground' (2008, p. 16). To the extent that that description is accurate, 'Piss Factory' is an undiluted expression of the poet's first aesthetics and poetics[8] before she was created a punk rock musician and star. Smith's 'nobody' ignominy recalls perhaps the state Jack Kerouac embodied before *On the Road* was published in 1957 and made him famous, thereby imposing stultifying conditions on his life and subsequent art (see Worden, 2009).

Smith dates her typescript version of 'Piss Factory' to 1972 (Smith, 2015a, p. 26). It is a long lyric about the experiences of the 16-year-old speaker-poet working in summer on an assembly line in a hot factory, repetitive work unrelieved by camaraderie or any perceived value except the pay cheque it earns. Smith has claimed the poem to be the most autobiographical and truthful of her works (Tosches, 1976), but, more accurately, it is a confessional poem; rather than the recounted story of a life – an autobiography – this poem follows the mind and emotions of the teller as she lives through her experience; it is not factual or literal so much as affectively impressionistic. It exudes what John Clellon Holmes termed 'poetic truth', an emotional truth versus an historical one, a quality he found dominant in Kerouac's work through the free associations in writing he advocated over slavish adherence to literal truth, even if that were possible to obtain: as Kerouac states in 'Essentials of Spontaneous Prose', the best writing is 'Not "selectivity" of expression but following free deviation (association) of mind into limitless blow-on-subject seas of thought, swimming in [a] sea of English with no discipline other than rhythms of rhetorical exhalation and expostulated statement' (Kerouac, in Charters, 1992, p. 57). All the versions of 'Piss Factory', but especially the one that Smith recorded with Sohl for Mer Records, are notable for the work's evident organization by 'free deviation (association) of mind' that Kerouac values, down to the telling interpretive signifier 'deviation': the writer embraces the deviance or nonconformity of the creating mind; this is the art Smith dedicated 'to the criminal' and like the criminals Kerouac took for heroic models for free confession (1959). Certainly 'Piss Factory' bears the fearlessness to be aberrant or anomalous that permits strong literary art in Kerouac's ethos. The work is constructed by techniques of pastiche, repetition (a rhythmic anaphora), dialogue and editorial intrusion. It includes its own poetics mandate in the poet's warning to herself – 'But no you gotta, you gotta (relate, babe) / You gotta find the rhythm within' – a formulation of the confessional imperative ('relate') combined with poetics ('rhythm within') that precedes the narrative of an episode with the factory 'floor boss'.

The opening stanza is an exposition of the scene: the oppressively hot factory, the numbing 'job in a piss factory inspecting pipe', the co-workers so benighted they are grateful for their oppression there, all the issues of exploited 'labor', including those of the young speaker: 'But me well I wasn't sayin' too much neither / I was a moral school girl hard-working asshole / I figured I was speedo motorcycle / I had to earn my dough, had to earn my dough'. The initially oblique 'speedo motorcycle', a trope for the impatient hustling young worker as a street machine, swerves further into pop culture in the reprimand of the floor boss: 'You doin' your piece work too fast / Now you get off your mustang sally / you ain't goin' nowhere, you ain't goin' nowhere'; the slangy order to conform (slow down) also suggests a comeuppance for the smug superiority of the young female worker – you get off your high horse, 'your mustang sally' – and is rendered in a double entendre that also evokes the 1966 pop song 'Mustang Sally' by the soul singer Wilson Pickett about a girl 'running all over town' who won't behave. The free association/deviation from reprimands by the floor boss and Dot Hook that the singer-poet turns into her own language of impudent song resistant to theirs of sour discipline is a way 'Piss Factory' 'unconsciously' reflects Kerouacian poetics: the structural swerves of mind and subjects of social context, as described, occur repeatedly to the end of the song; they are the 'free deviation[s] (association[s])' that comprise spontaneous composition. There is a narrative through line, but it runs through the mind of the poet-singer, not the tale as story. Another soulless encounter with 'hot shit Dot Hook', who threatens the singer ('if you don't get off your mustang sally / if you don't shake it up baby. "Shake it up, baby, Twist and shout"') is neutralized by its transformation into the language of pop-song sex, in the allusion to the Isley Brothers' 1962 hit song of that name, followed by that of the Beatles in 1963. This swerve into pop allusion comes through the threats and actions of the singer's co-workers who gang up on her and dunk her head in a toilet full of piss (Tarr, 2008, p. 16). The reality of economic exploitation and the fantasy of pop music mind intermingle in this account in a fashion that responds to Kerouac's manifesto for spontaneous composition to follow the mind in all its twists and deviations as the story is recounted.

The poem/song has two endings, one preserved on the Mer recording and the other on the typescript. Their variances provide another significant insight into the inferential, indirect influence that is possible among artists, and that is evident here between Kerouac and Smith. The recorded version of the song ends with the singer's defiance of the oppressions of the piss factory ('But I will never faint, I will never faint / They laugh and they expect me to faint but I will never faint / I refuse to lose, I refuse to fall down') in the chanted repeated vows, which open out to her confession of singularity. The singer is no 'Piss Factory' victim of mindless conformity. The prose poem version published in *Collected Lyrics 1970–2015* reads as follows, the version also more or less as printed elsewhere and as recorded on the Mer Records single in 1974:

...I got nothin' to hide here save desire And I'm
gonna go I'm gonna get out of here I'm gonna get on that train and go
to New York City and I'm gonna be somebody, I'm gonna get on that
train and go to New York City and I'm gonna be so bad. I'm gonna be
a big star and I will never return never return no never return, to burn
at this Piss Factory. And I will travel light Oh watch me now.

Smith, 2015a, p. 27

Here, the singer-poet triumphs over the 'Piss Factory' tortures and subordinations by
preserving her hidden desire. More explicitly, she envisions a revenge-future of star
success. The resolute poetic triumph evokes in reverse the close of Dylan's 'Just Like
Tom Thumb's Blues': 'I'm going back to New York City, I do believe I've had enough'
(*Lyrics*); this poet has learned that adventure in the hinterlands of love is dangerous.
The original version of Smith's song – the typescript version – ends with the evocation
of Rimbaud that instantiates the classic muse-poet in the ephebe poet's escape dirge.
In the typescript, following the gist of the lyrics quoted above, Rimbaud enters the
poet's mind and her song. She recounts in this poem the oft-told genesis anecdote of
the poet's 'salvation' through Rimbaud:

lucky i lifted rimbauds illuminations from the paper back forum. it was the face
on the cover see rimbauds hair his sailor face. faire than any boy on the block I
was seeing. my salvation my nosegay the words rocked sex smells coming on
like my brothers sheets before the bath what did i care what he was saying it was
the sound the music the way he was saying it his words over and over in my
skull ... i was getting my first brain fuck illuminations my salvation oh stolen
book no crime since has been so sweet no perfume ever to fill my nose no snow
no more light then the simple knowledge of you rimbaud ...

Smith, 2015a, p. 26; typescript

The nearly run-on prose suggests the pounding rising piano accompaniment Sohl
invents in the Mer Records track. But this passage is omitted from the prose poem
published in *Collected Lyrics* and from the song recorded in 1974 by Mer. In this
typescript version the poet does not stand alone, an escapee to New York City and
stardom; she is rescued in the 'salvation' of Rimbaud, whom she discovers by stealing
a used copy of *Illuminations* because she is drawn to his cover photograph, which is
lovingly recounted and linked to boy sex through the poet's brother's musky 'sheets
before the bath'. That is, the original version features rescue by the precursor muse-
poet; the revised version, produced two years later, features self-rescue by escape to
New York from the factory life to which the poet is born. Maturity is an internalization
of influences that permit self-invention and self-reliance in this narrative. Moreover,
Rimbaud offers poetics counsel; he triggers the singer-poet's attention to sound over
sense – 'what did i care what he was saying it was the sound the music the way he was

saying it his words over and over in my skull' – as well as an anaphoric beat felt in her body (skull), the classic Rimbaudian inheritance.

An influence of inference applies to Rimbaud in Smith's formulations: 'the incantatory language of Rimbaud's prose poems, which shaped Smith's sense of what poetry could be', Sharon DeLano reports, 'had also influenced the Beats and Dylan, who had begun reading the French Symbolists in the early sixties' (DeLano, 2002, p. 21). In this inferential influence, overlapping mutual admirations of Rimbaud substantiate the intuitive conviction of Smith's influence by Beat writers, by Kerouac, through Dylan. Smith's epigraph to the early poem 'babel field' (1978) is a homage to Rimbaud that may also express influence: '"we know how to give our whole life everyday." a. rimbaud' (Smith, 1978, p. 198).[9] The concluding verses of 'babel field' mix the Lord's Prayer with Smith's paean to Rimbaud: it ends 'I step up to the microphone / I have no fear' (p. 201), stopping short of the last line of the prayer, 'for thou art with me'. Kerouac's poem 'Rimbaud', published in 1960, is a long biography of the visionary poet told in a revisionary Bretonesque-Beat language that invents a literary genealogy through which Kerouac claims Rimbaud as Franco-American-ish through astute formulations of the poet and his poetics. 'Cities are bombarded as / he stares & stares & chews / his degenerate lip & stares / with gray eyes at / Walled France ... the Voyant is born, / the deranged seer makes his / first Manifesto, gives vowels colors / & consonants carking care' (1970, p. 33). Smith deliriously spins a homage to Rimbaud: 'Life is full of pain I push it through my brain / And I fill my nose with snow and go Rimbaud / Go Rimbaud go Rimbaud go Johnny go / And do the watusi oh do the watusi' ('Land of a Thousand Dances', Smith, 1998, p. 32), a homage that incorporates a sample of another Wilson Pickett hit of 1966, 'Land of a 1000 Dances', in which the death of Smith's Burroughsian Johnny is intercut with pop music lyrics, just as 'Mustang Sally' or 'Twist and Shout' appear in 'Piss Factory'. Dylan makes direct reference to Rimbaud in 'You're Going to Make Me Lonesome When You Go' from the break-up album *Blood on the Tracks* (1975), only a year after Smith's Mer Records single: 'Situations have ended sad / Relationships have all been bad / Mine've been like Verlaine's and Rimbaud' (*Lyrics*). With a turn on the trope 'brain fuck' from the 'Piss Factory' typescript (see above) that refers to Rimbaud, in the song 'La Mer (de)' Smith evokes Rimbaud in relinquishment and clearing him from her mind: 'I put my hand inside his cranium, oh we had such a brainiac-amour / But no more, no more I gotta move from my mind to the area / [Go Rimbaud go Rimbaud go Rimbaud]' Smith chants (Smith, 1998, p. 37; brackets in the original). In these works, homage and resistance to homage – '[Go Rimbaud go Rimbaud go Rimbaud]' also suggests an imperative 'leave Rimbaud' – is an expression of influence; at the same time as it pays respects or refuses to pay respects, the sample – or appropriation – internalizes the precursive source or artist. See Smith's possession by or appropriation of Ginsberg's work – her absorption of his influence in making her own work from his – as expressed in her homage 'Spell' in which she chants 'Footnote to Howl' over music by Oliver Ray (*Peace and Noise*, 1997). With Kerouac, Smith is often on a parallel track of imagery or idea in which the points do not meet but run together into infinity.

* * *

Kerouac's Lowell novels are tales of familial and regional origins, and recount the poignant disappointments and tragedies of a *bildungsroman*, or coming-of-age cycle. They are patently autobiographical and confessional stories strained through Kerouac's distinctive style in its earliest incarnation, closer to the dark 'New Vision' than to the effervescent 'Essentials of Spontaneous Prose'. The 'New Vision' conceived with Lucien Carr and Allen Ginsberg in 1944 was a manifesto of art and living inspired by Rimbaud and Nietzsche (Kerouac, 1995, pp. 80–1), a dark existentialism that paradoxically gave Kerouac, according to his biographer, the historian Dennis McNally, consolation for 'transient, illusory' life by 'celebrat[ing] the transcendental *act* of making art' (1980, pp. 66–7); art is salvific in the face of the mortal end. The 'New Vision' and its capacity for 'art [that] is the potential ultimate' solace (Kerouac, 1995, p. 82) is felt in the Lowell novels in one special existential determinant: the universal and yet explicitly personal genealogy of forerunners. The hero's begotten family and blood line of 'predecessor diers' (Kerouac, 1958/1976, p. 89) are the father and brother of *Visions of Gerard*, both gone before, objects of the artist's narrative commemorative revery-gaze. These familial forerunners – influences – offer the artist Kerouac in his guise as narrator Jack Duluoz 'the truth that is realizable in dead men's bones' that shapes his narrative and poetic art. For Kerouac, the first teaching and truth of the 'predecessor diers' is of death, the ultimate influence on style, writing method, practice and poetics. Kerouac writes – through Jack Duluoz – that 'death is the only decent subject, since it marks the end of illusion and delusion – Death is the other side of the same coin, we call now, Life' (Kerouac, 1958/1976, p. 123). Nietzsche's 'phrase "Art seducing me to a continuation of life"' (McNally, 1979/1980, p. 67) was an epigraph Kerouac placed above his writing desk, offering him a bulwark against self-destruction, what Patti Smith sang of in 'Redondo Beach' as 'sweet suicide'. While de facto suicide carried off her Beat novelist precursor, for Smith, the poet-punk rock successor, suicide was disarmed in the fantasy of her early lyric, 'Redondo Beach', given to be the fate of an imagined character substituted for the Smith sister who occasioned the song and did not die.

Smith notes that 'The words for "Redondo Beach" were written in 1971' (Smith, 1998, p. 10), and the song was first recorded on *Horses* in 1975. As Kerouac was concerned with the dead father and brother, characters in *Visions of Gerard*, Smith's poem is about a woman washed up on the shore of Redondo Beach, a 'victim of sweet suicide', who had been the object of a search before her body was discovered. Speaking in the first person, the poet laments the disappearance of a beloved other after they have 'the quarrel that sent you away', a girl, it is implied, who might be a lover – 'small and angel with apple blonde hair now ... Down by the ocean it was so dismal / I was just standing there with shock on my face / The hearse pulled away and the girl had died it was you' (Smith, 1998, p. 11). It is produced in a reggae beat, unexpected at this time in Smith's first recording (though quite popular with later punk musicians), and has a lilting nearly upbeat feel that opposes the dark lyrics of the lost girl, the 'victim of sweet suicide', the 'shock' on the beach with the recovery of her corpse. Smith has published accounts of the poem's actual circumstances, a quarrel between Smith and her younger sister Linda, who are sharing space in an apartment with Robert Mapplethorpe; Linda leaves/is sent away and Patti seeks her on Coney Island; but the ending is pacific: after Patti wrote the draft of a poem and had fallen asleep, Linda 'returned. I showed her what I had written' – the poem turned into the song 'Redondo Beach' – and 'we never quarreled again' (Smith, 1998, p. 10). The real life ends well – the sisters remain close – and the recorded song is popular and often performed. However, Smith fictionalizes the song considerably: Redondo Beach was known as a California beach that lesbians frequented (at the time); the antagonist of the poem-song is not a sister but, it is implied, a lover; and in the song she dies by 'sweet suicide', inspiring the grieving but oddly bouncing ska refrain 'You'll never return into my arms cause you are gone gone / Never return into my arms cause you are gone gone / Gone gone gone / Good-bye' (Smith, 1998, p. 11). But Linda Bianucci Smith does return and the sisterhood continues. The 'predecessor dier' – the existential influence – that Smith creates in her poem is fictive, unlike Kerouac's in *Visions of Gerard*; Smith makes her 'sister' a dead possible lover, which tautens the narrative and the pathos of the journey away from the beach. This transformation of a story that is contained in Kerouac's *Visions of Gerard* of the untimely death of a sibling, and its attendant guilt for the survivor sibling, masks any real influence the Kerouac Lowell novel may have, though an attentive reading of both reveals parallel congruences.

A second song on *Horses*, 'Kimberly', is explicitly concerned with a sister, but in this instance, she is a 'babe . . . in her swaddling clothes', a 'little sister' held by the speaker who protects the baby from apocalypse. In this case, the baby Kimberly is Smith's actual sister, and their witness of a lightning storm that strikes and burns a nearby barn is autobiographical; only its rendering is a literary invention on the order of a surreal Kerouacian nightmare. In 'notes, august 2, 1975', Smith describes a vivid day of great burning when she was twelve, in a kind of prose poem: 'Lightning struck. Her [Kimberly's] face lit up. Everything in flames. The world was turning all the destructive whims of nature. Rivers drying, rivers of salt remaining . . . The barn was crumbling. The bush was burning. And Kimberly was shining in my hands like a phosphorescent living doll' (*Complete*, 20). In the poem Smith sings on *Horses* (and publishes widely in her books, including *Collected*), the verses are less frantic and more assured and the speaker imagines herself: 'And I feel like some misplaced Joan of Arc / And the cause is you looking up at me'; the mutual gaze makes the poet a kind of martyr or saviour for the baby. The poem continues in repetitions and internal rhymes, and a chanting crescendo build-up, surreal and grounded at once – 'Looking deep in your eyes baby' (Smith, 1998, p. 22) – as the apocalypse showers flames around them.

Oh baby I remember the day you were born / It was dawn and the storm settled in my belly / And I rolled in the grass and I spit out the gas . . . And the sky split and the planets hit . . . Little sister the sky is falling / I don't mind I don't mind / Little sister the fates are calling on you / . . . As the bats with their baby vein faces / Burst from the barn in flames into the violent violet sky / And I fell on my knees and pressed you against me . . .

Smith, 1998, pp. 21–2

Memory and invention enjoy seamless interface, as in a Rimbaudian synaesthesia, and astral apocalypse is a dramatic vision, one far removed from Kerouac's sibling broodings, but expressed in similar ecstatic terms. In Smith, poet and baby sibling survive; in *Visions of Gerard*, the older brother dies of rheumatic fever in his crib as the younger Jack – both narrator and protagonist at once – watches helplessly. The poetics of Kerouac's novel are simple and profound, and lionize memory: the narrator, from his doubled point of view as a boy in the tale and adult poet narrator, warns 'I don't remember rationally but in my soul and mind' (Kerouac, 1958/1976, p. 16), suggesting a duality or divisible binary between the logical/rational and the affective (soul and mind), a binary complicated by the inclusion of 'mind' in opposition to the rational. This is a kind of rhetorical synaesthesia, like but unlike a Rimbaudian linguistic and imagistic synaesthesia; an expression of, but resistance to, influence. Gazing on his brother, his 'predecessor dier', the Kerouac narrator waxes with biblical metaphor, 'amazed and scared in the corner, as one might have felt seeing Christ in the temple bashing the moneychanger tables everywhichaway and scourging them with his seldom whip' (Kerouac, 1958/1976, p. 19). He is no Joan of Arc like Smith's hero, but a frightened witness to divine power and retribution. Kerouac elaborates the novel's meta-narrative perspective about the death that takes the nine-year-old older brother Gerard, the dark opposite version of Smith's sunny survivor conviction in 'Kimberly':

> All conditional and talk, what I have to say, to point it out – Miserable as a dull sermon on a dull rainy morning in a damp church in the North and Sunday to boot – We are baptized in water for no sanitary reason, that is to say a well-needed *bath* is implied – Praise a woman's legs, her golden thighs only produce black nights of death, face it –

Kerouac, 1958/1976, p. 42

Language – 'All conditional and talk' – religious talk, existential talk, all are contingent pacifiers that mask the mortality assigned to existence which derives from women and the 'golden thighs'. Just so, language fails the narrator: 'Words cant do it . . . Words cant do it, readers will get sick of it – because it's not happening to themselves' (Kerouac, 1958/1976, p. 86); words cannot express what is happening, although the vivid lyric of 'Kimberly', the 'barn in flames into the violent violet sky', begs otherwise.

Gary Snyder zeroed in on Kerouac's masterful poetics of the word, even as within *Visions of Gerard* the narrator despairs of them. Reading *Mexico City Blues*, Snyder experiences 'some constant surprise arising in the words, always something happening with the words. You can see the mind at work, see the mind in it. Each poem was complete in itself, each had a similar mode of movement, each like a little stanza born' (Ginsberg, 1992, p. iii). Reduced to the literary unit, Kerouac still engenders creative explosion. In her 1970 poem 'Oath', Smith sees words as powerful, not disempowered as in Kerouac's lament, but they are not for her the vehicle or containers of energy that Snyder recognizes. For Smith, 'words are just rules and regulations' ('Oath', recorded 1970, in Smith, 1998, p. 8) and may be – must be – overridden for free art's sake.

Still grounded in death and apocalypse, still riding a sibling-family theme but in a displaced form, 'Birdland' is about a son and father, Peter Reich and his father Wilhelm Reich, the Austrian American psychoanalyst much favoured by the first generation Beat writers, especially Kerouac and Burroughs, though for somewhat different reasons.[10] Smith has said the song was inspired by Peter Reich's autobiography, *A Book of Dreams* (1973). The father had died and the son thought he saw a spaceship that he wished to board because he believed his father was steering it and would reunite with him (Smith, 1998, p. 12), a sighting which turned out to be a flock of birds, suggesting the poem's title. Smith does not note that father and son would spend their nights searching for UFOs through telescopes and binoculars and attacking them with Wilhelm's 'cloudbusters'. The elder Reich wrote of the possibility that his own father had been from outer space (Reich, 1973; Turner, 2011). Smith's paean to the son grieving his dead father sombrely commemorates a universal experience of parental loss: 'His father died and left him a little farm in New England / All the long black funeral cars left the scene / And the boy was just standing there alone ... / Nobody there except for the birds around the New England farm ... coming together into the head of a / Shaman bouquet' (Smith, 1998, pp. 15–16). The hallucinogenic feeling of the poem's visions and of the poet's rendering of the bereft son's wrenching cries is overwhelming and alluring in its synaesthesia.

Of special interest are several connections to Kerouac implied in this drama of death. Smith's notes on 'Birdland' in *Complete* are about improvisation, a 'concept' that 'has long repelled and excited me, for it contains the possibilities of humiliation and illumination' (Smith, 1998, p. 12), and she recounts the improvisational composition of the lyric to 'Birdland' in the studio as it was being recorded, lauding the 'trust built between musicians, requiring communal selflessness in order to draw from the collective intelligence' (ibid.). Kerouac wrote *Visions of Gerard* alone in twelve nights by hand, from midnight to dawn, spontaneously (although he did reject all of one night's work) (McNally, 1979/1980, pp. 213–14). The two artists' practices embody the binary imago of Beat individualism versus rock music's necessary collectivity. Further, in an uncanny anticipation and overlap, in 'Essentials of Spontaneous Prose', Kerouac's manifesto of free writing and improvisation, the Beat writer cites Wilhelm Reich as an exemplar of the spontaneous prose process:

If possible write 'without consciousness' in semitrance (as Yeats' later 'trance writing') allowing subconscious to admit in own uninhibited interesting necessary and so 'modern' language what conscious art would censor, and write excitedly, swiftly, with writing-or-typing cramps, in accordance (as from center to periphery) with laws of orgasm, Reich's 'beclouding of consciousness'. *Come from within, out* – to relaxed and said,

Kerouac in Charters, 1992, p. 58

Kerouac's manifesto of trusting the writing mind – no revision, a rejection of self-censorship – contrasts with Smith's rejection of words' 'rules and regulations': for her the very smallest unit of writing, the word, a vehicle of writing, is inherently censorship itself. Kerouac's invocation of Reich, of the best writing occurring under 'beclouded' senses – evoking and repurposing Reich's cloudbuster device used in UFO-hunting with his son – and the orgasmic release in Kerouac's principles of spontaneous prose read ahead to Smith's paean to the son deprived of his father by death.

Smith's distinctive exposition about improvisation and collaboration is analogous to Kerouac's reference to orgasm and sexual satisfaction: the best writing, spontaneous and uncensored by the superego of the 'subconscious', is orgasmic, a visceral extemporaneity. Substantiating the link between writing and orgasm, Philip Shaw cites Smith's rather sensational comments in a 1972 interviewer: 'for me writing is a very physical process. I write with the same fervor Jackson Pollock used to paint . . . I learned this from Genet, who wrote in prison so he could turn himself on and masturbate – I'd sit at the typewriter until I felt sexy, then I'd go and masturbate to get high, then I'd come back in that higher place and write some more' (quoted in Shaw, 2008, pp. 62–3). This practice literalizes Kerouac's use of Reich as a metaphoric guide for writing spontaneous prose. Then again, as Ann Charters reports, Kerouac himself literalized this ethos: 'His whole artistic approach to the book [Lowell novel *Maggie Cassidy*] was simply to relive its confused days and long nights, almost as a Method actor would do, pushing himself into a state of heightened emotional intensity that he sustained with benzedrine' and orgasm in the night yard of his mother's home (Charters, 1974/1994, p. 184). The indirect connection, through Reich and cosmic UFO hunting, orgone boxes and theories of orgasm, bring Smith and Kerouac into juxtaposition and uncovers that both use actual sexual stimulation for a composition aid as well as an imago for free writing. Kerouac's *Visions of Gerard* commemorates death, family, spontaneous creation and improvisation, and piercing grief – all of which resonate with Smith's 'Birdland', of the informal, unofficial trilogy of 'familial' verses in *Horses*. She ends with a seductive, crooning and dirgelike 'Sha da do wop da shaman do way', a hypnotically repeated refrain of blessing and '50s pop culture ('do wop') in testament to improvised, live in-studio composition unto release in recording, if only momentarily, from consciousness and self-censorship, death and irrevocability. Her song feels eternal; Kerouac's narrative *Visions of Gerard* gets caught in its mourning, but is preceded by his having earlier composed 'Essentials of Spontaneous Prose' and charting a way to literary eternal freedom through the act of writing.

* * *

Patti Smith and Jack Kerouac face each other across a divide of history on a spectrum of twentieth-century American art and literature, the younger artist a white woman, defiant, mythologizing and self-mythologizing, the precursor artist a white man, imaginative, inventive, both from the working class of harsh northern urban factory cities. One is a post-war Baby Boomer, the other a member of the Second World War Greatest Generation; one was brought up a strict Jehovah's Witness, the other a strict Catholic; both rejected what Smith called 'rules and regulations' (Gross, 1975, p. 5; 'Oath' in Smith, 1998, p. 8), what Kerouac advocated as 'free deviation (association) of mind into limitless blow on subject seas of thought' (Charters, 1957/1992, p. 57). Both are themselves avatars of individualism and innovators of American art, twentieth century unto the twenty-first. And their mysterious spectral connections, the older writer influencing the younger through the 'air' she breathes, through the spiritual and almost phantasmal once- and even twice-removed charismatic sway of mutual artist friends and admirers tarrying between them, erase time's divide between Patti Smith and Jack Kerouac. Theirs is an existential artistic continuity, a poetics of unbound word and mind that is their legacy in literary influence.

Notes

1. Joe Tarr reports the way the Sex Pistols famously scorned their 2006 Rock and Roll Hall of Fame induction, posting on the group's website, 'Next to the Sex Pistols, rock and roll and that hall of fame is a piss stain. Your museum. Urine in wine. We're not coming. We're not your monkeys. If you voted for us, hope you noted you reasons. Your [sic] anonymous as judges but your [sic] still music industry people. We're not coming. Your [sic] not paying attention. Outside the shit stream is a real Sex Pistol' (2008, p. 98).

2. Note that Burroughs was dubbed the 'grandfather of punk' by Jim Fourrat, cited in the epigraph to this chapter.

3. These New York artists of the 1960s and 1970s often straddle several schools of influence and practice, as Waldman claims, and others – Laurie Anderson, Eileen Myles – show.

4. Defining Beat arts via the shared art, friendship, and culture 'hang-out factor' has been noted as such by Ginsberg, Regina Weinreich, Waldman, and others. See Johnson and Grace, 'Visions and Revisions of the Beat Generation' in *Girls Who Wore Black* (2002, pp. 3-4).

5. Cool hipsters that Leo Percepied depicted in *The Subterraneans*, especially Roxanne, seem to predict Patti Smith and the punk poetry-rock she brought into being out of the incantatory chants of Ginsberg and the scatted jazz recitations of Kerouac (Bockris and Bayley, 1999, p. 107). Roxanne was

   . . . a woman of 25 prophesying the future style of America with short almost crewcut but with curls black snaky hair, snaky walk, pale pale junky anemic face and we say junky when once Dostoevski would have said what? if not ascetic or saintly? but not in the least? but the cold pale booster face of the cold blue girl and wearing a man's white shirt but with the cuffs undone untied at the buttons so I remember her leaning over talking to someone after having slinked across the floor with flowing propelled shoulders, bending to talk with her hand holding a short butt and the neat little flick she was giving it to knock ashes but repeatedly with long long fingernails an inch long and also orient and snake-like . . .

Kerouac, 1958/1981, p. 18

6. See the 22 February 1998 obituary for Anton Rosenberg (1927–98) in the *New York Times* by Robert McGill Thomas, Jr, in which Rosenberg's illustrious career as a subterranean hipster provided a well known model for Kerouac's Julian Alexander of *The Subterraneans*.

7. For a more formal statement about her connection to Kerouac, see Patti Smith, liner notes to *One False Move Or I'm Gone*: 'It seems like he's always been in the air . . . Yet when I was asked to speak of him I had to search my conscience. I had never read his books. I knew him mostly second-hand through those who truly loved him . . . I knew Jack Kerouac through men.'

8. Smith's first chapbooks are *Seventh Heaven* (1972), *Kodak* (1972), *Witt* (1973) and *Babel* (1978). These are the most significant of her early poetry publications.

9. Smith's poem 'babel field' is strongly Rimbaudian. Synaesthesia abounds amid mystical misalignments of nouns and adjectives ('the columns of words. Words of sand-psalms / of love and guerre coursing through our veins. we are / the adrenal people. we need action. words we use up. / grind into powder like sex and death', Smith, 1978, p. 198) and surrealistic declamations ('i couldn't plug in anywhere and so I hid my amp in the / bushes and threw my guitar over my shoulder. it weighs / less than a machine gun and never runs out of ammunition') (ibid., p. 200).

10. Wilhelm Reich, the Austrian American psychoanalyst, was a member of the second generation of psychoanalysts after Sigmund Freud, and, in terms of Beat Generation significance, the originator of the orgone accumulator, of which William S. Burroughs was famously an advocate and user. Reich had a notable impact on Kerouac, especially expressed in *The Subterraneans*. There, narrator Leo Percepied rhapsodizes about 'the reading, the sudden, illuminated glad wondrous discovery of Wilhelm Reich, his book *The Function of the Orgasm*, clarity I had not seen in a long time', and protagonist Mardou Fox counters with her extreme distaste for the same: 'Mardou kept saying "O don't pull that Reich on me in bed, I read his damn book, I don't want our relationship all pointed out and f . . . d up with what HE said"' (pp. 64–5; elision in original). In Kerouac, then, Reich is an ambiguous and controversial, if tempting, figure. In Smith, in 'Birdland', Reich has a more mundane aura as the dead father of his grieving son Peter. Her treatment is familial in emphasis and more in line with the trope of 'predecessor diers' Kerouac develops in *Visions of Gerard*.

Bibliography

Bangs, L., 'Stagger Lee Was a Woman', *Creem*, February 1976.

Bangs, L., 'The White Noise Supremacists', in Greil Marcus (ed.), *Psychotic Reactions and Carburetor Dung*, New York: Vintage (1988), pp. 272–82.

Bloom, H., *The Anxiety of Influence: A Theory of Poetry*, New York: Oxford, 1973/1975.

Bockris, V. and R. Bayley, *Patti Smith: An Unauthorized Biography*, New York: Simon & Schuster, 1999.

Bracewell, M., 'Woman as Warrior and Mystic', *Guardian* (weekend supplement), 22 June 1996.

Burroughs, W. S., 'When Patti Rocked', *Spin*, April 1979/1988, www.oceanstar.com/patti/intervus/8804spin.html (accessed 13 June 2017).

Burroughs, W. S., 'Introductory Notes', in G. Corso, *Mindfield*, New York: Thunder's Mouth, 1989, pp. xvii–xix.

Charters, A., *Kerouac: A Biography*, New York: St Martin's Press, 1973, 1974/1994.

Colegrave, S. and Chris Sullivan, *Punk: The Definitive Record of a Revolution*, New York: Thunder's Mouth, 2001/2005.

DeLano, S., 'The Torch Singer', *The New Yorker*, 11 March 2002, pp. 48–63.

Dylan, B., *The Lyrics: 1961–2012*, New York: Simon & Schuster, 2016.

Frank, R. and Alfred Lesley (dir.), *Pull My Daisy*, 1959.

Ginsberg, A., 'Foreword: On Corso's Virtues', in G. Corso, *Mindfield*, New York: Thunder's Mouth, 1989, pp. xiii–xv.

Ginsberg, A., 'Introduction', *Pomes All Sizes*, Pocket Poet Series 48, San Francisco: City Lights, 1992, pp. i–x.

Gross, A., 'Introducing Rock 'n' Roll's Lady Raunch: Patti Smith', *Mademoiselle*, September 1975, www.oceanstar.com/patti/intervus/7509made.html (accessed 8 June 2017).

Johnson, R. C., '"You're putting me on": Jack Kerouac and the Postmodern Emergence', *College Literature* 27, no. 1 (Winter 2000): 22–38. Rpt. in Kostas Myrsiades (ed.), *The Beat Generation: Critical Essays*, New York: Lang, 2002.

Johnson, R. C., '"And then she went": Beat Departures and Feminine Transgressions in Joyce Johnson's *Come and Join the Dance*', in R. C. Johnson and Nancy M. Grace (eds), *Girls Who Wore Black: Women Writing the Beat Generation*, New York: Rutgers, 2002, pp. 69–94.

Johnson, R. C., 'Mapping Women Writers of the Beat Generation', in N. M. Grace and Ronna C. Johnson (eds), *Breaking the Rule of Cool: Interviewing and Reading Women Beat Writers*, Jackson: University Press of Mississippi, 2004, pp. 3–41.

Johnson, R. C. and N. M. Grace, 'Visions and Revisions of the Beat Generation', in R. C. Johnson and Nancy M. Grace (eds), *Girls Who Wore Black: Women Writing the Beat Generation*, New York: Rutgers, 2002, pp. 1–24.

Johnstone, N., *Patti Smith: A Biography*, London, Omnibus Press, 1997/2012.

Kerouac, J., 'Essentials of Spontaneous Prose', in A. Charters (ed.), *The Viking Portable Beat Reader*, New York: Viking, 1957/1992, 57–8.

Kerouac, J., *The Subterraneans*, New York: Grove, 1958/1981.

Kerouac, J., *Visions of Gerard*, New York: McGraw-Hill, 1958/1976.

Kerouac, J., 'Belief & Technique for Modern Prose', in A. Charters (ed.), *The Viking Portable Beat Reader*, New York: Viking, 1959/1992, pp. 58–9.

Kerouac, J., *Maggie Cassidy*, New York: McGraw-Hill, 1959/1978.

Kerouac, J., *Mexico City Blues: (242 Choruses)*, New York: Grove, 1959.

Kerouac, J., 'The Origins of the Beat Generation', in S. Donaldson (ed.), *On the Road: Text and Criticism*, New York: Viking, 1959/1979, pp. 357–67.

Kerouac, J., 'Are Writers Made or Born?', in *Writers' Digest XLII*, 1 January 1962. Reprinted in A. Charters (ed.), *The Portable Jack Kerouac*, New York: Viking, 1995, pp. 488–90.

Kerouac, J., *Scattered Poems*, San Francisco: City Lights, 1970/1972.

Kerouac, J., *Pomes All Sizes*, Pocket Poet Series 48, San Francisco: City Lights, 1992.

Kerouac, J., *Jack Kerouac: Selected Letters 1940–1956*, ed. Ann Charters, New York: Viking, 1995.

McNally, D., *Desolate Angel: Jack Kerouac, the Beat Generation, and America*, New York: McGraw-Hill, 1979/1980.

Reich, P., *A Book of Dreams.* New York: Harper & Row, 1973.

Rice, M., 'Mustang Sally', 1965, http://www.azlyrics.com/lyrics/wilsonpickett/mustangsally.html (accessed 19 June 2017).

Ricks, C., *Dylan's Vision of Sin*, New York: Ecco, 2004.

Shaw, P., *Horses*, New York: Bloomsbury, 2008.

Smith, P., *Witt*, New York: Gotham Book Mart, 1973/1994, p. 35.

Smith, P., *Babel,* New York: G. P. Putnam's Sons, 1978.

Smith, P., 'We Can Be Heroes', *Details*, July 1993.

Smith, P., *Early Work: 1970–1979*, New York: Norton, 1994.

Smith, P., *Patti Smith: Complete Lyrics, Reflections, Notes for the Future*, New York: Doubleday, 1998.

Smith, P., liner notes, *One Fast Move or I'm Gone: Kerouac's Big Sur*, dir. C. Worden, n.p., 2009.

Smith, P., *Just Kids*, New York: HarperCollins, 2010.

Smith, P., *Camera Solo.* New Haven, CT: Yale University Press, 2011.

Smith, P., *Patti Smith Collected Lyrics*, New York: HarperCollins, 2015a.

Smith, P., *M Train*, New York: Knopf, 2015b.

Tarr, J., *The Words and Music of Patti Smith*, Westport, CT: Praeger, 2008.

Tosches, N., 'A Baby Wolf with Neon Bones', *Penthouse*, April 1976.

Turner, C., 'Wilhelm Reich: The Man Who Invented Free Love', *Guardian*, 8 July 2011, pp. 370–6, 397–400, 406.

Warner, S., *Text and Drugs and Rock'n'Roll: The Beats and Rock Culture*, London: Bloomsbury, 2013/2014.

Wilentz, S., *Bob Dylan in America*, New York: Anchor, 2010/2011.

Discography

Smith, Patti, 'Hey Joe'/'Piss Factory', Mer Records, 1974.

Smith, Patti, *Horses*, Arista, 1975.

Smith, Patti, *Easter*, Arista, 1978.

Smith, Patti, *Land (1975–2002)*, Arista, 2002.

Filmography

One Fast Move or I'm Gone: Kerouac's Big Sur, dir. C. Worden, Kerouac Films, 2009.

Patti Smith: Dream of Life, dir. S. Sebring, Palm, 2008.

POEMS
Marc Zegans

Introduction

I wanted to say a bit about how I approached the two poems published here, with a particular eye toward relating this material to the larger project. My aim was to create poems that were distinct, that stood on their own feet, but were thematically and musically related in ways that enhanced each other and that would, with luck, resonate with the book's essays. Central to the project was a concern with musical influence: how was Kerouac shaped by music, and how did his writing, and his life more broadly lived, shape musical culture? Why did people who would become legendary singer-songwriters of the 1960s and 1970s pick up on Kerouac, and what did they find there that fostered their creativity? I've know about this influence for some decades, but have been somewhat perplexed as to the reasons why because he came so strongly out of the bop era. What was it in him, in the world and, specifically, his writing that produced this pattern of influence?

I decided to engage with this question by imagining the circumstances in which these rockers would have encountered Kerouac, what he might have meant to them and how his life and work might have affected them. To undertake this imaginative exercise, I returned to my own early and mid-teens, remembering both how I came upon Kerouac and how I imbibed and was inspired by Waits and Dylan and Mitchell and Springsteen, who came of age when Kerouac was in his prime. This early process of consideration opened doors to my own years in New England and Kerouac's meaning to me in that context, doors to the history of post-war America and where he fitted into this saga, doors into the making of music, the urge to the road and the way that Kerouac's distinct sounds came into his writing and thus to speak to the generation that followed in his wake.

In making the poems I wanted to get at things best got at through poetry. I found my path first in exploring how the music in Kerouac's poetic prose operated. As we know, he's famously quoted on his desire to create a 'spontaneous bop prosody'. Although my reading is not comprehensive, my experience of critical response to this idea over the years has been that people saw Kerouac's bop prosody either as a jazz-inspired, or perhaps a jazz-inflected, gesture rooted in imitative desire, or as a failed experiment. In this reading, 'bop prosody' represented either a broad gesture of how he saw literature in a modern jazz world, or an effort to fuse jazz with literature, as witnessed by the jazz and Beat recordings. From my perspective, neither account fully seemed to work. I imagine that some of this rather glib interpretation had to do with the television broadcast of Kerouac reading over Steve Allen's blues piano on television. While Allen is an accomplished pianist and the interaction has feel and moment, the music is sometimes poorly matched to Kerouac's words and vocal performance.

I chose to approach Kerouac's bop prosody as a question of craft: 'What was he doing?' I asked. I went in deep, took my skills as a spoken word artist and began exploring the rhythm and music of his language while listening both to his recordings and to 1940s bop. I began repeating his language one phrase at a time, until I could match and intuit his phrasing and style, then reduced this to the unadorned rhythm. I then went further, scatting his rhythms in nonsense syllables over bop recordings. As I did this, I came to understand how much bop was actually inflected in his language. He'd gone further in creating a truly novel prosody than I'd ever imagined, one that was both deeply inspired and quite difficult to reproduce in any meaningful sense, because it was so original. I suspect Kerouac's innovation was a line not followed by others, both because they failed to take the time to see what was going on, and because its method was so difficult to internalize. So that gave me a first challenge for this project: to make a poem that spoke to Kerouac's bop prosody, and that reflected its principles, but that was expressed in my voice not his. I needed a poem that brought forth the music that came into him, and I needed this poem to show how far this bop world that made Kerouac was from rock'n'roll and from its R&B precursors.

This difference of worlds led me to other poetically and historically important realizations. Three struck me as being crucial to understanding Kerouac's influence on the rock innovators who held sway, beginning in the 1960s. First, Kerouac went on the road as countless rock bands would do, but under very different circumstances. The America interstate highway system did not begin construction until nearly a decade after Kerouac's seminal journeys with Cassady. His travels were through a regional, idiosyncratic America tied together by rails and radio, but divergent, diverse and not easy to reach. His experience was more akin to that described by Che Guevara on his epic journey on his motorcycle, 'La Poderosa', through the vastness of South America, than that of the tour bus road warriors who defined the rock'n'roll lifestyle.

Second, rock'n'roll did not hit the radio until approximately six years after Kerouac went on the road. The teenagers who first danced to Elvis and Jerry Lee and the rest were ten years old when Kerouac went West. They were the older siblings of rockers who shaped the 1960s, and this is important. Why? Because *On the Road* sat unpublished for seven years after its completion, so it entered the minds, not of the first teenagers, but of the kids who had grown up in rock'n'roll, in a world of highways, and in a world where the nation had been fermenting its new and dynamic youth culture. They were acculturated to rock'n'roll and to the road when the book hit. Kerouac's bid for originality was, as a document, separated culturally from the conditions that spawned it, its cultural meaning shaped by its moment of introduction and by the age of the people who read it, mid-teens in 1957, who'd been born in 1942. They were five when he went on the road, and that matters intensely. I needed a poem that would speak to this insight about their age. The fact that I had come to Kerouac, at 15 or thereabouts, created a cross generational empathy that I could work with.

Finally, Kerouac's work and that of his rock'n'roll followers engages the vernacular, but engages it in varied ways. These ways matter to the songwriting methods they employed and to how these methods made their encounters with the vernacular both indelible and distinct. Yet this love of the vernacular formed them into a tribe, a wandering group of somewhat mismatched minstrels, a group of Traveling Wilburys if you like. The poems here follow these insights. They also take the music seriously and engage it consciously, winding its rhythms deeply into their structures.

'Passing tones' brings us into Kerouac's world in the form of a bop poem, developing his history in relation to a mythical ten-year-old who will become the first teenager infected by rock'n'roll in its seminal moment. The poem carries us into the history of road and highway and the map of America into which Kerouac's *On the Road* fell. The poem experiments with its language and sound, specifically in the improvisational sense that Kerouac felt was at the heart of the literature he wanted to invent. I run 'passing tones' in long lines and sentences, soloing through his world and the years, giving life to bop prosody as practice. Consistent with this fluid style, I've written this poem in lower case with the exception of a single capitalized 'America' – it's meant to have the spontaneity and flow of an improvised solo, dashed off, written on the fly.

The second poem, 'Mining the Vernacular', functions as a suite of three. It's about rock'n'roll, and Kerouac, and the hipster's relation to what is found in the town and on the road. I wanted this piece to have the youthful, make-it-up-as-you-go quality that fuelled rock'n'roll from its earliest days: the freshness, the inspired amateurism, the thrill of discovering a new sound that utterly changes one's life. I'm talking about the experience captured so well in that segment from *It Might Get Loud* when Jimmy Page plays 'Rumble', regresses into childhood and animates the effect that Link Wray generated in him as a young guitarist. I wanted to make this a vehicle for travelling into the vernacular as Springsteen, Waits, Dylan and Kerouac each encountered it, and as I experienced their worlds as a kid making things up. Behind this, I wanted a design and structure that accomplished more musically, and that imparted more layers and meaning than those achieved by these surface connections.

The suite of poems is structured as four sonnets divided into three sections (I here frame the term sonnet loosely – they're unrhymed, take neither Petrarchan nor Shakespearean form, but do consist of 14 lines each, are metred and have a turn). This tripartite partition follows the structure of a sonata – theme, development and recapitulation – the progress marked by the presence of 'a Jersey girl' in the first and in the last. Sonnet and sonata, poem and music, words and song, and three against four. Imagine this as quarter note triplets against straight eighths in a slow blues. There's a rhythmic tension here at that level of abstraction. But the sonnets break across the three sections – 1/2/1. So a one-sonnet movement, then two sonnets that depend on each other, as two verses in a song before the chorus or the bridge, and then a final sonnet. This isn't quite a square song, But there's an intro, a couple of verses, and a return to the beginning. There's no accident here. It was meant to fall that way.

The metre in the piece expands and becomes both more formal and more rarified as we move from one section to the next. The metre in section one is loose, felt, the line lengths vary. It's the music being made by a teenage boy and girl, who share an album in common and a feeling and not much else; they're clumsy, but alive. The metre in the second section's two sonnet-shaped stanzas is nominally pentameter, but they're written to play off the riffing in 4/4 that Waits does in his early work. Again, rhythm against rhythm against rhythm, making verse and music work with and off each other. The third and final section is written in hexameter, rarely used in English verse, expansive, capacious, tying these stories of minstrels and poets together into a larger quilt. If you were to graph the development of the metre, it would open like the horn on an old RCA Victor Victrola, as an amplifier of the local and the particular that we all share through our rock'n'roll heroes and the French-Canadian from Lowell who inspired them.

passing tones

sitting in lowell massachusetts six years before the making
of a teenager, the first one, who came about when elvis laid tracks
in 1953 memphis tennesee, some ten year old dreams in hiroshima
pictures of peacetime prosperity, and the footballer who left ma mere
and the memories of pa pere's print shop, merrimac overflown,
drowned paper in the flood, who went south like a bird from mill town
in winter to begin. but never finish, the columbia exposition . . . bound
for the marines . . . and unbound, flushed back into new york city where
he found auto-mat thief, laying back at the horn and hardart's, and
the gritty fedora filled mid-town street that he and the boys from
columbia scooted past on the way downtown to nights of be-bop
and run downs and run rounds and the big shouldered hudson that
cassady and he swooped into, like birds nesting in perpetual flight
in their criss-cross, east-west, rolling reverie of life on the american
vernacular freeway that remained unbuilt until 1956.

on the road, the rock 'n roll novel, the countercultural scroll of
beat, the beat, beatitude, the big beat blowing up from mexico
in hundred thousand watt glory – morrison's wasp – came out
of the scroll closet into, a shake rattle, rollin', maybelline, roll-over
beethoven world just jumpin' for that 1947 ten year old – big brother
to hendrix, dylan, manzarek mitchell and the poet minstrels of the
unborn sixties, who put it in the back pocket of their jeans and
carried it to glory in the unlimited, unbound, acid test explosion

of free love and expanding amplification, and poet heroes of
the fm radio, answer to the brill building record machine; not
knowing that this world onto which it imprinted its limitless road,
the road of countless rock 'n roll revues and tours of the almost
famous and one hit wonders on the teen circuit, was a hidden
harbinger, released into what was to come, when it had already
happened, because when jack and neal went on the road,
America had not been tied into an interstate knot, rock n' roll
hadn't happened and the future wasn't here yet, so no one
knew what to do, except for charlie parker and kenny clarke
and diz and thelonious and dexter and all those beboppers
playin' over the changes with that extra passing tone and
passin' it on in clubs to disaffected white boys needing to
get to that place between – hanging high on the note that lay
between
places.

Mining the Vernacular

The first time I heard Springsteen,
a Jersey girl in cutoffs
said, 'He's like Dylan, only worse,
but *The Wild The Innocent
& The E Street Shuffle*
makes me want to fuck him'
She pulled out *Greetings
from Asbury Park*,
a gaudy postcard
of a fantasy shore
laid it on the table
and sent it spinning.

'I hear you roll tight bones,'
she said, nuzzling my neck.

   * *

The wood-clad-washing-machine Hi Fi
was my portal to the vernacular
twenty-four hour diner and road stand
delivered straight from the mouth of Stone Man
where one afternoon I happened to hear

Kerouac on Record

ba-doom-ba-buh-doo-wah snaking out of
an upright bass, and ba-da-da-dum, from
a saxophone, fronting a piano
and the live-wire-swish of a brushed snare
opening a Tom Waits weather report
charting the condition of his mental health
as he began his journey into
the living residue of lost angels
stolen from an Edward Hopper painting.

It was at this moment that I recognized
the architecture that populated
the frenetic journeys of Kerouac
and Cassady as Dean Moriarty
transmitted on the unrolling scroll
by means of manic typewriter frenzy
being killed by fast food and shopping malls
still existed in the corners and cracks
of Los Angeles and San Francisco
too un-commercial to have been removed
by the promise of perpetual sameness
and that Tom Waits, hunter of the hipness
he imputed to his father's wild years
had snared it, in swizzle stick riffs on Nighthawks.

     * *

It always amused me that the essential song
About nostalgic romance on the Jersey Shore
The song about love you started remembering
Even as you were in the middle of a long kiss
The song that made girls who 'went down the shore' swoon
When Springsteen sang it with complete sincerity
And the kind of conviction that made you believe
Was written by Tom Waits, 'Sing sha-la-la-la-la-la'

If Waits was a hunter and Springsteen a romantic
Dylan was the barker in front of a sideshow
Conjuring the marvels that a thin dime would bring
Inventing a fantasy of America

Far better than life, a life Kerouac embraced
In the un-conjured moments that never return.

INTERVIEW 5: ALLEN GINSBERG
Pat Thomas

In 1984, I sat down with Allen Ginsberg in Rochester, NY, after one of Allen's musical performances – we discussed Kerouac and several bands who have written songs about him.

PT: How does the new wave/punk movement relate to Jack Kerouac and the Beats?

AG: We were a continuation of the old Bohemian movement – the '20s and all that. I think the hippies and then punk and new wave and all that is just a continuation of the old Bohemian movement. Every generation is a little bit wrong, but it's mostly right in trying to break out and start over again, and start at the ground and build something new and just not get smothered by the last generation's solidification of a fresh idea. I think it's great, that's why I was happy to work with the Clash [on their *Combat Rock* album].

PT: Have you heard the King Crimson album, *Beat*?

AG: Yeah, I did. I didn't think too much of the words.

PT: 'Neal and Jack and Me'

AG: Yeah, I didn't think the words were very inspired. I think the Clash's words were. Strummer's a better poet. I thought it was nice King Crimson cared, but on the other hand – Who was it?

PT: Adrian Belew actually wrote the lyrics.

AG: I didn't think the lyrics were that accurate or inspired. Did you?

PT: I did. I think he's genuinely into Kerouac.

AG: Yeah, but I don't think he got the rhetoric. He didn't get the Nazi milk* of Kerouac. He didn't get the outrageous purple hippopotamus or something.

---

*Interviewer's note: Allen Ginsberg took a particular fascination in the power of the oxymoron. As he once told a class: 'The best I ever heard was something like, well, in my own poetry, "hydrogen jukebox" […] but from students, the best I ever heard was "Nazi milk". Those two words don't seem to fit together and yet when you put together they make you laugh, because they're so opposite. Nazi – dark, sadistic or whatever, milk – the innocent.' Quoted in Jiří Zochr, PhD thesis, 'Allen Ginsberg in Olomouc: Allen Ginsberg's Lecture on Spontaneous Writing with Commentary', 2014, http://theses.cz/id/cwpo5i/Ji_Zochr_DP_2014.pdf (accessed 24 October 2017).

PT: I was really disappointed by Willie Alexander and the Boom Boom Band and 'Kerouac'. Now, to me, that was really uninspired.

AG: I know him [Willie Alexander] from Gloucester. Yeah, it's a littler group. They didn't have a big deal to do. I don't know who did ... well, Ramblin' Jack Elliott has a song or two, and so does David Amram.

PT: What do you think of the song 'Cassidy' by Bob Weir of the Grateful Dead?

AG: It's alright, they knew him. Actually, I never heard that until about a year ago. I went to a Grateful Dead concert and heard it. I hadn't been to any of their concerts since 1967, till 1982 or so.

PT: What do you think about the Grateful Dead, the 'Deadhead' movement?

AG: They obviously have a solid communal basis ... They've lasted so long, like a good marriage. That takes stability and sensibility to do. The bands that I listen to at the moment, Dead Kennedys, and I've heard Black Flag.

CHAPTER 19
TRAMPS LIKE THEM: JACK AND BRUCE AND THE MYTH OF THE AMERICAN ROAD

Simon A. Morrison

The only truth is music

Jack Kerouac, Desolation Angels, p. 136

A Side: Synergies

Track 1 – Intro

When rock star Bruce Springsteen appeared on BBC Radio 4's *Desert Island Discs* at the tail end of 2016 he did not mention author Jack Kerouac in the list of writers he would consider for his book choice on the island. Unlike then the friendship of Allen Ginsberg and Bob Dylan, or the overt and discernible creative influence of Jack Kerouac on music personalities such as Jerry Garcia and Tom Waits, there are – at least at first glance – fewer direct links that might be drawn between Jack Kerouac and Bruce Springsteen. However, although Kerouac is known principally as a writer, Springsteen as a musician, the crossover between the two is much more developed than one might initially suppose, especially when considering Springsteen's relationship to words; Kerouac's to music and the desire to *write musically*.

Track 2 – Motivation and methodology

In terms of a methodology, this chapter will function much like the two sides of a Springsteen LP. This A-Side is concerned with the synergies that might be found between Jack and Bruce. Having established these sartorial, aesthetic and mythologized connectives, the B-Side, or flip-side, will then move on to consider the impact that these two men, and the work they produced, have made on post-war American culture and wider society.

Academic research has taken place into the relationship of the Beat Generation to the counterculture that would follow in the later years of the 1960s. Equally, there has been research around Springsteen, notably Daniel Cavicchi's *Tramps Like Us: Music and Meaning Among Springsteen Fans*. However, that volume was published in 1998 and relates principally to the fans of Springsteen rather than the artist himself; there is no mention of Kerouac in the index, for instance. No more recent research has sought to draw these links between the two; however, even very light research reveals others within fan communities thinking along similar lines. The following is a thread from the Springsteen fan site, *Greasy Lake*:

> I guess I'm late to this party, but on my reading bucket list (if there is such a thing) has always been Jack Kerouac's *On the Road*. I know, I know, everyone should have read that, but somehow I reached my fifties without ever doing so. So, about a month or two ago, I bought it from Amazon, loaded it onto the iPad, and I've been carrying it around ever since. I finally actually started reading it today.
>
> I was really stunned almost immediately, by how obvious an influence Kerouac must have been on Springsteen! You will never convince me that Springsteen didn't devour this book at some early point in his life, and I think it had a profound influence on his early songwriting . . . I would go so far as to say even more than Dylan. The sentence here alone, from the end of chapter one, simply sounds like it should have a Springsteen soundtrack behind it:
>
> 'And in his excited way of speaking I heard again the voices of old companions and brothers under the bridge, among the motorcycles, along the wash-lined neighborhood and drowsy doorsteps of afternoon where boys played guitars while their older brothers worked in the mills.'
>
> Once again, I'm sure many people were already aware of this, but I was really struck by it.
>
> By the way, I'm only on Chapter 4, so no spoilers, please![1]

This *Greasy Lake* fan suggests Kerouac as a present-absence in Springsteen's world,[2] or a ghost presence that Jacques Derrida would detect as a cultural, spectral haunting. The influence of author on rock star is, therefore, one that is admittedly more nebulous but nonetheless impactful; there not merely in the lines but more obliquely in what might be inferred between the lines.

As readers of novels, and listeners of music, we are often, naturally, drawn out of these texts by an interest in context, in the lives of the actual writers and singers themselves. As such, the critical bent of this chapter will be the antithesis of a structuralist approach that would argue only the text matters. Instead, we need to reconnect text to context, a desire that is not voyeuristic but merely forged from an instinctive desire to understand the full picture. In the early stages of writing this chapter, for instance, Springsteen conducted several interviews to publicize his autobiography, the very candid and readable *Born To Run*. These included the BBC (for both *Desert Island Discs* and an hour-long TV special), the *Sunday Times*, the *Observer* and *Vanity Fair*. These articles have been invaluable in opening up possible routes of research – new roads of possibility and potential.

And of course we have the texts themselves, both the novels of Kerouac and the songs of Springsteen, both of which form vessels for working through their autobiographical concerns, which Springsteen himself calls his 'twisted autobiographies'.[3] *Vanity Fair*, meanwhile, calls Springsteen a 'born memorist', in line with Proust and indeed Kerouac,[4] and in his review of this autobiography, music writer David Hepworth writes 'Bruce Springsteen is all stories. His songs are stories.'[5] Principal among the stories analysed in this chapter will be perhaps the signature texts of these two creative forces: Kerouac's novel *On the Road*, and the Springsteen track 'Born to Run'. The three-word titles of each, anchored by the short middle word and the alliterative force of the final punch draws immediate parallels between the two. It is also worth noting at this early stage – although nothing more than a numerological circumstance – that, rather like George Orwell writing his signature novel in 1948 and reversing the last two numbers, *Born to Run*'s appearance in 1975 is similarly a reversal of the appearance of *On the Road* in 1957.

In now progressing to outline the cultural connective tissues that link these two icons of American post-war popular culture, these can broadly be defined in three ways. First, there are sartorial connections in the way the two men dress and present themselves; second, obvious thematic links between the musical and literary work of these two icons of American popular culture; finally, defined stylistic links in the free-flowing lyricism that defines the words and worlds of both men. Although these three areas provide the main focus for this account, other synergies may also be seen between the two: European heritage; a troubled relationship with patriotism and the American flag; family dynamics; Catholicism. More than these, however, this chapter will explore the ways Jack Kerouac was able to make literature powerful in a new and alluring way, and similarly how Springsteen was able to engage globally, musically, in a way that might perhaps never have happened without Kerouac's influence. The chapter will explore the reality, or perhaps the myth, of the American road and what inspirational power it held for these two men, leading perpetually, unendingly, towards a distant sense of a place called The American Dream, lying somewhere just out of reach, just over the horizon.

Track 3 – Sartorial links

This chapter will begin with the outward appearance of the two men, before venturing more towards their inner spirit. Kerouac – handsome, rugged, charismatic – had a style, even if it was unforced and unintended; functional, driven by necessity and affordability, rather than affectation. In now iconic photographs we see Kerouac in white T-shirts and blue jeans, or in boots and plaid work shirts, whether on the road or in more ascetic times, working the railroads. This was demonstrably a look adopted by Springsteen – the same jeans, Ts and work-shirt look that defined Kerouac's Beats – by the mid 1970s repositioned as Springsteen's 'tramps'. Kerouac himself predicted that this was a style that would be co-opted. In a June 1959 essay for *Playboy* magazine entitled 'The Origins of the Beat Generation', Kerouac envisaged how 'that Beat style and manners would inevitably be swept up in the restless tide of fashion', moving on to write of smooth professionals 'coming out nattily attired in Brooks Brothers jean-type tailoring and sweater style pull-ons, in other words, it's a simple change in fashion and manners, just a history crust'. And indeed his image would be used, perhaps even abused, for example in a 1993 Gap advert for khaki trousers. Kirkpatrick describes Springsteen at his now infamous 1972 live showcase at The Gaslight in Greenwich Village as 'equal parts Beat poet, motorcycle punk, and Bohemian gypsy' (Kirkpatrick, 2009, p.18), and this is a view taken up by Steve Turner in his excellent appraisal of Kerouac, *Angelheaded Hipster*:

> Bruce Springsteen, who shared with Jack a working-class East Coast Catholic upbringing, also shared his love of fast cars and the open American landscape. It is hard to imagine Springsteen existing without Jack. Even his stage clothing of a check shirt and blue jeans – once unthinkable attire for a performer – are straight out of *On the Road*.
>
> Turner, 1996, p. 21

These links between music and literary fashions were identified very early on. Writing in the March 1975 issue of *NME*, just before the release of the album *Born to Run*, UK music journalist Mick Farren notes how:

> In many respects the musical underground, which spanned such diverse artists as Charlie Parker, Hank Ballard and even Hank Williams, paralleled the moves that were being made by Kerouac and Mailer in the same way that Steinbeck and Fitzgerald paralleled Guthrie and Porter.
>
> Farren, 2010, p. 56

In the same piece, Farren extends these connections to draw specific parallels between Springsteen and the Beats, although interestingly references William S. Burroughs rather than Kerouac himself: 'What makes him a little suspect is the way his imagery is an amalgam of previous archetypes drawn from a range of classics that encompass Hubert Selby, Bill Burroughs, James Dean and, of course, Dylan' (Farren, 2010, p. 57).

Moving into the 1980s, and in considering the cover photo of Springsteen's 1984 album *Born in the USA*, these links remain solid; indeed, as the photo is taken from behind it might well be Kerouac himself who stands in white T-shirt and blue jeans, a red cap in his back right pocket as though working as a mountain-top fire lookout, or 'laying down the blacktop', like the character from that album's 'Working on the Highway'. Such sartorial connections even carry over to the flat woollen caps the pair also sported at various stages in their life. In his article 'The Real Thing – Bruce Springsteen', Simon Frith raises understandable and problematic questions inherent in Springsteen adopting what is essentially workwear: 'Worn jeans, singlets, a head band to keep his hair from his eyes – these are working clothes' (Frith, 2007, p. 249).

Here Frith refers to *Born in the USA* but issues of affectation remain true when Springsteen's income might suggest he could afford rather better clothes. On his own roadtrips, and in his own words, Springsteen also details a wardrobe of 'blue-jean shirtsleeves rolled down, sunglasses, gloves, boots, and jeans, and bandanas soaked in water completely covering our heads and faces' (Springsteen, 2016, p. 360). As recently as 2016, Michael Hann registers Springsteen's paint-spattered jeans when he meets the singer, and is forced to ponder 'if someone splattered the paint on for him, just to keep things looking blue collar' (Hann, 2016, p. 6).

There are two points to be made in Springsteen's favour here. First, in his autobiography, Springsteen himself admits to the apparent hypocrisy inherent in adopting American work apparel, almost audibly chuckling when writing, 'I'm a repairman. That's part of my job. So I, who's never done a week's worth of manual labor in my life (hail, hail rock'n'roll!), put on a factory worker's clothes, my father's clothes, and went to work' (Springsteen, 2016, p. 414). Second, Springsteen seems to exist in two physical modes: a skinnier Beat/tramp version in a vest and longer hair, and a more muscular iteration of later years when, although still in workwear, his clothes – according to Hann – are 'so casual they could only be expensive'. In a sense, Frith's headband has fallen; now to become the necktie more likely to be found running around Springsteen's neck in these later years. One is minded of the transformative effect the New York John Varvatos clothing store had on that other frayed and shabby icon of American culture – the very space it took over, previously known as the nightclub CBGBs.[6] Of course we will never know what Kerouac would have made of Springsteen. Kerouac's body changed too, though not in the more determined, sculpted way Springsteen has managed, but rather to become the pudgy, overweight frame of Kerouac's alcoholic last years. Of course, we will never know what Kerouac would have made of the New Jersey rock star; Springsteen's debut album – *Greetings From Asbury Park, NJ* – did not appear until four years after the author's death. But it would be good to think he would have approved. At least of the way the Boss dressed.

Track 4 – Thematic links

Thematic links run hard and true between the work of both Kerouac and Springsteen, a mythologizing interest in blue collar, small town America and the way it harbours past love affairs; male friendship; the open road and its (alleged) freedoms.

Part 1 – Small town, blue-collar American life: In terms of psychogeography, we must certainly stress the role of place on both creatives, especially as it undoubtedly is the same kind of place. Both Kerouac and Springsteen live with a haunting – the haunting sense of their past – the kind of place one wonders (admitting a UK perspective) even exists anymore, in the America of this following century. This is the small town, Anytown USA, that one finds located throughout popular culture. However, whether or not it physically exists on the map, small town America plays a fundamental psychogeographic role in the texts of Jack and Bruce, pulling them back home when, as we shall see, the call of the road was pulling them in altogether another direction.

Kerouac grew up in Lowell, Massachusetts, a redbrick town where his father worked as a printer. Around 270 miles away, Springsteen was born in Freehold, New Jersey, before moving to Asbury Park on the New Jersey shoreline. Perhaps the greatest expression of connection the two have to their hometowns is that Springsteen, even to this day, lives in Colts Neck, Monmouth County, the same county where his life began (notwithstanding, of course, the other homes he has in Florida and LA). Kerouac, meanwhile, is buried in a very modest grave in the Lowell cemetery.[7] One need not look far to discover the presence of their hometowns in the grooves of their records, the imprint of the words on the page: tracks like Springsteen's 'Growing Up', or tales of Kerouac's youth in works such as *Doctor Sax* (1959). Throughout, their own lives and experiences infuse their work. Kerouac's 1963 novel *Visions of Gerard*, for instance, was a eulogy to his older brother, who died aged nine. Meanwhile in his autobiography Springsteen talks of his own rather disjointed upbringing, at one point billeted with grandparents who were overly protective, perhaps making up for the early death of their own daughter. Both men had Catholic upbringings, born of European ancestry: Kerouac's French, Springsteen's principally Italian, although also Irish amongst others (yet Holland, from where the Springsteen name derives, seems of limited import).

Beyond the parameters of their own homes, gardens and streets, both tell stories of other average Americans leading average lives. Perhaps they even romanticize an America that they sense is passing, taking with it the American Dream that writers such as Norman Mailer also acknowledged was disappearing.[8] In *On the Road*, Kerouac necessarily implied, if not described, the home from where such blacktop adventures would originate. Meanwhile in his overview of Springsteen's signature song, Nick Hasted writes of 'the constituency "Born To Run" romanticized: the blue-collar car lovers and working stiffs that pop's post-psychedelic feyness left disenfranchised. He was the laureate of the greasers and the steel mill, the same dismissed whitebread Americans later lured by Reagan' (Hasted, 2005, p. 80).

Part 2 – The myth of Maggie/Mary: In their idealizing of their hometowns, a female presence also lurks in the shadows of the psyches and sidewalks of both men. A muse, invariably known as Mary (Springsteen) and exemplified by Maggie (Kerouac). Whether in prose or song, many stories of hometown life in an endless youth revolve around these arguably mythologized adolescent romances the pair had in their, also arguably, idealized hometowns. Kerouac penned *Maggie Cassidy*, published in 1959, detailing his high school relationship with Mary Carney. Springsteen refers many times to female characters, with Kirkpatrick locating 'Mary' in the figure of a Puerto Rican girl Maria Espinoza, who shared Springsteen's first teenage kiss. Content analysis reveals that the name appears in tracks including 'Mary's Place', 'Thunder

Road', 'Mary, Queen of Arkansas', 'The Rising', 'The River', 'Gypsy Biker', 'Bring On The Night' and 'Car Wash'. A typical example, from 'Thunder Road', runs:

The screen door slams
Mary's dress waves

Part 3 – Male friendship: Kerouac died in 1969, around the same time that Springsteen was stepping up his own music career, and of course they were destined never themselves to meet in the way, for instance, that Ginsberg and Dylan did. However, male friendships did develop and define both men. Kerouac, firstly, was defined by his friendship with Neal Cassady, *On the Road*'s Dean Moriarty to Kerouac's Sal Paradise. Indeed when many people think of *On the Road* – its energy and spirit – they often mistake the Kerouac role for that of Cassady; however, every buddy story needs the chronicler of their adventures, as well as the instigator, and Cassady was the spark, the real hero (or perhaps antihero) of the piece; Kerouac the Sancho Panza to his Don Quixote. Intriguingly, Kerouac conflates the name of his male friend with his childhood gal for the title of the novel *Maggie Cassidy*, and for some commentators that does suggest a certain queering of image. In photos we see Kerouac and Cassady arm in arm like romantic partners, and of course The Original Scroll publication of *On the Road* reveals the true level of homosexual engagement that was redacted from the better-known published version.

Springsteen's stage presence was also defined by his friendship with The Big Man – saxophonist Clarence Clemons – a relationship that, like Kerouac's, infused his creative and professional world. Here we find not only the displaced masculinity in being lower middle class, in dressing like workers, or living a peripatetic lifestyle, but also a keen interest and connection to African American culture, again touching on Mailer's notion of the 'The White Negro' in his 1957 essay. And that especially holds true for musicians, both artists captivated by the romance of the late-night wail of the saxophone, whether Lester Young blowing bebop jazz for 1940s night hawks, or the heartbreaking wail of Clemons' sax on 'Jungleland' some 30 years later.

These two friendships are key, and are perfectly encapsulated in two images: the much reproduced 1952 shot of Jack and Neal, shoulder to shoulder, and the black-and-white shot of Springsteen and Clarence Clemons that formed the gatefold cover of *Born to Run*. Asbury Park was riven by racial tension at this time, where interracial friendships such as this were not common, and, in semiotic terms, Springsteen makes key points with this image. Yes, it is him on the cover of his breakthrough LP, but open up the gatefold sleeve to get the full picture, and you will find he is, and in fact literally, leaning for support on the broad shoulders of his great friend. The photographer, Eric Meola, recalls:

When I showed the prints to Bruce, the cover shot was my favourite. It's the movement, the way they lean into each other. It gives the sense of the title, *Born to Run*. The album's about friendship, and it captured theirs, with the little impish grin on Bruce's face as he looks at Clarence, and the hand on his shoulder.

Hasted, 2005, p. 68

Cassady died in 1968, Kerouac just a year later. Clemons died in 2011, and on his next album – 2012's *Wrecking Ball* – Springsteen penned the following, beautiful words on the sleeve notes:

> We were united, we were strong, we were righteous, we were unmovable, we were funny, we were corny as hell and serious as death itself. And we were coming to your town to shake you and to wake you up. Together, we told an older, richer story about the possibilities of friendship that transcended those I'd written about in my songs and in my music. Clarence carried it in his heart. It was a story where the Scooter and the Big Man not only busted the city in half, but we kicked ass and remade the city, shaping it into the kind of place where our friendship would not be such an anomaly.[9]

It would be positive to think, or to hope at least, that America might be moving towards the place Springsteen envisaged.

Part 4 – The (myth of) the road: In his 2007 work, *Magic In The Night*, Rob Kirkpatrick writes:

> When Springsteen wrote and recorded the songs for *Born to Run*, he wasn't striving for realism: he aimed to explore the romance and mythology of American cities, American car culture, and rock'n'roll. He sought to portray larger-than-life characters and situations reminiscent of Sal Paradise's words in Jack Kerouac's *On The Road*.

Kirkpatrick, 2009, p. xv

Indeed a seam of romance runs through the works of both men, both a literal romance and an idealized romance of cities, late nights, lost loves and the road. Post-Second World War America's wide open spaces became a playground, where white middle-class Americans (particularly men) collectively became fascinated with the idea of 'escape' from the everyday, as a moment of authentic personal expression set against the quicksand of the domestic, the quotidian.

Escape can take different forms: hedonistic indulgence, long hair, style choices, connections made down the class ladder (Kerouac and itinerant criminal Herbert Huncke, for instance) and across the racial divide (Springsteen and Clemons). Escape also requires something key. Wheels. Here we also find a very particular aesthetic: traumatized Second World War veterans gathering in packs to cruise America on motorbikes, an aesthetic picked up in everything from the 1953 Marlon Brando film

The Wild One to the 1973 Springsteen track 'The Angel' to the 2016 Annie Leibovitz photoshoot Springsteen conducted with *Vanity Fair* magazine, featuring the singer sitting astride a powerful motorcycle. In his *Uncut* article, Nick Hasted agrees that '"Born To Run" was a song you could drive to; his sweat-soaked gigs were Friday night celebrations. Briefly, he made rock seem that simple' (Hasted, 2005, p. 82). Springsteen bought his first car the year he made 'Born to Run'. According to Kirkpartick (his description ringing out like a Springsteen lyric), it was 'a '57 Chevy with dual, four-barrel carbs, a Hurst on the floor, and orange flames painted across the hood';[10] a '57 Chevy, in fact, produced the same year *On the Road* was published.[11]

Kerouac's roadtrips with Cassady and others form the substance of *On the Road*; Springsteen also took many roadtrips with his own male friends, feeding into his songs. For both, the narrator is firmly entrenched in the action, whether that be Kerouac masquerading as Sal Paradise in *On the Road* or the narrator of 'Born To Run' making his impassioned call to Wendy, where:

> In the day we sweat it out on the streets of a runaway American dream
> At night we ride through the mansions of glory in suicide machines

One of the first original songs performed by Springsteen's first band, the Castiles, was titled 'Sidewalk', leading Kirkpatrick to comment, 'Even then, Springsteen's lyricism paralleled images of the road.'[12] The notion of the open road is certainly key in the minds of both men, and their texts, and must necessarily be front and centre of this account. However, is the story more nuanced than one might think? One must always question where, for instance, the road is leading. Is it, like the river in *Huckleberry Finn*, actually running towards greater danger? Physically, for both men the road often leads to California, the very end of the road in that great push west. In his review of the Cavicchi book, Jefferson Cowie falls back upon personal experience and reactions:

> Following groundwork laid by dissenting wanderers from Walt Whitman to Jack Kerouac, I pointed the car toward the west-bound side of the interstate. Rolling down the on-ramp toward California, I punctuated the last line of the song, as we always did, with head out the window and my voice straining to compete with Bruce's: 'It's a town full of losers / And I'm pulling out of here to win!'
>
> Cowie, 2001

In the *Vanity Fair* interview, Springsteen agrees: 'Where do people run? They run West,'[13] although in progressing to metaphysics one must question if there ever is a final direction ... or is being 'on the road' enough, in and of itself? One detects myth rolling like low mist across this blacktop. Myth because the American Dream was now the Runaway American Dream, both men needing a car and a road to chase it down, forever disappearing over the horizon. In the *New York Times* review of Springsteen's biography, Dwight Garner writes, 'Bruce Springsteen's song lyrics have injected more drama and mystery into the myths of the American road than any figure since Jack Kerouac' (Garner, 2016), and, in detailing the extended trips he took across America, Springsteen concurs: 'The road was my trusty shield against the truth' (Springsteen, 2016, p. 273). The *Uncut* article importantly adds the suffix '-er' to Springsteen's lyric to create 'The Runaway American Dreamer'. It transpires, for instance, that neither Jack nor Bruce were actually competent drivers. In the autobiography *Born to Run* we discover that Springsteen, like Kerouac, is often not the driver, not the alpha male, but rather the driven, offering the space and scope to function, once again, as observer. As Dwight Garner remarks, 'He did not exactly, when young and virile, ride through mansions of glory on suicide machines. He mostly stuck out his thumb. He'd been born to hitch' (Garner, 2016). Perhaps, in the final outcome, the myth is preferable.

In terms of process, and the creation of the two key texts for this chapter, Kerouac's three-week burst of energy in 1951 could not be more different than the six months it is estimated that it took Springsteen to assemble, arrange and record the track 'Born to Run', aged 24. Kerouac originally typed *On the Road* onto one single roll of paper which, when stretched out, itself resembled a road,[14] the words rolling as though spilt not spelt, out along a paper highway. In comparison, Springsteen agonized over that one track, knowing it was make-or-break. Springsteen himself recalls:

> The tension making that record I could never describe. It was killing, almost; it was inhuman. I hated it. I couldn't stand it. It was the worst, hardest, lousiest thing I ever had to do.[15]

And yet whether born to run or already on the road, and despite their very different births and deliveries into the world of popular culture, both texts would ultimately become the signature works for both men.

Track 5 – Stylistic links

In terms of its literature, there is a great commonality within the Beat and rock scenes. What links the cultures is the energy in the texts. Kerouac was accused of being a typist rather than a writer, using Benzedrine to fuel all-night binges of writing. His style of 'spontaneous prose' would, in turn, become an inspiration to later writers, such as the music critic Lester Bangs, as well as musicians, ironic when you consider that Kerouac himself wrote in a style that was intended to mimic the free form improvisational spirit of bebop jazz. The early Springsteen albums had a similarly free-flowing, loose lyricism that, according to Peter Gertenzang in *The Observer*, 'sounded like Chuck Berry had been secretly collaborating with Jack Kerouac',[16] while in the student newspaper of Boston University we hear how Springsteen's 'lyrics hold a longing and nostalgia akin to the great American poets of the beat generation: Jack Kerouac, Allen Ginsberg and William S. Burroughs' (Parkinson, 2016). First consider the famous passage from *On the Road*:

iconic, the titular song famously misunderstood and erroneously appropriated by the Reagan 1984 presidential election campaign as a jingoist rallying call. In response to Reagan singling him out in a speech, Springsteen sang the subversive track 'Johnny 99' at his very next show. Springsteen is still asking questions of his country, now increasingly compelled to answer them as well, following the election of Donald Trump in late 2016. Springsteen remains vocally supportive of Democratic presidential candidates including Bill Clinton and Barack Obama, very much part of the inner circle. For instance, we find Springsteen with Obama at the 2016 event to award him the Presidential Medal of Freedom, the nation's highest civilian honour. In addressing Springsteen, Obama details a collage of 'pool halls, bars, girls and cars, altars and assembly lines', while a White House press statement cites how 'The stories he has told, in lyrics and epic live concert performances, have helped shape American music and have challenged us to realize the American dream.' Here we find a new Camelot, an establishment of rebels.

The Stars and Stripes also features on several paperback covers of Kerouac novels,[19] although Kerouac would never go as far as to subvert its overt representative role, as the hippies were able to do in their own displays of semiotic occupation. As we have seen, the real driver (in every sense) of the Beat scene was Neal Cassady, evidently a fine writer who never slowed down to write much that survives to this day but instead burned like 'fabulous yellow roman candles exploding like spiders across the stars'.[20] Cassady blazed his own trail from the 1950s to 1960s, linking up with author Ken Kesey in La Honda, California, driving Kesey's Merry Pranksters across America on the bus Furthur. Kerouac left Cassady to get on with the business of becoming a Merry Prankster. There was little merry about Kerouac towards the end of his life, the author coping with the apparent contradiction inherent in the nonconformist-to-conformist trajectory by not coping with it at all. Instead he descended into a sloppy solipsism, and the right-wing bile and alcoholism that ultimately consumed and poisoned him. If Kerouac balked at the 1960s counterculture, and especially its hippies, he did at least acknowledge the decade's pop culture. In *Vanity of Duluoz* (1968), Kerouac's Proust-esque remembrance novel, he reports on his own visit to Liverpool during his time in the merchant marine, and makes his own connection from Beat to Beatles, reporting:

> Then we sailed down into the Irish Sea, laid anchor off Belfast, waited there for some British convoy boats, and crossed the Irish Sea that afternoon and night straight for Liverpool. 1943. The year the Beatles were born there, ha ha ha.
>
> Kerouac, 1982, p. 204

Maybe some mirth was left, but certainly it was in very short supply. And here we do find a note of divergence between the two men: in their relationship with their fans and with wider society. If they are both to be seen as part of the cultural iconography of post-war America, we must also recognize that Kerouac had issues with the influence he had, and could not control; Springsteen more comfortable with the man he would become, even if that is, perhaps, a role he adopts. Kerouac pulled down the shutters, moving from romantic outsider to angry, drunk, hippie-bating patriot, retreating into self-imposed exile, leaving his fans to camp out on his lawn. Springsteen welcomes his public to sing with him on his stage, a unique relationship with fans expertly explored in the Cavicchi book. And off stage, Springsteen sought help in battling his demons from the modern muses of psychiatry and contemporary medicine. Springsteen admitted to his depression. One can only wonder what might have happened if Kerouac had received the professional help Springsteen has had, and that he evidently needed. Ultimately, Springsteen wrote himself out of himself and into the world. In a spoken break in his performance of 'Growing Up' on the album *Live 1975–1985*, Springsteen recounts how his mother told him he 'should be an author, he should write books; that's a good life. You can get a little something for yourself.' Springsteen continues, 'me, I just wanted to play guitar' and yet 30 years later Adele Springsteen is proved right. Bruce wrote a book, confessed in the true spirit of Catholicism, and proved himself a capable writer. Kerouac instead wrote himself into a dark and fatal corner.

Track 7 – Preservation

As well as their impact on the society into which their books and novels were published and released, both have an enculturative role in terms of their stories moving forwards. It is the underground that pushes culture forward, from the bottom up; it is within the underground that genuine creative experiments flourish. Jazz, a black American music form, was taken further in the 1950s by the free-spirited energy of bebop. The likes of Thelonious Monk, Charlie Parker, Dizzy Gillespie and Miles Davis had the ability and vision to take jazz forwards on high-energy, tangential breaks and Kerouac aimed to write exactly as they played – spontaneously. His depiction of jazz clubs in novels like *On the Road* are arguably amongst the very best writing on music, and, as detailed, this improvised note rang through to the 1960s, picked up by the likes of everyone from Hunter S. Thompson to Bruce Springsteen. The 1960s rock scene was born from garages in New Jersey and beaches in California: long-haired, raucous, denim-clad. These music styles all share something: they are primarily concerned with innovation and experimentation, with mixing styles and influences to create something original, something essentially *modern*. Bebop was built around freewheeling solos. In rock music the improvised guitar solo became iconic. Whether sax or six string, both would take off and soar before inevitably, entropically, returning to the root, to *the road*, of the song. The spirit remained the same: Kerouac wrote texts musically, Springsteen wrote music with stories woven in.

So if you want to know about the bebop clubs of Harlem in the late 1940s and 1950s, you need only turn to the pages of a Kerouac novel and listen to the scansion and metre of his prose. If you want to know about small town American life, and the hopes and dreams and lives and loves of its people, you need only turn up the volume of a Springsteen song. For these reasons these songs and stories, taken together, stand as a fundamental and essential archive of American life in the second half of the twentieth century. And then into this century, *On the Road* continues to speak to generations of young people, an eternal shield guarding against the creeping pervasiveness of the parochial and ordinary. And as Springsteen says of 'Born to Run': 'A good song takes on more meaning as the years pass by' (Kamp, 2016, p. 130).

Outro (Coda)

So to bring the needle back to the beginning of this record, no, Bruce did not take Jack to his desert island. However, there is one – and only one – direct reference to Kerouac in Springsteen's autobiography and it contains a small, furry character revealing a stronger, if stranger, connection than perhaps he imagined.

Later in his life Springsteen would take long road-trips with friends, one of whom had broken up with his girlfriend and was clutching a teddy bear as Springsteen took a turn at driving. Springsteen explains: 'I try to explain to him the teddy is throwing a kink into our Kerouac *On the Road* cool, but Matt's committed to his bear, so we drive on' (Springsteen, 2016, p. 302). Springsteen failed to grasp, however, how close he was to the essence of Kerouac, in that moment with Matt's teddy bear. Kerouac ends *On the Road*, in a scene wholly reminiscent of a Springsteen song, going down to the river, 'on this old broken-down river pier watching the long, long skies over New Jersey', looking towards, in fact, Springsteen's home state. Kerouac contemplates how 'tonight the stars'll be out, and don't you know that God is Pooh Bear?' (Kerouac, 1987, p. 291). Maybe Jack was with Bruce all along.

Notes

1. *Greasy Lake*, 17 December 2013, https://www.greasylake.org/the-circuit/index.php?/topic/116941-jack-and-bruce/ (accessed 17 March 2017).

2. Please see Dick Hebdige, *Subculture: The Meaning of Style* (London: Methuen, 1983), p. 68.

3. Rob Kirkpatrick, *Magic In The Night: The Words and Music of Bruce Springsteen* (London: Souvenir Press, 2009), p. 18.

4. David Kamp, 'The Book of Bruce', *Vanity Fair*, October 2016, p. 130.

5. David Hepworth, 'I'm a poser. I'm good', *New Statesman*, 30 September–6 October 2016, p. 69.

6. The author conducted a research trip to New York in 2015 and was amused to find the site of the seminal CBGBs was indeed now an upmarket clothes store, where ripped jeans are now likely to costs hundreds of dollars.

7. The author has a print on the wall of his study that features Kerouac's grave, sat by which are Allen Ginsberg and Bob Dylan, a photograph taken by Ken Regan during Dylan's 1975–76 Rolling Thunder Revue.

8. See, for example, Norman Mailer's 1966 novel *An American Dream*.

9. *Wrecking Ball*, sleeve notes.

10. Kirkpatrick, 2007, p. 41.

11. Kirkpatrick cites the film *American Graffiti* and indeed that celebration of American cars and the 1950s had been in cinemas only the year before.

12. Kirkpatrick, 2007, p. 6.

13. Kamp, 'The Book of Bruce', p. 139.

14. The Original Scroll made a rare UK appearance at the Barber Institute of Fine Arts, Birmingham, in 2008, the first place the author came into contact with Simon Warner. They have since collaborated on many Beat-related projects, including *Still Howling* in Manchester, 2015, and a panel at the European Beat Studies conference in Manchester a year later.

15. Kirkpatrick, 2009, p. 48.

16. Peter Gertenzang, 'How Bruce Springsteen made *Born to Run* an American masterpiece', *Observer*, 25 August 2015.

17. Dwight Garner, 'Bruce Springsteen's Memoir: Riding Shotgun With the Boss', *New York Times*, 20 September 2016.

18. The author saw Springsteen at Hyde Park Calling in 2009, and at five or six other live shows, both indoors and outdoors, in London and Manchester.

19. This includes the author's copies of *Desolation Angels* and *The Dharma Bums*, whose cover images became the tattoos he now has on his upper arms.

20. Kerouac, *On the Road*, 1986, p. 11.

Bibliography

Cavicchi, D., *Tramps Like Us: Music and Meaning Among Springsteen Fans*, Oxford: Oxford University Press, 1998.

Frith, S., 'The Real Thing – Bruce Springsteen', in Theo Cateforis (ed.), *The Rock History Reader*, New York: Routledge, 2007.

Garner, D., 'Bruce Springsteen's Memoir: Riding Shotgun With the Boss', *New York Times*, 20 September 2016.

Hanley, J., 'Springsteen tops 2016's highest-grossing tours list', *Music Week*, 5 January 2017, http://www.musicweek.com/live/read/springsteen-tops-2016-s-highest-grossing-tours-list/067039 (accessed 12 October 2017).

Hann, M., 'American Idol', The New Review, *Observer*, 30 October 2016, p. 6.

Hasted, N., 'The Runaway American Dreamer', *Uncut*, November 2005.

Hebdige, D., *Subculture: The Meaning of Style*. London: Methuen, 1983.

Hepworth, D., 'I'm a poser. I'm good', *New Statesman*, 30 September–6 October 2016.

Hodgkinson, W., 'Why Bruce Springsteen finally wrote the story of his life', *The Times*, 19 September 2016.

Kamp, D., 'The Book of Bruce', *Vanity Fair*, October 2016.

Kerouac, J., *Vanity of Duluoz*, London: Granada, 1982.

Kerouac, J., *On the Road*, London: Penguin, 1986.

Kirkpatrick, R., *Magic In The Night: The Words and Music of Bruce Springsteen*, London: Souvenir Press, 2009.

Mailer, N., 1957. 'The White Negro', *Dissent* magazine, New York: University of Pennsylvania Press, 1957, https://www.dissentmagazine.org/online_articles/the-white-negro-fall-1957 (accessed 17 March 2017).

Marcus, G., *Mystery Train*, London: Omnibus, 1977.

Parkinson, E., 'Bruce Springsteen opens The Boss up with "Chapter and Verse"', *Daily Free Press*, 26 September 2016.

Springsteen, B., *Born To Run*, London: Simon & Schuster, 2016.

Turner, S., *Angelheaded Hipster: A Life of Jack Kerouac*, London: Bloomsbury, 2006.

Discography

Bruce Springsteen, *Greetings From Asbury Park, NJ*, Columbia, 1973.

Bruce Springsteen, *Born To Run*, Columbia, 1975.

Bruce Springsteen, *The River*, Columbia, 1980.

Bruce Springsteen, *Nebraska*, Columbia, 1982.

Bruce Springsteen, *Born In The USA*, Columbia, 1984.

Bruce Springsteen, *Live 1975–1985*, Columbia, 1986.

Bruce Springsteen, *Tracks*, Columbia, 1998.

Bruce Springsteen, *The Rising*, Columbia, 2002.

Bruce Springsteen, *Magic*, Columbia, 2007.

Bruce Springsteen, *Wrecking Ball*, Columbia, 2012.

Bruce Springsteen, *Chapter and Verse*, Columbia, 2016.

Filmography

Howl, dir. Rob Epstein and Jeffrey Friedman, Werc Werk Pictures, 2010.

Kill Your Darlings, dir. John Krokidas, Killer Films, 2013.

On The Road, dir. Walter Salles, MK2 Productions, 2012.

The Wild One, dir. László Benedek, Stanley Kramer Productions, 1953.

INTERVIEW 6: GRAHAM PARKER
Pat Thomas

I've long thought of Graham Parker's music as the missing link between Van Morrison and Elvis Costello – but I also foolishly thought that hiding behind those dark glasses was a man, who like Van Morrison, might be a bit of a curmudgeon. Nothing could be further from the truth! My conversation with Parker in early 2017 flowed easily and, since we were both Kerouac aficionados, we hit it off right away.

While many of you are familiar with Parker's inspired singing/songwriting (both with and without the Rumour), what you may not know is that Parker has recorded several of Kerouac's works – spoken word recordings in collaboration with Jack's buddy, musician David Amram.

Parker reads from Jack Kerouac's unpublished journals 1949–50 on the Japanese version of the Kerouac tribute CD *Kicks Joy Darkness*, produced by Jim Sampas. And on the *Jack Kerouac ROMnibus* (CD-ROM), Graham reads passages from *The Dharma Bums* and *Visions of Cody*, accompanied by David Amram, and there is also an audiocassette of the complete *Visions of Cody* book with original music by Amram.

Many musicians who began recording during the 1970s punk and new wave era had been beatniks and bohemians in their youth; Parker was no exception – and we dug into his 'Lonesome Traveller' roots during our discussion.

PT: I guess I'm going to start with the obvious, which is your first introduction to Kerouac that you remember.

GP: Well, I know a lot of people are experts, quite obsessed and read everything that some writers do, especially these people with Kerouac. I can't say that I am, really, but my introduction to the Beats in general was when I was only about 17 at my first job. There was a guy who fancied himself a bit bohemian. He lent me a copy of William Burroughs' *Junkie*. I'd never taken a drug at this point and I found it very weird and interesting. I think I read *Naked Lunch* and there was one called *The Soft Boys*, was it? Something like that. So, I read a few of those and at some point I guess in the '70s – very early, maybe even late '60s – I knew that there was this guy Jack Kerouac, so I'd read a bit about it. I'd picked up a few hints – you know, this is ancient times we're talking about here, when it was hard to find things out very easily. Because the whole, I guess, hippie thing was starting to come in, that those people were getting onto the radar of this next generation of bohemians as it were. So I picked up this book, I'm sure in a little bookstore, a paperback of Jack Kerouac's *Lonesome Traveler*. I read that and that's basically all I read by him. I didn't read *On the Road*. As far as poetry's concerned, I found it incomprehensible – whoever it's by. It doesn't do it for me. I've never even read Ginsberg's 'Howl'. I've seen clips of him reading from it, I think. It's never appealed to me but I loved this novel to pieces. It's only much later that I read that it was basically a bit cobbled together. It wasn't a novel that he wrote in one go. I read something like that – I'll have to back up and check on that to see. It wasn't like *On the Road*, which he wrote as a novel like *The Town and the City*. I think it was maybe some publishing idea … but anyway, to me, it flowed beautifully and I just loved [the] romantic idea, the railway earth and travelling somewhere with very little, getting jobs in exotic places, like working on the trains and cooking for himself with a little skillet in a tiny garret somewhere in San Francisco. I thought it was just a marvellous idea and because I was, by then, a certified freak, a hippie, and I'd left home by the time I was just about 18, I went to a place called Guernsey in the Channel Islands, spent some time there, hung out with freaks and listened to music of the times. Then I went back to England, did various jobs and then I was only about 20 or 22 when I went off to Paris. Got on the ferry and went to Paris with the backpack on, the guitar, got into playing and fingerpicking. I was really trying to learn to play properly, which I'd never actually done before despite the interest. So, I was developing that kind of artistic side of myself and it was starting to look like something, like it might go somewhere someday, you know. I got my first record deal when I was 25, I suppose, in 1975. Kerouac's book was very much part of that for me. I just felt that whole *Lonesome Traveler* thing. Hitchhiking to the ferry I took from Paris. I don't know whether I had a frying pan with me, but I might have done. [*Laughs*]. It was just fantastic. What I was doing is going to Paris; I stayed there for a while – very much with no money. Very, very little money – I'd just saved little bits, and found my way through Spain. It was just interesting going south of France by hitchhiking, maybe taking a train when I could afford it. I'd hitchhike and find myself in the middle of nowhere because the guy had to turn off somewhere else and then point off south to Spain, that way, and I'd sleep on the edge of the road. I woke up once on what turned out to be a triangle in the middle of a highway. It was empty at night, pitch black, and I just found some grass, put my sleeping bag there, woke up covered in snails to the sound of trucks roaring right next to me. So I did all those kinds of things and then I ended up in Morocco. Talk about the fellaheen, beatnik world. There it was: Morocco. I'd known that Burroughs had gone and it was part of the Marrakesh Express; you'd go there to smoke a lot of dope, basically. The idea of sitting with old blokes, Moroccans, and smoking with a clay pipe, you know? Very, very cheap pot. I didn't have much money there, and then when I ran out people said, 'Go to Gibraltar', which was a short ferry ride. I went there, found myself a place to crash, found a room full of bunks, which some slumlord was selling for a few shillings and I got a job on the decks. So it was very much a part of that, very much living the Kerouac dream, in a way. It was influential in that respect, and I was writing some songs that were a bit hippie, you know, they weren't quite right. They were a bit flowery and all that stuff but I could tell that some of the melodic structures were good. It was very much that *Lonesome Traveler* thing, on the road, so I think it must have had quite an influence in that respect.

Basically, that's it until much later in the '90s, I think, I met Jim [Sampas] who told me his history and the Kerouac connection and then he would put these productions on where I would go somewhere to Boston or somewhere and do a reading of Kerouac. The next thing I know, there were a lot of people like the Poetry Association getting hold of me and [asking], 'Can you read some poetry?' and I was like, 'I'm sorry, I'm just not into it.' I'd read one book by Kerouac, that's it, you know? I'd be back doing things, I did one at Town Hall with Ginsberg, Odetta, Thurston Moore, the usual suspects were all there. It was a grand night – Town Hall in New York. I didn't really know anything about David Amram whatsoever. I did not have any deep history, but Jim put me together with him and I found out about his history and went, 'Wow, that is impressive.' He'd actually played on stage with Kerouac. I mean, he really was there when that stuff was going on, the *Pull My Daisy* thing and all that. At some point, I think Viking put out a new edition of *On the Road* and finally I read the classic. It took me a long time; it was probably whenever they re-released that new edition. Because of the work I'd done with the spoken word of *Visions of Cody*. I think it was on cassette. There you go, I mean, somebody had just edited that. There was a paper in front of me, David and I would be in the studio and I would just sort pick out a way that I was going to read something, whether it was kind of a speed rap jive approach or a very slow, kind of melancholy approach, and he would find an instrument that worked and we'd do it in one take usually.

PT: Well, that's very Kerouac right there. You probably know the phrase, 'First thought, best thought'.

GP: Yes. Absolutely. If you can get the first take with music, with a song ... wow, it ain't going to get better. You try it again and you go, 'Nope, that ain't better.' We were very in sync with it. You know, I remember I felt like I was hanging on by my fingernails as I'm speed rapping something. Somehow we got through every piece and I don't remember stopping halfway through or anything, I don't remember doing that.

PT: I'm going to hit the rewind button and go back to your early journeys. I assume you're talking early '70s when you're cruising through Paris and Morocco?

GP: Yes, well, basically. I know it was '71, I believe, or '72 even – don't quote me. When I was there, there were these riots going on, marches, Angela Davis. I think that might have been '71 or '72 because years later I looked it up trying to figure out when did I do all these things ... I did not keep notes really well. Guernsey, that was about '68. I was turning 18 maybe when I'd just left home. I don't know whether I'd read Kerouac's book then. It might have been before the next trip. I came back to England and I think that's when I probably found it, probably '70 or something in a bookstore somewhere when that was actually released. These things get hazy but we're talking about a period from about '68 up to '73 perhaps when I was doing that, and then I came back to England and stayed at my parents' house and said, 'That's it for travelling, I'm not going to do it again until I get paid,' which was an incredibly rash statement but what it meant was is that now you're going to write songs, you're going to get a record deal and you're going to be famous so when you travel you're going to be getting paid to do it. So, somehow it worked, strangely. [*Laughs*] That's the time period we're talking about.

PT: I want to run this by you. Years ago I interviewed Ginsberg and we were talking about how there's a direct lineage from the Beats to the hippies to the punks, right? That it's a countercultural thing and one of the things that I found interesting is when you and Elvis Costello, Joe Jackson, the Sex Pistols – when you guys all sort of exploded on the scene within a year or two of each other, it was interesting to find out many years later that many of you had been, in fact, hippies.

GP: Absolutely, yeah, I was primo freak. I did whole acid trips and was healthy to someone, probably – mentally healthy, anyway – but managed to come out the other end of it. But absolutely – I had the hair . . . that's it. The travel thing was part of the freak idea and of course, there it was, we knew our predecessors were the Beats. They experimented with drugs, they got into meditation, they'd got their Eastern philosophies, they were doing that in, what, the '50s? Yeah. There you go. Totally different from my life in the '50s growing up. I was born in 1950. I was born in London but was only there for four years and grew up in the suburbs, so it was just a fascinating idea. It was nonconformity. That's what being a hippie was, it was . . . nonconformist and you gravitated toward an interest in Buddhism, and I'd got Jack Kerouac. There you go. You gravitated toward those things. They just seemed to be part of that freak culture. I don't think there were many freaks who didn't know William Burroughs or Jack Kerouac at least by name, on some level, or had read some of their works. Those books were circulated and it was very much that that precedent was there and we just fell into our own version of it, which came from the Beatles, and suddenly *Sgt. Pepper* and all those kinds of things . . . Jimi Hendrix, and the psychedelic thing. So yeah, definitely, the hippie thing was very much part of me before I reinvented myself once again and cut my hair brutally short and found myself singing music that was very un-hippie, in a way, my first records. Nobody seemed to know: they wouldn't have guessed the lineage.

PT: That's what I mean! It was fascinating to me to find out that many singer-songwriters of your generation – to us, we'd thought you guys sort of formed out of a hat two days earlier. We didn't realize that, oh no, these guys were listening to the same hippie rock that everybody else was five years ago but now they're doing – whatever we'd call it, new wave or punk or whatever, doesn't really matter – but you know what I mean.

GP: Yeah, I mean, I'd lay on the floor with the other cats in the room, stoned, tripping, whatever, listening to Floyd, Santana, even something very – must've been more like punk than punk – there wasn't punk then, per se, it wasn't a general type of music that we knew, of course, but this band – what was his name? David Peel?

PT: Oh, David Peel, yeah. I want to switch topics for a minute. To me, there's always been a very American influence in your music – you know, R&B, soul. Let's talk about that for a few minutes, about the Americanism, jazz and soul in your songwriting.

GP: Well, before even the Stones or the Beatles came along, we'd have the stereogram, this giant, beautiful wooden thing and you'd hear, even then, most of it was American music in the shape of Doris Day and Bing Crosby – classic songs like that. A lot of that stuff had a jazz feel to it and what really set me off and the people of my age group was that in 1962 I was 12 and in late '63 I was 14, the Beatles and the Stones. Some of my older cousins and their generation, Elvis Presley were more in their era and Buddy Holly, I guess – which I kind of liked. You'd hear it on the jukeboxes in the cafe, but it didn't really relate to me. When the Beatles and the Stones came, it was like now we've got our own music, our own bands and our own look. This is the stuff for us. The Stones' first album, in those days my parents could only afford one album now and again, and you went – just like in the hippie days – you went to other people's houses and listened to their albums and brought yours with you. You'd do things like that – it was before drugs and all that stuff – but it was the same kind of idea. Not everybody could buy every record because it was working class. The Stones album, for instance, the very first one, it's a history lesson. I was probably aware of a bit of Southern music and a bit of blues because in England, blues artists were revered, even in the '60s. Even before the Stones and the Beatles, I had people who were friends of mine, art college kids, and I hung out with them and they had a Sonny Bill Williamson record. It was like something from another planet. It was really the Stones where you looked at the credits on the Stones album and there's all these writers, 'Who is this C. Berry guy? Who's he?' Then there was the radio where you could pick up, only occasionally in the car, Radio Luxembourg or Radio Caroline, those pirate stations coming in and you'd hear Chuck Berry, you would hear Little Eva. Then radio opened up with the BBC Radio 1, which was a very tight playlist, very limited, but still, if the Four Tops had a hit, you'd hear it. It was, to me, that's where the Stones and Beatles came from. The Beatles were doing 'Please Mr. Postman', 'Twist and Shout', I mean, these guys didn't pull it out of nowhere! They had the same precedents. They were going to the Liverpool docks, the sailors were coming in with 45 singles of these acts and Mick Jagger was writing to Chess Records sending cheques or money orders and getting records. By that time, we had more record stores, our generation, so we could go and you'd just look through the racks – 'Can I afford this Lightnin' Hopkins record?' In the suburbs, even when I was 16, you could go and see Sonny Terry and Brownie McGhee in some cobble street town nearby, very nearby where I grew up in the county of Surrey. If you'd go to Guildford or somewhere like that or Woking, you'd see these kind of acts. I mean, the British blues bands came along, which I was very, very into – obsessed with – Peter Green, Chicken Shack, all those acts, John Mayall. That became a very fashionable thing, so I hadn't got into the freak music until I left home and everybody was listening to this incomprehensible music. We'd figured out that you've got to take this psychedelic stuff to understand it and you did and suddenly you became … 'Oh, okay, this is the stuff.' I couldn't listen to 12-bar blues or soul music for years. I couldn't stomach it! It sounded unbearably straight.

PT: One of the things that's great about Kerouac's writing, as you know, is that he captures the beautiful simplicity of having a breakfast in an American diner. The bacon, the eggs, obviously the road … so let's talk about the first couple of times you came to America, because you were suddenly seeing all these things that you had thought about. What was that like for you?

GP: Yeah, well, as I said, by then I was a musician, a professional, so it was an airplane, a rental van with the band in the back of the station wagon, touring and we stopped at all those places. I suppose – I can't remember distinctly, but I'm sure I thought, 'This is it, the Railroad Earth!', and we'd be in some very Beat places. I would even remember travelling across some part of America and it was like forest, it was beautiful, and there was some kind of restaurant that looked like a shack. We went in there and there were basically benches. There were American Indians, what they call Native Americans. Native Americans were in there eating and they were eating Mexican food, it was tacos. I was introduced to that kind of food and I remember afterward I was at a gig in New York, The Bottom Line, going out with Martin [Belmont], the guitarist for the Rumour, and we found some diner that just seemed to be a straight strip of chairs and you sat at the counter and there's these hotplates and they're whipping out the egg. I had one of the best burgers I've ever had – maybe because I was stoned or I'd done the gig and it was one of those munchies things at three in the morning – and it was full of cab drivers. There were all these Beat cab drivers and there I would definitely have remembered Kerouac and thought, 'Wow, I'm doing it – but I'm getting paid to do it!' [*Laughs*]

PT: Do you think your writing or your lyrics started to change once you came to America?

GP: Well, if you listen to *Howling Wind*, the first album, that was made before I'd gone to America, I believe. We did two tours in '76, that came out April in '76, so it's a good deal before new wave and punk exploded, you know? It was there in the music press and they were writing about CBGBs. There were people – writers – who didn't really like me much, they thought I was too old school music, they liked this punk thing happening at CBGBs and they relentlessly pushed it, but it didn't get any real play. But then the Ramones came over and, you know, that whole thing was building and it was mid-'77 when that hit. So I had like a year and a half where I had already established myself. I was playing theatres and all that kind of stuff but I suppose, yeah, going to America it would have been 'Yeah, you've got to do that. You've got to do it.' My manager, Charles, said, 'We've got to get you over there really quickly before other people are copying you.' That's literally what he said: 'There's going to be people copying you. We gotta get there.' So we went there very quickly, twice in '76, before there were going to be people allegedly copying me who went there. Basically, the people who came after me learnt from my mistakes probably. We were on Mercury Records and they had no other market for me and the Rumour. New wave and punk weren't a happening thing and in America the radio never really let punk catch on.

PT: I meant more like, for example, you've written a zillion songs before you've ever been to America, right? But then, as you start to tour America, maybe consciously or subconsciously, you're lyrics are now more perhaps influenced or inspired by the American landscape?

GP: Yeah, it's possible. It's possible. Again, because of the music that we listened to and I was obsessed with soul and all that stuff as I was writing my best songs, the songs that became *Howling Wind*, I was listening to all kinds of things but a lot of it came from that. I think America might have kicked it up even harder because *Heat Treatment*, the next record, came out – and I had already done one tour before that came out, maybe even two tours – I don't know the exact date, came out October '76, the same year. By then I was very into America – the idea of it and spending more time there. As a writer, it was very hard for me to look at it and say, 'Well, it was definitely because I was somewhere geographically.' I mean, one record I can say, geographically I was in upstate New York in a house with acreage and a barn and I'd go in the barn and I'd be writing songs and there'd be a deer outside my window and my daughter running by with a butterfly net and I'd write 'The Kid with the Butterfly Net' and that was in 1991 on a record called *Struck by Lightning*. That was really inspired by 'real' America but not in the way you might think, not in any tough, kind of street way because they would say things to you like, 'You're like Springsteen, aren't you? You're, like, streetwise, right?' and I was like, 'Well, I really like my mall – more like hotelwise, really!' A really long time ago I was on the street a bit more but now I'm protected. So there were some records like that but that's not in the way you think. It's not in the way that I was influenced by soul music more by being in America – I'd already got that. That was there already. I'd already had that bit, deep pot to draw water from.

PT: Well obviously at some point you move to Woodstock, you move to America, right?

GP: Yeah, I was kind of six months there, six months here, actually, with some holidays in between. It was still a bit of each. The place I'm in now in London, I've had since 1979. It was always back and forth, back and forth. One of the few things I did right was keep a place in London in a very upscale part of London, which is very lucky of me. But still, I'm renting a place in upstate New York in the country. I love the country and I did spend an awful lot of time in New York City and did have a loft there, one of those 2,000-square-foot spaces, brought an architect in and, you know, I had my first kid who was born in New York. She also went to kindergarten in England. It was very back and forth. Obviously, very privileged, I mean, as soon as I signed a record deal I became a very privileged person. It just is, it comes with the territory and I was very lucky, in fact, that record companies always kept you on for four albums even if you didn't become a megastar.

PT: That was the good ol' days.

GP: It was beautiful, man, my albums sold. My first accountant, who I'm still friends with, said to me the other day, 'God, you should have seen the cheques that came in,' because I wasn't paying much attention. I never knew I had money. 'You should have seen the cheques!' I mean, I was supposed to be a flop as a commercial artist. He said, 'Oh my God, those cheques that came in . . .' He sent figures to me and it was like, 'Holy shit!' Not quite the flop they still write me off as. It was a privileged time. And the '80s would give me even more silly amounts of money. I was supposed to be well finished by the '80s. In England, it's true I wasn't very popular, but America always stayed with me, the fans always stayed with me, even when I left the Rumour and made those albums. They didn't do it as bad as people feel and I'd tour and the places were packed. It was a wonderful thing, really. America has been great to me. You can't do an awful lot of solo gigs in England without wearing thin quickly. America is huge and some years I would do up to eight or ten gigs in a year in New Jersey alone, playing solo in all these little places I missed when I was with the band and, in some of them, I actually played with the band as well. It was very much the American idea of things has been very supportive for me. I guess it's there in the music; people know where it's coming from.

PT: Before we wrap this up, I just want to go back around to the projects that you've done with him for a moment. First thing you did was a Jack Kerouac CD rom and on that one you read from *The Town and the City*, *Visions of Cody* and *The Subterraneans*, and I know, of course, you worked with Amram. Any comments that you can remember from reading from those various, different pieces? Did you study up – did you sit in your room and practise? How did this all come about for you?

GP: Well, I read *The Town and the City* – the whole book – and it was quite a surprise to me. It was very stately and it didn't have what I would consider that frenetic, Beat, Benzedrine speed jive thing and it showed me the breadth of Kerouac's talent. Jim [Sampas] introduced me to these things. *The Subterraneans*, that was much more street stuff, wasn't it? *The Town and the City* was so stately and 'a very nice novel', but beautiful in its atmosphere – Lowell, Massachusetts, I seem to remember in it. So I did read some stuff. For *Visions of Cody*, I don't remember if I read the entire book or not. I had enough background to know that 'Cody' was that complete nutcase – what was his name?

PT: Neal Cassady.

GP: Yeah, Cassady.

PT: One of the things that's interesting about *Visions of Cody* – we're gonna geek out here for a moment – is that it's kind of an addendum to *On the Road*.

GP: Yeah, Cassady was in that, wasn't he, with a different name or whatever? He followed through with him a sort of obsession. He was obsessed with him a bit, wasn't he? He thought, 'This guy is the real deal, right?'

PT: That's right, and let's face it, there's sort of a bromance there, right?

GP: Yes, absolutely, it is. It is 'bromantic'. It made you not quite sure where Kerouac stood with this.

PT: Yeah, there's a little bit of a suggested – well, for lack of a better word – a suggested homoeroticism there, perhaps.

GP: Might well be, yeah. Of course, with Ginsberg, it was sort of open, really.

PT: Yeah, no suggestion. With Ginsberg, it's not suggested, it's open and full on.

GP: With Kerouac, it was one of those things that maybe a young man still not quite sure of his sexuality, or maybe he was 100 per cent heterosexual, but everyone's got a bit of the other chromosome, perhaps, and it was something that was probably lost in time. How Kerouac really felt about it, I don't know.

PT: Lastly, a piece that I've never heard but I think at the Town Hall in New York City you read some journals from '49 to '50 that were used on some Japanese version of *Kicks Joy Darkness*.

GP: Yeah, all these famous people got on the records so I got bumped to the Japanese copy. I think it was vinyl. Once you get Michael Stipe and Patti Smith, GP is gonna get bumped to the Japanese version. I don't know if I've even heard them myself. I remember that I killed it and it was good. It was something about North Dakota.

PT: Right. Well, I will say this: as far as know, you have the distinction of being the only Englishman who has done Kerouac audiobooks.

GP: Really? Isn't that funny. I was telling Jim, when is that going to come out on CD?

PT: It does need to be re-issued because we don't have cassette players.

GP: My fans, they wouldn't have known about it – there was no internet back then. It was not like something you could post on Twitter and on your website. Somebody had a website for me back then, but it wasn't like it is now. If you had a CD or a double CD out of that then, I could really push it for the hardcore fans – it's a hardcore fan thing . . . but they wouldn't know about it!

PT: I agree. For most of us, it would be like it was coming out for the first time.

GP: Yes, absolutely. I hope you can kick Viking Penguin into doing it.

CHAPTER 20
PUNK AND NEW WAVE
James Sullivan

To most who heard the new song, the name was unfamiliar. What exactly were those three drawled syllables? Was the song about a particular make of luxury sedan – a 'Cadillac'? Some heard it instead as an ode to a girl named 'Caroline'.

It had been only six years since Jack Kerouac's death, on 21 October 1969, of abdominal hemorrhaging, the writer having endured a long, slow, agonizing decline. Though his last published piece was a rambling essay for the *Chicago Tribune Magazine* called 'After Me, the Deluge', there was little evidence that Kerouac's influence was still coming down hard. By 1975, when Willie Alexander recorded his first single, 'Kerouac', an unabashed tribute to his favourite writer, many of his fellow performers on the emerging punk scene did not recognize the name.

Thirty-two at the time, already a veteran of a handful of Boston-based bands and a brief stint with a latter-day version of the Velvet Underground, Alexander was several years older than most of his peers in the fetid incubators of the punk scene – the Rathskeller in Boston, CBGBs and Max's Kansas City in New York. The day he took delivery on the first pressing of his debut 45 with his Boom Boom Band (first called, though the record company balked, the Rhythm Assholes) (Van Ness, 2013), Alexander brought the carton to the Brookline party house that was home to his friends in a Boston band called Reddy Teddy. The place, known as the Kilsyth Manor, had a reputation for debauchery. The members of Aerosmith, living at the time in a downmarket apartment building nearby, were regulars. On this day, the New York guitarist Johnny Thunders was in town.

The B-side of the single featured 'Mass Ave', an ode to one of Boston's main arteries, which would soon become Alexander's signature song. The A-side was 'Kerouac', the woozy tribute ballad that addressed the writer's memory as if he were still alive. The song wore its familiarity with and affection for Kerouac's work on its sleeve: 'Like your brother Gerard, whoa, now you're both saints / Let them call you what you want, oh, you ain't what you ain't'.

Thunders, as Alexander recalls, fixated on the line in which the singer tells Kerouac 'You're on the top of my shelf.' The guitarist, a notorious substance abuser, immediately pictured a medicine chest.

'What's that song about – cough syrup?' he asked. To him, the name sounded like a pharmaceutical brand. When Alexander explained the identity of the subject of the song, Thunders replied, 'Oh, he's a writer. Richard Hell would know about that.'

When Richard Hell was a boy of eight, he planned to run away with two friends. Growing up in Lexington, Kentucky, where his father had a job teaching psychology at the university, the boy – Richard Meyers, then – enjoyed the typical suburban upbringing of the 1950s. He played cowboys and Indians; his family took him and his sister to the drive-in movie theatre; once in a while they stood in line at a local amusement park called Joyland.

Mostly, however, he roamed the woods and neighbourhoods with his schoolmates. 'I grew up thinking men worked best in wandering small teams, usually two-man,' the future punk rock performer wrote in his autobiography (Hell, 2013, p. 9). 'You needed someone to conspire with, someone to help you maintain the nerve to carry out your ideas.'

On the night Richard was due to meet his friends at a midnight rendezvous by a cavemouth, to his surprise, his father told the boy he'd be happy to drive. If his friends were there, Richard could go with them.

They packed up Richard's pyjamas and his snacks and drove to the site in the darkness. To Richard's disappointment, the other boys didn't show up. Ernest Meyers drove his son home and tucked him into bed. A few weeks later, Ernest Meyers died of a sudden heart attack. A few weeks after that, his son wrote a story for school based on the night he wanted to run away. The dream he recalled from that night would become the name of his memoir, *I Dreamed I Was a Very Clean Tramp* (2013), years after he'd effectively ended his career in music, the field in which he made his name.

He didn't know it at the time, but young Richard's plan to escape his ordinary life occurred just weeks after the September 1957 publication of Jack Kerouac's *On the Road*, the book that captured the runaway restlessness of a generation of young men and women in post-war America.

Some years later the small Meyers family moved to Virginia. Richard's widowed mother found a boarding school in Delaware where her boy, already showing strong signs of rebellion, could complete his high school studies. There he met a classmate named Tom Miller, someone who might help Richard maintain the nerve to carry out his ideas. They were both 'inner-oriented people who didn't respect much convention' (Hell, 2013, p. 39), and they shared an interest in specific styles of music and writing and in a very wry brand of humour. After serving a suspension during his senior year, Richard returned to class and convinced Tom to join him on the train to Washington, DC. From there, they would hitchhike.

They were gone about two weeks. The travelling, as Richard would write elegantly, was a strong dose of his favorite feeling: 'of leaving myself behind for another world'.

A drug can do it; so can a new type of work, or falling in love, or just changing your appearance; but actually taking off and abandoning all your previous responsibilities and history and relationships is probably the most pure and exhilarating.

Hell, 2013, p. 43

At 17, he had undoubtedly already absorbed the imperative of perpetual motion that defined Kerouac's work.

After being expelled from high school for going missing, Richard moved to New York City, taking a series of odd jobs, as a Macy's stockboy, a cab driver and a bookstore clerk, among others. His old friend Tom Miller eventually moved to New York, and the two began plotting ways to become artists together. As Miller had been playing guitar for years, they settled on starting a rock band. Worried that their given names sounded 'hopelessly banal', they took on stage names. Meyers became Richard Hell, which to him sounded just right: 'assertive but negative without being too specific' (Hell, 2013, p. 119). Miller became Tom Verlaine, after the nineteenth-century French poet. (Hell has claimed he chose his own assumed surname before he and Miller landed on 'Verlaine'; any allusion to Arthur Rimbaud's *A Season in Hell* (1873), he says, is incidental.)

Hell had only rudimentary skill on his instrument, the electric bass, but he heard the tunes in his head, and he could certainly turn a phrase. One of the first songs he wrote for the new band (at first known as the Neon Boys, then Television) was called 'Blank Generation'. Driven by irreverence, it was a kind of parody once-removed – a flippant statement about generational impressions that owed a clear, if sideways, debt to 'The Beat Generation', which was itself a satire. That song was used as the title theme to a 1959 movie of the same name, a noirish crime film set in the 'weird, way-out world of the Beatniks'. The song was written by Rod McKuen, the songwriter and poet who would become a laureate of the middle class a decade later, with kitschy bestselling collections such as *Listen to the Warm* and *Lonesome Cities* (which won a Grammy Award as Best Spoken Word Recording for its album version in 1968). McKuen was also known for his English translations of songs by the Belgian pop singer Jacques Brel, including 'If You Go Away' and 'Seasons in the Sun'.

For 'The Beat Generation', McKuen (credited simply as 'Dor') teamed with a voice actor named Bob McFadden, with whom he'd also released a novelty single called 'The Mummy'. 'I belong to the Beat Generation,' McKuen recited, lingering on the 'beeeeat'. 'I don't let anything trouble my mind.' Though McKuen had performed his own poetry in San Francisco's coffeehouses and wine bars, he peppered the song with cheap jokes about beards, sandals and unemployment cheques – the cartoon effects that turned Kerouac's milieu into an overnight lampoon.

Hell performed 'Blank Generation' with both Television and the Heartbreakers, the band he formed with ex-New York Dolls Johnny Thunders and Jerry Nolan in the spring of 1975. According to Hell, Verlaine owned 'The Beat Generation' single, part of his collection of obscure novelty songs. 'The McKuen thing was an in-joke, a pretty obscure one,' Hell said in a 2013 interview with the UK magazine *Uncut* (Love , 2013). 'No one figured that out for ten years. But my sentiments and attitude were committed. Sometimes people refer to it as like lounge music, tongue-in-cheek. But it wasn't a joke to me.'

Craig Leon, who produced the sessions for the first EP by Richard Hell and the Voidoids, the punk band he formed after parting ways with the Heartbreakers, thought the connection to the Beat Generation made perfect sense: 'I always thought the New York thing in the 70s was a continuation of the Beat thing of the 40s and 50s, so it was very cool for him to take a bad, mass-produced novelty song about the Beat Generation and turn it around into a real anthemic thing,' said Leon, who, as a Sire Records staff producer, helped develop the early careers of the Ramones, Talking Heads, Blondie, and others. 'Richard was always a literary personality, someone who could paint the scene, similar to Kerouac in the 50s' (Love, 2013).

Marc Bell, the drummer who would eventually join the Ramones as Marky Ramone, was the Voidoids' original drummer. In his memoir *Punk Rock Blitzkrieg* (Ramone, 2015), he seconds the notion that Hell was influenced by the Beats. 'Richard had been taken by the rawness of the MC5 and the Stooges,' he writes. 'Lyrically, he was influenced by Jack Kerouac and the Beat Generation that began to emerge with the publication of *On the Road* in 1957. He also loved surrealist art and the decadent movement poems of Arthur Rimbaud and others from the late nineteenth century' (Ramone, 2015, p. 100). If some of their peers were unfamiliar with Kerouac, the Beat legacy was still undeniably alive in New York. When Hell signed a lease on an apartment in an old East Village tenement in 1975, Allen Ginsberg was a fellow resident of the building.

Like Kerouac, Hell was conflicted about representing an entire generation of his peers. He understood certain things about them, but he also understood it was ridiculous to put yourself in such a position. 'I felt like I had this psychological condition in common with my generation, the generation that followed flower children and Vietnam and which just felt overloaded, buzzed out, and with an awareness that honesty is more complicated than other rebellious generations had recognized,' he told the critics Robert Christgau and Carola Dibbell for the liner notes to a compilation of his work (*Spurts*, 2005). 'I did feel that this song was going to resonate with people whom I hadn't actually met yet, maybe they'd come introduce themselves to me. At the same time I knew it was ludicrous to expect people to proudly say "I belong to the blank generation". And that's how it turned out. It's not as if I think people are pretending to like it. They like it, but it's never been an anthem. It's too ambivalent. How can there be an ambivalent anthem?'

In truth, 'Blank Generation' was pure punk in its disdain for meaning. 'I was saying let me out of here before I was even born,' Hell yowls on the song's conversational opening line, as the band swings into a cheap high-hat rhythm that screams insincerity, even as Robert Quine's demented lead guitar sounds like the desperation of a choking victim. The chorus makes a declaration – 'I belong to the Blank Generation' – and then undermines it in the next breath: 'I can take it or leave it each time.'

Hell left it as often as he took it. Despite his formative influence on two of the most noteworthy bands of the American punk and new wave era – Television and the Heartbreakers – he left virtually nothing in the way of recordings with either. He parted ways with Sire Records months after the release of *Blank Generation*; the Voidoids would release one more album, five years later, called *Destiny Street*.

In the early 1990s, Hell did some recording with a group calling themselves Dim Stars, including guitarist Don Fleming and two members of Sonic Youth, Thurston Moore and Steve Shelley, with additional contributions from Quine, the Voidoids' exceptional, radical guitarist. For the past few decades, Hell has identified as a writer more than a musician. His junkie novel *Go Now* (1996), in which an alter-ego, Billy Mudd, drives across America in a 1957 DeSoto, was favourably compared to Irvine Welsh's *Trainspotting* (1993). Billy's 'sordid plunges' into sex, drugs and betrayal, wrote one critic, were 'rendered in a slit-eyed dryness worthy of Burroughs' (Hell, 1996).

In 1997, Hell was one of dozens of artists who took part in a marathon reading of *On the Road* to mark its 40th anniversary at the St Mark's Poetry Project, including Rick Moody, Taylor Meade and Joyce Johnson, one-time Kerouac paramour and author of *Minor Characters* (Hoban, 1997). Over the years Hell has tangled periodically with his literary influences, which, he suggests, ran more to the French Symbolists but undoubtedly included the poets of the post-war twentieth century.[1]

Hell got to the heart of his thoughts for Kerouac in typically roundabout manner in a piece he wrote on the late rock critic Lester Bangs for the *Village Voice* in 2003. In the essay, he considered the 'first thought-best thought' style of writing that Kerouac espoused (his 'bop prosody') as it manifested in the criticism of Bangs, a California native born in 1948 who was ready-made for the punk era. A hard drinker who adopted industrial, blue-collar Detroit as a second home during his years with *Creem* magazine, Bangs was part of the group of writers who first began using the term 'punk rock' to describe the hard rock bands of the early 1970s. When Kerouac died, Bangs wrote an appreciation for *Rolling Stone*, calling him 'a spiritual father of us all, as much as Lenny Bruce or Dylan'. He noted that Kerouac's generation of hipsters did not, in fact, epitomize 'cool'; instead, they ran hot, representing 'the apotheosis of American individualism and rascally exuberance' (in George-Warren, 1999, pp. 140–2).

Bangs and Kerouac seemed to share a specific trait, Hell wrote. They both became insufferable drunks in person. It was the writer's work, not the man himself, that you befriended.

Admitting that his distaste for Bangs while he was alive may have been 'that of the junkie for the lush', Hell characterized him as 'sweet like a big, clumsy puppy'. Bangs, who died of an accidental overdose of prescription pills and Nyquil in 1982, was a 'big, swaying, cross-eyed, reeking drooler … trying to corner me with incessant babble somewhere in the dark at CBGBs' (Hell, 2003). But as a writer, Bangs shared an appeal with Kerouac: 'that innocence and goodwill and drive to describe and be true to what matters in life. People like a writer's writing because they like the writer's company.' Hell continued, 'Writing is intimate and finally what draws you to an author's work is the shape of the mind and quality of feeling you find there, and Lester, like Kerouac, reads like a real good friend to a lot of people.'

Jim Carroll was barely a teenager when a mentor, the poet Ted Berrigan, took the young writer to visit with Kerouac, in Maine. The wan young New York City street kid, declared the King of the Beats, wrote better prose 'than eighty-nine percent of the novelists working today' (MacAdams, 2009).

He also wrote poetry. Some years later, when Kerouac died in 1969, Carroll took out his notebook and dedicated a poem to him. He called it 'Highway Report':

> *Kerouac is dead at 47*
> > *on radio*
> *and McCartney alive*
> > *(we lost)*   *and*
> *tragedy's just that and what to do but keep on going all in one line*

It's part of every man's dream, he continued,

> *to rise to the sky . . . to die, gone forever from*
> *American highways, where I nod today, missing nothing*
> *really . . . to disappear . . . at least for a time*
>
> *this clear October day.*

Carroll, 1993, pp. 69–70

By high school, Carroll was – as Kerouac had been – a prized athlete, an all-city selection as a basketball star. But he was also a secret heroin user. Hustling for dope money, he spent years working on *The Basketball Diaries*, the unflinching memoir about his double life that he would publish officially, to great acclaim, in 1978. 'There ain't much time left, you're born out of this insane abyss and you're going to fall back into it, so while you're alive you might as well show your bare ass,' as he once reasoned (Carter, 2009).

It was Berrigan, a fellow product of Irish Catholic culture who considered himself a late-period Beat writer, who inspired Carroll's best-known work. Berrigan had a poem called 'People Who Died', in which he recited a litany of friends, family and idols whom he'd lost, and the methods by which they succumbed: his father, his grandfather, his best friend's big brother (in combat in Korea), and two high school friends (in separate car crashes), as well as Frank O'Hara ('hit by a car on Fire Island, 1966'), Woody Guthrie ('dead of Huntington's Chorea in 1968') and Kerouac: 'died of drink & angry sickness . . . in 1969' (Berrigan, 1994, p. 56).

To try to outrun his heroin addiction, Carroll moved in the mid-1970s to Bolinas, a bohemian Northern California community. Poets made up a considerable portion of the local populace. At one point, Carroll lived in a cabin on property owned by Robert Creeley; in 1985, the poet Richard Brautigan would take his own life at his home there. In Bolinas, Carroll had written some poems with the idea of offering them as lyrics to rock musicians. When Patti Smith, his friend and one-time lover, brought him along to a gig in San Diego, a missed connection with an opening act led her to introduce Carroll onstage as 'the guy who taught me how to write poetry', with her own band backing him (Carter, 2009). Soon he was colluding with the members of a San Francisco band known as Amsterdam to form the Jim Carroll Band. They landed a recording contract with Atlantic Records with the support of the Rolling Stones' Keith Richards. The memorably colour-enhanced cover photograph of their debut album, *Catholic Boy* (1980), of the lanky Carroll with his arms slung around the shoulders of his parents, both of them looking bemused in overcoats, was taken by celebrity photographer Annie Leibovitz.

The Jim Carroll Band would eventually fulfil a three-album contract with Atlantic, following *Catholic Boy* with *Dry Dreams* (1982) and *I Write Your Name* (1984). The final album featured a cover of Lou Reed's 'Sweet Jane' and backing vocals by a number of guests, including the poet Anne Waldman, who helped found the Jack Kerouac School of Disembodied Poetics at the Naropa Institute in Boulder, Colorado. Waldman and Carroll had become friends, and over the years he occasionally travelled to Boulder to teach writing at the school.

Carroll's deep connection to Kerouac's work continued late into his life. In 1997, long after he'd effectively retired from his rock'n'roll career, he appeared on the tribute compilation *Kicks Joy Darkness*, performing the brief *Pomes All Sizes* piece 'Woman' with backing from Patti Smith Band guitarist Lenny Kaye and Sonic Youth's Lee Ranaldo. In 2003, Carroll appeared on an audiobook recording of *Doctor Sax and the Great World Snake*, a previously unpublished screenplay adaptation of Kerouac's mystical novel *Doctor Sax*. Other voice artists who contributed included Robert Creeley, Lawrence Ferlinghetti, Graham Parker and Grateful Dead lyricist Robert Hunter.

Carroll died at age 60 in September 2009, reportedly while sitting at his desk. A year later, Viking published his long-gestating novel *The Petting Zoo*, which tells the story of Billy Wolfram, a New York artist who suffers a breakdown brought on by his reaction to a museum exhibit of the Baroque portraiture of the Spanish painter Velazquez. Hell, who had occasionally shared stages with Carroll, both of them reading from their poetry – in a joint appearance in 1996 in Central Park, for instance, called 'Punks in the Park', and gigs in Boston and Toronto the following year – reviewed the book for the *New York Times*. Hell noted that the first small-press edition of *The Basketball Diaries* included a disclaimer that was conspicuously absent from later editions: the diaries were 'as much fiction as biography', Carroll wrote. 'They were as much made up as they were lived out. It all happened. None of it happened. It was me. Now it's you. "Nothing is true; everything is permitted".'[2]

Carroll was one of the great poets, Hell writes (others, he suggests, include 'Col. Tom Parker, Guillaume Apollinaire, Josef von Sternberg'). However much Carroll embellished his own legend, 'it beat working', Hell concludes. 'He lived in his head. Doesn't everyone? The difference is that he knew it.'

Hell recalled an excerpt from the work-in-progress which Carroll had presented in a staged reading, thrillingly, more than 20 years before his death. Though the passage was apparently cut from the finished version of *The Petting Zoo*, for Hell, it was critical to Carroll's story. In the vignette, Wolfram is riding a bus in the rain, sitting next to a young man who claims he's a writer. How many people have you disappointed? Billy Wolfram wants to know.

The kid thinks a moment, then replies, 'I'll say eight. Eight people'.
Billy gazes back. 'I've disappointed thousands', he says. 'Literally thousands'.

Willie Alexander first read *On the Road* as a teenager, upon its publication in 1957. 'And it just hit me,' he says. 'It coincided with what I was getting out of the radio at the time, jazz and rock'n'roll. I was totally into the music, and Kerouac was writing very excitingly about the music that was exciting me. I went through phases, Dixieland to swing to bebop. I could dig it. I wanted to play drums at the time, and I understood his concept of being like a horn, improvising, blowing.'

His family had an upright piano, and Alexander wanted to play like an Errol Garner, or a Thelonious Monk. Rehearsing Afro-Cuban jazz with some friends, he decided he needed a stage name, and quickly settled on calling himself Willie Loco. 'It turned out to be perfect for punk rock, because with a name like "Loco", you can do anything,' he would later recall (Van Ness, 2013).

In the mid-1960s, having dropped out of art school in Boston, he joined a friend at Goddard College in Vermont, where the music department had plenty of pianos, and his interest shifted from Latin jazz to the pounding rock'n'roll of Little Richard, Jerry Lee Lewis and Fats Domino. Though Alexander was leading a bohemian lifestyle, he didn't think of himself as a beatnik. 'Being called a beatnik was like being called a hippie [would soon be] – I didn't like that, either,' he says. 'Those were just categorizations.' Yet he devoured every new Kerouac book as it became available. 'I knew when you went to somebody's house and you saw a Kerouac book, you were friends,' he says. It was an instant bond.

Alexander formed his first band, the Lost, at Goddard, and they quickly became part of the emerging music scene in Boston, dubbed the 'Bosstown Sound' by record companies in search of the next geographical breeding ground. The Lost released three singles with Capitol Records, a relationship that led to touring opportunities as an opening act for James Brown, Sonny and Cher and the Beach Boys. When Capitol dropped the band in 1967, Alexander assembled another Boston band, this one called the Bagatelle. That led to an invitation to join the late-period Velvet Underground, a band that had made Boston a second home; as VU members John Cale, Lou Reed and Sterling Morrison departed, they were replaced in turn by Boston scene colleagues Doug Yule, Walter Powers and Alexander. That group would tour behind Yule's music for the final Velvet Underground studio album *Squeeze* (1973).

Alexander parlayed that disappointing experience into his defining role as an originator of his home city's punk-era scene. Willie 'Loco' Alexander and the Boom

Boom Band were a staple of the heyday at the Rat, and the bandleader's high-spirited, hard-drinking performances were heavily influenced by the nearly forgotten writer from nearby Lowell. Just as Kerouac claimed that his late brother Gerard was guiding his hand as he wrote, Alexander learned to turn off his editing mind and let the words – what he would come to call his 'Holy Babble' – flow.

'You just have to learn to trust,' he says. 'That's part of the rules I may have learned from him.' One of Kerouac's 'Essentials for Spontaneous Prose', he points out, is to remind yourself (sometimes in the face of conflicting evidence) that you're a genius all the time. The advice has served Alexander well.

In 2000, Alexander contributed a soundtrack, alongside the 'cool jazz' alto saxophonist Lee Konitz, to *Lowell Blues: The Words of Jack Kerouac*, a 30-minute tone-poem by Gloucester, Massachusetts, filmmaker Henry Ferrini. The short film now screens daily in the National Historical Park in Kerouac's hometown. More recently, Alexander recorded an album based on the poems of Vincent Ferrini, the filmmaker Henry's late uncle, who was a friend and foil to the poetry titan Charles Olson and the long-time poet laureate of their shared city of Gloucester.

Late in life, Kerouac twice travelled to Gloucester to visit with Olson, who'd once called him the country's finest writer. It was a pilgrimage of sorts. 'Olson and Kerouac would argue over the implications of residence and mobility,' as Iain Sinclair, the British author of *American Smoke: Journeys to the End of the Light* (2013), once said in a lecture, 'the great American neurosis about the daunting scale of the place where they found themselves, between Atlantic Ocean and the always difficult but seductive draw of the West' (Sinclair, 2013).

Jim Carroll went west, then returned to New York. There, as Kerouac did, he continued to grapple with his legacy as an East Coast 'Catholic boy' seeking the creative divine. Richard Hell still lives in the same building he moved into more than 40 years ago, when Ginsberg was his neighbour (Myers, 2013), still 'leaving [him]self behind' by means of art, new types of work and the constant urge to go, in whatever form that may take. Willie Alexander returned to Gloucester to live decades ago, the place where his family had owned a home when he was a boy, and he has remained there ever since, rummaging, as Kerouac did, his New England roots. For each of these artists, each influenced in his own way by the 'subterranean' Beat author, punk iconoclasm only meant another form of transcendence.

Notes

1. In his autobiography, he admits being embarrassed by his youthful passion for the poetry of Dylan Thomas: 'He was so overwrought and "poetic" . . . [w]hereas the New York poets I eventually came to love were wiseass goofs and collaging phraseologists, adorers of everyday details, never taking themselves too seriously' (Hell, p. 47).

2. That phrase inspired the title of one of the songs on *Catholic Boy* (Hell, 2010).

Bibliography

Berrigan, Ted, *Selected Poems*, New York: Penguin Books, 1994.

Carroll, Jim, *Fear of Dreaming: The Selected Poems of Jim Carroll*, New York: Penguin Books, 1993.

Carter, Cassie, 'About Jim Carroll', 14 February 2009, http://www.catholicboy.com/intro.php (accessed 17 March 2017).

George-Warren, Holly (ed.), *The Rolling Stone Book of the Beats: The Beat Generation and American Culture*, New York: Rolling Stone Press, 1999.

Hell, Richard, *Go Now*, New York: Simon & Schuster, 1996.

Hell, Richard, 'The Right to Be Wrong', *Village Voice*, 12 August 2003, http://www.villagevoice.com/news/the-right-to-be-wrong-6409816 (accessed 17 March 2017).

Hell, Richard, 'Hallucinatory Effects', *New York Times*, 10 December 2010, www.nytimes.com/2010/12/12/books/review/Hell-t.html?_r=0 (accessed 17 March 2017).

Hell, Richard, *I Dreamed I Was a Very Clean Tramp*, New York: Ecco/HarperCollins, 2013.

Hoban, Phoebe, 'The Night; Insomniacs for Kerouac', *New York Times*, 28 September 1997, http://www.nytimes.com/1997/09/28/style/the-night-insomniacs-for-kerouac.html (accessed 17 March 2017).

Love, Damien, 'The Making of . . . Richard Hell & the Voidoids' Blank Generation', *Uncut*, 7 June 2013, http://www.uncut.co.uk/features/the-making-of-richard-hell-the-voidoids-blank-generation-22461 (accessed 17 March 2017).

MacAdams, Lewis, 'Remembering Jim Carroll', *Los Angeles Times*, 16 September 2009, http://articles.latimes.com/2009/sep/16/entertainment/et-carroll16 (accessed 17 March 2017).

Myers, Marc, 'Richard Hell Finds His Peace in East Village Apartment', *Wall Street Journal*, 19 July 2013, https://www.wsj.com/news/articles/SB10001424127887323936404578581993025822864 (accessed 17 March 2017).

Ramone, Marky with Rich Herschlag, *Punk Rock Blitzkrieg: My Life as a Ramone*, New York: Touchstone/Simon & Schuster, 2015.

Sinclair, Iain, 'On the Back of the Elephant: Riding with Charles Olson', 10 January 2013, http://www.iainsinclair.org.uk/?s=charles+olson (accessed 17 March 2017).

Van Ness, Peter, 'Willie "Loco" Alexander', *The Noise*, 27 November 2013, http://thenoise-boston.com/2013/11/willie-alexander/ (accessed 17 March 2017).

Discography

Alexander, Willie and the Boom Boom Band, 'Kerouac', MCA, 1978.

The Jim Carroll Band, *Catholic Boy*, Atco, 1980.

The Jim Carroll Band, *Dry Dreams*, Atco, 1982.

The Jim Carroll Band, *I Write Your Name*, Atlantic, 1983.

Hell, Richard, *Spurts: The Richard Hell Story*, Sire/Rhino, 2005.

Hell, Richard and the Voidoids, 'Blank Generation', Sire, 1977.

INTERVIEW 7: JIM DEROGATIS ON LESTER BANGS

James Sullivan

Jim DeRogatis is the author of six books, including *Let It Blurt: The Life and Times of Lester Bangs, America's Greatest Rock Critic*, a biography of the late, Beat-inspired writer. A long-time rock critic for the *Chicago Sun-Times*, DeRogatis today is co-host of the syndicated radio show *Sound Opinions* and an English teacher at Columbia College, Chicago.

JS: Let's start by talking about Lester's infatuation with Jack Kerouac. How did he come to be a fan?

JD: You have to understand the incredibly strange upbringing Lester had. His mother was a hardcore Jehovah's Witness. The religion is unique among almost all religions in the history of mankind. There is no music in Jehovah's Witness celebrations or gatherings. Whether you're talking about pygmy tribes or the High Church of England, there's always music. Sometimes it's good, like the gospel church in Chicago, and sometimes it's only good at Christmas, like the Catholic Church I grew up in. But the Witnesses believed music was a window to the devil. So Lester grew up with no music, no art, no joy, no blood transfusions, no Christmas celebrations. No mourning of the dead. All these things that Jehovah's Witnesses believed at the time.

But he happened to have a lifeline. When you look at subcultures, often there's someone you need to be your guide, your Beatrice, whether you're joining the Hell's Angels or learning to smoke pot. Nobody knows how to inhale properly until a cool older cousin or a hip friend shows you.

Lester had an older nephew [Ben Catchings] playing the role of the older brother who was cool. He introduced him to comic books. Those were forbidden by the Witnesses – Lester had to hide them under his bed. When they were a little older, they'd go to the drugstore in El Cajon and shoplift records. He was a big fan of free jazz – bop, Coltrane, Coleman, Mingus. *Kind of Blue*. Lester was initiated into these alternative visions, and part of that was Kerouac and the Beats.

Ironically, Ben was never as hardcore a music fan as Lester would become, or as big a fan of the Beats as Lester would become. But that introduction to Kerouac would stick with Lester at age 13, when we all discovered *The Catcher in the Rye* and *On the Road*, right? And Lester went deep, as he did with anything. He was obsessive. When I teach my book in my 'Reviewing the Arts' class, I always point out that many of you may have nieces, nephews, cousins or younger siblings who may have a mom who never lets their kid have anything with sugar. Finally, they get to go trick-or-treating, and what do they do with that big bag of candy? They pig out, right? And I think that's what happened to Lester with Beat literature and music. He was denied these joys in his life, and he was finally discovering them. He lost many comic books – if his mother found them, she'd take them to the garbage furnace in the basement of their apartment complex and burn them. Which only made them sweeter.

He was a huge fan of Burroughs, *Junkie* and then the stranger stuff. He was a big fan of Allen Ginsberg, if a little less – you know, Allen was a little twee at times, but 'I've seen the best minds of my generation', okay, I'm down with that. But most of all Kerouac. I think it was that lust for life, 'Be here now', live-in-the-moment . . .

The other influence in Lester's life was his father, who died young. He burned to death in a fire, just about the most horrible death you could imagine. The mother, of course, did not mourn. If you are one of the 144,000 Jehovah has chosen to get into heaven – from the beginning of time, from Adam and Eve to the present, only 144,000 people, the rest are doomed. Which is not good odds. Basically, 'I'm in this world, I'm fucked, I'm denied all these pleasures. I may get into heaven, but the odds are not that good.' Boy, what a way to grow up.

His father was a drunk, not a religious person. His mother married him as a reclamation project. He was sort of a happy drunk. They'd take drives together and listen to the radio. Dad was a big believer in 'Be here now'. I don't think he was a literate or educated man – he'd done time in the Texas prison system. But one time, they were on a road trip, looking over the smog of southern California. Lester said 'Wow, what's that?' And his dad said, 'Well, I know it's really ugly, but it's also beautiful in a way.' That's kind of a nice encapsulation of that essential Kerouac, Beat, find-the-beauty-in-whatever.

The passages that always stick out to me in Kerouac are riding in the back of a truck, freezing your ass off while hitchhiking, and somebody has a jug of wine, and that's the greatest sip of wine you've ever had in your life. Or *Desolation Angels*, sitting in a lookout tower, watching for forest fires, and that cup of tea you have is the greatest cup of tea in the world. Nine out of ten people might say, 'I'm freezing my ass off, sitting in this tower, looking for something that's not gonna happen. What a shitty job.' For Kerouac and the Beats, the philosophy was, 'I am where I'm supposed to be. This moment is wonderful.'

So I think to have a horrible upbringing, a horrible home life, and to have this other philosophy dangled in front of you . . .

The other thing Lester was attracted to was the language. I had his high school and college transcripts. He was a shitty student. He just wanted to get out. The only thing he cared about was composition. He loved language from the time he was a young boy. The thing with Kerouac, that cool jazz he was listening to – if you go to his famous 'It's beat, it's the beat to keep', where in his prose he's mimicking what he's hearing on the stage in the San Francisco jazz clubs, and the rhythm of his prose is the rhythm of that jazz – I think that's what Lester got from Kerouac. He's loving the music, he's loving the prose. They are one and the same. They're two different artists taking the same approach in their own mediums. And I would contend – and the [Robert] Christgaus and [Greil] Marcuses, the Lester naysayers, or Lester minimizers, would disagree about what Lester was doing – you can say he's high on speed, writing paragraphs that had 450 words, or you can say the rhythm he is mimicking is the new rhythm of the MC5 or the Stooges, the Count Five. And I believe that at his best, that's what he was doing.

Have you ever seen the touring Beat exhibition? It opens with the Kerouac scroll that he famously wrote *On the Road* on, the teletype roll. To see that, that first paragraph, always meant a lot to me. But we forget – he may have written that in a burst of inspiration, but he edited it fastidiously. So Lester may have always written in a burst of speed-fuelled energy, but he cared about every word. He thought about the rhythms, the syntax, the metaphors. It only *looks* like it was blurted out. When you look at that prose and go deeper, as a scholar, an appreciator, or a reader, it's brilliant, and constructed as well as any of the best Beats.

Kerouac was dismissed infamously as 'It's not writing, it's typing.' And what I say to those people is 'Fuck you!' Let us open *On the Road* at random to any one page and read it. And it's poetry. The ending, the last paragraph, 'I look out across the landscape' – I mean, that's beautiful. It's poetry.

JS: Lester wrote Kerouac's obituary for *Rolling Stone*. To what extent do you think he knew what Kerouac's private life had become?

JD: I'm sure he did. He was a voracious reader of both high- and lowbrow culture. He liked gossip columns, and he also read Dostoevsky. I don't think that obituary is a particularly good piece of writing. I don't think it's particularly 'Bangsian'. You have to remember the caveat. As Philip Seymour Hoffman [playing Bangs] tells the young Cameron Crowe in *Almost Famous*, *Rolling Stone* will change what you write. I think much of Lester's writing in two stints for *Rolling Stone* is not Bangsian. It's over-edited, scrubbed of Bangs's prose flair. I don't think that was a piece he was particularly proud of. It doesn't read like Lester to me. It reads more like somebody at *Rolling Stone* who thinks they know more about the Beats because they're still in San Francisco.

JS: Richard Hell once wrote a piece for the *Village Voice* on his thoughts about Kerouac and Lester. He imagines Kerouac to be similar to Lester in that he could be pretty insufferable in person: 'I really miss Lester – not the guy who was a pain in the ass, in my face – but what I miss is the writing.'

JD: I have a couple thoughts on that. Richard Hell, when I interviewed him for my book, had little or nothing to say about Lester. I think that piece in the *Voice* was a revision. Lou Reed had nothing to say about Lester. Patti Smith had nothing to say.

Lester wrote about Lou Reed, that he was a great artist with a tremendous amount of empathy for the people who the rest of society doesn't give a shit about – druggies, addicts, transvestite hookers. But in person, Reed treated Lester like shit. His famous quote was 'I wouldn't shit in his nose.' The fundamental lesson in a long life of writing rock journalism is that 99.9 per cent of the time we should separate the art from the artist. You can be a miserable son of a bitch and make brilliant art. And you can be the nicest human being in the world and make pretty mediocre art. And we shouldn't let those things affect our appreciation of the art.

Lester never learned that. He was forever being deeply disappointed in life by people like Blondie, or Talking Heads. They liked him when he wrote nice things. Patti Smith – he was the best person in the world when he lauded her first album and helped make her a star. But he didn't like *Easter*, so fuck Lester. And I think that's Richard Hell. Lester loved [Robert] Quine and loved 'Blank Generation'. I'm sure if he met Kerouac it would've broken his heart. He met Bukowski, who I consider a latter-day Beat, though we can have a scholarly debate about that. He kind of liked Bukowski, but that's because they got drunk together.

JS: You wrote in your book that *The Subterraneans* actually meant more to Lester than *On the Road*, yes?

JD: Yeah. I don't know why. Probably because there's more music in *The Subterraneans*.

JS: What I remember is him talking about the black girlfriend, Mardou.

JD: Right. Well, Lester grew up perpetually, adolescently horny and completely unfulfilled, and he never progressed in adult relationships with women past the point of a frustrated 13-year-old boy. And he'd be the first to admit it. In fact, he did. Nothing I wrote could be more invasive than anything he wrote about himself, like the Beats. This is where I have a problem with Patti Smith. In her various autobiographical writing, she glosses over much of the difficulty in her life. But the Beats were about warts-and-all honesty, whether it was Burroughs talking about shooting his wife playing William Tell, or Kerouac, to a large degree, did not spare himself reasons for us to think he was an asshole. Kerouac didn't really give a shit about any of us liking him. I don't think any of the Beats did. Lester did the same thing. He'd confess tirelessly his own foibles and failures.

JS: But he wrote about not caring whether you liked him or not, and then in real life he did. He cared.

JD: Of course. I mean, I don't think any artist doesn't. [*Laughs*] They all want to be loved, whether it's a writer like Lester or a musician like Lou Reed or Patti Smith. They can quote verbatim the negative reviews, but the mountains of praise – that's just what's owed to them.

JS: Let me go back to Lester's mother being a Jehovah's Witness. Would it be making too much of the fact that both Lester and Kerouac obviously led shortened lives ruled by strong mothers? And both had arrested relationships with women.

JD: Yeah. I think you're onto something there. I don't think we'll ever know. I hate the school of biography where the writer plays armchair psychoanalyst.

JS: As I just did.

JD: No, no, it's a valid thing to talk about. I interviewed Lester's therapist, who was Joey Ramone's stepdad. He was reluctant to talk specifics but could talk generalities, and when I asked about the relationship with the mother, he pointed out something I'd already realized. Of the millions of words, the most personal, embarrassing failures – talking about his knee-jerk racism, or his priapism, or his angry outbursts at women, some of them violent – he confessed everything in his life, but he never wrote a word about his mother, the Jehovah's Witnesses or his father. What does that tell you? It's something he hadn't resolved. The novel that might've come out of it, that's pure speculation. Or he could have been a drunk. He could've been Nick Tosches or Richard Meltzer, his two closest peers.

JS: Is there a piece of writing of Lester's that strikes you as especially Kerouacian?

JD: You know, basically everything he did for *Creem* is Kerouacian. I would say Bangsian. He captured the fundamental lesson of Kerouac, to capture the energy and rhythm in your prose. I think the early stuff before he got to *Creem* is him trying to do that and not always succeeding – occasionally, but not always. By the time he got to New York, Christgau was a very good influence on him. What we're seeing is a new Lester, more academic in some ways, but still just as energetic. The prose style changes, becomes much more thoughtful, but there's still a lot of that kind of Beat, seemingly stream-of-consciousness. That's to belittle it. Like I said, I think those long passages of high-energy 'blurting' are actually very well thought-out, or then edited and honed. I think the Iggy Pop piece ['Of Pop and Pies and Fun'], and just before that, 'James Taylor Marked for Death', yeah, I think those are prime – if we consider the first-generation Beats, the Holy Trinity of Burroughs, Ginsberg and Kerouac, and then Ed Sanders and Bukowski as the second generation, I think Lester was actually a third-generation Beat.

CHAPTER 21
THE KEROUAC TRIBUTE RECORDINGS
Jim Sampas with Simon Warner

Introduction

When Simon Warner asked me speak about some of the Kerouac-related projects I produced over the years for *Kerouac on Record* I jumped at the opportunity. Not just because I'm proud of these accomplishments – and because they were so much fun to work on – but because I honestly feel, with the benefit of hindsight, that they are worthy of examination for what they show about Kerouac's legacy. Some of them have even become what they call 'evergreens' in the music industry – projects that stay alive and sell well for many years after they were released. As for my part in all of this, I see myself as equally conduit and creator, assisting in facilitating the sublime work of the many artists, recording engineers, actors, composers, musicians, who contributed to these six Kerouac projects, each of which was so lovingly created. As someone once said, 'Surround yourself with the people you admire and you'll GET the best results.'

The projects I'll speak of are: *Kerouac: Kicks Joy Darkness, A Spoken Word Tribute* (compilation album); *Jack Kerouac Reads On the Road* (album); *Doctor Sax and the Great World Snake* (multi-media CD and illustrated book set); *One Fast Move or I'm Gone: Kerouac's Big Sur* (documentary); *Big Sur* (feature film); and *Esperanza: Songs from Jack Kerouac's Tristessa* (compilation album).

Taken together, these projects have expanded and helped to continue the unfolding of a profoundly important author's work. They give us a chance to see his prose and poetry from a fresh perspective, and are a testament to how malleable great art can be. They confirm that if the work has depth, new versions of it – such as a posthumous collaboration with other artists – can be meaningful and produce amazing results. As my buddy Billy Conway of the band Morphine would say, when speaking of trying to make something good out of something mediocre, 'A lousy sandwich is a lousy sandwich.' You can put all the relish and toppings on it you want – in musical terms, reverb, effects, echo, backwards guitars – but it's still going to be a lousy sandwich. No matter what you do you can't transcend the fact that the underlying product is weak. Kerouac's work on the other hand is strong – and remarkable – and each of the Kerouac-related projects I've worked on confirms its power.

I was first introduced to Kerouac by my brother Tony who passed a copy of *On the Road* down to me when I was in my early teens. You see Jack Kerouac was our uncle, married to my father's sister, dear Aunt Stella. Years before, when I was around two, my mom used to bring me and my sister Christine to visit Aunt Stella and her then-reclusive husband Jack Kerouac, back when they were living here in Lowell on Sanders Avenue, across the city in the Highlands. Having been that young I can't remember it now, but according to Tony, on one of those visits when we pulled up to the kerb Jack was outside with arms wide open. My three-year-old sister and I ran over to him across the front lawn and he gave us a big bear hug greeting.

The first experiences that I remember with the poets and writers of the Beat Generation were at the time of Jack's funeral in 1969, when John Clellon Holmes, Allen Ginsberg and others stayed at my parents' house. Holmes wrote about it in his beautiful essay 'Gone In October', an excerpt of which was published in *Playboy* later that year. I was four years old then and do remember Allen hanging out with my brother on the third floor front corner room of our big Victorian home. In fact, Allen made such an impression on me that I drew a picture of him, which my brother Tony still has. For months after, I remember having dreams about Allen Ginsberg landing on our front lawn in a helicopter with an entourage of odd-looking, long-haired friends.

My first foray into producing music came when I was in my early twenties. Writing songs and performing in Boston where I lived, and recording music in various studios both there and in New York. Singing, playing guitar, working with session musicians, experimenting with sounds, was a highlight of my life. This all culminated in a recording session in Woodstock with a pretty amazing crew that, years before, I never would have imagined working with. Notable session players like Jerry Marotta (whom you may know from his work on Peter Gabriel's 'Red Rain' and Marc Cohn's 'Walking In Memphis'), Gary Burke (Joe Jackson's drummer) and Graham Parker, whose most popular album *Squeezing Out Sparks* was recently included in the top 25 albums of all time by *Rolling Stone*.

We recorded that album in a now-legendary recording studio where many popular albums were recorded, including The B-52s' *Cosmic Thing*. My session was sandwiched in between those of the popular Boston act Buffalo Tom and the Dave Matthews Band. What an experience this all was, in my early twenties working with musicians whose music I admired so.

Once my album was finished I started playing the Boston music circuit with a band I had assembled. Auditioning players, networking, working to get gigs in a competitive music scene. Shortly after the release of my album, I landed a gig opening up for one of the most popular Boston bands of the time – Letters To Cleo – in one of the biggest clubs in the area. A highly coveted prime time Friday night slot, with about 300 people in the audience. That gig helped get the album featured in the *Boston Phoenix*, wherein I was fortunate enough to have Brett Milano call me a 'promising writer'.

While living this fun musician lifestyle, in my alternate life I was holding down a day job. My work life was in a place far away from art, where creativity was nearly non-existent. But the skills I learned turned out to be valuable in my development as a producer. As security manager, a big part of my job was to call employees – late at night – and try to get them to fill in for other employees who had called in sick. Trust me, after working a long day for little money, those folks sure weren't happy to be woken up in the wee hours. So I developed some skills at the art of persuasion. And that – along with the hard knocks of going to Lowell High School – become invaluable to me as a producer.

The stakes can be high in artistic endeavours, and everyone is so invested in the outcome. You need to hold a few hands, and sometimes walk people back off a cliff, and be willing and able to also ask tough questions – about a musical performance, or an actor's performance, or an interviewee's delivery. You need to get the very best you can, based on what you feel is right for the project.

Make no mistake, a producer may have creative ideas they wish to implement but first and foremost you are a salesman. You are constantly selling ideas. At first I was selling my music to club managers in Boston. Later it would be to artists and their managers, to agents, lawyers and entertainment companies in Hollywood and New York. You need to know when to push on the pedal and when to let up – both with the company people to whom you are selling your ideas, and with the artists you work with. You are both captain and coach, working to put folks at ease, to inspire them, to lead and sometimes nudge them on, with excitement.

Over the years it's been my pleasure to 'sell' projects I believe in – projects about the Beatles, the Stones, the Cure, Dylan, Nirvana, Bessie Smith, the Smiths. My pitch in general is that with this particular project, I am going to bring credibility to your artist, your actor. The project may be more artistic than commercial. It may not earn them enough money to buy a house, but it will win them a certain kind of respect, on an artistic level, that they won't get for doing something more pop and splashy.

Of course, as a producer you have to believe in what you are selling. And while Kerouac is not known for creating writings with the bankable narrative structure of, let's say, John Grisham or Tom Clancy, we all know that Kerouac is a force to be reckoned with. Artists and musicians can't ignore that. And many agents and managers hold him in high regard themselves.

Even those of us who love his work would agree that not all of his novels should be made into films or song. For me it's been a matter of finding the stories that can be told on the screen or in music, that are filmic or musical, in a true-to-life way. Once the concept of a project has been established then I pitch it to the artists' reps, fostering the idea that their clients' involvement, playing a role in a film and creating a song for our project, will show another side of their talent. A given artist might be seen as risking something by taking on a project that is unusual for them, and if they are looking for longevity in their work they surely have to take some chances. And if you're going to take a chance, it makes sense to take it on something of quality, whether critics approve of your choice or not. Smart films, cerebral music, indie work – this is where creative people can try things and go places that the mass market may not be ready or willing to follow. In the end, critics will either embrace what you've done or reject it, so another attribute of a producer is thick skin. In the end, as Allen

Ginsberg remarked on getting bad reviews, and I'm paraphrasing, 'As long as you spell my name right, I don't care what you say about me.'

Among all the folks I call on in Hollywood there are some who don't know who Jack Kerouac is. But there are a great many who do. And it is often those people who open doors for you – maybe it's an assistant who read *On the Road* in college and tells the agent they work for, 'You really need to look at this.' It's important to get them to understand the cultural significance – that what I'm selling is very different from the usual cookie cutter roles. An agent will only take it to his or her client if the agent believes it will help the client's career in some meaningful way. Agents are the gatekeepers. They decide what the client even sees. And they work on a commission. So if there's very little money and no upside, the gate remains closed. There needs to be a factor lending credibility, or hipness, that will be of value to his or her client, to open that gate. The smart agents understand that keeping their client in the news, including being written about in hip music and film journals, is worth something. And if they have one eye on the bank book and another eye on the kind of prestigious indie awards and accolades that keep their client relevant, they'll take a risk, and get involved with an offbeat project.

Even among the agents who recognize the name Jack Kerouac, many know precious little about his work. Add to that that an agent may be weighing some big pay day project for their actor, and what I'm offering for a small indie feature is a fraction of that. Another project may have a big time director, a major studio, and they anticipate wide distribution. How can my project compete with that? The key is that I need to be able to articulate why my project is different, and steer the focus to its artistic merit and cultural importance.

Kerouac's influence on the arts is key in making my sales pitch. Of course, Kerouac is one of the most influential figures of the last century, and that his influence can be found in people of all walks of life and in every area of the arts. I mean really, would Hunter S. Thompson ever have created 'gonzo journalism' without Kerouac's 'spontaneous prose'? And what would rock lyrics have looked like without Kerouac and Ginsberg? Would the Beatles have spelled their name with an 'a' instead of an 'e' if John Lennon hadn't been reading Allen Ginsberg's poetry? The Doors are on record as saying their music never would have existed without Kerouac. And what of the folks who were influenced by the Doors? If the Doors had never existed, would *they*? And so on.

As for the creation of the projects I'll speak of here, in some ways they followed Kerouac's writing method in more ways than one. Recent scholarship has confirmed that Kerouac's work involved far more discipline than he's been given credit for, that there was tremendous preparation behind his 'spontaneous prose'. In *Mexico City Blues*, he wrote 'I want to be considered a jazz poet blowing a long blues in afternoon jam session on Sunday.' In jazz, even the most seasoned improvisational player looks down at his charts for the framework of the song. And the free-est improvisation is based a profound awareness of the underlying structure. Similarly, Kerouac's lyrical narrative riffs were grounded in a deep understanding of his craft. With words, funny, sad, dark and wild 'in tranced fixation . . . telling the true story of the world in interior monolog.'[1]

And that is the spirit in which we created many of the film and music projects. While there's preparation, for sure, spontaneity is key. In many cases, first and second takes were the only way we could get a project done, given budget constraints. There was no time, or money, for obsessing over a performance. And that's okay; there are also no overblown, overthought performances that make you cringe.

The opportunity to work on Kerouac projects, and find ways to honour his work and help it find new forms, was a wonderful opportunity for me, one I am profoundly grateful for.

Kerouac: Kicks Joy Darkness (1997)

My first internationally released production was *Kerouac: Kicks Joy Darkness*. The idea of doing a spoken word tribute to him occurred to me around 1994, but I had problems coming up with the right approach. I talked to Allen Ginsberg about it, and he was quite gracious in giving feedback and advice. I remember him saying emphatically, 'Stay away from *On the Road*, because it is overdone.' Around that time I started getting into Kerouac's poetry and became completely caught up in the playfulness, simplicity and beautiful rhythmic structure of his 'pomes', as he called them. They were self-contained and perfect for four-to-five-minutes' reading, a factor which sealed the idea for me. I would seek to have the world discover Kerouac's pomes and other more obscure works – like his novel *Visions of Cody* – through the voices of a diverse group of celebrated artists, musicians, poets, actors and writers.

Over the years, so many folks have commented on the musicality of Kerouac's writing. In the same way that jazz influenced Kerouac's aforementioned 'spontaneous prose' method, when he composed poetry he always had rhythm and cadence in mind. We can assume from the recordings Kerouac himself made that he really enjoyed reading the poems, or 'pomes', out loud, and it is surely by design that they flow so naturally when spoken. Like any writer, Kerouac had a strong desire to grab the reader's attention and keep the reader engaged, and I think he understood that the key was not just clever wordplay, but the musicality of the words, whether read aloud or in one's head.

The fact that the pomes have such a natural tempo and beg to be read out loud is yet another example of Kerouac's genius. In imagining *Kicks Joy Darkness* as an album, I saw that the pomes would be like songs, which would match well with the diversity of the many different voices. I was inspired by Kerouac's recordings with great jazz artists Al Cohn and Zoot Sims, who played behind his readings. This approach certainly registered with the contributors. Two of the poet/musicians of the group, Patti Smith and Jim Carroll, would later go on to make his pomes into songs, performing them with their own musical accompaniment.

As I explained the idea of the album to others, I faced much resistance. People would ask, 'Who is going to buy that?' But I knew that hundreds of highly-regarded artists possess dog-eared copies of Kerouac's books, and that his influence has thereby changed our culture. I wanted to create a great celebration of my uncle's work. And I'm pleased to say that *Kicks Joy Darkness* – with Johnny Depp, Allen Ginsberg, Michael Stipe, Eddie Vedder, Steven Tyler, Patti Smith, William S. Burroughs and Matt Dillon – went on to become the second-bestselling album of the biggest indie record label in America: Rykodisc.

Sadly, since we recorded that album, some of the contributors have passed away – Rob Buck, Warren Zevon, Joe Strummer, William S. Burroughs, Allen Ginsberg, Jeff Buckley and Mark Sandman. Rob Buck – the incredibly gifted guitarist for 10,000 Maniacs, who along with Natalie Merchant wrote 'Hey Jack Kerouac' – had a truly unique sound in a world where so many guitarists sound the same. I got to know him a bit. We would hang out at his apartment in East Village, literally across the street from St Mark's Church, the famous gathering station for New York poets. And we'd have long conversations on the phone. He had a comedian's wit – such a joy to hang with, the most positive person I've ever encountered. I spoke with him only a few days before he died, and, while he apparently was in the hospital at the time in need of a liver transplant, I had no idea. He may have said he wasn't feeling well, but that was it. Positive until the end.

Joe Strummer was an incredible influence on me as a kid. Chatting with him throughout the process of his creating the musical accompaniment for the Jack Kerouac recording on *Kicks Joy Darkness* was a real trip. Here was a guy whose every word I would hang onto, who helped me get through my teenage angst years and not be so absorbed in myself, and helped me see the world of politics outside of my city, my country, my small world – all through his music and ideas. I would later ask him to do an interview for a Mark Sandman documentary. In the context of Morphine's seminal work, he graciously talked about how originality and progression was so essential to art – that you can't live in the past, that you need to dive into the future. Which is where we were helping Kerouac's work to go. I just recently found out that Maggie Estep also passed away. I have such fond memories of our phone conversations; she had such an incredible wit. She once appeared at a spoken word event I produced in North Hampton and I gave her a ride from New York City. She played me what was the new Soul Coughing album *El Oso* and explained how the lyricist Mike Doughty wrote much of the album about her and cited examples as we drove along. Mike Doughty recently said that she helped him with his substance abuse problems, saying 'Maggie saved my life, and she did it by being interesting.'

Simon Warner speaks to Jim Sampas about Kicks Joy Darkness

SW: This was one of the most successful spoken word albums of all time and you must be very proud of the body recordings that were gathered for this project. Did its sales surprise you and why do you think people wanted to buy into the Kerouac myth in this way?

JS: This might sound odd, but I'm not sure if the sales surprised me, though they should have, as they were quite impressive. At the time I was a young and naive singer-songwriter. Knowing how much other musicians, and friends of all kinds, were into Kerouac's works I was just so sure folks would respond positively toward the project. When people did respond positively I was very excited, don't get me wrong, but not necessarily shocked.

With hindsight, the timing simply couldn't have been better. At that moment, the mid-'90s, the Kerouac estate was releasing Jack Kerouac works nobody had ever seen before. For instance, Ann Charters' brilliantly conceived and executed *Selected Letters of Jack Kerouac* with Viking showing a different, more personal side of Jack. With the vivid, personal, descriptions within the letters, we began to get a greater understanding of the man, who his friends were, and what made them tick. A bird's-eye view into Jack's life and the lives of those around him. While Kerouac had shown us his feelings, dreams and insecurities, for sure, in works such as *Big Sur*, *Desolation Angels* and *Book of Dreams*, the letters found him working out relationships, foibles; you see him as he tries to impress, console and occasionally get irate with those around him. With the publication of *Some of the Dharma* you get a greater sense of his Buddhist interests and philosophies, *Pomes All Sizes*, a better idea of his wit and humour.

When Jack Kerouac first arrived on the literary scene in the '50s, reviewers didn't always seem to get, and often ridiculed, what he was doing as a writer. It all came full circle for Jack in the 1990s and beyond. I believe it was, ironically, the popular writers of the '70s and '80s that Jack himself had influenced – the gonzo journalism of Hunter S. Thompson, the diaries of Jim Carroll, the memoirs of Brett Easton Ellis – that made Kerouac's own writings more accessible to critics in the '90s. In any case, instead of panning the new works coming to light, as reviewers often did in Kerouac's lifetime, this time around critics showered him with praises across the board.

Speaking to the success of *Kicks Joy Darkness*, in addition to the revival at hand, and the new works coming out, *Kicks* seems to have matched up well with other more understated, personal and poetic albums on the charts at that time, such as Elliott Smith, Damien Jurado, Aimee Mann and others.

In her lifetime, folks criticized my Aunt Stella (Kerouac) for not publishing more Kerouac writings in his archive. But truth be known, according to more than one experienced book editor I spoke with a couple years into the revival, to hold back for all those years was a brilliant move, whatever reason she had decided to do so might be. When these new Kerouac books hit the stand, thanks to Viking, City Lights Books, Grey Fox Press, a vacuum was being filled. *Kerouac: Kicks Joy Darkness* came on the heels of all of this, which helped make the album a big success, and the album may have in turn helped feed into the resurgence of Kerouac's works.

That's a great way of putting it, Simon, I do absolutely think people wanted to buy into the myth. Let's face it, Kerouac at the time of the release of *Kicks* was more of a cult phenomenon, than the major literary figure he is considered to be today. In the mid-'90s he was still a bit of a mystery, really an underdog writer. His everyday man persona and spontaneous, real to life, prose was devoured with great enthusiasm during this moment when artists in all areas – painting, music, literature – were getting back to the basics. The new, previously unpublished works, seemed to fit in well what was going on at the time such as the '90s artists gaining popularity, like Elliott Smith, painter George Condo, writer Bret Easton Ellis, who had a more understated approach, that turned out to be quite appealing to a wide audience.

SW: Could you tell something about the derivation of the title?

JS: I came across this quote in *On the Road*: 'At lilac evening I walked with every muscle aching among the lights of 27th and Welton in the Denver colored section, wishing I were a Negro, feeling that the best the white world had offered was not enough ecstasy for me, not enough life, joy, kicks, darkness, music, not enough night.' I thought 'life, joy, kicks, darkness, music' felt like a great title, and the product manager at Rykodisc, David Greenberg, rightfully further simplified it as *Kicks Joy Darkness* without commas, in keeping with Kerouac's tendency to write without punctuation.

SW: There is an interesting cover shot you chose for the album. Who took the image and what special spirit to feel was contained within the picture?

JS: Yes, there's a sense of movement and playfulness in that now iconic photo by Allen Ginsberg that works so incredibly well for a musical tribute to a free-spirited writer, and I think the image appealed to a younger audience. The handsome young Jack messing around.

SW: You recorded many of the items on the album yourself but sourced some existing material to incorporate into the running order. Can you tell us something about these processes involved in gathering individual pieces and which tracks did you feel were particularly satisfying from your point of view?

JS: Yes, there were many sources. After producing the two Kerouac tributes at the Middle East Cafe in Cambridge, MA, with Graham Parker, Jim Carroll and Morphine, I was asked to become the artistic director of the Kerouac tribute at New York's Town Hall in the mid-'90s. Thanks again to Kerouac's vast influence, we had such an amazing cast of characters there. So much so that *Vanity Fair* took notice and had Annie Leibovitz photograph the contributors outside the venue: Allen Ginsberg, Lawrence Ferlinghetti, David Amram, Gregory Corso, Graham Parker, Odetta and others all lined up with the backdrop of this historic theatre.

A mishap in recording the Kerouac tributes at Middle East Cafe, wherein the recording device malfunctioned, influenced me to take further measures to ensure that wouldn't happen again, and that we would have a recording of the utmost quality for this important event, being taped, in part, for the tribute album. We put together a top-notch recording set-up. A friend and notable recording engineer David Cook (10,000 Maniacs, the B-52s), who I had worked with as a singer-songwriter, provided a multi-track mobile recording truck he parked just outside the hall. A handful of the recordings for *Kicks Joy Darkness* came from this spectacular night of engaging readings.

But as with the Middle East tape recorder going on the fritz, the Town Hall night was not without problems. In the process of faxing Allen Ginsberg the Kerouac poem 'Brooklyn Bridge Blues', the last page stuck to the back of the second to last and as a result the final part never made it through. So Allen wasn't able to read the entire piece. As you might expect, he was very upset. To reconcile, backstage I asked him if he would like to choose the person to finish the reading of the poem and he said he would think about it, still visibly ticked off. Later he called to suggest singer-songwriter Eric Andersen, and I thought what a brilliant idea. Eric actually ended up finishing 'Brooklyn Bridge Blues' by recording a reading of the last part while walking over Brooklyn Bridge.

Lawrence Ferlinghetti's track on the album was recorded at Town Hall as well, and we later added new music of seminal '90s band Helium led by Mary Timony, who is still today a vibrant voice in indie rock with her bands Autoclave, Wild Flat, and more currently in critics' darling act Ex Hex. Mary spent an incredible amount of time mapping out the arrangement she composed for the piece, and the recording process went amazingly well thanks to the work she'd done before entering the studio. That is, until we started mixing, and there was yet another mishap. In the process of adding an overdub, the assistant engineer actually recorded over Lawrence's recorded voice from Town Hall. We were all a little freaked out, and the assistant felt horrible. I tried to console him, and in the process came up with an idea: if there was a set of headphones close enough to a microphone somewhere that might be bleeding into the recording from the music mix coming out of them, then perhaps we could sync Lawrence's reading with that. Sure enough, Mary's headphones were close to a mic and we ended up pushing the volume up on that one, and used it as our guide to get the reading back to where it should be. Another potential tragedy averted, and a captivating work created.

As for the process of taking other existing readings and creating music behind it, I think Johnny Depp's track, 'Madroad Driving', may be the most fascinating behind-the-scenes story. The original recorded reading was done for the *United States of Poetry* PBS documentary in which Johnny read from Kerouac's famous poem *Mexico City Blues*. Out-takes included *Visions of Cody* and I ended up taking that recording and having another notable '90s era band, Come, do music under it at the legendary recording studio of Fort Apache in Cambridge, MA. Of course, I would say this, I'm from Massachusetts, but this is the place that greatly influenced grunge, with heavy, and messy, guitar bands like the Pixies and Throwing Muses coming out of the Fort. In fact, as I understand it, Kurt Cobain insisted that Courtney Love record Hole's album *Live Through This* with Sean Slade and Paul Kolderie at Fort Apache because of the influence the Boston music scene had on Nirvana's work.

You can hear that grunge sound in the music of Come on the Depp track. After we finished the recording, while Johnny was very pleased with the musical accompaniment, he wasn't fully satisfied with his reading. So he ended up rereading over his previously recorded reading, at his studio in Los Angeles. While rock and pop vocalists 'double' their vocal all the time, and have done so since the '60s, this was a unique idea for a spoken word piece. The net result was an enchanting amalgamation of two voices, that I never heard before or since in a spoken word piece, that lends itself to the surreal imagery within the words.

Patti Smith's track, 'The Last Hotel', recorded at a Kerouac festival in Lowell, with Thurston Moore of Sonic Youth, and also with a member of her own band, Lenny Kaye, was one that we recorded live for the project. We didn't have to do much with that, save for working to accentuate her voice in the mastering process, to make it more present.

SW: You also worked with Lee Ranaldo, also of Sonic Youth, on this record. He's known to be a long-time Kerouac and Beat fan. How did the two of you collaborate on this project?

JS: Allen Ginsberg had told me that Lee was a big fan of Kerouac. Shortly after he mentioned that, I saw that Lee was playing the Middle East Cafe with an offshoot band of Sonic Youth. My friend Chris Porter booked the venue and I asked if he might introduce me to Lee during sound check. I told Lee my idea of a spoken word tribute to Jack and he immediately got it and said he would love to become involved. He in turn introduced me to Eddie Vedder and others who contributed, which was so crucial in the project's development, having the first highly praised artists sign on, so instrumental in getting all the others.

This reminds me of another episode involving trying to get an artist on board with the help of the Chris Porter. Chris would later manage another club in Boston, which Aerosmith opened up, named Mama Kin's. While nothing ever came of it, I tried the same tactic I did with Lee Ranaldo – showing up at, in this case, a Pogues concert at Mama Kin's to see if I could entice lead singer and songwriter Shane McGowan to become involved in the tribute. I waited outside his tour bus for someone to come out. A roadie soon walked down the bus stairs, and I asked if I could speak to the road manager. While the manager appeared to be giving me the brush off, as I waited for 45 minutes or so, out walks Shane McGowan, with the same roadie I spoke with earlier, whispering slyly, 'Come on, we're going to find a bar.' And there it is, I'm off to go have a drink with Shane McGowan. As we proceeded, a funny thing happened. At the sports bar at the top of Lansdowne Street, across the street from the historic Fenway Park, all of us were asked for IDs. Sure enough Shane did not have one. So they wouldn't let us in. Shane McGowan turned away by an overzealous bouncer! I said to Shane, I know someone who can get us in to a place to have a drink, and we went back to Mama Kins where I called Chris and he let us into the bar early.

Shane seemed to have a shyness that I have heard from friends of Jack Kerouac, such as Joyce Johnson, that Jack had as well. In fact, I think Shane feigned being tipsy to get folks to stay away from him. I say this, because even though I also thought he was pretty buzzed and was a little upset with myself for getting him in early to the bar as he had a show to put on, the moment he and I were alone he snapped out of it and spoke almost as if we were in a library somewhere, methodically going over all the questions he had listed in his head about this new project he had only just heard about. Though Shane did give me his phone number, in the end he wasn't able to particpate. I hope to work with him one day on a project. In fact, that reminds me I should check to see if that number still works for the next one.

SW: There was an expanded Japanese edition of the album. How did that come about and how do the two sets differ?

JS: There was a Japanese company that wanted to do an expanded edition with two CDs and accompanying small CD-size book with artwork and the writings and poems. Graham Parker did a magnificent reading of an unpublished 1949 journal of Jack Kerouac's at Town Hall, with musical accompaniment by one of America's greatest composers and close friend of Jack's, David Amram. But Graham's performance was too long for the American version and, to my ear, couldn't be edited without compromising the rest of the short journal story Jack was telling. So we included this stellar full version in the Japanese edition, along with a magnificent track by the United Future Organization, one of the pioneers of acid jazz in Japan, entitled 'Poetry And All That Jazz'. In that 'song', UFO used another Jack Kerouac recording and spiced it up with quite modern, hip hop influenced, music. The track, still to this day, is among my personal favourite Kerouac-related recordings or reimaginings.

SW: What do you think Jack Kerouac might have made of this collection?

JS: Well, that's the hardest question to answer. Since there were so many artists who, like Kerouac, were pushing the envelope in their own artistry, so incredibly devoted to their work, if nothing else I think he would have appreciated the effort. Allen Ginsberg once told me he felt that Jack would have liked the Clash. If that follows, perhaps he would have enjoyed Joe Strummer's music behind his reading of 'MacDougal Street Blues'. But who knows? We do know that Kerouac wanted his work to be widely distributed. To the degree that this project did get his work out to a younger audience, who may never have heard of him if it weren't for this, I imagine he might have liked that. My personal view is if we're able to further Kerouac's great work and legacy in meaningful ways without being in any way disrespectful, or tainting the work in any way (I suppose that is subjective), then we've accomplished the goal Kerouac himself set out to achieve, to have his work known by the masses. But I remain very open to other people's views as well.

Jack Kerouac Reads On the Road (1999)

The next project was *Jack Kerouac Reads On the Road*, also released by Rykodisc. I was working for the Kerouac Estate at this time, with executor John Sampas, my uncle. On the heels of the success of *Kerouac: Kicks Joy Darkness*, John and I were interested in the idea of creating a Jack Kerouac recordings project, and I was looking through the archive for material that might be right for such a project. For the 25th anniversary of Jack Kerouac's death I was scheduled to be interviewed by a Seattle radio station, and that day I was looking through a stack of Jack's albums, and came across a white-sleeved record jacket. The label on the vinyl itself said 'Charlie Parker' and nothing else. I took it downstairs and put it on the record player so John and I could listen to what we assumed would be a Parker recording. As it turned out, it was in fact the acetate master of legendary 28-minute lost recording of Jack Kerouac reading from *On the Road*. Our jaws dropped. We knew we had rediscovered something truly special.

As I mentioned, I'd worked with Lee Ranaldo of Sonic Youth on *Kicks Joy Darkness* and knew him to be a big fan. I asked him if he wanted to produce a new album of recordings with me. He of course loved the idea, and we set out to recruit the person we all felt would be perfect for the project, Kerouac's long-time friend and accompanist David Amram.

Watching David in the studio in Manhattan, listening to his old buddy Jack's voice coming out of the monitors, is one of the fondest memories I have. We decided to have David create a score behind some other beautiful unreleased home recordings of Jack, and he brought his jazz band along to help him. I had also asked John Medeski, of Medeski, Martin & Wood, to do an accompaniment behind a song called 'On the Road', which Jack wrote and recorded. And even though Jack's tempo was slightly off, John and guitarist Vic Juris managed to create a beautiful musical accompaniment that sounded as though they were in the room with Jack.

Later I asked Tom Waits to record a cover of the song 'On the Road'. After a little bit of arm twisting he agreed. The arm twisting was not because he didn't believe in the song, but that he, being such a big Kerouac fan, worried about doing it justice. He hired the famous rock act Primus to do the accompaniment. They recorded the song in the small town of Cotati, northwest of San Francisco, at Prairie Sun Recording Studio. (I would later record an artist at that studio, and you can literally wake up in the morning and get a fresh egg from under a chicken to start your day.) Waits is a perfectionist and apparently, as he explained later, he was a little bit nervous about how the song was coming together. He was sitting outside for a break on the steps of the recording studio when he saw a teenager riding his bicycle down the road. He called out 'Hey kid come over here!' The kid stopped and navigated his bike up the dirt driveway. Tom had him sit in the control room and listen to a rough mix of the song, which he reacted to well. I love all the different things that anecdote says about Tom Waits. The release of the album made news around the world and became quite a success.

Simon Warner speaks to Jim Sampas about Jack Kerouac Reads On the Road

SW: This is an eclectic collection, comprising spoken word pieces by Kerouac, new musical settings for his extended poems, contributions from important rock figures – like Tom Waits and Primus – and also vintage recordings of Kerouac singing himself in the manner of a crooner. Can I ask you some questions about the novelist's own vocal performances of standards on this album? How did you find these performances? Were they part of the Kerouac archive? Were they part of a lost body of work or just not well identified?

JS: I discovered the recordings within the Kerouac archive. They were on reel-to-reel tapes and acetate recordings those of which look identical to a vinyl album. Both the acetates and the reel-to-reels were in pretty good shape and seemed like they hadn't been touched since Jack himself put them in the boxes they were in. The one that helped create the most excitement surrounding this project, of course, was the legendary 'lost' recording of Jack reading *On the Road* which I believe Dave Moore had discovered had been recorded from various sources he had found about the making of the album. But no one could locate the tapes until I found the recording in the Kerouac archives. It was simply a piece of good fortune – the item was wrongly described but contained a real gem.

SW: Kerouac seemed to be a fan of the jazz standard and even the Broadway songbook. Would you agree?

JS: He was a devoted listener to jazz standard music, a huge fan of Frank Sinatra, Billie Holiday and others. In fact, he had many other reel-to-reel tapes, besides the ones where he recorded of himself reading, extensive recordings, and I believe maybe even compilations, that he made from vinyl records of jazz standards and other styles.

SW: When did Kerouac record the songs? He pops on a more than passable style as a romantic singer in that 1940s and 1950s tradition, recalling Sinatra, Bennett, Damone and other greats of the era. Did he go into the studio and work with an orchestra?

JS: Yes, I agree he had a pretty interesting voice that you do get a sense had been influenced by the folks you mentioned, but also had something else going on. He was indeed an incredibly talented spoken word reader and you can't help but wonder if he had pursued that path – as poet Maya Angelou did in the '50s or later Jim Carroll and Patti Smith in the '80s with even more success – he wouldn't have done well with it. But if you notice, unless there is a letter or journal note missing somewhere I don't know of, Jack doesn't seem to really talk much about the recordings after they were made, save for a letter I'll mention later, speaking of recording of an album but nowhere talking about how it came out. Which makes you wonder how seriously he took the idea of being a crooner, as we know he seemed to write about everything he was truly passionate about.

At the time of the release of *Jack Kerouac Reads On the Road*, we didn't list the artists involved because we couldn't seem to pinpoint who they were. However, your question has prompted me to go back over my notes, and dig a little deeper and I did come across some intriguing, though quite loose, leads that may or may not have be helpful in deterimining who these folks were.

Dave Moore recently reminded me that the crooner songs more than likely were recorded in the following manner. Jerry may have had instrumental recordings of various musicians he worked with in his studio. He believes, and I tend to agree, that Jerry had Jack sing to pre-recorded mixes of various arrangements of song by these bands he had recorded. To be clear, we have no idea at this point who was on the music that Newman had Jack sing to. However, there are a couple interesting references I came across in Kerouac's letters that may or may not have to do with these recordings, one to Neal Cassady and the other to Allen Ginsberg, both included in Ann Charters' *Jack Kerouac Selected Letters 1940 to 1965*. The Cassady letter apparently wasn't dated, but Ann notes that she thinks it was written 'before April 15, 1955'. In it, Jack writes, 'I am arranging a jam session to make an album for Jerry Newman's record company, with Allen Eager on tenor, for which, with written notes, I'll get 50 bucks, with which I'll buy a phonograph and $20 worth of records'. Kerouac further writes in the letter to Ginsberg, dated 23 August 1953, 'I must look up Keck[2] soon, tho I dont know him and dont particularly like Allen Eager and Tony Fuselli and assorted musicians of the Village, but Jerry, who had me yesterday at a long weekend of swim and Sandeman Port and beer and kids at private beach and cottage over barn, wants to pay me $25 for rounding up those guys (at Joe's Open Door, etc) and bringing them to a session, where concoctions and liquors are all set out for the gig. Can I do this? And $25 for program notes.'

Now around this time Jerry Newman's was also working with the Al Haig Trio comprised of Al Haig on piano, Bill Crow on double bass, and Lee Abrams on drums, releasing their work on his label Esoteric, including one entitled *The Al Haig Trio on 13 March 1954*. Again, I have I don't know if any of these musicians are on the Kerouac crooner songs, but I suppose a jazz historian or enthusiast could help to answer this lead by listening to the recordings to see if the characteristics of the musicianship might shed some light on the possibility that these artists were those on the tapes Kerouac sang to.

SW: So these were home recordings? Did he have a microphone? Did he have a tape recorder?

JS: According to Allen Ginsberg, and Kerouac's own letters, he would record in the back of Jerry Newman's record shop. Allen once told Newman's shop was on the corner of Greenwich and 7th in the Village. My guess is that since Newman was quite an accomplished recording engineer, and from listening to the recordings themselves, that Newman had put together a high quality mic and reel-to-reel set-up for Jack. Again, the recordings speak for themselves. And it's the setting that makes all the difference in the world. The record shop recordings did not involve a big recording studio set-up, with engineers, a producer in the room and nervous Jack. Instead these are incredibly intimate and uninhibited readings which often involve quite personal subject matter.

SW: Is this only the tip of an iceberg? Are there other Kerouac-as-crooner recordings we have not yet heard?

JS: While there are no other crooner songs, there are some other recordings from Newman's record shop, that haven't been made available yet.

SW: There are two fascinating tracks on the album which see the same song approached in a completely different fashion. Kerouac's own song 'On the Road' forms part of the package and then Tom Waits gives the piece a completely different reading. How did you feel about this intriguing contrast – the writer's maudlin introspection and the fierce swamp blues of the singer and band – in styles?

JS: There are actually three recordings of the 'On the Road' song. You may not know about the other more slowed down piano version that Tom Waits recorded at Prairie Sun in Cotati, CA in the same session as 'On the Road' with Primus. 'Home I'll Never Be' appears on the Waits compilation album *Orphans: Brawlers, Bawlers & Bastards* and it is such a heartfelt, beautiful rendering, that is as good as any of Tom Waits's greatest. The 'On the Road' song with Primus is a swampy, cocky, rendering that seemed to me as if it were written by Jack for Tom.

I absolutely love the contrast between the two and, as someone devoted to re-creating versions of songs for my covers label Reimagine Music, I find this to be particularly fascinating – the different takes on one song.

Immediately upon discovering the original Jack Kerouac version, I knew it was quite special. While the recording itself was a little rough around the edges, I think I like them all equally, Jack's version and Tom's two versions. Jack has a pretty fascinating singing voice and if you listen to it closely I swear the sound of his voice on this reminds me of the Velvet Uunderground. Guitarist Vic Juris and keyboardist John Medeski did a spectacular job creating the music behind the piece, especially since Jack was slightly offbeat and therefore difficult to sync with.

SW: Again, Lee Ranaldo played a part in this set of recordings. Once more, how did the two of you cooperate on the project?

JS: For *Jack Kerouac Reads On the Road*, Lee and I worked closely together on it, both giving feedback deciding the approach and what to do with the recordings. It's a pleasure to work with him, and he has such incredibly fascinating ideas.

SW: The album features remarkable cover images by major photographer and Beat associate Robert Frank. Please explain how this important artist – the two of them had worked together on *The Americans* and *Pull My Daisy*, hadn't they? – allowed his classic images to be utilized.

JS: Now I may be mistaken, as it has been a while, but as I recall this was result of reading somewhere that Kerouac wanted that now famous road photo of Robert Frank to be on the cover of a proposed *On the Road* album. I got in touch with Robert and he enthusiastically gave his blessing for the photo. Seeing as that photo in and of itself is such an iconic image, we were incredibly blessed to have his support.

SW: You also drew on a very hip album sleeve designer in Frank Olinsky, who had a strong track record of creating eye-catching indie rock album covers. Tell us a little more about this aspect.

JS: Frank Olinsky, as you say, has to be one of the most accomplished album designers on the scene today, having done albums of Sonic Youth, Paul Simon, Smashing Pumpkins, Joshua Redman and so many others. He and I collaborated on the design, in that I brought in and suggested many of the images – Robert Frank, Michael Stipe, and the reel-to-reel tapes the songs were recorded on, and liner notes of Douglas Brinkley – with Frank creating the overall placement of where each image should go within the package, and, for instance, coming up with the idea that Doug's liner notes should cover the entire inside of the spread to made it look like a scroll of Kerouac's. That package he created is among the best I have ever been involved with.

Doctor Sax and the Great World Snake (2003)

After these two musical projects, I moved on to *Doctor Sax and the Great World Snake*, a previously unpublished screenplay Kerouac wrote in 1967 based on his mystical, vision novel *Doctor Sax*. It's a haunting tale based on true reflections of his 1930s childhood growing up in this industrial milltown of Lowell, and he spins out a wildly imaginative dark cosmology, as 'concentrations of evil' gather – vampires, gnomes, spiders, werewolves of the soul, leerers at the gladheart of others – aspiring to destroy mankind. Dr Sax – alchemist of the night and friend of the children – is the caped crusader who stands against the darkness. According to Kerouac, the idea for Doctor Sax emerged as 'myth itself as I dreamt it in the fall of 1948'.

For this recording of *Doctor Sax and The Great World Snake* we used multiple voice textures and music that emulate the golden age of radio drama, which is the source period for the book. For this excursion into a bygone era I again sought out John Medeski, one of the most innovative jazz musicians working today, to compose the score. His music is spontaneous and real, only sparingly retouched by overdubs. To record the readings and music we seldom went beyond the second or third take, and in fact used mainly first and warm-up takes for the final cut.

Four great American poets read on that album, all of them personally connected to Kerouac. Robert Creeley narrates with eloquence, and reading for deep meaning. He draws us, willingly or not, into Kerouac's landscape. Jim Carroll captures both the small-town innocence of Jackie's character, and the melancholy reminiscence of Kerouac's voice. And the splendidly peculiar wizard, Lawrence Ferlinghetti – poet, painter and publisher – added 'ensemble actor' to his resumé. Kerouac's inspiration for Doctor Sax himself was the classic radio character 'The Shadow', and Grateful Dead lyricist Robert Hunter, inspired by this persona, has given us a Sax both crafty and compassionate.

The illustrations for the book that accompanied the recording were done by Richard Sala – drawing the underworld out from the darkness of Kerouac's childhood landscape, but not too far into the light. Strangely enough, it was the novel *Doctor Sax* that inspired a young Sala to seek out the pulp mystery magazines of The Shadow – which proved to be a major influence on his style. Again, jazz drove Kerouac, and it was with that improvisational, sometimes fevered, spirit we worked Kerouac's script into a hybrid art form combining sound and image.

Simon Warner speaks to Jim Sampas about Doctor Sax and the Great World Snake

SW: This is based on a Jack Kerouac screenplay derived from the novel *Doctor Sax*, isn't it? What did the author intend to do with this? It was never produced, was it, until you brought it to this recording?

JS: It appears Jack actually wanted his screenplay to be made into a film, and wrote it in order to help facilitate the process. It never came to fruition but I'm working to bring his dream to reality. Since we knew it would be the first time anyone would see the work, we wanted to do our best to created a stunning production. We released it as multi-media set of an illustrated book and two CDs of readings. The effort all seemed to pay off as it drew such great press attention including coverage on NPR, *Voice of America*, *The Jim Bohannon Show* and many others.

SW: How did it differ from the novel *Doctor Sax*, a fantastical and highly cinematic work of fiction, which perhaps may become a feature film some day?

JS: Jack didn't alter it that much at all. It seems it was more about editing than changing the story to fit the screen. However, there are detailed scene descriptions throughout. You get the sense he had a real vision for it. As for the storyline, it appears he simply worked to find the most cinematic opportunities within while also keeping the integrity of story arc. I think this is a perfect example of an artist so confident in, and with great reverence for, his own work. He didn't want to dress it up at all to make it more filmic, but wished rather to create something that could live in another medium as is.

SW: Tell us something about the way you attracted such a remarkable cast: Robert Creeley, Jim Carroll, Robert Hunter and Lawrence Ferlinghetti.

JS: *Doctor Sax and the Great World Snake* is such a magnificent and daring work of art I felt we needed a unique approach. Poets often do readings, of course, and therefore are entertainers to some degree, yet have different sensibilities from actors. Inspired by indie films, as well as old radio dramas, I sought out notable poets instead to create a poetic feel that I felt would suit the work.

Now that you mention it, looking back on how we were able to get four giants of poetry all together is quite impressive. I can't also help but consider, thinking on Ferlinghetti and Creeley, how it is at all these folks knew each other? The fact that lightning struck so many times around Kerouac and his talented circle of friends, well it's like considering how three young kids from Liverpool, along with Ringo, would happen to get together to form the greatest band of all time. Lawrence Ferlinghetti, Allen Ginsberg, Robert Creeley, Gregory Corso, and then of course there is William Burroughs. How did that happen?

I had worked with Jim Carroll and Robert Hunter, and actually produced an album of Lawrence Ferlinghetti's: *A Coney Island of the Mind*. So I not only knew them to be incredible talented spoken word readers, but that they were open to these sort of ideas.

The character that I selected for Lawrence was the Wizard, the dark soul within Jack's story that would usher the daemonic summit in Lowell. Knowing how entertaining he could be, embodying the fascinating characters within his poems, I sensed he would be the ultimate Wizard. In fact we recorded the parts for the Wizard during the recording sessions of the second Ferlinghetti album I would work on with him – *Pictures of the Gone World* – with David Amram in Francis Ford Coppola's tiny studio in San Francisco. Lawrence really got into the character and camped it up magnificently. I recorded Robert Creeley in a recording studio in Buffalo, New York. Robert had the most fascinating gaze, such a truly sweet soul. He had his parts down perfectly, and his commentary in between recordings, of fond memories of Jack, were priceless. Jack Kerouac once gave the glowing review of Jim Carroll's diaries that 'At 13 years of age, Jim Carroll writes better prose than 89 percent of the novelists working today.' Being very familiar with his voice, both as a fan and working with him on the tribute I mentioned at the Middle East, I thought Jim Carroll would do a great job with the young Jacky Duluoz. With his deep, endlessly fascinating voice, I also knew Robert Hunter would be the ultimate Doctor Sax. He did two long passes of the lines and we spliced the best parts together.

SW: How and where was it recorded?

JS: As you would imagine, from a practical standpoint, to get each of the long list of artists and poets into one studio would have been a gargantuan proposition. So we decided to record everyone in different locations and mix it all together once all the pieces were in place. Then, when all were in, recording engineer Jim Keegan edited down the readings into one stereo mix, with some help from me editing the lines – which I found to be quite a time consuming, laborious process. Then we took that recording to Applehead Recording Studio in Woodstock, and in keeping with Kerouac's writing aesthetic, famed jazz musician John Medeski would record and arrange a quite spontaneously conceived, improvisational score with the help of three other session musicians: Eric Hippe on saxophone, Mike Rivard on acoustic bass and electric bass and Kenney Wollesen on drums and percussion. I have to say I have such fond memories of this experience, quite a lovely time, and back in the day when there were bigger recording budgets. We had big dinners with a chef, and John had his wine broker ship some of the finest wine I have ever had straight to the studio door. The resulting recordings that John and crew lovingly conceived, in my view, are a truly engaging, jazz tinged musical accompaniment, among the finest I have ever heard.

SW: Will the original screenplay ever see the light of day in a theatre situation or could it be the basis of a movie in the future?

JS: Yes, I hope to produce a film version. Right now we are hard at work on what may become the next Kerouac film, adapted from the storyline just after *Sax* entitled *Maggie Cassidy*, with a screenplay by the accomplished, award-winning screenwriter Chris Sparling (*The Sea of Trees, Buried*), which, as a period piece set in the '40s (Chris moved it up a decade), I hope will prove to the world a Kerouac film can be made on a bigger scale, and that *Doctor Sax* will become the next in line.

One Fast Move or I'm Gone: Kerouac's Big Sur (2009)

The way the documentary film *One Fast Move or I'm Gone: Kerouac's Big Sur* came together is interesting. I became friendly with a producer and director team Curt Worden and Gloria Bailien based in Providence, Rhode Island. We came up with the idea together, wanted to do something truly unique together with it. So, instead of the typical documentary route, wherein you encapsulate a person's entire life, we opted to focus on one work. We felt that *Big Sur* really gave us a sense of who Jack Kerouac was.

In other works the light had been shown squarely and almost exclusively on his friends. In this one he dug deep into his own soul and seemed to be writing himself out of his own dilemma and inner demons.

A great many artists have had to deal with the downsides of fame, and many have had substance abuse problems. In that regard alone we knew this work would resonate. And it surely did, with Tom Waits, Sam Shepard and Patti Smith all coming on board. But an idea alone does not a project make, and I had to seek out investment. That process went incredibly fast, and from the moment we had the idea to the time we were on the ground in Big Sur shooting was only a matter of months. I was able to secure enough investment for us to have a great deal of flexibility, including a full theatrical film crew, and you can see the result for yourself on Netflix.

When it came to the music for the film, I'd been listening to a great deal of Americana and alt-country music, much of which, like Kerouac's work, is grounded in tales of the American heartland. Given the cadence, rhythm and intimacy of the prose of *Big Sur*, I thought this particular novel would lend itself to song with the right collaborator. I'd met one of the pioneers of alt-country, Jay Farrar, associated with both the bands Uncle Tupelo and Son Volt, by working with him years ago when I produced an album paying tribute to Bruce Springsteen's *Nebraska*. I had read that Jay had been influenced by Kerouac's spontaneous prose, and that he used a similar method in songwriting. Ben Gibbard, of Death Cab for Cutie, is one of his generation's best lyricists, and his playful enunciation and unique singing style drew me towards him.

While Ben and Jay's music differs in style, I just had a feeling that these two could create a fascinating blend of music together. I asked Jay to write a series of songs using the prose of *Big Sur* as lyrics. So when you hear any song in the film, it actually draws on Kerouac's words from *Big Sur*. There was a US theatrical release of the film, as well as a music tour with Jay and Ben. And the album and film probably broke a record that year for the number of spots about it that aired on NPR. I've never had so many of my friends call me to tell me how much they loved the album and film, and this inspired me to work a feature film based on *Big Sur*.

Simon Warner speaks to Jim Sampas about One Fast Move or I'm Gone

SW: This is a remarkable documentary, made to commemorate the 40th anniversary of Kerouac's death, full of dramatic vistas and atmospheric settings in San Francisco and on the Californian coast. How did director Curt Worden find locations that were contemporary but still suggested those West Coast places at the turn of the 1960s?

JS: Yes, Curt and the team did a fabulous job scouting out locations. He's a well-travelled documentarian, familiar with so many places around the world, and seemed to have a good sense of what might work in New York, San Francisco and Big Sur from the get go. He also had help from the acclaimed cinematographer for *One Fast*

Move, Richard Rutkowski (*Iron Man, Jack Ryan*), in selecting the best settings. An incredible amount of time and effort went into the cinematography, as you can see. I've had so many folks tell me this is, by far, the best Beat related documentary and those words means a great deal to me as there have been so many great ones.

SW: Again, there was some amazing contributions from a rich gallery of significant artists – Lawrence Ferlinghetti, Sam Shepard, Patti Smith, Tom Waits and others. What were the logistics of assembling such an impressive line-up?

JS: This again is a perfect example of the profound influence Kerouac has had on so many different actors, artists, musicians everywhere. Three of the folks you mention had worked on other Kerouac related projects and Sam Shepard I met as a very young child when he made a pilgrimage to Lowell to see Kerouac's birthplace, so I knew him to also be a fan. We did have to get strategic with logistics working within budget so we were recording folks close to where they were within our shooting schedule. Sam Shepard insisted that he would not speak on the Kerouac work itself but would only read passages from *Big Sur* for the film because he didn't believe it was his place to give his own impressions of the work, that it spoke for itself. His reading of course is a highlight of the documentary. Since Tom and I had gotten to know each other over the years, while Gloria Bailen did an incredible job on the interviews of all the subjects in the film, I did the Tom Waits one, and what a thrill that was. The perspectives of everyone involved in the project are endlessly fascinating to me. Having worked with Dar Williams, Tom Waits, Patti Smith, I had developed a rapport with them which I think was helpful. Years before, Donal Logue and I would frequent the same pub in Cambridge, MA, a melting pot of creative artists like Donal from the area such as members of the seminal Boston rock bands Mission of Birma, the Volcano Sons, Bullet Lavolta and others. I feel that Donal wouldn't mind me saying what I'm about to, as he seems to be very supportive of folks with substance abuse issues. Donal himself had a real drinking problem in his early twenties, around the time I knew him. This seemed to give him a greater awareness, that others may not have, of precisely what was going on with Jack during the events of *Big Sur*.

SW: Tell us something about the soundtrack by Ben Gibbard, of Death Cab for Cutie, and Uncle Tupelo and Son Volt's Jay Farrell. How did you involve them? How did they end up working as a duo on the recording?

JS: I'd been listening to a great deal of alt.country music, much of which, as with Kerouac's work, grows out of rural, backwoods America. I had worked with Jay Farrar and Son Volt on the album *Badlands: A Tribute To Bruce Springsteen's Nebraska* and was a big admirer of his work, especially Uncle Tupelo, the band that many rock journalists cite as having started the whole alt.country music phenomenon. I had also read that he used a similar method of writing as Kerouac, creating songs in short bursts, and that clinched it for me, and I rang him up. Given the cadence, rhythm and intimacy of the prose of *Big Sur*, I thought this *Big Sur* would lend itself so well to song with the right collaborator. For me, Jay was the ideal person for this role.

I was familiar with Ben Gibbard's remarkable work, in both the Postal Service and Death Cab For Cutie, and do feel he is among the greatest vocalists and lyricists of our time, with his heady lyrics and playful enunciation. While he struck me as someone well read, what I hadn't realized was he was actually a huge admirer of Kerouac. In fact, in my many years working to attract artists to projects, I don't think I've ever received a more positive first response for Ben being involved in the documentary interview side of this. Immediately upon receiving word from me for a request for an interview with Ben, before he was involved in the album, his management said something to the effect of 'Ben not only wants you to know he is up for being there for the dates you mentioned in San Francisco but that if he does have anything on his schedule during that period we're pushing everything aside for this.'

While Jay and Ben's music is quite different, I just had a sense they would create a fascinating blend. They really hit it off as well, and worked incredibly efficiently as if they'd known each other for years and years.

SW: Whose idea was it to use the text from *Big Sur* verbatim as lyrical source?

JS: I came up with that idea, and the inspiration for it was Patti Smith and Jim Carroll's pieces for *Kicks Joy Darkness*, where they turned the pomes (as Jack called them) into songs with amazing results. I'm sure I also had Billy Bragg and Wilco's *Mermaid Avenue* in mind, wherein, thanks to Nora Guthrie, they took previously unpublished lyrics of Woody Guthrie and created songs from them.

Jay absolutely loved the idea, and later would say it was a liberating experience not having to come up with lyrics but using someone else's. In fact, this may sound hard to believe, and I can't help but wonder what Kerouac would have thought of this, but Jay actually wrote all the songs for the album in one three-day burst of inspiration. Truly amazing.

SW: I know you were very happy with the results. How do you think the artists achieved a balance between a country roots sound and the fictional passages they adopted? How did their musical compositions dovetail so well with the actual text of the novel?

JS: It all sounds so incredibly natural to me, as if the lyrics were Jay's and not from a book by Kerouac, he and Ben embody the spirit of the work so well. This is particularly remarkable because as a songwriter Jay didn't alter the words whatsoever to fit the melodies, with only one exception that he asked me [about] before he did, leaving out just one single word. One word. I don't know how that is possible but there it is. Just for curiosity's sake I once did a search of lyrics using a Word doc transcription of the entire novel of *Big Sur*. And all words, are, in fact, verbatim.

While I had never heard Ben sing a style of music anything like what we have here, Ben and Jay's voices, however different they may be, blend together so well. And as it turns out, Kerouac's words match the sensibilities and alt.country feel of the album beautifully. In fact, I'm not sure if you agree, but some almost sound as though they are old traditional songs, something that you've heard before.

Big Sur (2013)

Since *Big Sur* is a particularly introspective, nonlinear, work, where the dialogue and inner thoughts are the prevailing force, I knew I needed to get an independent, groundbreaking, director at the helm. One who wouldn't shy away from experimentation. I had been blown away by the Polish Brothers' work – *Twin Falls Idaho* and *Astronaut Farmer* – and sought out Michael Polish to direct. I was incredibly surprised to hear from Michael's manager that he would absolutely be interested in the project as he had been thinking about optioning the novel himself. As with illustrator Richard Sala, it turns out that Kerouac had been an important influence on Polish.

In today's world of contrived narratives, Kerouac's works, such as *Big Sur*, are, as films, more in line with the great indie features, with less linear structure and more of a real-life foundation: films like *Stranger in Paradise* and *Easy Rider*. In fact, the *New York Times* wrote that *Big Sur* 'cracks the code of how to adapt Jack Kerouac for the screen'. They went on to say, 'The secret is deceptively simple: Go to the source and stay there. The hot-wired energy and spontaneity of the Beat mystique are embedded in writing that distills its feverish essence better than any hyped-up action.'

Simon Warner speaks to Jim Sampas about Big Sur

SW: Filming Jack Kerouac's fiction for the big screen has proved a considerable challenge. Walter Salles' 2010 version of *On the Road* received a very mixed critical response. The version of *Big Sur* you produced appeared to fare much better. Why did you feel you wanted to return to the subject of *Big Sur* so quickly after the *One Fast Move* documentary? Did making the doc give you a better insight as to how the novel could become a feature film?

JS: Yes, after getting such a great sense of the narrative structure and how Jack is so awfully brave to put forth his trials and inner demons so eloquently to the page, it seemed to me so many people could relate to what he was going through – the overnight success, and pressures therein, the fall from flight – that's what sealed it for me. The response that I saw going to film festivals showing *One Fast Move*, how engaged the audience was, I knew we had something here. But look, I had never created a feature film before so I needed feedback. And when I reached out to the director I felt would be the best match for the project, Michael Polish, one of the most celebrated indie film directing teams, the Polish Brothers, with their left-of-centre productions of *Astronaut Farmer*, *Twin Falls Idaho*, *Northfork*, the response was quite encouraging. Shortly after getting a proposal to Michael, his manager called and said 'Michael can't believe you're asking him to become involved in directing *Big Sur*. He recently read the novel and actually wanted to option it, work toward making this into a film.' Of all the books in the world it just so happens that this was the one Michael, one of my favourite directors, wanted to be his next film project. What are the chances of that? As a producer of music, I also knew you had to be practical, try to create a fertile atmosphere for success, one that would attract people who could help get you financing, as after all, in this case we weren't talking about a John Grisham novel, but a dark tale of a man on the edge. *One Fast Move* had proven to me that we had a good chance, again with the right director, the right bait, we could get the best acting talent out there involved. And sure enough we did in Jean-Marc Barr, Kate Bosworth, Josh Lucas, Anthony Edwards, Rahda Mitchell and others.

SW: Tell us something about director Michael Polish's approach and about the actors who took on the key roles in the movie.

JS: Michael insisted we get the story as close to the book as was humanly possible. In fact he used the exact dialogue from the text, making very few alterations if any. He said, let's tell Jack's story the way it is, no need to embellish, it is all there. And that is precisely what he did. At one point we were looking at big name actors to play Jack, and again, this being a Kerouac-related project, three A-list actors became seriously interested. But then my producer partner Orian Williams suggested Jean-Marc Barr. The three of us watched his work, and interviews, and decided immediately that he was our Jack. After seeing how much Jean-Marc actually looked like Kerouac, in addition to being an actor with stellar credentials, we quickly agreed if we had a big name, with a recognizable face, that person, who the audience would recognize immediately, would take them out of the story. Michael wanted the world to be introduced to Jack himself. As if to foreshadow what was ahead, long before we made any announcement of the film, and with virtually no one knowing we were making a film based on *Big Sur*, Michael and a very enthusiastic Jean-Marc went to scout the locations to shoot the scenes in San Francisco, not often done by the way, with actor in tow. And sure enough, as Michael and Jean-Marc were walking down Columbus Street near the infamous Beat location of City Lights Books, where it all started, a man in a convertible driving by pointed his finger at Jean-Marc and shouted 'Jack Kerouac!' True story.

Later, after the film was out, Kerouac's close friend and former girlfriend, esteemed writer Joyce Johnson, said to me 'Jean-Marc Barr is the Jack I knew.' The ultimate compliment made even more incredible to me knowing Joyce to be someone who never pull punches, says what she really feels.

Michael also felt the region of Big Sur, one of the most majestic places on earth, should become a major character within the film. The tension between the beauty and the solitude of a man on the edge of a nervous breakdown is palable when you take the film in. Another interesting anecdote, about the region, is that shortly before filming there was one of those huge mudslides that closed down the route from San Francisco, so the film crew had to drive several hours extra around to the other side of the disaster in order to start filming at Big Sur. Also, just after the very last take at the end of the film, no sooner had Michael shouted the words 'Cut, that's it,' than there was a wild downpour with the crew racing to get the cameras and equipment in the trucks to shelter. Had that last take not gone as well as it did, there would have been days before another chance to complete. As if someone up above was watching over the production.

SW: Could you tell us about the soundtrack by members of the National? How did that come about and what are your feelings about the score that resulted?

JS: Michael, and all the producers were big fans of the National, especially Michael, and so we reached out to them and they enthusiastically signed on. In the process of creating the score, Michael would send Aaron and Bryce Dessner footage and they would create the score to match. I just love what they did with it, incredibly minimal, but with their singular, evocative musical vision, that I think fans of the National would appreciate, as well as anyone else into great scores.

Esperanza: Songs from Jack Kerouac's Tristessa (2013)

Esperanza would be my next Kerouac endeavour. After seeing how well the meditative aspects of *Big Sur* worked for *One Fast Move*, particularly how effectively Jay Farrar was able to channel Kerouac thoughts into song, I felt the personal nature of his novel *Tristessa* could also evoke ideas and feelings within the artists.

Kerouac scholars have since found that Esperanza was Tristessa's given name. Upon completing the album and considering a title for it, I mentioned this to my daughter Chloe, nine years old at the time. She said, 'Why don't you name the album *Esperanza*?' 'What a truly a brilliant idea,' I said. And so I did.

In the end, it was the darkness within *Tristessa* that did actually become the perfect palette for 19 acclaimed singer-songwriters and bands: William Fitzsimmons, Tim & Adam, Gregory Alan Isakov, Peter Bradley Adams, Alela Diane, Wintersleep, Marissa Nadler, Joshua James, Lee Ranaldo (of Sonic Youth), Hey Rosetta!, Will Dailey, Willy Mason, Matt Costa, the Low Anthem, Neal McCarthy with Barbara Kessler, and Tony Dekker with Hanne Hukkelberg.

And sure enough, they did channel the bleak emotions of the novel into something vivid and intense. But I also wanted a few songs influenced by the light Kerouac wrote of, underscoring his urge to live within and beyond the despair he found in Mexico. Some created their pieces using the text as lyrics; others found inspiration within the subtext of the novel itself. What I hoped to achieve was a discovery, pointing folks toward this lesser known Kerouac novel while placing their finger on the pulse of the best in indie rock today.

The Kerouac projects I produced are a testament not only to the endurance of his writings, but also to the widespread influence he had – and continues to have – on people in all walks of life, and artists of every stripe. It's hard to imagine what the world would be like without Jack Kerouac, how different art culture would be, without the inspiration he provided. He taught a whole world of writers and artists to stop thinking and overanalyzing. To work from the heart. To make it real.

Simon Warner speaks to Jim Sampas about Esperanza

SW: This album was based on a Kerouac novella based in Mexico City and entitled *Tristessa*. What made you turn to this somewhat dark story as a source for a musical response?

JS: The *Tristessa* story is something everyone can relate to, especially these days when it seems we all know someone with substance abuse issues. There's an incredible struggle going on throughout, as Jack falls madly in love with someone really incapable of returning those feelings in a truly meaningful way. The artists seemed to relate to both the downward spiral we are seeing played out, and the tug of war Jack is going through, wondering should he stay and try to help Tristessa or should he leave and save himself from the heartbreak. I had the artists pick out different sections of the novella, making this project similar to a concept album, or even a musical, in that there is a story being told through the music, and each piece of the puzzle or song is important to that narrative. Some used the actual text for lyrics; others created lyrics inspired by the story.

SW: The record principally featured an impressive body of new young artists, although established figures like William Fitzsimmons and, once more, Lee Ranaldo were also participants. How did you identify the fresh talent and narrow down the contributors who would take part in the final version?

JS: In my view, we are at another high point of talented artists on the music scene. There is a plethora of incredibly talented recording artists of all genres out there right now. My job was to simply find the ones who matched the project – artists who had shown themselves to be unafraid of delving into serious subject matter, themes that challenge the listener.

SW: How did you feel yet another new generation of rock artists took to the notion of adapting classic Beat literature in this fashion?

JS: Well let's put it this way, in this particular case, and trust me it doesn't always happen this way, having produced tributes to several iconic artists in the past, the ratio of folks who said yes vastly outweighed the ones who passed. And many of the ones who said no, did so only because they had other engagements. The excitement for this one was palpable: from the managers to the artists, everyone seemed to get it, understand that they were about to embark on something set apart from the rest of the projects they were being pursued for. So in that sense, this one is a perfect example of the popularity of Beat literature on yet another generation. I'm not wild about this phrase because it is so overused, but the beat absolutely goes on. And on.

SW: Do you have favourites from the album you would like to pick out?

JS: While I honestly think all the recordings on this album are equally as good, here are three that jump out right this second. The first is Joshua James's song 'Esperanza'. Joshua once commented on the project, 'I was asked to read a novel by the infamous Jack Kerouac entitled *Tristessa*. And, seeing as how Tristessa was a Spanish speaker I felt it necessary to write the song in Spanish.' The two others are Peter Bradley Adams's 'She Has To Come Down' and Gregory Alan Isakov's 'O' City Lights'.

Sleeve notes for the album *Esperanza* (2016), featuring songs inspired by the Kerouac novella *Tristessa* (1960)

Simon Warner

Trembling and chaste: the long sadness of the Mexico City night

Jack Kerouac, the leading light of that maverick pack of 1950s writers who forged the so-called Beat Generation and sparked a social and cultural revolution in the process, is best known for his exhilarating lust for life, expressed in a series of high-octane novels that distilled his adventures and his hopes. In books like *On the Road*, *The Dharma Bums* and *Desolation Angels*, he transformed his own picaresque autobiography into thrilling, foot-to-the-floor fiction.

Yet if Kerouac's image as freewheeling spirit, unfettered hobo, hitchhiking hero of the open road, has been enduring, his motivations, his obsessions, were far more complex. For every vivacious celebration of everyday wonder, he was drawn also to the darker recesses of experience: the plight of the human soul, the early realization that 'we're all going to die'.

His concerns were tied intimately to his early Catholic upbringing, religious foundations that would both inspire and taunt him for every day of his short 47 years. Through the Church he was touched and tainted by God, by the saints, by the Virgin Mary, and threatened constantly by the bony tendrils of his own festering mortality.

There are few examples in his large body of writing that better represent the dolorous yin to the effervescent yang of the novelist's worldview than his 1960 novella *Tristessa*, a story which actually reflects on experiences he had endured around half a decade before in the seething cauldron of Mexico City, a burgeoning mid-century metropolis on the cusp of the primitive and the modern, a chaotic termite hill of the devotional and the damned.

Tristessa is a morphine-addicted prostitute with whom he falls in love. Kerouac's narrator is first hopelessly drawn to this frail and exotic angel of the streets, then returns a year on to discover she has gone into inevitable decline. Few accounts of love can be so haunted by the shadow of approaching tragedy, and the writer, we can assume, only escapes the ultimate conclusion to this fated affair by moving on, his usual default when things became just too difficult to manage.

Yet the relating of this shadowy romance is touched with a terrible beauty. Kerouac's prose is jagged, brittle and broken, staccato phrases punctured by long dashes, a spontaneous combustion of compassion and terror. Amid this Boschian nightmare of rainy alleys, disease and squalor, the novelist still weaves a tapestry that almost pre-empts the wonders and mysteries of Latin American magical realism.

There are many recognizable features, too: Kerouac's Franciscan affection for animals is a regular motif – the cat, the dove, the chicken earn tender mentions – and the magnetic pull of the mystical, whether Christian or Buddhist, infuses the account, too.

Further, another notable figure from the writer's gallery of real-life associates drift in and out of the Mexican night, but the individual called Bull is based not on Kerouac's long-time friend William Burroughs but rather another exiled addict, William Garver. Here dubbed Old Bull Gaines, he is a key protagonist in the curious love triangle as the drama unfolds.

Tristessa is an important, and truthful, part of the myth of Duluoz, the name the writer often adopted for the central character in this cycle of confession. This particular tale is harsh but it is vivid; it has both the brilliant and garish colours of neon midnight and the sepia tones of eternal sadness. But if it is frequently bleak, it is honest and moving, and for all its bitter tears, fundamentally humane.

Now, on this remarkable album, 12 rising artists and bands, working in a range of genres, respond to the novella – taking on its themes as inspiration, adopting its very words as a lyrical source. Almost 60 years after Kerouac's doomed tryst in 'the Nirvana glare of Saturday night', these songs offer a contemporary take on a less celebrated, but no less rich, slice of the writer's kaleidoscopic canon.

Notes

1. From Jack Kerouac, 'Belief in Technique Modern Prose' (See Appendix II).

2. 'Bill Keck was one of the "subterraneans" whom Kerouac met around the San Remo and Fugazzi bars, New York, summer 1953. Keck was a jazz musician, playing guitar and a recording date with trumpeter Tony Fruscella (1959)', according to the entry in Dave Moore's indispensable 'Character key to Kerouac's Duluoz Legend'. See: http://www.beatbookcovers.com/kercomp/ (accessed 17 October 2017).

APPENDIX I: 'ESSENTIALS OF SPONTANEOUS PROSE'[1]

Jack Kerouac

SET-UP The object is set before the mind, either in reality, as in sketching (before a landscape or teacup or old face) or is set in the memory wherein it becomes the sketching from memory of a definite image-object.

PROCEDURE Time being of the essence in the purity of speech, sketching language is undisturbed flow from the mind of personal secret idea-words, blowing (as per jazz musician) on subject of image.

METHOD No periods separating sentence-structures already arbitrarily riddled by false colons and timid usually needless commas – but the vigorous space dash separating rhetorical breathing (as jazz musician drawing breath between outblown phrases) – 'measured pauses which are the essentials of our speech' – 'divisions of the sounds we hear' – 'time and how to note it down.' (William Carlos Williams)

SCOPING Not 'selectivity' of expression but following free deviation (association) of mind into limitless blow-on-subject seas of thought, swimming in sea of English with no discipline other than rhythms of rhetorical exhalation and expostulated statement, like a fist coming down on a table with each complete utterance, bang! (the space dash) – Blow as deep as you want – write as deeply, fish as far down as you want, satisfy yourself first, then reader cannot fail to receive telepathic shock and meaning-excitement by same laws operating in his own human mind.

LAG IN PROCEDURE No pause to think of proper word but the infantile pileup of scatological buildup words till satisfaction is gained, which will turn out to be a great appending rhythm to a thought and be in accordance with Great Law of timing.

TIMING Nothing is muddy that runs in time and to laws of time – Shakespearian stress of dramatic need to speak now in own unalterable way or forever hold tongue – no revisions (except obvious rational mistakes, such as names or calculated insertions in act of not writing but inserting).

CENTER OF INTEREST Begin not from preconceived idea of what to say about image but from jewel center of interest in subject of image at moment of writing, and write outwards swimming in sea of language to peripheral release and exhaustion – Do not afterthink except for poetic or P. S. reasons. Never afterthink to 'improve' or defray impressions, as, the best writing is always the most painful personal wrung-out tossed from cradle warm protective mind-tap from yourself the song of yourself, blow! – now! – your way is your only way – 'good' – or 'bad' – always honest ('ludi – crous'), spontaneous, 'confessionals' interesting, because not 'crafted.' Craft is craft.

STRUCTURE OF WORK Modern bizarre structures (science fiction, etc.) arise from language being dead, 'different' themes give illusion of 'new' life. Follow roughly outlines in outfanning movement over subject, as river rock, so mindflow over jewel-center need (run your mind over it, once) arriving at pivot, where what was dim-formed 'beginning' becomes sharp-necessitating 'ending' and language shortens in race to wire of time-race of work, following laws of Deep Form, to conclusion, last words, last trickle – Night is The End.

MENTAL STATE If possible write 'without consciousness' in semi-trance (as Yeats' later 'trance writing') allowing subconscious to admit in own uninhibited interesting necessary and so 'modern' language what conscious art would censor, and write excitedly, swiftly, with writing-or-typing-cramps, in accordance (as from center to periphery) with laws of orgasm, Reich's 'beclouding of consciousness.' Come from within, out – to relaxed and said.

Notes

1. Jack Kerouac, 'The Essentials of Spontaneous Prose', *Evergreen Review* 2, no. 5 (Summer 1958).

APPENDIX II: 'BELIEF AND TECHNIQUE FOR MODERN PROSE'[1]

Jack Kerouac

1. Scribbled secret notebooks, and wild typewritten pages, for yr own joy
2. Submissive to everything, open, listening
3. Try never get drunk outside yr own house
4. Be in love with yr life
5. Something that you feel will find its own form
6. Be crazy dumbsaint of the mind
7. Blow as deep as you want to blow
8. Write what you want bottomless from bottom of the mind
9. The unspeakable visions of the individual
10. No time for poetry but exactly what is
11. Visionary tics shivering in the chest
12. In tranced fixation dreaming upon object before you
13. Remove literary, grammatical and syntactical inhibition
14. Like Proust be an old teahead of time
15. Telling the true story of the world in interior monolog
16. The jewel center of interest is the eye within the eye
17. Write in recollection and amazement for yourself
18. Work from pithy middle eye out, swimming in language sea
19. Accept loss forever
20. Believe in the holy contour of life
21. Struggle to sketch the flow that already exists intact in mind
22. Dont think of words when you stop but to see picture better
23. Keep track of every day the date emblazoned in yr morning
24. No fear or shame in the dignity of yr experience, language & knowledge
25. Write for the world to read and see yr exact pictures of it
26. Bookmovie is the movie in words, the visual American form

27. In praise of Character in the Bleak inhuman Loneliness

28. Composing wild, undisciplined, pure, coming in from under, crazier the better

29. You're a Genius all the time

30. Writer-Director of Earthly movies Sponsored & Angeled in Heaven

Notes

1. Jack Kerouac, 'Belief and Technique for Modern Prose', *Evergreen Review* 2, no. 8 (Spring 1959).

APPENDIX III: JACK KEROUAC: AN ANNOTATED DISCOGRAPHY

Dave Moore

1949: The John Clellon Holmes Acetates (October)[1, 2]

1. Disc 5B. 33 1/3 rpm, 10″ acetate (6 mins)

    (i)   Kerouac and Seymour Wyse riffing to an unidentified recording.

    (ii) Kerouac and Wyse riffing 'Lover Come Back to Me'.

    (iii) Kerouac and Wyse riffing 'Hot House'.

    (iv) Kerouac and Wyse riffing 'Always'.

2. Disc 6B. 33 1/3 rpm, 10″ acetate (8 mins)

    (i)   Kerouac and Wyse riffing 'Fine and Dandy'.

    (ii) Kerouac and Wyse riffing and singing 'All the Things You Are'.

    (iii) Kerouac and Wyse riffing 'Cherokee'.

    (iv) Kerouac and Wyse riffing and singing 'Pennies From Heaven'.

3. Disc 7B. 33 1/3 rpm, 10″ acetate (6 mins)

    (i)   Kerouac, Wyse and Lee Nevels riffing 'I've Found A New Baby'.

    (ii) Kerouac and Wyse riffing to a Lester Young recording.

4. Disc 10B. 33 1/3 rpm, 10″ acetate (8 mins)

    (i)   Kerouac, Wyse and Nevels riffing 'Ornithology'.

    (ii) Kerouac, Wyse and Nevels riffing 'Groovin' High'.

    (iii) Kerouac, Wyse and Nevels riffing an unidentified number.

    (iv) Kerouac, Wyse and Nevels riffing 'Euphoria'.

5. Disc 11A. 33 1/3 rpm, 10″ acetate (9 mins)

    (i)   Kerouac reads from an early, unedited draft of *The Town and the City* – the football game sequence, described in Book 3, Chapter 7 of the published book.[3]

    (ii) Kerouac and Allen Ginsberg conversation: 'What is a pippione?'[4]

    (iii) Ginsberg and Holmes conversation: 'The microphone, Blake, Shakespeare'.

    (iv) Kerouac and Seymour Wyse riffing 'Pennies From Heaven'.[5]

6. Disc 13B. 33 1/3 rpm, 10″ acetate (3 mins)

   (i)   The Three Tools (Kerouac, Wyse, Holmes) perform an a cappella riff, 'Logic'.

7. Disc 14A. 33 1/3 rpm, 10″ acetate (7 mins)

   (i)   Kerouac and Wyse riffing to Sarah Vaughan's recording of 'Body and Soul'.

   (ii) Kerouac and Wyse riffing 'Always'.

   (iii) Kerouac and Wyse riffing 'Lover Come Back to Me'.

8. Disc 15A. 33 1/3 rpm, 12″ acetate (20 October 1949) (9 mins)

   (i)   Kerouac, Wyse and Holmes riffing 'The Absolute'.[6]

   (ii) Kerouac, Wyse and Holmes riffing 'I Can't Get Started'.

   (iii) Kerouac, Wyse and Holmes riffing and whistling 'Ghost of a Chance'.

9. Disc 15B. 33 1/3 rpm, 12″ acetate (20 October 1949) (7 mins)

   (i)   Jack Kerouac reads two selections from *Hamlet* ('in a new manner'), with background music, including Lester Young's 'Jumping With Symphony Sid' (1947).[6]

10. Disc 20A. 33 1/3 rpm, 8″ acetate (7 mins)

   (i)   Kerouac and Wyse riffing 'Hot House'.

   (ii) Kerouac and Wyse riffing 'Groovin' High'.

   (iii) Kerouac and Wyse riffing 'Lover Come Back to Me'.

These recordings were made on an acetate-cutting machine left in John Clellon Holmes' New York apartment by his brother-in-law. The blank discs were provided by Seymour Wyse, who worked with Jerry Newman in a record shop. Another acetate survives (Disc 9), dating from the same period, and containing recordings of eight of Allen Ginsberg's earliest poems (as subsequently published in *The Gates of Wrath*) on a 9-minute, 10″, 33 1/3 rpm disc.[7]

1950: Ann Bradford interview (March) (5 mins)

Kerouac interviewed about his recently published novel, *The Town and the City*. Broadcast by radio station WLLH, Lowell, on 15 March.

1952: The Cassady Tape (18 mins)

   (i)   Neal Cassady reading from Proust (*Swann's Way*), with pronunciation corrected by Jack Kerouac.

   (ii) Kerouac singing 'A Foggy Day in London Town' and 'My Funny Valentine'.

(iii) Kerouac humming an improvised jazz riff.

(iv) Kerouac reading from *Doctor Sax* – Book 6, Chapter 5 of the published book – with Neal making encouraging sounds.

(v) Kerouac, Neal and Carolyn Cassady discuss William Burroughs, as transcribed in the tape section of *Visions of Cody* (McGraw-Hill, p. 236). 'He'll disintegrate in the heat of the tropics; that's bound to be what'll happen.'

(vi) Neal (discussing Philip Lamantia?): 'He's a . . . he doesn't do nothing, does he? He just stays home . . .' Another fragment from the tape section of *Visions of Cody* (p. 204).

This recording comprises several different layers, over-recorded on the same tape. Items (i) to (iv) are the later recordings, made at the Cassady's home in San Jose, around September 1952. Items (v) and (vi) were recorded at their previous home in Russell Street, San Francisco, around February 1952. These fragments are all that survive of the tapes that Jack, Neal and Carolyn recorded together. Jack recorded over some of the others with records for the Cassady children.[8] 'A Foggy Day' can be heard in the background of the Robert Hunter track 'Have you ever seen anyone like Cody Pomeray?' included on the CD *Kerouac: Kicks Joy Darkness*, Rykodisc RCD 10329 (1997).

1953: John Clellon Holmes Tape (January) (5 mins)

(i) Holmes and Ginsberg greet Kerouac after his return to New York from the West Coast. *Doctor Sax*, Mexico and California are discussed. 'This is what Carolyn and I drink all the time. But not port, you understand – tokay. And Neal shudders, and says "Ugh!" when he looks at us, because of his father.'

(ii) Kerouac and Holmes riffing to Thelonious Monk's recording of 'Round Midnight'.

1958: Mike Wallace Interview (January)

Kerouac interviewed by Mike Wallace, CBS-TV, New York City. Kerouac presents the mysticism and religion of the Beat generation. He explains that love will cause a mystical religious revival in modern Western society.

1958: John Wingate Interview (March) (30 mins)

Kerouac interviewed by John Wingate, *Nightbeat*, Channel 7, ABC-TV, New York City. On this, his second appearance on *Nightbeat* (the first was in September 1957), Jack responds to Wingate's question 'What is a "mainliner"?' by singing 'Skyliner'.

1958: *Poetry for the Beat Generation*, Dot 3154, Hanover HML 5000 (March) (37 mins)

Kerouac LP, with Steve Allen, piano. Fourteen readings, from 'October in the Railroad Earth', *Mexico City Blues*, 'Orizaba 210 Blues', 'Orlanda Blues', 'MacDougal Street Blues' and *Old Angel Midnight*, recorded in New York. Reissued by Rhino Records as part of *The Jack Kerouac Collection* (4 LP or 3 CD set, 1990).

1958: *Readings by Jack Kerouac on the Beat Generation*, Verve MGV-15005 (March) (42 mins)

Kerouac LP, with seven readings, from *Desolation Angels*, *San Francisco Blues*, *Mexico City Blues*, *Old Angel Midnight*, 'History of Bop', *The Subterraneans* and *Visions of Cody*, recorded in New York. Reissued by Rhino Records as part of *The Jack Kerouac Collection*. According to producer Bill Randle, material for another two albums was recorded at this session, but never issued, including an *On the Road* set, for which the search continues. Some of this *On the Road* material, a reading by Kerouac of his 'Jazz of the Beat Generation', was found on two acetate discs and released on the CD *Jack Kerouac Reads On the Road*, Rykodisc RCD 10474 (1999). Also on one of the acetates was Kerouac's reading of a short poem, 'Hooray For Zoot Sims', which is probably chorus 32 of Kerouac's 'Orlanda Blues'. This track is as yet unissued.

In 2007 a tape emerged which contained extracts from the master tapes of this Verve album. Most of the tracks included extra content to that on the issued album, including spoken introductions by Kerouac to each track and extra sections of the *Desolation Angels*, *San Francisco Blues* and *Mexico City Blues* readings. The date of recording is given on the tape box as 2 March 1958.[9]

1958: June Havoc Interview (30 mins)

Kerouac interviewed by June Havoc, Radio station WOR, New York City.

1958: Ben Hecht Interview (17 October) (30 mins)

Kerouac interviewed by Ben Hecht, Channel 7, ABC-TV, New York City. Hecht tries to get Kerouac to speak out against the President and the Pope, but Jack insisted he wanted to speak *for* things, like the crucifix, the Star of Israel, Mohammed, Buddha and Bach. A 15½-minute extract has been issued by Rhino Records as part of *The Beat Generation* set (1992).

1958: Brandeis University Lecture (6 November) (12½ mins)

A talk by Kerouac, given as part of the forum 'Is There a Beat Generation?', held in the Hunter College Playhouse, New York. It includes readings of the poems 'To Harpo Marx' and the 230th chorus of *Mexico City Blues*. Issued by Rhino Records as part of *The Jack Kerouac Collection*. The talk was subsequently published in an enlarged and edited form as 'The Origins Of the Beat Generation' in *Playboy*, June 1959.

1959: *Pull My Daisy* Soundtrack (Spring) (25 mins)

Kerouac narrated the soundtrack over this movie by Robert Frank and Alfred Leslie, which starred Allen Ginsberg, Gregory Corso, Peter Orlovsky, Larry Rivers, David Amram and others. The soundtrack recording was made in three takes at Jerry Newman's studio, New York, and the final version was spliced together from all three takes.[10]

1959: *Blues and Haikus*, Hanover HM 5006 (July) (47 mins)

Kerouac LP, with Al Cohn (tenor sax, piano) and Zoot Sims (tenor sax), recorded in New York. Readings from five works: *American Haikus*, *San Francisco Blues*, 'Hard Hearted Old Farmer', 'The Last Hotel' (from *Tangiers Blues*) and *Some of the Dharma*. This session has been reissued by Rhino Records as part of *The Jack Kerouac Collection*. Rhino discovered the original master tapes in unmarked boxes at EMI's Abbey Road studios in London and have released the complete session, including the previously unissued 'Old Western Movies' (in three takes) and 'Conclusion of the Railroad Earth'. These tracks are presented in stereo, as are also 'Hard Hearted Old Farmer' and 'The Last Hotel/Some of the Dharma', while the remaining two readings, 'American Haikus' and 'Book of Blues' are in the mono of the original release. Studio talk between Jack, the musicians and producer Bob Thiele is preserved on the Rhino release. Also discovered on the master tape and included on the Rhino release were a few extra lines in the middle of one of the choruses of *San Francisco Blues* which were excised for the original 1960 release.

1959: Steve Allen Show (16 November) (6 mins)

Kerouac on *The Steve Allen Plymouth Show*, NBC-TV, Los Angeles, for a fee of $2,000. Allen interviews Kerouac, while playing the piano, and accompanies him as Kerouac reads (as Allen believes) from *On the Road*. What Jack is actually reading are two sections from Part 3 of the then unpublished *Visions of Cody* (McGraw-Hill, pp. 295,

368) followed by the final paragraphs of *On the Road*. The readings only (3½ mins) were issued by Rhino Records as part of *The Jack Kerouac Collection*. (The complete session also exists as a colour video.)

1960: *Doctor Sax / Old Angel Midnight* (60 mins)

A recording made by Kerouac, at his home in Northport, Long Island, for his girlfriend of the time, Lois Sorrells. Readings are from *Doctor Sax*, Book 6, Chapters 1, 2 and 3; *Old Angel Midnight*, Sections 52–6; *Doctor Sax*, Book 6, Chapters 4, 5, 6 and 12; *Old Angel Midnight*, Sections 66–7. The intermingling of material in this way was arranged by Kerouac as a form of oral cut-up technique. Kerouac reads against the sound of Frank Sinatra on the hi-fi, from two albums, *No One Cares* and *In The Wee Small Hours*. The *Doctor Sax* readings were used to great effect on the soundtrack of Richard Lerner's movie *What Happened to Kerouac?* (1986), and in BBC TV's *Kerouac* (*Arena*, February 1988). At the end of the tape, Jack is heard talking to his guest (Leroi Jones?): 'End of record, end of record ... Turn off the tape. Leroi, turn off the tape!'

1960: *San Francisco Blues* (29 mins)

Another home recording for Lois Sorrells, and probably a continuation of the above session. A reading of the complete *San Francisco Blues*, although choruses 1 to 14 are missing from the tape in circulation. Also recorded to the backing of a Sinatra album (*In The Wee Small Hours*). Halfway through, Memere may be heard admonishing Jack's guest (Leroi?): '... You've been here all day!'

1960: More Home Recordings

(i) 'MacDougal Street Blues' (2:48).

   Reading by Kerouac, with overdubbed bass, synth and guitar by Joe Strummer. Released on the CD *Kerouac – Kicks Joy Darkness*, Rykodisc RCD 10329 (1997).

(ii) 'Orizaba 210 Blues' (9:34).

(iii) 'Washington D.C. Blues' (17:46).

(iv) 'On the Road' (2:18).

Readings by Kerouac, with Sinatra playing in the background. First 13 choruses of 'Orizaba 210 Blues' and the as yet unpublished 'Washington D.C. Blues'. Both included on the CD *Jack Kerouac Reads On the Road*, Rykodisc RCD 10474 (1999), with music soundtracks by David Amram added in order to cover up the sound of Sinatra. The

CD also included Kerouac singing his song 'On the Road', as well as a cover by Tom Waits with Primus.

1961: Jerry Newman Session (13 mins)

Kerouac, high, singing against backing tapes in Jerry Newman's studio, New York. The songs attempted are 'Ain't We Got Fun', 'Come Rain Or Shine', 'When A Woman Loves A Man' and 'Leavin' Town'. Jack dedicates the songs to 'sweet Jerry Newman, my angel', and to a girlfriend who is present in the studio, 'lovely, beautiful, skinny, shapely Sue Evans' (included on the CD *Jack Kerouac Reads On the Road*, Rykodisc RCD 10474 (1999)).

1962: Charles Jarvis Interview (8 October) (25 mins)

Kerouac interviewed by Professor Charles Jarvis and James Curtis, in the series *Dialogues in Great Books*, radio station WCAP, Lowell. Topics include his mother and his brother Gerard, writers and writing. 'Once God moves the hand, you go back and revise – it's a sin!' Many quotes from the interview are included in Jarvis's book *Visions of Kerouac* (1973). The third edition of the book (1997) included a complete transcription of the interview.

1963: Gregory Corso Interview (Summer) (90 mins)

Kerouac interviewed by Gregory Corso at Jack's home, in Northport. Jack is accused of unconcern for the welfare of blacks, compared with his apparent love for them as expressed in *On the Road*. 'I meant every word,' Kerouac replies.

1964: Harvard University (March) (65 mins)

Kerouac was invited to give a reading in Harvard University's Lowell House common room. A recording of the event was made, and Kerouac can be heard talking with the students and reading from 'Mexico City Blues' (230th Chorus) and 'Orlanda Blues' (10th Chorus).

1964: Northport Library Interview (14 April) (150 mins)[11]

Kerouac interviewed for the Northport Public Library, in the art studio of his friend Stanley Twardowicz. The interviewers include Miklos Zsedely, then assistant director of the library, James Schwaner, David Roberts and Twardowicz. Topics covered were Kerouac's family history, his travels in Europe (France and England), painting, writers and writing, Beats, belief, religion and God. Most of the interview was transcribed in *Athanor* 1–3 (1971–2), and a small fragment later appeared in *Street Magazine* (1975).

1964: Northport Library Interview (13 August) (115 mins)

Miklos Zsedely continued his interview shortly before Kerouac left Northport for St Petersburg, Florida. Stanley Twardowicz and his wife Ann participated in the interview which again took place in Twardowicz's studio. More relaxed than the April interview, the discussion ranged from Catholicism to broken relations with Ginsberg to the reasons behind the Florida move.

1964: Party Tape (August 26) (50 mins)[12]

Recording of a party, with Lawrence Smith and Stanley Twardowicz, at Kerouac's house, in Northport, on the eve of his intended return to Florida. Jack talks about the Kennedys, his time in the Navy and his disappointment – with his own life and with America.

1964: Warhol Session (Summer) (10 mins)

Dialogue with Kerouac, Ginsberg, Corso, Peter Orlovsky, Taylor Mead, Gerard Malanga and Andy Warhol, during the filming of *Couch* at The Factory, New York. Included on the Gerard Malanga CD *Up From The Archives*, Sub Rosa SR170 (1999).

1965: 'The Midnight Ghost' (Autumn) (60 mins)

Kerouac recorded at his home in St Petersburg, Florida, plucking Cliff Anderson's guitar and performing a talking blues, describing a ride on the Zipper freight train from San Francisco to Los Angeles.

1967: CBC-TV Interview (7 March) (20 mins)

Kerouac interviewed by Fernand Seguin on *Le Sel de la Semaine*, CBC-TV, Montreal, Canada. The interview was conducted in French, and covered his Lowell childhood, spontaneous prose and the Beats. 'If you were twenty years old today, would you do the same as you have already done?' 'Well I've already done it, and I'm fed up.' A transcription in French and English has been published in Quebec as *Les Avant-Dire* 3 (September 1987). (A black and white video also exists of this programme.)

1967: Christmas Tape (December)

Kerouac at a Christmas party at the house of Manuel 'Chiefy' Nobriga, Lowell, teaching carols to Nobriga's little boy.

1968: William Buckley Interview (3 September) (50 mins)

Kerouac discusses 'Hippies' with William F. Buckley Jr, Ed Sanders and Lewis Yablansky, on Buckley's *Firing Line* TV show, New York City. 'Hey Ed, I was arrested two weeks ago, and the policeman said "I'm arresting you for decay."' (This programme also exists as a colour video.)

1968–9: *Vanity of Duluoz* (62 mins)

A home recording by Kerouac, in St Petersburg, Florida, reading the first eight chapters, from Book 1, Part 1 to Book 2, Part 1. A sad, drunken affair. Jack concludes by singing 'Ain't Nobody's Business' and 'Cigarettes and Whiskey'.

1968–9: *Mexico City Blues* (115 mins)

Another home recording, possibly from the same session as above. Kerouac is heard reading the introduction and Choruses 1 to 112. A radio, tuned to WFLA, Tampa, is playing music in the background.

1968–9: *Satori in Paris* (130 mins)

Yet another home recording at St Petersburg. Kerouac reads the complete 38 chapters of his book.

1969: 'Jack's Last Tape' (85 mins)

St. Petersburg, Florida. Kerouac sings, whistles and scats along to the radio, and plays harmonica. Songs include 'Love is a Many Splendoured Thing', 'Are You Lonesome

Tonight', 'Night and Day' and 'The Sound of Music'. He is also heard talking with his wife, Stella. The complete session is analysed by Gerald Nicosia in *Memory Babe*.

Other tapes of Kerouac from the 1960s exist, according to Nicosia. Tony Sampas, Kerouac's brother-in-law, supposedly has dozens of hours of Jack reading and rapping on various subjects, and Chiefy Nobriga, a bookie, had a tap on his phone and recorded several hours of Jack's drunken calls to his house. Further details of these recordings will hopefully emerge at a later date. Seymour Wyse has also reported that his brother, the late Dr Derek Wyse, had some recordings of Kerouac on acetate discs.

Kerouac has also written about a recording session at party at the Lynbrook, NY, house of his pianist friend Tom Livornese on New Year's Eve, 1947. 'We had a recording machine and made mad jazz records all night, singing and riffing with the piano – "How High the Moon" and "Lover" and "Born to be Blue," etc. Some of it is actually great jazz.'[13] None of these recordings are known to have survived.

A collection of material relating to Kerouac was recently acquired by the Rose Library of Emory University (Atlanta, Georgia). The collection includes many of the audio tapes listed above, as well as other recordings of Kerouac reading from his work and talking with friends.

Notes

1. Barbara Rodrigues, 'John Clellon Holmes, Recordings, 1949–1951 and 1968', Kent, OH: Kent State University Library, 1996.

2. Dave Moore, 'The John Clellon Holmes Acetates', Kent, OH: Kent State University Library, 2001.

3. Dave Moore, '*The Town and the City* – Extracts from an Early Draft', *Moody Street Irregulars* 14 (Spring 1984). Includes a transcription of this item.

4. Dave Moore, 'A Beat Conversation, 1949', *Moody Street Irregulars* 11 (Spring/Summer 1982). Includes a transcription of this item, as well as a background to the acetate recordings, by John Clellon Holmes.

5. Jack Kerouac, *The Subterraneans*, New York: Grove Press, 1958, p. 68): 'Before, I'd with Ossip Popper sung bop, made records, always taking the part of the bass fiddle thum thum to his phrasing.'

6. Jack Kerouac, October 1949 journal, in Jack Kerouac, *Windblown World: The Journals of Jack Kerouac 1947–1954*, New York: Viking, 2004, p. 237: 'On Thurs. night Holmes and Seymour and I made some astounding "prophetic" voice-music recordings that sound like [Lennie] Tristano's "Intuition". I did a few boyishly sad Hamlet soliloquies.'

7. George Dowden, *A Bibliography of the Works of Allen Ginsberg, 1943–1967*, San Francisco: City Lights, 1971.

8. Carolyn Cassady, 'Kerouac and Women', Naropa Institute, Boulder, CO, 27 July 1982.

9. Andrew Sclanders, *Beat Books Catalogue* 45 (February 2007).

10. Blaine Allan, 'The Making (and Unmaking) of *Pull My Daisy*', *Film History* 2 (1988): 185–205. Abridged version in *Moody Street Irregulars* no. 22/23 (Winter 1989–90).

11. Barbara Johnson, 'Jack Kerouac: Unique & Primary Items', Northport-East Northport Public Library.

12. Pat Fenton, *Jack Kerouac's Last Night in Northport*, Coventry, UK: Beat Scene Press, 2012.

13. Jack Kerouac, letter to Allen Ginsberg, 2 January 1948, in *Jack Kerouac: Selected Letters 1940–1956*, ed. Ann Charters, New York: Viking, 1995.

Bibliography

Charters, Ann, *A Bibliography of Works by Jack Kerouac*, New York: Phoenix Bookshop, 1975.

Jarvis, Charles, *Visions of Kerouac: The Life of Jack Kerouac*, Ithaca, NY: Ithaca Press, 1974.

McNally, Dennis, *Desolate Angel: Jack Kerouac, the Beat Generation, and America*, Boston: Da Capo Press, 1983.

Milewski, Robert *Jack Kerouac: An Annotated Bibliography of Secondary Sources, 1944–1979*, Metuchen, NJ: Scarecrow Press, 1981.

Nicosia, Gerald, *Memory Babe: A Critical Biography of Jack Kerouac*, New York: Grove Press, 1983.

Also consulted were Robert Milewski's *Jack Kerouac: Annotated Bibliography of Secondary Sources*, Dennis McNally's *Desolate Angel*, and Charles Jarvis's *Visions of Kerouac*.

APPENDIX IV: TRIBUTE ALBUM DISCOGRAPHY

Jim Sampas

Various Artists – *Kerouac: Kicks Joy Darkness (A Spoken Word Tribute With Music)* (1997)

1. Morphine, 'Kerouac' (2:54)
Recorded and Mixed by Mark Sandman.
Drums: Billy Conway.
Voice: Mark Sandman.
Music by Billy Conway and Mark Sandman.
Words by Mark Sandman.

2. Lydia Lunch, 'Bowery Blues' (1:55).
Recorded by Lydia Lunch.
Performer: Lydia Lunch.
Words by Jack Kerouac.

3. Michael Stipe, 'My Gang' (2:23).
Recorded and Mixed by Tom Lewis.
Voice, organ (Vox Jaguar): Michael Stipe.
Music by Michael Stipe.
Words by Jack Kerouac.

4. Steven Tyler, 'Dream: "Us Kids Swim Off a Gray Pier . . ."' (1:34).
Recorded and Mixed by Kevin Shirley.
Assistant Engineer: Rory Romano.
Voice and Backing Vocals: Steven Tyler.
Words by Jack Kerouac.

5. Hunter S. Thompson, 'Letter to William S. Burroughs & Ode to Jack' (1:41).
Recorded by George Tobia, Jr.
Voice: Hunter S. Thompson.
Words by Jack Kerouac and Hunter S. Thompson.

6. Maggie Estep and The Spitters, 'Skid Row Wine' (5:51).
Recorded and Mixed by Ingo Krauss and Roy Mayorga.
Assistant Engineer: Sal Mormando.
Drums: Louis Echavarria.
Bass: Bill Bronson.
Guitar: Tim Bradlee.
Vocals: Mark Ashwill.
Voice: Maggie Estep.
Music by Bill Bronson, Louis Echavarria, Maggie Estep, Mark Ashwill and Tim Bradlee.
Words by Jack Kerouac.

7. Richard Lewis, 'America's New Trinity Of Love: Dean, Brando, Presley' (6:06).
Recorded and Mixed by Daniel Messerli.
Voice: Richard Lewis.
Words by Jack Kerouac.

8. Lawrence Ferlinghetti and Helium, 'Dream: "On a Sunny Afternoon . . ."' (2:04).
Recorded by David Cook, Ann Pope, Dan McLaughlin and Owen Burkett.
Mixed by Dan McLaughlin, Jim Sampas and Mary Timony.
Guitar (Ghost): Ash Bowie.
Keyboards, Xylophone, Vocals: Mary Timony.
Voice: Lawrence Ferlinghetti.
Music by Helium.
Words by Jack Kerouac.

9. Jack Kerouac and Joe Strummer, 'MacDougal Street Blues' (2:48).
Bass, Synth, Guitar: Joe Strummer.
Electronics (Beatbox): Richard Norris.
Recorded and Mixed by Joe Strummer.
Music by Joe Strummer.
Words by Jack Kerouac.

10. Allen Ginsberg, 'Brooklyn Bridge Blues (Choruses 1–9)' (5:47).
Recorded by David Cook.
Mixed by Chris Anderson and Jim Sampas.
Voice: Allen Ginsberg.
Words by Jack Kerouac.

11. Eddie Vedder, Campbell 2000 and Sadie 7, 'Hymn' (3:12).
Recorded and Mixed by 13 Anthony.
Bass: Sadie 7.
Guitar: Campbell 2000.

Voice: Eddie Vedder.
Music by Eddie Vedder.
Words by Jack Kerouac.

12. William S. Burroughs and Tomandandy, 'Old Western Movies' (2:32).
Recorded and Mixed by Brian Smith and Jerry Gottus.
NYC Music Coordinator: Josh Rabinowitz.
Accordion: Gil Goldstein.
Double Bass: John Patatucci.
Percussion: Bashiri Johnson and John Arrucci.
Guitar: James Liebow.
Keyboards: Tomandandy.
Voice: William Burroughs.
Music by Tomandandy.
Words by Jack Kerouac.

13. Juliana Hatfield, 'Silly Goofball Pomes' (4:02).
Recorded and Mixed by David Cook.
Guitar: Gregory Hormel.
Voice: Juliana Hatfield.
Music by Gregory A. Hormel.
Words by Jack Kerouac.

14. John Cale, 'The Moon' (3:01).
Recorded and Mixed by John Cale.
Voice and Keyboards: John Cale.
Music by John Cale.
Words by Jack Kerouac.

15. Johnny Depp and Come, 'Madroad Driving . . .' (3:28).
Come Recorded and Mixed by Tim O'Heir.
Johnny Depp Recorded and Mixed by Bruce Witkin.
Drums and Percussion: Kevin Coultas.
Bass: Tara Jane O'Neil.
Guitar, Carinet, Vibraslap: Thalia Zedek.
Guitar and Zither (Marxophone): Chris Brokaw.
Voice: Johnny Depp.
Music by Come.
Words by Jack Kerouac.

16. Robert Hunter, 'Have You Ever Seen Anyone Like Cody Pomeray? . . .' (2:36).
Recorded by Robert Hunter.
Backing Vocals (Background Scat Singing, Playing On Cassette player): Jack Kerouac.
Voice and Tape (Jack Kerouac Playing On The Cassette Player In Hunter's Car):
    Robert Hunter.
Words by Jack Kerouac.

17. Lee Ranaldo and Dana Colley, 'Letter to John Clellon Holmes' (3:48).
Recorded by Pete Weiss.
Mixed by Dana Colley, Jim Sampas and Pete Weiss.
Saxophone: Dana Colley.
Voice: Lee Ranaldo.
Music by Dana Colley and Lee Ranaldo.
Words by Jack Kerouac.

18. Anna Domino, 'Pome on Doctor Sax' (1:45).
Recorded and Mixed by Anna Domino.
Music by Anna Domino.
Voice and Keyboards: Anna Domino.
Words by Jack Kerouac.

19. Rob Buck and Danny Chauvin, 'Mexico Rooftop' (1:25).
Guitar: Rob Buck.
Saxophone: Tony White.
Voice: Danny Chauvin.
Music by Daniel Chauvin and Rob Buck.
Words by Jack Kerouac.

20. Patti Smith with Thurston Moore and Lenny Kaye, 'The Last Hotel' (3:47).
Recorded and Mixed by Lonnie Bedell.
Guitars: Lenny Kaye, Patti Smith and Thurston Moore.
Voice: Patti Smith.
Music by Patti Smith.
Words by Jack Kerouac.

21. Warren Zevon and Michael Wolff, 'Running Through – Chinese Poem Song' (3:34).
Recorded and Mixed by Duncan Aldrich.
Piano: Michael Wolff.
Voice: Warren Zevon.
Music by Michael Wolff.
Words by Jack Kerouac.

22. Jim Carroll with Lee Ranaldo, Lenny Kaye and Anton Sanco, 'Woman' (2:25).
Recorded and Mixed by Warton Tears.
Guitars: Lee Ranaldo and Lenny Kaye.
Keyboards: Anton Sanco.
Voice: Jim Carroll.
Music by Anton Sanco, Lee Ranaldo and Lenny Kaye.
Words by Jack Kerouac.

23. Matt Dillon with Joey Altruda, Joe Gonzalez and Pablo Calogero, 'Mexican Loneliness' (3:19).
Recorded and Mixed by Danny Caccavo.
Cigars at sessions provided by George Tobia, Jr.
Bass: Joey Altruda.
Percussion: Joe Gonzalez.
Saxophone: Pablo Calogero.
Voice: Matt Dillon.
Music by Joe Gonzalez, Joey Altruda and Pablo Calogero.
Words by Jack Kerouac.

24. Inger Lorre and Jeff Buckley, 'Angel Mine' (5:24).
Recorded and Mixed by Hillary Johnson.
Guitar, Sitar, Voice Saxophone and Voice: Jeff Buckley.
Voice, Guitar, Keyboards: Inger Lorre.
Music by Inger Lorre.
Words by Jack Kerouac.

25. Eric Andersen, 'Brooklyn Bridge Blues (Chorus 10)' (1:59).
Recorded by Eric Andersen.
Voice: Eric Anderson.
Words by Jack Kerouac.

Recorded at Hi-N-Dry, Rockit Studios, Avatar Studios, Harold Dessau Recording, Nevessa Productions Mobile Recording Studio, Fort Apache, The Woodshed, Heckfield, The Garage, Los Angeles, Light Of Day Studios, Avalon Studios, Pollywood Studios, Fun City, This Way Studios, Spa Recording Studios.
Mixed at Hi-N-Dry, Rockit Studios, Avatar Studios, Harold Dessau Recording, Fort Apache, The Woodshed, Heckfield, The Garage, Los Angeles, Zippah Studios, Light Of Day Studios, Fun City, This Way Studios, Spa Recording Studios.

Produced by Jim Sampas.
Associate Producer: Lee Ranaldo.
A&R (Voices Series / Product Management): David Greenberg.

Package Design: Barbara Longo.
Illustration (Skid Row Wine – Drawing): Ralph Steadman.
Mastered by Danny Caccavo.
Kerouac Legal Representation: George Tobia, Jr.
Research by Barbara Longo and Sonya Kolowrat.
Photography by Allen Ginsberg.
Record Label: Rykodisc.
Original Release Date: 8 April 1997.

Various Artists – *Jack Kerouac Reads On the Road* (1999)

1. Jack Kerouac, 'Ain't We Got Fun'.
Recorded and Mixed by Jerry Newman.
Instrumentation by Unknown Ensemble.
Tape transfer by Sean Slade.
Vocals: Jack Kerouac.
Written by Egan, Whiting and Sammy Kahn.

2. Jack Kerouac, 'On the Road (Jazz of the Beat Generation)' (28:40).
Recording Transfer by Greg Calbi and Steve Fallone.
Voice: Jack Kerouac.
Words by Jack Kerouac.

3. Jack Kerouac, 'On the Road' (2:16).
Recorded and Mixed by Danny Lawrence.
Assistant Engineer: James Harned.
Arranged by Victor Juris and John Medeski.
Recording Transfer by Jim Sampas.
Guitar: Victor Juris.
Hammond organ: John Medeski.
Voice: Jack Kerouac.
Words by Jack Kerouac.

4. Jack Kerouac, 'Come Rain or Shine' (3:37).
Recorded and Mixed by Jerry Newman.
Instrumentation by an Unknown Ensemble.
Lyrics by Johnny Mercer.
Music by Harold Arlen.
Recording Transfer by Sean Slade.
Vocals: Jack Kerouac.

5. Jack Kerouac, 'Orizaba 210 Blues' (9:34).

Recorded and Mixed by Danny Lawrence.

Assistant Engineer: James Harned.

Recording Transfer: Jim Sampas.

Performer, French Horn, Piano, Shanai, Goblet Drum (Dumbek), Drums (Frame Drum), Flute (Lakota), Tin Whistle (Penny), Ocarina, Congas, Percussion: David Amram.

Voice: Jack Kerouac.

Music by David Amram.

Words by Jack Kerouac.

6. Jack Kerouac, 'When a Woman Loves a Man' (2:54).

Recorded and Mixed by Jerry Newman.

Instrumentation by an Unknown Ensemble.

Recording Transfer by Sean Slade.

Written by Bernard D. Hanighen, Gordon Jenkins and John H. Mercer.

Vocals: Jack Kerouac.

7. Jack Kerouac, 'Leavin' Town' (3:00).

Recorded and Mixed by Jerry Newman.

Instrumentation by an Unknown Ensemble.

Recording Transfer by Sean Slade.

Written by George Handy and Jack Segal.

Vocals: Jack Kerouac.

8. Jack Kerouac, 'Washington D.C. Blues' (17:43).

Recorded and Mixed by Danny Lawrence.

Assistant Engineer: Danny Harned.

Performed by the David Amram Ensemble.

Drums, Bongos: Johnny Almendra.

Congas: Candido.

Bass: Victor Venegas.

Alto Saxophone: Jerry Dodgion.

Bassoon: Jane Taylor.

Guitar: Victor Juris.

Oboe, English Horn: Ronald Roseman.

Hammond B3 Organ: John Medeski.

Viola: Midhat Serbagi.

Piano, French Horn, Shanai, Goblet Drum (Dumbek), Penny Whistle: David Amram.

Vocals: Jack Kerouac.

9. Tom Waits and Primus, 'On the Road' (3:58).
Recorded by Biff Daws.
Mixed by Bernd Bergdorf.
Second Engineer: Jeff Sloan.
Upright Bass and Percussion: Les Claypool.
Guitar, Percussion: Larry LaLonde.
Percussion: Brain.
Saxophone: Ralph Carney.
Vocals, Guitar, Percussion: Tom Waits.
Music by Jack Kerouac and Tom Waits.
Words by Jack Kerouac.

Produced by Jim Sampas and Lee Ranaldo.
A&R (Voices Series): David Greenberg.
Art Direction, Design: Frank Olinsky.
Additional Digital Editing by Lee Ranaldo.
Liner Notes: Douglas Brinkley.
Mastered by Greg Calbi.
Assistant Mastering Engineer: Steve Fallone.
Photography by Robert Frank (Front And Back Covers).
Photography by David Greenberg (Macro Images).
Photography by Michael Stipe (Shack And Train Station).
Record Label: Rykodisc.
Original Release Date: 14 September 1999.

Various Artists – *Doctor Sax and the Great World Snake* (2003)

Piano, Hammond B3 Organ, Keyboard Strings and Mellotron: John Medeski.
Drums, Percussion: Kenny Wollesen.
Acoustic Bass, Electric Bass, Effects, Sintir: Mike Rivard.
Saxophone: Eric Hipp.

Narrated by Robert Creeley.

Voice Actors:
Baroque: Graham Parker.
Blanche, Nin: Anne Emerick.
Dicky: Bill Janovitz.
Doctor Sax: Robert Hunter.
Gene: Jim Sampas.
GJ: John Keegan.

Jacky Duluoz, Voice, Count Condu, Boaz, Butcher, Man 1, Parakeet, Man 2: Jim Carroll.
Lousy: Ellis Paul.
Ma, Mother, Woman: Kristina Wacome.
Pa: Jim Eppard.
The Wizard: Lawrence Ferlinghetti.
Vamp: Kate Pierson.
Wizard's Wife, Woman 2: Maggie Estep.

Music by John Medeski.
Words by Jack Kerouac.

Produced and Directed Jim Sampas.

Mixed at Applehead.
Mastered By Mike Fossenkemper at Mastered at Turtle Tone Studios.
Design by Ron Valdes.
Design Layout by Jim Sampas, Phil Hopkins, Ralph Stevens and Ron Valdes.
Book introduction by Jim Sampas.
Text transcribed by Jim Sampas.

Recorded by Brandon Mason, Chris Bittner, Chris Caswell, Fran Flannery, Jeff Philips, Mike Birnbaum, Mike Rorick and Scott Harding.
Mixed by Scott Harding.
Digital Editing: John Keegan and Jim Sampas.
Illustrations by Richard Sala.
Liner Notes: Douglas Brinkley and Jim Sampas.
Mastered by Alex Theoret at Turtle Tone Studios.
Recorded at Audio Magic, Applehead Recording, Hot Sound, Allaire Studios, Madhouse Productions, American Zoetrope and Gargoyle Studio.
Mixed at Applehead Recording.
Editorial Assistance by David Stanford.
Editorial Consultant: Paul Marion.
Musical Research and Archival Recordings: Glen Howard.
Research by Tony Sampas.

SPECIAL MULTIMEDIA EDITION includes:

- 2 CD audio version of screenplay.
- Unabridged original screenplay text.
- 74 Illustrations

John Medeski appears courtesy of Blue Note Records.
Kate Pierson appears courtesy of Warner/Reprise Records.

Ellis Paul appears courtesy of Rounder Records.
Label: Gallery Six.
Format: 2 × CD, Book.
Released: 7 October 2003.

Jay Farrar and Benjamin Gibbard – *One Fast Move or I'm Gone: Music from Jack Kerouac' s Big Sur* (2009)

1. 'California Zephyr' (2:23).

2. 'Low Life Kingdom' (3:20).

3. 'Willamine' (4:00).

4. 'All in One' (2:07).

5. 'Breathe Our Iodine' (2:58).

6. 'These Roads Don't Move' (3:06).

7. 'Big Sur' (3:24).

8. 'One Fast Move or I'm Gone' (4:16).

9. 'Final Horrors' (2:39).

10. 'Sea Engines' (3:30).

11. 'The Void' (2:58).

12. 'San Francisco' (3:58).

Composer, Guitar (Acoustic), Harmonica, Lap Steel Guitar, Liner Notes, Organ, Percussion, Piano, Primary Artist, Slide Guitar, Producer and Vocals: Jay Farrar.

Composer, Drums, Guitar (Acoustic), Guitar (Electric), Piano, Primary Artist, Producer and Vocals: Ben Gibbard.

Producer, Executive Producer: Jim Sampas.

Mixed by Paul Q. Kolderie.

Bass, Engineer, Mixing: Aaron Espinoza.
Pedal Steel: Brad Sarno.
Bass, Engineer, Guitar (Electric), Lap Steel Guitar, Piano, Producer: Mark Spencer.
Music by Jay Farrar.
Words by Jack Kerouac (except 'Williamine' and 'The Void').
Music by Jay Farrar and Benjamin Gibbard.
Words by Jack Kerouac.
and
'One Fast Move or I'm Gone'
Music by Benjamin Gibbard.

Words by Benjamin Gibbard.
Record Label: Atlantic Records.
Released: 20 October 2009.

Various Artists – *Esperanza: Songs from Jack Kerouac's Tristessa* (2013)

1. William Fitzsimmons and Tim & Adam, 'First Page of Kerouac's Tristessa' (1:09).
2. Tim & Adam, 'Billie Holiday Eyes' (4:11).
3. Gregory Alan Isakov, 'O' City Lights' (2:40).
4. Peter Bradley Adams, 'She Has to Come Down' (4:44).
5. Alela Diane, 'We Are Nothing' (2:13).
6. Wintersleep, 'Father Time' (4:03).
7. Marissa Nadler, 'Tristessa's Song' (4:00).
8. Joshua James, 'Esperanza (Spanish Version)' (2:33).
9. Lee Ranaldo, 'Middle Page of Kerouac's Tristessa' (1:05).
10. Will Dailey, 'Broke My Calm' (2:27).
11. Hey Rosetta!, 'Sad Animals' (5:51).
12. Willy Mason, 'I Have Known Love' (2:21).
13. Matt Costa, 'Shadows of Autumn' (4:35).
14. The Low Anthem, 'Numbers in Nirvana' (2:53).
15. Neal McCarthy and Barbara Kessler, 'Esperanza (English Version)' (2:38).
16. Tony Dekker and Hanne Hukkelberg, 'Last Page of Kerouac's Tristessa' (1:40).

Produced by Jim Sampas.
Executive Producer: George Sampas.
Co-Produced by David Greenberg and Tom Waltz.
Mastered by Tom Waltz at Waltz Mastering.
Record Label: Reimagine Music.
Released: 17 September 2013.

APPENDIX V: JACK AND NEAL ON RECORD

Dave Moore and Horst Spandler

A list of recordings which relate to Jack Kerouac and/or Neal Cassady. The qualification for inclusion is that the item must either refer directly to Jack or Neal, or quote from their work.

Artist	Track title	Date	Jack/Neal	Album (if any)
Dizzy Gillespie	'Kerouac' (improvisation on 'Exactly Like You', named in 1953)	1941	J	*The Harlem Jazz Scene –1941*
Allen Ginsberg	'The Green Automobile'	1954	N	*Holy Soul Jelly Roll*
Allen Ginsberg	'Howl' (for Carl Solomon)	1956	N	*Holy Soul Jelly Roll*
Allen Ginsberg	'Sunflower Sutra'	1956	J	*Holy Soul Jelly Roll*
Ella Fitzgerald	'Like Young'	1959	J	*Get Happy*
The Nervous Set cast	'Fun Life'	1959	J	*The Nervous Set*
Lenny Bruce, Steve Allen	'All Alone'	1959	J	*Swear to Tell the Truth* (movie soundtrack)
André Previn	*The Subterraneans* (movie soundtrack music)	1960	J	*The Subterraneans*
André Previn	'Like Blue'/'Blue Subterranean' (from *The Subterraneans* movie)	1960	J	*Like Blue*
Linda Lawson	'Like Young'	1960	J	*Introducing Linda Lawson*
Don Morrow	'Kerouazy'	1961	J	*Grimm's Hip Fairy Tales*
Perry Como	'Like Young'	1961	J	*For the Young at Heart*
Charles Laughton	*The Dharma Bums* (extract)	1962	J	*The Story-Teller*
The Barrow Poets	*Mexico City Blues* (104th Chorus)	1963	J	*An Entertainment of Poetry and Music*

Artist	Track title	Date	Jack/Neal	Album (if any)
Paul Simon	'A Simple Desultory Philippic'	1965	J	*The Paul Simon Song Book*
David Amram	'Summer in the West' (from *Lonesome Traveller*)	1965	J	*A Year in Our Land*
Bob Dylan	'Desolation Row'	1965	J	*Highway 61 Revisited*
Bob Dylan	'Just Like Tom Thumb's Blues'	1965	J	*Highway 61 Revisited*
Eric von Schmidt	'Lolita'	1967	J	*Take a Trip with Me*
Paul Jones	'Tarzan, etc...'	1967	J	*Love Me, Love My Friends*
Joki Freund Quintett and Harald Leipnitz	'Mordsspektakel'	1967	J	*Amerika (Europa?) – Ich Rede Dich An!*
Joki Freund Quintett and Harald Leipnitz	'Charlie Parker' (240th Chorus)	1967	J	*Amerika (Europa?) – Ich Rede Dich An!*
Grateful Dead	'That's It for the Other One'	1968	N	*Anthem of the Sun*
Four Jacks And A Jill	'Master Jack'	1968	J	*Jukebox Hits Of 1968, Vol. 2*
David Amram, Lynn Sheffield	'Pull My Daisy'	1971	J	*No More Walls*
Allen Ginsberg	'On Neal's Ashes'	1971	N	*Holy Soul Jelly Roll*
Michel Corringe	'Kerouac Jack'	1971	J	*En Public*
Bob Weir	'Cassidy'	1972	N	*Ace*
Aztec Two-Step	'The Persecution & Restoration of Dean Moriarty'	1972	J&N	*Aztec Two-Step*
David Amram	'East and West'	1973	J	*Subway Night*
David Amram	'The Fabulous Fifties'	1973	J	*Subway Night*
Gary Farr	'Breakfast Boo-Ga-Loo'	1973	J	*Addressed to the Censors of Love*
Road	'Come Back Jack Kerouac'	1973	J	*Road*
Mott the Hoople	'The Wheel of the Quivering Meat Conception'	1974	J	*Brain Capers*

Artist	Track title	Date	Jack/Neal	Album (if any)
Donovan	'Age Of Treason'	1974	J	7-Tease
Ramblin' Jack Elliott	'912 Greens'	1974	J	Live In Utah
Willie Alexander	'Kerouac'	1975	J	Willie Loco Boom Boom Ga Ga
Doobie Brothers	'Neal's Fandango'	1975	N	Stampede
Al Stewart	'Modern Times'	1975	J	Modern Times
Jethro Tull	'From a Dead Beat to an Old Greaser'	1976	J	Too Old to Rock 'n' Roll
David Amram	'Pull My Daisy' (live)	1976	J	Summer Nights, Winter Rain
Willie Alexander	'Kerouac'	1976	J	Live at The Rat
Tom Waits	'Jack & Neal'	1977	J&N	Foreign Affairs
Willie Alexander	'Kerouac'	1978	J	Willie Alexander and the Boom-Boom Band
Sylvain Lelièvre	'Kérouac'	1978	J	Sylvain Lelièvre
Pataphonie	'Kerouac' (instrumental)	1978	J	Le Matin Blanc
The Cooper Brothers	'Old Angel Midnight'	1978	J	The Dream Never Dies
Jack Nitzsche	Heart Beat (movie soundtrack music)	1979	J&N	Heart Beat
Dexy's Midnight Runners	'There, There, My Dear'	1980	J	Searching for the Young Soul Rebels
Allen Ginsberg	'The Shrouded Stranger'	1980	J	Allen Ginsberg in Wuppertal: Poems and Songs
Allen Ginsberg	'Pull My Daisy'	1980	J&N	Allen Ginsberg in Wuppertal: Poems and Songs
Allen Ginsberg	'Prayer Blues: For John Lennon'	1980	J	Allen Ginsberg in Wuppertal: Poems and Songs
Allen Ginsberg	'Howl' (including 'Footnote to "Howl"')	1980	J&N	Allen Ginsberg in Wuppertal: Poems and Songs

Artist	Track title	Date	Jack/Neal	Album (if any)
Grateful Dead	'Cassidy'	1981	N	*Reckoning*
Godley & Creme	'Snack Attack'	1981	J	*Ismism*
Ramblin' Jack Elliott	'912 Greens'	1981	J	*Kerouac's Last Dream*
Mark Murphy	'Parker's Mood' (including *Subterraneans* extract)	1981	J	*Bop for Kerouac*
Mark Murphy	'Ballad of the Sad Young Men' (including *On the Road* extract)	1981	J&N	*Bop for Kerouac*
Bauhaus	'Kick in the Eye'	1981	J	*Mask*
Emil Mangelsdorff Quartett	'Blues for Allen' (i.e. Allen Ginsberg's 'Footnote to "Howl"')	1981	J&N	*Das Geheul*
Emil Mangelsdorff Quartett	'Rosengärten' (excerpt from Ginsberg's 'Howl')	1981	N	*Das Geheul*
Van Morrison	'Cleaning Windows'	1982	J	*Beautiful Vision*
David Amram	'This Song's for You, Jack'	1982	J	*This Song for Jack* (movie soundtrack)
King Crimson	'Neal and Jack and Me'	1982	J&N	*Beat*
Wah!	'The Story of the Blues – Part 2'	1982	J	*The Way We Wah!*
Blue Oyster Cult	'Burnin' for You'	1982	J	*E.T.I.*
Charlélie Couture	'La Route (Oui Mais Kérouac est Mort)'	1982	J	*Quoi Faire*
David J.	'With the Indians Permanent'	1983	J&N	*Etiquette of Violence*
Graham Parker	'Sounds Like Chains'	1983	J	*The Real Macaw*
Steve Tilston	'B Movie'	1983	J	*In for a Penny . . . In for a Pound*
The Smiths	'Pretty Girls Make Graves'	1984	J	*The Smiths*
The Icicle Works	'When It All Comes Down'	1985	J	*Seven Singles Deep*
The Long Ryders	'Southside of the Story'	1985	J&N	*Looking for Lewis & Clark* (10″ single)
Van Morrison	'Cleaning Windows'	1985	J	*Live at the Grand Opera House Belfast*

Artist	Track title	Date	Jack/Neal	Album (if any)
Bob Dylan	'Something's Burning, Baby'	1985	J	*Empire Burlesque*
King Crimson	'Neal and Jack and Me' (live)	1985	J&N	*The Noise-Frejus 82*
It's Immaterial	'Driving Away from Home' (Dead Man's Curve mix)	1986	J	*Ed's Funky Diner* (12″ single)
Minor Characters	'1972'	1986	J	*Minor Characters* (7″ EP)
Andy Summers	'Search for Kerouac' (instrumental)	1986	J	*Down and Out in Beverly Hills*
David Carradine	'Reading from *On the Road*'	1986	J&N	*On the Road* (double cassette)
East Buffalo Media Association	'Sea' (from *Big Sur*)	1986	J	*Sea*
East Buffalo Media Association	'Mantra for Kerouac'	1986	J	*Sea*
Jesse Garon & the Desperadoes	'The Rain Fell Down'	1986	J	*A Cabinet of Curiosities*
The Go-Betweens	'The House That Jack Kerouac Built'	1987	J	*Tallulah*
Marillion	'Torch Song'	1987	J	*Clutching at Straws*
10,000 Maniacs	'Hey Jack Kerouac'	1987	J	*In My Tribe*
The Panic Brothers	'Bivouac'	1987	J	*In the Red*
Hobo	'Üvöltés (Howl) – Carl Solomonért – részletek' (Hungarian)	1987	N	*Üvöltés*
Pierre Flynn	'Sur la Route'	1987	J	*Le Parfum du Hasard*
Richard Séguin	'L'Ange Vagabond'	1988	J	*Journée d'Amerique*
Beatnik Beatch	'Beatnik Beatch'	1988	J	*Beatnik Beatch*
David Amram	'Pull My Daisy'	1988	J	*Pull My Daisy and Other Jazz Classics*
Crash Harmony	'(Mexico) Jack Kerouac Is Dead'	1988	J	(Wesleyan University radio tape)
Roger Manning	'Pearly Blues'	1989	J	*Roger Manning*
Billy Joel	'We Didn't Start the Fire'	1989	J	*Storm Front*

Artist	Track title	Date	Jack/Neal	Album (if any)
Eric Andersen	'Ghosts upon the Road'	1989	J&N	Ghosts upon the Road
The Washington Squares	'(Did You Hear) Neal Cassady Died?'	1989	J&N	Fair and Square
Mark Murphy	'San Francisco' (including Big Sur extract)	1989	J&N	Kerouac Then and Now
Mark Murphy	'November in the Snow' (including On the Road extract)	1989	J&N	Kerouac Then and Now
Ramblin' Jack Elliott	'912 Greens'	1989	J	Legends of Folk
Jackson Sloane	'Jack Kerouac Said'	1989	J	Old Angel Midnight
The Beastie Boys	'3-Minute Rule'	1989	J	Paul's Boutique
Mike Heron	'Mexican Girl'	1989	J	The Glen Row Tapes
Robert Kraft	'The Beat Generation'	1989	J&N	Quake City
Steve Earle	'The Other Kind'	1990	J	The Hard Way
Everything But The Girl	'Me and Bobby D'	1990	J	The Language of Life
Adam Ant	'Anger Inc.'	1990	J	Manners and Physique
R.B. [Morris] and the Irregulars	'Spy in My Brain'	1990	J&N	Local Man
Les David Vincent	'Kerouac Way'	1990	J	Ourouni
Tynal Tywyll	'Jack Kerouac' (in Welsh)	1990	J	'Jack Kerouac'/'Boomerang' (single)
Elliott Murphy	'Ballad of Sal Paradise'	1990	J&N	Affairs, etc.
Van Morrison	'On Hyndford Street'	1991	J	Hymns to the Silence
Pete Wylie and Wah!	'Don't Lose Your Dreams'	1991	J	Infamy
Allen Ginsberg	Reading from The Dharma Bums	1991	J	The Dharma Bums (double cassette)
A House	'Endless Art'	1991	J	I Am the Greatest
John Gorka	'The Ballad of Jamie Bee'	1991	J	Jack's Crows
Suzanne Vega	'Cassidy'	1991	N	Deadicated: A Tribute to the Grateful Dead

Artist	Track title	Date	Jack/Neal	Album (if any)
R.E.M.	'Kerouac No. 4'	1991	J	*Outtakes of Time* (bootleg)
Mingus Dynasty	'Harlene'	1991	J	*Next Generation Performs Mingus*
Terry Riley	'*Mexico City Blues* Suite' (224th, 204th and 216th-B Choruses)	1991	J	*June Buddhas*
Frisco Jenny	'La Balada de Dean Moriarty'	1991	N	*El Dolor del Escorpion*
Tom Parker	Reading *The Dharma Bums* (unabridged)	1992	J&N	*The Dharma Bums* (5 cassettes or 6 CDs)
Jerry Jeff Walker	'The Man He Used to Be'	1992	J	*Hill Country Rain*
Sweet Lizard Illtet	'Mutiny Zoo'	1992	J	*Sweet Lizard Illtet*
STS	'Unterwegs'	1992	J	*Auf Tour*
Everything But The Girl	'Me and Bobby D'	1992	J	*Acoustic*
Jasmine Love Bomb	'An Announcement'	1992	J	*Fun With Mushrooms*
Loudon Wainwright III	'Road Ode'	1993	J	*Career Moves*
Jawbreaker	'Boxcar'	1993	J	*24 Hour Revenge Therapy*
United Future Organization	'Poetry and All That Jazz'	1993	J	*United Future Organization*
Naked Soul	'You, Me and Jack Kerouac'	1993	J	*Visiting Your Planet*
Barrence Whitfield with Tom Russell	'Cleaning Windows'	1993	J	*Hillbilly Voodoo*
10,000 Maniacs	'Hey Jack Kerouac' (live)	1993	J	*MTV Unplugged*
'Ranger Will' Hodgson	'Smokin' Charlie's Saxophone'	1993	J&N	Unissued studio recording
Colin Vearncombe	'Call of the Narc'	1993	J	*Don't Take the Silence Too Hard* (CD single)
Dashboard Saviors	'Sal Paradise'	1993	J	*Spinnin On Down*
Dave Graney 'n' The Coral Snakes	'Maggie Cassidy'	1993	J	*Night of the Wolverine*

Artist	Track title	Date	Jack/Neal	Album (if any)
Michael Smith	'Ballad of Elizabeth Dark'	1993	J	*Time*
Allen Ginsberg and Philip Glass	Song #11 from 'The Green Automobile'	1993	N	*Hydrogen Jukebox*
Looking For Adam	'Sal Paradise'	1993	J	*Bombshell Marie*
The Zimmermans	'Love Saxophone'	1994	J	*Cut*
Peter Droge	'Straylin Street'	1994	J	*Necktie Second*
Weezer	'Holiday'	1994	J	*Weezer*
Bad Religion	'Stranger Than Fiction'	1994	J	*Stranger Than Fiction*
Hersch Silverman	'The Jack Kerouac Blues'	1994	J	*Channel Nine with Hersch Silverman*
Divine Comedy	'The Booklovers'	1994	J	*Promenade*
Lee Ranaldo	'Spring'	1994	J	*Envisioning*
Jawbreaker (outro: JK w. Steve Allen)	'Condition Oakland'	1994	J	*24 Hour Revenge Therapy*
Matthew Good	'Euphony'	1994	J	*Euphony*
Tom Parker	Reading *On the Road* (unabridged)	1995	J&N	*On the Road* (7 cassettes or 9 CDs)
Loudon Wainwright III	'Cobwebs'	1995	J	*Grown Man*
Dmitri Matheny	'The Myth of the Rainy Night'	1995	J	*Red Reflections*
Terrell	'Toystore'	1995	J&N	*Angry Southern Gentleman*
Graham Parker with David Amram	Reading from *The Town and the City*	1995	J	*A Kerouac ROMnibus*
Graham Parker with David Amram	Reading from *Visions of Cody*	1995	J&N	*A Kerouac ROMnibus*
Graham Parker with David Amram	Reading from *The Subterraneans*	1995	J	*A Kerouac ROMnibus*
Michael McClure	Reading from *Mexico City Blues*	1995	J	*A Kerouac ROMnibus*
Ann Charters	Reading from *Mexico City Blues*	1995	J	*A Kerouac ROMnibus*

Artist	Track title	Date	Jack/Neal	Album (if any)
Daniel Lavoie	'Nantucket'	1995	J	Ici
Eric Taylor	'Dean Moriarty'	1995	J&N	Eric Taylor
Jon Hassell	'Sulla Strada'	1995	J	I Magazzini
Reg E. Gaines	'Ode to Jack Kerouac'	1995	J	Sweeper Don't Clean My Street
Fatboy Slim	'Neal Cassady Starts Here' (with voice of Ken Babbs)	1995	N	Santa Cruz (12″ single)
Tony Imbo	'Streaking The Days Asunder'	1995	J	Reinventing Man – Outtakes
Daniel Amos	'The Glory Road'	1995	J	Songs Of The Heart
Cracker	'Big Dipper'	1996	J	The Golden Age
Graham Parker with David Amram	Reading from Visions of Cody	1996	J&N	Visions of Cody (double cassette)
Allen Ginsberg	Reading Mexico City Blues	1996	J	Mexico City Blues (double cassette)
Holy Barbarians	'Bodhisattva'	1996	J	Cream
David Byrne	'It Goes Back' (from 'Origins of Beat Generation')	1996	J	Off Beat: A Red Hot Sound Trip
Mike Heron	'Mexican Girl'	1996	J	Where the Mystics Swim
Aztec Two-Step	'The Persecution & Restoration of Dean Moriarty'	1996	J&N	Highway Signs: 25th Anniversary Concert
Fun Lovin' Criminals	'Come Find Yourself'	1996	J	Come Find Yourself
The Gathering Field	'Lost In America'	1996	J	Lost In America
The Gathering Field	'Are You an Angel?'	1996	J	Lost In America
The Gathering Field	'Midnight Ghost'	1996	J	Lost In America
I Mother Earth	'Hello Dave'	1996	J	Scenery and Fish
BR5-49	'Bettie, Bettie'	1996	J&N	Live From Robert's (EP)

Artist	Track title	Date	Jack/Neal	Album (if any)
Mike Plume Band	Various	1996	J	*Jump Back Kerouac*
Major Nelson	'Living Like Kerouac'	1996	J	*Big Stir*
The Bloodhound Gang	'Asleep At The Wheel'	1996	J	*One Fierce Beer Coaster*
Carolyn Cassady	Reading from *Off The Road*	1996	J&N	*Women of the Beat Generation* (4 cassettes)
ruth weiss	Reading from *Nobody's Wife* (by Joan Haverty)	1996	J	*Women of the Beat Generation* (4 cassettes)
Joyce Johnson	Reading from *Minor Characters*	1996	J	*Women of the Beat Generation* (4 cassettes)
Mary Norbert Körte	Reading from *Trainsong* (by Jan Kerouac)	1996	J	*Women of the Beat Generation* (4 cassettes)
Anne Waldman	'I Am The Guard!'	1996	J	*Women of the Beat Generation* (4 cassettes)
Zachary Richard	'Massachusetts'	1996	J	*Coeur Fidèle*
Steve Shapiro	'Sal's Paradise'	1996	J	*Vibe Out*
Holy Barbarians	'It Ain't Over Yet (For Jack Kerouac)'	1997	J	*Beat.itude, A New Jazz Beat*
Morphine	'Kerouac'	1997	J	*B-Sides and Otherwise*
Various Artists	Various readings from Kerouac's work	1997	J	*Kerouac: Kicks Joy Darkness*
Graham Parker with David Amram	Reading from Kerouac's unpublished journals,1949–50	1997	J	*Kerouac: Kicks Joy Darkness* (Japanese edition)
Matt Dillon	'The Thrashing Doves'	1997	J	*Kerouac: Kicks Joy Darkness* (Japanese edition)
Lydia Lunch	'How to Meditate + Mexican Loneliness'	1997	J	*Kerouac: Kicks Joy Darkness* (Japanese edition)
Belle and Sebastian	'Le Pastie de la Burgeoisie'	1997	J	*3..6..9 Seconds of Light*

Artist	Track title	Date	Jack/Neal	Album (if any)
Subincision	'Kerouac'	1997	J&N	*Subincision*
Silent Bear	'Kerouac's Child'	1997	J	*River Drum Child*
Patti Smith	'Spell' (i.e. 'Footnote to "Howl"' by Allen Ginsberg)	1997	J&N	*Peace and Noise*
Bob Martin	'The Old Worthen'	1997	J	*The River Turns the Wheel*
Bob Martin	'Stella Kerouac'	1997	J	*The River Turns the Wheel*
RatDog	'Cassidy'	1997	N	*Furthur More*
Umka	'Kerouac (Treplo)'	1997	J	*Dozhili, Mama*
Various Artists	'The Last Time I Committed Suicide' (soundtrack music and talk)	1997	N	*The Last Time I Committed Suicide*
X Generation	'Sal's Paradise'	1997	J	*Kerouac's Legacy*
X Generation	'Nebraskan Dawn (Dedicated to Cody)'	1997	N	*Kerouac's Legacy*
Beat Hotel	'Beathotel'	1997	J	*Beathotel*
DJs Wally & Swingsett	'Smoking Up The Music'	1997	J	*Dog Leg Left*
Conrad	'Jack Kerouac'	1997	J	*Conrad*
The Dinner Is Ruined	'I Ain't No Neal Cassidy'	1997	N	*Elevator Music for Non-Claustrophobic People*
The Lord High Fixers	'Sal Paradise Delegation'	1997	J	*Group Improvisation That's Music*
Headswim	'Old Angel Midnight'	1997	J	*Despite Yourself*
Olesen-Olesen	'Jack Kerouac I Jylland'	1997	J	*Indenlands Udenbys*
Sportfreunde Stiller	'On the Road – Unterwegs'	1998	J&N	*Thonträger*
Dr. John	'John Gris'	1998	J (?)	*Anutha Zone*
Umka	'Kerouac (Treplo)' (live)	1998	J	*Live in Fakel*
Mike Heron and Robin Williamson	'Mexican Girl'	1998	J	*Bloomsbury 1997*
Jim Dunleavy	'Lonesome Travelers'	1998	J	*Steady Rollin'*

Artist	Track title	Date	Jack/Neal	Album (if any)
David Amram	'This Song's for You, Jack'	1998	J	*Rebels* (documentary soundtrack)
Tom Parker	Reading *Big Sur* (unabridged)	1998	J&N	*Big Sur* (4 cassettes or 5 CDs)
Jeremy Gloff	'Kerouac's Dead'	1998	J	*Jeremy Gloff, 1998, Vol. 9*
Beekler	'Dean Moriarty'	1998	N	*In Layman's Terms*
Richard Bicknell	'Dean Moriarty'	1998	N	*Mayflower*
Ron Whitehead	'The Other'	1998	J	*Tapping My Own Phone*
Ron Whitehead	'San Francisco, May 1993'	1998	J	*Tapping My Own Phone*
Ron Whitehead	'Asheville'	1998	N	*Tapping My Own Phone*
Five Iron Frenzy	'Superpowers'	1998	J	*Our Newest Album Ever*
David Nelson	'Kerouac'	1999	J&N	*Visions under the Moon*
Tom Waits with Primus	'On the Road'	1999	J	*Jack Kerouac Reads On the Road*
Guy Clark	'Cold Dog Soup'	1999	J	*Cold Dog Soup*
R.B. Morris	'Distillery'	1999	J	*Zeke and the Wheel*
Hot Sauce Johnson	'Jack Kerouac'	1999	J	*Truck Stop Jug Hop*
Richard Thompson	'Sibella'	1999	J	*Mock Tudor*
Patti Smith	'Spell' (live)	1999	J&N	*Gung Ho Giveaway*
Robert Briggs	Lawrence Ferlinghetti, Jack Kerouac, Gary Snyder, Allen Ginsberg	1999	J	*Poetry and the 1950s: Homage to the Beat Generation*
Michael Johnathon	'Kerouac Alley'	1999	J	*The Road*
Christian Brückner	'Beat-Glückselig' (from 'Origins of the Beat Generation')	1999	J&N	*Brückner Beat*
Mary Gauthier	'Drag Queens In Limousines'	1999	J	*Drag Queens In Limousines*
Helen Shapiro	32nd Chorus from *Orlando Blues*	1999	J	*Jazz Poetry*

Artist	Track title	Date	Jack/Neal	Album (if any)
Ian Dury	'Skid Row Wine'	1999	J	*Beat Poetry* (2 CDs)
Anne Waldman	'Hymn'	1999	J	*Beat Poetry* (2 CDs)
Anne Waldman	'Pome on Doctor Sax'	1999	J	*Beat Poetry* (2 CDs)
David Alpher	'Tribute to Kerouac'	1999	J	*American Reflections*
Josh Lamkin	'Kerouac's Advice'	1999	J	*UNCA Music Biz*
Gregory Wiest et al.	Chorus 172 (from *Mexico City Blues*)	1999	J	*Beat*
Frank Muller	Reading *On the Road* (unabridged)	1999	J&N	*On the Road* (10 CDs or 8 cassettes)
Alexander Adams	Reading *On the Road* (unabridged)	1999	J&N	*On the Road* (9 CDs or 8 cassettes)
Blue Room	'Jack Kerouac'	1999	J	*Into the Night*
Guy Forsyth	'Children of Jack'	1999	J	*Can You Live Without*
Root 88	'Jack Kerouac'	1999	J	*Root 88*
Jonathan Marosz	Reading *The Dharma Bums* (unabridged)	2000	J&N	*The Dharma Bums* (5 cassettes)
Grover Gardner	Reading *Orpheus Emerged* (unabridged)	2000	J	*Orpheus Emerged* (3 CDs)
Kevn Kinney	'Kerouac'	2000	J	*The Flower and the Knife*
Kurt Elling	'The Rent Party'	2000	J	*Live in Chicago*
Leona Naess	'Charm Attack'	2000	J (?)	*Comatised*
Umka	'Kerouac (Treplo)'	2000	J	*Dandelion Cinema*
Brian Hassett	'All of Us'/'Hearing Shearing' (including *On the Road* extract)	2000	J	Live at CBGB's, NYC, 12 April
Guy Clark	'Cold Dog Soup' (live)	2000	J	Austin City Limits performance
The Mighty Manatees with David Amram	'Smokin' Charlie's Saxophone'	2000	J&N	Live at Bitter End, NYC, 22 April
Ralph	'Goodbye Jack. Kerouac'	2000	J	*This Is for the Night People*

Artist	Track title	Date	Jack/Neal	Album (if any)
Ralph	'Pull My Daisy'	2000	J	This Is for the Night People
Cosmic Rough Riders	'Ungrateful'	2000	J	Deliverance
Matt Dillon	Reading On the Road (unabridged)	2000	J&N	On the Road (10 CDs)
Barenaked Ladies	'Car Seat'	2000	J	Maroon
Phased 4°F	'Jack-Off All Trades'	2000	J	Painfield (10" EP)
Allan Taylor	'Kerouac's Dream'	2000	J	Colour To The Moon
The Spanish Armada	'Baby Fever' (Kerouac mix)	2000	J	Brave New Girl
Shawn Mullins	'North On 95'	2000	J	Beneath The Velvet Sun
Bell X1	'Beautiful Madness'	2000	J&N	Neither Am I
Flanagan Ingham Quartet	'Textile Lunch on Moody St.' (Suite – 4 tracks)	2000	J	Textile Lunch
David Amram et al.	Various	2001	J&N	Spirit: A Tribute to Jack Kerouac
Graham Cournoyer	'One For Jack'	2001	J	One For Jack
Anne Waldman	'Jack Kerouac Dream'	2001	J	Alchemical Elegy
John Gorka	'Oh Abraham'	2001	J	The Company You Keep
Michael Ubaldini	'Old Angel Midnight (Song to Kerouac)'	2001	J	American Blood
Tony Imbo	'Streaking The Days Asunder' (remix)	2001	J	Reinventing Man
Don Michael Sampson	'Come On Jack'	2001	J	Black Flower
Zwan	'Freedom Ain't What It Used To Be'	2001	J	Honestly (CD single)
Ron Whitehead	'Psychic Supper'	2001	J	Hozomeen Jam (EP)
Railroad Earth	'Railroad Earth'	2001	J	The Black Bear Session
Tuba Stockholm	'Dean Moriarty'	2001	N	I Feel American
Migala	'Kerouac'	2002	J	Diciembre, 3a.m.

Artist	Track title	Date	Jack/Neal	Album (if any)
Dale Morningstar	'2000 Kerouac Girl'	2002	J	*I Grew Up On Sodom Road*
John Hasbrouck	'Kerouac Alone in Des Moines'	2002	J	*Ice Cream*
Curse, with David Amram and Marc Ribot	'Pull My Daisy'	2002	J	'Pull My Daisy'/'Graveyard Shuffle' (single)
Valerie Lagrange	'Kerouac'	2002	J	*Fleuve Congo*
Our Lady Peace	'All For You'	2002	J	*Gravity*
David McMillin	'The Legend of Jack Kerouac'	2002	J	*Where I Belong*
Spitznagel	'Kerouac's Treehouse'	2002	J	*Under the Plane*
Kenn Kweder	'Jack Kerouac'	2002	J	*Kwederology Vol. 1*
Kenn Kweder	'Cassady's Bible'	2002	N	*Kwederology Vol. 1*
Chris Keup	'Close Your Eyes Maggie Cassidy'	2002	J	*The Subject of Some Regret*
BAP	'Schluss, Aus, OK!'	2002	J	'Schluss, Aus, Okay' (CD single)
Goodman County	'Kerouac Sings the Blues'	2002	J	*Pictures from a Moving Vehicle*
Richard Meltzer et al.	'Kerouac Never Drove, So He Never Drove Alone'	2002	J	*The Tropic of Nipples*
Atika	'Kaip Keruakas kelyje'	2002	J	*Karve ir kosmonautai*
Robert Creeley et al.	*Doctor Sax and the Great World Snake* (Kerouac's screenplay)	2003	J	*Doctor Sax and the Great World Snake* (2 CDs)
Ramblin' Jack Elliott	'912 Greens'	2003	J	*Live At Tales From The Tavern*
Eric Andersen	'Beat Avenue'	2003	J	*Beat Avenue*
Allan Taylor	'The Beat Hotel'	2003	J	*Hotels and Dreamers*
Spitalfield	'I Loved The Way She Said L.A.'	2003	J	*Remember Right Now*
Steve Lacy	'Wave Lover' (from 'Lucien Midnight')	2003	J	*The Beat Suite*

Kerouac on Record

Artist	Track title	Date	Jack/Neal	Album (if any)
Steve Lacy	'Jack's Blues'	2003	J	*The Beat Suite*
Alfred Howard	'Kerouac Incarnate'	2003	J	*14 Days of the Universe in Incandescent Bloom*
Jack Shea, JD Caioulet, & J Sanderson	'On the Road'	2003	J	*Who Owns Jack Kerouac?* (movie soundtrack)
Jack Shea, JD Caioulet, & J Sanderson	'Jack Reaches God'	2003	J	*Who Owns Jack Kerouac?* (movie soundtrack)
Ron Whitehead & David Amram	'To Dream In Kerouac's Playground'	2003	J	*Kentucky Blues*
Ron Whitehead & David Amram	'Amram's Kentucky Rap'	2003	J	*Kentucky Blues*
Julie Geller	'The American Night (Kerouac's Song)'	2003	J	*This Road*
Mars Arizona	'Railroad Song'	2003	J	*Love Songs from the Apocalypse*
Reckless Kelly	'Desolation Angels'	2003	J	*Under the Table & Above the Sun*
Dayna Kurtz	'Just Like Jack'	2003	J	*Postcards From Downtown*
Rusted Root	'Jack Kerouac'	2004	J	*Rusted Root Live*
Seedy Gonzales	'Kerouac & Burroughs'	2004	J	*Seedy Gonzales*
Walter T. Ryan	'Burnin' (Like a Kerouac Coyote)'	2004	J	*Underdog American Music*
Max Joshua Klaooerman	'In Spiteful Dedication Jack Kerouac'	2004	J	*This Side of Everywhere: Poet's Monday*
Mark Boucot	'Cassady's Ashes'	2004	N	*Mark Boucot*
Mark Boucot	'Beatific Nights'	2004	J	*Mark Boucot*
Manual & Syntaks	'Sal Paradise'	2004	J	*Golden Sun*
Kevn Kinney	'Epilogue Epitaph In A Minor'	2004	J	*Sun Tangled Angel Revival*

Artist	Track title	Date	Jack/Neal	Album (if any)
Erin Jordan	'Road to Eureka'	2004	J	Land of Milk and Honey
Styrofoam (feat. Ben Gibbard)	'Couches in Alleys'	2004	J	Nothing's Lost
The Go-Betweens	'The House That Jack Kerouac Built'	2004	J	Live in London
Garagecow Ensemble	'I Never Slept With Allen Ginsberg'	2004	J	Saint Stephen's Dream
Matt Merten	'Jack Kerouac'	2004	J	Matt Merten
Manual & Syntaks	'Sal Paradise'	2004	J	Golden Sun
Tom Russell	'Border Lights'	2005	J	Hotwalker: Charles Bukowski & A Ballad For Gone America
Tom Russell	'Harry Partch, Jack Kerouac, Lenny Bruce'	2005	J	Hotwalker: Charles Bukowski & A Ballad For Gone America
Bap Kennedy	'Rock and Roll Heaven'	2005	J&N	The Big Picture
Bap Kennedy	'Moriarty's Blues' (with voice of Carolyn Cassady)	2005	J&N	The Big Picture
Gang 90	'Jack Kerouac'	2005	J	Sexual Life of the Savages
Rock N Roll Monkey and the Robots	'Toss it Back Like Kerouac'	2005	J	Detroit Trauma
Ron Whitehead	'Searching For David Amram'	2005	J	Closing Time
Ron Whitehead	'Allen Ginsberg: The Bridge', Parts 2 and 3	2005	J	Closing Time
Ron Whitehead	'From Hank Williams' Grave'	2005	J&N	Closing Time
Ron Whitehead	'Calling The Toads'	2005	J	Closing Time
Jimmy LaFave	'Bohemian Cowboy Blues'	2005	J	Blue Nightfall
Laura Ranieri	'Like Kerouac'	2005	J	Southbound
Sage Francis	'Escape Artist'	2005	J	A Healthy Distrust
The Clients	'Dharma Bum'	2005	J	Straycat

Kerouac on Record

Artist	Track title	Date	Jack/Neal	Album (if any)
The Green Revolution	'Jack Kerouac Was A Filthy Liar'	2005	J	As Far As Twenty Pesos Can Go
Denny Brown	'Kerouac "On the Road"'	2006	J&N	No Middle Ground
Haiku	Various tracks with a selection from Kerouac's haiku	2006	J	The Kerouac Project
Jeff Root	'Kerouac King Kong'	2006	J	Kerouac King Kong
Jim Dickinson	'Maggie Cassidy'	2006	J	Fishing with Charlie and Other Selected Readings
Jonathan Byerley	'I Got Over Kerouac'	2006	J	Hymns and Fragments
Mads Oustal	På kjøret (On the Road in Norwegian)	2006	J&N	På kjøret (10 CDs)
Milagro Saints	'Kerouac'	2006	J	Let It Rain
Orko	'Hello Dean Moriarty'	2006	N	Creating Short Fiction
The Daisy Cutters	'Second Hand Kerouac'	2006	J	Lines and Sinkers (The E.P. Years)
The Hold Steady	'Stuck Between Stations'	2006	J	Boys and Girls in America
Tom Waits	'Home I'll Never Be'	2006	J	Orphans: Brawlers, Bawlers & Bastards
Tom Waits	'On the Road'	2006	J	Orphans: Brawlers, Bawlers & Bastards
Top Models	'Kerouac'	2006	J	To the Maximum
Mike Macharyas	'Jack Kerouac'	2006	J	Mary J. Blige
Ronnie Elliott	'Jack's St. Pete Blues'	2006	J	Tales Of Drink And Debauchery
Beekler	'Dean Moriarty'	2007	N	In Layman's Terms
Jocelyn Arem	'Kerouac'	2007	J	What the Mirror Said
Mark Handley & The Bone Idols	'Jack Kerouak AKA Anywhere But Here'	2007	J	The Land of Song
Michael Hansonis	Unterwegs (On the Road in German, abridged)	2007	J&N	Unterwegs (6 CDs)

Artist	Track title	Date	Jack/Neal	Album (if any)
Mudvayne	'On the Move'	2007	J	*By the People, for the People*
Steven Light & the Black Sand	'Cassady'	2007	N	*Sweet Transmission*
The Weather Underground	'Neal Cassady'	2007	N	*Psalms & Shanties*
Will Patton	'On the Road'	2007	J&N	*On the Road* (9 CDs)
Tim Minchin	'Inflatable You'	2007	J	*So Live* (DVD)
Robert Creeley	'Jack's Blues'	2007	J	*Really!!*
The Brian Wilson Shock Treatment	'Jack Kerouac, I Don't Know You'	2007	J	*The Hammer Of The Metal Gods*
Jacob Johnson	'Me And Jack Kerouac'	2007	J	*Est. 1986*
Joe Cassady and the West End Sound	'Jack Kerouac'	2007	J	*What's Your Sign?*
	On the Road (Penguin Readers simplified text)	2008	J&N	*On the Road* (Penguin Readers audio CD)
BAP	'Wat für e' Booch'	2008	J&N	*Radio Pandora (Plugged)*
Blackwater Tribe	'Jack Realized Beat'	2008	J	*Blackwater Runs Deep*
Clifton Roy & Folkstringer	'Kerouac's Folksong'	2008	J	*Where the Rock Meets the Rail*
Danny Campbell	*Wake Up – A Life of the Buddha*	2008	J	*Wake Up: A Life of the Buddha* (5 CDs)
David Anderson	'Recollections of Neal Cassady'	2008	N&J	*Layover in Reno*
Five Iron Frenzy (live)	'Superpowers'	2008	J	*Proof That the Youth are Revolting*
Individual	'Kerouac'	2008	J	*Fantastic Smile*
John Ventimiglia	'*On the Road*: The Original Scroll'	2008	J&N	*On the Road* (10 CDs)
Joy Askew	'Kerouac'	2008	J	*The Pirate of Eel Pie*
Ray Porter	*And the Hippos Were Boiled in Their Tanks*	2008	J	*And the Hippos Were Boiled in Their Tanks* (4 CDs)

Kerouac on Record

Artist	Track title	Date	Jack/Neal	Album (if any)
Steve Allee Sextet	'Kerouac' (instrumental)	2008	J	*New York in the Fifties* (soundtrack)
Swallows	'Kerouac'	2008	J	*Songs for Strippers (and Other Professions)*
The Areola Treat	'Kerouac'	2008	J	*The Areola Treat*
The Five Corners Quintet, feat. Mark Murphy	'Kerouac Days in Montana'	2008	J	*Hot Corner*
The Maple State	'Starts with Dean Moriarty'	2008	N	*Say Scientists*
Tim Young Band	'Kerouac'	2008	J	*The Cost*
Van Bluus (vcl. Horst Spandler)	'White Boy Blue'	2008	J	*White Boy Blue*
William S. Burroughs	'Speaking of Jack Kerouac'/ various readings	2008	J	*A Spoken Breakdown*
Yer Cronies	'Kerouac'	2008	J	*When I Grow Up*
Josh Young	'Run Away With Me'	2008	J	*Josh Young*
Roy Zimmerman	'I Approve This Message'	2008	J	*Thanks For The Support*
S.D. Ineson	'Jack Kerouac'	2008	J	*Far Wanderer*
Skin On Glass	'Sal Paradise'	2008	J	*Skin On Glass*
Roger Holzheimer	'Ghost Of Kerouac'	2008	J	*Rough Hewn Heart*
BAP	'Unterwegs'/'Blue in Green'	2009	J&N	*Live und in Farbe*
BAP	'Wat für e' Booch'	2009	J&N	*Live und in Farbe*
Chris Hickey	'Kerouac'	2009	J&N	*Razzmatazz*
Frank Turner	'Poetry of the Deed'	2009	J	*Poetry of the Deed*
Jay Farrar & Benjamin Gibbard	Various tracks /soundtrack	2009	J	*One Fast Move Or I'm Gone: Music From Kerouac's Big Sur*
Tereu Tereu	'Neal Cassady'	2009	N	*All That Keeps Us Together*
The Low Anthem	'Home I'll Never Be'	2009	J	*Oh My God, Charlie Darwin*
Wreak Havoc	'Kerouac's Ghost'	2009	J	*Abandon Everything*

Artist	Track title	Date	Jack/Neal	Album (if any)
Chuck Perrin	'It Ain't Over Yet (For Jack Kerouac)'	2009	J	Beat.itude – the Holy Barbarians
Bob Martin	'Jack Kerouac'	2009	J	Live At The Bull Run
Bob Martin	'Stella Kerouac'	2009	J	Live At The Bull Run
Admiral Freebee	'Alibies'	2009	J&N	Admiral Freebee
The Rub-Touch Propellor	'Jack Kerouac'	2009	J	I Don't Wanna Suffer, Man
Tereu Tereu	'Neal Cassady'	2009	N	All That Keeps Us Together
R.B. Morris	'Spy In My Brain'	2010	J&N	Spies Lies and Burning Eyes
R.B. Morris	'Father Fisheye'	2010	J	Spies Lies and Burning Eyes
Felix Goeser/ Florian von Manteuffel	Und die Nilpferde kochten in ihren Becken (And the Hippos Were Boiled in Their Tanks)	2010	J	Und die Nilpferde kochten in ihren Becken (4CDs)
Billy Koumantzelis	Various narrations	2010	J	On the Lowell Beat: My Time With Jack Kerouac
The 757s	'Kerouac'	2010	J	Last Laugh
Papa Razzi and the Photogs	'Jack Kerouac Celebrated a Group of Irresponsible Dudes'	2010	J	Songs About Great Literary Giants
Brooke Fraser	'Jack Kerouac'	2010	J	Flags
Thieves and Villains	'Song For Dean Moriarty'	2010	N	South America
Andrew McConathy	'Dean Moriarty's Blues'	2010	N	Light of the Eye
Vera, The Ghost	'Kerouac'	2010	J	Memories Like Photographs
Jamnesia2	'Cassady & Kerouac'	2010	J&N	Three Seconds Of Silence
Nick Blaemire	'Run Away With Me'	2010	J	The Unauthorized Autobiography Of Samantha Brown

Artist	Track title	Date	Jack/Neal	Album (if any)
Florian Soyka	'Run Away With Me'	2010	J	Showbühne Live
The Killer B's	'Jack Kerouac Kinda Day'	2010	J	Love Is A Cadillac, Death Is A Ford
Frank Hammond Quartet	'For Jack Kerouac'	2010	J	142nd Street
B. Willie Dryden	'Jack Kerouac'	2010	J	Carolina Prophet
Bill Mallonee	Various tracks 'inspired by the writings of Jack Kerouac'	2011	J	Hearts Crossing The Center Line
Michael Arden	'Run Away With Me'	2011	J	My First Mistake
Crow Song	'Dean Moriarty'	2011	N	Junebugs And Journeymen
Mort Weiss and Peter Marx	'Readings of Kerouac'	2011	J	Mort Weiss Meets Bill Cunliffe
The Indescriptibles	'Kerouac's Road'	2011	J	Never 2 Late
Keith Price Quintet/ Trio	'Theme for Kerouac (A Poet Hops a Midnight Freight)'	2011	J	Gaia/Goya
Red Cortez	'Neal Cassady'	2011	N	EP Two
Admiral Freebee	'Old Angel Midnight'	2011	J	Wreck Collection: The Singles
Doron Braunshtein	'Jack Kerouac'	2011	J	The Obsessive Poet
Astronauta Pinguim	'Manana, Jack, Manana (To Jack Kerouac)'	2011	J	Zeitgeist/Propaganda
TiRon & Ayomari	'Jack Kerouac'	2011	J	A Sucker For Pumps
Keith Price Quintet/Trio	'Theme For Sal Paradise'	2011	J	Gaia/ Goya
Alanna Eileen	'Cassady and Kerouac'	2012	J&N	Single
C.P. Carrington	'Phantom Thumb'	2012	J	The Valley
C.P. Carrington	'Neal Cassady', Parts 1 and 2	2012	N	The Valley
C.P. Carrington	'Counting Tracks'	2012	N	The Valley
Spielgusher	'Kerouac'	2012	J	Spielgusher
Gustavo Santaolalla et al.	Various artists, movie soundtrack music	2012	J&N	On the Road: Original Motion Picture Soundtrack

Artist	Track title	Date	Jack/Neal	Album (if any)
Get Dead	'Kerouac's Teeth'	2012	J	*Tall Cans And Loose Ends*
John Ellis	'Jack Kerouac's Blues'	2012	J	*Rural*
Paul Webb & Sloane Spellman	'D'aujourd'hui Kerouac'	2012	J	*Paz & Sloaney: The One and Only*
Tamara Colonna	'Hey Jack Kerouac'	2012	J	*Born To Ride*
Diversion Tactics	'Kerouac'	2012	J	*The Boot Vinyl Archives*
The Crookes	'Sal Paradise'	2012	J	*Hold Fast*
Ray Porter	Reading *The Sea is My Brother* (unabridged)	2012	J	*The Sea is My Brother* (MP3/CD)
Sean Taylor	'Cassady'	2012	N	*Love Against Death*
Treatment Bound	'Kerouac's Ghost'	2012	J	*Another Round*
Eric Miller	'The Ghost Of Jack Kerouac'	2012	J	*City Lights*
Fervid	'Kerouac'	2012	J	*Little Massacre*
Jeremy Siskind	'What Is That Feeling? (For Jack Kerouac)'	2012	J	*Finger-Songwriter*
The Pocket Gods	'I'm Not Jack Kerouac'	2012	J	*Psychedelic Moonswamp, Vol. 1*
The Lord High Fixers	'Sal Paradise Delegation'	2012	J	*Group Improvisation . . . That's Music*
Martin Schmiddi Schmidt and Olaf Rupp	'Sal Paradise'	2012	J	*Three Sides Of A Coin #1*
Martin Schmiddi Schmidt and Olaf Rupp	'Dean Moriarty'	2012	N	*Three Sides Of A Coin #1*
Brent David Foster	'Ghost Of Jack Kerouac'	2013	J	*23*
Wolf Cub	'Kerouac'	2013	J	*Love High*
Hannes Wader and Allan Taylor	'Kerouac's Dream'	2013	J	*Old Friends in Concert*
Rod Stewart	'Brighton Beach'	2013	J	*Time*
Tim Grimm	'King Of The Folksingers'	2013	J	*The Turning Point*

Artist	Track title	Date	Jack/Neal	Album (if any)
Roger Alan Wade	'Fighting For The Sweetness'	2013	J	*Scenic City Roots (Live)*
Various Artists	Various songs and readings	2013	J	*Esperanza: Songs From Jack Kerouac's Tristessa*
Tony Adams	'Jack Kerouac, Jack!'	2013	J	*Miles Of Blu*
Kerry Kearney	'Jack Kerouac ('Bout Time We Get Away)'	2013	J	*Got Wood? The Acoustic Collection*
Estricalla	'Sal Paradise Eta Dean Moriartyren 17'	2013	J&N	*Triple Asalto Mortal*
Steve Dalachinsky and Dave Liebman	'The Leaves Are Changing (for Jack Kerouac)'	2014	J	*The Fallout Of Dreams*
Morrissey	'Neal Cassady Drops Dead'	2014	N	*World Peace Is None Of Your Business*
Gary Calamar	'She's So Mid-Century'	2014	J	*You Are What You Listen To* (EP)
ERRI	'Jack Kerouac'	2014	J	*I Passi*
Island Wren	'Jack Kerouac'	2014	J	*Fountain* (EP)
Emma Minturn	'Neal Cassady Man'	2014	N	*Emma Minturn*
Michael Bowman	'Ghost Of Neal Cassady'	2014	N	*Lyin', Cheatin', Stealin'*
Papa Razzi and the Photogs	'Sal Paradise Needs To Get A Job'	2014	J	*Famous Fictional People*
Papa Razzi and the Photogs	'Dean Moriarty Is A Deadbeat Loser'	2014	N	*Famous Fictional People*
Mexiko	'Dean Moriarty'	2014	N	*A Punk Rock Symphony in D Major*
Rina Mushonga	'Dean Moriarty'	2014	N	*The Wild, The Wilderness*
Elliott Murphy	'The Ballad Of Sal Paradise'	2014	J	*Affairs*
The Waterboys	'Long Strange Golden Road'	2015	J	*Modern Blues*
Nadine Shah	'Fool'	2015	J	*Fast Food*
Tommy Castro and the Painkillers	'Ride'	2015	J	*Method To My Madness*

Artist	Track title	Date	Jack/Neal	Album (if any)
John McCullagh and The Escorts	'Sal Paradise'	2015	J	New Born Cry
The Earthmen	'The House That Jack Kerouac Built'	2016	J	College Heart
The Kevin Hall Fan Club	'You're Damn Right, Jack Kerouac'	2016	J	A Race To The Starting Line
Landlines	'A Shred Of Dean Moriarty Kinship'	2016	N	Logical Fallacies
Van Morrison	'In Tiburon'	2016	J&N	Keep Me Singing
Jesu and Sun Kil Moon	'Twenty Something'	2017	J&N	30 Seconds To The Decline Of Planet Earth

Thanks to Ralph Alfonzo, Dan Barth, Adrien Begrand, Frank Bor, Jonathan Collins, Richard Cooper, Rick Dale, Diane De Rooy, Johan Deruyck, Neil Douglas, Evad Fromme, Giorgio Gelmini, Brian Hassett, Tbonesteak Leebo, John Low, Richard Marsh, Tony Marshall, Ron McGregor, Chris Moore, Frances Moore, Michael Powell, Joseph Price, Stephen Ronan, Horst Spandler, Jeff Taylor, Matt Theado and Simon Warner.

NOTES ON CONTRIBUTORS

Co-Editors

Simon Warner is a writer, lecturer and broadcaster. He is Visiting Research Fellow in Popular Music at the University of Leeds, UK, and takes a particular interest in the ways in which rock music and the Beat Generation writers share an association. His books on this connection include *Howl for Now* (2005) and *Text and Drugs and Rock'n'Roll: The Beats and Rock Culture* (2013). He also co-organized the Kerouac 50th anniversary conference 'Back On the Road' in Birmingham in 2008 and the Allen Ginsberg live celebrations *Howl for Now* in Leeds in 2005 and *Still Howling* in Manchester in 2015.

A music journalist, Warner was a live rock reviewer for the *Guardian* in the early 1990s and wrote the 'Anglo Visions' column for the webzine *Pop Matters* between 2001 and 2005. He makes regular contributions on popular music topics to BBC radio, and has also been a judge on several occasions in the US Association of Alternative Newsweeklies' Music Criticism Award.

In 1990, he embarked on, then attained, the world's first MA in Popular Music Studies at Liverpool University and, from 1994, taught rock history and culture, emphasizing ideas of political resistance, on various campuses. He was awarded his PhD by the University of Leeds in 2010.

Warner's work has appeared in a number of collections including *Remembering Woodstock* (2004), *Centre of the Creative Universe: Liverpool and the Avant Garde* (2007), *The Summer of Love: The Beatles, Art and Culture in the Sixties* (2008) and *Countercultures and Popular Music* (2014).

Jim Sampas is a music and film producer, and Literary Executor of the Estate of Jack Kerouac. Jack Kerouac was his uncle, married to his Aunt Stella Kerouac, and he was introduced to Kerouac's writings at a young age.

Sampas has produced several projects based on Kerouac's works, including spoken word and music albums *Kerouac: Kicks Joy Darkness* (with Michael Stipe, Eddie Vedder, Patti Smith, Johnny Depp and others), *Kerouac Reads On the Road* (featuring material recorded by Tom Waits with Primus), *Doctor Sax and the Great World Snake* (with Robert Creeley, Lawrence Ferlinghetti, Jim Carroll and others), Jay Farrar and Benjamin Gibbard's *One Fast Move or I'm Gone: Music from Kerouac's Big Sur* and *Esperanza: Songs from Kerouac's Tristessa* (with William Fitzsimmons, Wintersleep, Joshua James and others), and the films *One Fast Move Or I'm Gone: Kerouac's Big Sur* (with Tom Waits, Sam Shepard, Patti Smith and others) and *Big Sur* (with Jean-Marc Barr, Kate Bosworth, Radha Mitchell, and music score by Aaron Desner and Bryce Dessner of The National).

For the other projects Sampas has produced, he set his sights on other major cultural figures, who, like Jack Kerouac, have had widespread impact, and brought new meaning, to music, film, literature or art culture. These include tribute albums to Bruce Springsteen, the Cure, Bob Dylan, the Beatles, the Smiths, the Police, Nirvana, David Bowie, Bessie Smith and the Rolling Stones.

Sampas's projects have been covered on the radio programmes *Weekend Edition*, *Morning Edition*, *Here and Now* and *All Things Considered* on National Public Radio, as well as The Westwood One's *Jim Bohannon Show* and the US Government's *Voice of America*. His work has also been reviewed in *People Magazine*, *Newsweek*, *CNN*, the *New York Times*, *Pitchfork*, the *Chicago Tribune*, the *Washington Post*, the *Los Angeles Times*, *Entertainment Weekly*, *Rolling Stone* and others.

Essayists and interviewers

Larry Beckett's poetry ranges from songs and brief lyrics to blank sonnets and book-length narrative works which form a sequence, *American Cycle*, inspired by our history, legends and music, written over 47 years. *Paul Bunyan* (2015) was published by Smokestack Books, and *Wyatt Earp* (2018) is forthcoming from Alternating Current Press. *Songs and Sonnets* (2002) was published by Rainy Day Women Press, and *Beat Poetry* (2012), an anthology with extensive commentary, is out from Beatdom Books. He has restored the *Tao Te Ching* in *The Way of Rain*, and translated Tang dynasty poets Li Po and Li Shang-yin.

Mark Bliesener is Director of BandGuru Management and Consulting. He has years of daily experience in the music business as a performer (1966–76), music critic (1976–78), publicist (1978–88) and personal manager since 1989. Bliesener has received 16 Gold and Platinum record awards from artists whose careers he has managed, including Alan Parsons, Lyle Lovett, Big Head Todd and the Monsters and the Nitty Gritty Dirt Band. He coined the band name 'Dead Kennedys', is the author of *The Complete Idiot's Guide to Starting a Band* and is the organizer of Denver's annual Neal Cassady Birthday Bash.

Jim Burns is a poet and critic who over the past 50 years has written extensively about the jazz of the 1940s and 1950s, and about the writers of the Beat Generation, in *Jazz Journal*, *Jazz Monthly*, *Blues and Rhythm*, *Beat Scene* and other publications. He has published several collections of essays and reviews, including *Artists, Beats and Cool Cats* (2014), *Anarchists, Beats and Dadaists* (2016) and *Paris, Painters, Poets* (2017).

Douglas Field is senior lecturer in twentieth-century American literature at the University of Manchester and a frequent contributor to the *Times Literary Supplement*. He is the author, most recently, of *All Those Strangers: The Art and Lives of James Baldwin* (2015) and the co-editor, with Jay Jeff Jones, of *An Aesthetic of Obscenity: Five Novels by Jeff Nuttall*. Field co-curated the exhibition *Off Beat: Jeff Nuttall and the International Underground* (2016–17), also with Jay Jeff Jones.

Holly George-Warren is a two-time Grammy nominee and an award-winning writer and editor named one of the top women music critics 'you need to read' by Flavorwire. com. She is the author of numerous books, including *A Man Called Destruction: The Life and Music of Alex Chilton* (2014); *Public Cowboy No. 1: The Life and Times of Gene Autry* (2007); and a forthcoming biography of Janis Joplin. She is also the co-writer of *The Road to Woodstock* (2009) (with Michael Lang) and *It's Not Only Rock 'n' Roll* (1992/2013) (with Jenny Boyd), and the editor of *The Rolling Stone Book of the Beats* (1999). She teaches at the University of New York New Paltz.

Michael Goldberg is a novelist, editor, digital music pioneer and an animal rights activist. He has written extensively about Bob Dylan. His interview subjects have included Tom Waits, Patti Smith, Frank Zappa, Nicholas Ray, Captain Beefheart, Professor Longhair, Muddy Waters, Townes Van Zandt, James Brown, Lou Reed, John Cale, the Sex Pistols, the Clash and the Ramones. Goldberg was a Senior Writer and Associate Editor at *Rolling Stone* magazine for a decade. He founded the first web music magazine, the award-winning *Addicted To Noise*, in 1994, and was a Senior Vice-President at the *SonicNet* music site. Goldberg's novels include *True Love Scars* (2014), *The Flowers Lied* (2016) and *Untitled* (2017). Kerouac biographer Dennis McNally described Goldberg's fiction as 'Kerouac in the 21st Century'. A collection of his music features and essays, *Addicted To Noise*, will be published in 2018.

Nancy M. Grace is the Virginia Myers Professor of English at the College of Wooster, Ohio. She holds an MA and PhD from Ohio State. Professor Grace teaches courses in twentieth-century American and British Literature, Beat Studies, James Joyce, Journalism, Women's and Gender Studies, and Literary Theory. She is the author of *Jack Kerouac and the Literary Imagination* (2007), co-editor/author of *Breaking the Rule of Cool* (2004) and co-editor of *Girls Who Wore Black* (2002), the *Journal of Beat Studies* and the new Beat Studies book series for Clemson University Press. Grace is a two-time winner of the Choice Top 100 Books-of-the-Year award. Currently, she is developing a book on *Teaching Beat Generation Writers* for the Modern Language Association's Options Series and is serving as a consultant on Julie Dash's documentary *Travel Notes of a Geechee Girl*. She has directed the College of Wooster's Program in Writing and the Center for Diversity and Global Engagement in addition to serving as administrator for the Five Colleges of the Ohio Teagle Foundation-funded project on creative and critical thinking.

Brian Hassett is the author of *The Hitchhiker's Guide to Jack Kerouac* (2015) and a major contributor to *The Rolling Stone Book of The Beats* (2000). He has been published in the *New York Times*, the *Village Voice*, *Penthouse*, *High Times* and many other magazines and newspapers. Hassett experienced over a hundred Grateful Dead shows between 1980 and 1995, and caught every incarnation since. He first became involved in producing Acid Tests at age 15, toured with the Rolling Stones at 20, and by 21 had become friends with many of the Beats and Merry Pranksters. He is currently 'on the road' with original Prankster George Walker, bringing Jack and Neal to life in a spoken-word-theatre-comedy-improv act.

Marian Jago is currently a lecturer in jazz and popular music at the University of Leeds, UK. Her research interests include jazz ethnography, scene study, jazz as cultural practice, and American popular music of the mid-twentieth century. She maintains a particular interest in the music and pedagogical approaches of Lee Konitz and Lennie Tristano. Jago has published on a variety of jazz topics for the *Journal of Jazz Studies*, *Jazz Perspectives*, the *Jazz Research Journal* and the *Journal of the Art of Record Production*, among others.

Ronna C. Johnson is Lecturer in English and American Studies at Tufts University in Medford, MA, USA, where she has been Director of Women's Studies. She holds an MA from University of Michigan-Ann Arbor and a PhD from Tufts University. She has written about Jack Kerouac, Joyce Johnson, Lenore Kandel, Brenda Frazer and Gregory Corso, and presented papers on Diane di Prima, emphasizing gender and radical proto-feminist politics in Beat movement discourses. Johnson is currently writing *Inventing Jack Kerouac: Reception and Reputation 1957–2007* for Camden House Press and has published *Breaking the Rule of Cool: Interviewing and Reading Women Beat Writers* with Nancy M. Grace (2004), a sequel to their book *Girls Who Wore Black: Women Writing the Beat Generation* (2002). Johnson is a founding member of the Beat Studies Association and co-founder and co-editor of the *Journal of Beat Studies* and the new Beat Studies book series from Clemson University Press/ Liverpool University Press. Her latest essays are 'Gregory Corso's Dada-Surrealist-Absurd Beat Plays', in *Beat Drama: Playwrights and Performances of the 'Howl' Generation*, edited by Deborah R. Geis (2016), and 'Beats and Gender', in *The Cambridge Companion to The Beats*, edited by Steven Belletto (2016).

Jay Jeff Jones is a writer, editor and creative director. He has worked in alternative culture, as well as the mainstream, including major newspapers, small presses, underground magazines and fringe/guerrilla theatre in San Francisco, London, British Columbia, New York and Manchester. Jones was the editor of the literary quarterly *New Yorkshire Writing* (1977–9) and author of *The Lizard King* (1991), a multi-produced, semi-abstracted biographical play about Jim Morrison. With Douglas Field, he curated the John Rylands Library/University of Manchester exhibition, *Off Beat – Jeff Nuttall and the International Underground* (2016–17) and co-edited (also with Field) *Aesthetics of Obscenity: Five Novels by Jeff Nuttall* (2017).

Jack Kerouac was a novelist born in Lowell, Massachusetts, in 1922. He headed to New York City in 1939 shortly before taking up a football scholarship at Columbia University. A broken leg put paid to his sporting aspirations, but opened up opportunities to pursue his ambitions as a writer. In 1950, he published his debut novel, *The Town the City*, but it would be his 1957 publication, *On the Road*, that would catapult him into the bestseller lists and to national fame as his literary network of friends and fellow poets, dubbed the Beat Generation, achieved acclaim and notoriety in almost equal measure. In the years that followed, he would publish a sequence of novels based on his own picaresque experiences, but the 1960s would prove an unhappy period as his increasing reliance on alcohol affected his creative abilities and his relationships with former associates. He was frustrated by the links made between his books and their alleged influence on the anti-war counterculture, an issue which caused animosity with one-time allies like Allen Ginsberg. He died, aged 47, in Florida in 1969.

A. Robert Lee, formerly of the University of Kent at Canterbury, UK, retired as Professor of American Literature at Nihon University, Tokyo, in 2011. His publications include *Designs of Blackness: Mappings in The Literature and Culture of Afro-America* (1998); *Multicultural American Literature: Comparative Black, Native, Latino/a and Asian American Fictions* (2003), which won the 2004 American Book Award; *United States: Re-Viewing American Multicultural Literature* (2009); *Gothic to Multicultural: Idioms of Imagining in American Literary Fiction* (2009); and *Modern American Counter Writing: Beats, Outriders, Ethnics* (2010). His further Beat interests are reflected in *The Beat Generation Writers* (1996) as editor, and a wide range of book chapter and journal essays on transnational Beat authorship.

Paul Marion is the author of several collections of poetry, including *Union River: Poems and Sketches* (2017), and editor of the work of young Jack Kerouac, *Atop an Underwood: Early Stories and Other Writings* (1999). His book *Mill Power* (2014) tells how Lowell, Massachusetts, was named a national park that preserves the story of the American Industrial Revolution. As a government programmes manager, he helped develop the *Jack Kerouac Commemorative*, a sculptural tribute by Ben Woitena with thousands of words sandblasted into granite pillars in a downtown park in the author's hometown.

Peter Mills has published books on Van Morrison (*Hymns To The Silence*, 2010), Samuel Beckett (*Beckett at Reading*, 2001) and The Monkees (*The Monkees, Head and the 60s*, 2016) the last of which was praised by Bob Rafelson and Jack Nicholson. He has also published shorter studies of, amongst others, Jake Thackray, national anthems and the Durutti Column. He was singer and lyricist for Innocents Abroad, who made two albums, *Quaker City* (1987) and *Eleven* (1989). He is currently Senior Lecturer in Media and Popular Culture at Leeds Beckett University.

Dave Moore lives in Bristol, UK, and is the author of many articles on the Beat writers. Founding editor of *The Kerouac Connection* magazine (1984–2000), he compiled and annotated *Neal Cassady: Collected Letters, 1944–1967* for publication by Penguin (2004). Dave also writes on mystery and crime fiction as well as jazz and blues, and is the author of *The Kerouac Companion* (2010), which includes a definitive guide to the 600-plus characters in Kerouac's *Duluoz Legend*, and other Beat works. Dave also runs the Yahoo discussion forum, Kerouac Studies, and is administrator of three Facebook groups: Jack Kerouac, The Beat Generation, and Jazz of the Beat Generation.

Simon A. Morrison is a writer and academic, currently working as Programme Leader for the Music Journalism degree at the University of Chester. Author of the book *Discombobulated* (2010) – a collection of Gonzo columns penned for *DJmagazine* and published in the UK and US by Headpress – Simon has reported on the music scene everywhere from Beijing to Brazil; Moscow to Kosovo. He edited Ministry of Sound's *Ibiza* magazine and has also produced and presented on television and radio. Now working within academe, Morrison has contributed to previous Bloomsbury books including *How To Write About Music* (2015) and *DJ Culture in the Mix* (2013), as well as various academic publications including the *Journal of Popular Music*. His research interest lies in the intermedial intersection of words and music and he has presented this research at conferences across Europe.

Michael J. Prince is an associate professor of American Literature and Culture at the University of Agder in Kristiansand, Norway. His recent scholarship includes works on the Beat poets, comics and graphic novels, science fiction and film adaptations. Together with his colleague, Frida Forsgren, he has contributed to and edited *Out of the Shadows: Beat Women Are Not Beaten Women* (2015). He is author of *Adapting the Beat Poets: Burroughs, Ginsberg, and Kerouac on Screen* (2016).

Jonah Raskin is the author of 14 books, including biographies of Jack London, Allen Ginsberg and Abbie Hoffman. He has a PhD from the University of Manchester where he studied with Frank Kermode. His BA and MA are from Columbia, a school he attended because Ginsberg and Kerouac had been there. A performance poet, Raskin is the author of seven poetry chapbooks and performs his work with jazz musicians. His first teaching job was at Winston State College in North Carolina, his second at the State University of New York at Stony Brook and his third at Sonoma State University where he taught for 30 years in both the English Department and Communication Studies. He has been a book reviewer and a book critic for the *San Francisco Chronicle* and the *Santa Rosa Press Democrat*. Raskin is currently a staff reporter for *Valley of the*

Moon magazine and writes about everything the editor assigns him, from drug addiction and wine tasting rooms to bicycles and baseball. He has just written his first murder mystery titled *Dark Land, Dark Mirror*, which was published in 2017. Among his other books are *For The Hell of It: The Life and Times of Abbie Hoffman* and *American Scream: Allen Ginsberg's "Howl" and the Making of the Beat Generation*.

Horst Spandler, from Nuremberg, Germany, is a recently retired grammar school teacher of German, English, ethics and music. He did German and American Studies at the University of Erlangen, where he received a Fulbright Scholarship that enabled him to study American literature at Colorado University in Boulder. Having been an admirer of Beat Generation writers since his mid-teens, this academic opportunity enabled him to take lessons on this subject by Allen Ginsberg at Naropa's Jack Kerouac School of Disembodied Poetics in 1977, including some personal contact with Ginsberg, Peter Orlovsky and Gregory Corso. An avid collector of Beat books, part of his collection of editions of Kerouac's *On the Road* – now numbering more than 160 – were exhibited in Chicago, San Francisco, Karlsruhe and elsewhere. He collects the music of Kerouac and Neal Cassady on record and is also a translator of work by Kerouac and ruth weiss. He has published a number of essays and articles concerning them and other Beats.

James Sullivan is the author of four books, including biographies of James Brown, *The Hardest Working Man* (2008), and George Carlin, *7 Dirty Words* (2010), as well as a forthcoming title on protest music and American social movements. He is a long-time contributor to the *Boston Globe* and a former music critic at the *San Francisco Chronicle*, and he has written for *Rolling Stone*, *The Atlantic* and more.

Matt Theado is a professor of American Studies at Kobe City University of Foreign Studies in Japan. He holds a PhD from the University of South Carolina where he studied with Matthew Bruccoli and James Dickey. He has published two books, *Understanding Jack Kerouac* (2000) and *The Beats: A Literary Reference* (2003), as well as articles on Kerouac's *On the Road* typescript scroll, on Kerouac's relationships with Hollywood and with country music, and other topics. He currently serves as Book Review editor of the *Journal of Beat Studies*.

Pat Thomas is a writer and reissue producer. He is the author *of Listen, Whitey! The Sights & Sounds of Black Power 1965–1975* (2012) and *Did It! Jerry Rubin, From Yippie to Yuppie – An American Revolutionary* (2017). Thomas is also the co-curator of *Invitation to Openness: The Jazz & Soul Photography of Les McCann 1960–1980*. He compiled the Allen Ginsberg three-CD box set of Ginsberg's singing/songwriting, *The Last Word on First Blues* (2016), and two Ginsberg CDs of William Blake poems set to music (2017), *The Complete Songs of Innocence And Experience*. He was a consultant to the PBS documentary film *The Black Panthers: Vanguard of the*

Revolution (2015) and has lectured at USC, Evergreen State College (Olympia, Washington state) and the Universities of Copenhagen, Oslo and East London.

Marc Zegans is a poet and creative development advisor with a deep-seated interest in the Beats and in rock'n'roll culture. He is the author of four collections of poems – *Boys in the Woods* (2016), *The Book of Clouds* (2016), *The Underwater Typewriter* (2015) and *Pillow Talk* (2008) – and two spoken word albums, *Marker and Parker*, with the late jazz pianist Don Parker (2010), and *Night Work* (2007). His poem 'P(un)k Poets', which is included in *The Underwater Typewriter*, and which publicly premiered at the 111 Minna Gallery in San Francisco as part of the *40th Anniversary of Punk Rock Renaissance Festival*, is a contemporary answer to 'Howl'. Marc has performed everywhere from the Bowery Poetry Club to the American Poetry Museum. He lives near the coast in Northern California. His work may be found at www.marczegans.com.

INDEX

Index

Index